Scottish Civic Government Licensing Law

4th edition

Scottish Civic Government Licensing Law

4th edition

By

Andrew M Hajducki QC

and

Steven L Stuart QC

W. GREEN

THOMSON REUTERS

First edn 1994
Second edn 2002
Third edn 2009

Published in 2016 by
W. Green
21 Alva Street
Edinburgh EH2 4PS
Part of Thomson Reuters (Professional) UK Limited
(Registered in England & Wales, Company No.1679046.
Registered Office and address for service: 2nd floor,
1 Mark Square, Leonard Street, London EC2A 4EG)

http://www.wgreen.thomson.com

Typeset by YHT Ltd
Printed and bound in Great Britain by CPI Group (UK) Ltd,
Croydon, CR0 4YY

ISBN 978-0-414-03165-4

A catalogue record for this title is available
from the British Library

PREFACE TO THE FOURTH EDITION

Since publication in the autumn of 2009 of the third edition of this work there have been many changes in the legislation upon which the book is based and although some of these alterations are of a minor nature many are not and have been major and of considerable importance. The Civic Government (Scotland) Act 1982, which forms the basis of the system of local government licensing over a whole range of activities administered by councils, is now some third of a century old and although there are those who would criticise it as being antiquated and being no longer fit for purpose there are perhaps more who regard the Act as amended as forming a well thought out and effective code to use for the governance of the system of administering this wide and increasingly important area of the law. The principle that the elected local members are the best persons to reflect the opinions and aspirations of those covered by the activities to be licenced in their administrative area has invariably been followed and the courts regard their duty as being that of serving the purpose of ensuring that the law is properly and fairly applied in accordance with the legislation and its interpretation.

The main changes brought in since the 2009 edition of the book and the chief reason for the delay in producing the new edition have been found in many provisions of the Criminal Justice and Licensing (Scotland) Act 2010 and the Air Weapons and Licensing (Scotland) Act 2015 as well as those occasioned by the centralisation of the police and fire services in Scotland and the fact that sexual entertainment venues and theatres are now included in the activities covered by the 1982 Act while houses in multiple occupation have been removed and the law covering scrap metal dealers, private hire cars and have been radically amended as well as a myriad of other alterations to the existing legislation. Other changes will, no doubt, be made in the forthcoming years but the present authors hope that this fourth edition will still prove to be a valuable *vade mecum* to the legal practitioner, licensing authorities and all of those who use and value it as it has been over the past 21 years or so. We have attempted to state the law as it stands at the current time and have included the amendments introduced by the 2015 Act and have indicated whether or not the they are yet to be brought into effect at a later date. Once again we would like to thank all our colleagues and friends in the legal profession who have found time to discuss many of the sometimes obscure issues raised by the legislation and decided cases (with particular thanks to Scott Blair and Robert Skinner) and to the clerks of the sheriff court in Edinburgh, Glasgow and elsewhere and of course the very considerable help that we received from Morag Ferguson and the other always helpful staff of the Advocates' Library in Edinburgh.

Parliament House
Edinburgh

AMH and SLS
February 2016

CONTENTS

TABLE OF CASES

TABLE OF STATUTES

TABLE OF SCOTTISH STATUTES

TABLE OF STATUTORY INSTRUMENTS

TABLE OF SCOTTISH STATUTORY INSTRUMENTS

INTRODUCTION

What is civic government licensing?

For the purposes of this work, the term "civic government licensing" is used to denote the licensing functions of local authorities in Scotland that are not concerned with alcohol, betting and gaming, social work or environmental matters. The bulk of such licensing is regulated by the Civic Government (Scotland) Act 1982 (the 1982 Act), but there are two principal groups of "mainstream" licensing provisions that are outwith that Act by reason of being contained in statutes that apply also to England and Wales and have been modified for Scotland. These groups comprise: (a) cinema licences; and (b) licences connected with the regulation and use of domestic and wild animals covering such topics as the breeding and sale of dogs and the administration of zoos.

With a few statutory exceptions, civic government licensing is a devolved function in terms of the Scotland Act 1998 and the subordinate legislative functions previously dealt with by the Secretary of State are now devolved to Ministers of the Scottish Government. These functions of the Secretary of State were transferred by virtue of the Scotland Act 1998 (Transfer of Functions to the Scottish Ministers etc.) (No.2) Order 1999[1] although there are a handful of civic government licensing functions that are specifically reserved to the UK Government and these are dealt with in the annotations below.

Historical background to the 1982 Act

Although the granting by local bodies of licences to permit and regulate various forms of trading and commercial activities had been a feature of Scots law since medieval times, it was only with the passing of the 1982 Act that anything like a national, uniform code of licensing law and procedure, similar to that which had applied for many years to regulate the sale and consumption of liquor and the carrying out of betting, was brought into being. With the exception of a few activities mentioned later in this introduction, virtually all of the "mainstream" licensing that local authorities had carried out and supervised prior to the 1982 Act coming into force was brought within the ambit of a single, regulatory, statutory provision. As a result of that, both practitioners and the courts were faced with a new code of law and practice which they had to consider and apply with little guidance available from either the previous legislation or the case law which had evolved thereunder.

Immediately before the radical reform of Scottish local government, instituted by the coming into effect of the Local Government (Scotland) Act 1973 (the 1973 Act), the bodies which were responsible for administering those licensing provisions that then existed were a diverse collection of local authorities whose archaic and often arcane structure reflected a haphazard system of piecemeal reform of institutions whose origins were part of the fabric of Scottish history: despite the reforms instituted by the passing of the Local Government (Scotland) Act 1929. Numerically, the largest category of these bodies were the burghs, which were classified for historical reasons as royal burghs, burghs of barony or regality, and the parliamentary and police burghs. Their uniformity largely consisted of the fact that they were

[1] Scotland Act 1998 (Transfer of Functions to the Scottish Ministers etc.) (No.2) Order 1999 (SI 1999/3321).

all nominally urban settlements although their size varied between large towns, such as Paisley, through to small settlements, such as Pittenweem and Tobermory. For all of these 196 burghs the principal licensing legislation was found in the Burgh Police (Scotland) Acts 1892 to 1911, a monument to Victorian efforts to provide a civic code of sorts which—despite their diversity and their often archaic provisions—remained in use in an amended and reduced form until local government reorganisation. A brief valedictory account of the history and working of the Burgh Police Acts at the very end of their existence can be found in an article by Wilson Finnie, 1981 J.L.S. 447, and the everyday working of the Acts can be traced in textbooks such as Sir William Edward Whyte's *Local Government in Scotland.*[2] Among the principal licensing and regulatory provisions contained within the Acts were those which related to the licensing of porters, messengers, chimney sweepers, golf caddies, shoe blacks and the vendors of newspapers and small wares, but perhaps of greater importance and permanence were the provisions concerning the licensing of hackney carriages, i.e. taxis, and brokers, i.e. second-hand dealers, which have found a parallel in the current legislation, together with other activities which are now enshrined in national legislation, such as the operation of omnibuses and theatres. The Burgh Police Acts also provided for the extension of certain of its provisions to the "county landward" areas, i.e. the rural districts outwith the burghs and these areas were also covered by their own local legislation, by remnants of the common law and other general legislation, although it should be noted that local licensing as such was never seen as having an important role to play in the regulation of the affairs of these districts.

Not all of the urban areas of Scotland were, however, covered by the Burgh Police Acts, and in particular the "five burghs" of Edinburgh, Glasgow, Aberdeen, Dundee and Greenock were all exempt from the licensing provisions in the Acts. These "five great central towns of Scotland" (in the words of AJ Balfour when the application of the Burgh Police Acts was being debated in the House of Commons prior to its introduction) managed to stay outwith the scheme of the Acts altogether and, although a procedure was provided whereby these burghs could adopt parts of the Acts if they so chose, they all opted to remain administratively unique, so that in consequence each had its own distinct, local Act to provide for, inter alia, the regulation and licensing of such activities as it was thought necessary to control. In their final forms, this legislation is to be found in the Greenock Corporation Act 1909, the Aberdeen Corporation (General Powers) Order Confirmation Act 1938, the Dundee Corporation (Consolidated Powers) Order Confirmation Act 1957, the Glasgow Corporation (General Powers) Order Confirmation Act 1960 and the Edinburgh Corporation Order Confirmation Act 1967. It is perhaps interesting to note that the Edinburgh Act, being the most recent statute, contains many parallels with the present legislation, including amongst its general licensing provisions the licensing of places of public entertainment, public shows, billiard rooms, brokers and pawnbrokers, cabs, pleasure boats, street traders, window cleaners and special hours restaurants. In addition to the activities covered by the Burgh Police Acts and the local legislation, the local authorities had a number of other licensing functions to discharge. Councillors who were also members of the licensing courts also had duties to perform in relation to liquor and gaming licences and this jurisdiction, now exercised by them qua the local

[2] Sir William Edward Whyte, *Local Government in Scotland*, 2nd edn (London: William Hodge, 1936).

licensing board, is now regulated by the Licensing (Scotland) Act 2005 (published separately: see Jack Cummins, *Licensing (Scotland) Act 2005*[3]).

On 16 May 1975 the Local Government (Scotland) Act 1975 came into effect, implementing the principal recommendations of the Wheatley Commission, and sweeping away the burghs, corporations, counties and other paraphernalia of the historical and haphazard system of local government in the country. They were replaced by a two-tier system of district and regional councils, with the exception of the Western Isles, Orkney and Shetland, where unitary, all-purpose local authorities were set up in the form of islands councils. It had already been felt that this radical reform should also be accompanied by a systematic reform of local legislation, and to this end the Secretary of State had, on 2 May 1972, set up a working party whose remit was:

> "To examine the powers available to local authorities in Scotland for the administration of civic government in their areas under the Burgh Police (Scotland) Acts 1892 and 1903, other related enactments and corresponding local Acts; and to make recommendations regarding: (i) the provision to be made ... for transferring existing regulatory powers to the new regional and district authorities, the terms in which a new general byelaw-making power should be framed ... and (ii) the longer-term action to be taken—including the repeal or modification of obsolete provisions and the standardisation of administrative powers—to prepare a civic government code for Scotland and the content of such a code."

Pending any resolution of the long-term aspects of any reform, the 1973 Act provided for the interim continuation in effect of the Burgh Police and local Acts until the end of 1979, with an overall power of extension or modification where necessary being given to the Secretary of State in terms of ss.225 and 229 of the 1973 Act. This meant that the new district and islands councils (and, to a very limited extent, the regional councils) became the new licensing authorities, responsible for the licensing and regulatory functions previously exercised under the Burgh Police and local Acts. The powers given to the Secretary of State were only used sparingly to extend taxi licensing to cover the whole area of the "five burghs" and into 21 other districts. The existing provisions were extended by s.5 of the Local Government (Scotland) Act 1978, which put the expiry date back to the end of 1982, and were further extended until the end of 1984 by the transitional provisions contained within ss.134 and 135 of the 1982 Act.

The working party submitted their report to the Secretary of State in January 1976 and consultations took place thereafter between the government and interested parties resulting in the publication in July 1980 of a white paper entitled *Proposals for a Code of Civic Government in Scotland—A Consultation Paper*,[4] which, somewhat unusually, included a draft Bill as an appendix. This draft was modified and, following both the response to the white paper and the recommendations of the *Report of the Committee of Inquiry into Local Government in Scotland*,[5] published in January 1981, it reappeared as the Civic Government (Scotland) Bill. Lively debate in

[3] Jack Cummins, *Licensing (Scotland) Act 2005*, 3rd edn (Edinburgh: W. Green, 2015).

[4] *Proposals for a Code of Civic Government in Scotland—A Consultation Paper* (HMSO, 1980), Cmnd.7958.

[5] *Report of the Committee of Inquiry into Local Government in Scotland* (HMSO, 1981), Cmnd.8115.

Parliament then followed and certain amendments and clarifications were carried out before, on 28 October 1982, the Civic Government (Scotland) Act 1982 received the Royal Assent and subsequently came into force on the appointed days.

The Civic Government (Scotland) Act 1982

The preamble to the Act states that it is:

> "An Act to make provision as regards Scotland for the licensing and regulation of certain activities; for the preservation of public order and safety and the prevention of crime; for prohibiting the taking of and dealing with indecent photographs of children; as to certain powers of constables and others; as to lost and abandoned property and property in the possession of persons taken into police custody; as to the rights and duties of the owners and users of certain land, buildings and other structures; as to the making by local authorities of byelaws; and to enable them to make management rules applying to land or premises under their control; as to certain other functions of local authorities and their officers; as to the time when the Burgh Police (Scotland) Acts 1892 to 1911 and certain local statutory provisions cease to have effect; and for connected purposes."

This is reflected in its content and structure.

The Act, unlike Caesar's Gaul, was divided into nine parts and these deal, respectively, with general provisions for licensing (Pt I), the licensing and regulation of particular activities (Pt II), the control of sex shops (Pt III), offences and powers of constables (Pt IV), public processions (Pt V), lost and abandoned property (Pt VI), property in the possession of persons taken into police custody (Pt VII), buildings (Pt VIII) and miscellaneous and general matters (Pt IX), while the four schedules to the Act deal with further provisions as to the general system of licensing and the control of sex shops as well as minor and consequential amendments and repeals. For the purposes of the present book, which is only concerned with licensing matters, only Pts I, II and III, those sections of Pt IX that have a relevance to licensing, and Schs 1 and 2 are dealt with both in this introduction and in the annotations that follow. The 1982 Act applies to the whole of Scotland, and so far as the licensing provisions are concerned, it came into force on 1 July 1984 by virtue of para.3 of the Civic Government (Scotland) Act 1982 (Commencement) Order 1983.[6] Transitional provisions are dealt with in ss.136 and 137 of the Act but these are not contained in this edition as they are now only of historic interest.

Part I of the Act deals with general matters that apply to all licences covered by the Act and consists of ss.1–8, together with Sch.1. These general matters, which apply to all licences covered in Pt II, include identification of the licensing authority, provisions relating to the discharge of their functions and other powers connected with inspection, enforcement and offences, together with certain definitions which have a general application to Pts I and II. Schedule 1 contains the procedures to be used in the administration of the licensing system and appeals therefrom, in contrast to the initial scheme of the Bill, and to the Licensing (Scotland) Act 1976 which includes procedural matters within the main body of the Act rather than relegating them to a separate schedule. Part II of the Act deals with the specific types of

[6] Civic Government (Scotland) Act 1982 (Commencement) Order 1983 (SI 1983/201).

activity which are covered by licensing provisions and covers both the procedure by which licensing authorities can resolve to make certain activities subject to licensing and the actual types of licence themselves. Part III of the Act covers the control of sex shops and sexual entertainment venues and contains, in Sch.2, a separate code of procedure for licensing these activities. Parts III–VIII do not concern licensing matters but Pt IX deals, inter alia, with certain general matters such as offences by bodies corporate, the application of the Act to the Crown, expenses and interpretation.

The Act has been amended and modified throughout its 33 year history and now contains provisions that were not even contemplated back in the 1980s but is generally felt to be workable and "fit for purpose" in its present form. The Scottish Government stated in 2015 that it had no plans to fundamentally review the Act as it was "reviewed only some 10 years ago and found fit for purpose", a view generally held by practitioners and local authorities not anxious to see any radical changes in the way in which "civic licensing" (as it has been inelegantly recently dubbed) was conducted—Scottish Parliament Local Government and Regeneration Committee, 3rd Report (2014) para.36. There were those who disagreed with this view and officials of both Glasgow and Edinburgh city councils, two of the largest councils in Scotland, are on record putting forward the views that "consolidation or revision of the Act is required to improve the licensing service that is delivered to businesses and communities we serve" and, more bluntly, "the 1982 Act has probably passed its sell-by date". It is undoubtedly true that the 1982 Act is now much expanded and added to since it originally came into force and has a plethora of increasingly confusingly numbered new sections, subsections and paragraphs added and is now a more difficult (but by no means impossible) document to follow and it may be that consolidation will one day be necessary once many of the difficult questions now raised by the alterations in technology and business practices involving many of the activities licensed under the Act have been resolved to the satisfaction of those who deal with this complex area of the law.

The two most recent and fundamental changes to the 1982 Act are found in three omnibus and seemingly disparate pieces of legislation, namely the Custodial Sentences and Weapons (Scotland) Act 2007 (the 2007 Act), the Criminal Justice and Licensing (Scotland) Act 2010 (the 2010 Act) and the Air Weapons and Licensing (Scotland) Act 2015 (the 2015 Act). The civic government licensing provisions of the first two of these Acts are now in force and those of the 2015 Act are due to come into force in the next few months and, for the purposes of this edition of the book, will be assumed to be current shortly after publication and each amendment made by the Act is separately noted in the relevant note as to either be in force already or noted as not to be in force as at 1 January 2016 as the necessary commencement order has not been passed at that date. For sections not yet in force the existing sections of the Act not yet superseded are set out in the Appendix on pp.415–444. The 2007 Act introduced an important new licensing scheme for dealers in knives and swords while the 2010 Act made a number of changes both to the substantive and procedural aspects of the law. The 2015 Act however was probably the most fundamental amendment to the 1982 Act in that it amended or introduced changes dealing with a number of areas of the law and not only made procedural changes but also substantially amended substantive areas of the law relating to licensed activities including metal dealers and others and has brought about a new category of licensing dealing with sexual entertainment venues and brought theatre licensing under the aegis of the 1982 Act. Other recent statutory alterations have removed licences for houses in multiple occupation from the provisions of the 1982 Act and have taken into account the recent centralisation of both the police and fire and rescue services in Scotland and a myriad of other pieces of legislation involving penalties, fire safety, charities, taxis and private hire cars and other matters have made changes to the relevant areas of licensing and it should be noted that these modifications and amendments have been made by a mixture of primary and secondary legislation.

A number of helpful circulars that set forth the Secretary of State's and the Scottish Ministers' views, or the experience of the way in which authorities were applying the Act, were issued by the relevant departments or ministers and relevant parts of such guidance are quoted from in the text and notes to the Act as appropriate. Some subordinate legislation has been passed in connection with the licensing provisions of the Act, principally in relation to taxis and private hire cars, tattoo and skin piercing, knife dealers and booking offices and this is set out after the annotated sections of the Act. Given that the 1982 Act is, on the whole, a well-drafted and workable piece of legislation it seems likely that it will continue in force for the foreseeable future, albeit in a piecemeal and often amended form.

The licensing authority

At the time that the 1982 Act was passed, the licensing authorities for all civic government licensing purposes comprised the 53 district councils and three islands councils constituted under the provisions of the 1973 Act in accordance with the proposals of the working party, although in the case of taxi licensing, the view was expressed that it would have been more appropriate for this function to be exercised by the regional councils qua highways authorities. The district/regional two-tier system of local government in Scotland subsisted for some 20 years but, by the early 1990s, political pressures (spurred on by a perceived "unworkability" of the system and a desire to "streamline" local government on a more cost-effective basis) led to the issue by the Scottish Office in June 1991 of the first of several consultative documents namely *The Structure of Local Government in Scotland: the Case for Change: Principles of the New System*.[7] The final proposals were published in a white paper in June 1993, *Shaping the Future—The New Councils*,[8] and formed the basis for the Local Government etc. (Scotland) Act 1994 (the 1994 Act) which received the Royal Assent on 3 November 1994. Changes were made and, from the public point of view, the most contentious issues appear to have been the desires of former counties to retain their autonomy, e.g. Clackmannan and East Lothian, and the allegations of gerrymandering in the drawing of council boundaries in the west. In 1995 elections were held for the new unitary authorities which were to be elected as "shadow" authorities, whilst the existing districts and regions remained in power until 31 March 1996. Not surprisingly, the three existing islands councils, already functioning as unitary authorities, were left in place, albeit with a minor name change in the case of the Western Isles. From 1 April 1996, the 29 new councils constituted in terms of ss.1 and 2, described in Sch.1 of the 1994 Act, along with the Orkney Islands, the Shetlands Islands, and the Western Isles Councils, became the new licensing authorities in respect of all functions previously carried out by the former authorities.

---

[7] *The Structure of Local Government in Scotland: the Case for Change: Principles of the New System* (HMSO, 1991).
[8] *Shaping the Future—The New Councils* (HMSO, 1993), Cm.2267.

Although the licensing authority is the council itself compared with the "licensing board" for alcohol licences granted under the Licensing (Scotland) Act 2005, s.56 of the Local Government (Scotland) Act 1973 provides for the delegation of, inter alia, the licensing power to committees, subcommittees or even an individual office, and in practice virtually all licensing matters are, in fact, delegated to a committee (known variously as "the licensing committee", "the general purposes committee", etc.). Decisions are reached by a collective exercise of the committee's discretion.[9] Minor, non-contentious matters are sometimes dealt with by a single officer whose actions are reported to the committee, although formal ratification thereof is not required. The actual administration of the licensing system, however, varies between different authorities although most have adopted the pattern of committees recommended in the Paterson Report in Working Group on Scottish Local Government Management Structures, *The New Scottish Local Authorities, Organisation and Management Structures*.[10] There are no provisions for statutory quarterly meetings, as in the case of licensing boards, and how and when applications are dealt with is an administrative matter for the authority, subject only to certain time constraints, such as those laid down in s.3 of the 1982 Act. The licensing authority must adhere to the provisions of the 1982 Act and to the procedure laid out therein and it cannot seek to depart from this by, for instance, attempting to rely on their general subsidiary powers in terms of s.69(1) of the 1973 Act. For the purposes of Pt III licences for sex shops and sexual encounter venues it should be noted that the expression "local authority" replaces the expression "licensing authority" even though in reality the expressions may well be synonymous.

Mandatory and optional licences

Licences issued under the 1982 Act fall into two basic categories: "mandatory" licences and "optional" licences, although these terms are somewhat misleading as both types are mandatory from the point of view of the person who seeks to carry out a particular activity to which they apply. The distinction refers to whether or not the licensing authority has any discretion as to whether or not it may regulate and licence a particular activity. In relation to certain activities, a licensing authority has no choice and must therefore regulate and licence any person carrying on that activity within its area. These "mandatory" licences presently cover five types of activity, namely the licensing of metal dealers, indoor sports entertainment centres, houses in multiple occupation, skin piercing and tattooing and knife dealers, although the metal dealers would have become an optional activity if the provisions of the Bill leading to the 2010 Act had been fully enacted. A further activity, the licensing of taxi booking offices, is mandatory if a licensing authority has passed a resolution to licence taxis and private hire cars. All other activities presently covered by the Act are "optional", i.e. the licensing authority may opt to implement licensing of these activities or not, following a resolution by them to do so and compliance thereafter with the provisions of s.9 of the Act. The "optional" activities cover, at present, taxis and private hire cars and the drivers of the same, second-hand dealers, boat

---

[9] See *Piper v Kyle and Carrick DC*, 1988 S.L.T. 267, and *Di Ciacca v Lorn, Mid Argyll, Kintyre and Islay Divisional Licensing Board*, 1994 S.C. 151; 1994 S.L.T. 1150.

[10] Paterson Report in Working Group on Scottish Local Government Management Structures, *The New Scottish Local Authorities, Organisation and Management Structures* (HMSO, 1973).

hire, street traders, market operators, public entertainments, late hours catering and window cleaners (and, under Pt III of the Act, sex shops). The various specific types of licence are dealt with later in this introduction.

Part II of the Act not only lists these categories but also defines each activity, and it is only if a person carries on an activity within the area to which the licensing requirement applies (which, in the case of an "optional" activity, may not necessarily be the whole of the area within the jurisdiction of the licensing authority) that they will require a licence. In the case of an "optional" activity, the licensing authority may resolve to restrict the categories of activity which could fall within a general heading, e.g. they could resolve that a second-hand dealer's licence would only be needed by persons trading in a particular commodity or class of goods.

It is perhaps worth repeating the views of the Secretary of State, in relation to the scope of the optional licences, which are quoted in Scottish Development Department (SDD) Circular 6/1983, Appendix A, para.2.5, where it is said that

> "he shares the view expressed in Parliament that licensing for the optional activities should be introduced only where it is shown to be *necessary* to prevent crime, to preserve public order and safety, or to protect the environment. The purpose of licensing is not to restrict trade or competition. It follows that before introducing licensing, authorities should pay particular attention to the views of the Chief Constable and the traders likely to be concerned before proceeding to the resolution, and they should be satisfied that the introduction of licensing under the Act will contribute to the amelioration of the nuisance complained of. In the Secretary of State's view the only instance of a prima facie case for almost universal licensing is that of the taxi and hire car trades—but even here the authorities in the most remote and highly populated areas may feel that licensing throughout their area is unnecessary".

It is also worth observing that any resolution should be concerned solely with the desire to regulate and control licensed activities, and not with any attempts at "social engineering", e.g. an attempt to license brothels as s.41 public entertainments in the guise of sauna and massage parlours,[11] or an attempt to refuse a temporary public entertainment licence to a circus when an authority disapproved of the concept of performing animals, notwithstanding the 1925 Act which regulated the same.[12] In *Stewart v Perth and Kinross District Council*[13] conditions on a second hand dealer's licence were held to be invalid because they were an attempt to deal with consumer protection issues and in *McCluskey v North Lanarkshire Council*,[14] an attempt by the Council to place restrictions on street trading close to schools was deemed to be ultra vires because it was felt to be contrary to the Government's policy to promote the benefit of healthy eating and lifestyles for schoolchildren—in the words of Lord Hope in *Stewart* such issues were a matter for Parliament to enforce through primary legislation to apply throughout the country rather than a matter for licensing authorities to apply in their own areas. Where a licence was refused inter alia because a

[11] *Scanlan v City of Edinburgh DC*, 1995 S.L.T. (Sh Ct) 89.
[12] *Gerry Cottle's Circus v City of Edinburgh DC*, 1990 S.L.T. 235.
[13] *Stewart v Perth and Kinross District Council*, 2004 S.C. (HL) 71.
[14] *McCluskey v North Lanarkshire Council* [2016] S.C. Ham 3.

licensing authority took into account a government policy on drinking and driving see *BP Express Shopping Ltd v Perth & Kinross Licensing Board.*[15]

Additional activities

The Secretary of State retained a power under the 1982 Act to designate any additional activity as an "optional" activity (s.44) and although this power has, to date, only been used on one occasion it nevertheless permits a flexibility which enables them to meet any particular needs or evils which were unforeseen at the time that the 1982 Act was drafted. The purpose of this provision was stated thus in SDD Circular 6/1983 at paras 2.113–2.114 of Appendix A:

> "This section will allow new developments in trade or entertainment to be regulated where necessary on grounds of crime protection, environmental health, or protection of public safety. It will also be possible for the Secretary of State to standardise existing district and islands council licensing by repealing existing licensing provisions in other enactments and drawing the activities therein covered with the scope of the Civic Government (Scotland) Act licensing system. The powers in this section will be used only where broad public consensus exists that control or standardisation is necessary to protect the public and the Secretary of State (via the Scottish Ministers) will consider each suggestion for a section 44 Order carefully on its own merits. He has no plans to use the powers in the foreseeable future; and in any case would not want to use the powers unless absolutely necessary, until the other provisions of this Part have been in force for some years and have settled down. He would not normally consider suggestions from individual local authorities for extension, unless endorsed by the Convention [of Scottish Local Authorities] in the light of precise evidence of the abuses which it was thought necessary to regulate."

This power is now exercised by the appropriate Minister of the Scottish Government in terms of the Scotland Act 1998 and have been exercised in the case of tattooing and skin piercing establishments and booking offices.

Licensing procedure

Schedule 1 to the Act sets forth the procedural code to be followed in relation to licences issued or sought under Pts I and II of the Act. Applications for the grant or renewal of a licence must be made in compliance with the provisions of para.1 of the Schedule and the procedure to be followed by the licensing authority upon receipt of an application is set forth in para.2. Interested parties are allowed to make objections and representations in relation to the grant or renewal of a licence and there is provision for applicants to be heard by the licensing authority, who can also carry out their own investigations into relevant matters.

Procedure at any hearing is at the discretion of the authority. They may decide to hear evidence or simply proceed upon the basis of ex parte submissions. The emphasis is on disposal of business expeditiously with a minimum of formality[16]; both are liquor licensing cases but the same

[15] *BP Express Shopping Ltd v Perth & Kinross Licensing Board*, 2005 S.L.T. 862.

[16] *JAE (Glasgow) Ltd v City of Glasgow District Licensing Board*, 1994 S.C. 290; 1994 S.L.T. 1164 (approved in *Chief Constable, Strathclyde Police v North Lanarkshire Licensing Board*, 2004 S.C. 304; 2003 S.L.T. 1268).

approach would be applied in respect of hearings under the 1982 Act. Note, however, that the Scottish Ministers are now empowered to make regulations as to procedure to be followed at or in connection with hearings before the authority including rules of evidence, representation and expenses (Sch.1 para.18(8)). See also discussion in respect of art.6(1) of the European Convention on Human Rights at pp.20–22 below. Provided that the statutory provisions have been complied with, the authority must reach a final decision on the application within a stated time (s.3) and may then grant or renew a licence; grant it, but make it subject to certain specified conditions; or refuse the application which failing a deemed grant will be made. Provision is made for the prescribing of mandatory licence conditions by the Scottish Ministers and for authorities determining standard conditions to apply to licences granted by them (ss.3A and 3B). An authority must refuse the application if the applicant, manager or controller of the activity is not a fit and proper person, or if the premises are not suitable or convenient, or if there is any other good reason for refusing the application: Sch.1 para.5(3).

Commonly licensing authorities formulate policies to deal with particular classes of applications, even if only to achieve a degree of consistency in dealing with applications. Such policies could and do cover, for example, the opening hours of premises operating under late hours catering licences, a requirement that all vehicles operating as taxis be wheelchair accessible or a limit on the number of taxi licences to be issued in the context of s.10(3) of the Act. Conditions to be attached to particular licences may be standard in terms of policies adopted by the authority. The lawfulness of such policies will be judged against the statutory context against which they are formulated and applied. They should relate to and not be inconsistent with the purpose of the statutory provisions under which the authority's discretion is exercised. Generally there is no objection to the application of lawful policies to applications provided that they are not so rigidly applied as to fetter the authority's discretion. The authority must always consider individual applications on their merits and be prepared to listen to arguments that the policy in question should not be applied to a particular case.[17]

There is a restriction on successive applications being made. The duration of a licence is normally three years, although the authority can grant a licence for a shorter period and may also grant a temporary licence. A licence can be issued to any person, including a body corporate, provided that he, she or it is not deemed unfit. A licence holder must notify the licensing authority of a material change of circumstances. Provisions are made for the variation and suspension of licences, whether as a result of a complaint or not, the surrender of a licence and other administrative matters, including the temporary transfer of a licence to an executor and the keeping by the local authority of a register of all applications. Reasonable fees can be levied by the licensing authority but there is no set level of fee—special provisions apply in respect of fees for taxis and private hire cars and their drivers by virtue of s.12 of the Act.

A licence may in itself not be enough

One important qualification in respect of the ability of a licence holder to practice their particular activity must be made, however. The mere possession of a current licence may not entitle one per se to carry out any particular activity and it may be necessary to obtain planning permission, the

[17] *Sneddon v Renfrewshire Council* [2009] CSIH 40; 2009 S.C. 539; 2009 S.L.T. 563; *Elder v Ross and Cromarty District Licensing Board*, 1990 S.L.T. 307.

consent of a landlord, or to comply with environmental or health standards. In addition, other licensing legislation may have to be taken into account—for instance, if alcohol is being sold, plays being put on or gaming machines operated—and this particularly affects public entertainment licences. This matter is dealt with further in relation to the annotations to s.41 of the 1982 Act; see also *JE Sheeran (Amusement Arcades) Ltd v Hamilton DC.*[18] Another example is provided by boat hire licences, where licence holders are also bound by regulations made under the Merchant Shipping Act and the codes of conduct issued by the UK Maritime and Coastguard Agency. The Civic Government (Scotland) Act 1982 does not confer any particular rights as between individual license holders or persons in the same trade, and a licensed tradesman cannot interdict an unlicensed person who is carrying on the trade in defiance of the statutory requirement to be licensed. In *Reid v Mini-cabs*,[19] it was said that the Dundee Local Act of 1957 was designed to be a code for the municipal government and administration of Dundee for the benefit of its citizens and that no right of civil action was conferred on licensed operators of hackney carriages. A statutory licence will not excuse any negligence on the part of a licensee, see, e.g. *Hazard v Glasgow Pavilion*,[20] or the perpetration of any nuisance, see, e.g. *Reid v Aberdeen City Council*[21] (noise levels emanating from a licensed animal boarding establishment). Nor will it excuse any breach of the criminal law, see, e.g. *Reynolds v Normand*,[22] where a street trader was prosecuted for noise pollution in respect of an ice cream van's chimes.

Activities licensed under the 1982 Act

The various activities that are covered under Pts II and III of the 1982 Act are listed in alphabetical order as boat hire; booking offices; indoor sports entertainment centres; knife dealers; late-hours catering; market operators; metal dealers and itinerant metal dealers; public entertainments; salmon dealers; second-hand dealers; sex shops; sexual entertainment venues; skin piercing establishments; street traders; taxi and private hire car operators and drivers; and window cleaners. The greatest number of such licences are granted in respect of taxis while the number of licences and their economic importance in the other categories vary according to the nature of the geographic and economic and the social make up of the areas for which the licensing authorities are responsible.

Taxis and private hire car operators

Although optional activities all licensing authorities in Scotland now have resolutions in place for compulsory licensing of taxis and private hire cars and their drivers. A "taxi" is a hire car that can be hailed in a public place for a journey beginning there and then, and is thus distinguishable from a "hire car" that, in effect, has to be pre-booked and cannot ply for hire. The policy behind the provisions relating to taxis and private hire vehicles to draw a clear distinction between operation as a taxi and as a private hire car has been acknowledged by the Inner House.[23] Special provisions apply to a

---

18 *JE Sheeran (Amusement Arcades) Ltd v Hamilton DC*, 1986 S.L.T. 289.
19 *Reid v Mini-cabs*, 1966 S.C. 137; 1966 S.L.T. 166.
20 *Hazard v Glasgow Pavilion*, 1994 G.W.D. 13-850.
21 *Reid v Aberdeen City Council*, 2000 G.W.D. 37-1413.
22 *Reynolds v Normand*, 1995 G.W.D. 14-801.
23 *Spring Radio Cars Ltd v Glasgow City Council* [2014] CSIH 21; 2014 S.C. 529; 2014 S.L.T. 393.

hybrid category of vehicle, namely a taxi-bus—see the general note to s.10 for an explanation of this. Prior to the 1982 Act, taxis were covered by provisions relating to "hackney carriages" and "cabs" found in the Burgh Police and local Acts, but it was rightly recognised that a single uniform code was required in relation to such an important category of activity. This is one of the "optional" categories of licence, but a licensing authority must, if it seeks to introduce such licensing, license both taxis and hire cars and cannot choose merely to license one or other of these categories of vehicle. Once a hire car has been licensed as such, it cannot operate as a taxi. It is the operator of a taxi or hire car who requires a licence, and the licensing authority may have a guideline for the optimum number of such licences which should be granted—s.10(3) and restrictions can now be placed on the number of private hire car licences that that the licensing authority chose to issue. A licence relates to a particular vehicle and the authority must be satisfied in relation to the size, type and design of the vehicle. Powers exist for the testing and inspection of vehicles and the taximeter devices therein, and the level of fees charged for taxi or hire car licences must reflect the expenses incurred by the local authority in the carrying out of their taxi licensing functions.

Other specific provisions apply to taxis and hire cars. Vehicles other than taxis must not carry misleading taxi signs. Special powers apply to the operation of taxis outwith the area of a licensing authority, to cross-border journeys to England and Wales, and in respect of taxis from those countries journeying into Scotland. Sections 17 and 18 deal with the fixing by the licensing authority of a level of taxi fares and a system of appeal therefrom, and s.19 makes provision for taxi stances. The Scottish Ministers have the power to impose certain conditions on both taxi and hire car licences and driving licences and mandatory and standard conditions may also be imposed on licences. The separation of hire vehicles between taxis and private hire cars is still to be maintained although the government may well be reviewing the existence of the dual system in the future, It should be noted that the definition of both types of vehicle refers to motor vehicles of a certain carrying capacity for passengers and thus horse-drawn vehicles, stretch limousines, party buses and similar vehicles and bicycle based rickshaws and the like can only be licensed under the provisions relating to street traders.

Taxi and private hire car drivers

In addition to taxi and hire car licences, the drivers of those vehicles will require a separate licence issued in terms of s.13 and, if those persons are driver-owners, then they will require this licence in addition to the s.10 licence covering their vehicle. Various criteria are laid down in s.13 in relation to the fitness of a person to be a taxi driver or a private hire car driver in addition to the general requirement for any person seeking any form of licence to be a fit person by reason of para.5(3) of Sch.1. The licensing authority can require drivers of both types of vehicle to submit to medical examination and also to a "knowledge" test.

Booking offices

Where premises are used for the carrying on of a business of taking bookings from the public for the hire of taxis and/or private hire cars, the persons running that business will require a licence and certain mandatory records must also be kept. Licences are not required: (a) where less than four vehicles are involved; and (b) where the local authority do not require taxi and private hire licences, i.e. where no s.9 resolution in respect of them has been passed. This form of licensing, introduced under s.44 by the Civic Government (Scotland) Act 1982 (Licensing of Booking Offices) Order,[24] came into effect on 16 November 2009. Whether the existence of mobile phone and computer apps will eventually render this category of licence as otiose is another matter and the validity of internet apps that, in effect, book outwith the licensed area may also require reconsideration.

Market operators

This form of optional licensing activity contained in s.40 of the Act covers the operators of private markets (with the exception: (a) of those operated by local authorities and charities; and (b) agricultural markets for the sale of livestock, fodder or grain). It does not cover individual stallholders who accordingly do not require a separate licence. Potentially the most contentious forms of market, the car boot sale and one-day sale, are also covered.

Public entertainments

This optional licensing activity contained in s.41 of the Act covers places to which the public are admitted or in which the public may use facilities, upon payment, for the purposes of entertainment and recreation, but excluding athletic or sports grounds, premises licensed for alcohol or gaming, places for which s.41A licences are required, cinemas, and certain other categories but theatres (which formerly required a licence granted under the Theatres Act 1968) are now included under s.41. The specific categories of activity to be licensed must be clearly specified in terms of s.9(5)(b) of the Act:

> "In other words, a general resolution to license all places of public entertainment would be invalid. Authorities must instead specify all classes. The purpose of this provision—which was inserted in the light of Parliamentary discussion, was to ensure that the resolution did not inadvertently catch such functions as, say, sheepdog trials, or bird shows which might come within 'public entertainment' as defined in the section but which have no or negligible crime prevention, environmental or public safety implications."[25]

Previously, only a haphazard system of licensing of public entertainment had existed, although Edinburgh had a fairly comprehensive code in the Edinburgh local Act, ss.363–376, which included separate licensing for billiard rooms.

Indoor sports entertainment

This form of licence applies to indoor sports centres in terms of a substituted s.41A to the 1982 Act (introduced by the Fire Safety and Safety of Places of Sport Act 1987, as a result of the Popplewell Inquiry following the disastrous fire at the Valley Parade Ground of Bradford Football Club in May 1985). Sections 41A and 41 public entertainment licences are mutually

[24] Civic Government (Scotland) Act 1982 (Licensing of Booking Offices) Order 2009 (SSI 2009/145).
[25] SDD Circular 6/1983, Appendix A, para. 2.102.

exclusive. The purpose of indoor sports entertainment licences is primarily to enable the licensing authority to have greater control over these premises, for reasons of safety. This is a mandatory rather than optional activity.

Late-hours catering

These optional licences are required by all places serving food, whether on a "sit-in" or "carry-out" basis, between 23:00 and 05:00, if the licensing authority have made a s.9 resolution to license such premises. Conditions may be imposed, such as a restriction on opening hours, and it has proved in practice to be a particularly effective means of controlling late-night disturbances to restrict the opening hours of such premises so that they close prior to public houses, thus preventing inebriated persons from roaming the streets in search of food. Other than during the above-mentioned hours, s.42 licences have no effect and if premises are licensed to sell liquor under the Licensing (Scotland) Act 2005 then a s.42 licence will not additionally be required. Much of the current legislation is derived from the "Special Hours Restaurants" provisions, contained in ss.425–432 of the 1967 Edinburgh Act. For the text relating to late hours catering licences see pp.122–124 below.

Boat hire

Under s.38 of the Act the hirer of a boat for pleasure, recreational, educational or sporting purposes, or a person who uses a boat to carry for reward 12 or fewer persons for these purposes, will need a licence to do so provided that the licensing authority have passed a s.9 resolution to this effect—see pp.54–57 below. The basis for licensing this form of activity was found in s.304 of the Burgh Police (Scotland) Act 1892 although a more modern code was enacted in ss.402–404 of the Edinburgh Corporation Confirmation Act 1967. The 2004 Task Group report indicated that notwithstanding the need for pleasure vessels to comply with a number of statutory requirements made in Merchant Shipping Act subordinate legislation, they considered that this form of licensing should remain.

Knife dealers

This activity became a mandatory form of licensing from September 2009 and is to be found in the new ss.27A–27S of the Act which were inserted into it by the 2007 Act. They control the sale of certain types of knife, dagger and sword and these provisions are designed to prevent what was perceived to be the dangers inherent in the purchase and unlawful use of such potentially fatal items.

Metal dealers

This is a mandatory class of activity contained in ss.28–37 of the Act and the new sections added or amended by the 2015 Act. The provisions relating to dealers in scrap and redundant metal products were tightened up to make dealers more accountable and to stop the increasing problem of those who attempted to sell on stolen and illegally obtained scrap items to metal dealers and to control methods of payment and the records kept by dealers so that accountability and the tracing of illegally obtained items could be made. Travelling scrap merchants (referred to as "itinerant metal dealers" require a separate licence and they are required to keep specific receipts and invoices. A licence enables them to trade anywhere in Scotland. Separate licences are required for metal dealers, second-hand dealers and itinerant metal dealers, and if a person carries on more than one type of these activities they will require more than one licence. Metal dealers' and itinerant metal dealers' licences are covered by ss.28–37 of the Act.

Second-hand dealers

These are another "optional" type of licence but the authority must, when making their s.9 resolution, specify the exact categories of activity that are to be licensed under this head. Pawnbrokers, wholesalers, charities, finance houses and dealers, to whom second-hand goods are only an incidental part of their business, are all automatically exempt. The authority may require the recording of transactions and there are specific provisions governing the disposal of stock in trade, in order to try and curb the resale of stolen goods. The origins of such licensing were found in ss.433–453 of the Burgh Police (Scotland) Acts (1892) dealing with brokers and pawnbrokers, and in several of the local Acts, e.g. Pt XXXI of the 1957 Dundee Act.

Salmon dealers

This activity, covering dealers in salmon and sea trout (all migratory fish of the species *salmo salar* and *salmo trutta*) may be introduced as an additional activity in terms of s.44 of the 1982 Act, by virtue of s.20(1) of the Salmon Act 1986 but, as yet, no order has been passed under subss.20(2) and (3) of the 1986 Act to activate salmon dealers' licences and unless there is still perceived to be a need to licence salmon dealers it is unlikely that such a system will be introduced.

Sex shops

In terms of Pt III of the Act (which has a sole section, s.45) the district or islands council may, by resolution, introduce licensing for sex shops (as defined in Sch.2 para.2). Although licensing of this activity follows a similar pattern to that of the activities covered in Pts I and II of the Act, general provisions and procedure for licensing of sex shops are contained separately in Sch.2 which applies only to sex shops (whereas general provisions, etc. for Pt II activities are contained in Pt I and Sch.1). Control of sex shops was introduced virtually simultaneously in both England and Wales (by Sch.3 of the Local Government (Miscellaneous Provisions) Act 1982) and Scotland and was designed to meet a perceived problem which planning legislation alone could not cope with. In Scotland, however, sex shop licensing has been used comparatively little. The text of the relevant licensing provisions is set out at pp.126–127 below and the procedure at pp.185–208 below.

Sexual entertainment venue

This new category of licence was introduced by the 2015 Act in response to the decision of the Inner House in *Brightcrew Ltd v City of Glasgow Licensing Board*,[26] which decided that the appropriate form of such licensing was under the 1982 Act rather than alcohol licensing legislation. The interpretation of the venues and activities covered are set out in the new s.45A of the Act and apply to those categories of events listed in the section.

---

[26] *Brightcrew Ltd v City of Glasgow Licensing Board* [2011] CSIH 46; 2012 S.C. 67; 2012 S.L.T. 140.

Skin piercing and tattooing

Licences for businesses carrying on the activities of skin piercing and tattooing were introduced as a mandatory form of licence in 2006, following upon extensive consultation with the trade, community and health groups. The primary objective was to introduce consistent controls in order to manage and reduce the risks faced by potential clients in relation to health and specifically the transmission of blood borne viruses such as HIV and Hepatitis B and C. An "additional activity" in terms of s.44(1)(b) of the 1982 Act, they were introduced by the Civic Government (Scotland) Act 1982 (Licensing of Skin Piercing and Tattooing) Order 2006.[27] It should be noted that in Sch.1 of the Order certain important amendments are made to the procedure set forth in Sch.1 to the 1982 Act and that these amendments only cover skin piercing and tattooing licences.

Street traders

This is an optional activity and applies to persons selling or offering to sell goods and services in a public place, whether from a kiosk, vehicle, moveable stall or otherwise—the text of the relevant provisions is set out at pp.112–116 below. A s.39 licence is not required by persons selling newspapers, milk or coal; pedlars—provided that they are peddling at the time; persons participating in a public charitable collection; nor for any activity covered by another section of the Act or other legislation. Where a street trader sells food from a vehicle, kiosk or moveable stall then they are required to comply with the provisions of the Food Safety Act 1990. The origins of street traders' licences are to be found in byelaws made latterly under s.201 of the Local Government (Scotland) Act 1973, local legislation such as ss.405–408 of the Edinburgh Act, and Pt XXVIII of the 1957 Dundee Act.

Window cleaners

There was no general provision in respect of window cleaners requiring a licence prior to 1982 other than in local Acts, for example, s.409 of the 1967 Edinburgh Act, but the working party recommended that this be introduced as an optional activity under the 1982 Act:

> "This provision is in the interests of crime prevention—because window cleaners are unique amongst street traders in normally needing access to the inside and back of domestic premises. If a licensing authority resolves, in terms of section 9, to adopt the licensing provisions of this section then it may do either throughout the whole of its area, or only parts of it. During parliamentary discussion there was a generally expressed view that licensing of window cleaners was likely to be necessary only in major conurbations—and authorities will wish to consult the Chief Constable for their area before deciding whether or not to introduce licensing. In the Secretary of State's view, licensing should be introduced where there is firm evidence of abuses by unlicensed window cleaners and licensing can be justified on crime prevention grounds."[28]

[27] Civic Government (Scotland) Act 1982 (Licensing of Skin Piercing and Tattooing) Order 2006 (SSI 2006/43).

[28] SDD Circular 6/1983, Appendix A, paras 2.110–2.111.

Civic licensing standards officers

The 2015 Act introduced a new Pt 3A and s.45G of an officer responsible for certain duties relating to civic government licensing functions based on the model of such officers operating under the provisions of the Licensing Act 2005.

Appeals under the 1982 Act

A comprehensive appeals procedure is set out in Sch.1 to the Act. Paragraph 17 of the Schedule provides for the notification of decisions and the giving of reasons therefor, while para.18 provides for a relevant person (defined in para.17(4)) to take an appeal by way of summary application to the sheriff in relation to a grant or renewal of a licence, consent to a material change, the variation of conditions or the suspension of a licence. Section 50 of the Sheriff Courts (Scotland) Act 1907 provides that in a summary application the sheriff fixes a hearing and summarily disposes of the matter giving their decision in writing—see also the Act of Sederunt (Summary Applications, Statutory Applications and Appeals etc. Rules) 1999.[29] The sheriff may only uphold an appeal if the licensing authority, in reaching its decision, erred in law, based its decision on an incorrect material fact, acted contrary to natural justice or exercised its discretion in an unreasonable manner. The sheriff may hear evidence in the appeal and if they uphold the appeal then they may remit the case with reasons back to the licensing authority for its reconsideration to reverse or modify the decision of the licensing authority. On a point of law an appeal lies from the sheriff to the Court of Session. Thereafter appeal to the UK Supreme Court is possible subject to s.40 of the Court of Session Act 1988. Where there is no stateable ground of appeal and objectors persist therein, such objectors do not have any immunity against proceedings for abuse of process.[30]

Judicial review

In *West v Secretary of State for Scotland*,[31] Lord President Hope, delivering the opinion of the court, explained the principles under which applications for judicial review were properly made (at [412]–[413]):

> "1. The Court of Session has power, in the exercise of its supervisory jurisdiction, to regulate the process by which decisions are taken by any person or body to whom a jurisdiction, power or authority has been delegated or entrusted by statute, agreement or any other instrument.
>
> 2. The sole purpose for which the supervisory jurisdiction may be exercised is to ensure that the person or body does not exceed or abuse that jurisdiction, power or authority or fail to do what the jurisdiction, power or authority requires."

It was explained that the jurisdiction applies to the acts or decisions of any administrative body or person with similar function. Clearly it would apply to acts or decisions of a licensing authority under the 1982 Act. The Lord President went on (at [413]) to explain:

---

[29] Act of Sederunt (Summary Applications, Statutory Applications and Appeals etc. Rules) 1999 (SI 1999/929).

[30] *Asheden Ltd v Amber Entertainments Ltd*, 1996 S.C.L.R. 520.

[31] *West v Secretary of State for Scotland*, 1992 S.C. 385.

> "An excess or abuse of jurisdiction may involve stepping outside it, or failing to observe its limits, or departing from the rules of natural justice, or a failure to understand the law, or the taking into account of matters which ought not to have been taken into account. The categories of what may amount to an excess or abuse or jurisdiction are not closed, and they are capable of being adapted in accordance with the development of administrative law."

The categories are similar to some of the statutory grounds of appeal under para.18 of Sch.1 to the 1982 Act. Judicial review is not an appeal procedure and the court cannot review the decision or act complained of on its merits. Procedure is regulated by Ch.58 of the Act of Sederunt (Rules of the Court of Session 1994).[32] It is provided that judicial review does not apply to an application made or which could be made by way of appeal or review under and by virtue of any enactment (r.58.3(2)). This would include an appeal under para.18 of Sch.1 to the 1982 Act. Accordingly, a person who has a right of appeal under the statute must avail themselves of that remedy and cannot challenge the decision by judicial review.

In order to be entitled to bring proceedings for judicial review a person must demonstrate standing on the basis of sufficient interest in the matter. A broad approach should be taken. What amounts to sufficient interest will depend on the circumstances of each case. It will include persons directly affected by the decision in question and those having a reasonable concern in the matter.[33] In the light of this, previous cases applying the former test of title and interest including some noted hereafter must be viewed with caution. There must be a real issue and not an academic one.[34] In *Inverness Taxi Owners and Drivers Association v Highland Council*,[35] the petitioners sought to challenge the decision of the respondent authority to amalgamate the former district council areas into a single licensing area and to impose no limit on the number of taxi licences to be issued. The court held that the petitioners had no title to raise the petition. It is doubtful whether under the new test of standing, based on sufficient interest, the same result would now be reached. The 1982 Act did not confer an "amorphous right" to object to such decisions in the absence of a relevant application for a licence.[36] The availability of the statutory appeal procedure in relation to individual applications does not restrict the availability of judicial review.

---

[32] Act of Sederunt (Rules of the Court of Session 1994) (SI 1994/1443).

[33] *AXA General Insurance Co Ltd v Lord Advocate* [2011] UKSC 46; 2012 S.C. (UKSC) 122; *Walton v Scottish Ministers* [2012] UKSC 44; 2013 S.C. (UKSC) 67, per Lord Reed in both cases.

[34] *Scottish Old Peoples' Welfare Council, Petitioners*, 1987 S.L.T. 179, per Lord Clyde at 186.

[35] *Inverness Taxi Owners and Drivers Association v Highland Council*, 1999 S.L.T. 1316.

[36] See *PTOA Ltd v Renfrew DC*, 1997 S.L.T. 1112.

An obvious case for judicial review would be that of a refusal of a temporary licence where the right of appeal under para.18 of Sch.1 is excluded—see para.7(5) and *Gerry Cottle's Circus v City of Edinburgh DC*.[37] Another would be the decision to recall the suspension of a licence (para.10(6)). Other non-exhaustive examples include: a challenge to the terms or competency of a s.9 resolution; a challenge by a taxi operators' association to a licensing authority's decision to increase the number of taxi licences issued[38]; and a challenge to a deemed grant of licence in terms of s.3(4) of the 1982 Act by objectors to an application for grant of a licence.[39] In *Docherty v City of Edinburgh Council*,[40] it was held that certain guidance in a guidance note issued by the authority in respect of a policy relating to corporate applications for taxi licences was not a decision open to challenge by way of judicial review. Note that there still has to be a live and real issue involved (*Marco's Leisure Ltd v West Lothian Licensing Board*,[41] where judicial review of the refusal of an entertainment licence was sought, but the date of the proposed performance had passed). In *Spring Radio Cars Ltd v Glasgow City Council*,[42] the petitioners challenged the council's refusal under s.10(2) of the Act to grant their application to have a particular make and model of vehicle added to the list of approved vehicles for use as a private hire car on the basis that it had already been approved for use as a purpose built taxi cab. The challenge failed, the court holding, inter alia, that the purpose of the 1982 Act so far as relating to private hire cars and taxis was to make a clear distinction between the operation of the two types of vehicle and to seek to avoid confusion between the two in the public mind. The council's approach did not undermine or contravene that approach.

Human Rights Act 1998 and the European Convention

The Human Rights Act came into force on 2 October 2000 and incorporated the European Convention for the Protection of Human Rights and Fundamental Freedoms into domestic law. Under s.6(1) of the Act it is unlawful for a public authority to act in a way which is incompatible with a Convention right. That does not apply where as a result of primary legislation the authority could not have acted differently or the authority was acting to give effect to or enforce provisions of or under primary legislation which cannot be read or given effect to in a way which is compatible with Convention rights (s.6(2)). A licensing authority exercising its functions under the 1982 Act is a public authority and, therefore, subject to the provisions of s.6 of the Act. This means that it should carry out its functions in a manner and to achieve a result which is compatible with the Convention.[43]

So far as possible primary and subordinate legislation must be read and given effect to in a way which is compatible with Convention rights (s.3(1)). The House of Lords (and now the UK Supreme Court), the High Court of Justiciary and the Court of Session but not the sheriff court are empowered

[37] *Gerry Cottle's Circus v City of Edinburgh DC*, 1990 S.L.T. 235.

[38] *City Cabs (Edinburgh) Ltd v City of Edinburgh DC*, 1988 S.L.T. 184, cf. the *PTOA Ltd* and *Inverness Taxi Owners* cases; an appeal against a decision of the traffic commissioner in respect of taxi fares (*City of Glasgow DC v Traffic Commissioner for the Scottish Traffic Area*, 1992 S.L.T. 873; 1990 S.C.L.R. 737.

[39] *Monklands District Independent Taxi Owners Association v Monklands DC*, 1996 S.L.T. 182.

[40] *Docherty v City of Edinburgh Council*, 2000 S.C. 598; 2001 S.L.T. 291.

[41] *Marco's Leisure Ltd v West Lothian Licensing Board*, 1994 S.L.T. 129.

[42] *Spring Radio Cars Ltd v Glasgow City Council*, 2014 S.L.T 393.

[43] *Belfast City Council v Miss Behavin' Ltd* [2007] UKHL 19; [2007] 1 W.L.R. 1420, per Lord Neuberger at [87].

to make a declaration of incompatibility of such legislation with Convention rights. A person who claims that a public authority has acted or proposes to act in a way that is unlawful under s.6(1) may bring proceedings against the authority in the appropriate court or tribunal—to be determined by rules—or rely on the Convention right or rights in any legal proceedings but only if they are or would be a victim of the unlawful act (s.7(1)). For proceedings by way of judicial review only a victim has title and interest to sue (s.7(4)). Legal proceedings are defined (s.7(6)) and would include any appeal to the sheriff under para.18(1) of Sch.1 to the 1982 Act. The court may grant such relief or remedy in respect of an unlawful act as it considers just and appropriate (s.8(1)). That includes an award of damages by a court having power to do so. Accordingly, the sheriff hearing an appeal under para.18 by summary application procedure has no power. Time will reveal the extent of any impact which the Act and Convention rights will have on civic government licensing and procedure. It is proposed to consider briefly some of the provisions which, it may be anticipated, will have some effect.

Article 6(1) of the Convention provides:

> "In the determination of his civil rights and obligations ... everyone is entitled to a fair and public hearing ... by an independent and impartial tribunal established by law."

For art.6 to have application there must be a "contestation" or dispute over civil rights and obligations. This may relate to the existence of a right or its exercise. Proceedings in respect of the withdrawal of an alcohol licence have been held to be subject to art.6[44] as it involved the right to continue to run a restaurant business. Accordingly, an application for a licence or renewal of a licence under the 1982 Act or any determination as to whether to suspend such a licence would be subject to art.6, where there was any dispute on the matter in the form of objections, adverse representations and an adverse determination by the authority. The content of art.6(1) quoted above is already reflected to some extent in the principles of procedural fairness or natural justice developed by the courts. It has been said in the context of challenges to the impartiality of judges under the Convention that where there is any legitimate doubt or reasonable apprehension as to their impartiality they should withdraw.[45] In *Porter v Magill*,[46] the House of Lords held that in determining an issue of apparent bias the appropriate test was whether the fair minded and informed observer, having considered the relevant facts, would conclude that there was a real possibility that the tribunal was biased (Lord Hope at [103]). That test, which Lord Hope said was consistent with Scots law is likely to be adopted. If a tribunal proceeded to determine a case against that background that would, obviously, be a good ground of challenge.

Issues in relation to art.6 may arise where members of the authority are members of an organisation which has objected to an application for a licence or lodged a complaint leading to proceedings in which suspension is considered.[47] While the authority has, in terms of para.4(2) of Sch.1, a

---

44 *Tre Traktorer AB v Sweden* (1989) 13 E.H.R.R. 309.

45 *Hoekstra v HM Advocate (No.2)*, 2000 J.C. 391; *Hauschildt v Denmark* (1989) 12 E.H.R.R. 266; and *Mahmood v West Dunbartonshire Licensing Board*, 1998 S.C.L.R. 843, where a test of whether the circumstances would create in the mind of a reasonable man the suspicion that justice was not impartial was applied.

46 *Porter v Magill* [2001] UKHL 67; [2002] 2 A.C. 357.

47 *Blusins Ltd v City of Dundee Licensing Board*, 2001 S.L.T. (Sh Ct) 176.

discretion to give an applicant and objectors an opportunity to be heard before reaching a decision, it might be thought that where there is a clear factual dispute it would be appropriate, and, perhaps, necessary in order to secure a fair hearing, to allow evidence to be led.[48] Whether this would be the case would depend on the nature and extent of any dispute and its materiality to the determination. In *Catscratch Ltd v City of Glasgow Licensing Board (No.2)*,[49] Lord Johnston having held that there had been no unfairness in a licensing board hearing in respect of the ability of a licence holder to respond through their solicitor to an objector's assertions, stated that in what was a relatively routine application, the hearing of evidence would be unnecessarily cumbersome and was not essential to natural justice where the licence holder's position had been properly stated. Similar views in *JAE* were approved by the Inner House in *Chief Constable, Strathclyde Police v North Lanarkshire Licensing Board.* In these circumstances, it may be suggested that it is unlikely that in an ordinary case, it would be regarded as necessary that the authority should hear evidence. Furthermore, it must be stressed that art.6(1) simply requires a fair hearing. It does not prescribe the form of such a hearing or the procedure to be followed.

In *R (on the application of Alconbury Developments Ltd) v Secretary of State for the Environment, Transport and the Regions*,[50] which concerned, inter alia, a planning appeal called in by the Secretary of State, the House of Lords recognised that some administrative decisions affecting civil rights were taken by ministers answerable to elected bodies and that where such decisions were subject to review by a court regard had to be paid to the two stages of the process. Accordingly, although the initial decision maker may not be independent and impartial, the crucial question was whether there was sufficient judicial control to ensure determination by such a tribunal subsequently. It was also made clear that European Court jurisprudence did not require such control to involve a rehearing of an application by an appeal on the merits. The powers of the court in judicial review to review the legality of a decision or a decision and the procedure followed was sufficient to enforce compliance under art.6(1). Reference was made to the decision of the European Court in *Chapman v United Kingdom*[51] in which it was held that judicial review jurisdiction which enabled challenge on the ground that the decision was perverse, irrational, had no basis on the evidence or had been made with reference to irrelevant factors or without regard to relevant factors afforded adequate judicial control. It may be noted that in *Kaplan v United Kingdom*,[52] the Commission observed that to provide a full right of appeal on the merits of every administrative decision affecting private rights would be inconsistent with the approach of the courts in most of the contracting states. These decisions, particularly, *Alconbury*, provide strong pointers as to how the courts would deal with art.6 challenges relative to decisions by licensing authorities.

Under the 1982 Act an appeal may be upheld if the sheriff is satisfied that the authority have erred in law, based their decision on an incorrect material fact, acted contrary to natural justice or exercised their discretion in an unreasonable manner (para.18(7) of Sch.1 to the Act). Those provisions do

---

[48] *Hamid v City of Glasgow Licensing Board*, 2001 S.C. 398; 2001 S.L.T. 193; (2001) 18 S.L.L.P. 8; *JAE (Glasgow) Ltd v City of Glasgow District Licensing Board.*

[49] *Catscratch Ltd v City of Glasgow Licensing Board (No.2)*, 2002 S.L.T. 503.

[50] *R (on the application of Alconbury Developments Ltd) v Secretary of State for the Environment, Transport and the Regions* [2001] UKHL 23; [2001] 2 All E.R. 929.

[51] *Chapman v United Kingdom* (2001) 10 B.H.R.C. 48.

[52] *Kaplan v United Kingdom* (1980) 4 E.H.R.R. 64.

not, in terms, confer full power to review the decision of the authority on its merits (cf. s.44(2) of the Firearms Act 1968 as amended). In so far as *Alconbury* indicated that it would not be necessary for any appeal to provide a full review on the merits, it would appear that para.18(7) of Sch.1 would provide sufficient judicial control. In *Chapman*, a planning case, the complaint was that the High Court could not review a question of fact. It was held that in the specialised area of town planning law full review of the facts may not be required by art.6. Quaere whether licensing decisions would necessarily fall into the same category. For example, in hearings to consider the possible suspension of a licence following a complaint from, say, the chief constable, it may be said that the authority is acting in a quasi-judicial capacity. The problem may be thought to relate to the limited ground for interference with the decision in respect to factual matters. However, it is to be noted that in so far as an appeal may be allowed on the ground that it was "based on an incorrect material fact" that is potentially a wide ranging ground of review. It opens to challenge the factual basis of the decision. It enables the appellant to argue that the authority got it wrong on the facts as disclosed in any written reasons. The reference to the fact being "material" simply excludes as a ground of challenge errors in respect of trivial or immaterial facts, which is not a material restriction on the court's jurisdiction. One would not expect any court to overturn a decision on the ground of such an error. In any event, it is submitted that *Alconbury* and the other authorities mentioned support the contention that the para.18(7) grounds of appeal constitute sufficient judicial control.

Where, however, an issue may be thought to arise is in respect of the fact that unless one can bring the case within para.18(7) the sheriff would not be entitled to interfere with an opinion or judgment formed by the authority on the basis of factual material, where it was impossible to isolate any incorrect fact. Paragraph 5(3) of Sch.1 obliges an authority to refuse an application if they reach an "opinion" on certain matters. Even there, however, it would still be possible to argue that a decision had been reached on the basis of an incorrect material fact since that may cover an erroneous interference from otherwise correct facts.[53] Beyond that, *Alconbury* suggests that in relation to matters of opinion for the decision maker it is not appropriate that judicial control go as far as to permit review of such decisions. Ultimately, whether the court has full jurisdiction will turn on the specific grounds of challenge advanced in particular cases. In terms of disposal, the sheriff has wide powers given that they can reverse or modify the decision of the authority. It might be thought that there would be an issue as to whether in a case of bias or impropriety there was sufficient judicial control in that a remit would be back to the authority whose conduct was in issue, but it is submitted that the answer in such a case would be for the court to reverse the decision and determine the application itself. The same approach would fall to be taken where the means of challenge had to be by way of judicial review. The supervisory jurisdiction of the Court of Session is concerned to see that bodies subject to it do not exceed their jurisdiction. The merits of the decision are not within the scope of this jurisdiction. Nevertheless, in judicial review, it is possible to challenge a decision on the ground that there is no factual basis for a decision where one is required.

Another provision in the Convention which may have some impact on civic government licensing is art.1 of the First Protocol to the Convention. It provides:

---

[53] *Art Wells (t/a Corals) v Glasgow District Licensing Board*, 1988 S.C. 289.

> "Every natural or legal person is entitled to the peaceful enjoyment of his possessions. No one shall be deprived of his possessions except in the public interest and subject to the conditions provided for by law ... The preceding provisions shall not, however, in any way impair the right of a State to enforce such laws as it deems necessary to control the use of property in accordance with the general interest."

Possessions for the purposes of the article cover economic interests and assets. This includes the economic interest or goodwill associated with operating an activity or business under a licence—*Tre Traktorer*. While it is probably an academic issue, it is questionable whether a licence per se is a property right or possession protected by the article. In *R (on the application of Nicholds) v Security Industry Authority*,[54] a challenge was mounted by door supervisors to new licensing criteria prepared by the respondents which would have prevented them from obtaining the required licences. They argued that their existing "permissions" to work in the security industry were possessions for the purposes of art.1. The High Court was of the opinion that the permissions were not possessions and had no monetary value. They were neither marketable nor obtained at a market price and as such could not be possessions.[55] In *Malik* the permissions were not licences but it may be that the reasoning could be applied to licences issued under the 1982 Act which are not legally marketable although they are undoubtedly of economic value in the sense of enabling the holder to operate a business or provide a service. However, future income is not generally protected by this article.[56]

Article 1 only protects existing rights and certain legitimate expectations. It does not give any right to acquire something that one does not already hold.[57] Accordingly, it is unlikely that an unsuccessful applicant for a licence under the 1982 Act could invoke art.1 in any appeal. In *Belfast City Council v Miss Behavin' Ltd*[58] where an application for a sex shop licence had been refused by the respondent authority, two of the judges in the House of Lords expressed opinions that art.1 was engaged. Lord Hoffmann did so on the basis of an assumption (without deciding) doubtfully to the effect that a person who is denied the right to use their premises as a sex shop is thereby derived of their possessions (at [10]). However, both judges referred to *Iskcon*, which is to a different effect. Whilst any premises that are used for an activity to which a licence relates are, of course, a possession, it is to be stressed that without the necessary licence they cannot be used for the conduct of that activity. There is no existing right so to use the premises. It is the licensing regime which restricts that use.

Suspension of a licence to carry out a particular activity would, for example, involve an interference with the peaceful enjoyment of the licence holder's property and a temporary deprivation of the licence itself and may involve considerations as to whether or not such a course of action or interference is justified in terms of the qualifying provision at the end of

---

[54] *R (on the application of Nicholds) v Security Industry Authority* [2006] EWHC 1792 (Admin); [2007] 1 W.L.R. 2067.

[55] See also *R (on the application of Malik) v Waltham Forrest NHS Primary Care Trust* [2007] EWCA Civ 265; [2007] 1 W.L.R. 2092.

[56] *Malik*; *R (on the application of Countryside Alliance) v Attorney General* [2006] EWCA Civ 817; [2007] Q.B. 305.

[57] *Di Ciacca v Scottish Ministers*, 2003 S.L.T. 1031, see also *Iskcon v United Kingdom* (1994) 18 E.H.R.R. CD 133.

[58] *Belfast City Council v Miss Behavin' Ltd* [2007] UKHL 19; [2007] 1 W.L.R. 1420.

art.1. This could, of course, be an issue in the case of revocation. It may be observed that in *R (on the application of Royden) v Wirral MBC*,[59] the High Court held that a council's policy to remove a restriction on the number of licensed taxis did not involve any interference with a licensed driver's right to peaceful enjoyment of their possessions. The property in the licence was inherently liable to such deregulation. In *Gudmunsson v Iceland*[60] it was pointed out that the fact that a licence was ordinarily granted subject to conditions, breach of which could lead to withdrawal, meant that there could be no legitimate expectation that the holder would continue to hold their licence; in that regard it may be also noted that licences under the 1982 Act are of limited duration and that renewal may be refused if the grounds in para.5(3) of Sch.1 are made out.

Any interference must be lawful, and justified by the public interest. There must be a reasonable degree of proportionality between the means used and the ends sought to be achieved in order to ensure a fair balance between the interests of the individual and the community.[61] In the Supreme Court case of *Bank Mellat v HM Treasury (No.2)*,[62] Lord Reed set out what had to be determined to demonstrate proportionality. First, was the objective of the measure sufficiently important to justify the limitation of the protected right? Secondly, is the measure rationally connected to the objective? Thirdly, could a less intrusive measure have been adopted without unacceptably compromising achievement of the objective? Fourthly, balancing the severity of the measure's effect on the rights of the person to whom it applies against the importance of the objective, to the extent that the measure will contribute to its achievement, does the former outweigh the latter? Further the European Court of Human Rights has recognised that national authorities have a wide range of appreciation in implementing social policies and that their judgment as to the public interest will be respected unless it is manifestly without reasonable foundation (*James*). This point was reinforced in *Belfast City Council v Miss Behavin' Ltd*[63] where Lord Hoffmann referred to the wide margin of appreciation accorded to national governments that, in turn, was translated to broad powers of judgment granted to local authorities under statute such as in respect of licensing. He observed that if the authority exercises its powers rationally and in accordance with the statute it would require very unusual facts for it to amount to a disproportionate restriction on Convention rights (at [16]). It is worth noting that in the same case it was made clear that in addressing proportionality, the issue is not one of whether the authority has actively considered the terms of the relevant Convention provision but whether there has been a violation. If the authority has exercised its powers rationally and in accordance with the relevant statutory provisions and its decision could not be described as disproportionate, it would not matter if there had been no express reference to Convention rights in any reasons. Given the extent to which matters are left to the judgement of authorities, it cannot be assumed that a decision, say, to revoke a licence is disproportionate because the lesser sanction of suspension was available.

Paragraph 18(7) does not contain any ground of appeal on the ground that the decision is disproportionate. This may be contrasted with the position in respect of review hearing decisions under s.131(3)(b) and 131(4)

---

59 *R (on the application of Royden) v Wirral MBC* [2002] EWHC 2484 (Admin).
60 *Gudmunsson v Iceland* (1996) 21 E.H.H.R. CD89.
61 *James v United Kingdom* (1986) 8 E.H.R.R. 123.
62 *Bank Mellat v HM Treasury (No.2)* [2013] UKSC 39; [2014] A.C. 700.
63 *Belfast City Council v Miss Behavin' Ltd* [2007] UKHL 19; [2007] 1 W.L.R. 1420.

of the Licensing (Scotland) Act 2005. While, for the reasons referred to above, this issue is only likely to arise in respect of revocation and suspension, the absence of any reference to it in the Schedule does not mean that it is not relevant. There can be little doubt that if raised the court would be bound to address it.

Another article which may be relevant to civic government licensing is art.8(1) which provides that everyone has the "right to respect for private and family life and home". There is to be "no interference" with this right but, again, there is an exception where it is in accordance with the law and necessary in a democratic society in the interests of various considerations, including public safety, the economic well being of the country and the protection of the rights and freedoms of others. This may raise issues in relation to the effect of licensed activities on a person's home. At present, the authority must refuse an application where they are of the opinion that the premises are not suitable or convenient for the conduct of the activity having regard to the location and character of the premises and to public order, public safety and public nuisance considerations (para.5(3)(c)) of Sch.1). In relation to character and location, amenity to neighbouring properties is relevant.[64] Article 8(1) broadens the considerations to be taken into account. This may be limited in its practical effect in so far as the authority is able to demonstrate in their reasons that they have weighed up these considerations.

Activities licensed under other legislation

There are a number of other types of mainstream civic government licences which are not covered by the 1982 Act but the control of which are devolved to the Scottish Government and these areas of licensing are dealt with in full annotated form in this work. These fall into two groups, namely: (a) licences relating to cinemas; and (b) licences for the regulation and use of animals. These licensing provisions are largely found in statutes that apply to England and Wales and, with modifications, to Scotland as well, but it should be noted that only those parts of the relevant legislation which are applicable to Scotland have been reproduced in this edition (and omissions noted as such). Many of the provisions of these Acts are similar to those of the 1982 Act and although many of the annotations made in respect of the 1982 Act can also be applied to those Acts, care should be taken to make sure that the provisions are in fact comparable. The relevant licensing authorities, in all cases, are the councils constituted in terms of s.1 of the Local Government etc. (Scotland) Act 1994.

Cinema licences

The relevant legislation for cinemas licensed in Scotland is the Cinemas Act 1985, a statute that consolidated the previous Cinematographic Acts which dated back to Edwardian times. A licence is required for premises used for commercial film exhibitions and subsists for one year but certain premises and exhibitions are exempt from the licensing requirement. A cinema does not require a licence under s.41 of the 1982 Act.

---

64 *William Hill (Scotland) Ltd v Kyle and Carrick District Licensing Board*, 1991 S.L.T. 559.

Animal businesses licences

At the time of writing various forms of activities relating to the breeding, sale, housing and welfare of domestic and wild animals are subject to licensing by the local authority. The statutory basis for such licensing is to be found in a variety of Acts dating from 1925 to 1999 that, in the main, relate to the whole of the UK. Since devolution all animal licensing legislation is now the preserve of the Scottish Parliament. Following upon extensive consultation, the Animal Health and Welfare (Scotland) Act 2006 was enacted and in ss.26 and 27 of the Act a power was given to the Scottish Ministers to make secondary legislation for the eventual replacement or modification of the existing animal licensing regime—to date only the Licensing of Animal Dealers (Young Cats and Young Dogs) (Scotland) Regulations 2009[65] dealing with the dealing in young cats and dogs has been passed and given that the existing legislation already makes provision for the welfare of the animals concerned and that there are other areas of concern relating primarily to the welfare of farm animals the Acts annotated in this edition of this work are likely to remain in force for the foreseeable future.

Animal boarding establishments

The operator of a kennel or cattery where other people's animals are boarded (otherwise than ancillary to another business, e.g. the boarding of guests' pets by a hotel keeper) requires a licence under the provisions of the Animal Boarding Establishments Act 1963 and conditions can be placed thereon to ensure the safety and welfare of the boarded animals. A licence runs for one year. The origins of these provisions are not clear but a similar power was contained in an English local Act, the Huddersfield Corporation Act 1956.

Animal dealing (young cats and dogs) licence

With effect from 31 March 2009 a person dealing in young cats and young dogs (i.e. kittens and puppies less than 84 days old) requires an animal dealing licence in terms of the Licensing of Animal Dealers (Young Cats and Young Dogs) (Scotland) Regulations 2009, secondary legislation made under the enabling provisions in the 2006 Act (see above)—the text of the Regulations is set out at pp.401–412 below.

Dangerous wild animals

The keeper of a dangerous wild animal (defined in the Schedule to the Act) is required to have a licence issued in terms of the Dangerous Wild Animals Act 1976 by the local authority in whose area the animal is normally kept. Licences run for one year and there are provisions relating to safety and welfare. This Act provides for the usual enforcement powers plus a somewhat draconian power allowing for the seizure and disposal of animals without compensation.

Dog breeding and rearing establishments

The keeper of a place where dogs are bred or raised for commercial gain (defined as a place where two or more bitches are kept for the purposes of breeding for sale, or where a business of rearing puppies for sale is carried

---

[65] Licensing of Animal Dealers (Young Cats and Young Dogs) (Scotland) Regulations 2009 (SSI 2009/141).

on) requires a licence granted under the Breeding of Dogs Act 1973. Note, however, that the above definition applies only to Scotland as a result of amendments made by the Civic Government (Scotland) Act 1982 and that it is now substantially different to that applicable to England and Wales. A licence runs for one year and the licensing authority must have regard to the health, safety and well being of the dogs kept therein. A power of entry and inspection to unlicensed premises (similar to that for licensed premises in terms of the 1973 Act) is conferred by the Breeding of Dogs Act 1991. Further welfare provisions, designed to address public concern over "puppy farms" are to be found in the Breeding and Sale of Dogs (Welfare) Act 1999. The text of the 1973 licensing provisions is set out at pp.322–331, the 1991 Act at pp.383–385 and the 1999 Act at pp.386–391, while two statutory instruments relating to the latter Act are found at pp.398–399 (licensing records) and p.400 (identification tags) below.

Guard dog kennels

The Guard Dogs Act 1975 makes provision for a system of licensing for kennels at which guard dogs are kept. Although the majority of the sections of the Act were brought into force in February 1976 by the Guard Dogs Act (Commencement No.1) Order 1975[66] the licensing provisions were not and although they were originally provided in response to great public concern at the time it now seems unlikely that, given that the Government has no current plans to introduce this legislation, they will ever be brought into force. Accordingly, the guard dog kennel licensing provisions are not contained in this work.

Performing animals

A person who exhibits or trains any performing animal must be registered with the local authority for the area in which they reside in terms of the Performing Animals (Regulation) Act 1925. Registration must include specified details of the animals and the performance. If a person has no fixed abode then, in Scotland, registration must be made with one of four specified.

Pet shops

A person who carries on a business of selling animals as pets, whether in a shop or in private premises, requires a licence granted under the provisions of the Pet Animals Act 1951. "Animals" for the purposes of the Act do not include pedigree animals or the offspring of one's own pets. A licence runs for one calendar year. The Westminster Government is currently considering legislation for pet shops and animal fairs which will require shops and fairs and internet pet sales to adopt an approved code of practice, to give purchasers written advice of the welfare needs of the animals being sold and (for new entrants to the trade) a mandatory requirement to have a member of staff with suitable animal welfare qualifications and this legislation may be applied to Scotland by means of the Sewell motion procedure.

[66] Guard Dogs Act (Commencement No.1) Order 1975 (SI 1975/1767).

Riding establishments

The keeper of a business where horses are kept for either or both the purposes of letting them out for hire on payment or using them in return for payment for providing instruction in riding requires a licence granted in terms of the Riding Establishments Act 1964 as amended by the Riding Establishments Act 1970. Licences run for one year although provisional licences valid for up to six months can be granted under the 1970 Act. Stringent conditions relating to the health, welfare and safety of horses are attached to licences. The origin of such licensing dates from a statute of 1939 which only applied to England and Wales.

Zoos

Where animals are kept for exhibition to the public (other than in a circus or pet shop) and members of the public are admitted on more than seven days in the year, the operator of such premises must have a licence granted in terms of the Zoo Licensing Act 1981. No doubt because of changing public attitudes in relation to the welfare and exploitation of animals, the Act contains a very comprehensive licensing code. A licence runs for four or six years and the Secretary of State is given power to specify standards of zoo practice. Extensive amendments to the 1981 Act were made by the Zoo Licensing Act 1981 Amendment (Scotland) Regulations 2003 (SSI 2003/174) giving effect to the conservation measures that zoos are now required to make conform to art.3 of Directive 1999/22 relating to the keeping of wild animals in zoos [1999] OJ L94/24—these are all incorporated into the text of the principal Act and the regulations are accordingly not included.

Procedure for dealing with theatre, cinema and animal licence applications

The procedure for making applications, their consideration, the grant and refusal of licences, their duration, etc. is to be found in the individual statutes applicable to each type of licence and these are annotated below. Apart from performing animals there are no prescribed application forms and each licensing authority will issue its own (which failing applications should be in writing and give all necessary information as may be reasonably required). The licensing authority can (and in certain circumstances must) impose conditions upon any licence granted, subject of course, to the proviso that they must be reasonable, i.e. the *Wednesbury* test. It should, however, be noted that there is no requirement that a licensing authority need give reasons for its decision when notification of that decision is being given to the applicant (cf. the 1982 Act Sch.1 para.17)—this was highlighted in a case involving the Riding Establishments Act where the sheriff (AL Stewart) commented that

> "if there had been provision for me to require the first defenders to state reasons for their refusal of the pursuer's application, I should certainly have availed myself of it".[67]

Appeals

A right of appeal against the grant or refusal of any application, or the imposition of any conditions thereon, will normally lie open to the parties subject to the particular provisions of each Act. This right is sometimes said

[67] *McKay v Dundee City Council* unreported 22 February 1999 Dundee Sheriff Court.

to be exercisable by "a person aggrieved". In Scotland this is a familiar phrase in terms of planning legislation and, unless the contrary is indicated, denotes the applicant and any person with a genuine grievance who is prejudiced by the decision.[68] There is a difference between *feeling* aggrieved and *being* aggrieved, and to be entitled to object or appeal as "an aggrieved person" one has to demonstrate some external basis, such as a denial or affront to one's expectations or rights, for feeling upset: *Cumming* at 229. It may be relevant that such a person has failed to avail themselves of the right to object in terms of a particular statute; the nature of the grounds on which they claim to be aggrieved may also be relevant. In a licensing context "person aggrieved" has, in England, been held to include the licensing authority itself.[69]

Any right of appeal provided by the individual Acts lies to the sheriff having jurisdiction over the licensing authority or area. Unless there is provision to the contrary, appeals are made by way of summary application pursuant to the Summary Applications, Statutory Applications and Appeals etc. Rules 1999[70]—in *McKay v Dundee City Council* the sheriff, after highlighting what he perceived to be certain weaknesses in the Riding Establishments Acts comments that

> "unfortunately the 1964 Act appears to contain no provision granting the Court of Session power to make procedural rules in such appeals. Perhaps this is something to which the Scottish Parliament might direct its attention in due course".

The standard grounds of appeal derived from general principles of administrative law apply and conform to the grounds found in Sch.1 para.18 of the 1982 Act.

It should be noted that the fact that reasons for a decision need not be given do not necessarily give rise to an appeal on the basis of unreasonableness[71] that

> "the absence of reasons for a decision where there is no duty to give them cannot of itself provide any support for the suggested irrationality of the decision. The only significance of the absence of reasons is that if all other known facts and circumstances appear to point overwhelmingly in favour of a different decision, the decision-maker who has given no reasons cannot complain if the court draws the inference that he had no rational reason for his decision".

This passage was adopted in *McKay v Dundee City Council.*

With the exception of any Act which provides that the decision of the sheriff is final, e.g. s.18(6) of the Zoo Licensing Act 1981, there is a right of appeal on a point of law from the final judgment of the sheriff to the sheriff

[68] See, e.g. *Attorney General of the Gambia v N'Jie* [1961] A.C. 617 PC (West Africa); *Cumming v Secretary of State for Scotland*, 1993 S.L.T. 228; *MacKenzie's Trustees v Highland RC*, 1994 S.C. 693; 1995 S.L.T. 218; and *Lardner v Renfrewshire DC*, 1997 S.C. 104; 1997 S.L.T. 1027.

[69] *Cook v Southend BC* [1990] 2 W.L.R. 61 CA (Civ Div); and see also the case of *City and County of Swansea v Davies* unreported 16 June 2000 QBD, discussed in David M Daycock, "Who qualifies as a person aggrieved?" (2000) 43(Oct.) L.R. 9.

[70] Summary Applications, Statutory Applications and Appeals etc. Rules 1999 (SI 1999/929).

[71] See *Bass Taverns Ltd v Clydebank District Licensing Board*, 1995 S.L.T. 1275 at 1277F–1277G where the court approved of the opinion of Lord Keith of Kinkel in *R v Secretary of State for Trade and Industry Ex p. Lonhro Plc* [1989] 2 All E.R. 609 HL at 620f–620g.

principal and, provided that the sheriff principal certifies the cause as suitable for such an appeal, a further right of appeal applies from their final judgment to the Court of Session—Sheriff Courts (Scotland) Act 1971 s.38 as amended by s.18(4) of the Law Reform (Miscellaneous Provisions) Act 1985. There would not seem to be any reason in principle why such an appeal could not reach the Supreme Court. Note that there is no direct right of appeal from the sheriff to the Court of Session and that any appeal from the sheriff principal requires their certification. However, in *McKay v Dundee City Council*, Sheriff Principal Wheatley held that an appeal from the sheriff to the sheriff principal was incompetent where the original appeal before the sheriff had been on the basis that the licensing authority had not exercised their discretion in a reasonable manner. A further appeal was held to be incompetent since: (a) the jurisdiction of the sheriff was a statutory one in terms of the Riding Establishments Act 1964; (b) the sheriff was acting in an administrative capacity; and (c) that the reference in the Act to "sheriff" in the singular and not "Sheriff Court" was of significance. This decision, which seems to run contrary to that in *Rodenhurst v Chief Constable of Grampian Police*[72] (a case that was cited but not distinguished in *McKay*) will no doubt be regarded by practitioners as being somewhat controversial but it is understood that the parties do not intend to challenge it.

In certain cases, particularly where there are no apparent alternative statutory remedies to exhaust, a decision of the licensing authority may be challengeable by way of judicial review—see generally above.

Enforcement, offences and penalties under the 1982 Act and other legislation

In order to have an effective system of civic government licensing, it is necessary to have means of enforcing the various statutory provisions, and, to this end, each Act, to a greater or lesser degree, provides for policing by way of powers of entry and inspection, the power to suspend, vary, cancel or modify an existing licence, the power to refuse a new licence on the basis of an applicant not being a fit and proper person (e.g. where there have been persistent breaches of the terms of a licence as in *Stewart v Perth and Kinross DC*[73]), the creation of a number of specific statutory offences, and the power to disqualify a person from holding a licence for a contravention of the particular Act or an analogous one.

A common provision in all civic government licensing Acts is to give rights of entry and inspection into licensed and unlicensed premises and each Act specifies by whom such rights can be exercised. Rights of enforcement cannot be exercised by unauthorised persons, e.g. officers of a third party organisation.[74]

An expression that arises in the context of rights of entry and inspection is that of "at all reasonable times". What this constitutes will depend on the particular circumstances of a case, but relevant factors would include the normal opening hours of a business, the degree of urgency, the nature of a suspected breach, etc. An example of the use of this expression in an English licensing context is found in *Small v Bickley*.[75] Another common phrase is, "wilfully [or intentionally] obstructs or delays". This connotes mens rea and, in the case of "obstructs", an act of the same character as an assault, so that,

72 *Rodenhurst v Chief Constable of Grampian Police*, 1992 S.C. 1; 1992 S.L.T. 104.
73 *Stewart v Perth and Kinross DC*, 1996 G.W.D. 3-165.
74 *Spook Erection Ltd v City of Edinburgh DC*, 1995 S.L.T. (Sh Ct) 107.
75 *Small v Bickley* [1870] 40 J.P. 119.

accordingly, some physical feature is necessary[76]; in the case of "delays" there does not need to be any physical element so that, for instance, the deliberate giving of misleading or false information to delay an inspection might be enough.

Statutory offences are created in general for the carrying out of an unlicensed activity, where such a licence is required, e.g. s.7(1) of the 1982 Act; for contraventions of the terms and conditions of a licence, e.g. s.7(2); and for obstructing inspections, e.g. s.7(4). In addition, there are a large number of specific offences for contraventions of particular provisions of Acts, e.g. ss.21, 24, 26, 27, 34, 35 and 38 of the 1982 Act. All the offences are to be tried summarily in the sheriff court.

Certain of the statutory offences created impose strict liability, but the majority require mens rea. The usual criminal standard of proof is required, i.e. proof beyond reasonable doubt.

In many of the Acts there is a statutory defence if the accused can show that they exercised all due diligence to prevent the commission of the offence since in certain circumstances it would be clearly unfair for a licence holder to be vicariously liable for all the acts and omissions of their employees where they have, in fact, exercised due diligence in attempting to comply with the particular provisions. They could do so, e.g. by properly instructing and supervising their employees. "To exercise due diligence to prevent something from being done is to take all reasonable steps to prevent it."[77] The onus of proof of this and other statutory defences is upon the accused and the standard of proof is the normal civil standard, i.e. the balance of probabilities—see *HM Advocate v Mitchell (Ian Urquhart)*[78]; *McNeish v Stevenson*[79]; and, in relation to the effect of the European Convention on Human Rights see *Mclean v Carnegie*.[80] For a general discussion of vicarious liability for criminal offences see Gerald H Gordon's *Criminal Law of Scotland*.[81]

There are a number of other expressions which are commonly found in sections of civic government licensing statutes dealing with offences, and these are dealt with as follows:

(a) "Having reasonable grounds for suspecting" and "having reasonable grounds to believe": here the grounds for such suspicion or belief would have to be based upon reason and not merely a capricious whim or fancy. "Reason" can be derived from observation, an anonymous tip off, or any other source.[82]

---

76 *Curlett (James Hull) v McKechnie*, 1938 J.C. 176.

77 Per Lord Diplock in *Tesco Supermarkets Ltd v Nattrass* [1972] A.C. 153 HL at 203C; see also *Byrne v Tudhope*, 1983 S.C.C.R. 337; *Gorman v Cochrane* (1977) S.C.C.R. Supp. 183; *Alex Munro (Butchers) Ltd v Carmichael*, 1990 S.C.C.R. 225; *Ahmed v MacDonald*, 1994 G.W.D. 14-890; *Davenport v HM Advocate*, 1994 G.W.D. 40-2392; and *First Quench Retailing Ltd v McLeod*, 2001 S.L.T. 372 and *Feeney (Terrence) v Harvie* [2014] HCJAC 84; 2014 S.C.L. 677.

78 *HM Advocate v Mitchell (Ian Urquhart)*, 1951 J.C. 53.

79 *McNeish v Stevenson*, 1969 S.L.T. 229.

80 *Mclean v Carnegie* [2005] HCJAC 72; 2006 S.L.T. 40; [2005] L.L.R. 448.

81 Gerald H Gordon, *Criminal Law of Scotland*, edited by Michael GA Christie, 3rd edn (Edinburgh: SULI/W. Green, 2000), Vol.1, paras 8–38 onwards.

82 See, e.g. *McNicol v Peters*, 1969 S.L.T. 261; *Copeland v McPherson (Andrew)*, 1970 S.L.T. 87; and *Dryburgh (David Ronald) v Galt*, 1981 S.L.T. 151. Two English licensing examples are provided in *R v Banks (Frank Herbert)* [1916] 2 K.B. 621 and *R v Harrison (Douglas Percy)* [1938] 3 All E.R. 134.

(b) "Knowingly": denotes some form of personal knowledge on the part of the licensee—see *Noble (James Morrison) v Heatly*[83] (in which the English doctrine of delegation was expressly rejected); and not a wilful shutting of one's eyes to a fact.[84]

(c) The use of the expression "which he knows" implies that the person making the statement has actual knowledge of the facts being spoken to.

(d) "Knowingly or recklessly" implies, in addition to the above, a disregard for the consequences of such a statement, e.g. making a representation which at the time was untrue, but might have become true at a later date, and vice versa.[85] Leaving a blank space on an application form might constitute knowingly or recklessly making a false declaration.[86]

(e) "Recklessly" implies that a person making the statement has no regard to the truth or falsity of their statement, shuts their eyes to the fact or purposely abstains from enquiring into them.

Fines and penalties

All of the above statutory offences are punishable by fines (with, in certain cases, terms of imprisonment as an alternative). The levels of fines are expressed in two ways, namely: (a) fines on five specified standard scales; and (b) in other cases, in monetary terms. Originally all Acts specified monetary fines, but, in the case of most of these sums, these were replaced with references to standard scales of maximum fines by virtue of the amendments made in ss.289E–289G of the Criminal Procedure (Scotland) Act 1975 brought into effect by s.54 of the Criminal Justice Act 1982. The purpose of these amendments was to allow for the effects of inflation and allow variations to be made to reflect the current value of money. The current levels, by virtue of s.225 of the Criminal Procedure (Scotland) Act 1995, are as follows:

Level 1 £200; Level 2 £500; Level 3 £1,000; Level 4 £2,500; Level 5 £5,000.

Section 225(4) gives the Secretary of State power to substitute new amounts for the above sums by way of Order. In respect of certain penalties described as "exceptionally high maximum fines", e.g. the £20,000 maximum fines prescribed for operating an unlicensed sex shop (1982 Act Sch.2 para.19(3)), or for carrying out an unlicensed public entertainment or being in breach of public entertainment conditions (1982 Act s.7(1)(a), (2)(a)); these monetary fines remain in place, but, once again, they can be altered to take account of changes in the value of money, etc. by the Secretary of State by Order, made in terms of s.226 of the 1995 Act—in reality the level of fines has not been so increased.

The fact that a statutory offence has been committed does not mean that a common law offence cannot be charged. In *Normand v Robinson (Keith)*,[87] which involved the case of a "rave" in a derelict building. Averments specifying defects in the premises, which had a clear bearing on the safety of

[83] *Noble (James Morrison) v Heatly*, 1967 S.L.T. 26.

[84] See *Knox (Thomas) v Boyd*, 1941 J.C. 82; *Bunting v Procurator Fiscal, Glasgow* unreported 5 July 1997 Glasgow Sheriff Court; and *Kearney v Vannet*, 2000 G.W.D. 9-325.

[85] See *Herron v Lunn Poly (Scotland) Ltd*, 1972 S.L.T. (Sh Ct) 2.

[86] See *Buchmann v Normand*, 1994 S.C.C.R. 929.

[87] *Normand v Robinson (Keith)*, 1994 S.L.T. 558.

persons attending the event, were sufficient to give rise to a charge of culpable and reckless conduct against the organisers of the event, notwithstanding the fact that the rave would have required a licence under s.41 of the 1982 Act. The court, albeit with some hesitation, came to the view that the sheriff (who dismissed the common law complaint as being irrelevant) erred in law since the fact that the Crown might have brought charges under the 1982 Act was no reason for concluding that it might not also proceed under common law.

CIVIC GOVERNMENT ACT LICENSING PROVISIONS

General references in the annotations:

"the 1982 Act"—Civic Government (Scotland) Act 1982.
"the 1994 Act"—Local Government etc. (Scotland) Act 1994.
"2004 task group report"—report of Scottish Government task group set up to review the licensing provisions of the 1982 Act.
"the 2007 Act"—Custodial Sentences and Weapons (Scotland) Act 2007.
"the 2010 Act"—Criminal Justice and Licensing (Scotland) Act 2010.
'the 2015 Act"—Air Weapons and Licensing (Scotland) Act 2015.
"the 2015 report"—Scottish Government Local Government and Regeneration Report on 2015 Bill.

Civic Government (Scotland) Act 1982

ARRANGEMENT OF SECTIONS

PART I

LICENSING—GENERAL PROVISIONS

PART II

LICENSING AND REGULATION—PARTICULAR ACTIVITIES

Licensing and regulation of taxis and private hire cars

Licensing and regulation of second-hand dealers

Licensing and regulation of knife dealers

Licensing and regulation of metal dealers

Miscellaneous licences

Part III

Control of sex shops and sexual entertainment venues

Part 3A

Civic licensing standard officers

[Parts IV–VIII omitted.]

Part IX

Miscellaneous and general

SCHEDULES

Schedule 1

Licensing—further provisions as to the general system

SCHEDULE 2

CONTROL OF SEX SHOPS AND SEXUAL ENTERTAINMENT VENUES

[Schedules 2A, 3 and 4 omitted.]

An Act to make provision as regards Scotland for the licensing and regulation of certain activities; for the preservation of public order and safety and the prevention crime; for prohibiting the taking of and dealing with indecent photographs of children; as to certain powers of constables and others; as to lost and abandoned property and property in the possession of persons taken into police custody; as to the rights and duties of the owners and users of certain land, buildings and other structures; as to the making by local authorities of byelaws; and to enable them to make management rules applying to land or premises under their control; as to certain other functions of local authorities and their officers; as to the time when the Burgh Police (Scotland) Acts 1892 to 1911 and certain local statutory provisions cease to have effect; and for connected purposes.

[28th October 1982]

PART I

LICENSING—GENERAL PROVISIONS

Application of Parts I and II of this Act

1. This Part of this Act shall have effect with respect to the licensing of the activities for which licences are required under Part II of this Act.

DEFINITION
"licence": s.8.

GENERAL NOTE
Part I of the Act (ss.1–8, together with Sch.1) contains the uniform licensing code applicable in respect of all licences which are, or may be, required for the activities specified in Pt II of the Act and this section provides the necessary link between Pts I and II which would otherwise remain unconnected. Note that, despite the misapprehension of the Appeal Court in *Rees v Lees*, 1996 S.C.C.R. 601, Pts I and II have no application to Pt III (sex shop and sexual entertainment venues) licences.

Licensing authorities

2.—[1](1) For the administration of licensing in relation to the activities in connection with which licences are required under Part II of this Act there shall be a licensing authority for the area of each local authority.

[1](2) The licensing authority shall be the local authority within whose area the activity is, or is to be, carried on.

[1](3) Notwithstanding subsection (2) above, a local authority shall not be exempt from any requirement to have a licence or any other obligation under this Part or Part II of this Act and a licensing authority shall have power to entertain and dispose of an application by a local authority for a licence or in respect of a licence held by them.

NOTE
1. As amended by the Local Government etc. (Scotland) Act 1994 (c.39) Sch.13 para.129(2) (effective 1 April 1996).

DEFINITION
"licence": s.8.

GENERAL NOTE
This section identifies the licensing authority which is to grant and administer licences which are or may be necessary for the activities specified in Pt II of the Act.

Subsection (1)

The appropriate authority will normally be the council within whose jurisdiction the particular activity to be licensed takes place or is to take place, but there are certain exceptions to this general proposition in the case of immediately adjoining areas—see, e.g. ss.15, 16 and 38—and of itinerant metal dealers—see notes to s.32(2) below.

Subsection (3)

This subsection provides that a council, who themselves are responsible for a particular activity covered by Pt II of the Act, will require to obtain a licence for this activity from themselves qua licensing authority, e.g. a council-run boat hiring operation will require a s.38 licence in the same way as any similar privately run business. The application for such a licence would then be processed, and determined in accordance with all of the relevant provisions of the Act in the normal manner. Note, however, that the licensing authority do not require a market operators' licence—see notes to s.40(4) below.

Discharge of functions of licensing authorities

3.—[1](1) For the purpose of the discharge of their functions under this Part of this Act, every licensing authority must—

(a) consider each relevant application made to them within the period of 3 months beginning with the date on which the application was made, and

(b) subject to the following provisions of this section, reach a final decision on the application within the period of 6 months beginning with the end of 6 months beginning with the end of the 3 month period referred to in paragraph (a).

(2) On summary application by the licensing authority within the 6 month period referred to in subsection (1) above, the sheriff may, if it appears to him that there is good reason to do so, extend that period as he thinks fit.

(3) The applicant shall be entitled to be a party to a summary application under subsection (2) above.

[2,3](4) Where the licensing authority have failed to reach a final decision on the application before the expiry of—

(a) the 6 month period referred to in subsection (1) above, or

(b) such further period as the sheriff may have specified on application under subsection (2) above,

the licence shall be deemed to have been granted renewed or, as the case may be, varied on the date of such expiry.

[4](4A) A licence deemed to have been granted or renewed under subsection (4) is—

(a) in the grant of a temporary licence, to remain in force for the duration of the period sought in the application (up to a maximum period of 6 weeks), or

(b) in any other case, to remain in force for a period of one year.

[4](4B) A variation of the terms of a licence deemed to have been granted under subsection (4) is to have effect for the remaining period of the licence.

[4](4C) Subsections (4) and (4B) do not effect—

(a) the powers of revocation under section 7(6)(a),

(b) paragraph 8(5) of Schedule 1 (which relates to renewals of existing licences),

(c) the powers of variation under paragraph 10 of that Schedule, or

(d) the powers of suspension and revocation under paragraphs 11 and 12 of that Schedule.

[5](5A) The deemed grant, renewal or variation of the terms of a licence under subsection (4) is, for the purposes of Schedule 1, to be treated as a decision of the licensing authority to grant, renew or vary the terms of a licence.

[5](5B) For the purposes of this section, a "relevant application" is an application under paragraphs 1, 7 or 10 of Schedule 1.

NOTES

1. As substituted by the Air Weapons and Licensing (Scotland) Act 2015 (asp 10) Pt 3 s.77(2)(a) (date yet to be appointed).

2. As amended by the Air Weapons and Licensing (Scotland) Act 2015 (asp 10) Pt 3 s.77(2)(b) (date yet to be appointed).

3. As amended by the Criminal Justice and Licensing (Scotland) Act 2010 (asp 13) Pt 8 s.172(2) (effective 28 March 2011).

4. As inserted by the Air Weapons and Licensing (Scotland) Act 2015 (asp 10) Pt 3 s.77(2)(c) (date yet to be appointed).

5. Subsections (5A) and (5B) substituted for subs.(5) by the Air Weapons and Licensing (Scotland) Act 2015 (asp 10) Pt 3 s.77(2)(d) (date yet to be appointed).

DEFINITIONS
"licence": s.8.
"licensing authority": s.2.

GENERAL NOTE

Section 3 deals with the discharge by the licensing authorities of their functions, and imposes statutory time limits upon the processing and determining of applications. It also provides in certain circumstances for the deemed grant of a licence when these time limits have not been adhered to. For a practical example of the problems arising out of statutory time limits and of the interrelation of the various *Monklands* cases cited below, see Andrew M Hajducki, "Taxi! A licensing saga from the Monklands", 1996 S.L.T. (News) 85. Section 3 was amended by s.172(2) of the 2010 Act. Various amendments have been made to the section by the 2015 Act and are intended, according to the Explanatory Notes to the Bill that resulted in the 2015 Act, "to modernise the language to provide greater clarity of the requirement to consider an application within three months and then reach a final decision within a further six months".

Subsection (1)

Applications are "made" on the date upon which the written application for the licence in terms of Sch.1 para.1 is received by the licensing authority—i.e. time will run from the date of receipt by the authority and not the date upon which the application form was completed or signed. A final decision is reached when the licensing authority are satisfied in relation to any conditions to be imposed and grant the licence and not, for instance, the date upon which the licence document is delivered to the applicant in terms of Sch.1 para.5(7). In *City of Edinburgh Council v Salteri*, 2007 S.C. 463 the Inner House held that the critical time limit was not the three-month one but the six-month period within which a final decision must be taken. There was no penalty for failure to consider within the former period. Once the decision has been made, the authority are *functus quoad* the grant of the licence, and they cannot purport thereafter to hold a second hearing to determine the application in respect of which they have already granted the licence, if they proceeded originally upon a factual error, or even if the applicant lied to them. This might, of course, provide grounds for subsequently suspending or revoking the licence—see, e.g. *Thomson v City of Glasgow District Council*, 1992 S.L.T. 805, where the licensing authority sought unsuccessfully to invoke their general subsidiary powers under s.69(1) of the Local Government (Scotland) Act 1973 to allow them to arrange a rehearing in circumstances where a taxi licence had been granted but not yet issued. In the case of licences for skin piercing and tattooing, the period allowed of the reaching of a final decision is 12 months, not six—see Schedule para.2(a) to the Civic Government (Scotland) Act 1982 (Licensing of Skin Piercing and Tattooing) Order 2006 (SSI 2006/43) below. An appeal to the sheriff principal and thereafter to the Court of Session from a sheriff's refusal to extend the period is competent—*City of Edinburgh Council v Salteri*, 2007 S.C. 463.

Subsection (2)

The discretionary power of the sheriff to grant an extension is limited to situations where a "good reason" exists for so doing. The authority must put forward a reason which can be described as "good" and persuade the sheriff to exercise his discretion to grant the application. The entitlement to seek an extension should be regarded as "a relief to be exercised in exceptional circumstances"—*Salteri*, 2007 S.C. 463 at [13] and [14]. In *City of Edinburgh Council v 3 Maxblack LLP*, 2005 S.L.T. (Sh Ct) 86, it was held this covered the situation where the licensing authority were unable to decide an application within the six-month period because they were awaiting a consultant's survey into the question of unmet demand for the purposes of s.10(3) of the Act in terms of which an authority may refuse the application on the ground that there was no significant unmet demand for the services of taxis. However, in the *Salteri* case the Inner House held that the "self-imposed burden" of undertaking such a survey and consulting upon its results, whatever procedural problems this gave rise to, could not amount to a "good reason" for not determining an application within six months. It would thus appear that it is only in unusual circumstances where the inability to decide within the statutory period is not due to any fault (in its widest sense) on the part of the authority that an extension should be granted. This might cover an inability to complete necessary investigations under para.4 of Sch.1. While a relevant consideration may be that to refuse an extension of time could result in the denial to objectors of any recourse or opportunity to make their representations (see

Monklands District Council v Bennett unreported 8 December 1994 Airdrie Sheriff Court), it would appear from the decision in *Salteri* that attention is directed towards the sufficiency of the reason put forward by the authority for the inability to timeously determine the application.

An application for an extension is made on the day when it is lodged with the sheriff clerk or a member of their staff (*Monklands DC v McGhie*, 1995 S.L.T. (Sh Ct) 52; *Fife Council v Watters* unreported 27 February 2006 Kirkcaldy Sheriff Court). However in *Cunninghame DC v Payne*, 1988 S.L.T. (Sh Ct) 21, where an application for an extension was made within the six-month period, but the sheriff's interlocutor granting the same was pronounced after the expiry of that period, it was held that the effective date for the purpose of calculating whether the application had been made timeously was the date of citation of the summary application and not the date upon which the application was eventually granted or refused. It is submitted that the view in the first-mentioned cases accords with the wording of the subsection and common sense and is to be preferred. Nothing in the wording of this subsection excludes the general rule in computation of time excluding the day from which time runs. There is no discretion to extend the time period within which an application can be made as the timetable is not directory but mandatory and failure to adhere to it results in a deemed grant of the licence—*Monklands DC v McGhee*, 1995 S.L.T. (Sh Ct) 52. In the case of skin piercing and tattooing licences the period allowed of the reaching of a final decision is 12 months, not six—see note to subs.(1) above.

Subsection (3)

This provision exists because the applicant may, of course, have a direct interest in the failure of a summary application to the sheriff made by the licensing authority, given the implications of subs.(4)—see, e.g. *Cunninghame DC v Payne*, 1988 S.L.T. (Sh Ct) 21.

Subsection (4)

Such a licence would be identical to one obtained in the conventional manner subject to mandatory and standard licence conditions in terms of ss.3A and 3B and with a duration limited to one year, as opposed to the normal three-year period provided for in Sch.1 para.8(2). Deemed licences were formerly granted "unconditionally" until the 2010 Act removed this word following the recommendation of the 2004 Report of the Task Force which recognised that the effect of granting an unconditional deemed licence was that other traders who were subject to attached conditions and who were granted licences in the normal manner "were trading at a disadvantage". Where another application is lodged by a person during the year that a deemed licence is in force, the latter will continue in force until a final decision on the second application has been reached—see Sch.1 para.8(5). For the meaning of "final decision" see note to subs.(1) above. Note that the terms of this subsection are clear and unambiguous and that they cannot be read subject to any qualification—*Monklands District Independent Taxi Owners Association v Monklands DC (No.2)*, 1997 S.L.T. 7. In the case of licenses for skin piercing and tattooing the period allowed of the reaching of a final decision is 12 months, not six—see note to subs.(1) above.

Subsection (4A)

This provides that a deemed grant or renewal shall in the case of a temporary licence remain in force for the period sought up to a maximum of six weeks or in the case of all other licences for a period of one year.

Subsection (4B)

A variation shall only have effect for the remaining duration of the licence. This subsection was added as a clarification that a licence granted under these provisions is not immune to the separate powers of a licensing authority to vary, suspend or revoke licences.

Subsection (4C)

Deemed grants or renewals or variations are subject to the same powers of revocation, objections and representations, variation and suspension as all other licences.

Subsections (5A) and (5B)

These subsections provided that once a licence is deemed to have been granted, the obligation is upon the licensing authority to issue and deliver it to the applicant. For an unsuccessful attempt by objectors to interdict the licensing authority from issuing deemed licences, see *Monklands District Independent Taxi Owners Association v Monklands DC*, 1996 S.L.T. 182; 1995 S.C.L.R. 547.

Mandatory licence conditions

[1]**3A.**—(1) The Scottish Ministers may by order made by statutory instrument prescribe conditions conditions to which licences granted by licensing authorities under this Act are to be subject.

(2) Different conditions may be prescribed under subsection (1)—

(a) in respect of different licences, or different types of licence,

(b) otherwise for different purposes, circumstances or cases.

(3) No order may be made under subsection (1) unless a draft of the statutory instrument containing the order has been laid before and approved by resolution of the Scottish Parliament.

(4) Subsection (1) does not affect any power of the Scottish Ministers under this Act or any other enactment to prescribe—

(a) to which licences granted by licensing authorities under this Act are to be subject, or

(b) to be imposed by licensing authorities in granting or renewing licences under this Act.

(5) The following conditions are referred to in this Part and Part 2 of this Act as "mandatory conditions"—

(a) conditions prescribed under subsection (1),

(b) conditions prescribed under any power referred to in subsection (4), and

(c) conditions imposed, or required to be imposed, by any provision of this Part or Part 2 of this Act.

(6) In this section and section 3B, references to licences granted by licensing authorities include references to—

(a) licences renewed by licensing authorities, and

(b) licences deemed by virtue of section 3(4) to be granted or renewed by licensing authorities.

NOTE

1. As inserted by the Criminal Justice and Licensing (Scotland) Act 2010 (asp 13) Pt 8 s.172(3) (effective 28 March 2011).

DEFINITIONS

"licence": s.8.
"licensing authority": s.2.

GENERAL NOTE

The 2004 Task Force report concluded that the imposition of standard as opposed to individualised conditions to a deemed grant "would act as an incentive to licensing authorities to ensure that applications were processed quickly and efficiently". This section allows by statutory instrument the imposition of mandatory conditions to be applied to both new, renewed and deemed grants and allows in s.3A(2) these mandatory conditions to be tailored for different types of licence and different circumstances.

Standard licence conditions

[1]**3B.**—(1) A licensing authority may determine conditions to which licences granted by them under this Act are to be subject.

(2) Conditions determined under subsection (1) are referred to in this Part and Part 2 as "standard conditions".

(3) Different conditions may be determined under subsection (1)—

(a) in respect of different licences, or different types of licence,

(b) otherwise for different purposes, circumstances or cases.

(4) A licensing authority must publish, in such manner as they think appropriate, any standard conditions determined by them.

(5) Standard conditions shall have no effect—

(a) unless they are published, and

(b) so far as they are inconsistent with any mandatory conditions.

(6) Subsection (1) is subject to paragraph 5(1A)(a) of Schedule 1 to this Act.

NOTE

1. As inserted by the Criminal Justice and Licensing (Scotland) Act 2010 (asp 13) Pt 8 s.172(3) (effective 28 March 2011).

DEFINITIONS

"licence": s.8.

"licensing authority": s.2.

GENERAL NOTE

This section enables licensing authorities to introduce standard licensing conditions in respect of all or individual licensed activities and these standard conditions will also apply to licences deemed to have been granted to renewed licences and those granted under s.3(4)(a). In effect many licensing authorities already have "standard conditions" for certain categories of licence but s.3B(4) requires them to be published in such manner "as they think appropriate". The standard conditions can be disapplied by the local authority at its discretion.

Further provisions as to licensing

4. Schedule 1 to this Act (which contains further provisions as to licensing and regulation in relation to the activities in connection with which licences are required under Part II of this Act) shall have effect.

DEFINITION

"licence": s.8.

GENERAL NOTE

The detailed further provisions relating to licensing required for activities covered by Pt II are contained in Sch.1 of the Act, and this section acts as a link to bring the Schedule into effect.

Rights of entry and inspection

5.—[1,2](1) Without prejudice to any other provision of this Act, an authorised officer of the licensing authority, an authorised civilian employee or a constable may, for the purposes specified in subsection (2) below, at any reasonable time—

(a) enter and inspect any premises, vehicle of vessel used or to be used for an activity in relation to which a licence is in force or has been applied for under this Act;

(b) require production of and inspect any equipment, plant, apparatus or stock-in-trade which is or is to be kept or used in connection with any such activity;

(c) require production of and inspect any records or other documents required by or under this Part or Part II of this Act to be kept by the holder of the licence and take copies of or extracts from any such record or document.

(2) The purposes referred to in subsection (1) above are—

(a) where a licence is in force—

(i) seeing whether the terms of the licence are being complied with and, if they are not, obtaining information in respect of such non-compliance;

[3](ii) obtaining information relevant to the question whether the terms of the licence should be varied under paragraph 10 of Schedule 1 to this Act or whether the licence should be renewed or, under paragraph 11 or 12 of that Schedule, suspended or revoked; or

(b) where the grant of a licence has been applied for, obtaining information relevant to the question whether the application should be granted.

(3) Any person who—

[1,2](a) being a person for the time being in charge of any premises, vehicle or vessel, fails without reasonable excuse to permit a constable, an authorised civilian employee or an authorised officer of a licensing authority who, in pursuance of subsection (1) above, demands to do so to enter or inspect the premises, vehicle or vessel or obstructs the entry thereto of a constable or such an employee or officer, in pursuance of that subsection;

[1,2](b) being a person in respect of whom powers are exercised under subsection (1) above, on being required under that subsection to do so by a constable, authorised civilian employee or an authorised officer of the licensing authority fails without reasonable excuse to produce any equipment, plant, apparatus or stock-in-trade or to permit a constable or such an employee or officer, in pursuance of that subsection, to inspect any equipment, plant, apparatus or stock-in-trade;

[1,2](c) being a holder of a licence, on being required by a constable, authorised civilian employee or an authorised officer of the licensing authority in pursuance of subsection (1) above, to produce any records or other document required by or under this Part or Part II of this Act to be kept by the holder of a licence, fails without reasonable excuse to produce them shall be guilty of an offence and liable, on summary conviction, to a fine not exceeding level 3 on the standard scale.

[2](4) An authorised officer of a licensing authority, an authorised civilian employee or a constable may require any person who the officer, employee or constable has reasonable ground to believe is carrying on an activity which requires to be licensed to produce his licence within 5 days of being required to do so.

[3](5) Any person who, having been required under subsection (4) above to produce a licence, fails without reasonable excuse to do so within the period of 5 days specified in that subsection shall be guilty of an offence and liable, on summary conviction, to a fine not exceeding level 1 on the standard scale.

[1,2](6) An authorised officer of a licensing authority or authorised civilian employee shall not be entitled to exercise the powers which he may exercise under subsection (1) or (4) above until he has produced his authorisation—

(a) in relation to the exercise of powers under subsection (1)(a) above, to the person for the time being in charge of the premises, vehicle or vessel; and

(b) in any other case, to the person in respect of whom the powers are to be exercised.

(7) A constable who is not in uniform shall not be entitled to exercise the powers which he may exercise under subsection (1) or (4) above until he has produced his identification—

(a) in relation to the exercise of powers under subsection (1)(a) above, to the person for the time being in charge of the premises, vehicle or vessel; and

(b) in any other case, to the person in respect of whom the powers are to be exercised.

NOTES

1. As amended by the Fire (Scotland) Act 2005 (Consequential Modifications and Savings) Order 2006 (SSI 2006/475) Sch.2 para.1 (effective 1 October 2006).

2. As amended by the Criminal Justice and Licensing (Scotland) Act 2010 (asp 13) Pt 8 s.173 (effective 13 December 2010).

3. As amended by the Air Weapons and Licensing (Scotland) Act 2015 (asp 10) Pt 3 s.78 (date yet to be appointed).

DEFINITIONS

"authorised civilian employee": s.8.
"licence": s.8.
"licensing authority": s.2(2).
"premises": s.8.
"standard scale": see Introduction p.32 above.
"vessel": s.133.

GENERAL NOTE

This section empowers the police, an authorised civilian employee and authorised officers of licensing and fire authorities to enter and inspect premises, vehicles or vessels of a licence holder or applicant for a licence. In addition, this section gives the officers a power to require the production of certain equipment and records from those persons, and to require them to produce a licence within a specified period, and a variety of summary statutory offences are created in relation thereto. All of these powers were introduced with the primary objective of ensuring that the licensing provisions of the 1982 Act are properly complied with, and to avoid any evasion thereof. Section 5(1) and 5(3) were amended by the Fire (Scotland) Act 2005 and references to an authorised civilian employee were added by s.173 of the 2010 Act.

Subsection (1)

An "authorised officer" is a person who has been authorised in writing by the licensing authority to exercise either generally or specifically, the powers contained within this section and who is at the material time acting within the scope of their employment. A "reasonable time" would be determined by a subjective test depending on the nature of the activity, the place at which it is carried out and the circumstances of the applicant (see Introduction, p.30 above). Provided that the powers are thus exercised for the purposes specified in subs.(2), and the authorisation or identification required by s.5(6) and (7) is produced, the authorised officers would appear to have very wide powers indeed. Note, however, that no powers are given to any other persons, e.g. inspectors of the Office of Fair Trading: see *Spook Erections Ltd v City of Edinburgh DC*, 1995 S.L.T. (Sh Ct) 107.

Subsection (2)

This subsection provides a limitation in respect of the purposes for which the powers are granted, and these powers cannot be exercised for any other purpose.

Subsection (3)

For "obstructs" see Introduction pp.30–31 above.

Subsection (6)

This subsection requires the authorised officer or employee to produce a written authorisation to the person in charge or the licence holder, before they exercises their powers under s.5 and until this is produced they are not entitled to exercise the powers.

Subsection (7)

Likewise, a plain-clothes police officer must produce their warrant card (i.e. their formal identification document) before exercising their powers under s.5.

Powers of entry to and search of unlicensed premises

6.—(1) If a justice of the peace or sheriff is satisfied by evidence on oath that there is reasonable ground for suspecting that—

[1](a) an activity in respect of which a licence under this Act (other than a knife dealer's licence) is required is being carried on in any premises, vehicle, or vessel; and

(b) no such licence is in force,

he may grant a warrant authorising any constable to enter and search the premises, vehicle or vessel specified in the warrant.

(2) A constable may use reasonable force in executing a warrant granted under subsection (1) above.

(3) A constable who is not in uniform shall produce his identification if required to do so by any person in or upon any premises, vehicle or vessel which the constable is about to enter, is entering or has entered under the powers conferred under subsection (1) above, and if he has been so required to produce his identification, he shall not be entitled to enter or search the premises, vehicle or vessel or, as the case may be, remain there or continue to search the premises, vehicle or vessel until he has produced it.

(4) Any person who fails without reasonable excuse to permit a constable in pursuance of a warrant granted under this section to enter and search any premises, vehicle or vessel or who obstructs the entry thereto or search thereof by a constable shall be guilty of an offence and liable, on summary conviction, to a fine not exceeding level 3 on the standard scale.

NOTE

1. As amended by the Custodial Sentences and Weapons (Scotland) Act 2007 (asp 17) Pt 3 s.59 (effective 1 June 2010).

DEFINITIONS

"licence": s.8.
"premises": s.8.
"standard scale": see Introduction p.39 above.
"vessel": s.133.

GENERAL NOTE

Section 6 provides for powers of entry to, and search of premises where activities are being carried on which require a licence, but in respect of which a licence is not in force. Although the purpose of this section is similar to that of s.5, note that the powers are given only to constables in possession of a warrant, and that reasonable force may be used in the exercise of that warrant.

Subsection (1)

The reasonable grounds must result from the justice or sheriff being satisfied as a result of evidence given on oath—see Introduction above. In the case of licences for skin piercing and tattooing, this subsection is amended so as to insert the words "(or an authorised officer of the licensing authority)" after the word "constable"—see para.3 of the Civic Government (Scotland) Act 1982 (Licensing of Skin Piercing and Tattooing) Order 2006 (SSI 2006/43) below.

Subsection (2)

This subsection was amended in the case of licences for skin piercing and tattooing in the same manner as subs.(1) above.

Subsection (3)

See note to subs.(1) above relating to skin piercing and tattooing.

Subsection (4)

See note to subs.(1) above relating to skin piercing and tattooing.

Offences, etc.

7.—[1](A1) Any person who without reasonable excuse does anything for which a licence is required under Section 27A without having such a licence is guilty of an offence and liable—

(a) on summary conviction for imprisonment for a term not exceeding 12 months or a fine not exceeding the statutory maximum or both;

(b) on conviction on indictment to imprisonment for a term not exceeding 2 years or a fine or both.

[1](1) Any person who without reasonable excuse does anything for which a licence is required under any provision of Part II of this Act other than section 27A without having such a licence shall be guilty of an offence and liable, on summary conviction,

[2](a) in the case where the licence so required is a metal dealer's licence, an itinerant metal dealer's licence or a public entertainment licence, to a fine not exceeding £20,000 or to imprisonment for a term not exceeding months or to both; and

(b) in any other case to a fine not exceeding level 5 on the standard scale.

(2) If a condition attached to a licence is not complied with, the holder of the licence shall, subject to subsection (3) below, be guilty of an offence and liable, on summary conviction,—

[1](a) in the case where the licence is a public entertainment licence and the condition is attached under section 41(3)(b) of this Act, to such fine or imprisonment as is mentioned in subsection (1)(a) above (or to both);

[1,2](aa) in a case where the licence is a knife dealer's licence, to fine not exceeding level 5 on the standard scale;

[2](ab) in the case where the licence is a metal dealer's licence or an itinerant metal dealer's licence, to such fine or imprisonment as is mentioned in subsection (1)(a) (or to both), and

[1](b) in any other case to a fine not exceeding level 3 on the standard scale.

(3) It shall be a defence for a person charged with an offence under subsection (2) above to prove that he used all due diligence to prevent the commission of the offence.

[1](4) Any person who, in making an application under this Part of this Act to the licensing authority, makes any statement which he knows to be false

or recklessly makes any statement which is false in a material particular shall be guilty of an offence and liable, on summary conviction, to a fine not exceeding level 4 on the standard scale.

(5) Any person who, being the holder of a licence—

(a) fails without reasonable excuse to notify the licensing authority of a material change of circumstances in accordance with paragraph 9(1) of Schedule 1 to this Act;

(b) without reasonable excuse makes or causes or permits to be made any material change in any premises, vehicle vessel in contravention of paragraph 9(2) of Schedule 1 to this Act;

(c) fails without reasonable excuse to deliver his licence to the licensing authority in accordance with paragraph 13(2) of Schedule 1 to this Act,

shall be guilty of an offence and liable, on summary conviction, to a fine not exceeding, in the case of an offence under paragraph (a) or (b) above, level 3 on the standard scale and in the case of an offence under paragraph (c) above, level 1 on the standard scale.

(6) Where a holder of a licence is convicted of an offence under section 5 (other than subsection (5) thereof), 6 or this section, the court by which he is convicted may, in addition to any other penalty which the court may impose, make an order in accordance with one or both of the following paragraphs—

(a) that the licence shall be revoked;

(b) that the holder of the licence shall be disqualified from holding a licence for a period not exceeding 5 years.

(7) Where the holder of a licence is convicted of an offence under this section, an extract of such conviction and sentence (if any) shall, within 6 days after the date of the conviction, be transmitted by the clerk of the court to the licensing authority which granted the licence.

(8) A person may appeal against an order under subsection (6) above in the same manner as against sentence and the court which made the order may, pending the appeal, suspend the effect of the order.

(9) A person may, at any time after the expiry of the first year of his disqualification under subsection (6) above, apply to the court which ordered the disqualification to remove it, and, on such application, the court may by order remove the disqualification as from such date as may be specified in the order or refuse the application, and, in either case, may order the applicant to pay the whole or any part of the expenses of such application.

(10) Where an offence is alleged to have been committed under subsection (2) above by an employee or agent named in a licence, proceedings in respect of that offence may be instituted against the joint licence holder who is the employer of the employee or principal of the agent, whether or not proceedings have been instituted against the employee or agent.

NOTES

1. As amended by the Custodial Sentences and Weapons (Scotland) Act 2007 (asp 17) Pt 3 s.59 (effective 1 June 2010).

2. As amended by the Air Weapons and Licensing (Scotland) Act 2015 (asp 10) Pt 3 s.66 (effective 1 September 2016).

DEFINITIONS

"licence": s.8.

"standard scale": see Introduction p.32 above.

GENERAL NOTE

This section creates several statutory summary offences which arise from the failure to observe the provisions and requirements of Pts I and II of the Act (including Sch.1), and provides the penalties applicable on conviction. The offences relate to the failure to have an appropriate licence, failure to observe the conditions of a licence already granted and certain other matters. Apart from the financial penalties, the court may also order the revocation of an existing licence or the disqualification of an existing licence holder. With the exception of subs.(3), the standard of proof is that normally required in criminal trial procedure, i.e. beyond a reasonable doubt—e.g. *Heatherstone v Wilson*, 1993 G.W.D. 23-1464, where the High Court held that findings that the accused had an out of date licence, that on the date libelled he was not the holder of a current licence and that he was serving customers, were sufficient to establish that he was in contravention of the section in relation to unlicensed street trading. Since licence holders can be individuals, partners or bodies corporate, the offences created impose liability on the holder of the licence, a joint licence holder (s.7(10)), and the directors of a body corporate and office holders of unincorporated associations—see notes to s.130 below and for a general discussion of the application of vicarious liability see Gerald H Gordon, *Criminal Law of Scotland*, edited by Michael GA Christie, 3rd edn (Edinburgh: SULI/W. Green, 2000), Vol.1, paras 8–38 onwards. Note that this section does not apply to Pt III of the Act (i.e. to sex shops) for which separate statutory offences are created. Notwithstanding the clear terms of s.7(1), the appeal court in *Rees v Lees*, 1996 S.C.C.R. 601 erroneously upheld a conviction under s.7(1) of a person charged with carrying on the activity of an unlicensed sex shop although, in fairness, this error did not appear to have been noticed by either the Crown or the appellant!

Subsection (A1)

This subsection was added to make the penalty for trading as an unlicensed knife dealer subject to imprisonment of up to one or two years depending on the manner in which the unlicensed dealer was tried; in addition there is a higher level of fine which can be imposed in addition to or in substitution of imprisonment—both reflect the aim of preventing knives from falling into the wrong hands. This section was added by s.59(3) of the 2007 Act.

Subsection (1)

The activity for which a licence is required under Pt II may be one for which licensing is mandatory or optional (see notes to s.9, below) but, in the case of the latter, further specification of the categories of activity for which a licence is required may be needed. This specification must be stated clearly in terms of the resolution made under s.9 to license that particular form of activity in order that, inter alia, a person will know whether or not they are likely to be committing an offence under this subsection—see, e.g. *Normand v Norris*, 1992 G.W.D. 1-41. Note that the offences created are not those involving strict liability, in that a reasonable excuse is permitted as a defence, so that if, say, a person trades without a licence but under a genuine mistake of fact, the court will be able to consider the effect of this on his mens rea. This amendment introduced these markedly higher penalties in order to deal with the perceived problem of unlicensed "festivals" or other events which were attracting young persons and where the existing penalties were disproportionate to the profits being made by the promoters thereof. For an example of the approach of the courts to the level of fines levied under subs.(1)(a) see *Knowles v Lees*, 1994 G.W.D. 2085; and under subs.(1)(b) see *Joseph Dunn (Bottlers) Ltd v MacDougall*, 1987 S.C.C.R. 290 (street trading), *Jackson v Friel*, 1996 G.W.D. 25-1448 (private hire car), *McKenzie v Friel*, 1998 G.W.D. 13-676 (operation of vehicle as taxi without licence) and *Huwaish v Vannet*, 1999 G.W.D. 22-1067 (unlicensed public entertainment). Subsection 1(a) was further amended and subs.(2)(ab) was added by s.62A of the 2015 Act.

Subsection (2)

This subsection creates an offence of non-compliance with the conditions imposed upon a licence, subject to the statutory defence contained in subs.(3). Subsection (2)(a) was added by s.2(2) of the Entertainments (Increased Penalties) Act 1990 and applies only to conditions relating to the limitation of those attending public entertainment licences—see note to subs.(1), above. For some of the considerations which might be applicable in sentencing under the 1990 Act see the obiter comments of Watkins LJ in *Mendip District Council v Glastonbury Festivals Ltd* [2003] L.L.R. 90 at 96.

Subsection (3)

For the statutory defence of "due diligence" see Introduction p.32 above. A joint licence holder is held to be in a similar position to that of an employer—see note to subs.(10) below.

Subsection (4)

This also applies to statements made under the provisions of Sch.1. A false statement, even if made without the requisite degree of knowledge or recklessness necessary to establish the statutory offence, may, of course, result in the invalidation of the application or, if already granted before the misrepresentation came to light, in the suspension or revocation of the licence—see *Thomson v City of Glasgow District Council*, 1992 S.L.T. 805, the notes to s.3(1) above and Introduction p.32 above. It was held to be a contravention of this subsection where an application form for a licence stated that each question must be answered and an applicant left blank a space for "previous unspent convictions" and signed a declaration at the end of the form that the particulars on the form were true whereas he had previous unspent convictions: see *Buchmann v Normand*, 1994 S.C.C.R. 929. The wording, "which you knew to be false or recklessly made a statement" is essential to the offence—see *Kearney v Vannet*, 2000 G.W.D. 9-325.

Subsection (5)

A "material change in circumstances" is one which affects the licence holder or the activity licensed or the premises, vehicle or vessel licensed in a material way, i.e. a change of such significance as to be likely to influence the licensing authority in determining how they would exercise their powers under the Act. It includes a change in the particulars given or referred to in the application for the grant, or the most recent application for the grant, or the most recent application for the renewal of the licence—Sch.1 para.9(8).

Subsection (6)

This subsection provides the court with additional powers in relation to offences created by ss.5, 6 and 7 of the Act. The powers to revoke or disqualify, however, are only available when it is the holder of the licence who commits an offence, so that where a person was convicted of street trading without a licence but had obtained the required licence between the dates upon which the offence was committed, and the date upon which his complaint called in court, it was held incompetent to disqualify him from holding a licence for a period of two years—*Gregan v Tudhope*, 1987 S.C.C.R. 57.

Subsection (7)

The purpose of this subsection is to make the licensing authority aware of the sentence of the court, since this may well influence them to exercise their own powers to revoke, vary, impose conditions, etc.

Subsection (8)

The orders made under subs.(6) above have the same effect as the sentence of the court for the purposes of an appeal, accordingly the court may suspend their effects pending the determination of the appeal.

Subsection (9)

The circumstances that might influence the court here would be similar to those which would apply when a driver disqualified from driving under the provisions of the Road Traffic Act 1988 reapplied for their licence—note that the disqualification cannot be removed within the first year.

Subsection (10)

This subsection gives a power to bring proceedings against a joint licence holder for the acts and omissions of their employee or agent—see notes to subs.(3) above.

Interpretation of Parts I and II

8. In this Part and in Part II of this Act except where the context otherwise requires—

[*As repealed by the Police and Fire Reform (Scotland) Act 2012 (asp 8) Sch.8 para.1 (effective 1 April 2013).*]

[1]"authorised civilian employee" means a person—

[2](a) appointed by the Scottish Police Authority under section 26(1) of the Police and Fire Reform (Scotland) Act 2012 (asp 8), and

(b) authorised by the chief constable of the Police Service of Scotland

[2]"chief constable" means the chief constable for the purposes of sections 5 and 11 of this Act;

[*As repealed by the Police and Fire Reform (Scotland) Act 2012 (asp 8) Sch.8 para.1 (effective 1 April 2013).*]

"licence" means a licence granted under this Part and Part II of this Act, and cognate expressions shall be construed accordingly;

"premises" includes land.

NOTES

1. As amended by the Criminal Justice and Licensing (Scotland) Act 2010 (asp 13) Sch.8 s.173 (effective 13 December 2010).

2. As amended by the Police and Fire Reform (Scotland) Act 2012 (asp 8) Sch.7 para.6 (effective 1 April 2013).

GENERAL NOTE

These are all important definitions which apply throughout Pts I and II of the Act unless specific sections give a different meaning—e.g. "premises" in s.41A. Further definitions of a general application throughout the Act are given in s.130. Note that for the purposes of Pts I and II (excluding s.41A) "premises" includes land so that open-air activities are also covered by the Act. This section has been amended in its current form by the Police and Fire Reform (Scotland) Act 2012 and by s.173 of the 2010 Act which also defines "enactment" when s.10 comes into force. In the case of licensing of skin piercing and tattooing this section has been amended by para.2(b) of the Civic Government (Scotland) Act 1982 (Licensing of Skin Piercing and Tattooing) Order 2006 (SSI 2006/43).

PART II

LICENSING AND REGULATION—PARTICULAR ACTIVITIES

Application of sections 10 to 27 and 38 to 44

9.—(1) Sections 10 to 27 (except section 20), any regulations made under the said section 20, and sections 38 to 43 (except section 41A) of this Act and any order made under section 44(1)(a) of this Act (which sections regulations and order are in this section called the "optional provisions") shall have effect in the area of a licensing authority only if and insofar as the authority have so resolved in accordance with subsections (2) to (8) below.

(2) A licensing authority may, in accordance with this section, resolve that, as from a day specified in the resolution (which must not be before the expiration of the period of nine months beginning with the day on which the resolution was made) any activity provision for the licensing and regulation of which is made by the optional provisions shall require to be licensed in accordance with the provisions of this Act relating to that activity and shall be regulated by those provisions.

(3) Subject to subsections (4) and (5) below, a resolution under this section may be made—

(a) in relation to all or any of the activities referred to in subsection (2) above;
(b) in relation to the whole or any part of the area of the licensing authority;
(c) in relation to—
  (i) all classes of an activity referred to in any of the optional provisions; or
  (ii) all such classes subject to exceptions; or
  (iii) any particular such class or classes.

(4) A licensing authority may not make a resolution under this section relating to any of the activities provision for the licensing and regulation of which is made in sections 10 to 23 of this Act (that is to say the operation of a vehicle as a taxi, the operation of a vehicle as a hire car, the driving of a taxi and the driving of a hire car) unless it relates to all these activities

(5) A resolution made under this section by the licensing authority relating to—
(a) the activity provision for the licensing and regulation of which is made in sections 24 to 27 of this Act (that is to say the carrying on of business as a second-hand dealer) shall specify the particular class or classes of that activity which shall thereby fall to be licensed and regulated;
(b) the activity provision for the licensing of which is made in section 41 of this Act (that is to say the use of premises as a place of public entertainment) shall specify the place or places, or class or classes thereof, which shall thereby fall to be licensed

(6) A licensing authority shall not make a resolution under this section unless they have—
(a) published in a newspaper or newspapers circulating in their area the terms of the proposed resolution together with a notice stating—
  (i) that they intend to make the resolution; and
  (ii) that representations about the resolution may be made in writing to the authority within 28 days of the first publication of the notice; and
(b) considered any representations so made.

(7) A licensing authority, before proceeding to make a resolution under this section, may make such modifications to the proposed resolution as they think fit in the light of representations made to them about it provided such modifications do not extend its scope.

(8) The licensing authority shall, as soon as they have made a resolution under subsection (2) above, publish in a newspaper or newspapers circulating in their area—
(a) the terms of the resolution so made; together with
(b) a notice stating—
  (i) that with effect from the date specified as that on which the resolution comes into effect it will be an offence under section 7(1) of this Act to do without a licence whatever the resolution specifies as being an activity requiring to be licensed; and
  (ii) that applications for licences in respect of the activity will be considered by the authority after the expiry of one month after the date of the making of the resolution.

(9) A resolution under this section may be varied or rescinded by a subsequent resolution made in like manner except that, in relation to the time when it takes effect, a resolution under this subsection
(a) varying a resolution under this section so as to reduce its scope; or

(b) rescinding a resolution under this section shall take effect on such date as may be specified in it being any date subsequent to the making of the resolution.

(10) Anything which must or may be done under or by virtue of Part I or this Part of this Act may, at any time after the making by the licensing authority of the resolution, be done so far as may be necessary or expedient for the purpose of giving full effect to the resolution at or after the time it takes but no application for a licence in respect of an activity requiring to be licensed in consequence of the resolution shall be considered by the authority until the expiry of one month after the making of the resolution.

DEFINITIONS

"licensing authority": s.2.
"licence": s.8.

GENERAL NOTE

This section, which was drafted to give licensing authorities the greatest possible discretion in regulating and licensing matters, is of considerable importance in that it provides for the division of activities to be licensed into two separate categories, namely: (i) those activities for which it is mandatory for licensing authorities throughout Scotland to license ("mandatory" activities); and (ii) those activities for which individual licensing authorities have a discretion as to whether or not to license ("optional" activities). In order to invoke licensing for the "optional" activities, a licensing authority must make a proper resolution to do so and follow the procedure laid down in this section, once they have done so and the licensing provisions have come into effect, it is then mandatory for a person carrying on those activities within the specified area to hold a licence for that activity. In general, resolutions may be made to cover all or any of the optional activities and they may relate to the whole or any part of the licensing authority area, and they may also relate to all classes or any particular class within the activity covered by the relevant sections of the Act. For the transitional provisions made in respect of s.9 resolutions by the 1994 Act, see notes to subs.(9) below.

Subsection (1)

This subsection provides for the division of activities between the "mandatory" and "optional" categories. In effect, all activities are covered by the optional provisions with the exception of knife dealers (ss.27A onwards), metal dealers and itinerant metal dealers (ss.28–37), and places of indoor sports entertainment (s.41A). The optional provisions can be invoked only if the procedures contained in subss.(2)–(8) of this section have been followed and, if no resolution has been passed, then licences will not be required for any of the particular optional activities. Note that the licensing authorities may pass only resolutions relating to the activities covered by the Act and that they cannot seek to license activities that are not covered in this Act or under any other statutory provision. Should they wish to license any other activity not covered by the Act then they must try to persuade the appropriate minister of the Scottish Government to introduce new optional categories in terms of s.44(1)(a)—see, Introduction p.9 above. This subsection was amended by s.44(3) of the Fire and Safety of Places of Sport Act 1987.

Subsection (2)

This provision gives a minimum period of nine months' grace from the passing of the resolution to license a particular activity, before a licence will be required. The purpose of this notice, is to allow those trading in whichever particular sphere to be covered by the licensing, to adapt their businesses so as to meet any licensing requirements.

Subsection (3)

A resolution may cover any or all of the optional activities, i.e. all of them or any one of them or a combination of optional activities subject, in the case of taxis and private hire cars, to the provisions of subs.(4), below. A resolution may cover the whole or any part of the geographical area covered by the licensing authority and thus may take into account demographic factors—

e.g. limiting the licensing requirement to the urban or suburban areas within the area of an authority—the geographical area must be clearly specified, e.g. by reference to discernible localities such as electoral wards or to areas delineated on a map. A resolution may cover all or any part of an activity specified in the Act, subject to the special provisions relating to second-hand dealers and public entertainment licences contained in subs.(5) below; thus a window cleaner's licence may be required only for, say, domestic premises.

Subsection (4)

This is a qualification to subs.(3)(a) and provides that, in respect of taxis, private hire cars, taxi drivers and private hire car drivers, it is an "all or nothing" provision. Taxis and hire cars provide, in effect, a single service and to license one without the other might lead to unfair competition and circumvention of the licensing requirements.

Subsection (5)

In the case of both second-hand dealers and places of public entertainment, the resolution must specify clearly the categories of activity covered and a general, unspecific resolution is not enough. Thus, a resolution could state, e.g. "general second hand books, bicycles, clothing" or "discotheques, dance halls, exhibition centres". Care should be exercised to avoid expressions such as, "massage parlours and sauna establishments" since these can be construed conjunctively, which may not have been the intention of the licensing authority—*Normand v Norris*, 1992 G.W.D. 1-41—see also the interesting case of *Scanlan v City of Edinburgh District Council*, 1995 S.L.T. (Sh Ct) 89 in relation to a possibly ulterior motive in a s.9 resolution.

Subsection (6)

This is to enable the views of the public and other interested persons to be taken into account. Note that they have to consider any representations, from whatever source: "In the Secretary of State's view it will usually be desirable to consult the Chief Constable (on whose advice the decision, in principle, to license will no doubt be based) and the appropriate trade associations *before the draft resolution is published*" (Scottish Development Department Circular 6/1983, Appendix A, para.2.7).

Subsection (8)

It is, however, the terms of the resolution rather than the terms of the advertisement which govern whether or not a licence is required—see *Normand v Norris*, 1992 G.W.D. 1-41.

Subsection (9)

This subsection gives a power to vary or rescind a resolution by way of a subsequent resolution with the proviso in relation to the date of it taking effect. Special provision was made by para.3 of the Local Government (Transitional Provisions) (Scotland) Order 1995 (SI 1995/1878) in respect of "shadow authorities" taking steps prior to 1 April 1996 to apply to vary or rescind after that date as a resolution.

Subsection (10)

In effect, this provides that the licensing authority may process applications and issue post-dated licences to come into effect on the due day, in terms of the period commencing one month after the passing of the resolution and ending on the day before the due date.

Licensing and regulation of taxis and private hire cars

Taxi and private hire car licences

10.—(1) A licence, to be known as a "taxi licence" or, as the case may be, a "private hire car licence", shall be required for the operation of a vehicle as—

(a) a taxi; or
(b) a private hire car.

(2) A licensing authority shall not grant or renew a taxi licence or private hire car licence unless they are satisfied that the vehicle to which the licence is to relate is suitable in type, size and design for use as a taxi or private hire car, as the case may be, and is safe for that use, and that there is in force in relation to the vehicle such a policy of insurance or such security as complies with Part VI of the Road Traffic Act 1972.

(3) Without prejudice to paragraph 5 of Schedule 1 to this Act, the grant of a taxi licence may be refused by a licensing authority for the purpose of limiting the number of taxis in respect of which licences are granted by them if, but only if, they are satisfied that there is no significant demand for the services of taxis in their area which is unmet.

[2](3A) Without prejudice to paragraph 3 of Schedule 1, the grant of a private hire car licence may be refused by a licensing authority if, but only if, they are satisfied that there is (or, as a result of granting the licence, could be) overprovision of private hire car services in the locality (or localities) in the area in which the private hire car is to operate.

[2](3B) it is for the licensing authority to determine the localities within their area for the purposes of sub-section (3A) and in doing so may determine that the whole of their area is a locality.

[2](3C) In satisfying themselves as to determine where there is, or would be overprovision for the purposes of subsection (3A) in any locality, the licensing authority must have regard to—

(a) the number of private hire car licences operating in the locality, and
(b) the demand for private hire car services in the locality.

[1](4) A vehicle shall, for the purposes of subsection (2) the grant of above, be treated by a licensing authority—

(a) as being suitable in type, size and design if it complies with regulations in that regard made by the Secretary of State under section 20(2) of this Act in respect of their area and
(b) as not being so suitable if it does not so comply.

(5) A taxi licence or private hire car licence shall extend to the operation of a vehicle substituted for the vehicle in respect of which the licence was granted or, as the case may be, last renewed if the licensing authority are as respects the substitute vehicle satisfied as to the matters specified in subsection (2) above, and where a taxi licence or private hire car licence extends under this subsection to a substitute vehicle, subsection (6) below shall not apply in respect of the vehicle replaced by the substitute vehicle.

(6) Subject to subsection (5) above, the holder of a taxi or private hire car licence shall within 28 days of his selling or otherwise disposing of the vehicle to which the licence relates deliver to the licensing authority his licence and any licence plate or other thing which has been issued by the licensing authority for the purpose of indicating that the vehicle is a taxi or, as the case may be, private hire car, and if without reasonable excuse he fails to do so he shall be guilty of an offence and liable, on summary conviction, to a fine not exceeding level 2 on the standard scale.

NOTES

1. As amended by the Disability Discrimination Act 1995 (c.50) Pt V s.39(2) (effective 5 February 2003).

2. As inserted by the Air Weapons and Licensing (Scotland) Act 2015 (asp 10) Pt 3 s.63 (date yet to be appointed).

DEFINITIONS

"licensing authority": s.2(2).
"private hire car": s.2.

"standard scale": see Introduction p.32 above.
"taxi": s.23.

GENERAL NOTE

Taxi and private hire car licences are, from a numerical and economic point of view, the most important of the categories of "optional" activities covered by the 1982 Act and the provisions which apply to them are covered by ss.10–23. Certain of these provisions apply to taxi-buses, which are taxis being used under a special licence to provide a local service within the meaning of reg.3 of the Local Services (Operation by Taxis) (Scotland) Regulations 1986 (SI 1986/1239) and unless otherwise stated at the end of the general note to each section, it should be assumed that these provisions do apply thereto. A resolution in terms of s.9 must be passed before taxi and private hire cars require licences, and such a resolution can specify the areas or particular types of activity for which licences will be required—e.g. limiting the requirement for licences to the City of Perth or having a system of separate airport taxi licences. However, if a licensing authority makes a resolution to introduce taxi licensing (and it is understood that in fact all licensing authorities in Scotland have now made such licensing mandatory) then they must license and regulate both taxis and private hire cars since, in essence, the two types of vehicle provide a similar service. Taxis, however, have additional powers in that they can pick up passengers in public places without prior booking. Drivers of taxis and private hire cars require separate licences issued under the provisions of s.13 and thus an "owner-driver" will need both a s.10 and a s.13 licence if they do not drive their taxis personally. Different considerations may apply in respect of an operator's and a driver's licence, and a person may be deemed unfit under the provisions of Sch.1 para.5(3)(ii) to hold a driver's licence but fit to hold an operator's licence—see, e.g. *McDowall v Cunninghame DC*, 1987 S.C.L.R. 587; cf. *Middleton v Dundee City Council*, 2001 S.L.T. 287. An operator's licence can be refused if the applicant is deemed unfit because of their general disregard for the law, but if this is to be a relevant consideration then it must be related to the law concerning the suitability of the vehicle, lack of insurance, etc. and not the applicant qua driver. It is an offence to operate a taxi or private hire car without a licence in terms of s.7(1) (see, e.g. *Jackson v Friel*, 1996 G.W.D. 25-1448) but it should be noted that, in certain circumstances, an additional licence or permit may be required to operate a taxi in a particular place if byelaws require such a licence or permit—examples are railway stations, where such permits are issued by the station operator (Network Rail or Scotrail), and airports where byelaws issued under s.63 of the Airports Act 1986 may require such a permit provided, of course, that the byelaws are not ultra vires—see *Cinnamond v British Airports Authority* [1980] 2 All E.R. 368; *Perth General Station Committee v Ross* (1897) 24 R. 44; the case of *Casey v Edinburgh Airport Ltd* unreported 23 February 1989 OH; *Fulton v Lees*, 1992 S.C.C.R. 923 and *Gordon v Lees*, 1994 G.W.D. 5-261.

Subsection (1)

Although "taxi" and "private hire car" are defined in the Act, "operation" is not but, having regard to the later provisions of the Act, it would appear to equate with the notion of, "to make available for the use as". In relation to private hire cars in England and Wales s.80(1) of the Local Government (Miscellaneous Provisions) Act 1976 defines "operate" as, "to make provision for the invitation or acceptance of bookings for such a vehicle in the course of business". The applicant for a licence, however, does not have to exercise direct control over the operation of the vehicle. The relationship between a non-natural person who is an applicant (e.g. a limited company) and the person responsible for the day to day management of the company may be governed by contract—see, e.g. *Intascot Plc v Inverclyde DC*, 1992 G.W.D. 21-1238, where the competency of a taxi franchising agreement was considered.

Subsection (2)

This subsection, which was designed to provide for the safety of both passengers and other road users, places three separate requirements upon the operators of taxis and private hire cars and provides that the licensing authority must be satisfied in respect of all three of these requirements before granting a licence. The first requirement is that the vehicle is suitable in type, size and design for its purpose and by virtue of both subs.(4) of this section and s.20(2) of the Act the Secretary of State may, by order, specify the types, sizes and specifications of vehicles for all or individual licensing areas which a licensing authority shall treat as suitable for their area. At present, some licensing authorities impose restrictions on the types of taxis to be used (usually limiting them to the well-known types of classic "London" taxi such as the FX4, Metrocab, etc.), and Perth and Kinross District Council place an age limit upon vehicles. An attempt by way of judicial review to challenge the policy of a Welsh licensing authority in relation to an age limit on taxis was unsuccessful in that it could not be shown that such a policy was either irrational or an unreasonable fettering of discretion—*R v Swansea City Council Ex p. Jones* [1997] 2 C.L. 432. Some authorities specify that vehicles shall be suitable for use by disabled persons (but see notes to s.20 below). In *Sneddon v Renfrewshire Council*, 2009 S.L.T. 563, the Inner House made it clear that the authority in exercising their discretion under this subsection was bound to have regard to the suitability of a vehicle sought to be licensed as a taxi for use by an identifiable class of persons likely to use it, namely the wheelchair bound, and to that end they were entitled to develop a policy as licensing authority which recognised the need to secure provision of taxis suitable for use by wheelchair users and which was implemented by a standard condition requiring taxi vehicles to be wheelchair accessible. The specification requirement is separate from the requirement to be satisfied: (a) in relation to safety of the vehicle (powers being contained in s.11 in relation to the inspection and testing of individual vehicles for, inter alia, their safety) and the issue of safety refers to the use of the vehicle as a hire car as opposed to whether the vehicle is per se safe as a vehicle—see *Chaffeur Bikes Ltd v Leeds City Council* [2005] EWHC 2369; and (b) in relation to a proper certificate of insurance being in force—the reference to Pt VI of the Road Traffic Act 1972 is now superseded by Pt VI of the Road Traffic Act 1988. There are, of course, other grounds upon which a taxi or private hire car licence can be refused—see para.5 of Sch.1 and, e.g. *McDowell v Cunninghame DC*, 1987 S.C. 217; 1987 S.L.T. 662; 1987 S.C.L.R. 587. In general it is a matter for the licensing authority to make their decisions under this subsection according to local conditions and circumstances (*R v Bournemouth Council ex p Thompson*) but they must make sure that the distinction between taxis and private hire cars are clear to the public and any specification of vehicle types must not place vehicles manufactured outwith the UK at a disadvantage to domestic vehicles under art.34 of the Treaty on Functioning of the European Union—see *Spring Radio Cars v Glasgow City Council*, 2013 S.L.T. 491 (Outer House) and 2014 S.L.T. 393 (Inner House).

Subsection (3)

This subsection, amended by Transport Act 1985 Sch.7, which does not apply to private hire cars, allows a licensing authority to refuse a taxi licence for the purpose of limiting the number of taxis, provided that they are satisfied that there is no significant unmet demand for taxis in their area. In *Barclay v Renfrewshire Council* unreported 3 April 2001 Extra Division, it was made clear that "grant" in s.10(3) does not include the renewal of an already existing taxi licence so that an authority cannot exercise their power in terms of s.10(3) at the time when it was no longer available to them, namely upon an application for renewal of an existing licence. It was held that when considering an application for renewal of a deemed grant under s.3(4), the authority are not entitled to have regard to a policy which had been determined subsequent to the licence coming into force. Note the use of "may", i.e. the power is permissive and discretionary—see *Douglas v City of Glasgow DC*, 1996 S.L.T. 713. The purpose of this power is to prevent a situation where it becomes impossible for licensed taxi operators to provide a proper service on economic or other grounds due to an excessive number of licences. "It is for licensing authorities to decide what evidence of no significant unmet demand would be sufficient to satisfy them that they may refuse a licence so as to limit licence numbers" (para.2.22 of Appendix A to Scottish Development Department Circular 6/1983, as substituted by Scottish Development Department Circular 25/1986), but there is no onus on the licensing authority in an appeal to establish the lack of significant demand: *Thomson v Motherwell DC*, 1989 S.C.L.R. 175. "Demand" can only be meaningfully expressed by reference to the overall demand in an area and this would refer to the whole population and not to a significant minority such as the disabled (who may, in any event, be catered for separately by the powers contained in s.20(2A) below—*Davies v Renfrewshire Council*, 2005 S.L.T. 445). If a licensing authority have decided in advance upon an optimum number of licences to be granted, this can be only a guideline and the authority must satisfy themselves, at the time of determining the application, whether it is still applicable as being sufficient to meet the demand. "Two things stand out [in relation to s.10(3)]. First, the use of the phrase 'if, but only if' emphasises how tightly this discretion is drawn. Secondly ... the committee's assessment must be made in relation to the situation at the time when the application falls to be considered ... In other words when making their decision the committee required to be aware of the current demand for the services of taxis and to be satisfied that there was no significant unmet demand for those services"—Lord President

Rodger in *Coyle v City of Glasgow Council*, 1998 S.L.T. 453. He went on to say that to that end they must keep the matter of demand under review. Licensing authorities must not fetter that discretion by adopting an inflexible policy—see *Aitken v City of Glasgow DC*, 1988 S.C.L.R. 287 at 293; *City Cabs (Edinburgh) Ltd v City of Edinburgh DC*, 1988 S.L.T. 184; *Shennan v City of Glasgow DC*, 1994 S.L.T. 440; *Doyle v City of Glasgow DC*, 1995 S.L.T. 327; *Douglas*, 1996 S.L.T. 713 and *Dundee Taxi Cab Co Ltd v Dundee City Council*, 2005 S.L.T. 401. The fact that there may be no significant demand that was met does not mean that an application should be automatically refused, since the licensing authority still have to consider it and address themselves as to whether there are circumstances that require the case to be looked at independently of their general policy on numbers—for instance by considering the needs of the disabled: *Davies v Renfrewshire Council*, 2005 S.L.T. 445. The area referred to is that of the local authority as a whole and does not refer to any administrative zones within that area—see *PTOA Ltd v Renfrew DC*, 1997 S.L.T. 1112. For the purposes of subs.(3) an authority may instruct from time to time a survey and report on the demand for taxis within their area. The results will inform decisions as to whether to maintain a limit on numbers of taxi licences to be issued and what that limit should be. This will, in turn, provide a basis for refusal under this subsection. However, in *City of Edinburgh Council v Salteri*, 2007 S.C. 463, the authority's adoption of such a limit resulted, in the circumstances of the case, in their being unable to obtain an extension of time under s.3(2) which they had sought in order to allow them to address the results of a survey report on demand. The court's view was that this was a self-imposed burden that did not amount to a good reason for granting an extension. For examples of attempts to judicially review licensing authorities decisions to refuse to impose limits, see *Inverness Taxi Owners and Drivers Association v Highland Council*, 1999 S.L.T. 1316 and *Falconer v South Ayrshire Council*, 2002 S.L.T. 1033. Subsection 10(3) was amended by s.139(2) of the Transport Act 1985.

Subsection (3A)

This provision, without prejudice to subs.(3), which applies only to taxis, enables but does not require the licensing authority to refuse to grant a private hire car licence application on the ground that they are satisfied that there already exists (or will exist if the licence is granted) an overprovision of private hire car facilities in the area or locality where the car is to operate. This is a different standard to that in subs.(3), which deals with unmet demand, and there is apparent method of establishing either a cap should be imposed and how overprovision is to be established. This subsection and the two following subsections were all added by s.60 of the 2015 Act and as at 1 January 2016 subss.(3A) and (3B) were yet not in force.

Subsection (3B)

This gives the licensing authority discretion to determine the locality or localities within the area to which subs.3(A) will apply.

Subsection (3C)

The licensing authority must have regard to two factors, namely: (a) the number of private hire cars operating there; and (b) the demand for private hire car services. As at 1 January 2016 this subsection was not yet in force.

Subsection (4)

See note to subs.(2) above. "This power to prescribe types and other characteristics of vehicles is intended primarily as a reserve power to be used if there is evidence of authorities imposing too specific or expensive types on the local trade with consequent increased costs for the public. It would not prevent a local authority from refusing a licence if the vehicle was unsuitable (provided that those alleged defects were not an inseparable part of the type, size or design)"—para.2.21 of Appendix A to Scottish Development Department Circular 6/1983, as substituted by Scottish Development Department Circular 25/1986. This subsection was amended by s.39(2) of the Disability Discrimination Act 1995 in order that the Secretary of State can make requirements in relation to disabled persons.

Subsection (5)

These provisions relate to substituted vehicles, which must comply with the requirements of subs.(2) above, i.e. the licensing authority must be satisfied as to their suitability, safety and insurance cover.

Subsection (6)

This subsection requires delivery of the licence plate or other distinguishing mark issued by the licensing authority, within 28 days of the sale or disposal of a licensed vehicle. This is to prevent misuse and evasion of the licensing requirements, as a licence plate is personal to the operator and is non-transferable between operators. Note, however, that it can be transferred between vehicles if one has been substituted for another in terms of subs.(5) above.

Inspection and testing of vehicles

11.—(1) The holder of a taxi or private hire car licence shall present the taxi or private hire car for inspection and testing by or on behalf of the licensing authority within such period and at such place as they may by notice reasonably require.

[1](2) An authorised officer of a licensing authority (as respects a taxi or private hire car licensed for the area of the authority) an authorised civilian employee or a constable shall have power at any reasonable time to inspect and test, for the purpose of ascertaining its fitness, a licensed taxi or private hire car or, for the purpose of testing its fitness or accuracy, any taximeter and if he is not satisfied as to the safety of the taxi or private hire car for the carriage of passengers or as to the fitness or accuracy of the taximeter he may by notice in writing—

(a) require the holder of the taxi or private hire car licence to make the taxi, private hire car or taximeter, as the case may be, available for further inspection at such reasonable time and place as may be specified in the notice;

[1](b) suspend the licence until such time as an authorised officer of the licensing authority, an authorised civilian employee or a constable is so satisfied:

[1]Provided that, if an authorised officer, employee or constable is not so satisfied before the expiration of a period of 28 days from the date of the suspension of the licence, the said licence shall, by virtue of this subsection, be deemed to have been suspended by the licensing authority under paragraph 11 of Schedule 1 to this Act.

NOTE

1. As amended by the Criminal Justice and Licensing (Scotland) Act 2010 (asp 13) Pt 8 s.173 (effective 13 December 2010).

DEFINITIONS

"authorised civilian employee": s.8.
"taxi licence": s.10(1).
"private hire car licence": s.10(1).
"licensing authority": s.2(2).

GENERAL NOTE

This section contains powers to be used in the public interest to inspect and test taxis and private hire cars, in order both to test for the safety of the vehicles themselves, and also to check the taximeters, if fitted. Where vehicles do not satisfy the examiners there are powers for further tests to be carried out and for licences to be automatically suspended, where vehicles are not up to the required standard.

Subsection (1)

This empowers a licensing authority to require a vehicle to be inspected and tested, upon the giving of reasonable notice, and is supplementary to any powers given to the police in respect of general road traffic legislation. The words, "by or on behalf" mean that the licensing authority can delegate the inspecting and testing function to an independent agency, such as a commercial garage or, as in the example of the City of Edinburgh, the police.

Subsection (2)

This subsection enables spot checks to be carried out on taxis and private hire cars and is in addition to any powers given by s.5(2). Note that if the authorised officer is not satisfied as to the safety of the vehicle, or the fitness or accuracy of the taximeter, then he can require a further inspection and suspend the licence until he is so satisfied with the proviso that if the licence is suspended and the officer is not so satisfied, within 28 days, the licence will be deemed to be suspended under the provisions of para.11 of Sch.1. For "authorised officer" and "reasonable time" see notes to s.5(1) above. For an explanation of "taximeter" see note to s.21(5).

Fees for taxi and private hire car licences

12. A licensing authority shall charge such fees in respect of taxi and private hire car licences and applications for such licences as may be resolved by them from time to time and shall seek to ensure that the total amount of such fees is sufficient to meet the expenses incurred by them in carrying out their functions under sections 10 to 23 (other than section 19) of this Act in relation to such licences.

DEFINITIONS

"licensing authority": s.2(2).
"taxi and private hire car licences": s.10(1).

GENERAL NOTE

Licensing authorities are specifically required, in terms of this section, to charge such fees in respect of taxi and private hire car licences and applications for the same, as will meet the costs of the operation of ss.10–23 of the Act (with the exception of s.19, which deals with taxi stances). This provision, which is separate from the more general provisions as to fees contained in para.15 of Sch.1 and applicable to all other Pt I and II activities, is designed to prevent any cross-subsidy between the taxi and private hire car and other types of licensing activity. It was introduced because it was envisaged that there might be fairly substantial fees incurred in respect of the testing and inspection of vehicles (particularly, if carried out on an agency basis) and in the administration of applications for licences. Fees are chargeable on both the application for and the granting of licences (including renewals) and the licensing authority is under a duty to ensure that the total amount recovered in such fees will meet the relevant costs, including the "spot-check" inspections. "Differing levels of fees should bear an obvious relationship to costs incurred (for example, a taxi driver's licence involving a 'knowledge' test should cost more than a 'private hire' driver's licence) and the Secretary of State expects that authorities will ensure that the costs are kept to the minimum, and that the basis for the fees charged should be explained to the local trade organisations, who should be consulted well before charges or adjustments are proposed. It may often be convenient to adjust charges at the same time as taxi fares are reviewed"—para.2.25 of Appendix A to Scottish Development Department Circular 6/1983, as substituted by Scottish Development Department Circular 25/1986. A local authority can charge vehicle inspection fees whether or not a licence is granted. "Parliament could not have intended that the local authority or those who repeatedly presented first-class vehicles should subsidise those who repeatedly failed" (*Kelly v Liverpool City Council* [2003] L.L.R. 197).

Taxi and private hire car driving licences

13.—(1) A licence, to be known as a "taxi driver's licence" or, as the case may be, a "private hire car driver's licence", shall, subject to subsection (2) below, be required for driving or otherwise having charge of a taxi or private hire car.

(2) A private hire car driver's licence shall not be required by the holder of a taxi driver's licence for driving or otherwise having charge of a private hire car whilst in operation as such.

[1](3) A licensing authority shall not grant a licence to any person under this section unless that person has held, throughout the period of 12 months immediately prior to the date of his application, a licence authorising him to drive a motor car issued under Part III of the Road Traffic Act 1988 or a licence which would at the time of his application entitle him to such a licence without taking a test, not being a provisional licence.

(4) A licensing authority may, at any time, for the purposes of satisfying themselves that he is physically fit to drive a taxi or, as the case may be, private hire car, require an applicant for or holder of a taxi driver's licence or private hire car driver's licence to submit to medical examination, at their expense, by a medical practitioner nominated by them.

[2](5) A licensing authority may require an applicant for a taxi driver's licence or a private hire car driver's licence to take a test of his knowledge of the area to which the licence is to relate, of the layout of roads in that area and such other matters relating to the operation of a taxi or, as the case may be, private hire car as the authority consider desirable, and the authority may refuse to grant a licence to a person who does not satisfy them that he has adequate knowledge of any of these matters.

(6) If a person holding a licence under this section ceases for any reason to be authorised by law to drive on a road the vehicle to which the licence relates, the licence shall cease to have effect.

NOTES

1. As amended by the Criminal Justice and Licensing (Scotland) Act 2010 (asp 13) Pt 8 s.174 (effective 11 November 2011).

2. As inserted by the Air Weapons and Licensing (Scotland) Act 2015 (asp 10) Pt 3 s.64 (date yet to be appointed).

DEFINITIONS

"licensing authority": s.2(2).
"private hire car": s.23.
"taxi": s.23.

GENERAL NOTE

Where a licensing authority require taxis and private hire cars to be licensed under the provisions of s.10, they are required also to license the drivers thereof, who require to hold a separate licence under this section. It is an offence for such drivers to drive while unlicensed—s.7(1). Section 13 gives the licensing authority powers to satisfy themselves as to the fitness or suitability of a driver to hold such a licence, in respect of certain specified matters, and it should be noted that these powers are without prejudice to the provisions of para.5(3) of Sch.1. Different considerations may apply in respect of the fitness of a person to hold a s.10 and a s.13 licence—see *McDowall v Cunninghame DC*, 1987 S.C.L.R. 587; cf. *Middleton v Dundee City Council*, 2001 S.L.T. 287. Examples of unfitness to hold a s.13 licence include the incurring of a speeding conviction (*Piper v Kyle and Carrick DC*, 1988 S.L.T. 267), a multiplicity of previous convictions under the Road Traffic Act 1972 (*Holmes v Hamilton DC*, 1987 S.C.L.R. 407), a conviction for a sexual offence (*Francey v Cunninghame DC*, 1987 S.C.L.R. 6), and two previous convictions for assault and breach of the peace (*Ranachan v Renfrew DC*, 1991 S.L.T. 625); cf. *Cashley v City of Dundee DC*, 1993 S.C. 543; 1994 S.L.T. 1111; 1994 S.C.C.R. 6—for a general discussion of the exercise of the powers under para.5(3) of Sch.1 and the applicability of the Rehabilitation of Offenders Act 1974, see the notes to that paragraph.

Subsection (1)

"Otherwise having charge of" is not defined in the Act and it is difficult to see what meaning these words can have in this context—they do not refer to an "operator", who is covered in s.10. An owner-driver will require both a s.10 and s.13 licence.

Subsection (2)

The holder of a taxi driving licence will be able also to drive a private hire car without the need for a separate private hire car driver's licence but the converse does not apply. It follows therefore that no person would ever need to hold both a taxi and a private hire car driver's licence simultaneously.

Subsection (3)

Without prejudice to any other requirement (such as the fitness of an applicant in terms of para.5 of Sch.1), an applicant for a s.13 licence must have held a full car driver's licence for a continuous period of 12 months immediately prior to making their application—thus, if they only passed their driving test six months before or was disqualified from holding a driving licence for even one month during the preceding year, then they will not be eligible to hold a s.13 licence.

Subsection (4)

This subsection provides for the examination of an applicant for or holder of a licence by a nominated medical practitioner at any time, so as to enable a licensing authority to be satisfied as to their physical fitness. The cost of examinations are to be met by the licensing authority, who nevertheless are required to cover the same in the levels of licence fees by virtue of s.12. "It is not expected that such examinations would be automatic—bearing in mind that applicants will already be holders of ordinary driving licences and it is anticipated that they will be required by authorities only where there are specific grounds for concern about the medical fitness of the applicant or the driver—on age, accident or health record"—para.2.28 of Appendix A to Scottish Development Department Circular 6/1983, as substituted by Scottish Development Department Circular 25/1986.

Subsection (5)

This subsection provides for the so called "knowledge" tests to ensure that the applicant is familiar with local topography, road names and other matters—of particular importance in areas where tourists or foreigners may be using taxis. For a case involving the adequacy of an applicant's knowledge and the standard of the tests, see *McIntosh v City of Edinburgh DC*, 1993 G.W.D. 33-2148, in which it was held that although the standard was high in terms of detailed knowledge required, the test was reasonable having regard to the great influx of visitors to the city annually, and to the recent pass rate of applicants. This provision, which it should be noticed is a power rather than a requirement placed on licensing authorities, was originally only applied to taxi drivers but was extended to private hire car drivers by s.61 of the 2015 Act—the 2015 report noted that "it had been suggested that private hire car drivers, who are pre-booked, have the ability to prepare for journeys in advance and can utilise satellite navigation facilities. Set against this we are aware of limitations in such systems particularly in urban areas and the need for a degree of flexibility in routes to take account of conditions and traffic problems". The tests applied to both categories of driver may be identical or separate and it is interesting to note that despite the existence of apps and other navigation devices the 2015 Act has extended the knowledge test requirements perhaps in response to the apparent unreliability of such devices! Of different standards although given the above it is difficult to see what justification could be advanced for a lower test for private hire car drivers than that imposed for taxi drivers.

Subsection (6)

This subsection would apply to persons who are disqualified from driving by the courts for driving offences (including those disqualified under the "totting-up" provisions), and also persons who become unfit to hold a driving licence by reason of physical infirmity or other condition, and whose driving licence is revoked under the provisions of s.92 of the Road Traffic Act 1988.

Signs on vehicles other than taxis

14.—(1) Subject to subsection (2) below, there shall not be displayed on or in a private hire car any word, sign, notice, mark, illumination or other feature which may suggest that the vehicle is available for hire as a taxi.

(2) Subsection (1) above does not apply in relation to any licence plate or other thing issued by the licensing authority for the purpose of indicating that the vehicle to which it relates is a private hire car or in relation to any sign required by virtue of section 21 of the Vehicles (Excise) Act 1971.

(3) Any person who—

(a) drives a vehicle in respect of which subsection (1) is contravened; or

(b) causes or knowingly permits that subsection to be contravened in respect of any vehicle,

shall be guilty of an offence and liable, on summary conviction, to a fine not exceeding level 3 on the standard scale.

DEFINITIONS

"licensing authority": s.2(2).
"private hire cars": s.23.
"standard scale": see Introduction above.
"taxis": s.23.

GENERAL NOTE

These provisions, which relate to private hire cars only, make it an offence to display signs which suggest that the vehicle is available for hire as a taxi. The section does not apply to taxis or taxi-buses.

Subsection (1)

For an interesting example where a licensing authority attempted to impose such a condition on a licensed airport taxi see *Ingram v City of Aberdeen DC*, 1995 G.W.D. 40-2096. The test to be applied in deciding whether or not a sign does suggest that the vehicle is available as a taxi is to look at the vehicle itself and ask as a matter of common sense whether or not the sign suggests that the vehicle is in fact a taxi—*Yakha v Tee* [1984] R.T.R. 122.

Subsection (2)

This subsection exempts signs, etc. that are advertisements, or which merely carry the name of the operator firm (provided, of course, that this is not misleading by including words such as "taxi" within the name), or which are licence plates issued by the licensing authority for the purpose of identifying the vehicle as a private hire car. "The Secretary of State regards basic advertisements that a vehicle is a taxi or private hire car—such as displays of the name of the firm and its telephone number—as generally being in the public interest, because it permits ready identification"—Scottish Development Department Circular 6/1983, para.2.29 of Appendix A, as substituted by Scottish Development Department Circular 25/1986.

Subsection (3)

"Causes or knowingly permits"—see Introduction p.32 above. The driver of such a vehicle is, accordingly, guilty of an absolute offence—subs.(3)(a)—but the operator of the vehicle must have actual knowledge that the vehicle was to be used in contravention of s.13(2), i.e. that it displayed the signs referred to when it was in use. In respect of "causing", the person charged must possess some degree of control or authority to order or direct the use of the vehicle by another—see *Hunter (James) v Clark*, 1956 J.C. 59, per Lord Russell at 66, and the discussion on "causing and permitting" in Gerald H Gordon, *Criminal Law of Scotland*, 2nd edn (Edinburgh: SULI/W. Green, 1978), para.8–66. Also see p.32 above.

Operation of taxis outside licensing areas

15.—(1) A licensing authority, with the agreement of another licensing authority, may name destinations or classes of destinations in the area of the other authority and, with the agreement aforesaid, fix scales under section 17 of this Act for journeys from their area by taxis licensed by them to such destinations or classes thereof.

(2) The conditions to which a taxi or taxi driver's licence are subject shall continue to apply while the taxi or its driver is engaged in such a journey.

(3) Nothing in this section or in Part I of this Act enables a condition to be imposed in a taxi driver's licence requiring him to make any journey to a destination outside the area in respect of which he is licensed.

DEFINITIONS

"licensing authority": s.2(2).
"taxi": s.23.

GENERAL NOTE

This section makes provision for licensing authorities to fix fare scales for destinations outwith their area in respect of taxis licensed by them. The section does not apply to private hire cars or taxi-buses.

Subsection (1)

This provision was intended to be used for destinations that were outwith the licensing authority's area but nevertheless the destination of frequent hirings thereto, e.g. to railway stations, airports or ferry terminals in adjacent districts. The provisions apply only when the licensing authority for the destination area have consented to their use. When invoked, the same provisions apply as to "domestic" fares (i.e. ss.17, 18).

Subsection (2)

Thus, the conditions of, e.g. a West Lothian taxi licence still apply when it is making a journey to Edinburgh Airport.

Subsection (3)

A taxi driver cannot be compelled to make a cross-boundary journey and any condition imposed to that effect would be ultra vires.

Journeys in England and Wales by vehicles and drivers licensed under this Act

16.—In section 75 of the Local Government (Miscellaneous Provisions) Act 1976 (saving for certain vehicles from requirements of Part II of that Act as to private hire vehicles), after subsection (2) there shall be inserted—

"(2A) Where a vehicle is being used as a taxi or private hire car, paragraphs (a), (b) and (c) of section 46(1) of this Act shall not apply to the use or driving of the vehicle or the employment of a person to drive it if—

(a) a licence issued under section 10 of the Civic Government (Scotland) Act 1982 for its use as a taxi or, as the case may be, private hire car is then in force, and

(b) the driver holds a licence issued under section 13 of that Act for the driving of taxis or, as the case may be, private hire cars.

In this subsection, 'private hire car' and 'taxi' have the same meaning as in sections 10 to 22 of the Civic Government (Scotland) Act 1982.".

GENERAL NOTE

This section was designed to cover journeys made by Scottish taxis and private hire cars to destinations in England and Wales (e.g. the railway stations at Carlisle and Berwick-upon-Tweed) and to enable them to pick up passengers there, without the need for a separate English local authority licence granted under the parallel English legislation. It achieves this end by adding a new subsection to the Local Government (Miscellaneous Provisions) Act 1976 (which applies only to England and Wales) which exempts taxis, private hire cars and their drivers licensed under ss.10 and 13 of the 1982 Act from the provisions of the 1986 Act, which make it an offence to pick up passengers in an area to which the 1976 Act applies. Thus, taxis and private hire cars licensed in Scotland can pick up passengers in England, provided that the hiring was made by request in the area in which they are licensed (e.g. by a phone call made from a house in Annan). It does not allow vehicles to ply for hire in England and does not apply to unlicensed vehicles which are, in any event, not allowed to pick up passengers in England. For the reciprocal arrangements applying to English and Welsh taxis see s.21(3).

Taxis fares

17.—(1) The fares for the hire of taxis in any area and all other charges in connection with the fire of a taxi or with the arrangements for its hire shall be not greater than those fixed for that area under this section and section 18 of this Act.

[1](2) It licensing authority must fix scales for the fares and other charges mentioned in subsection (1) within 18 months beginning with the date on which the scales came into effect.

[1](3) In fixing scales under section (2) the licensing authority may—

(a) alter fares and other charges,

(b) fix fares or other charges at the same rates.

[1](4) Before fixing scales under subsection (2), the licensing authority must review the scales in accordance with subsection (4A).

[1](4A) In carrying out a review the licensing authority must—

(a) consult with persons or organisations appearing to them to be, or be representative of, the operators of taxis operating within their area;

(b) following such consultation—

(i) review the existing scales, and

(ii) propose new scales (whether at altered rates or the same rates),

(c) publish those proposed scales in a newspaper circulating in its area—

(i) setting out the proposed scales,

(ii) explaining the effect of the proposed scales,

(iii) proposing a date on which the proposed scales are to come into effect, and

(iv) stating that any person may make representations in writing until the relevant date, and

(d) consider any such representations.

[1](4B) In subsection (4A) (iv) "the relevant date" is a date specified by the licensing authority failing at least one month after the first publication by the authority of the proposed scales.

[1](4C) After fixing scales under subsection (2), the licensing authority must give notice in accordance with subsection (4D).

[1](4D) The licensing authority must—

(a) set out, and explain the effect of, the scales as fixed,

(b) notify the persons named in subsection (4E) of—

(i) the date on which the scales as fixed are to come into effect, and

(ii) the rights of appeal under section 18.

[1](4E) Those persons are—

(i) all operators of taxis operating within their area, and

(ii) the persons and organisations consulted under section (4A)(a).

[1](5) Notice shall be given for the purposes of subsection (4D)(b) above by—

(a) its being sent by recorded delivery letter to the last known address of the persons and organisations referred to in subsection (4E) above so as to arrive there, in the normal course of post, not later than seven days after the scales are fixed under subsection (2) above; or

(b) personal service of the notice upon those persons within that time.

NOTE

1. As amended by the Criminal Justice and Licensing (Scotland) Act 2010 (asp 13) Pt 8 s.174 (effective 11 November 2011).

DEFINITIONS

"licensing authority": s.2(2).
"taxi": s.23.

GENERAL NOTE

This section makes it mandatory for the licensing authority to fix maximum fares in relation to taxi hires, and provides for a regular review of the same. The section does not apply to private hire cars or to taxi-bus operation, since the latter will be subject to control only if, and in so far as they are the subject of any subsidy agreement or other formal agreement for the provision of a service.

Subsection (1)

"All other charges" include charges for the carriage of additional passengers, dogs, waiting times, holiday and night-time supplements, etc. in other words, all charges which passengers will be obliged to pay in connection with the hire of the taxi. Any charges not catered for in the list fixed by the local authority cannot lawfully be rendered, e.g. a surcharge for paying by credit card collected by the driver if such a charge is not included in those specified on the list. Note that the charges listed are maximum charges and, in theory and provided that no contrary stipulation is made in any licensing condition, taxi operators are free to charge less than the scale charges provided that this does not result in any potential disturbance. Note that no additional charges may be made for the carriage of a guide dog, hearing dog or assistance dog—see the Taxi Drivers' Licences (Carrying of Guide Dogs and Hearing Dogs) (Scotland) Regulations 2003 (SSI 2003/73)—see pp.217–220 below. It does not include charges for hires to destinations outwith the licensing area, unless the provisions of s.15 have been invoked. The fares fixed are the *maximum* fares although there would be no objection, in principle, to taxi operators or drivers undercutting or waiving any of the charges. It is an offence in terms of s.21(5) of the Act to charge more than the prescribed amounts.

Subsection (2)

The 18 month period is a maximum and licensing authorities can review at more frequent intervals if they so wish. Note that the consultation and intimation procedures detailed below will result in any reviews having to be initiated, so as to give adequate time for the procedures to be followed and completed prior to the expiry of the 18 month period.

Subsection (3)

There are three duties here that are incumbent on the licensing authority. The first is to consult with persons or organisations representative of the taxi operators within their area, although it should be noted that it is not a duty to consult with every individual operator of a taxi, notwithstanding the rights of the latter to make an appeal in terms of s.18(1). The second duty is to give notice by advertising in local newspapers and to invite representations from any person. The third duty is to consider any representation duly lodged with them—the effect of this is that all timeous representations must be considered, but it is not mandatory to consider late representations. All three duties must be fulfilled before the revised charges can take effect.

Subsection (4)

Notice has thus to be given to the persons consulted in terms of subs.(3)(a) of the new charges (or the fact that the charges are unchanged) and those persons have to be informed of their rights of appeal in terms of s.18(1)—note that the persons who lodge representations in terms of subs.(3)(c) do not have to be so informed.

Subsections (4A)–(4E)

These subsections were added by s.174(3) of the 2010 Act and set out the method by which the proposed scales are to be calculated, how they are to be advertised, to whom they should be notified and consulted with and other matters.

Subsection (5)

This lays down a very precise timescale for the giving of notice and if there is any uncertainty, personal service would be preferable—the provisions are, perhaps, archaic in the age of electronic communication!

Appeals in respect of taxi fares

18.—[1](1) Any person mentioned in subsection (1A) may, within 14 days of notice being given under section 17(4C), appeal against those scales to the traffic commissioner for the Scottish Traffic Area as constituted for the purpose for the Public Passenger Vehicles Act 1981.

[1](1A) Those persons are—

(a) any person who operates a taxi in an area for which scales have been fixed under section 17(2)

(b) any person or organisation appearing to the traffic commissioner to be representative of such taxi operators.

(2) The traffic commissioner may hear an appeal under this section notwithstanding that it was not lodged within the time mentioned in subsection (1) above.

[1](3) On an appeal under subsection (1) above, the traffic commissioner may—

(a) confirm or alter the scales; or

(b) decline to proceed—

(i) at any stage in the appeal, if he considers the case for the appellant and is not representative of the view of a substantial proportion of the operators of taxis operating in the area of the licensing authority;

(ii) if less than two years have elapsed since they decided an appeal against a decision of the same authority in respect of the same scale, and he considers it inappropriate that he should consider the matter again.

(4) An appeal under this section shall have the effect of suspending the decision referred to in subsection (1) above under the date when the appeal is abandoned or, as the case may be, when notice is given to the appellant advising him of its disposal.

(5) Where he alters scales under subsection (3)(a) above, the traffic commissioner may substitute a different date for the coming into effect of these scales.

(6) The Secretary of State may by order made by statutory instrument make rules as to procedure in relation to appeals under this section.

(7) The decision of the traffic commissioner on an appeal under this section shall be final.

(8) The traffic commissioner shall give notice of his decision in writing to the appellant and to the licensing authority and notice shall be given to the appellant by—

(a) its being sent by recorded delivery letter to his last known address or, as the case may be, to them so as to arrive, in the normal course of post, not later than five days after his decision; or

(b) personal service of the notice on the appellant within that time.

(9) [*As repealed by the Criminal Justice and Licensing (Scotland) Act 2010 (asp 13) Pt 8 s.174 (effective 11 November 2011).*]

(10) A licensing authority shall pay the expenses incurred under this section by the traffic commissioner in relation to appeals under this section.

(11) [*As repealed by the Tribunals and Inquiries Act 1971 (c.42) Sch.1 Pt 11.*]

NOTE

1. As amended by the Criminal Justice and Licensing (Scotland) Act 2010 (asp 13) Pt 8 s.174 (effective 11 November 2011).

DEFINITIONS

"licensing authority": s.2(2).

"taxi": s.23.

"traffic commissioner": s.4 of the Public Passenger Vehicles Act 1981, as amended by s.3 of the Transport Act 1985.

GENERAL NOTE

This section provides a right of appeal by any taxi operator to the Traffic Commissioner for the Scottish Traffic Area, in respect of the scales of fares and charges, and any review thereof made by the licensing authority in terms of s.17. Section 18 does not apply to private hire cars or taxi-buses. Section 18(11) was repealed by Sch.1 para.62 of the Tribunals and Inquiries Act 1992.

Subsection (1)

This applies to any licensed taxi operator in the area and not just to persons who were consulted or who made representations in terms of s.17(3).

Subsection (1A)

This was added by s.174(4) of the 2010 Act.

Subsection (2)

Since the timescale laid down in subs.(1) is a tight one (and, in certain circumstances, may give a party only nine days in which to lodge an appeal), the commissioner is given a discretionary power to hear late appeals.

Subsection (3)

This subsection was the subject of adverse judicial comment by the Inner House in the case of *City of Glasgow DC v Traffic Commissioner for the Scottish Traffic Area*, 1990 S.C.L.R. 737 where it was described as badly drafted, lacking logical order, containing errors in syntax and having been poorly amended by the 1985 Act—an example of the latter is found in the first line where "them" is left unaltered despite its lack of meaning in the new context. In terms of subs.(3), the commissioner can proceed in one of three ways, namely they can decline to hear the appeal (subs.3(b)) or hear the appeal and either confirm the scales or alter them (subs.(3)(a)). If they decide to hear the appeal, then the original scales continue to apply in the meantime (see subs.(4)), and they are entitled to consider all of the scales and charges, and alter or otherwise deal with all or part of them, notwithstanding that the appeal may only have been concerned with one particular charge or charges, the rationale behind this being the interdependence of the component parts of the scale or scales. Subsection 3(b) contains two quite separate and unrelated powers, which enable the commissioner to exercise a discretionary power to decline to hear an appeal. In terms of subs.(3)(b)(i) they may "at any stage in the appeal" (i.e. up until the final determination thereof), decline to hear an appeal if they consider that the appellant's case is not representative of a substantial proportion of the local taxi operators, "as the coming into effect of the scales is delayed while an appeal is being dealt with, an appeal by an unrepresentative minority would mean that the rest of the trade was denied charging fares with which it was content. While 'substantial proportion' is not defined, it is assumed that it will be more than one-third of operators"—para.2.39 of Appendix A to Scottish Development Department Circular 6/1983 (as substituted by Scottish Development Department Circular 25/1986). In the case cited above, however, it was held that the question of whether or not the appellants were representative of a substantial proportion of the operators was a matter of fact for the commissioner and that their decision thereon should not be lightly interfered with. By reason of the wording of the subsection, the commissioner does have a discretion to proceed with the appeal even if they do not consider that the appellants are representative of a substantial proportion of operators, e.g. where a very small number of operators might have a legitimate and important interest in seeking a particular amendment of the scales that bears upon their own highly unusual circumstances—see *City of Glasgow DC v Traffic Commissioner for the Scottish Traffic Area*, 1990 S.C.L.R. 737. An example of circumstances which might give rise to an exercise of the commissioner's discretion not to hear an appeal in terms of subs.(3)(b)(ii), would be where the appellants wished to run the same argument in an appeal that they had run in one heard in the previous year, and there had been no material change in circumstances in the intervening period.

Subsection (4)

The effect of this subsection is that while the appeal is still pending, the revised scales are suspended and the original scales still remain in force.

Subsection (5)

This is an additional power to that contained in subs.(3)(a).

Subsection (6)

Prior to the Transport Act 1985 coming into force these were contained in Scottish Development Department Circular 1/1984.The rules have now been amended and are contained in a statutory instrument, namely the Licensing and Regulation of Taxis (Appeals in Respect of Taxi Fares) (Scotland) Order 1985 (SI 1985/2025) which is set out at pp.209–212 below.

Subsection (7)

There is no appeal from his decision other than by way of judicial review—see *City of Glasgow DC v Traffic Commissioner for the Scottish Traffic Area*, 1990 S.C.L.R. 737.

Subsection (8)

Although the licensing authority must meet the commissioner's expenses (but not the appellant's) they must, by virtue of s.12, recover the same out of the general fees for taxi, etc. licences and applications and ultimately therefore these expenses will be paid for by way of fares.

Publication and coming into effect of taxi fares

[1]**18A.**—(1) Following the fixing of scales by a licensing authority under section 17(2) the licensing authority must—

(a) determine the dates on which the scales are to come into effect, and
(b) publish the scales in accordance with subsections (3) to (5)

(2) The scales may come into effect no earlier than seven days after the date on which they are published.

(3) The licensing authority must—

(a) give notice of the scales by advertisement in an newspaper circulating in its area, and

(b) specify in that advertisement the date on which the scales are due to come into effect

(4) The authority must give notice of the scales—

(a) where no appeal has been lodged under subsection (1) of section 18, as soon as is practicable after the expiry of the period of 14 days mentioned in that subsection,

(b) where such an appeal has been lodged, as soon as practicable after determination of that appeal.

(5) For the purposes of subsection (4), an appeal is determined on the date which the appeal is abandoned or notice given to the appellant of its disposal.

NOTE

1. As inserted by the Criminal Justice and Licensing (Scotland) Act 2010 (asp 13) Pt 8 s.174 (effective 11 November 2011).

GENERAL NOTE

This section sets out how new scales are to be advertised and when they will come into effect.

Taxi stances

19.—(1) A licensing authority may, after consultation with persons or organisations appearing to them to be, or be representative of, the operators of taxis operating in their area, appoint stances for taxis for the whole or any part of a day in any road within their area or on any land owned by the authority, or, with the consent of the owner, on any land owned by him.

(2) A licensing authority may—

(a) erect and illuminate signs,

(b) cause lines or marks to be made on roads; indicating the limits of taxi stances.

(3) A licensing authority may from time to time, after consultation as mentioned in subsection (1) above, vary the number of taxis permitted to be at each stance and alter the position of such stances or revoke the appointment thereof.

(4) Before appointing any stance for taxis or varying the number of taxis permitted to be at each stance, the licensing authority shall give notice to the chief constable of the area in which the stance is situated and shall also give public notice of the proposal by advertisement in at least one newspaper circulating in their area and shall take into consideration any objections or representations in respect of such proposal which may be made to them in writing within 28 days of the first publication of such notice.

(5) Nothing in this section shall empower a licensing authority to appoint any taxi stance so as unreasonably to prevent access to any premises or, without the consent of the roads authority to appoint any taxi stance on any road or erect or illuminate any sign there or cause any line or mark to be made on any road.

DEFINITIONS

"licensing authorities": s.2(2).
"premises": s.8.
"road": s.133.

"roads authority": s.133.
"taxi": s.23.

GENERAL NOTE

This section provides a discretionary power for licensing authorities to provide taxi stances (ranks) in their respective areas provided that they obtain the necessary prior consents, consult the appropriate trade organisations and other representatives, give notice to the police and the public and do not obstruct access to any premises. This section does not apply to private hire cars. For the views of the Joint Advisory Group on Hire Cars in relation to the parking of taxis and private hire cars see Scottish Development Department Circular 25/1986 para.16. Subsection 19(5) was amended by s.87(1) of the Roads (Scotland) Act 1984 and subs.19(6) by s.156(3) of the same Act. The owner of a stand on private land can impose conditions on its use—*Jones v First Great Western Ltd* [2015] R.T.R. 3.

Regulations relating to taxis and private hire cars and their drivers

20.—(1) Notwithstanding paragraph 5(2) of Schedule 1 to this Act, the Secretary of State may by regulations provide that licensing authorities shall, in relation to taxi, private hire car, taxi drivers' or private hire car drivers' licences, impose such conditions or classes of conditions as may be prescribed in the regulations and shall not impose such other conditions or classes of conditions as may be so prescribed and may provide that such conditions shall be imposed or, as the case may be, shall not be imposed for different areas or classes of areas; and different conditions or classes of conditions may be prescribed in relation to different categories of taxi or private hire car.

[1](2) The Secretary of State may by regulations prescribe types, sizes and designs of vehicles for the purposes of section 10(4) of this Act and, in doing so, may prescribe different types, sizes or designs of vehicles in respect of different areas.

[2,3](2A) Without prejudice to the generality of subsections (1) and (2) above, regulations under those subsections may make such provision as appears to the Secretary of State to be necessary or expedient in relation to the carrying in taxis of disabled persons (within the meaning of section 6 of the Equality Act 2010) and such provision may in particular prescribe—

(a) requirements as to the carriage of wheelchairs, guide dogs, hearing dogs and other categories of dog;
(b) a date from which any such provision is to apply and the extent to which it is to apply; and
(c) the circumstances in which an exemption from such provision may be granted in respect of any taxi or taxi driver,

and in this subsection—

"*guide dog*" means a dog which has been trained to guide a blind person;
"*hearing dog*" means a dog which has been trained to assist a deaf person; and
"*other categories of dog*" means such other categories of dog as the Secretary of State may prescribe, trained to assist disabled persons who have disabilities of such kinds as he may prescribe.

[3,4](2AA) The Scottish Ministers may by regulations make such provision as appears to them to be necessary or expedient in relation to the carrying in private hire cars of disabled persons (within the meaning of section 6 of the Equality Act 2010 and such provision may in particular prescribe—

(a) requirements as to the carriage of guide dogs, hearing dogs and other categories of dogs;

(b) a date from which any such provision is to apply and the extent to which it is to apply; and

(c) the circumstances in which an exemption from such provision may be granted in respect of any private hire car or private hire car driver, and in this subsection "guide dog", "hearing dog" and "other categories of dog" have the same meaning as in subsection (2A) above.

[4](2AB) Regulations under subsection (2AA) above may provide for the creation of offences and for making offenders liable on summary conviction to a fine not exceeding level 3 on the standard scale.

[4](2AC) Regulations under subsection (2AA) above shall be made by statutory instrument subject to annulment in pursuance of a resolution of the Scottish Parliament.

[1](3) Regulations under subsection (1) or (2) above shall be made by statutory instrument subject to annulment in pursuance of a resolution of the Scottish Parliament.

NOTES

1. As amended by the Local Government in Scotland Act 2003 (asp 1) Pt 8 s.49 (effective 1 April 2003).

2. As inserted by the Disability Discrimination Act 1995 (c.50) Pt 5 s.39(3) (effective 5 February 2003).

3. As amended by the Equality Act 2010 (c.15) Sch.26(1) para.7 (effective 1 October 2010).

4. As inserted by the Private Hire Vehicles (Carriage of Guide Dogs etc.) Act 2002 (c.37) s.2 (effective 31 March 2004).

DEFINITIONS

"disabled person": Disability Discrimination Act 1995 s.1(2).
"licensing authority": s.2(2).
"private hire car": s.23.
"taxi": s.23.
"taxi and private hire car licences": s.10.
"taxi driver's or private hire car driver's licences": s.13.

GENERAL NOTE

Two quite separate powers are given to the Secretary of State in relation both to taxis and private hire cars (and also taxi-buses) and these are to impose regulations upon licensing authorities with regard to prescribed conditions—s.20(1); and to specify types, sizes and designs of vehicles—s.20(2); and to make provision for the carriage of disabled persons, wheelchairs, guide dogs, etc.—see s.20(2A). In addition, a set of recommended model licensing conditions has been produced for taxis and private hire cars and their drivers; these are extremely comprehensive and can be found in full set out as Annex B to Scottish Development Department Circular 25/1986; they were drawn up after extensive consultations with the trade and the licensing authorities. Their adoption is not mandatory and it is the prerogative of the licensing authority to adopt such of the conditions as they think appropriate although there is, of course, some merit in having national uniform conditions which each authority would adopt, subject only to any peculiar local considerations.

Subsection (1)

These powers are additional to the power of the licensing authority to impose conditions in terms of para.5(2) of Sch.1 and the Secretary of State has exercised these powers in the Licensing and Regulation of Taxi and Private Hire Cars and their Drivers (Prohibited and Required Conditions) (Scotland) Regulations 1986 (SI 1986/1238). These regulations, which replace those contained in SI 1983/1029, provide for five prohibited conditions. Paragraph 3(a) of the regulations prohibits the restriction of a taxi in one mode of operation only, i.e. limiting it for exclusive use (the "classic" taxi operation), shared use ("carriage at separate fares"), taxi-bus operations, etc. The other paragraphs contain the original four prohibitions relating to restrictions on the number of vehicles for which a licence holder may hold licences, requirements that the licence holder has to reside in the area, the banning of radios and the prevention of licence holders engaging in any other employment or business. In the case of taxi-buses, para.4 imposes certain mandatory conditions. In addition, regulations have been made by the Secretary of State in respect of taxi-bus operations—the Local Services (Operation by Taxis) (Scotland) Regulations 1986 (SI 1986/1239).

Subsection (2)

The power is intended as a reserve power to be used in addition to the licensing authority's powers under s.10(2) only if there was evidence of the specification by licensing authorities of unnecessarily expensive vehicle types in particular areas—see para.2.47 of Appendix A to Scottish Development Department Circular 6/1983, as substituted by Scottish Development Department Circular 25/1986. It has, so far, not been exercised.

Subsection (2A)

This subsection allows the Secretary of State to introduce regulations for the carrying of disabled passengers, wheelchairs, guide dogs and hearing dogs. A "common sense" approach to the 1995 Act definition was expected by the Minister for Social Security and Disabled People and some guidelines are given in Sch.1 to that Act. In relation to taxis, the Minister stated that the requirements for accessibility would not apply, in the first instance, to existing vehicles since, "we have no intention of introducing the requirements over such a period as would undermine the viability of the taxi trade". No regulations in relation to wheelchairs have, to date, been made by the Secretary of State in relation to Scottish taxis—a delay which, given the general dilatory implementation of the Act as a whole, is not altogether surprising. For an indication of what regulations in Scotland might be expected to contain see the parallel legislation applicable to England and Wales and set out in ss.32–38 of the 1995 Act—this includes detailed provision relating to exemptions. In terms of Sch.5 Pt II para.E5 of the Scotland Act 1998 this function has been reserved to the UK Parliament. It is, however, proposed that such functions be devolved to the Scottish Ministers by an order to be made under s.63 of the 1998 Act. In the interim licensing authorities have been advised that they should await the new regulations before approving new types of accessible taxi types.

Regulations have, however, been made under this subsection in respect of the carriage of wheelchairs, guide dogs, hearing dogs and other categories of dogs. The definition of "assistance" dog is found in reg.2(2) of the Taxi Drivers' Licences (Carrying of Guide Dogs and Hearing Dogs) (Scotland) Regulations 2003 (SSI 2003/73)—see pp.217–220 below, which applies to taxis. Provisions relating to the carrying of assistance dogs in private hire cars are found in the Private Hire Cars (Carrying of Guide Dogs and Hearing Dogs (Scotland) Regulations 2004 (SSI 2004/88).

Subsections (2AA)–(2AC)

These subsections were added by the Private Hire Vehicles (Carriage of Guide Dogs etc.) Act 2002 and the wording was altered by Sch.26 of the Equality Act 2010.

Offences

21.—(1) If any person—

(a) operates, or permits the operation of, a taxi within an area in respect of which its operation requires to be but is not licensed or the driver requires to be but is not licensed, or

(b) picks up passengers in, or permits passengers to be picked up by, a private hire car within an area in respect of which its operation requires to be but is not licensed or the driver requires to be but is not licensed, that person shall be guilty of an offence and liable, on summary conviction, to a fine not exceeding level 4 on the standard scale.

(2) Subsection (1) above does not apply to the operation of a taxi or private hire car within an area in respect of which its operation or its driver is not licensed if the request for its hiring was received by its driver

(otherwise than in a public place from the person to be conveyed in it, or a person acting on his behalf, for a journey beginning there and then) whilst—

(a) in the area or in that part thereof in respect of which its operation and its driver are licensed;

(b) engaged on hire on a journey which began in that area or part or will end there; or

(c) returning to that area or part immediately following completion of a journey on hire.

(3) Subsection (1)(b) above does not apply to the operation of a vehicle within an area in respect of which its operation or its driver is not licensed if there are in force—

(i) in respect of the vehicle, a licence under section 37 of the Town Police Clauses Act 1847 (licensing of hackney carriages) or section 48 of the Local Government (Miscellaneous Provisions) Act 1976 (licensing of private hire vehicles); and

(ii) in respect of its driver, a licence under section 46 of the said Act of 1847 (licensing of hackney carriage drivers) or, as the case may be, section 51 of the said Act of 1976 (licensing of drivers of private hire vehicles).

(3A) Subsection (1)(b) does not apply to the operation of a vehicle within an area in respect of which its operation or its driver is not licensed if there are in force—

(a) in respect of the vehicle, a licence under section 7 of the Private Hire Vehicles (London) Act 1998; and

(b) in respect of its driver, a licence under section 13 of that Act.

(4) If any person, being the holder of a taxi licence or private hire car licence in respect of a vehicle, permits another person who does not have a current taxi driver's licence or private hire car driver's licence, as the case may be, to operate the vehicle as a taxi or, as the case may be, a private hire car he shall be guilty of an offence and liable, on summary conviction, to a fine not exceeding level 4 on the standard scale.

(5) If any person demands fares or other charges in respect of the hire of a taxi or for the hire of a private hire car which is fitted with a taximeter in excess of the scales established under sections 17 and 18 of this Act, he shall be guilty of an offence and liable on summary conviction, to a fine not exceeding level 4 on the standard scale.

(6) If any person without good cause breaks the seal on a taximeter or operates or drives a taxi or private hire car knowing that the seal on its meter has been broken, he shall be guilty of an offence and liable, on summary conviction, to a fine not exceeding level 4 on the standard scale or to imprisonment for a period not exceeding 60 days or to both.

(7) If any person, without reasonable excuse, causes or permits any vehicle other than a taxi to wait on any stance for taxis during any period for which that stance has been appointed by a licensing authority under section 19 of this Act, he shall be guilty of an offence and liable, on summary conviction, to a fine not exceeding level 2 on the standard scale.

(8) Notice of the effect of subsection (7) above shall be indicated by such traffic signs as may be prescribed as authorised for the purpose by the Secretary of State in pursuance of his powers under section 54 of the Road Traffic Regulation Act 1967.

DEFINITIONS

"private hire car": s.23.
"public place": s.133.
"standard scale": see Introduction p.32 above.

"taxi": s.23.

GENERAL NOTE

This section provides for a number of statutory offences that are in addition to the general offences specified in s.7.

Subsection (1)

A number of separate offences are created in this section namely: (a) of operating or permitting the operation of (i.e. as a booking office or app or other device) a taxi within an area which it does not hold a licence for or in which its driver is not licenced; or (b) a private hire car picking up or permitting such a car to pick up passengers (e.g. again by a booking office or app or other device) within an area in which it and its driver are not licenced. In subs.(1)(a) "operate" includes both picking up pre-booked passengers and plying for hire, i.e. picking up passengers in a public place where those passengers have not pre-booked, and a private hire car driver would be guilty of an offence under s.21(1)(a) if they had plied for hire as a taxi. It is an offence for a private hire car driver to pick up passengers in an area for which they did not have a s.13 licence. In *Braintree DC v Howard* [1993] R.T.R. 193, where a private hire car operator operated his business from a base at a caravan outside of a district, but obtained bookings from a telephone number within the district answered by his wife who then telephoned him to confirm the booking, and who accepted such bookings to take passengers on journeys within the district, it held that he was guilty of the offence of operating an unlicensed private hire car business. A private hire car driver does not "operate" within a district merely by advertising in a directory circulating within the district. If their offices and facilities for accepting bookings were outside it, the determining factor was whether they had made provision to invite or accept bookings in the district in general. The word "operate" did not refer to a place where bookings must reach but the place at which such provision had been made—see *Windsor and Maidenhead RBC v Khan (t/a Top Cabs)* [1994] R.T.R. 87 and *Kingston Upon Hull Council v Wilson* (1995) 23 L.R. 17. An operator is only permitted to use taxis and private hire cars licensed by the authority in whose area they operate and cannot use those licensed by an adjacent authority; this also applies to drivers: see *Dittah v Birmingham City Council* [1993] R.T.R. 356. For a case involving the transfer of bookings from one operator to another see *Shanks v North Tyneside BC* (2001) 47 L.R. 9. For a discussion of the concept of "permitting", see Gerald H Gordon, *Criminal Law of Scotland* (1978), para.8–73. These offences are additional to those in s.7(1) but, when used, are to be a substitute for them—s.7(1) makes it an offence to carry out an unlicensed activity "without reasonable excuse", whereas this section imposes a strict liability offence. For examples of how the court has dealt with unlicensed vehicles, see *Jackson v Friel*, 1996 G.W.D. 25-1448 (private hire car); *McKenzie v Friel*, 1998 G.W.D. 13-676 (taxi).

Subsection (2)

This subsection provides that an offence under s.21(1) will not have been committed in certain specified circumstances, namely, where the request for hire was received by the driver outwith the "home area", i.e. the area in which car and driver are licensed, but otherwise than in a public place for a journey beginning immediately (e.g. by phone call to a booking office in their home area), provided that it was whilst: (a) they were in the home area or any part thereof in which the driver and car was licenced—which in any event they would have been entitled so to do; (b) they were at the relevant time engaged in a journey which had begun in the home area or was to end in the home area; or (c) they were returning to the home area or part of it immediately following completion of a journey or hire.

Examples of: (a) might be if an Edinburgh taxi or private hire car was booked in Edinburgh for a journey beginning there but due to end in, say, Aberdeen; or (b) if they received a request while on that journey but was asked to undertake a new journey thereafter; and (c) if they were returning to Edinburgh immediately following completion of that journey and asked to undertake a new journey within the home area. It should be noted that these are said to be exceptions to the general rule in s.21(1) and cannot properly be used as an excuse to trade in another area in which the driver and car and the car were not licenced so that, e.g. an Edinburgh licenced car and driver if undertaking a journey from Edinburgh to Aberdeen could not on arrival spend a whole day on subsequent local journeys within the Aberdeen area for different customers who had not pre-booked and they or their office could not accept such bookings.

Subsection (3)

This section provides exemptions for vehicles licensed in England and Wales in respect of journeys to Scotland—see s.16 for reciprocal Scottish vehicle exemptions.

Subsection (3A)

Prior to the insertion of this subsection private hire vehicles in London were unlicensed. This subsection was added by Sch.1 para.3 of the Private Hire Vehicles (London) Act 1988.

Subsection (4)

This applies only if the vehicle is being used as a taxi or private hire car. This subsection applies also to taxi-buses.

Subsection (5)

This subsection only creates an offence if an attempt is made to charge in excess of the amount which appears on the taximeter of a taxi or a private hire car if a taximeter is fitted to it. A taximeter is "a device that works together with the signal generator to make a measuring instrument; with the device measuring duration, calculating distance with on the basis of a signal delivered by the distance signal generator; and calculating and displaying the fare to be paid for a trip on the basis of the calculated distance or of the measured duration of the trip, or of both": reg.2(1) of the Measuring Instruments (Taximeter) Regulations 2006 (SI 2006/2304) applicable to Scotland. A lesser fare can be charged by arrangement and fares applicable to private hire cars are subject only to prior agreement and those hiring a private hire car are responsible for paying reasonable rates therefore. In *Transport for London v Uber London Ltd* [2015] EWHC 2918 (Admin) it was held that the Uber app and similar hand-held apps did not constitute taximeters so that fares calculated in that manner were not to be equipped with taximeter fares. Note also that it is an offence to charge more than the sums on the taximeter or to impose additional charges or premiums other than those provided for in the scales.

Subsection (6)

Note that taximeters require to be tested in terms of s.11(2)(a) and must not be tampered with.

Subsection (7)

For "causes and permits" see notes to s.14(3) above, and Introduction p.32 above.

[1]Exemptions

22.—(1) Nothing in sections 10 to 21 (with the exception of subsection (7) of section 21) of this Act shall—

(a) apply to a vehicle used for bringing passengers or goods within and taking them out of an area in respect of which the vehicle is not licensed as a taxi or a private hire car in pursuance of a contract for the hire of the vehicle made outside the area if the vehicle is not made available for hire within the area;

(b) apply to a vehicle while it is being used in connection with a funeral or wedding;

(2) The Scottish Ministers may by regulations specify further circumstances in which sections 10 to 21 (with the exception of subsection (7) of Section 21) are not to apply.

(3) Regulations under subsection (2)—

(a) may make transitional, transitory and saving provision,

(b) are subject to the negative procedure.

NOTE

1. As amended by the Air Weapons and Licensing (Scotland) Act 2015 (asp 10) Pt 3 s.65 (effective 1 December 2015).

DEFINITIONS
"private hire car": s.23.
"taxi": s.23.

GENERAL NOTE

This section was amended by s.65 of the 2015 Act which added subss.(2) and (3) and removed the previous exemption which allowed exemption for vehicles carrying passengers under a contract allows contract for its exclusive hire for a period of not less than 24 hours as it as felt that in so doing a "level playing field was created". Examples of work that may now fall within the Act are given in the 2015 report as executive work where a car is hired to transport an individual between meetings over the course of the day and airport transfers where a car is hired to transport customers on a longer journey meaning that the car can only be used for that journey during the day—the example was given of a hiring from Glasgow Airport to Iona.

Taxi-buses are also exempt. The saving does not permit exempt vehicles from waiting at a taxi stance.

Subsection (a) applies to vehicles picking up passengers as the homeward part of a prearranged "to and fro" journey starting from outside the area, e.g. a taxi requested to collect a passenger arriving at a railway station in an area adjacent to that in which the taxi was licensed: *Britain v ABC Cabs (Camberley)* [1981] R.T.R. 395 and *Adur DC v Fry* [1995] C.L.Y. 3148. Section 22(1)(b) excludes wedding and funeral cars. This section on came into force on 1 December 2015—see Air Weapons and Licensing (Scotland) Act 2015 (Commencement No.1) Order 2015 (SSI 2015/382).

Interpretation of sections 10 to 22

23.—(1) In sections 10 to 22 of this Act—

"*taxi*" means a hire car which is engaged, by arrangements made in a public place between the person to be conveyed in it (or a person acting on his behalf) and its driver for a journey beginning there and then; and

"*private hire car*" means a hire car other than a taxi within the meaning of this subsection.

(2) In subsection (1) above, "hire car" means a motor vehicle with a driver (other than a vehicle being a public service vehicle within the meaning of section 1(1)(a) of the Public Passenger Vehicles Act 1981) which is, with a view to profit, available for hire by the public for personal conveyance.

(3) Notwithstanding that a vehicle in respect of which there is a licence for its operation as a taxi is, on any occasion, engaged as a hire car otherwise than in the manner referred to in subsection (1) above, the enactments relating to its operation as a taxi, and to the driving of it as such (including any such enactments in this Act) shall nonetheless apply in relation to it; and that other manner of engagement on that occasion shall not of itself cause the operation or driving of the licensed taxi to be regarded for the purposes of this Act as the operation or driving of a private hire car within the meaning of subsection (1) above.

DEFINITION
"public place": s.133.

GENERAL NOTE

This is an extremely important section for it provides the definitions of "taxi" and "private hire car".

Subsection (1)

Both a taxi and a private hire car are "hire cars" (see subs.(2)) that can be pre-booked but only a taxi can "ply for hire" or pick up passengers without a prior pre-booking in a public place for a journey beginning then and there, and it can be signalled to stop by a member of the public in the street, at a station, outside a hotel or indeed at any location that would be a "public place" within the meaning of s.133, or can be picked up by a passenger at a taxi stance. Where the driver of a private hire car, clearly marked as such, was approached by a potential customer who asked whether they were free and they answered that they were, it was held that they were plying for hire as a taxi: see *Nottingham City Council v Woodings* [1994] R.T.R. 72; [1993] C.O.D. 350; see also *DPP v Computer Cab Co Ltd* [1995] C.O.D. 361; *Eastbourne BC v Stirling* [2000] 12 C.L. 49911 (where the forecourt of a railway station was held to be a street for the purposes of English legislation relating to taxis); where a driver positioned his vehicle so that the offer of its use was "projected to and addressed to" people in the street, he was considered to be plying for hire—*White v Cubitt* [1930] 1 K.B. 443 and *Smith v Hughes* [1960] 1 W.L.R. 830. The difference between taxis and private hire cars has been said to be an important one and the public should be able to recognise which form of vehicle is being hired (*Spring Radio Cars Ltd v Glasgow City Council* [2013] CSOH 15; 2013 S.L.T. 491 OH; [2014] CSIH 21; 2014 S.C. 529; 2014 S.L.T. 393 IH; *Central Taxis (Tollcross) Ltd v City of Edinburgh Council* unreported 23 March 2013 Edinburgh Sheriff Court) although it is said that the licensing requirement of both "is to safeguard the public from potential harm such as may befall the unwary who accept transport in unlicensed vehicles and unlicensed drivers". Little guidance is given as to what "a journey beginning then and there" means in respect of private hire cars but it is generally held that such vehicles require to be "pre-booked" with the operator or booking office but not with the driver (see *Central Taxis* case). The expression pre-booking is used in the government circular 25/286, para.2.59 and the Scottish Government's *Taxi and Private Hire Car Licencing: Best Practice Guidance for Local Authorities*, 2nd edn (Scottish Government, 2012) and the words appear on the sticker attached to private hire car doors but nothing is said in the circular or guides as to whether the pre-booking cannot be instantaneous or made at the location of the private hire car. The Law Commission of England and Wales in its *Report on Taxi and Private Hire Services* (The Stationery Office, 2014), Law Com. No.347 at para.13.19 recognised that the speed at which a pre-booking can be made blurs the distinction, that no minimum time requirement is applicable and that it is a question of fact as to whether the booking is made for a journey beginning then and there. The 2015 report said at para.320 that "[we] are in no doubt that if a licensing system was now designed it would be a single regime applying to both taxis and private hire cars and their respective drivers. We accept the majority view that change would be disruptive to operators and the licensing authorities" and that a further review was necessary but in the interim made the changes found in ss.10(3A) and (3B) and 13(5). The fares and charges are fixed under s.17. A private hire car cannot be engaged in a public place but the fares therefor are freely negotiable between the operator and customer.

Subsection (2)

Note that "a view to profit" and "available for hire by the public for personal conveyance" are prerequisites for both types of vehicle—thus a private car carrying voters to the polling station for no financial reward, a voluntary taxi service for say the disabled and a free lift given to a hitchhiker are all activities falling outwith this definition. A "free" taxi service taking passengers home from a public house or club will probably be regarded as falling within the definition of "taxi" since it is designed to contribute to the commercial viability or attractiveness of those premises and is therefore being conducted "with a view to profit". A vehicle being used to convey pet animals to a veterinary surgeon, even if on rare occasions the owners of the pets are also being conveyed, does not fall within the definition of hire car—see *R (on the application of Arun DC) v Spooner* [2007] EWHC 307 (Admin); [2007] L.L.R. 200. The statutory exemption mentioned refers to public service vehicles with more than eight seats, i.e. buses, minibuses and coaches. Note also that the definition of "hire car" specifically means "a motor vehicle"—thus horse-drawn vehicles and pedestrian drawn vehicles such as trishaws and rickshaws and pedicabs are not taxis (cf. the position in England—see *R v Cambridge City Council Ex p. Lane* [1998] T.L.R. 615 and *Bugbugs Ltd v Transport for London* [2007] EWHC 2987 (QB); [2008] L.L.R. 247). Sedan chairs would also be are all excluded from this definition and cannot be "hire cars". However the operation of such conveyances as quasi-taxis would require a street trader's licence since the plying for hire would constitute the offering of a service within the meaning of s.38(2)(b) of the Act—an example is of pedicabs where a s.38 licence was refused on safety grounds: *Birrell v Glasgow City Council* [2015] CSIH 21; such vehicles as stretch limousines and party buses and fire engines could also be licenced under s.38. Quaere whether a motorcycle can properly be described as a taxi—see *Chaffeur Bikes Ltd v Leeds City Council* [2005] EWHC 2369 (Admin).

Subsection (3)

Where a taxi is used on occasions as a private hire car, e.g. where it is booked for a specific journey, it is still held to be being operated as a taxi for the purposes of the Act.

Licensing and Regulation of Second-hand Dealers

Second-hand dealer's licences

24.—(1) Subject to subsection (3) below, a licence, to be known as a "second-hand dealer's licence", shall be required for carrying on business as a second-hand dealer.

(2) In this section and in sections 25 to 27 and 36 of this Act "second-hand dealer" means a person carrying on a business as a dealer in second-hand goods or articles of any description.

(3) A second-hand dealer's licence shall not be required for carrying on—

(a) the business of a pawnbroker (that is to say, a person who, under a regulated agreement under the Consumer Credit Act 1974, takes an article in pawn);

(b) a business as a wholesale dealer purchasing exclusively from second-hand dealers licensed under this Act;

[1](c) the business of a charity (that is to say, a body which is entered in the Scottish Charity Register);

(d) a business as a dealer in second-hand goods or articles incidentally to another business not being that of a dealer in such goods or articles;

(e) a business either of financing the acquisition of goods by means of hire-purchase agreements, conditional sale agreements or credit sale agreements (as defined in section 189(1) of the Consumer Credit Act 1974) or of financing the use of goods by means of hiring agreements.

(4) Without prejudice to paragraph 5 of Schedule 1 to this Act, a licensing authority may, after consultation with the chief constable, attach conditions to a second-hand dealer's licence requiring the keeping of records in relation to the dealer's stock-in-trade; and conditions so attached may, without prejudice to the authority's power under this subsection, include provision as to—

(a) the information to be included in these records;

(b) their form;

(c) the premises where they are to be kept; and

(d) the period for which they are to be kept.

(5) A second-hand dealer acquiring a second-hand motor vehicle for the purpose of its re-sale in the course of his business shall keep a record of the mileage reading on the vehicle's odometer when he acquired it.

(6) Any person who contravenes subsection (5) above shall be guilty of an offence and liable, on summary conviction, to a fine not exceeding level 3 on the standard scale.

(7) It shall be a defence for a person charged with an offence under subsection (6) above to prove that he used all due diligence to prevent the commission of the offence.

NOTE

1. As amended by the Charities and Trustee Investment (Scotland) Act 2005 (asp 10) Sch.4(1) para.5(a) (effective 1 April 2006).

GENERAL NOTE

A second-hand dealer's licence is required by a person who carries on business as a second-hand dealer, provided that the licensing authority have passed a resolution to implement this "optional" category of licence in terms of s.9, and that the resolution specifies the particular class or classes of the activity that they require to be licensed and regulated—s.9(5)(a) (see note to that subsection, p.57). The term "second-hand dealer" is defined in subs.(2) and certain statutory exclusions are listed in subs.(3). The licensing authority is given powers to attach certain conditions to a licence and there is a special provision relating to second-hand car dealers; a statutory offence and defence thereto are created in respect to this special provision. For cases involving the fitness of a person to hold a second-hand dealer's licence, see *White v City of Edinburgh DC*, 1993 G.W.D. 36-2348 and *Stewart v Perth and Kinross DC*, 1996 G.W.D. 3-165.

Subsection (1)

The requirement for a licence applies to the proprietor or proprietors of the business—thus, partners would be required to hold a licence but not employees.

Subsection (2)

This is a wide definition which is, of course, qualified by the exemptions in subs.(3) below and also by the fact that the goods must fall within the particular class or classes of items covered in the licensing authority's resolution (see s.9(5)(a)). There is no definition given of "second-hand" so that one would probably have to adopt a standard dictionary definition of, "not new, having previously been worn or used by another" and one could therefore differentiate between chain store "seconds" and "remaindered" books on the one hand, and clothing that had already been worn and old books on the other; shop-soiled items, if not previously sold to a customer, would not be "second-hand". "Dealer" is also not defined but would encompass a person who trades in these goods in the ordinary course of business, as contrasted with a person disposing of their own surplus goods through, say, the medium of a classified advertisement or car boot sale, provided that this did not form part of a business. There is no necessity for the goods to have been acquired by the dealer for money or money's worth, so long as they sell them for such—thus, a person who acquires old building materials from demolition sites free of charge but subsequently sells them to the public would be a "dealer". The person who buys and "does up" cars and then sells them, but does not use them for their own use in the interim, would probably fall within the description of a "dealer", but in such a case the court would probably examine the exact nature of the person's activities and determine the matter according to all the surrounding facts and circumstances—at the end of the day, a "common sense" approach would have to be adopted. It should be noted that where a second-hand dealer also trades in metal (defined in s.37(1)), they require also a separate licence for that activity, in addition to the s.24 licence—see s.36.

Subsection (3)

This subsection lists the specific categories of dealers who are expressly excluded from the requirements to hold a licence, namely: (a) pawnbrokers; (b) wholesalers who purchase only from licensed second-hand dealers (such as persons who buy antiques in bulk for shipment to America or Germany); (c) charities—thus charity shops, which would normally be covered by the definition in subs.(2) above, are exempted; the definition was amended by Sch.4 para.5(s) of the Charities and Trustee Investment (Scotland) Act 2005; (d) dealers who trade in second-hand goods incidentally to another business—the classic example would be that of dealers in new "white goods" who take, e.g. old fridges and washing machines from customers in exchange for a discount on new items bought from them ("trade-in" or "part-exchange" deals), but where these dealers do not themselves directly sell these second-hand goods on to other customers; and (e) financiers.

Subsection (4)

This subsection provides that, after consultation with the chief constable and without prejudice to the general powers in Sch.1 para.5, the licensing authorities can impose conditions relating to stock-in-trade records of a second-hand dealer and can prescribe the appropriate form of those records. This is obviously a useful power in relation to the recovery of stolen property, and particularly so in relation to certain categories of goods, which are over-represented in theft statistics, such as electronic equipment. Note the similar, but mandatory, provisions in relation to stock recording imposed on metal dealers (s.30) and itinerant metal dealers (s.33).

Subsections (5) and (6)

These provisions were inserted to counteract the notorious practice of "clocking" of cars, and are designed to be applied in addition to any offences and penalties arising out of the sale of a "clocked" vehicle to a third party. For "level 3 on the standard scale" see Introduction p.32 above.

Subsection (7)

For the defence of "due diligence" see p.31 above.

Disposal of stock-in-trade

25.—(1) Subject to subsections (2) and (3) below and section 27 of this Act, a second-hand dealer shall not dispose of any item of his stock-in-trade until the expiry of 48 hours (excluding any time on Saturdays or Sundays) after he acquired it.

(2) Subsection (1) above shall not apply to any article acquired by the dealer in a public roup and disposed of by him without being brought to his place of business.

(3) A licensing authority may, on granting a second-hand dealer's licence or at any time thereafter, on application by the dealer and after consultation with the chief constable, order that subsection (1) above shall not apply to the disposal by the dealer of any item, or any specified item or class of items, of his stock-in-trade or any specified part of it.

(4) An order under subsection (3) above may—

(a) be made subject to such conditions as the authority think fit;

(b) relate to stock-in-trade or items thereof still to be acquired by the dealer to whom the order relates; or

(c) be varied or revoked at any time by the licensing authority.

(5) In subsection (3) above, "specified" means specified in an order under that subsection.

(6) A holder of a second-hand dealer's licence may appeal to the sheriff against a decision of the licensing authority under this section and paragraph 24(3) to (9) and (11) and (12) of Schedule 1 to this Act shall, with any necessary modifications, apply to an appeal under this subsection.

(7) Any person who contravenes subsection (1) above shall be guilty of an offence and liable, on summary conviction, to a fine not exceeding level 3 on the standard scale.

GENERAL NOTE

In order to prevent stolen goods and the like from being sold on by a second-hand dealer before, say, police inquiries have been completed, a 48 hour period is imposed following upon the acquisition of the goods by the dealer and, with certain exceptions, they are forbidden from disposing of the goods during that period.

Subsection (1)

The 48 hour period does not run at the weekends so that goods acquired at, say, 17:00 on a Friday cannot be disposed of until 17:00 on the following Tuesday. Section 27(2) provides for the substitution of a seven day period in certain circumstances.

Subsection (2)

This would cover the common situation whereby a dealer may have bought a mixed lot at a public roup, which contained goods they did not wish to retain and which they immediately sold on to another dealer or a member of the public.

Subsections (3)–(6)

These subsections provide that the 48 hour period can be waived by the licensing authority in certain specified circumstances, and can apply to goods not yet acquired by the dealer (subs.4(b)). The reference in subs.(6) to para.24(3)–(9), (11) and (12) would appear to be erroneous in that there is no such paragraph in the Schedule and should, in fact, refer to para.18, which is the appropriate paragraph dealing with appeals.

Subsection (7)

Note that this would appear to create an absolute offence and that the defence of due diligence is not provided for—cf. s.24(7) above. For "standard scale" see Introduction p.32 above.

Sellers of second-hand goods; offences, etc.

26.—(1) Any person who, when selling anything to a second- hand dealer, gives the dealer a false name or address shall be guilty of an offence and liable, on summary conviction, to a fine not exceeding level 3 on the standard scale.

(2) If anything is offered to a second-hand dealer in the course of his business and he has reason to believe that it has been stolen or otherwise unlawfully obtained he may, subject to subsection (3) below, detain the person offering it and a constable may arrest that person and take possession of it.

(3) Nothing in subsection (2) above authorises a second-hand dealer to detain a person longer than is reasonably necessary for obtaining the attendance of a constable.

(4) No civil liability shall arise as a result only of the detention in good faith of a person under subsection (2) above.

GENERAL NOTE

Section 26 creates an offence if a seller of second-hand goods gives a licensed dealer a false name and address, and powers are given to dealers to detain persons offering goods which appear to be stolen or unlawfully obtained.

Subsection (1)

This offence would appear to be an absolute one provided, of course, that the details given were "false". It is, however, not an offence to refuse to give one's name and address but this may cause the dealer to invoke their powers under subs.(2). For fine levels see Introduction, above.

Subsection (2)

Powers are given to the dealer to detain persons for a reasonable period so that the attendance of the police may be obtained and a constable may thereafter arrest the would-be seller and take possession of the goods. "Has reason to believe" implies a genuinely held belief based upon reason and not a mere fanciful notion or view formed by malice.

Subsection (3)

This would be a matter for the facts and circumstances of each case and different considerations might apply in a rural area, as distinct from a city.

Subsection (4)

Thus, the dealer, if acting in good faith, would not be liable in an action for damages for false or wrongful imprisonment; if they used undue force in detaining a person, then both criminal and civil liability might follow.

Functions of the court in relation to second-hand dealers convicted of offences

27.—(1) Where a second-hand dealer is convicted of an offence relating to second-hand dealing, the court by which he is convicted may make any order which it is competent to make under section 7(6) of this Act and an extract of such conviction and sentence (if any) shall, within 6 days after the date of the conviction, be transmitted by the clerk of the court to the licensing authority which granted the licence.

(2) Where a second-hand dealer is convicted—

(a) of an offence relating to second-hand dealing; or

(b) of an offence which in the opinion of the court is an offence involving dishonesty,

the court may, in addition to any other order which it is competent to make, order that he shall not dispose of any second-hand goods acquired by him until the expiry of a period of 7 days after their acquisition.

(3) In making an order under subsection (2) above, the court shall specify a period not exceeding 2 years for which it is to remain in force, but the court may revoke such an order at any time on the application of the person to whom it relates.

(4) Any person who fails to comply with an order made in relation to him under subsection (2) above shall be guilty of an offence and liable, on summary conviction, to a fine not exceeding level 4 on the standard scale or to imprisonment for a period not exceeding 60 days or to both.

GENERAL NOTE

Further provisions are made here in respect to second-hand dealers who have been convicted of offences relating to second-hand dealing.

Subsection (1)

The offences relating to second-hand dealing can be both those contained in this part of the Act, e.g. ss.24(6) and 25(7) or a crime, such as theft or reset of goods, which relate to their second-hand dealing, e.g. knowingly buying stolen goods or being art and part in the theft of second-hand goods that they then offers for sale. The orders that the court may make, pursuant to s.7(6), are the revocation of the licence and the disqualification from holding a licence for a period not exceeding five years. The transmission of the extract conviction to the licensing authority is an administrative measure that ensures that the licensing authority are aware of such a conviction and order.

Subsection (2)

This allows the court to extend the 48 hour period, provided for automatically in s.25(1), to seven days but note that there is no apparent exclusion of Saturdays and Sundays in the reckoning of the seven day period, so presumably a normal week between, say, 17:00 on Friday 1 and 17:00 on Friday 8 (i.e. the time at which the seven day period expires) is intended. Subsection (2)(b) extends the scope of this power to any offence involving dishonesty, whether or not it was connected with second-hand dealing so that, e.g. a licensed antique dealer who stole a car would fall within the ambit of the subsection.

Subsection (3)

The court must specify the period during which the "seven-day rule" is to apply, and it cannot be greater than two years from the date of its imposition and it is subject to revocation at the discretion of the court upon the application of the dealer for such a revocation.

Subsection (4)

This provides an increased penalty for contravention of the "seven-day rule"; cf. s.25(7), with imprisonment as an option. For "level 4 on the standard scale" see Introduction p.32 above.

Licensing and regulation of knife dealers

Knife dealers' licences

[1]**27A.**—(1) A licence, to be known as a "knife dealer's licence", is required for carrying on business as a dealer in any article mentioned in subsection (2).

(2) Those articles are—

[2](a) knives (other than folding pocket knives whose blades do not exceed 3.5 inches (8.91 centimetres) in length or knives designed for domestic use);

[2](aa) daggers (other than kirpans or skean dhus whose blades do not exceed 3.5 inches (8.91 centimetres) in length;

(b) knife blades (other than those designed for domestic use);

(c) swords;

(d) any other article—

(i) which has a blade; or

(ii) which is sharply pointed,

and which is made or adapted for use for causing injury to the person.

(3) A knife dealer's licence shall, in addition to specifying the activity which the dealer engages in, specify the premises in or from which the activity is to be carried on.

(4) In subsections (1) and (3), "dealer" means a person carrying on a business which consists wholly or partly of—

(a) selling;

(b) hiring;

(c) offering for sale or hire;

(d) exposing for sale or hire;

(e) lending; or

(f) giving,

to persons not acting in the course of a business or profession any article mentioned in subsection (2) (whether or not the activities mentioned in paragraphs (a) to (f) are carried out incidentally to a business which would not, apart from this section, require a knife dealer's licence).

(5) In subsection (4), "selling", in relation to an article mentioned in subsection (2)—

(a) includes—

(i) selling such an article by auction;

(ii) accepting goods or services in payment (whether in part or in full) for such an article; but

(b) does not include selling (by auction or otherwise) such an article by one person on behalf of another;

and "sale" is to be construed accordingly.

(6) For the purposes of subsection (4), an article is not to be treated as being exposed for sale if it is exposed for sale (by auction or otherwise) by a person other than the owner.

(7) The Scottish Ministers may by order modify subsection (2) so as to—

(a) add articles or classes of article;

(b) amend descriptions of articles or classes of article;

(c) remove articles or classes of article.

(8) The Scottish Ministers may by order—

(a) modify subsection (4) so as to modify the definition of "dealer";
(b) specify descriptions of activity which are not to be taken to be businesses for the purposes of that subsection (or that subsection as modified).

(9) The power in subsection (8)(a) includes in particular power to add descriptions of business—an example is given in subs. (2) and (4) above

NOTES

1. As inserted by the Custodial Sentences and Weapons (Scotland) Act 2007 (asp 17) Pt 3 s.58 (effective 1 November 2007).

2. As inserted by the Knife Dealers (Exceptions) Order 2009 (SSI 2009/218) art.2(b) (effective 1 September 2009).

DEFINITION

"premises": s.27H.

GENERAL NOTE

This section creates a new form of licence known as a knife dealers' licence which is required by a dealer (defined as a person who carries on a business which consists wholly or partly of selling, hiring, offering for sale or hire, lending or giving certain types of specified weapons to persons not acting in the course of a business or profession). Sections 27A–27F was introduced by s.58 of the 2007 Act in response to a perceived increase in knife and other related weapon related crime in Scotland.

Subsection (1)

Knife dealer is further detailed in subs.(4).

Subsection (2)

The articles specified in this subsection are those which are commonly misused with often fatal results such as knives, knife blades, swords and any other article that has a blade or is sharply pointed and is made or adapted for causing injury to the person. Note the exceptions for short-bladed folding pocket knives (e.g. pen knives), knives and knife blades designed for domestic use and daggers worn as part of a national or ceremonial dress in the form of a skean dhu in Highland dress and a kirpan worn by Sikhs as a religious symbol—Knife Dealer's (Exceptions) Order 2009 (SSI 2009/218) art.2.

Subsection (3)

Notice that the premises from which the activity is carried on has to be specified and premises includes a vehicle or vessel.

Subsection (4)

A dealer does not include a person who does not carry on a business or profession of dealing in the specified objects (i.e. a one-off sale) or one who does not deal with the general public (i.e. a person who sells such items to another dealer by way of trade). In addition no dealer's licence is required where a qualified fencing teacher hires, lends or gives a fencing sword to a person learning the sport—Knife Dealer's (Exceptions) Order 2009 (SSI 2009/218) para.3. Also excluded are qualified teachers of archery and water sports taking part in or in the vicinity of recognised competitions—see Knife Dealer's Licence (Miscellaneous) (Scotland) Order 2010 (SSI 2010/311) art.2; see also the Knife Dealer's (Miscellaneous) (Scotland) Order 2010 (SSI 2010/311) which excludes knifes used in water sports, and those used in historical re-enactments—Knife Dealer's Licence (Historical Re-enactment Events) (Scotland) Order 2011 (SSI 2011/263).

Subsection (5)

This subsection defines "selling" to include selling by auction or accepting such items in payment but excludes selling an item on behalf of another.

Subsection (6)

An article is not exposed for sale if it is exposed for sale by a person other than the owner (i.e. a sale on commission).

Subsection (7)

Subordinate legislation made in terms of s.27S can modify the list of items to which the licensing provisions apply and this was done originally by the Knife Dealers (Exceptions) Order 2009 (SSI 2009/218).

Subsection (8)

A similar provision applies to the definition of dealer or the descriptions of activity covered by the licensing provisions.

Applications for knife dealers' licences: notice

[1]**27B.**—(1) A licensing authority must cause public notice to be given of every application made to them for the grant or renewal of a knife dealer's licence.

(2) Sub-paragraph (8) of paragraph 2 of Schedule 1 applies to the giving of public notice under subsection (1) as it applies to the giving of public notice under sub-paragraph (7) of that paragraph.

NOTE

1. As inserted by the Custodial Sentences and Weapons (Scotland) Act 2007 (asp 17) Pt 3 s.58 (effective 1 November 2007).

GENERAL NOTE

This deals with the public notice that is to be given by the licensing authority where an application is made to them for the grant or renewal of a licence.

Knife dealers' licences: conditions

[1]**27C.**—(1) In granting or renewing a knife dealer's licence, a licensing authority—

(a) must attach to the licence such conditions as are specified (in particular or in general) by order by the Scottish Ministers;

(b) may, without prejudice to section 3B and paragraph 5 of Schedule 1, attach to the licence different conditions in relation to different articles or different classes of article;

(c) may, without prejudice to that section and paragraph, attach to the licence conditions for or in connection with—

(i) the keeping of records by the holder of the licence;

(ii) the storage of articles mentioned in section 27A(2); and

(iii) the display of such articles.

[2](2) An order under subsection (1)(a) may provide for different conditions to apply to different articles or different classes of article.

NOTES

1. As inserted by the Custodial Sentences and Weapons (Scotland) Act 2007 (asp 17) Pt 3 s.58 (effective 1 November 2007).

2. As amended by the Criminal Justice and Licensing (Scotland) Act 2010 (asp 13) Pt 8 s.172 (effective 28 March 2011).

3. To be repealed by the Criminal Justice and Licensing (Scotland) Act 2010 (asp 13) Pt 8 s.172 (date yet to be appointed).

GENERAL NOTE

This section allows a local authority to specify the conditions which may be attached to the grant or renewal of a knife dealers' licence and, without prejudice to the powers contained in Sch.1 para.5, different conditions may be attached to different articles or classes or articles. Note that licensing authorities have to treat as mandatory such conditions as are specified in secondary legislation made under the provisions of s.27S. The Scottish Ministers have used this power to make mandatory conditions in the Knife Dealers (Licensing Conditions) Order 2013 (SSI 2013/22) below—in respect of information and records, the display of relevant articles and notices to be displayed and certain additional mandatory conditions apply in respect of swords.

Provision of information to holder of knife dealer's licence

[1]**27D.**—(1) Subsection (2) applies where the holder of a knife dealer's licence ("the dealer")—

(a) is required by the licence to obtain information of a type specified in the licence from a person; and

(b) the dealer requests (whether orally, in writing or otherwise) the information from the person.

(2) A person, or any person acting on behalf of the person, who knowingly or recklessly provides false information in response to a request under subsection (1)(b) is guilty of an offence and liable on summary conviction to a fine not exceeding level 3 on the standard scale.

NOTE

1. As inserted by the Custodial Sentences and Weapons (Scotland) Act 2007 (asp 17) Pt 3 s.58 (effective 1 November 2007).

DEFINITION

"standard scale": Introduction p.32 above.

GENERAL NOTE

This section requires a person (usually the person selling or buying the article) from whom the dealer is under an obligation as part of their licence condition to obtain information from to supply that information and if the person gives false information then they have committed an offence. For "knowingly or recklessly" see Introduction p.32 above.

Knife dealers' licences: warrants to enter, search and seize articles

[1]**27E.**—(1) Subsection (2) applies if a justice of the peace or sheriff is satisfied by evidence on oath that—

(a) subsection (3) applies; and

(b) subsection (4) or (5) applies.

(2) The justice of the peace or sheriff may grant a warrant authorising a constable or an authorised officer—

(a) to enter and search the premises specified in the warrant; and

(b) to seize and remove any relevant article.

(3) This subsection applies if there are reasonable grounds for suspecting that a person (the "suspect") is carrying on in any premises an activity in respect of which a knife dealer's licence is required under section 27A.

(4) This subsection applies if no knife dealer's licence is in force in respect of the activity.

(5) This subsection applies if a knife dealer's licence is in force in respect of the activity but there are reasonable grounds for suspecting that the suspect has failed, or is failing, to comply with a condition of the licence.

NOTE

1. As inserted by the Custodial Sentences and Weapons (Scotland) Act 2007 (asp 17) Pt 3 s.58 (effective 1 November 2007).

DEFINITION

"authorised officer": s.27H.

GENERAL NOTE

This section allows a constable or authorised officer to obtain a warrant to enter, search and seize certain articles provided that there are: (a) reasonable grounds for suspecting that an activity is being carried out for which a knife dealers' licence is required (for "reasonable grounds" see Introduction p.31 above); (b) no licence is in force at that time; or (c) that a licence is in force but there are reasonable grounds for suspecting that a condition is or has not been complied with.

Powers of constables and authorised officers

[1]**27F.**—(1) A constable or an authorised officer may use reasonable force in executing a warrant granted under section 27E(2).

(2) Where a constable who is not in uniform is about to enter, is entering or has entered any premises under the powers conferred under section 27E(2) he must, if required to do so by a person in or upon the premises, produce his identification.

(3) Where an authorised officer is about to enter, is entering or has entered any premises under the powers conferred under section 27E(2) he must, if required to do so by a person in or upon the premises, produce his authorisation.

(4) If a constable has been required to produce his identification under subsection (2) he is not entitled to enter or search the premises or, as the case may be, remain there or continue to search the premises until he has produced it.

(5) If an authorised officer has been required to produce his authority under subsection (3), he is not entitled to enter or search the premises or, as the case may be, remain there or continue to search the premises until he has produced it.

(6) Any person who—

(a) fails without reasonable excuse to permit a constable, or an authorised officer, acting in pursuance of a warrant granted under section 27E(2) to enter and search any premises; or

(b) obstructs the entry to, or search of, any premises by a constable or an authorised officer so acting, is guilty of an offence and liable on summary conviction to a fine not exceeding level 3 on the standard scale.

(7) Any relevant article which has been seized and removed under a warrant granted under section 27E(2) may be retained until the conclusion of proceedings against the suspect.

(8) For the purposes of subsection (7), proceedings in relation to a suspect are concluded if—

(a) he is found guilty and sentenced or otherwise dealt with for the offence;

(b) he is acquitted;

(c) proceedings for the offence are discontinued;

(d) it is decided not to prosecute him.

(9) In this section, "suspect" is to be construed in accordance with section 27E(3).

NOTE

1. As inserted by the Custodial Sentences and Weapons (Scotland) Act 2007 (asp 17) Pt 3 s.58 (effective 1 November 2007).

DEFINITIONS
"authorised officer": s.27H.
"relevant article": s.27H.
"standard scale": see Introduction p.32 above.

GENERAL NOTE
This section gives constables and authorised officers certain powers to enforce the licensing provisions.

Subsection (6)

For "obstructs" see Introduction p.31 above.

Power to inspect documents

[1]**27G.**—(1) Subsection (2) applies where—
(a) a constable or an authorised officer has reasonable grounds for suspecting that an activity in respect of which a knife dealer's licence is required under section 27A is being carried on; and
(b) no such licence is in force in respect of the activity.

(2) The constable or authorised officer may—
(a) require a relevant person to produce any records or other documents connected with the activity,
(b) inspect any such records or documents, and
(c) take copies of, or extracts from, any such records or documents.

(3) A relevant person who—
(a) is required under subsection (2) to produce records or documents; and
(b) fails without reasonable excuse to do so,

is guilty of an offence and liable on summary conviction to a fine not exceeding level 3 on the standard scale.

(4) Before exercising the power conferred by subsection (2)—
(a) a constable who is not in uniform must produce his identification to the relevant person;
(b) an authorised officer must produce his authorisation to the relevant person.

(5) For the purposes of this section, a person is "relevant" if the constable or authorised officer has reasonable grounds for believing that the person has access to the records or documents.

NOTE
1. As inserted by the Custodial Sentences and Weapons (Scotland) Act 2007 (asp 17) Pt 3 s.58 (effective 1 November 2007).

DEFINITIONS
"authorised officer": s.27H.
"standard scale": see Introduction p.32 above.

GENERAL NOTE
This section gives a constable or authorised officer power to seek the production of certain documentation and to inspect or copy such documents.

Subsection (1)

For "reasonable grounds" see Introduction p.31 above.

Sections 27E to 27G: interpretation

[1]**27H.**—(1) In sections 27E and 27F—

"premises" includes a vehicle or vessel;

"relevant article" means an article mentioned in any of paragraphs (a) to (d) of subsection (2) of section 27A.

(2) In sections 27E to 27G, "authorised officer" means an officer of a licensing authority authorised by the authority for the purposes of section 27E, 27F or, as the case may be, 27G.

NOTE

1. As inserted by the Custodial Sentences and Weapons (Scotland) Act 2007 (asp 17) Pt 3 s.58 (effective 1 November 2007).

GENERAL NOTE

This section gives important definitions of "premises", "relevant articles" and "authorised officers" for the purposes of knife dealer's licences.

Forfeiture orders

[1]**27J.**—(1) Subsection (2) applies where a person ("the offender") is convicted of an offence under subsection (A1) or (2) of section 7 in relation to a relevant article—

(a) seized by virtue of a warrant granted under section 27E(2); or

(b) in the offender's possession or control at the relevant time.

(2) The court by which the offender is convicted may make an order for forfeiture (a "forfeiture order") in respect of the relevant article.

(3) The court may make a forfeiture order—

(a) whether or not it also deals with the offender in respect of the offence in any other way; and

(b) without regard to any restrictions on forfeiture in any enactment.

(4) In considering whether to make a forfeiture order, the court must have regard to—

(a) the value of the relevant article; and

(b) the likely financial and other effects on the offender of the making of the order (taken together with any other order that the court contemplates making).

(5) In this section—

"relevant article" means an article mentioned in any of paragraphs (a) to (d) of subsection (2) of section 27A;

"relevant time" means—

(a) the time of the offender's arrest for the offence; or

(b) the time of his being cited as an accused in respect of the offence.

NOTE

1. As inserted by the Custodial Sentences and Weapons (Scotland) Act 2007 (asp 17) Pt 3 s.58 (effective 1 November 2007).

GENERAL NOTE

Further powers are given to deal with unlicensed dealers in relevant articles by means of forfeiture of these items subject to certain conditions.

Effect of forfeiture order

[1]**27K.**—(1) A forfeiture order under section 27J(2) operates to deprive the offender of any rights he has in the property to which it relates.

(2) The property to which a forfeiture order relates must be taken into the possession of the police.

(3) The court by which the offender is convicted may, on the application of a person who—

(a) claims property to which a forfeiture order relates; but

(b) is not the offender from whom it was forfeited,

make an order (a "recovery order") for delivery of the property to the applicant if it appears to the court that he owns it.

(4) An application under subsection (3) must be made—

(a) in such manner as may be prescribed by Act of Adjournal; and

(b) before the end of the period of 6 months beginning with the date on which the forfeiture order was made.

(5) An application may be granted only if the applicant satisfies the court that—

(a) he had not consented to the offender's having possession of the property; or

(b) he did not know, and had no reason to suspect, that the offence was likely to be committed.

(6) If a person has a right to recover property which, by virtue of a recovery order, is in the possession of another, that right—

(a) is not affected by the making of the recovery order at any time before the end of the period of 6 months beginning with the day on which the order is made;

(b) is lost at the end of that period.

(7) The Scottish Ministers may by order make provision for or in connection with the disposal of property forfeited under a forfeiture order in cases where—

(a) no application under subsection (3) has been made before the end of the 6 month period beginning with the day on which the forfeiture order was made; or

(b) no such application has succeeded.

(8) An order under subsection (7) may in particular make provision for—

(a) dealing with any proceeds from the disposal;

(b) investing money; and

(c) auditing accounts.

NOTE

1. As inserted by the Custodial Sentences and Weapons (Scotland) Act 2007 (asp 17) Pt 3 s.58 (effective 1 November 2007).

GENERAL NOTE

The effect of a forfeiture order is to deprive an offender of their property rights to the forfeited property but this section makes provision for non-offenders to recovery that property in certain circumstances. Subsection (3) is subject to the Knives etc. (Disposal of Forfeited Property) (Scotland) Order 2010 (SSI 2010/214).

Offences by partnerships

[1]**27L.**—Where an offence committed by a partnership under—

(a) section 5 (in so far as the offence relates to a knife dealer's licence);

(b) section 7 (in so far as the offence so relates);

(c) section 27D;

(d) section 27F; or

(e) section 27G,

is proved to have been committed with the consent or connivance of, or to be attributable to any neglect on the part of, a partner, the partner as well as the partnership is guilty of the offence and is liable to be proceeded against and punished accordingly.

NOTE

1. As inserted by the Custodial Sentences and Weapons (Scotland) Act 2007 (asp 17) Pt 3 s.58 (effective 1 November 2007).

GENERAL NOTE

Provided that a partner in a partnership consented or connived in one of the statutory offences listed or the offence is attributable to their neglect, they as well as the partnership may be guilty of that offence.

Appropriate licence required

[1]**27M.**—Where a person carries on a business which—

(a) by virtue of section 24 requires a second-hand dealer's licence; and

(b) by virtue of section 27A requires a knife dealer's licence,

the person requires the appropriate licence in respect of each activity.

NOTE

1. As inserted by the Custodial Sentences and Weapons (Scotland) Act 2007 (asp 17) Pt 3 s.58 (effective 1 November 2007).

GENERAL NOTE

Where a second-hand dealer is also a dealer in knives then they will need both a second-hand dealers' and a knife dealer's licence but not if they deal only with new knives.

Remote sales of knives, etc.

[1]**27N.**—(1) This section applies where, in connection with the sale of an article mentioned in section 27A(2)—

(a) the premises (the "relevant premises") from which the article is dispatched in pursuance of the sale are not the same as those where the order for the article is taken (the "sale premises"),

(b) the relevant premises are in Scotland, and

(c) the sale premises are not in Scotland.

(2) For the purposes of this Act the sale of the article is to be treated as taking place on the relevant premises.

NOTE

1. As inserted by the Custodial Sentences and Weapons (Scotland) Act 2007 (asp 17) Pt 3 s.58 (effective 1 November 2007).

GENERAL NOTE

Where a relevant article is dispatched from premises in Scotland but the sale took place elsewhere at a location outwith Scotland then the sale is deemed to have taken place in Scotland at the dispatch premises.

Sales and dispatches in different local authority areas

[1]**27P.**—(1) Subsection (2) applies where, in connection with the sale of an article mentioned in section 27A(2)—

(a) the relevant premises are situated in the area of a local authority, and

(b) the sale premises are situated in the area of another local authority which, by virtue of section 2(2), is the

licensing authority in respect of the taking of the order for the article.

(2) For the purposes of this Act, the sale of the article is to be treated as taking place—

(a) on the relevant premises, and

(b) on the sale premises.

(3) In this section, "relevant premises" and "sale premises" have the same meanings as in section 27N.

NOTE

1. As inserted by the Custodial Sentences and Weapons (Scotland) Act 2007 (asp 17) Pt 3 s.58 (effective 1 November 2007).

GENERAL NOTE

Where the article is dispatched from premises different from those in which the sale took place and those premises are in different licensing authority areas then the sale will be deemed to have taken place in both areas.

Duty to avoid conflict between conditions of licences

[1]**27Q.**—(1) Subsection (2) applies where an application is made to a licensing authority for the grant or renewal of a second-hand dealer's licence by the holder of a knife dealer's licence issued by that authority.

(2) In granting the application, the licensing authority must not impose any condition which conflicts, or is inconsistent, with a condition of the knife dealer's licence.

(3) Subsection (4) applies where an application is made to a licensing authority for the grant or renewal of a knife dealer's licence by the holder of a second-hand dealer's licence issued by that authority.

(4) In granting the application, the licensing authority must, in accordance with paragraph 10 of Schedule 1, vary the terms and conditions of the second-hand dealer's licence to avoid any conflict or inconsistency with the terms or conditions of the knife-dealer's licence.

NOTE

1. As inserted by the Custodial Sentences and Weapons (Scotland) Act 2007 (asp 17) Pt 3 s.58 (effective 1 November 2007).

GENERAL NOTE

This section places a duty on a licensing authority to avoid conflict between the conditions placed on the grant or renewal of a knife dealer's licence.

Offences in relation to knife dealers' licences: exceptions

[1]**27R.**—The Scottish Ministers may by order provide that an offence under—

(a) section 5 (in so far as the offence relates to a knife dealer's licence);

(b) section 7 (in so far as the offence so relates);

(c) section 27D;

(d) section 27F; or

(e) section 27G,

is subject to such exceptions as may be specified in the order.

NOTE

1. As inserted by the Custodial Sentences and Weapons (Scotland) Act 2007 (asp 17) Pt 3 s.58 (effective 1 November 2007).

GENERAL NOTE

No such order has yet (as of February 2016) been made in terms of ss.27R and 27S.

Orders under sections 27A to 27R

[1]**27S.**—(1) Any power conferred by section 27A(7), 27A(8), 27C(1)(a), 27K(7) or 27R to make orders is exercisable by statutory instrument.

(2) Subject to subsection (3), a statutory instrument containing an order under any of those sections is subject to annulment in pursuance of a resolution of the Scottish Parliament.

(3) A statutory instrument containing an order under section 27R may not be made unless a draft of the instrument has been laid before, and approved by resolution of, the Scottish Parliament.

NOTE

1. As inserted by the Custodial Sentences and Weapons (Scotland) Act 2007 (asp 17) Pt 3 s.58 (effective 1 November 2007).

GENERAL NOTE

The following statutory instruments have been made under this section namely the Knife Dealers (Licence Conditions) Order 2009 (SSI 2009/217) and the Knife Dealers (Exceptions) Order 2009 (SSI 2009/218).

Licensing and Regulation of Metal Dealers

GENERAL NOTE TO SECTIONS 28–37

These sections have, with the exception of been modified, replaced or by the 2015 Act but as at 1 February 2016 only certain sections have come into force—those sections of the 2015 Act relating to metal dealers that are now in force are noted in the appropriate sections. Until the appropriate commencement orders have been made in respect of the other sections readers are therefore referred to the Appendix at p.421 where the law currently in force as of 1 January 2016 is set out together with explanatory notes.

Metal dealers: licensing and regulation

28.—[1](1) A "metal dealer's licence", shall be required for carrying on business as a metal dealer.

[2](2) A metal dealer's licence shall not be required by a person in relation to whom there is in force a warrant under section 29(1) or (4) of this Act (referred to in subsection (3) below and in sections 30 to 37 of this Act respectively as "*an exemption warrant*" and "*a temporary exemption warrant*").

[2](3) Sections 30 to 36 of this Act shall not apply to a person in relation to whom an exemption warrant or temporary exemption warrant is in force.

(4) A metal dealer's licence shall, in addition to specifying the activity which he engages in, specify the premises in or from which the activity is to be carried on.

NOTES

1. As amended by the Air Weapons and Licensing (Scotland) Act 2015 (asp 10) Pt 3 s.67 (effective 1 September 2016).

2. As repealed by the Air Weapons and Licensing (Scotland) Act 2015 (asp 10) Pt 3 s.67 (effective 1 September 2016).

DEFINITIONS

"metal": s.37.
"metal dealer": s.37.
"premises": s.8.

GENERAL NOTE

Sections 28–37 deal with the regulation and licensing of metal dealers and the licences required are mandatory, i.e. they do not require a resolution by the licensing authority to give effect to the licensing of this activity. Subject to certain listed exceptions, metal dealers require a licence that specifies both the activity and the premises which are to be licensed. The provisions relating to metal dealers were extensively amended by the 2015 Act in response to a perceived increase in thefts and sale as scrap of metal-related objects such as drain covers, building materials, plaques, memorial tablets, statutes, electric and services cables and essential railway signalling cables and it was felt that the sale value of these objects was often grossly under their actual replacement value and the disruption, danger and emotional impact caused by their theft but as at 1 February 2016 s.28 as amended by the 2015 Act is not yet in force. For the s.28(2) and (3) still applicable on that date see Appendix p.422.

Subsection (1)

With the exception of persons who are in possession of an exemption or temporary exemption warrant, granted in terms of s.29, all metal dealers require a licence and it is an offence for such persons to trade in metals without a licence—s.7(1).

Subsection (4)

The licence must specify both the particular activity in which the metal dealer is engaged and the premises from which they trade; it is limited to trading from those premises—cf. "itinerant metal dealer", s.32.

Metal dealers' exemption warrants

29. [*Repealed by the Air Weapons and Licensing (Scotland) Act 2015 (asp 10) Pt 3 s.67 (effective 1 September 2016).*]

GENERAL NOTE

This section was repealed by s.67 of the 2015 Act. Formerly a metal dealer who had an annual turnover in excess of £1,000,000 was eligible to receive an exemption warrant but it was felt that to remove the exemption would strengthen the system and ensure that the same high standards would apply industry-wide—2015 report, para.340.

Keeping of records

30. [*Repealed by the Air Weapons and Licensing (Scotland) Act 2015 (asp 10) Pt 3 s.68 (effective 1 September 2016).*]

GENERAL NOTE

This section was repealed by s.68 of the 2015 Act and replaced by the new ss.33A–33E. As at 1 February 2016 the 2015 Act repealing this section is not yet in force so until 1 September 2016 the existing law relating to the keeping of records is, see Appendix p.421.

Retention of metal

31. [*Repealed by the Air Weapons and Licensing (Scotland) Act 2015 (asp 10) Pt 3 s.68 (effective 1 September 2016).*]

GENERAL NOTE

This section was repealed by s.68 of the 2015 Act and metal dealers are no longer required to retain metal acquired within the course of the business for a period of 48 hours. It was felt that this would allow a metal dealer to dispense with the so called "tag-and-hold" provision which was felt to be impractical for many dealers, would mean that metal could be processed quickly (which might be required for the safe operation of the site) and was no longer necessary in view of the new provisions introduced by the 2015 Act. As at 1 February 2016 the 2015 Act repeal has not yet been brought into force so the retention of metal provisions still apply, see Appendix p.422, but this will change as of 1 September 2016.

Itinerant metal dealers

32.—(1) A licence, to be known as an "itinerant metal dealers licence" shall be required for carrying on business as an itinerant metal dealer.

(2) An itinerant metal dealer's licence shall have effect so as to permit the licence holder to carry on business as an itinerant metal dealer anywhere in Scotland.

DEFINITION

"itinerant metal dealer": s.37.

GENERAL NOTE

A separate category of mandatory licence is provided for, which was designed to licence and regulate the travelling scrap merchant and it is an offence to so trade without such a licence—s.7(1).

Subsection (1)

The essence of an itinerant metal dealer is that they travel from place to place and have no "metal store" (defined in s.37), i.e. a person who keeps the metal with them in their van or lorry, until they disposes of it to another party; if they have a fixed place of business then they are a "metal dealer" subject to the licensing requirements of s.28. A person who combines the trades of a "metal dealer" and "itinerant metal dealer" will require a licence for each activity—s.36.

Subsection (2)

A licence issued by any one licensing authority will have effect throughout Scotland so that, e.g. an itinerant metal dealer with a s.32 licence issued by South Ayrshire Council would not require another s.32 licence if they were to carry on their trade in, say, Fife or West Lothian.

Receipts and invoices: itinerant metal dealers

33. [*Repealed by the Air Weapons and Licensing (Scotland) Act 2015 (asp 10) Pt 3 s.70 (effective 1 September 2016).*]

GENERAL NOTE

This section was repealed by s.70 of the 2015 Act. As at February 2016 the 2015 Act was not brought into effect but will be brought into force in September 2016 and so the receipt and invoice provisions was still in force, see Appendix p.425.

[1]Acceptable forms of payment for metal.

33A.—(1) A metal dealer or an itinerant metal dealer may pay for metal only by a method of payment specified in subsection (2).

(2) The methods of payment are—

(a) by means of a cheque which under section 81A of the Bills of Exchange Act 1882 is not transferable, or

(b) by electronic transfer of funds to a bank or building society account in the name of the payee.

(3) If a metal dealer or an itinerant metal dealer pays for metal otherwise than in accordance with subsection (1), the dealer and each of the persons listed in subsection (4) (if any) commit an offence.

(4) The persons are—

(a) in a case of payment being made by a metal dealer at a place of business of the dealer, the person with day to day management of the place,

(b) in any case, any person who, acting on behalf of the metal dealer or the itinerant metal dealer, makes the payment.

(5) It is a defence for a metal dealer, an itinerant metal dealer or a person described in subsection (4)(a) who is charged with an offence under this section to prove that the dealer or, as the case may be, person—

(a) made arrangements to ensure that the payment was to be made only in accordance with subsection (1), and

(b) took all reasonable steps to ensure that those arrangements were complied with.

(6) A person who commits an offence under this section is liable, on summary conviction, to a fine not exceeding level 5 on the standard scale.

(7) The Scottish Ministers may by regulations—

(a) amend subsection (2) so as to add, amend or remove methods of payment, and

(b) make such consequential modification of section 33B or 33C(3) as they consider appropriate.

(8) Regulations under subsection (7) are subject to the affirmative procedure.

(9) In this section, "place of business" means a place of business operated by a metal dealer in the ordinary course of that dealer's business as a metal dealer.

NOTE

1. As inserted by the Air Weapons and Licensing (Scotland) Act 2015 (asp 10) Pt 3 s.69 (effective 1 September 2016).

DEFINITIONS

"bank or building society account": s.33B.
"itinerant metal dealer": s.37(1).
"metal": s.37(1).
"metal dealer": s.37(1).

GENERAL NOTE

This section was inserted by the 2015 Act s.69. It was noted in the 2015 report (para.344 et seq) that the banning of cash payments for metal would remove much of the incentive for metal crime and that substantial reduction in the number of offences would result and that this had been noted in England and Wales when a similar ban had been implemented under the Scrap Metal Dealers Act 2013. This section deals with a ban on all payments other than those made by means of a recognised method of payment (subss.(1) and (2)), the creation of an offence if the section is breached (subs.(4) and (6)) and that subsequently regulations may be made.

[1]Acceptable forms of payment: meaning of "bank and building society account"

33B.—(1) In section 33A(2)(b), "bank or building society account" means an account held with a bank or a building society.

(2) For the purposes of subsections (1) and (4)—

(a) "bank" means an authorised deposit-taker that has its head office or a branch in the United Kingdom, and

(b) "building society" has the same meaning as in the Building Societies Act 1986.

(3) In subsection 2 (a), "authorised deposit-taker" means—

(a) a person who has permission to accept deposits under Part 4A of the Financial Services and Markets Act 2000 (but see subsection (4) for Exclusions),

(b) an EEA firm of the kind statement in paragraph 5(b) of Schedule 3 to that Act that has permission under paragraph 15 of that Schedule (as a result of qualifying for authorisation under paragraph 12(1) of that Schedule).

(4) The reference in subsection (3)(a) to a person who has permission to accept deposits under Part 4A of the Financial Services and Markets Act 2000 does not include—

(a) a building society,

(b) a society registered as a credit union under the Co-operative and Community Benefit Societies Act 2014 or the Credit Unions (Northern Ireland) Order 1985 (S.I. 1985/1205 (N.I. 12)),

(c) a friendly society within the meaning given by section 116 of the Friendly Societies Act 1992, or

(d) an insurance company within the meaning of section 275 of the Finance Act 2004.

NOTE

1. As inserted by the Air Weapons and Licensing (Scotland) Act 2015 (asp 10) Pt 3 s.69 (effective 1 September 2016).

GENERAL NOTE

This section was inserted by the 2015 Act s.69 and provides additional explanations of the acceptability of s.33A payments.

[1]Requirement to keep records

33C.—(1) This section applies where a metal dealer or an itinerant metal dealer ("the dealer"), in the course of the dealer's business—

(a) acquires any metal (whether or not for value), or

(b) processes or disposes of any metal (by any means).

(2) In respect of any metal acquired, the dealer must record the following information—

(a) the description and weight of the metal,

(b) the date and time of the acquisition of the metal,

(c) if the metal is acquired from another person—

(i) the name and address of the person,

(ii) the means by which the person's name and address was verified,

(d) the price, if any, payable in respect of the acquisition of the metal, if that price has been ascertained at the time when the entry in the record relating to that metal is to be made,

(e) the method of payment of the price (if applicable),

(f) where no price is payable for the metal, the value of the metal at the time when the entry is to be made as estimated by the dealer,

(g) in the case of metal delivered to the dealer by means of a vehicle, the registration mark (within the meaning of section 23 of the Vehicle Excise and Registration Act 1994) borne by the vehicle.

(3) Where the dealer has paid for metal, the dealer must keep a copy of—

(a) the cheque, or

(b) the document evidencing the electronic transfer of funds.

(4) In respect of any metal processed or disposed of, the dealer must record the following information—

(a) the description and weight of the metal immediately before its processing or disposal,

(b) in the case of metal which is processed, the process applied,

(c) in the case of metal disposed of by sale or exchange—

(i) the consideration for which it is sold or exchanged,

(ii) the name and address of the person to whom the metal is sold or with whom it is exchanged, and

(iii) the means by which the person's name and address was verified,

(d) in the case of metal disposed of otherwise than by sale or exchange, its value immediately before its disposal as estimated by the dealer.

(5) The dealer must—

(a) keep separate records in relation to—

(i) metal acquired, and

(ii) metal processed or disposed of,

(b) record the information immediately after the metal is acquired, processed or disposed of,

(c) keep a copy of any document produced by a person to verify that person's name or address, and

(d) retain information recorded or documents kept under this section for a period of not less than 3 years beginning with the date on which the information was recorded or document obtained.

(6) The Scottish Ministers may by regulations—

(a) specify the means by which a person's name and address may be verified for the purposes of this section,

(b) require further information to be recorded about any metal acquired, processed or disposed of by metal dealers or itinerant metal dealers.

(7) Regulations under subsection (6)—

(a) may make different provision for different purposes, and

(b) are subject to the negative procedure.

NOTE

1. As inserted by the Air Weapons and Licensing (Scotland) Act 2015 (asp 10) Pt 3 s.69 (effective 1 December 2015 for the purpose of inserting s.33C of the 1982 Act, but only for the purpose of making regulations under s.33C(6); not yet in force otherwise).

DEFINITIONS

"metal dealer": s.37(1).
"itinerant metal dealer": s.37(1).
"metal": s.37(1).

GENERAL NOTE

This section was inserted by the 2015 Act s.69. "We support the enhanced record keeping requirements and in particular the move to impose new conditions on itinerant metal dealers. These measures will establish an audit trail , making it easier to investigate metal crime and acting as a deterrent to criminals"—2015 report, para.262. Subsection (2) gives details of the information to be recorded, the method of payment and further details if the metal was processed or disposed of—in other words information which will enable the audit trail to be followed.

Subsection (6) came into force on 1 December 2015—Air Weapons and Licensing (Scotland) Act 2015 (Commencement No.1) Order 2015 (SSI 2015/382). The rest of this section was not yet in force by February 2016.

[1]**Form of records**

33D.—(1) A metal dealer or an itinerant metal dealer ("a dealer") must record the required information—

(a) in books with serially numbered pages, or

(b) by means of a device for storing and processing information.

(2) Where a dealer records the required information in books, the dealer must use separate books for recording the required information about—

(a) metal acquired, and

(b) metal processed or disposed of.

(3) Where a dealer uses a device for storing and processing information, the dealer must, by means of the device or otherwise, keep details of all modifications made in the records kept by the device.

(4) Where a dealer is required to keep a copy of a document under section 33C, it is sufficient for the dealer—

(a) to keep an electronic copy of the document, and

(b) in relation to a document verifying a person's name or address, keep only one copy of the document.

(5) In this section, "required information" means the information about metal acquired, processed or disposed of that a dealer is required to record under or by virtue of section 33C(2), (4) or (6).

NOTE

1. As inserted by the Air Weapons and Licensing (Scotland) Act 2015 (asp 10) Pt 3 s.70 (effective 1 September 2016).

GENERAL NOTE

This section was inserted by the 2015 Act s.70 and provides for the form in which the records and details of them are kept.

[1]Metal dealers to keep records of each place of business

33E.—(1) A metal dealer must keep separate records of the required information in relation to—

(a) each place of business operated by the dealer, and

(b) any metal acquired, processed or disposed of otherwise than at such a place of business.

(2) Where a metal dealer records the required information in books, the dealer must not, at any time at a place of business, use more than—

(a) one book for recording the required information about metal acquired, and

(b) one book for recording the required information about metal processed or disposed of.

(3) In this section—

"*place of business*" means a place of business operated by a metal dealer in the ordinary course of that dealer's business as a metal dealer,

"*required information*" means the information about metal acquired, processed or disposed of that a dealer is required to record under or by virtue of section 33C(2), (4) or (6).

NOTE

1. As inserted by the Air Weapons and Licensing (Scotland) Act 2015 (asp 10) Pt 3 s.70 (effective 1 September 2016).

DEFINITIONS

"metal dealer": s.37(1).

Offences relating to metal dealing

34.—(1) Any metal dealer or itinerant metal dealer who disposes of metal to a person apparently under the age of 16 or who acquires metal from such a person, whether that person is acting on his own behalf or on behalf of another person, shall be guilty of an offence and liable, on summary conviction, to a fine not exceeding level 3 on the standard scale.

(2) In any proceedings for an offence under subsection (1) above, it shall be a defence to prove that the person to whom it is alleged the metal was

disposed of or from whom it is alleged it was acquired was 16 years of age or over at the time.

[1](2A) Any metal dealer or itinerant metal dealer who fails to comply with a requirement of sections 33B, 33C or 33D commits an offence and is liable, on summary conviction, to a fine not exceeding level 3 on the standard scale.

[1](3) Any metal dealer or itinerant metal dealer who knowingly or recklessly produces any information or document which the dealer is required to keep under section 33B, which is false or misleading in a material particular shall be guilty of an offence and liable, on summary conviction, to a fine not exceeding level 4 on the standard scale(4) Any person who, when selling metal to or purchasing metal from a metal dealer or itinerant metal dealer, gives the dealer a false name or address shall be guilty of an offence and liable, on summary conviction, to a fine not exceeding level 3 on the standard scale.

NOTE

1. As inserted by the Air Weapons and Licensing (Scotland) Act 2015 (asp 10) Pt 3 s.70 (effective 1 September 2016).

DEFINITIONS

"itinerant metal dealer": s.37.
"metal dealer": s.37.
"metal": s.37.
"standard scale": see Introduction p.32 above.

GENERAL NOTE

This section, which was amended by the 2015 Act s.70, applies both to metal dealers and itinerant metal dealers, creates certain additional statutory offences, namely those of acquiring metal from or disposing of metal to young persons, of making false records and the giving of false names and addresses to dealers.

Subsection (1)

A dealer must, therefore, neither acquire metal from nor dispose of it to a person (whether acting as an agent or principal) who is apparently under the age of 16 years, i.e. a person who appears to the dealer to be under 16. This provision derives from s.20 of the Children and Young Persons (Scotland) Act 1937 and s.443 of the Burgh Police (Scotland) Act 1892. Quaere on whom is the onus of proof that the person is apparently under 16—cf. *Lockwood v Walker*, 1909 2 S.L.T. 400; *Paton v Wilson*, 1988 S.L.T. 634.

Subsection (2)

A statutory defence is provided here if that person was, in fact, 16 or older.

Subsection (3)

"False information" would be information which is, in any material sense, untrue; "knowingly or recklessly"—see Introduction p.31 above. Both this offence and that created by the following section had no parallel in previous legislation.

Functions of the court in relation to metal dealers convicted of offences

35.—(1) Where a metal dealer or itinerant metal dealer is convicted of an offence relating to his business as such, the court by which he is convicted may make any order which it is competent to make under section 7(6) of this Act and an extract of such conviction and sentence (if any) shall, within 6 days after the date of the conviction, be transmitted by the clerk of the court to the licensing authority which granted the licence.

(2) Where a metal dealer is convicted—

(a) of an offence relating to his business as such; or
(b) of any offence which in the opinion of the court is an offence involving dishonesty,

the court may, in addition to any other order which it is competent to make, order that he shall not dispose of or process any metal acquired by him until the expiry of a period of 7 days after its acquisition.

(3) In making an order under subsection (2) above, the court shall specify a period not exceeding 2 years for which it is to remain in force, but the court may revoke such an order at any time on the application of the person to whom it relates.

(4) Any person who fails to comply with an order made in relation to him under subsection (2) above shall be guilty of an offence and liable, on summary conviction, to a fine not exceeding level 4 on the standard scale or to imprisonment for a period not exceeding 60 days or to both.

(5) A licensing authority receiving, by virtue of subsection (1) above, an extract of conviction and sentence (if any) of an itinerant metal dealer shall notify all other licensing authorities of the particulars of the conviction.

DEFINITIONS

"itinerant metal dealer": s.37.
"metal dealer": s.37.
"metal": s.37.
"standard scale": see Introduction p.32 above.

GENERAL NOTE

The court is empowered by this section to impose further penalties and orders upon metal dealers and itinerant metal dealers convicted of certain offences.

Subsection (1)

This gives the court the power, upon convicting a metal dealer or itinerant metal dealer of an offence relating to their business as such (e.g. theft or reset of metal for dealing purposes or a contravention of ss.30(8) or 33(5)), to make one of the orders contained in s.7(6), namely, revocation of the licence and/or a disqualification from holding a licence for a period of up to five years, and the court must inform the licensing authority of any such conviction and sentence passed by them (including any order made under subs.(2) below).

Subsection (2)

This applies only to metal dealers (since there is no minimum period of retention of metal imposed upon itinerant metal dealers) and gives the court a discretionary power to substitute seven days for the 48 hour period contained within s.31(1).

Subsection (3)

The court must specify the period (up to a maximum of two years) for which such an order is to run and they have the power to revoke the order if the dealer so applies to them.

Subsection (5)

Because an itinerant metal dealer's licence applies throughout Scotland (s.32(2)), a stringent requirement is put upon the authority who issued that licence to notify all other Scottish licensing authorities of convictions, orders and sentences imposed by a court and notified to them under subs.(1) above.

[1][**Register of metal dealers and itinerant metal dealers**

35A.—(1) The Scottish Ministers may by regulations make provision for and about the establishment, keeping and maintaining of a register of metal dealers and itinerant metal dealers.

(2) Regulations under subsection (1) may, in particular, make provision—
(a) about who is to keep and maintain the register,
(b) requiring the provision of information to the person who keeps the register,
(c) specifying the information to be included in the register in relation to each person who holds a licence as a metal dealer or itinerant metal dealer,
(d) about the form and publication of the register,
(e) for the charging of fees in such circumstances as may be specified in the regulations.

(3) Regulations under subsection (1) may—
(a) make incidental, supplementary, consequential, transitional, transitory or saving provision,
(b) modify this or any other enactment.

(4) Regulations under subsection (1) which contain provision which adds to, replaces, or omits any part of an Act are subject to the affirmative procedure.

(5) Otherwise, regulations under subsection (1) are subject to the negative procedure.]

NOTE

1. As inserted by the Air Weapons and Licensing (Scotland) Act 2015 (asp 10) Pt 3 s.71 (date yet to be appointed).

GENERAL NOTE

This section was inserted by the 2015 Act s.71 and gives the Ministers the power to maintain a register of all metal dealers and itinerant metal dealers with the information that might be required such as the name or trading name of the business, contact details, the place of business and details of the licence held.

Appropriate licence required

36. Where a person carries on business as a second-hand dealer and as a metal dealer and as an itinerant metal dealer or as any two of these kinds of dealer he shall require the appropriate licence in respect of each activity.

DEFINITIONS

"itinerant metal dealer": s.37.
"metal dealer": s.37.
"metal": s.37.
"second hand dealer": s.24(2).
"standard scale": see Introduction p.32 above.

GENERAL NOTE

A person who combines business activities as a second-hand dealer and metal dealer and/or itinerant metal dealer, or as a metal dealer and itinerant metal dealer, will require a licence for each of the two or three categories of activity carried on by them by way of business; and, if they deal in more than one licensing authority area, they will require a licence for each area, subject only to the s.32(2) proviso relating to the validity of an itinerant metal dealer's licence being valid throughout Scotland.

Interpretation of sections 28 to 26

37.—(1) In sections 28 to 36 of this Act—
[1]"*itinerant metal dealer*" means a person who
(a) carries on a business which consists wholly or substantially of buying and selling for scrap—
(i) metal articles that are old, broken, warn out or defaced, or

(ii) partly manufactured articles that are made wholly or partly from metal,

(b) collects articles of the kind described in paragraph a (i) and (ii) by means of visits from, place to place, and

(c) disposes of such articles without causing them to be kept in a metal store or other premises (including by disposing or giving custody of the articles to a person who keeps a metal store.

"*metal*" means any metal (including any precious metal) and any alloy of any metals, whether old or new and includes manufactured articles, whether old or new, made wholly or partly of metal, of any of the materials commonly known as hard metal or of cemented or sintered metallic carbides;

"*metal dealer*" means a person carrying on business in terms of subsection (2) below but does not include an itinerant metal dealer within the meaning of this subsection;

"*metal store*" means a place where metal is received or kept in the course of a metal dealer's business;

"*processing*", in relation to metal, includes melting down and any process whereby the composition or form of the metal or of any article which is made of the metal is altered so as to make it substantially less identifiable than before the process, and "process" and "processed" shall be construed accordingly.

[1](2) For the purposes of sections 28 to 36, a person carries on business as a metal dealer if the person—

(a) carries on a business which consists wholly or substantially of buying or selling for scrap—

(i) metal articles that are old, broken, worn out or defaced, or

(ii) partly manufactured articles that are wholly or partly from metal, or

(b) carries on business as a motor salvage operator (so far as that does not fall within paragraph (a).

(3) For the purposes of subsection (2)(b), a person who carries on business as a motor salvage operator if the person carries on a business which consists wholly or substantially of—

(a) recovering salvageable parts from motor vehicles for re-use or sale and selling or disposing of the rest of the vehicle for scrap,

(b) buying significantly damaged motor vehicles and subsequently repairing or reselling them, or any of the activities mentioned in paragraphs (a) or (b).

NOTE

1. As inserted by the Air Weapons and Licensing (Scotland) Act 2015 (asp 10) Pt 3 s.72 (effective 16 March 2016 for purposes specified in SSI 2016/85 Sch.1 subject to transitional provisions specified in SSI 2016/85 arts 4 and 6; 1 September 2016 otherwise).

GENERAL NOTE

These definitions were amended by and subss.(2) and (3) were inserted by the 2015 Act s.66B. Definitions are provided here for terms which appear in ss.28–36 of the Act, i.e. the sections which deal with the licensing and regulation of metal dealers and itinerant metal dealers—note that the two types of dealer are mutually exclusive in the definitions. The concept of the metal being for "scrap" is an important one and therefore persons, such as metal stockholders or the manufacturers of products using metals (even though they may dispose of surplus or waste metal arising out of the manufacturing process), would not be caught within this definition.

[1]Exemptions

37A.—(1) the Scottish Ministers may by regulations make provision specifying circumstances in which the provisions of sections 28 to 37 are not to apply.

(2) Regulations under subsection (1)—

(a) may make transitional, transitory or saving provision,

(b) are subject to the negative procedure.

NOTE

1. As inserted by the Air Weapons and Licensing (Scotland) Act 2015 (asp 10) Pt 3 s.73 (effective 1 December 2015).

GENERAL NOTE

This section was inserted by the 2015 Act s.73 and gives the Ministers the power to exclude by regulations sections of the Act that may not apply in certain stated circumstances.

Miscellaneous Licences

Boat-hire licences

38.—(1) Subject to the provisions of this section, a licence under this Act, to be known as a "boat hire licence", shall be required for the use of a vessel, in the course of a trade or business carried on in or from any place within the area of a licensing authority, for the purpose of—

(a) letting it on hire; or

(b) carrying for reward 12 or fewer passengers, for pleasure, recreational, educational or sporting purposes.

(2) A boat hire licence may relate to one or more vessels or classes of vessel and shall specify—

(a) the vessels or the classes of vessels to which it relates; and

(b) the maximum number of vessels or of each class of vessel which may be used under the licence.

(3) A boat hire licence shall extend to the use of any vessel added to or substituted for a vessel to which the licence relates if—

(a) the additional or substitute vessel is of identical type to a vessel of a class to which the licence relates; and

(b) the maximum number referred to in subsection (2)(b) above is not exceeded.

(4) A boat hire licence shall not be required in respect of the use—

[1](a) of any vessel in respect of which there is in force a passenger certificate, load line certificate or load line exemption certificate under the Merchant Shipping Act 1995;

(b) for a continuous period of over 24 hours, of any vessel having overnight sleeping accommodation;

(c) of any vessel for the purpose of instruction or training in seamanship;

(d) of any vessel exclusively for fishing in non-tidal waters;

(e) of any vessel—

(i) on any inland waterway; or

(ii) at any harbour owned or managed by the British Waterways Board; or

(f) of any vessel with the consent of the harbour authority (within the meaning of the Harbours Act 1964) in any harbour owned or managed by them.

(5) Before granting an application to grant or renew a boat hire licence a licensing authority may require the application to produce a certificate in respect of each vessel to which the application relates issued by a person appearing to the authority to be suitably qualified for the purpose of issuing such a certificate stating that the vessel is suitably designed, constructed, maintained and equipped and in a safe condition for the purpose for which, and the place or waters in which, it is to be used.

(6) Without prejudice to paragraphs 5(3), 11 and 12 of Schedule 1 to this Act a licensing authority shall—

(a) refuse an application to grant or renew a boat hire licence;

(b) suspend a boat hire licence in accordance with the said paragraph 12,

to the extent that it relates to any vessel which is in their opinion not in a safe condition for the purpose for which, and the place or waters in which, it is to be or, as the case may be, is being used.

(7) Without prejudice to paragraph 5 of Schedule 1 to this Act, a licensing authority, on granting an application for the grant or renewal of a boat hire licence, shall attach conditions—

(a) fixing the maximum number of persons which may be carried in the vessel;

(b) specifying inland waters in their area, the inland waters adjacent to inland waters in their area and the tidal waters

within which each vessel or class of vessel to which the application relates may be used.

(8) The holder of a boat hire licence shall effect and maintain in force in relation to every vessel to which the licence relates a policy of insurance to the satisfaction of the licensing authority and complying with subsection (9) below, and shall not reduce the amount or extent of the cover specified in the policy without the prior approval of the authority.

(9) A policy of insurance complies with this subsection if it insures such person, persons, or classes of persons as may be specified in the policy in respect of any liability which may be incurred by him or them in respect of the death of or bodily injury to any person caused by, or arising out of, the use of the vessel.

(10) Any person who, being the holder of a boat hire licence, uses or causes or permits any other person to use a vessel to which the licence relates without having in force in relation to that vessel a policy of insurance in accordance with subsection (8) above shall be guilty of an offence and liable, on summary conviction, to a fine not exceeding level 4 on the standard scale.

(11) Where—

(a) a vessel in respect of which a boat hire licence is in force is used—

(i) within the territorial waters of the United Kingdom adjacent to Scotland; and

(ii) within any inland waters or waters specified in the licence under subsection (7)(b) above; but

(iii) outwith the area of the licensing authority which granted or last renewed the licence; and

(b) all persons carried in the vessel embark initially from places within the area of the authority,

it shall not be necessary to have in force in respect of that use of the vessel a boat hire licence granted by any other licensing authority and the conditions subject to which the licence is held shall continue to apply to such use.

NOTE

1. As amended by the Merchant Shipping Act 1995 (c.21) Sch.13 para.67 (effective 1 January 1996).

GENERAL NOTE

Boat hire forms the subject matter of the first of the "miscellaneous" category of licences in the Act and is another "optional" activity, licensing for which may be instituted by the local authority throughout their area, or in parts, and for all categories of boats or restricted to certain classes only. The requirement to licence applies only to small vessels used for certain specified purposes on inland and tidal waters and the primary purpose thereof is to provide protection for the safety of members of the public who use the craft. It was stated that it was the Secretary of State's intention to issue advice to local authorities on the types of licensing conditions which it was felt would be appropriate to apply in relation to boat hire licences but, to date, this has not been done (Scottish Development Department Circular 6/1983, Appendix A, para.2).

Subsection (1)

The requirement only covers "vessels" (defined in s.133) which are let on hire in the course of a business, or carry 12 or fewer passengers for reward, for pleasure, recreational, educational or sporting activities, which might all be thought to involve inexperienced members of the public being passengers or in charge—the classic example would be that of the "trip round the bay". It does not include use by persons carrying out professional surveying from a boat, or uses specified in subs.(4). Within the range of vessels carrying 12 or less passengers there can, of course, be a wide variation and s.38 applies to a diverse selection of vessels including dinghies, yachts, rowing and motor boats, "pedaloes", punts, single-seat canoes, hovercraft and any other kind of related water craft.

Subsection (2)

The licensing authority have a discretionary power to issue licenses for more than one vessel or for classes of craft where they feel that this would be more appropriate than one applicant having to hold a number of separate licences—e.g. in the case of rowing boats in a park—subject to the licence specifying the vessels, classes or numbers to which it relates.

Subsection (3)

This sensible administrative provision provides for the addition or substitution of identical craft when vessels are, say, being repaired or where demand justifies further boats to be hired; it is subject to the limits specified in subs.(2)(b).

Subsection (4)

This subsection lists types of vessels which are excluded from the licensing requirements, namely:

- (a) boats which carry 12 or less passengers but which require certificates under the Merchant Shipping Acts—these are vessels which proceed more than 15 miles from their point of departure or more than three miles from land and therefore are subject to the Department of Trade licensing requirements;
- (b) vessels with overnight sleeping accommodation used for more than 24 hours, e.g. yacht charters;
- (c) training vessels, e.g. those used in sailing schools;
- (d) fishing vessels in non-tidal waters—this might be thought to be a curious exception given that coastal fishing hires are not excluded but it was thought that to extend the licensing provisions to fresh water would be an unduly burdensome requirement and unjustified in the case of, say, boats used for a day's fishing on the loch;
- (e) British Waterways Board territory—the board have their own regulatory powers on canals, etc.;
- (f) in harbours controlled by harbour authorities within the meaning of s.57(1) of the Harbours Act 1964.

This subsection was amended by Sch.13 of the Merchant Shipping Act 1995.

Subsection (5)

This contains a discretionary power to require a certificate of suitability relating to design, construction, maintenance and equipment and fitness for a specific purpose and was primarily inserted in relation to larger or older craft used at sea (although the requirement can be applied to any craft as the licensing authority think proper). The suitable qualifications of the person issuing the certificate are not specified and although a subjective test is therefore to be applied it is suggested that there are certain "obvious" classes of qualified persons such as boatbuilders, marine surveyors and naval architects and, possibly, suitably experienced seamen.

Subsection (6)

This subsection imposes a mandatory requirement on the licensing authority to refuse to grant or renew, or to suspend, a licence where a vessel is unsafe for the purpose, place or waters where it is to be used, and any consideration of safety would presumably include equipment carried as well as the condition of the boat.

Subsection (7)

This is another mandatory requirement and provides that the licensing authority shall attach conditions which limit both the number of passengers to be carried and the areas of operation. The specification of the areas can cover areas where the local authority would not normally have jurisdiction, such as where parts of a loch fall within different local government areas (e.g. Loch Lomond) or inshore areas lying between the foreshore and the three mile limit (beyond which, of course, the Merchant Shipping Act requirements would apply)—there would, of course, be nothing to stop boats being limited to a tidal area less than the three mile limit, e.g. within an area bounded by the headlands of a bay or as far out as, say, the Bass Rock, provided that these areas were properly specified in the licence.

Subsections (8)–(10)

It is mandatory for a licensee to effect and maintain suitable third party insurance cover in relation to every vessel covered by the licence and for the risks specified in subs.(9) and, although there is no restriction on the insurer, the policy must be to the satisfaction of the licensing authority. It is an offence not to have such insurance cover in operation. For "level 4 on the standard scale" see Introduction p.32 above.

Subsection (11)

This provision covers journeys made in another licensing area and, to avoid unnecessary duplication, where the passengers have all embarked initially from a place within the licensing authority area and the vessel is still within the area specified in the licence by virtue of subs.(7)(b), although in a different local authority area, a licence will not be needed for that second area—e.g. if a boat licensed by the City of Edinburgh was permitted to operate in an area which included the Fife shores of the Firth of Forth, then separate licences would not be required from the Fife Council.

Street traders' licences

39.—(1) Subject to subsection (3) below, a licence, to be known as a "street trader's licence", shall be required for street trading by a person, whether on his own account or as an employee.

(2) In this section "street trading" means doing any of the following things in a public place—

(a) hawking,
selling or offering or exposing for sale any article;

(b) offering to carry out or carrying out for money or money's worth any service,

to any person in the public place and includes doing any of these things there in or from a vehicle or in or from a kiosk or moveable stall not entered in the valuation roll except where it is done in conjunction with or as part of a retail business being carried on in premises abutting the public place.

(3) A street trader's licence shall not be required for—

(a) the sale of newspapers only;

(b) the sale of milk by or on behalf of a person registered under regulations made under section 19 of the Food Safety Act 1990;

(c) the sale of coal, coke or any solid fuel derived from coal or of which coal or coke is a constituent;

(d) any activity in respect of which a certificate under the Pedlars Act 1871 has been granted;

(e) any activity in respect of which a licence is required under this Act apart from this section; or

(f) organising or participating in a public benevolent collection (within the meaning of section 84 of the Charities and Trustee Investment (Scotland) Act 2005 (asp 10).

[1,2](4) Where an application for a street trader's licence is made in respect of an activity which—

(a) consists of or includes food business within the meaning of section 1(3) of the Food Safety Act 1990; and

(b) involves the use of a vehicle, kiosk or moveable stall,

the licensing authority shall, without prejudice to paragraph 5(3) of Schedule 1 to this Act, refuse the application unless there is produced to them a certificate by the food authority (for the purposes of section 5 of the Food Safety Act 1990) mentioned in subsection (4A) stating that the vehicle, kiosk or moveable stall complies with such requirements as the Scottish Ministers may be order make by statutory instrument specify.

[2](4A) A food authority referred to in subsection (4) is a food authority in Scotland which, in respect of the activity mentioned in that subsection—

(a) has registered the establishment that carries out or intends to carry out the activity for the purposes of Article 6.2 of the Regulation EC No. 852/2004 of the European Parliament and the Council of 29 April 2004 on the hygiene of foodstuffs, or

(b) where no such food authority has registered the establishment for those purposes, a food authority which is—

(i) the licensing authority to which the application mentioned in subsection (4) in respect of the activity is made, or

(ii) another licensing authority to which an application for a street trader's licence in respect of the activity is made or has been made.

[1](5) Any order under subsection (4) may specify requirements by reference to provision contained in another enactment.

[1](6) A statutory instrument containing an order made under subsection (4) is subject to annulment in pursuance of a resolution of the Scottish Parliament.

NOTES

1. As amended by the Criminal Justice and Licensing (Scotland) Act 2010 (asp 13) Pt 8 s.175 (effective 28 March 2011).

2. As amended by the Regulatory Reform (Scotland) Act 2014 (asp 3) Pt 4 s.56 (effective 30 June 2014).

DEFINITIONS

"public place": s.133.

GENERAL NOTE

Street trading is one of the "optional" activities, licensing for which may be brought into effect by resolution of the licensing authority pursuant to the provisions of s.9, and the requirement for licensing can be restricted to particular forms of street trading or to particular geographical areas. A licence is required for persons who are self-employed or employees in order that they may carry on specified activities involving the selling or offering of services from a pitch, stall, vehicle or kiosk in a public place; certain activities are, however, automatically exempt in terms of s.39(3). Additional provisions relate to the sale of food. Some disquiet was initially caused by the all embracing definition of "street trading" contained within s.39(2) and it has been stated that the licensing authority should introduce licensing for street trading only in those areas of activity and those neighbourhoods for which they consider regulation is required—Scottish Development Department Circular 28/1985. Note that the 2010 Act made provision for the introduction of a "social responsibility levy" to be imposed on street traders but as yet no such levy has been introduced.

Subsection (1)

The reference to "person" must be qualified by the fact that a street trader's licence cannot be granted to a person under the age of 17 years, although local byelaws may permit such persons to be employed as such by their parents—Children and Young Persons Act 1937 s.30. Local education authorities may also make byelaws regulating or prohibiting street trading by persons under the age of 18 years—Children and Young Persons Act 1963 s.35(2). The use of the wording, "whether on his own account or as an employee" would appear to cover every possible situation in which a person could trade in a public place so that in *McInnes v Tudhope*, 1987 S.C.C.R. 368, a person who had been assisting an unlicensed trader to sell goods from a van in order to gain work experience and whose only form of remuneration had been gifts of sweets and lemonade from the proprietor was held nevertheless to have been engaged in street trading, notwithstanding the absence of sufficient evidence, by which the court could conclude that at the material time she had been an employee and accordingly she required a licence. A "minder" who serves customers would also require a street trader's licence—*Heatherstone v Wilson*, 1993 G.W.D. 23-1464.

Subsection (2)

The definition of "street trading" is a wide one and includes specifically "hawking" (a hawker being a person who travels about selling their goods with a horse and cart or vehicle, and technically distinguishable from a pedlar who carries their goods on their person), "offering for sale" (the subject of judicial comment in *Wiles v Maddiston* [1943] 1 All E.R. 315; *Fisher v Bell* [1961] 1 Q.B. 394; *British Car Auctions v Wright* [1972] 3 All E.R. 462; and *Pharmaceutical Society of Great Britain v Boots Cash Chemists (Southern) Ltd* [1953] 1 All E.R. 482) and "exposing for sale" (see below). Examples of "street trading" include the sale of services such as street photography (*McIver v Robertson*, 1950 J.C. 56); trading from vehicles such as mobile shops and fish and chip vans; trading from moveable stalls (e.g. *Normand v Alexander*, 1994 S.L.T. 274); trading from a suitcase; trading by laying out tee-shirts on top of a cloth laid on the pavement (*Prentice v Normand*, 1983 G.W.D. 34-2191); the selling of flowers from a barrow (e.g. *Chichester District Council v Wood* [1997] 5 C.L. 442); trading from kiosks, provided that they are not structures for which local business rates would be payable or are activities being carried out as part of a business conducted from premises abutting a public place (e.g. the window of a seaside cafe through which ice creams are sold to passers-by); plying for hire of non-motorised conveyances in a quasi-taxi mode (cf. *Birrell v Glasgow City Council* [2015] CSIH 21, pedicab) and trading on a street corner by holding out a tray of cigarette lighters and calling out to passers-by to come and purchase them (*Prentice v Normand*, 1994 S.C.C.R. 55)—in the latter case it was held that a "pitch" as such was not a necessary element. Street trading includes sales by roundsmen (who are excluded from the parallel English legislation) and the expression "exposing for sale" can result in the conviction of an unlicensed trader whether or not a sale actually took place see, e.g. *Wheat v Brown* [1892] 1 Q.B. 418; *Clark v Strachan*, 1940 J.C. 29; *McIver v Robertson*, 1950 J.C 29; and *Major v Normand*, 1996 S.L.T. 297. In *Joseph Dunn (Bottlers) v MacDougall*, 1987 S.C.C.R. 290, it was held that street trading had taken place where members of the public could, on request, make purchases from a lemonade lorry which at the material time was engaged upon a delivery run along public roads. Thus, a local authority mobile library, which had a small selection of withdrawn books for sale, would also need a s.39

licence! A person who displays a "for sale" notice in the window of their car when that car is being used and is either being driven or parked for the owner's convenience is not engaged in "offering for sale" for the purposes of street trading—*Onasanya v London Borough of Newham* [2007] L.L.R. 37. Provided that a person actually serves customers then they are trading—in *Heatherstone v Wilson*, 1993 G.W.D. 23-1464 the fact that the person was mainly present to see that his companion did not suffer harassment was not a defence because he also had served customers. "Offering to carry out" in subs.(2)(b) would include canvassing for orders for themselves or on behalf of another person. There is no necessity for the trading to be regular or over a lengthy period of time and provision is made in Sch.1 para.7 for the granting of licences to cover particular events or seasons. Note that any street trading will require a licence—there is no de minimis rule or provision such as that applied to second-hand dealers in terms of s.24(3)(d). A licence can specify a particular area in which trading can take place or an exclusion zone, see *Cameron v Fife Council*, 2005 S.L.T. (Sh Ct) 115.

Subsection (3)

A number of specific exclusions are listed in this subsection, either because they are activities which are covered by other sections of this Act or in other legislation, or because they are activities for which the government did not consider regulation and licensing to be appropriate—e.g. subs.(3)(a)—because to do otherwise might have been thought to be an attempt to limit the freedom of the press particularly in the case of fringe political or religious material.

The exclusions are as follows:

(a) The sale of newspapers—see above, p.112. This would not include the sale of items such as postcards, tourist souvenirs, etc. unless excluded by the s.9 resolution.

(b) The exclusion does not automatically entitle a milk roundsman to undertake the sale of the normal ancillary items such as butter, yoghurt and fruit juice without the need for a s.39 licence, although there would be nothing wrong with a licensing authority having excluded these items when they were making the s.9 resolution.

(c) The sale of coal, coke and solid fuel.

(d) Pedlars—their activities, which have given rise to a certain amount of recent case law, are already covered by ss.4 and 5 of the Pedlars Act 1871, as amended by s.2 of the Pedlars Act 1881, and they require a pedlar's certificate issued under these Acts. A "pedlar" is defined as

> "any hawker, pedlar, petty chapman, tinker, caster of metals, mender of chairs or other person who, without horse or other beast bearing or drawing burden, travels and trades on foot and goes from town to town or to other men's houses, carrying to sell or exposing for sale any goods, wares or merchandise immediately to be delivered, or offering for sale his skill in handicraft".

Three cases from Glasgow illustrate the difference between a pedlar and a street trader. In *Normand v Alexander*, 1994 S.L.T. 274, a pedlar who, on a regular basis, trundled his stall on wheels to a site at St Enoch Square and, having reached that site then proceeded to sell goods therefrom, was held to be street trading at those times and therefore required a s.39 licence. In *Prentice v Normand*, 1983 G.W.D. 34-2191, the High Court held that a trader who held a pedlar's licence and who spread out T-shirts for sale to passers-by on a canvas cloth on the pavement for periods not exceeding 20 minutes was held to be street trading and thus required as s.39 licence, and it was stressed that it was the nature of the activity rather than its duration which was important. In a second case involving the same accused, namely, *Prentice v Normand*, 1994 S.C.C.R. 55, he was convicted of a contravention of s.7(1), having been observed by police officers standing in a street and calling out to passers-by to purchase cigarette lighters that were on a tray which he was holding. It was held by the High Court that it was not part of the legitimate activities of a pedlar to stop and call out to passers-by since it was the essence of peddling that he go to where his customers would be, to transact with them. In an English case, *Watson v Malloy* [1988] 1 W.L.R. 1026, persons who moved from place to place selling gift wrapping from portable stands were held not to have been trading as pedlars—per Hutchison J "a pedlar is one who trades as he travels as distinct from one who merely travels to trade". In the English case of *Chichester DC v Wood* [1997] 5 C.L. 442, where a flower seller with a moveable barrow was held to be a street trader, Blofeld J undertook a useful review of all the relevant English and Scottish authorities in relation to street trading and pedlars. He concluded therefrom that a pedlar might use a van to convey their goods to a place, provided that they then go on foot to sell their wares; they must travel to their customers rather than let them come to them; they must trade as they travel, rather than travel to trade; they must be a pedestrian; if a seller, rather than a mender, they must sell reasonably small goods; they may have a small means of assistance such as a trolley, but the use of a stand or barrow and the attendance on people to approach the seller would suggest that they intended to remain in one place and would thus be regarded as being a street trader. Further English examples include *Tunbridge Wells BC v Dunn* (1997) 95 L.G.R. 775 (where a trader who travelled from town to town, had no stand, and never stopped for longer than 20 minutes was held to be a pedlar); *Stevenage BC v Wright* (1997) 95 L.G.R. 404 (where a trader who sold wrapping paper from a large shopping bag at his feet for up to an hour at a time was held to be a street trader); and *South Tyneside MBC v Jackson* [1998] E.H.L.R. 249 (where a trader was not a pedlar because the purpose of moving his wheeled unit was merely an attempt to avail himself of the statutory pedlar defence rather than seek the attention of other potential customers); and see also *Islington LBC v Panico* [1973] 1 W.L.R. 1166 and *Croydon LBC v Braddon* [2002] EWHC 1961 for consideration of casual sales by roundsmen. The reason for the sudden upsurge in case law involving pedlars is not unconnected with the ease with which a pedlar's, as opposed to a street trader's, licence can be obtained.

(e) Activities covered by other sections of the Act—examples of this include taxis and boat hirers, itinerant metal dealers and public entertainments. If a specific licence is or would be required under another section of the Act then a s.39 street trader's licence would not be required provided, of course, that the person was not in fact acting as a street trader in relation to activities not covered by the above licences—e.g. *Thomson v Kirkcaldy DC*, 1987 S.L.T. 372, where a travelling showman was held not to require a street trader's licence in order to operate an amusement stall at the Links Market (a funfair held in the street) where, on the facts put forward, a public entertainment licence in terms of s.41 would have been more appropriate for the activity being carried on.

(f) A public charitable collection—since this activity is fully covered by the provisions of ss.84–92 of the Charities and Trustee Investment (Scotland) Act 2005.

Sections 3(b) and (4) were amended by the Food Safety Act 1990 ss.54 and 59; s.3(f) was amended by the Charities and Trustee Investment (Scotland) Act 2005 Sch.4.

Subsection (4)

This subsection places further controls on trading activities which involve food and is designed to ensure that high standards of food hygiene are complied with in order to minimise the obvious dangers of exposing the public to the sale of contaminated food. This subsection was amended by para.25(b)(i) of the Food Safety Act 1990, which replaces all previous references to the now superseded regulations made under the Food and Drugs (Scotland) Act 1956. The definition of a "food business" in the 1990 Act is "any business in the course of which commercial operations with respect to food or food sources are carried out", while "food", although not defined, is held to include drink (including water), chewing gum, ingredients used in the preparation of food and "articles and substances of not nutritional value which are used for human consumption", such as slimming aids. Food intended solely for pets or wild animals is excluded. Note that the subsection requires the food trading to involve the use of a vehicle, kiosk or stall and presumably the sale of food by a person merely standing in the street would not be covered. The reference to para.5(3) of Sch.1 to the 1982 Act is included because it might otherwise be thought that it was mandatory to grant a licence using the criteria of this subsection. "Food authority" was substituted for the original "islands or district council" by para.25(b) of the Food Safety Act 1990 and, in Scotland, a food authority is the council as constituted under s.2 of the Local Government etc. (Scotland) Act 1994, unless functions in certain areas have been assigned to a port local authority in terms of s.172 of the Public Health (Scotland) Act 1897—see ss.5(2) and (3) of the 1990 Act and Sch.13 para.163(1) of the 1994 Act. Enforcement of functions covered by the 1990 Act is the responsibility of the environmental health officers of those authorities.

This subsection however does not allow a licensing authority to make a decision based on any consideration other than one based on hygiene standards so, for instance, it would be ultra vires to make a decision based on, say, nutrition or diet considerations—*McCluskey v North Lanarkshire Council* 27 November 2015 Hamilton Sheriff Court.

Subsections (5) and (6)

These subsections were added by the 2010 Act s.175.

Market operators' licences

40.—(1) Subject to subsection (2) below, a licence, to be known as a "market operator's licence", shall be required for carrying on a private market.

(2) A market operator's licence shall not be required for carrying on either of the following—

(a) functions held by charitable, religious, youth, recreational, community, political or similar organisations;
(b) markets held only for the sale of livestock, fodder or grain.

(3) In addition to any other condition which may be included, a licence in respect of a private market shall include conditions as to—

(a) the regulation of days and hours of opening;
(b) the provision of adequate toilet facilities;
(c) the layout of the site or premises on which the market is to be held;
(d) the maintenance of order and public safety.

(4) In this section, "private market" means a market, whether covered or not, carried on by any person other than a local or public authority at which goods are offered by more than one seller for sale by retail to the public.

GENERAL NOTE

This section introduced for the first time the concept of a "market operator's licence" and once again this is a category of licence which can be issued if the licensing authority resolve to do so by virtue of s.9. It applies to all "private markets" (defined in subs.(4)), which are, in effect, commercial ventures run by an entrepreneur as opposed to, e.g. local authority markets, such as traditional burgh markets and includes car boot sales (see 2004 Task Group report, para.7.2). The 2010 Act did not include the sections in the Bill that would have removed the exemptions for charities and non-commercial markets.

Subsection (1)

The licence is granted to the *operator* of the market, and not the individual stallholder, and any requirements or conditions imposed are therefore the responsibility of the operator themselves and they will, in effect, have to ensure that the stallholders comply therewith. The stallholders will not, for the purpose of trading in the market, require to have street trader's licences by virtue of s.39(3)(e). A market operator has been held to include a tenant of a disused warehouse who entered into an agreement with a number of traders who paid them a weekly sum to use the premises to sell from in return for which they paid rates, heating, lighting and cleaning bills in relation to the whole premises—*Normand v Campbell*, 1988 S.C.C.R. 142.

Subsection (2)

Non-commercial and agricultural markets that might otherwise fall within the definition of "private market" in subs.(4) are specifically excluded from the provisions of s.40.

Subsection (3)

The four mandatory matters in relation to which conditions must be applied all relate to matters of public interest and safety. The licensing authority can impose other conditions provided that they can be justified in relation to the general scheme of this part of the 1982 Act—i.e. matters which relate to environmental and crime prevention and which cannot be otherwise regulated by the mechanism of the Town and Country Planning Acts. Thus, a licensing authority could not refuse a licence because they did not approve of the principle of private markets (see *Gerry Cottle's Circus v City of Edinburgh DC*, 1990 S.L.T. 235), or because they wished to limit competition or, say, protect traditional high street shopping in the area (Scottish Development Department Circular 6/1983) and note the English case of *East Staffordshire BC v Windridge Pearce (Burton-upon-Trent)* [1993] E.G.C.S. 186. In *Spook Erection Ltd v City of Edinburgh DC*, 1995 S.L.T. (Sh Ct) 107, the licensing authority was concerned with perceived problems relating to counterfeit goods and dubious stallholders and as a result attempted, under pressure from the Office of Trading Standards, to impose certain conditions on the holder of a s.40 licence. It was held by the court that five of these conditions were to be deleted for the following reasons, namely: (1) the condition that the operator give rights of entry and access to the Office of Trading Standards officers and that he comply with their reasonable directions and requirements was void because it was not for the licensing authority to add to the powers of a statutory body such as the Office of Trading Standards where no such powers had been given to them in terms of s.5 of the Act and that this condition was not imposed merely to assist the Office of Trading Standards officers in respect of their pre-existing powers; (2) the condition that the Office of Trading Standards officers are entitled to inspect a register kept by the operator whenever the market was open, was void because this would constitute a far leading power which the authority could not grant; (3) the condition that the operators do not permit "fly-pitches" was void both for uncertainty (there being no generally accepted definition of "fly-pitch"), and because the consequence of such a breach upon the operator was as severe one; (4) the condition that the operator obtain "proof of identity" of those requiring pitches was void because there was no explanation given of what steps an operator had to take to ascertain identity, and in any event, if this condition were read to be a lesser requirement upon an operator (i.e. not putting an absolute duty to obtain a true identification of the stallholder), then it was still void because it was a condition that the operator had to keep a register of stallholder's particulars; and (5) the condition that the operator was to ensure that all stallholders displayed their names and addresses within the stall was void because the condition sought to impose an absolute duty on the operator. In general, while it was clear from the licensing authority's statement of reasons why they had sought to impose these five conditions, it did not appear that they had anywhere considered or evaluated the operator's objections to these proposed conditions.

Subsection (4)

This is a fairly wide ranging definition, which includes open and covered markets and the concept of retail selling by more than one stallholder. For a discussion of the nature of market stalls and shops see *White v Kilmarnock and Loudon DC*, 1990 S.C.L.R. 771. Car boot sales, if organised on a commercial basis, would clearly fall within the ambit of s.40. Local authorities are entitled to establish and hold markets and provide market buildings in terms of s.27 of the Local Government and Planning (Scotland) Act 1982 and are thus excluded from the provisions of s.40.

Public entertainment licences

41.—(1) A licence, to be known as a "public entertainment licence", shall be required for the use of premises as a place of public entertainment.

[3](2) In this section, "place of public entertainment" means any place where members of the public are admitted or may use any facilities for the purposes of entertainment or recreation but does not include—

(a) an athletic or sports ground while being used as such;

(aa) premises
in respect of which a licence is required under section 41A of this Act while such premises are being used for the purposes mentioned in that section;

[5](ab) a sexual entertainment venue (as defined in section 45A) in relation to which Schedule 2 (as modified for the purposes of section 45B) has effect, while being used as such.

(b) an educational establishment while being used as such;

(c) premises belonging to or occupied by any religious body while being used wholly or mainly for purpose connected with that body;

[3,4](d) premises licensed under the Cinemas Act 1985;

[3](e) premises in which there is a club gaming permit (within the meaning of Section 271 of the Gambling Act 2005 (c.19) or a prize gaming permit)within the meaning of section 289 of that Act of 2005;

[1,3](f) licensed premises within the meaning of the Licensing (Scotland) Act 2005 (asp 16) in which public entertainment is being provided during licenced hours within the meaning of that Act;

[3](g) premises in which machines for entertainment or amusement are being provided incidentally to the main purpose or use of the premises where that main purpose or use is not where that main purpose or use is not as a place of public entertainment; or

[3](h) such other premises as the Scottish Ministers may by order made by statutory instrument specify.

[3](2A) A statutory instrument containing an order made under subsection 2(h) is subject to annulment in pursuance of a resolution of the Scottish Parliament.

[2](3) Without prejudice to section 3B of and paragraph 5 of Schedule 1 to this Act, a licensing authority may attach conditions to a public entertainment licence—

(a) restricting the use of the premises to a specified kind or specified kinds of entertainment or recreation;

(b) limiting the number of persons to be admitted to the premises;

(c) fixing the days and times when the premises may be open for the purposes of the entertainment or recreation;

[4](3A) In relation to a public entertainment licence which authorises the use of premises for the performance of plays, no condition may be attached to the licence, as to the nature of the plays which may be performed, or the manner of performing plays, under the licence.

[4](3B) Subsection (3A) does not prevent a licensing authority from attaching by virtue of section 3B or in accordance with subsection (3) or paragraph 5 of Schedule 1, any condition which they consider appropriate on the grounds of public safety.

(4) In this section, "educational establishment" has the meaning given by paragraphs (i) and (ii) of the definition of that expression in section 135(1) of the Education (Scotland) Act 1980 but includes a university and a theological college.

NOTES

1. As amended by the Licensing (Scotland) Act 2005 (asp 16) Sch.6 para.6 (effective 1 September 2009).

2. As amended by the Criminal Justice and Licensing (Scotland) Act 2010 (asp 13) Pt 8 s.172 (effective 28 March 2011).

3. As amended by the Criminal Justice and Licensing (Scotland) Act 2010 (asp 13) Pt 8 s.176 (effective 1 April 2012).

4. As inserted by the Air Weapons and Licensing (Scotland) Act 2015 (asp 10) Pt 3 s.76 (date yet to be appointed).

5. As inserted by the Air Weapons and Licensing (Scotland) Act 2015 (asp 10) Pt 3 s.74 (effective 1 December 2015).

DEFINITION

"premises": s.8.

GENERAL NOTE

This section of the Act provides for an "optional" scheme of licensing of public entertainments which are not defined other than by a list of activities which are specifically excluded therefrom. Whether or not any particular activity can constitute "entertainment" is an open question, but this would appear to be a matter within the discretion of the local authority—see e.g. *Bannatyne's Health Club (Aberdeen) Ltd v City of Aberdeen Licensing Board* (2000) 17 S.L.L.P. 11. The licensing authority, when making a resolution to adopt a scheme of s.41 licences *must*, in terms of s.9(5), clearly specify the categories of activity covered and should avoid expressions which could be construed conjunctively if this is not the intention—see, e.g. *Normand v Norris*, 1992 G.W.D. 1-41. As an example, the City of Edinburgh District Council resolved in 1983 to cover "saunas and massage parlours, health clubs, gymnasiums, billiard halls, video machine parlours, circuses, funfairs, variety shows, dance halls, discotheques, concert halls and ice rinks". It was the first category which gave rise to the difficulties in *Normand v Norris*, 1992 G.W.D. 1-41. There are limits, however, to the licensing authorities' powers to licence public entertainments, e.g. they cannot licence activities which would otherwise be illegal or immoral: see the interesting case of *Scanlan v City of Edinburgh DC*, 1995 S.L.T. (Sh Ct) 89 where, it was alleged, brothels were being licensed as public entertainments under the guise of saunas and massage parlours. A common law offence may also be committed by the holder of an unlicensed public entertainment, if there is culpable and reckless conduct on the part of the organisers thereof, e.g. a "rave" in a derelict building—*Normand v Robinson*, 1994; S.L.T. 588.

Subsection (1)

Note here that it is the premises (including land) that requires the licence and it is thus not transferable to other premises by the licence holder unless they seek a variation therefor. It is also important to note that the key factor is the *use* of the premises *as a place of public entertainment*, i.e. the current use to which the premises are being put is the key factor, not any original purpose for which they may have been constructed or adapted.

Subsection (2)

It is noted that authorities may not wish to licence certain types of free event, such as gala days and school fetes, but the task group felt that the decision on whether to licence these events should rest with the authority. The requirement for the event to be paid for by money or monies' worth was removed by the 2010 Act so free events are now covered. Note, too, that the purpose of the facility must be for the purpose of entertainment and recreation and thus, if another form of licence under the 1982 Act would be more appropriate, then a s.41 licence might not be needed—see *Thomson v Kirkcaldy DC*, 1987 S.L.T. 372 and subs.(2)(g) below.

There are a number of types of premises specifically exempted from the provisions of s.41 namely:

- (a) Athletic or sports grounds while being used as such—thus, a rock concert on a cricket ground will not automatically be exempt from a s.41 licence if such activities are covered by a s.9 resolution. While no definition is given of an athletic or sports ground, "sport" is defined for the purposes of indoor sports entertainment licences in s.41A(4).
- (aa) Indoor sports grounds. These are now covered by s.41A of the Act; this clause was added by s.44(5) of the Fire Safety and Safety of Places of Sport Act 1987.
- (ab) Sexual entertainment venues covered by Pt III of the Act.
- (b) Educational establishments as defined in subs.(4) below. If, however, the school hall is being hired out for, say, activities in connection with an arts festival run by an outside body then it will require a licence if a s.9 resolution applies to the activity taking place there.
- (c) Premises used by religious bodies—thus, the church youth club would be excluded from requiring a public entertainment licence, provided that they were not staging a public performance of a play or an entertainment to which the public were to be admitted on payment; an evangelical meeting, coffee morning or other discreet festivity would probably not require a s.41 licence! Note, however, that if the church hall is being hired out to an outside body for an exhibition, review or discotheque, then it may well be an activity for which a licence is required.
- (d) Cinemas will require a licence granted under s.1 of the Cinemas Act 1985 and premises licensed under Pt II of the Gaming Act 1968 will require a licence granted under the appropriate statutes.

(e) Premises to which s.16 of the Lotteries and Amusements Act 1976 applies—in effect, these are premises where there are, "amusements with prizes other than by machines". This paragraph does not otherwise exempt *amusement arcades* where amusement with prizes machines, i.e. one-arm bandits, fruit machines and their more sophisticated modern cousins, are kept, provided that the licensing authority have made a s.9 resolution to licence such premises. Note that a licence for an amusement arcade with amusement with prizes machines in terms of Pt IV of the Gaming Act 1968 will be required and that planning permission is usually a prerequisite for the operation of such premises—see *JE Sheeran (Amusement Arcades) Ltd v Hamilton DC*, 1986 S.L.T. 289; "Amusement centres, planning morals and planning practice" (1985) J.P.L. 5; and *Stair Memorial Encyclopaedia*, CM Brend and DW Williams, Reissue 7, *Entertainment*, para.8–18.

(f) Premises licensed under the Licensing (Scotland) Act 2005—note that there are two qualifications, namely: (i) that public entertainment is being provided; and (ii) that it is during the licensed hours.

(g) Incidental amusements—no indication is given as to the degree of incidence but an example might be a single video machine or pinball machine in the corner of a cafe.

Subsection (3)

This subsection allows certain additional conditions to be imposed without prejudice to the generality of Sch.1 para.5, namely: (a) a restriction of the types of activity to be carried on in particular premises, e.g. for safety reasons or to minimise disruption to neighbouring businesses or residents, and this can be used additionally to any planning powers—*JE Sheenan (Amusement Arcades) Ltd v Hamilton DC*, 1986 S.L.T. 289: for an example of the restriction of noise levels for a "rave" see *Cumnock and Doon Valley DC v Dance Energy Associates Ltd*, 1992 G.W.D. 25-1441; (b) a restriction in the number of persons using the premises for, say, fire safety purposes; and (c) a restriction of hours or days of operation. Special conditions may be applied where hypnosis is being used for the purpose of entertainment—Hypnotism Act 1952 and suggested appropriate conditions in Home Office Circular 28/53. Conditions would have to be reasonable and cannot be used as a pretext for banning an activity which the licensing authorities find morally or politically offensive—see, e.g. *Gerry Cottle's Circus v City of Edinburgh DC*, 1990 S.L.T. 235.

Subsection (3A)

Prior to the 2015 Act coming into force a mandatory licence was required from the licensing authority under the Theatres Act 1968 for the performance of a single play or a number of plays at a venue irrespective of whether performed by amateurs or professionals but the 2015 report noted that it would allow greater flexibility and a reduction in costs if the 1968 Act was abolished in respect of its licensing provisions and the matter was dealt with by replacing it with an optional scheme of licensing authority public entertainment licensing. Note that this applies to the premises (i.e. theatres) rather than individual plays and that no restriction may be placed on the nature of plays to be performed there or the manner in which they are to be performed. The 1968 Act still applies in respect of certain sections dealing with powers of entry and inspection and obscenity, racial hatred and public records of scripts.

As of February 2016 this subsection and subs.(3B) following were not yet in force and theatre licensing is still subject to the 1968 Act.

Subsection (3B)

Note that the licensing authority can attach conditions relating to public safety but otherwise cannot restrict performances by way, for instance, of attempting any form of censorship.

Subsection (4)

Thus, in effect, all primary, secondary and tertiary places of education are brought within the ambit of the exclusion in subs.(2)(b) above.

Indoor sports entertainment licences

41A.—(1) Subject to subsection (2) below, a licence to be known as an "indoor sports entertainment licence" shall be required for the use of premises as a place of public sports entertainment.

(2) Subsection (1) above shall not apply to any occasion on which the entertainment of the public by the sport is not the principal purpose for which the premises are used but this provision does not apply in relation to a sports complex.

(3) Without prejudice to paragraph 5 of Schedule 1 to this Act, a licensing authority may attach conditions to an indoor sports entertainment licence—

(a) restricting the use of the premises to a specified kind of specified kinds of public sports entertainment;

(b) limiting the number of persons to be admitted to the premises;

(c) fixing the days and times when the premises may be open for the purposes of public sports entertainment.

(4) In this section—

"*premises*" means any permanent or temporary building and any tent or inflatable structure and includes a part of a building where the building is a sports complex but does not include a part of any other building;

"*public sports entertainment*" means any sporting event to which the public are invited as spectators;

"*sporting event*" means any contest, exhibition or display of any sport;

"*sports complex*" means a building—

(a) which provides accommodation and facilities for both those engaging in sport and spectators; and

(b) the parts of which are so arranged that one or more sports can be engaged in simultaneously in different parts of the building; and

"*sport*" includes any game in which physical skill is the predominant factor and any form of physical recreation which is also engaged in for purposes of competition or display, except dancing (in any form).

GENERAL NOTE

This section was inserted into the 1982 Act by s.44(1) of the Fire Safety and Safety of Places of Sport Act 1987 and s.44(2) of the 1987 Act provides that "indoor sports entertainment licences" will replace public entertainment licences where the form of entertainment comes within the definition of activities covered by s.41A; and s.41 licences, which would properly fall within the ambit of the new section, when renewed, become s.41A licences. Indoor sports entertainment licences do not require a resolution in terms of s.9 since they are the one class of "miscellaneous licence" which is mandatory rather than optional.

Subsection (1)

"Public sports entertainment" and "premises" are both defined in subs.(4).

Subsection (2)

The licence is restricted to the use of the premises for the specified purposes and, with the exception of "sports complexes" (defined in subs.(4)), premises where the entertainment of the public by the sport is not the principal purpose for the use of the building (e.g. a town hall used for a wrestling match) are excluded from the provisions of s.41A.

Subsection (3)

All conditions imposed must, of course, be reasonable (Sch.1 para.5) and restrictions on the sports, number of spectators and opening times may be specified. It is usual to have conditions relating to staff, overcrowding, safety, fire precautions, electricity and lighting and other matters necessary for public safety and order—in the case of the City of Edinburgh, 28 separate conditions are imposed, all of which fall within the above categories.

Subsection (4)

"Premises"—this is a more detailed definition than that contained in s.8 and is necessary: (a) to restrict land, restrict it to indoor places only; and (b) to limit it to parts of sports complexes but to exclude parts of any other buildings, e.g. town halls. "Public sports entertainment" involves the public being "invited" to spectate and implies that the advertisement or intimation of the event is given to the public; note that there is no mention of "money or money's worth" as in s.41. "Sporting event" has a meaning wider than a game or match and includes tournaments as well as non-competitive events. A training session might fall within the definition if the public were "invited" to view it. "Sports complex" means a building (but presumably not a tent or inflatable structure—cf. definition of "premises") where sportsmen and spectators are given facilities and where one or more sports can be engaged in simultaneously; it is perhaps easier to visualise this fast-growing category of building than to actually describe it! "Sport" would presumably include games such as snooker but exclude chess, even though many might regard cerebral games as a form of sport; note the exclusion of dancing in any form—thus dance championships, displays or marathons fall outwith s.41A but might require a public entertainment licence under s.41.

Late hours catering licences

42.—[2](1) A licence, to be known as a "late hours catering licence", shall be required for the use of premises between the hours of eleven o'clock in the evening and five o'clock the following morning for the sale to or consumption by the public of food.

[2](2) The reference in subsection (1) above to the sale of meals or food is a reference to food for consumption on as well as off the premises in which it is sold.

[2](3) Without prejudice to paragraph 5 of Schedule 1 to this Act, a licensing authority may attach conditions to a late hours catering licence fixing the days and hours during which the premises may be open for business, and different days and hours may be fixed for the sale of food for consumption on the premises from those fixed for the sale of food for consumption off the premises.

(4) A late hours catering licence shall not be required in respect of—

[1](a) the use as such of licensed premises within the meaning of the Licensing (Scotland) Act 2005 (asp 16); or

(b) premises being used in accordance with a public entertainment licence.

(5) A licensing authority may, on application made to them, exempt the use of premises requiring a late hours catering licence from the requirement to have such a licence—

(a) in respect of any particular occasion; or

(b) during a specified period not exceeding 2 months in any period of 12 months.

(6) The licensing authority may attach conditions to an exemption granted under subsection (5) above, and the provisions of Part I of this Act relating to the attaching of conditions to licences and subsection (3) above shall apply to the attaching of conditions to exemptions under this subsection.

[2](7) In this section "food" has the meaning given in section 1 of the Food Safety Act 1990 (c.16).

NOTES

1. As amended by the Licensing (Scotland) Act 2005 (asp 16) Sch.6 para.6 (effective 1 September 2009).
2. As amended by the Criminal Justice and Licensing (Scotland) Act 2010 (asp 13) Pt 8 s.177 (effective 1 October 2012).

GENERAL NOTE

This is an "optional" class of licence which is only brought into effect by a resolution of the licensing authority in terms of s.9 and applies to premises used by the public for the consumption of refreshments between the specified hours. The primary purpose of this type of licence is to preserve the amenity of an area and it was the Secretary of State's view that licensing would be appropriate if there was a likelihood of noise, litter or other disturbance in primarily residential areas and that a blanket application throughout the whole of a local authority area was unlikely to be necessary or appropriate—Scottish Development Department Circular 6/1983. In practice, it has proved to be a useful method of preserving late night peace in many areas and the police and licensing authorities believe that conditions attached to s.42 licences have led to a reduction in disturbances and petty crime. The task group noted that "the principal justification for licensing such premises related to the potential for large numbers of people leaving pubs, night clubs, etc. late at night to cause a disturbance, and that this potential exists regardless of whether the food or drink being sold has been cooked or pre-prepared in any way". An establishment in possession of a s.42 licence will, of course, have to comply with planning and environmental health legislation.

Subsection (1)

The requirement only applies to premises open between 23:00 and 05:00 and thus a cafe which does not open during these hours does not require a s.42 licence. The wording "use of the premises" would cover the situation of a restaurant where diners begin their meals before 23:00 but do not finish them by that hour, i.e. the sale might have occurred before 23:00 but if the consumption continues after this time then a licence will be required: cf. the English case of *Amin v DPP*, *The Times*, 9 April 1993 DC; [1993] C.L.Y. 2596. The applicant must have some continuing interest in the premises for which they seek a s.42 licence: see, e.g. *Shahin v Roxburgh DC*, 1996 S.L.T. 457. Note that a sale is not a necessary part of the definition—cf. subs.(2). Scottish Development Department Circular 6/1983 suggests that "meals or refreshments" cover part-meals such as chips or coffee and s.177 of the 2010 Act altered the definition of "meals and refreshments" to cover "food" so as to include late night grocers and such establishments as 24 hour supermarkets and garage shops.

Subsection (2)

This subsection makes it clear that "carry out" establishments are also covered but cf. subs.(1)—in this subsection a "sale" is envisaged—presumably the licensing authority could make it clear in a s.9 resolution that, say, charitable "soup kitchens", etc. are to be excluded.

Subsection (3)

Any conditions must be reasonable and cannot apply to any period outwith the specified hours of 23:00 to 05:00. This power is additional to the general powers in Sch.1 para.5. An example of a "reasonable" condition was that applied in *Christoforou v City of Glasgow DC*, 1989 G.W.D. 10-447 where the opening hours were restricted to midnight because of noise problems experienced by neighbouring residents. In practice, many licensing authorities impose a general condition that premises must close at a specified time to prevent late night revellers from pubs and discotheques from wandering the streets in search of food and although individual premises might be allowed to stay open (e.g. a 24 hour garage that sells hot snacks to road users) it is at least arguable that if one establishment is allowed to remain open substantially later than others in the same town then this may defeat the whole reason for the restriction. There must, however, be a reason for such conditions—see *Richmond Inns Ltd v City of Aberdeen DC* unreported 11 June 1996 Aberdeen Sheriff Court. A licensing authority should not fetter its discretion by adopting an inflexible policy and should consider each case on its merits and any apparent discrimination against one particular premises could be challengeable—see, e.g. *Ali v Banff and Buchan DC*, 1990 G.W.D. 18-1017 and notes to Sch.1 para.5 below.

Subsection (4)

To prevent duplication, premises licensed to sell alcohol in terms of the Licensing (Scotland) Act 2005, and those for which public entertainment licences under s.41 are in force are specifically excluded. A street trader with a s.39 licence might need a s.42 licence if they were operating a business that included meals and refreshments supplied after 23:00—e.g. the proprietor of a nocturnal mobile fish and chip van could need both a s.39 and a s.42 licence.

Subsections (5) and (6)

These subsections allow a relaxation for special events such as local festivals but the power is limited to either a "one-off" situation or a specific period not exceeding two months in any period of 12 months. The licensing authority can, however, attach normal licensing conditions notwithstanding the fact that they have exempted the premises.

Subsection (7)

Note that food is defined and the 2010 Act abolished the old definition of "meals and refreshment"—see note to s.39(4) above.

Window cleaners' licences

43.—A licence, to be known as a "window cleaner's licence" shall be required for carrying on the trade of, or being employed as, a window cleaner.

GENERAL NOTE

This is an "optional" activity that the licensing authority may resolve to licence in terms of s.9 and the requirements may be limited to a particular geographical area, such as the largest town in a mainly rural district. No definition of "window cleaner" is given although it can be inferred that it is designed to cover a person who is a window cleaner by trade as opposed to someone who may incidentally clean windows as part of more general cleaning duties within a particular building or a person who cleans windows in, say, a single large institution. Employers and employees are both covered (see note to s.39(1)) and no special requirements or mandatory conditions are laid down, although a licensing authority may impose reasonable conditions under the provisions of Sch.1 para.5. For an example of a condition placed upon a window cleaner under the now repealed Edinburgh Act see *Ross v City of Edinburgh DC*, 1977 S.L.T. (Sh Ct) 39, where a window cleaner convicted of a sexual offence against a young girl had a condition imposed upon him prohibiting him from window cleaning in the area in which the offence had occurred. The condition was upheld by the court which held that the authority were justified in imposing a condition "for the preservation of good order in the district". A recent case involving a s.43 licence is *Rose v Falkirk DC*, 1994 G.W.D. 15-961.

The 2004 Licensing Task Group recommended, at para.11.6 of their report, that in order to minimise the burden on the window cleaning trade

> "model conditions of licence should be drawn up, perhaps by SOLAR [the Society of Local Authority Legal Officers and Administrators], to enable licensing authorities to consider the merits of entering into agreements with neighbouring authorities to avoid the need for window cleaners to have to obtain multiple licences when operating in more than one licensing authority area".

Additional activities

44.—(1) The Secretary of State may, by order made by statutory instrument, designate any activity other than one of those specified in this Part of this Act—

(a) as an activity for which, subject to a resolution of the licensing authority in relation to it under section 9 of this Act, a licence shall be required and which, subject to such a resolution, shall be regulated in accordance with the provisions specified in the order; or

(b) as an activity for which a licence shall be required and which shall be regulated in accordance with the provisions specified in the order.

(2) An order made under this section may provide—

(a) that Part I of this Act, with such modifications if any as may be specified in the order, shall have effect for the purposes of the licensing of the activity designated by the order;

(b) for the regulation of the activity designated by the order;

(c) for the repeal or modification of any enactment which provides (whether consistently or not) for the same matter as the order;

(d) without prejudice to any provision of Part I of this Act which has effect, with or without modification, by virtue of paragraph (a) above, for the creation of offences and for making offenders liable, on summary conviction, to imprisonment for a period not exceeding 60 days or such lesser maximum period as may be specified in the order or to a fine not exceeding level 3 on the standard scale or such lesser maximum fine as may be so specified or to both such fine and such imprisonment.

(3) No order shall be made under this section unless a draft of it has been laid before and approved by a resolution of each House of Parliament.

GENERAL NOTE

At the time when the 1982 Act was being drafted it was thought desirable to include a provision whereby new activities could be brought within the ambit of the licensing provisions of the Act in order to preserve a flexible approach to new developments, trends or needs. This section, therefore, provides the machinery whereby additional activities can be incorporated within the main part of the Act with any modifications that are thought necessary. The functions of the Secretary of State in this section are now dealt with by the appropriate Minister of the Scottish Executive—Scotland Act 1998.

Subsection (1)

The activity covered must be an additional one (i.e. not one already covered by the Act) and not merely a break away from or subdivision of an existing activity, which may explain why indoor sports entertainment licences, which previously fell within the ambit of s.41, were not deemed suitable to include as s.44 additional activities; it would, however, be quite possible to add a new activity which was previously licensed pursuant to another unconnected Act. Additional activities can be either optional (requiring a resolution from the licensing authority under s.9) or mandatory and are to be introduced into the Act only by statutory instrument.

Subsection (2)

This provides that Pt I of the 1982 Act (including Sch.1) may be applied by the subordinate legislation so as to preserve the uniform code of civic licensing but that modifications may be made and that additional offences may be created. Any other enactment may be repealed or modified by the order.

Subsection (3)

A resolution of each House of Parliament to approve the draft order was formerly required before it can be brought into effect. The position is now regulated by the Scotland Act 1998.

Part III

[1]Control of sex shops and sexual entertainment venues

NOTE

1. As amended by the Air Weapons and Licensing (Scotland) Act 2015 (asp 10) Pt 3 s.76 (date yet to be appointed).

Control of sex shops

45.—[1](1) A local authority may resolve that Schedule 2 to this Act shall have effect in their area; and if they do so resolve that Schedule shall have such effect as from the day specified in that behalf in the resolution (which must not be before the expiration of the period of one month beginning with the day on which the resolution is passed).

[1](2) A local authority shall, not later than 28 says before the day specified in the resolution for the coming into effect of Schedule 2 to this Act in the authority's area, publish notice that they have passed a resolution under this section in a newspaper circulating in their area.

(3) The notice shall state the general effect of that Schedule.

NOTE

1. As amended by the Local Government etc. (Scotland) Act 1994 (c.39) Sch.13 para.129 (effective 1 April 1996).

DEFINITIONS

"premises": s.8.
"sex shop": Sch.2 para.2(1).

GENERAL NOTE

Part III consists of this section and the three additional sections added by the 2015 Act which allows local authorities to control the number and location of sex shops within their area. It is an "optional" system and licensing becomes mandatory only when the licensing authority resolve to make it such in terms of s.45(1), thereafter it is an offence to operate a sex shop without a licence—Sch.2 para.19(1). This part of the Act is entirely separate from Pts I and II and Sch.1 and none of the provisions contained therein apply to sex shops which have their own separate code of procedure in Sch.2.

Subsection (1)

The local authority resolution will bring the necessity for sex shops to be licensed into effect on the day specified in the resolution, which must not be before the expiration of one month from the date upon which the resolution was passed. It is an "all or nothing" provision, i.e. they can resolve only to licence all the sex shops in the whole of their area.

Subsections (2) and (3)

The local authority must publish a notice stating the general effect of the provisions of Sch.2 in a newspaper circulating in the area affected, not later than 28 days prior to the licensing provisions coming into effect. These are mandatory provisions—see similar English legislation applied in *R v Birmingham City Council Ex p. Quietlynn Ltd* (1985) 83 L.G.R. 461; *Sheptonhurst Ltd v Newham LBC* (1985) 84 L.G.R. 97; and *Quietlynn Ltd v Portsmouth City Council* [1988] Q.B. 114.

Licensing of sexual entertainment venues: interpretation

[1]**45A.**—(1) This section applies for the purposes of the interpretation of section 45B and Schedule 2 (as modified for the purposes of section 45B).

(2) "*Sexual entertainment venue*" means any premises at which sexual

entertainment is provided before a live audience for (or with a view to) the financial gain of the organiser.

(3) For the purposes of that definition—

"*audience*" includes an audience of one,

"*financial gain*" includes financial gain arising directly or indirectly from the provision of the sexual entertainment,

"*organiser*", in relation to the provision of sexual entertainment premises, means—

(a) the person ("A") who is responsible for—

(i) the management of the premises, or

(ii) the organisation or management of the sexual entertainment, or

(b) where A exercises that responsibility on behalf of another person (whether by virtue of a contract of employment or otherwise), that other person,

"*premises*" includes any vehicle, vessel or stall but does not include any private dwelling to which the public is not admitted,

"*sexual entertainment*" means—

(a) any live performance, or

(b) any live display of nudity,

which is of such a nature that, ignoring financial gain, it must reasonably be assumed to be provided solely or principally for the purpose of sexually stimulating any member of the audience (whether by verbal or other means).

(4) For the purposes of the definition of "sexual entertainment", "display of nudity" means—

(a) in the case of a woman, the showing of (to any extent and by any means) her nipples, pubic area, genitals or anus,

(b) in the case of a man, the showing of (to any extent and by any means) his pubic area, genitals or anus.

(5) Sexual entertainment is provided if (and only if) it is provided (or allowed to be provided) by or on behalf of the organiser.

(6) References in Schedule 2 (as modified for the purposes of section 45B) to the use of any premises by a person as a sexual entertainment venue are to be read as references to their use by the organiser.

(7) The following are not sexual entertainment venues—

(a) a sex shop (within the meaning of paragraph 2(1) of Schedule 2),

(b) such other premises as the Scottish Ministers may by order specify.

(8) An order under subsection (7)(b) may make different provision for different purposes.

(9) Premises at which sexual entertainment is provided as mentioned in subsection (2) on a particular occasion ("the current occasion") are not to be treated as a sexual entertainment venue if sexual entertainment has not been provided on more than 3 previous occasions which fall wholly or partly within the period of 12 months ending with the start of the current occasion.

(10) For the purposes of subsection (9)—

(a) each continuous period during which sexual entertainment is provided on the premises is to be treated as a separate occasion, and

(b) where the period during which sexual entertainment is provided on the premises exceeds 24 hours, each period of 24 hours (and any part of a period of 24 hours) is to be treated as a separate occasion.

(11) The Scottish Ministers may by order provide for—

(a) descriptions of performances, or

(b) descriptions of displays of nudity,

which are not to be treated as sexual entertainment for the purposes of this section.

(12) An order under subsection (7)(b) or (11) is subject to the negative procedure.

NOTE

1. As inserted by the Air Weapons and Licensing (Scotland) Act 2015 (asp 10) Pt 3 s.76 (effective 1 December 2015 for the purpose of inserting s.45A of the 1982 Act, but only for the purpose of making regulations under s.45A(7)(b) and (11); not yet in force otherwise).

GENERAL NOTE

Sections 45A–45E were added by the 2015 Act s.68 in the light of the decision in *Brightcrew Ltd v City of Glasgow Licensing Board* [2011] CSIH 46; 2011 S.C. 67; 2012 S.L.T. 140, which held that licensing boards could only regulate such establishments in relation to matters concerned with the sale of alcohol rather than matters dealing with the safety of the premises and those who work there. Sexual entertainment venues are licenced in England and Wales under the Policing and Crime Act 2009 and their licensing in Scotland had already been under consideration by a working group set up in 2005 by the Scottish Ministers. The proposals which led to the 2015 Act provisions were somewhat controversial with views on the one hand that since such establishments existed they should be regulated and were necessary to attract such things as business conventions to Scotland's cities and the opposite view was that they should not be encouraged as they perpetrated outdated and unacceptable attitudes towards the degradation of women. The 2015 report at para.456 sets out the view of the Zero Tolerance charity: " ... in a civilised society in which our people and communities support and respect each other some choices are curtailed in the interests of al". Paragraph 457 says: "The Scottish Government's policy on violence against women defines stripping, lap dancing and pole dancing as commercial sexual exploitation and therefore violence against women. This is because 'these activities have been shown to be harmful for the individual women involved and have a negative impact on the position of all women through the objectification of women's bodies'"; and in para.458 it was remarked that the Cabinet Secretary when asked why sexual entertainment venues had not been banned by the Scottish Government given the harm caused by the commercial exploitation of women said:

> "What we are doing is giving local authorities the power to licence the venues and to determine what the number of them should be. If a local authority believes that the desirable number is zero, there is a process that it can do so to achieve that."

This type of licence is an optional activity for which a s.9 resolution must be passed.

Subsection(2)

This means that the sexual entertainment be live and for the direct or indirect financial benefit of the organiser.

Subsection (3)–(5)

These provide that the entertainment, apart from financial gain of the organisers, is to the sole or principal purpose of sexual stimulation of members of the audience. Private premises where events were held are excluded as are those where the entertainment is provided without the knowledge of the organiser (e.g.in para.460 "a strip-o-gram booked to attend a group in a pub"), and artistic as opposed to sexual entertainment although the latter may in practice be difficult to define.

Subsection (6)

It is also suggested in para.465 of the 2015 report that

> "we note that nothing in the licensing regime would serve to permit or mitigate illegal activity if offences are being committed e.g. brothel keeping, trading in prostitution or the use of the premises for unlawful intercourse".

Subsection (9) and (10)

This excludes venues used on not more than three occasions within a one year period and specifies the way in which such use would be calculated. The 2015 report states at para.475 that in the Cabinet Secretary's view

> "the exemption was included largely to reflect the fact that there could be unintended occasions on which a venue finds that it might have required an additional licence. It would be difficult for us to regulate such situations or to understand the full extent of that activity, and the exemption provision is an attempt to strike a balance".

[1][Licensing of sexual entertainment venues

45B.—(1) A local authority may resolve that Schedule 2 (as modified for the purposes of this section) is to have effect in their area in relation to sexual entertainment venues.

(2) If a local authority passes a resolution under subsection (1), Schedule 2 (as so modified) has effect in their area from the day specified in the resolution.

(3) The day mentioned in subsection (2) must not be before the expiry of the period of one year beginning with the day on which the resolution is passed.

(4) A local authority must, not later than 28 days before the day mentioned in subsection (2), publish notice that they have passed a resolution under this section.

(5) The notice must—

(a) state the general effect of Schedule 2 (as modified for the purposes of this section), and

(b) be published electronically or in a newspaper circulating in the local authority's area.

(6) For the purposes of this section, paragraphs 1 and 3 to 25 of Schedule 2 apply with the following modifications—

(a) references to a sex shop are to be read as references to a sexual entertainment venue,

(b) references to the use by a person of premises, vehicles, vessels or stalls as a sexual entertainment venue are to be read as references to their use by the organiser,

(c) in paragraph 1—

(i) in sub-paragraph (b)—

(A) the word "or" immediately following paragraph (i) is omitted,

(B) paragraph (ii) is omitted, and

(ii) sub-paragraph (c) is omitted,

(d) in paragraph 7—

(i) in sub-paragraph (2), at the beginning insert "Subject to subparagraph (3A),", and

(ii) after sub-paragraph (3) insert—

"(3A) If a local authority consider it appropriate to do so in relation to an application, the local authority may dispense with the requirement to publish an advertisement under sub-paragraph (2) and may instead publish notice of the application electronically.

(3B) Publication under sub-paragraph (3A) must be not later than 7 days after the date of the application.

(3C) The applicant must also, not later than 7 days after the date of the application—

(a) send a copy of the application to each person or body listed in the local authority's determination under sub-paragraph (3D), and

(b) submit to the local authority a certificate stating that the applicant has complied with this sub-paragraph.

(3D) For the purposes of sub-paragraph (3C), a local authority must—

(a) from time to time determine the persons or bodies who must receive a copy of the application, and

(b) publicise the determination in such manner as they consider appropriate.",

(e) in paragraph 9—

(i) in sub-paragraph (5)(c)—

(A) after the word "in" insert "the local authority's area or",

(B) after the word "for" insert "their area or",

(ii) after sub-paragraph (5) insert—

"(5A) For the purposes of sub-paragraph (5)(c), a local authority must—

(a) from time to time determine the appropriate number of sexual entertainment venues for their area and for each relevant locality, and

(b) publicise the determination in such manner as they consider appropriate.",

(iii) after sub-paragraph (6) insert—

"(6A) A local authority may refuse an application for the grant or renewal of a licence despite the fact that a premises licence under Part 3 of the Licensing (Scotland) Act 2005 is in effect in relation to the premises, vehicle, vessel or stall to which the application relates.",

(f) in paragraph 12(2)(b), for "shorter" substitute "other",

(g) in paragraph 19(1)(e), for the words from "without" to the end of paragraph (e) substitute "knowingly permits any person under the age of 18 to enter the sexual entertainment venue—

(i) at a time when sexual entertainment is being provided, or

(ii) without reasonable excuse, at any other time,", and

(h) in paragraph 25, in each of sub-paragraphs (1)(a) and (2), for "45" substitute "45B".

(7) In carrying out functions conferred by virtue of this section, a local authority must have regard to any guidance issued by the Scottish Ministers.]

NOTE

1. As inserted by the Air Weapons and Licensing (Scotland) Act 2015 (asp 10) Pt 3 s.76 (date yet to be appointed).

GENERAL NOTE

This section contains modifications to Sch.2 when, and only when, it is dealing with a sexual entertainment venue.

[1][Statements of policy in relation to sexual entertainment venues

45C.—(1) This section applies where a local authority passes a resolution under section 45B(1).

(2) The local authority must prepare a statement of their policy with respect to the exercise of their functions in relation to the licensing of sexual entertainment venues (a "SEV policy statement").

(3) In preparing a SEV policy statement, a local authority must—

(a) consider the impact of the licensing of sexual entertainment venues in their area, having regard, in particular, to how it will affect the objectives of—

(i) preventing public nuisance, crime and disorder,

(ii) securing public safety,

(iii) protecting children and young people from harm,

(iv) reducing violence against women, and

(b) consult such persons or bodies as they consider appropriate.

(4) The local authority must publish the SEV policy statement at the same time and in the same manner as they publish the notice of the resolution under section 45B(4).

(5) The local authority must—

(a) from time to time review the SEV policy statement and make such revisions as they consider appropriate (if any), and

(b) publish the revised statement in such manner as they consider appropriate.

(6) Subsection (3) applies to a review of a SEV policy statement as it applies to preparing such a statement.

(7) In exercising their functions in relation to the licensing of sexual entertainment venues, a local authority must have regard to their SEV policy statement or revised statement.

(8) In this section—

"*children*" means persons under the age of 16,

"*young people*" means persons aged 16 or 17.]

NOTE

1. As inserted by the Air Weapons and Licensing (Scotland) Act 2015 (asp 10) Pt 3 s.76 (date yet to be appointed).

GENERAL NOTE

Where a licensing authority has by s.9 resolution decided to licence sexual entertainment venues it must at the same time as it passes the resolution produce and publish a policy document which considers how the policy will affect the four objectives in subs.(3)(a) and consult with such persons as they consider appropriate. If at any time the policy statement is reviewed they must then publish any amended statement.

[1][**Deemed grant of applications**

45D.—(1) For the purpose of the discharge of their functions under this Part, every local authority must—

(a) consider each relevant application made to them within the period of 3months beginning with the date on which the application was made, and

(b) subject to the following provisions of this section, reach a final decision on the application within the period of 6 months beginning with the end of the 3 month period referred to in paragraph (a).

(2) On an application by the local authority within the 6 month period referred to in subsection (1)(b), the sheriff may, if it appears that there is a good reason to do so, extend that period as the sheriff thinks fit.

(3) The applicant is entitled to be a party to proceedings on an application under subsection (2).

(4) Where the local authority have failed to reach a final decision on the application before the expiry of—

(a) the 6 month period referred to in subsection (1)(b), or

(b) such further period as the sheriff may have specified on application under subsection (2), the licence is deemed to have been granted, renewed or, as the case may be, varied on the date of such expiry.

(5) A licence deemed to have been granted or renewed under subsection (4) is to remain in force for the period of one year.

(6) A deemed variation of the terms of a licence deemed under subsection (4) is to have effect for the remaining period of the licence.

(7) Subsections (4) and (6) do not affect—

(a) the powers of revocation under paragraph 13 of Schedule 2, and

(b) the powers of variation under paragraph 15 of that Schedule.

(8) The deemed grant, renewal or variation of the terms of a licence under subsection (4) has the same effect, for the purposes of Schedule 2, as a decision of the licensing authority to grant, renew or vary the terms of a licence.

(9) For the purposes of this section, a "relevant application" is an application under paragraph 6 or 15 of Schedule 2.

(10) In Schedule 1 (licensing: further provisions as to the general system), in paragraph 10, after sub-paragraph (5) insert—

"(6) Sub-paragraph (5) does not apply to a deemed variation of the terms of a licence under section 3(4)."

(5) In Schedule 2 (control of sex shops and sexual entertainment venues), in paragraph 15, after sub-paragraph (4) insert—

"(4A) Sub-paragraph (4) does not apply to a deemed variation of the terms of a licence under section 45D(4).".]

NOTE

1. As inserted by the Air Weapons and Licensing (Scotland) Act 2015 (asp 10) Pt 3 s.77 (date yet to be appointed).

GENERAL NOTE

This has certain similarities to deemed grants under s.3.

[1]Mandatory licence conditions

45E.—(1) The Scottish Ministers may by order prescribe conditions to which licences granted by local authorities under this Part are to be subject.

(2) Different conditions may be prescribed under subsection (1)—

(a) in respect of different licences or different types of licence,

(b) otherwise for different purposes, circumstances or cases.

(3) An order under subsection (1) is subject to the affirmative procedure.

(4) Subsection (1) does not affect any other power of the Scottish Ministers under this Act or any other enactment to prescribe conditions—

(a) to which licences granted by local authorities under this Part are to be subject, or

(b) to be imposed by local authorities in granting or renewing licences under this Part.

(5) The following conditions are referred to in this Part as "mandatory conditions"—

(a) conditions prescribed under subsection (1),

(b) conditions prescribed under any power referred to in subsection (4), and

(c) conditions imposed, or required to be imposed, by any provision of this Part.

(6) In this section and section 45F, references to licences granted by local authorities include references to—

(a) licences renewed by local authorities, and

(b) licences deemed by virtue of section 45D to have been granted or renewed by local authorities.

NOTE

1. As inserted by the Air Weapons and Licensing (Scotland) Act 2015 (asp 10) Pt 3 s.76 (effective 1 December 2015 for the purpose of inserting s.45E of the 1982 Act, but only for the purpose of making regulations under s.45E(1); not yet in force otherwise).

GENERAL NOTE

Again this has similarities to mandatory conditions granted under s.3A.

[1][Standard licence conditions

45F.—(1) A local authority may determine conditions to which licences granted by them
under this Part are to be subject.

(2) Conditions determined under subsection (1) are referred to in this Part as "standard conditions".

(3) Different conditions may be determined under subsection (1)—

(a) in respect of different licences or different types of licence,

(b) otherwise for different purposes, circumstances or cases.

(4) A local authority must publish, in such manner as they think appropriate, any standard conditions determined by them.

(5) Standard conditions have no effect—

(a) unless they are published, and

(b) so far as they are inconsistent with any mandatory conditions.

(6) Subsection (1) is subject to paragraph 9(1A) of Schedule 2.".]

NOTE

1. As inserted by the Air Weapons and Licensing (Scotland) Act 2015 (asp 10) Pt 3 s.80 (date yet to be appointed).

GENERAL NOTE

This has certain similarities to standard condition provisions granted under s.3B.

Part 3A

Civic licensing Standards Officers

[1][Civic licensing standards officers

45G.—(1) Each local authority must appoint for their area one or more officers (a "civic licensing standards officer")—

(a) to exercise, in relation to the authority's area, the general functions conferred on civic licensing standards officers by virtue of section 45H, and

(b) to exercise any other functions that may be conferred on such an officer by virtue of this or any other enactment.

(2) A civic licensing standards officer appointed by a local authority is taken to be an authorised officer of the authority for the purposes of Parts 1 to 3.

(3) A person may hold more than one appointment under subsection (1) (so as to be a civic licensing standards officer for more than one local authority area).

(4) Nothing in this section prevents an officer of a local authority other than a civic licensing standards officer from being an authorised officer of the authority for a purpose of Parts 1 to 3.

(5) In this Part, a reference to a local authority includes a reference to that authority acting as the licensing authority for their area and a reference to an authorised officer of a local authority (however expressed) is to be construed accordingly.]

NOTE

1. As inserted by the Air Weapons and Licensing (Scotland) Act 2015 (asp 10) Pt 3 s.82 (date as yet not appointed).

GENERAL NOTE

This section was modelled on the success of the licensing standards officers created under the Licensing (Scotland) Act 2005 with regard to alcohol licences and provides that the licensing authority may appoint one or more officers who are then also "authorised officers" within the meaning of the 1982 Act.

[1][**General functions of a civic licensing standards officer**

45H.—(1) The general functions of a civic licensing standards officer are—

(a) to provide to any interested person information and guidance concerning the operation of Parts 1 to 3 in the officer's area,
(b) to supervise the compliance by the holder of a licence granted under Parts 1 to 3 in the officer's area with—
  (i) the conditions of the licence, and
  (ii) the other requirements of Parts 1 to 3,
(c) to provide mediation services for the purposes of avoiding or resolving disputes or disagreements between—
  (i) the holder of a licence granted under Parts 1 to 3 in the officer's area, and
  (ii) any other person,

concerning any matter relating to compliance with the conditions of the licence or the other requirements of Parts 1 to 3.

(2) The function under subsection (1)(b) includes, in particular, power for a civic licensing standards officer, where the officer believes that a condition to which the licence is subject has been or is being breached—

(a) to give a notice to the holder of the licence requiring such action to be taken to remedy the breach as may be specified in the notice, and
(b) to refer the breach to the local authority which granted the licence for consideration at a meeting of the authority.

(3) A civic licensing standards officer may only refer a breach of a condition under subsection (2)(b) if—

(a) the officer has given notice under subsection (2)(a) and the holder of the licence has failed to comply with it, or
(b) the officer considers that it is appropriate for the breach to be referred to the authority without such a notice being given.

(4) In this section, a reference to an officer's area is a reference to—

(a) the local authority area for which the officer is appointed under section 45G(1), or
(b) where the officer is appointed for more than one local authority area, the area for which the officer is exercising a function at the relevant time.".]

NOTE

1. As inserted by the Air Weapons and Licensing (Scotland) Act 2015 (asp 10) Pt 3 s.82 (date yet to be appointed).

GENERAL NOTE

This section sets out the general functions of the civic licensing standards officer in respect of among other things providing information and guidance, supervising compliance with conditions and mediating between license holders and others for the purpose of avoiding disputes.

[*Sections 46 to 109 omitted.*]

PART IX

MISCELLANEOUS AND GENERAL

[*Sections 110 to 129 omitted.*]

General

Offences of bodies corporate

130.—(1) Where an offence under this Act or any regulation or byelaw made under this Act which has been committed by a body corporate is proved to have been committed with the consent or connivance of, or to be attributable to any neglect on the part of, a director, manager, secretary or other similar officer of the body corporate, or a person purporting to act in any such capacity, he as well as the body corporate shall be guilty of that offence and shall be liable to be proceeded against and punished accordingly.

(2) Where the affairs of a body corporate are managed by its members, subsection (1) above applies in relation to the acts and defaults of a member in connection with his functions of management as if he were a director of the body corporate.

GENERAL NOTE

This section, which is in similar terms to s.67(5) of the Licensing (Scotland) Act 1976, applies, inter alia, to licence holders who are bodies corporate and imposes individual criminal responsibility upon those persons who are capable of influencing the decisions of that body, i.e. the director, manager, secretary or similar officer or any person who purports to act in that capacity. In the case of a club, those who exercise management functions in the manner of a company director are caught by these provisions.

Application to Crown

[1]**131.** The provisions of Parts VI and VIIA and sections 120 to 123 of this Act apply to the Crown as provided in those provisions but otherwise this Act shall not bind the Crown.

NOTE

1. As amended by the Police Property Act (c.30) s.6 (effective 19 May 1997).

GENERAL NOTE

Thus the licensing provisions of the Act do not apply to the Crown.

Expenses

132. There shall be defrayed out of moneys provided by Parliament any increase attributable to the provisions of this Act in the sums payable out of moneys so provided under any other enactment.

Interpretation

133. In this Act, except where the context otherwise requires—

[2]"*enforcing authority*" has the meaning given by section 61(9) of the Fire (Scotland) Act 2005 (asp 5);

[1]"*local authority*" means a council constituted under section 2 of the Local Government etc. (Scotland) Act 1994 (c.39);

"*proper officer*" shall be construed in accordance with section 235(3) of the Local Government (Scotland) Act 1973;

"*public place*" means any place (whether a thoroughfare or not) to which the public have unrestricted access and includes—

(a) the doorways or entrances of premises abutting on any such place; and

(b) any common passage, close, court, stair, garden or yard pertinent to any tenement or group of separately owned houses; and

"*public road*", "*roads authority*" and "*road*" have the same meanings as in the Roads (Scotland) Act 1984;

"*vessel*" means any kind of water-craft including a hovercraft within the meaning of the Hovercraft Act 1968 but not including a vessel in Her Majesty's service.

NOTES

1. As amended by the Local Government etc. (Scotland) Act 1994 (c.39) Sch.13 para.129 (effective 1 April 1996).

2. As amended by the Fire (Scotland) Act 2005 (Consequential Modifications and Savings) Order 2006 (SSI 2006/475) Sch.1 para.11 (effective 1 October 2006).

GENERAL NOTE

This section provides certain definitions used throughout the Act unless the context otherwise requires.

"Local authority"—this definition was substituted for the original by Sch.13 para.21 of the Local Government etc. (Scotland) Act 1994.

"Public place"—literally, any place to which the public have unrestricted access including doorways, entrances, etc. of buildings and land adjoining the place; cf. definition of "public place" in s.10(2) of the Dangerous Dogs Act 1991 and see *Paterson v Ogilvy*, 1957 S.L.T. 354, *McGeachy v Normand*, 1994 S.L.T. 429 and *Vannet v Burns*, 1998 S.C.C.R. 414. On the English interpretation of the phrase "to which the public have access" see *West Berkshire DC v Parne* [2009] L.L.P. 381.

"Public road", etc.—this clause was added by s.156(1) of and Sch.9 para.87 to the Roads (Scotland) Act 1984. A "road" is any way over which there is a public right of passage (by whatever means) and includes the roadside verge or any temporary or permanent bridge over which, or any tunnel through which, the road passes and a reference to road includes any part thereof; see also the amendments to this basic definition caused by s.168(2) of and Sch.8 para.94(b) to the New Roads and Street Works Act 1991. "Public road" is a road which the "roads authority" have a duty to maintain. For consideration of the definition of road in a number of recent criminal cases see *Beattie v Scott*, 1991 S.L.T. 873; 1990 S.C.C.R. 435; *Alston v O'Brien*, 1992 S.L.T. 856; 1992 S.C.C.R. 238; *Young v Carmichael*, 1993 S.L.T. 167; 1991 S.C.C.R. 332; and *Thomson v MacPhail*, 1993 S.L.T. 225; 1992 S.C.C.R. 466.

"Vessel"—a hovercraft is defined in s.4(1) of the Hovercraft Act 1968 as

> "a vehicle which is designed to be supported when in motion wholly or partly by air expelled from the vehicle to form a cushion of which the boundaries include the ground, water or other surface beneath the vehicle".

Quaere whether water craft include hydrofoils, sea planes and amphibious craft.

Postponement of repeal of Burgh Police (Scotland) Acts and local statutory provisions

134.—(1) The repeal of—

[*As repealed by the Statute Law (Repeals) Act 1993 (c.50) Sch.1(X) para.1 (effective 5 November 1993).*]

(b) the local statutory provisions to which subsection (6) of section 225 of the Local Government (Scotland) Act 1973 applies, which by virtue, respectively, of

(i) subsection (1) of section 229 of the said Act of 1973; and

(ii) the said subsection (6),

falls to take place at the end of 1982 shall, subject to subsection (2) below, sections 135 and 137 of this Act and any order thereunder, be postponed until the end of 1984 and in each of the said subsections, at the beginning there shall be inserted the words "Subject to sections 134(2), 135 and 137 of the Civic Government (Scotland) Act 1982 and any order under these sections," and for the words "1982" there shall be substituted the words "1984".

135. [*As repealed by the Statute Law (Repeals) Act 1993 (c.50) Sch.1(X) para.1 (effective 5 November 1993).*]

Consequential, transitional and supplementary provisions

136.—(1) Anything done or treated by virtue of any enactment as having been done under any provision of the Burgh Police (Scotland) Act 1892 to 1911 or under any local statutory provision to which subsection (6) of section 225 of the Local Government (Scotland) Act 1973 applies which could be done by or under any provision of this Act shall, on the repeal of the provision of the said Burgh Police (Scotland) Acts 1892 to 1911 or of the local statutory provision, be treated as having been done under the provision of this Act.

(2) The Secretary of State may by order make such incidental, consequential, transitional or supplementary provision as may appear to him to be necessary, proper or expedient for the general or any particular purpose of this Act or in consequence of any of the provisions thereof or for giving full effect thereto and nothing in any other provision of this Act shall be construed as prejudicing the generality of this subsection.

(3) Without prejudice to section 13 of the Interpretation Act 1978 (anticipatory exercise of statutory powers) anything which must or may be done under any provision of Part I or II of this Act may, notwithstanding that that provision is not in force, be done for the purposes of giving full effect to that provision at or after the time when it comes into force and the Secretary of State may, in making transitional provision by order under subsection (2) above, modify any provision of Part I or II of this Act for the purposes of this subsection.

(4) An order under subsection (2) above—

(a) may be made at any time, whether before, at the same time as or after the commencement of any provision of this Act to which the provision made by the order relates;

(b) shall be made by statutory instrument subject to annulment in pursuance of a resolution of either House of Parliament.

Citation, commencement, repeals and extent

137.—(1) This Act may be cited as the Civic Government (Scotland) Act 1982.

(2) This Act, other than sections 134 to 136 and subsections (1) above, (3) to (6) and (9) below and this subsection, shall come into force on such date or dates as the Secretary of State may by order made by statutory instrument appoint and different dates may be appointed under this section for different provisions of this Act or for different purposes of the same provision.

(3) An order under subsection (2) above shall of itself have the effect of repealing—

(a) any provision of the Burgh Police (Scotland) Acts 1892 to 1911;

(b) any local statutory provision (whether or not subject to an order under section 225(6) of the Local Government (Scotland) Act 1973 (exemption from and postponement of repeal of local statutory provision))

to the extent that the provision provides for any matter which is also provided for (whether consistently or not) by or under any provision of this Act commenced by that order.

(4) A repeal under subsection (3) above shall take effect on the date of commencement of the provision of this Act the commencement of which gives rise, under that subsection, to that repeal.

(5) In this section "local statutory provision" means—

(a) a provision of a local Act, the Bill for which was promoted by a local authority;

(b) a provision of an Act confirming a provisional order made on the application of a local authority;

(c) a provision of an order made on such an application which was subject to special parliamentary procedure,

not being a provision relating to a statutory undertaking or a protective provision for the benefit of any person.

(6) In subsection (5) above, "statutory undertaking" means any railway, light railway, tramway, road transport, water transport, canal, inland navigation, ferry, dock, harbour, pier or lighthouse undertaking, any market undertaking, or any undertaking for the supply of electricity, gas, hydraulic power, water or district heating.

(7) The enactments specified in Schedule 3 to this Act shall have effect subject to the amendments there specified.

(8) The enactments mentioned in Schedule 4 to this Act are hereby repealed to the extent specified in the third column of that Schedule.

(9) This Act (except section 16, which applies to England and Wales) applies to Scotland only.

GENERAL NOTE

This section provides, inter alia, for the implementation of the Act and its extent.

Subsection (2)

Apart from the sections and subsections listed here, the licensing provision of the Act were brought into force by virtue of the Civic Government (Scotland) Act Commencement Order 1983 (SI 1983/201) as amended by SI 1984/573 and SI 1984/774 as follows: Pts I and II (ss.1–44), and Sch.1 for certain purposes only, on 1 April 1983, and fully on 1 July 1984; Pt III (s.45) and Sch.2 on 1 April 1983.

Subsections (7) and (8)

For reasons of space, Schs 3 and 4 have been omitted but, for the purposes of licensing, the repeals were of a fairly minor nature and are dealt with in the notes to the specific sections of this Act.

Subsection (9)

This is the section which deals with journeys in England and Wales by vehicles and drivers licensed under this Act and which accordingly inserts a new subsection into s.75 of the Local Government (Miscellaneous Provisions) Act 1976.

SCHEDULE 1

LICENSING—FURTHER PROVISIONS AS TO THE GENERAL SYSTEM

GENERAL NOTE

This Schedule sets out the procedural provisions in respect of the licensing system introduced by Pt I of the Act. These provisions apply to the licensing and regulation of the particular activities covered by Pt II of the Act. Briefly, the Schedule consists of a self-contained procedural code in respect of applications for the grant and renewal of licences, objections and representations in relation thereto, disposal of applications, the nature of licences, variation and suspension of licences, fees for applications, notification of decisions on applications and the giving of reasons for such decisions and appeals.

Applications for the grant and renewal of licences

1.—(1) An application to a licensing authority for the grant or renewal of a licence shall be—
- (a) made in writing in such form as may be determined by the licensing authority;
- (b) signed by the applicant or his agent; and
- (c) accompanied by such fee as the authority may charge under paragraph 15 below.

(2) An application under sub-paragraph (1) above shall specify—
- (a) the kind of licence in respect of which the application is made;
- [1](b) where the applicant is a natural person, his full name, address and date and place of birth and where the applicant himself is not to be carrying on the day-to-day management of the activity in relation to which the application is made, the full name, address and date and place of birth of any employee or agent who is;
- (c) where the application is made by or on behalf of a person other than a natural person,
  - (i) the full name of the person;
  - (ii) the address of its registered or principal office;
  - [1](iii) the names and private addresses and dates and places of birth of its directors, partners of other persons responsible for its management; and
  - [1](iv) the full name, address and date and place of birth of any employee or agent who is to carry on the day-to-day management of the activity in relation to which the application is made;
- (d) the address of the premises, if any, in or from which and the area in which the activity is to be carried on; and
- (e) such other information as the authority may reasonably require.

(3) Where the application relates to a licence for an activity which is wholly or mainly to be carried on in premises, it shall contain one or other of

the following declarations by the applicant, that is to say, a declaration that he is complying with paragraph 2(2) below or a declaration by him that he is unable to do so because he has not such rights of access or other rights in respect of the premises as would enable him to do so, but that he has taken such reasonable steps as are open to him (specifying them) to acquire those rights and has been unable to acquire them.

NOTE

1. As amended by the Criminal Justice and Licensing (Scotland) Act 2010 (asp 13t) Pt 8 s.178 (effective 28 February 2011 for purposes specified in SSI 2010/413 Sch.1; not yet in force otherwise).

DEFINITIONS

"licence": s.8.
"licensing authority": s.2(2).
"premises": ss.8, 41A(4).

GENERAL NOTE

Paragraphs 1 and 2 lay down the procedures to be followed by an applicant in seeking the grant or renewal of a licence and the action which is to be taken by a licensing authority upon receiving an application. Provided that the appropriate procedures have been followed then it is for the licensing committee rather than the clerk or other official, to decide whether or not the application is competent—*Datelock Ltd v Bain*, 1998 S.L.T. 381; *Kelvinside Community Council v Glasgow District Licensing Board*, 1990 S.L.T. 725. Additional information required was added by the 2010 Act s.178(2).

Subparagraph (1)

This provision requires that an application be signed by the applicant or their agent but otherwise the form of the application is left to the discretion of the particular authority. There is thus no statutory form of application for licences under the Act. The application must be accompanied by the specified fee (see pp.168–169 below). In the event of the relevant fee not being tendered, the authority would be justified in rejecting the application.

Subparagraph (2)

This sets out the details that must be specified in the form by the applicant or their agent. In addition to the kind of licence being sought, disclosure is required of the name and address of the applicant, any director, partner and manager of a non-natural applicant, or any person carrying on day to day management of the activity in respect of which the licence is sought, either in the case of an application by a natural person or a non-natural person. In other words, the person(s) "behind" the applicant or who are to be responsible for management must be designed. The premises from which and the area in which the activity is to be carried out must also be specified. In addition, the authority is empowered to request such other information as may reasonably be required. This would allow an authority to request information which is considered to be relevant to an application for a particular licence in its area, always providing that there was some reasonable basis for doing so, having regard to the nature of the licence for which application is made and the activity in respect of which it is sought.

Subparagraph (3)

This provides that where the activity is to be wholly or mainly carried on in premises, the application must contain a declaration that the applicant is complying with para.2(2), which requires display of a notice of application at or near the premises or a declaration that they have taken reasonable steps to acquire rights of access to enable them to comply but have been unable to do.

2.—[2](1) A licensing authority shall, as soon as an application for the grant or renewal of a licence is made to them, send a copy of the application to the chief constable and, where the activity is wholly or mainly to be carried on—

(a) in premises to which Part 3 of the Fire (Scotland) Act 2005 (asp 5) applies, the enforcing authority;

[3](b) in any other premises, the Scottish Fire and Rescue Service.

(2) Where an application is for the grant or renewal of a licence in relation to an activity wholly or mainly to be carried on in premises, the applicant shall, for a period of 21 days beginning with the date on which the application was submitted to the licensing authority, display a notice complying with sub-paragraph (3) below at or near the premises so that it can conveniently be read by the public.

(3) The notice shall state—

(a) that application has been made for a licence;

[1](b) the particulars required under paragraph 1(2) above to be specified in the application (other than the date and place of birth of any person);

(c) that objections and representations in relation to the application may be made to the licensing authority in accordance with paragraph 3 below;

(d) the effect of paragraph 3(1) to (3) below.

(4) Where an application contains a declaration that the applicant is complying with sub-paragraph (2) above, the applicant shall, as soon as possible after the expiry of the period of 21 days referred to in that sub-paragraph, submit to the licensing authority a certificate stating that he has so complied.

(5) An applicant shall not be treated as having failed to comply with sub-paragraph (2) above if the notice was, without any fault or intention of his, removed, obscured or defaced before the 21 days referred to in that sub-paragraph have elapsed, so long as he has taken reasonable steps for its protection and, if need be, replacement; and if he has cause to rely on this sub-paragraph, his certificate under sub-paragraph (4) above shall state the relevant circumstances.

(6) Where an application contains a declaration that the applicant is complying with sub-paragraph (2) above, and—

(a) he fails to submit the certificate required by sub-paragraph (4) above;

(b) in the circumstances referred to in sub-paragraph (5) above, he has not, in the opinion of the licensing authority, taken reasonable steps for the protection or, as the case may require, replacement of the notice; or

(c) the licensing authority is, at any time before they reach a final decision on the application, satisfied that the notice was not displayed in accordance with this paragraph,

they may require the applicant to display the notice again for a period of 21 days beginning with such date as they may specify and the provisions of this paragraph shall apply in respect of such display as they apply in respect of display under sub-paragraph (2) above.

(7) The licensing authority—

(a) shall, in accordance with sub-paragraph (8) below, cause public notice to be given of every application made to them for the grant or renewal of a licence falling within a prescribed class;

(b) shall, in accordance with sub-paragraph (8) below, cause public notice to be given of an application made to them for the grant or renewal of a licence in relation to an activity wholly or mainly to be carried on in premises if the application contains a declaration that the applicant has been unable to comply with the requirements of sub-paragraph (2) above;

(c) may, if they think fit, cause public notice to be given, in accordance with sub-paragraph (8) below, of any application for the grant or renewal of a licence which is made to them and notice of which they are not obliged to give under this sub-paragraph.

(8) Public notice of an application shall be given for the purposes of sub-paragraph (7) above by publication of a notice in a newspaper or newspapers circulating in the area of the authority stating—

[1](a) the particulars required under paragraph 1(2) above to be specified in the application other than the date and place of birth of any person;

(b) that objections or representations in relation to the application may be made to the licensing authority in accordance with paragraph 3 below; and

(c) the effect of paragraph 3(1) to (3) below.

(9) The Secretary of State may, by order made by statutory instrument subject to annulment in pursuance of a resolution of either House of Parliament, prescribe a class or classes of licences for the purposes of sub-paragraph (7) above.

NOTES

1. As amended by the Criminal Justice and Licensing (Scotland) Act 2010 (asp 13) Pt 8 s.178 (effective 28 February 2011 for purposes specified in SSI 2010/413 Sch.1; not yet in force otherwise).

2. As amended by the Fire (Scotland) Act 2005 (Consequential Modifications and Savings) Order 2006 (SSI 2006/475) Sch.1 para.11 (effective 1 October 2006).

3. As amended by the Police and Fire Reform (Scotland) Act 2012 (asp 8) Sch.7(2) para.53 (effective 1 April 2013).

DEFINITIONS

"licensing authority": s.2.
"enforcing authority": s.133.
"licence": s.8.
"premises": ss.8, 41A(4).
"chief constable": s.8.

Subparagraph (1)

This requires the authority to send a copy of the application to the chief constable and, in respect of an activity to be carried on in premises, to either the enforcing authority or the Scottish Fire and Rescue Service as the case may be.

Subparagraph (2)

This provides, in respect of activities wholly or mainly to be carried on in premises, for public notice being given of the application at or near the premises. The notice must be given as from the date of submission of the application. Subparagraph (3) requires the notice to state various details namely that the application has been made; the para.1(2) particulars; that objections and representation may be made and the general requirements for the making and entertaining of objections and representations detailed in para.3(1)–3(3). Paragraph 2(4) requires that the applicant certify that they have complied with para.2(2).

Subparagraph (5)

This provides for the not infrequent situation of a notice being defaced or removed within the statutory period for display. It is provided that such an occurrence does not involve non-compliance with para.2(2) if the applicant took reasonable steps to protect the notice and, if need be, to replace it. Quite what would be considered to be reasonable protection must depend on all the circumstances, including the location of the notice.

Subparagraph (6)

This provides for the consequences of failure to submit a certificate in terms of para.2(4) and a failure, in the opinion of the authority, to take reasonable steps in terms of para.2(5) or the situation where the authority, prior to reaching a final decision on the application, is satisfied that the notice was not properly displayed. In these circumstances, the authority is empowered to require that the notice be displayed for a further 21 days.

Subparagraph (7)

This requires that public notice be given by the authority of any application for grant or renewal of a licence within a prescribed class, or an application for grant or renewal of a licence to be carried out for an activity wholly or mainly in premises where the applicant states that they were unable to display a notice at or near the premises. The authority is also empowered in any other case in which it thinks fit to give public notice of the application.

Subparagraph (8)

This specifies how public notice is to be given. This is broadly as for a notice under para.2(3).

Subparagraph (9)

This explains that a prescribed class for the purposes of para.2(7) is one prescribed by statutory instrument.

Objections and representations

3.—(1) Any objection or representation relating to an application for the grant or renewal or a licence shall, subject to sub-paragraph (2) below, be entertained by the licensing authority if, but only if, the objection or representation—

(a) is in writing;

(b) specifies the grounds of the objection or, as the case may be, the nature of the representation;

(c) specifies the name and address of the person making it;

(d) is signed by him or on his behalf;

[1](e) was made to them within 28 days of whichever is the later or, as the case may be, latest of the following dates—

(i) where public notice of the application was given under paragraph 2(7) above, the date when it was first so given;

(ii) where the application relates to a licence for an activity which is wholly or mainly to be carried out in premises and the authority have specified a date under paragraph 2(6) above, that date;

(iii) in any other case, the date when the application was made to them.

(2) Notwithstanding sub-paragraph (1)(e) above, it shall be competent for a licensing authority to entertain an objection or representation received by them before they take a final decision upon the application to which it relates if they are satisfied that there is sufficient reason why it was not made in the time required under that sub-paragraph.

(3) An objection or representation shall be made for the purposes of sub-

paragraph (1) above if it is delivered by hand within the time there specified to the licensing authority or posted (by registered or recorded delivery post) so that in the normal course of post it might be expected to be delivered to them within that time.

[2](3A) Where a licensing authority have determined to accept objections and representations by means of an electronic communication under paragraph 16A, an objection or representation is made for the purpose of sub-paragraph (1) of this paragraph if it is sent—

(a) to the authority by means of an electronic communication which complies with the determination, and

(b) within the time specified in sub-paragraph (1).

[2](3B) Sub-paragraph (3A) is without prejudice to sub-paragraph (3).

(4) The licensing authority shall send a copy of any relevant objection or representation (within the meaning of paragraph 19 below) to the applicant to whose application it relates.

NOTES

1. As amended by the Criminal Justice and Licensing (Scotland) Act 2010 (asp 13) Pt 8 s.178 (effective 28 February 2011 for purposes specified in SSI 2010/413 Sch.1; not yet in force otherwise).

2. As amended by the Air Weapons and Licensing (Scotland) Act 2015 (asp 10) Pt 3 s.83 (date yet to be appointed).

DEFINITIONS

"licensing authority": s.2.

"relevant objection or representation": Sch.1 para.19.

GENERAL NOTE

This paragraph sets out the regulations for the making of relevant objections and representations in respect of applications for the grant and renewal of licences. As to whether or not children can make valid objections, see "Objectionable Children", James A Scott (2000) 15 S.L.L.P. 24.

Subparagraph (1)

This sets out the criteria which must be satisfied before an authority is obliged to entertain an objection or representation. If they are satisfied, the authority must consider the objection and representation. Objections must be properly considered and cannot be repelled at a stage before the licensing authority knows whether or not they are well founded (*Mitchell v Edinburgh City Council*, 2004 Hous. L.R. 59). It has been explained that in order to be treated as a valid objection, the word "objection" need not be used in the relevant document (*Centralbite Ltd v Kincardine and Deeside District Licensing Board*, 1990 S.L.T. 231). However, it must be possible to ascertain from the terms of the document that opposition to the application is being maintained. It has been stressed that the requirements set out in this subsection must be strictly observed (*Kilmarnock and Loudoun DC v Noble Organisation*, 1993 S.L.T. 759; *Little v East Ayrshire Licensing Board* (1998) 11 S.L.L.P. 8). The most significant criterion is that the ground of objection or nature of the representation must be "specified". A bald assertion without explanation is not enough. In the *Kilmarnock* case, for example, the Inner House held that the words, "Kilmarnock does not need a bigger arcade (Plaza converted into amusements)" at the head of each page of a petition did not specify a ground of objection. Grounds of objection will usually cover the grounds for refusal specified in para.5(3) below but need not be so limited. If an objection or representation is patently irrelevant the authority would be expected to exclude it from their consideration of the application and should so rule at the outset of the hearing—*Noble v City of Glasgow DC*, 1993 S.L.T. 800, where it was held that it was a matter of construction whether or not any particular document had the character of an objection or representation relating to the relevant application. The authority is also entitled to have regard to productions accompanying any competent objection, in so far as they support a relevant and competent objection. Note, however, that an objection must be both specific and contain a proper basis for concluding that the refusal of a licence would fall within the terms of Sch.1 para.5(3)—*Singh v Glasgow Licensing Board*, 1998 S.C. 830.

This subsection was altered to make the relevant time 28 days—2010 Act s.174(e).

Subparagraph (2)

Prior to reaching a final decision on an application the authority are entitled to entertain an objection which has not been timeously made, if they are satisfied that there is sufficient reason why it was not so made. This is a matter for the authority to determine. The authority are not entitled automatically to entertain late objections. They must satisfy themselves as to sufficiency of the reason for lateness and explain why they have decided to entertain the objection (*Speedlift Auto Salvage Ltd v Kyle and Carrick DC*, 1992 S.L.T. (Sh Ct) 57). In *Coyle v Glasgow City Council* [2012] CSIH 33; 2012 S.L.T. 1018, it was held that the authority was entitled to be satisfied that there was sufficient reason for an objection not having been made timeously where the police had awaited the outcome of criminal proceedings which were relevant to the application. The police had previously advised the authority that certain matters required investigation before any comment could be made on the suitability of the applicant. This provision would clearly exclude objections where there had been a wilful failure to submit it timeously and would clearly entitle the authority to exclude an objection lodged late through carelessness.

Subparagraph (4)

This subparagraph requires copies of relevant objections or representations to be sent to the applicant. This is of relevance in relation to the disposal of applications (paras 4(2), (3)).

Disposal of applications for the grant and renewal of licences

4.—(1) In considering an application for the grant or renewal of a licence, a licensing authority may make such reasonable inquiries as they think fit and include the results of these inquiries in matters they take into account, but where they intend so to include any of these results they shall notify the applicant of that intention.

[1](2) A licensing authority may, before reaching a final decision upon such an application, give the applicant and any person who has made a relevant objection or representation (within the meaning of paragraph 19 below) in relation to the application an opportunity to be heard by the authority and, where they propose to do so, shall, within such reasonable period (not being less than 14 days) of the date of the hearing, notify the applicant and each such person of that date.

(3) A licensing authority shall not reach a final decision upon such an application—

(a) in relation to which a relevant objection or representation (within the meaning of paragraph 19 below) has been made to them or in relation to which they intend to take into account any result of their inquiries under sub-paragraph (1) above; and

(b) in respect of which they have not, under this paragraph, given the applicant and any person who has made any such objection or representation an opportunity to be heard,

unless they have given the applicant an opportunity to notify them in writing of his views on such objection or representation or, as the case may be, result within such reasonable period (not being less than 7 days) as they may specify.

(4) The period referred to in sub-paragraphs (2) and (3) above shall begin with the date when the notification given by the licensing authority for the purpose of sub-paragraph (2) or, as the case may be, (3) is delivered to the person concerned and, when it is sent by post, it shall be treated as being delivered at the time when it might be expected to be delivered in the normal course of post.

NOTE

1. As amended by the Criminal Justice and Licensing (Scotland) Act 2010 (asp 13) Pt 8 s.178 (effective 28 February 2011 for purposes specified in SSI 2010/413 Sch.1; not yet in force otherwise).

DEFINITIONS

"licensing authority": s.2.
"licence": s.8.
"relevant objection or representation": Sch.1 para.19.

GENERAL NOTE

This paragraph deals with the procedures for consideration of applications.

Subparagraph (1)

The authority is not restricted to a role of determining applications purely on the basis of the material before it in the form of the relevant application and any objections or representations thereto. It is empowered to make reasonable inquiries and may take into account in reaching its decision the result of those inquiries, always provided that before doing so the applicant is notified. The nature of such inquiries is not limited except that they must be reasonable. In *Douglas v City of Glasgow DC*, 1996 S.L.T. 713, the Inner House held that the authority erred in not giving the applicant the opportunity to comment on the fact that where the maximum amount of taxi licences set by them had been exceeded by three, that they had an expectation that the total would be reduced by surrender, etc. The failure to advise the applicant of these matters was held to be a breach of para.4(1).

Subparagraph (2)

There is no obligation incumbent on the authority to give an applicant a right to be heard in respect of their application. The same is true of an objector or a person making a representation. If the authority decides not to hold a hearing, that decision is not appealable (cf. paras 17(1) and 18(1), below). The authority may permit such persons to be heard. If they do, they must give parties not less than seven days notice of the hearing. This time limit is mandatory: see *Monklands Independent Taxi Owners Association v Monklands DC (No.2)*, 1997 S.L.T. 7. Failure to give such notice would be an error in law, such as to justify the upholding of an appeal against any refusal of an application (*Aitken v City of Glasgow DC*, 1988 S.C.L.R. 287). If a hearing is allowed there is no right to insist on leading evidence in support of the application: see *JAE Glasgow Ltd v City of Glasgow District Licensing Board*, 1994 S.L.T. 1164. In that case relating to an application under the Licensing (Scotland) Act 1976 Lord Cullen accepted that the Act envisaged applications being heard and disposed of expeditiously and with a minimum of formality and that the Board had a discretion to proceed on the basis of any relevant material including submissions and objections. These observations were approved by the Inner House in *Chief Constable, Strathclyde Police v North Lanarkshire Licensing Board*, 2003 S.L.T. 1268 at [22]. It is considered that the same approach would be adopted in relation to applications made under the 1982 Act. In *Hamid v City of Glasgow Licensing Board* (2001) 18 S.L.L.P. 8, the sheriff held that no reasonable board could have reached a decision on whether the applicant was a fit and proper person without considering that it was necessary to hear evidence. In the light of what was said in the *JAE* and *North Lanarkshire Licensing Board* cases it is submitted that this decision cannot be supported. Even where there is a dispute over what may be a material fact, that does not mean that evidence requires to be heard in order to resolve the issue. At the hearing the committee are entitled to take into account hearsay evidence even though this might not stand up to scrutiny in court—see, e.g. *McCool v Rushcliffe BC* [1998] 8 C.L. 355; *Scanlan v City of Edinburgh DC*, 1995 S.L.T. (Sh Ct) 89 and, in respect of reliance on information supplied by the police that the applicant had been involved in unspecified serious criminal activity see *Anderson v Security Industry Authority* [2011] G.W.D. 11-268.

In *O'Doherty v Renfrewshire Council*, 1998 S.L.T. 327, the issue was posed as to whether the public had been wrongly excluded from a meeting at which an application had been determined having regard to the provisions of ss.50A and 50E of the Local Government (Scotland) Act 1973. It was argued for the authority that exclusion was justified, because the meeting would involve disclosure of "exempt information" in the form of information "relating to any particular applicant for or recipient of, any service provided by the authority". The court considered that this was a finely balanced issue, but it did not require to decide it, because the applicant was not a person entitled to raise the issue. In practice certain authorities have now adopted a practice of holding "pre-hearings" where they consider representations for and against their receiving further details of spent convictions. Note also that the decision as to whether or not a licensing authority should continue a hearing to allow an applicant to be personally represented at a hearing is one for their discretion—*Sneddon v West Dunbartonshire Council*, 1998 G.W.D. 34-1766. In *Heavenbrook Ltd v City of Glasgow Licensing Board* (2008) 40 S.L.L.P. 22, the sheriff held that the Board should have adjourned a hearing where technical information on noise was introduced on behalf of an objector in the course of submissions. Where the objection had related to noise issues, it may be suggested that it was for the applicant to be in a position to respond to whatever might be said by an objector (*McAllister v East Dunbartonshire Licensing Board*, 1998 S.C. 748; followed in *Chief Constable, Strathclyde Police v North Lanarkshire Licensing Board*, 2003 S.L.T. 1268) and that the Board were entitled in the exercise of their discretion to refuse to adjourn. However it does appear from the sheriff's judgment that the material introduced was not foreshadowed in the letter of objection. On that basis the sheriff's decision is explicable.

Subparagraph (3)

While there is, as has been noted, no obligation on the authority to give an applicant a hearing, if a relevant objection or representation has been made or the authority intend to take into account any result of their inquiries then, if no hearing is to be afforded the applicant, they must be given the opportunity to give their views in writing on the objection, etc. within a period of not less than seven days. Again, failure to give the required period for submission of views would amount to an error in law with the consequences noted in respect of the previous subparagraph. In *Jolly v Hamilton DC*, 1992 S.L.T. 28, the court stated that if the authority had realised that notification under this paragraph had not worked, the authority should still permit the applicant to express their views, and a failure to do so would amount to a failure to exercise discretion rendering the authority's decision liable to be quashed; *Douglas v City of Glasgow DC*, 1996 S.L.T. 713.

Subparagraph (4)

This subsection provides for the calculation of the periods referred to in subparas (2) and (3). The first date of the period is the date of delivery of the notification with a deeming provision in respect of postal intimation (*Dolan v City of Glasgow DC*, 1990 S.C.L.R. 553).

5.—(1) Where an application for the grant or renewal of a licence has been made to a licensing authority they shall, in accordance with this paragraph—

[2](a) grant or renew the licence;

(b) [*As repealed by the Criminal Justice and Licensing (Scotland) Act 2010 (asp 13) Pt 8 s.172 (effective 28 March 2011).*]

(c) refuse to grant or renew the licence.

[2](1A) In granting or renewing a licence in addition to any mandatory or standard conditions to which the licence is subject. under sub-paragraph 1(a), a licensing authority may (either or both)—

(a) disapply or vary any standard conditions so far as is applicable to the licence,

(b) impose conditions.

[1,2](2) Subject to sub-paragraph (2A) the conditions referred to in sub-paragraph (1A)(b) above shall be such reasonable conditions (other than conditions relating to the amount of rent or other charges which may be imposed upon occupiers of the house) as the licensing authority think fit and, without prejudice to that generality, may include—

(a) conditions restricting the validity of a licence to an area or areas specified in the licence; and

(b) in relation to the grant of a licence, where that licence is intended to replace an existing licence, a condition requiring the holder of the existing licence to surrender it in accordance with paragraph 13 below.

[2](2AA) A variation under sub-paragraph (1A)(a) or conditions imposed under sub-paragraph (1A) (b) shall have no effect so far as it is inconsistent with any mandatory condition to which the licence is subject.

[1,4](2ZA) The conditions referred to in sub-paragraph (1A)(b) above shall not relate to any matter in relation to which requirements or prohibitions are or could be imposed by virtue of Part 3 of the Fire (Scotland) Act 2005 (asp 5).

(3) A licensing authority shall refuse an application to grant or renew a licence if, in their opinion—

(a) the applicant or, where the applicant is not a natural person, any director of it or partner in it or any other person responsible for its management, is either—
  (i) for the time being disqualified under section 7(6) of this Act, or
  (ii) not a fit and proper person to be the holder of the licence;

(b) the activity to which it relates would be managed by or carried on for the benefit of a person, other than the applicant, who would be refused the grant or refusal of such a licence if he made the application himself;

(c) where the licence applied for relates to an activity consisting of or including the use of premises or a vehicle or vessel, those premises are not or, as the case may be, that vehicle or vessel is not suitable or convenient for the conduct of the activity having regard to—
  (i) the location, character or condition of the premises or the character or condition of the vehicle or vessel;
  (ii) the nature and extent of the proposed activity;
  (iii) the kind of persons likely to be in the premises, vehicle or vessel;
  (iv) the possibility of undue public nuisance; or
  (v) public order or public safety; or

(d) there is other good reason for refusing the application;

and otherwise shall grant the application.

(4) A licensing authority shall not, in a case where a certificate falls to be submitted to them under paragraph 2(4) above, reach a final decision under this paragraph in respect of the application to which the certificate relates until it has been so submitted.

(5) A licensing authority shall in accordance with sub-paragraph (6) below, notify their decision under sub-paragraph (1) above to—

(a) the applicant;

(b) the chief constable;

(c) any person who made a relevant objection or representation (within the meaning of paragraph 19 below) in relation to the application; and

[1](d) where the application was for a licence for an activity wholly or mainly to be carried on—
  (a) in premises to which Part 3 of the Fire (Scotland) Act 2005 (asp 5) applies, the enforcing authority;
  [3](b) in any other premises, the Scottish Fire and Rescue Service.

(6) Notification shall be made under sub-paragraph (5)(a), (b) or (d) above within 7 days of the decision to be notified by sending to the person concerned written notice of the decision and under sub-paragraph (5)(c)

above either by so doing or by publishing, within that time, in a newspaper circulating in the area of the licensing authority, notice of the decision.

(7) A licensing authority shall make out and deliver a licence to every person to whom a licence is granted or whose licence is renewed by the authority, and shall when requested by any such person and on payment of such fee as they may charge under paragraph 15 below, make out a duplicate of any licence issued under this sub-paragraph and certify such duplicate to be a true copy of that original licence; and any document purporting to be so certified by the proper officer of the authority shall be sufficient evidence of the terms of that licence.

(8) Where a licensing authority grant a licence in respect of which an employee or agent has been named under paragraph 1(2)(b) or (c)(iv) above, the licence shall be granted jointly in the names of the applicant and of the employee or agent, and in such a case any reference in this Schedule or in Part I or II of this Act to the holder of a licence includes a reference to one or both of those persons, as the case may require.

NOTES

1. As amended by the Fire (Scotland) Act 2005 (Consequential Modifications and Savings) Order 2006 (SSI 2006/475) Sch.1 para.11 (effective 1 October 2006).

2. As amended by the Criminal Justice and Licensing (Scotland) Act 2010 (asp 13) Pt 8 s.172 (effective 28 March 2011).

3. As amended by the Police and Fire Reform (Scotland) Act 2012 (asp 8) Sch.7(2) para.53 (effective 1 April 2013).

4. As amended by the Air Weapons and Licensing (Scotland) Act 2015 (asp 10) Sch.2 Pt 3 para.5 (date yet to be appointed).

DEFINITIONS

"licensing authority": s.2.
"licence": s.8.
"chief constable": s.8.
"enforcing authority": s.133.
"premises": ss.8, 41A(4).
"proper officer": s.133.
"vessel": s.133.

GENERAL NOTE

This paragraph deals with the important matter of the disposal of applications.

Subparagraph (1)

The authority's powers are clearly set out: namely to grant or renew, unconditionally or conditionally; or to refuse. Where the authority has concerns in respect of the activity for which a particular licence is sought, it should not refuse the application where those concerns could be adequately addressed by an appropriate condition being attached to a licence (*GA Estate Agency v City of Glasgow DC*, 1991 S.L.T. 16).

Subparagraph (1A)

Following the introduction of the concept of mandatory and standard conditions, this allows, as before, the imposition of conditions to the licence by the authority including the disapplication or variation of any standard conditions which would otherwise apply.

Subparagraph (2)

The requirement that conditions must be such reasonable ones as the authority think fit would, in any event, have been implied had it not been specifically stipulated. The power to impose "such reasonable conditions" gives a wide discretion to the authority but it is not unlimited. The scope of the words must be ascertained from their context (*Stewart v Perth and Kinross Council*, 2004 S.C. (H.L.) 71). In that case it was held by the House of Lords that a condition purporting to regulate the terms on which second-hand dealers traded with customers as distinct from controlling the activities of dealers in respects such as the premises they use, the manner in which they use them or the type of goods in which they deal, were ultra vires. It was concluded that Parliament had not intended the licensing system to be used in this way. Consumer protection was properly to be achieved by primary legislation and not through licensing conditions which could have arbitrary and material consequences for consumers and dealers. The conditions were not justified by the specific power under s.24(4) to attach conditions requiring the keeping of records in relation to stock-in-trade; see also *McCluskey v North Lanarkshire Council* [2016] S.C. HAM 3 when an attempt to prohibit street trading by snack vans seeing certain foods close to schools was held to be ultra vires. On reasonableness, see also *Ingram v City of Aberdeen DC*, 1995 G.W.D. 40-2096 and *R v Blackpool BC Ex p. Red Cab Taxis Ltd* (1994) 158 J.P. 1069. Any proposed conditions should, of course, be lawful and not contrary to the provisions of the Act: see *Baker v City of Glasgow DC*, 1981 S.L.T. 320; *Spook Erection Ltd v City of Edinburgh DC*, 1995 S.L.T. (Sh Ct) 10. Conditions should not be unnecessarily wide. They should not be so vague, imprecise or uncertain in their terms as to render them unenforceable: see *Spook Erection*, discussed at p.117 above. Conditions should not endanger the very continuance of the licensed activity: see *Classic Cinema Ltd v Motherwell DC*, 1977 S.L.T. (Sh Ct) 69. There is nothing wrong in an authority approving standard conditions for particular types of licences provided that the authority are prepared to listen to arguments that they should not be applied, or that they should be varied in particular cases (*Sneddon v Renfrewshire Council*, 2009 S.L.T. 563).

Non-exhaustive specification of the type of condition which may be imposed is given as follows:

(a) First, the validity of a licence may be restricted to a specified area or areas. The area may be wide or narrow. For example, in the case of a street trader's licence, it could be restricted to an identifiable area of ground on a particular street.

(b) In the case of a grant of a licence intended to replace an existing one, it may be a condition that the existing one be surrendered. This is an obvious condition designed to prevent the holder operating under two licences, perhaps relating to different premises and areas.

Subparagraph (2AA)

This introduces a necessary prohibition on variation or imposition of a condition inconsistent with any applicable mandatory condition. This provision was inserted by the 2010 Act s.172(6)(d). Confusingly, it is to be renumbered as subpara.(2ZA) by the 2015 Act Sch.2 Pt 3 para.4(2)(a)(i) when it comes into force.

Subparagraph(2A)

This provision was added by the Fire (Scotland) Act 2005 (Consequential Modifications and Savings) Order 2006 (SSI 2006/475) Sch.1 para.11(6)(b)(ii).

Subparagraph (3)

An application *must* be refused if, in the opinion of the authority, any of the grounds therefore in subpara.(3)(a)–(d) exist; otherwise the application is to be granted (with or without conditions). It has been observed that in relation to licensing "there is a balance to be struck between the legitimate interests of the applicant and those of the public who may be affected by the activity for which the licence is required", and that in respect of the system of the Act designed to achieve this the "open ended list of grounds for refusal" in para.5(3) gives "some flexibility to the system" (*Noble Organisation Ltd v Kilmarnock and Loudoun DC*, 1993 S.L.T. 759, per Lord President Hope at 762).

While the authority is bound to refuse an application if, in its opinion, any or all of the specified grounds are made out, there must, of course, be some material before the authority on the basis of which they could properly reach such an opinion. However if there is such material it is for the authority to decide on its sufficiency and quality and the appropriate weight to attach to it—*Ferguson v Dundee City Council* [2006] CSIH 51 at [7]. Nevertheless, it is always necessary for the authority to balance factors which would support refusal against relevant mitigating factors (*Ritchie v Aberdeen City Council*, 2012 S.L.T. 869). In a case where it is proposed to refuse on more than one of the grounds, it is not considered necessary to vote separately on each of these grounds (*Mohammed v City of Glasgow Licensing Board*, 1998 S.C.L.R. 426; cf. *Din v City of Glasgow District Licensing Board*, 1996 S.L.T. 363).

Subparagraph 3(a)(i): Where the applicant or, in the case of a non-natural applicant, any director is disqualified in terms of s.7(6) of the Act, the application is to be refused. As with the other grounds for refusal, it applies if "in their opinion" the ground is made out. However, disqualification is clearly a matter of fact.

Subparagraph 3(a)(ii): It is for the authority to satisfy themselves on the material before them that the applicant is not a fit and proper person. It is not for the applicant to establish to the satisfaction of the authority that they are a fit and proper person. There is no onus upon them (*J&J (Inns) Ltd v Angus District Licensing Board*, 1992 S.L.T. 930; *Din v City of Glasgow District Licensing Board*, 1995 S.C. 244; 1996 S.L.T. 363; *Allied Domecq Retailing Ltd v City of Glasgow Licensing Board*, 1999 G.W.D. 8-403; *Ferguson v Dundee City Council* [2006] CSIH 51). The inversion of the practical onus of proof does not entitle the applicant to ignore any objections or adverse reports made to a licensing authority: *Chief Constable of Strathclyde Police v North Lanarkshire Licensing Board*, 2003 S.L.T. 1268—"where criticisms were made of the conduct of the applicant it behoved the applicant to investigate the matter complained of and to lay an explanation before the board". In the case of a non-natural applicant, the reference to any director, partner or any person responsible for management obviates the need to take the approach sanctioned by the court in relation to liquor licensing, in *Fereneze Leisure Ltd v Renfrew District Licensing Board*, 1992 S.L.T. 604, and the board is entitled to consider the character and reputation of a person who controls the company such as a director or shareholder. There must be a proper basis for reaching a decision on whether a person is a fit and proper person to hold a licence. There must be an element of personal responsibility or culpability before a person can be deemed to be unfit—*Ward v Dundee City Council*, 1999 S.L.T. (Sh Ct) 56. A failure to adhere to the conditions of a licence could justify an authority in reaching a conclusion that the applicant was no longer a fit and proper person. However breach of a condition of a licence would not per se justify a conclusion of unfitness without an element of culpability, which would depend on the circumstances of the particular case including the nature of the condition itself. Persistent breaches would, however, be more likely to indicate culpability. In *Hamid v City of Glasgow Licensing Board*, 2001 S.C. 398, it was held that one could not infer unfitness in the form of a serious lack of management and control or lack of professional judgment from the mere fact that a sale of alcohol to a person under 18 had taken place at the hands of an employee. In that case the court referred to the absence of moral guilt or no lack of due diligence on the part of the licence holder.

Frequently, previous convictions, if relevant, will have a bearing on this issue. The weight to be attached to such convictions in determining whether an applicant is a fit and proper person is a matter for the authority (*Ranachan v Renfrew DC*, 1991 S.L.T. 625). In *McDowall v Cunninghame DC*, 1987 S.C.L.R. 587, it was held that a conviction for speeding could be of no relevance in respect of an application for a taxi licence, although it would be relevant in respect of an application for a taxi driver's licence. However, in *Middleton v Dundee City Council*, 2001 S.L.T. 287, the court pointed out that Parliament had left decisions on whether a person was a fit and proper person to local committees. The court should be slow to lay down hard and fast rules of general application as to matters which are or are not relevant. In that case the authority had taken account of a number of convictions for driving offences and concluded that the applicant had displayed complete disregard for road traffic legislation and scant regard for authority. On that basis they considered that he was not a fit and proper person to be the holder of a taxi licence. The court held that the authority had material before them on the basis of which they were entitled to reach the conclusion which they reached. It was pointed out that the authority was not considering the convictions from the point of view of fitness to drive but looking at whether in the light of all the material the applicant was a fit and proper person. It was noted that in *McDowall* there was no suggestion that the convictions were looked at as in any way indicating the nature of the applicant's character. In *Fife Regulation and Licensing Committee v Ewing* [2011] CSIH 45; 2011 S.L.T. 1250 it was held that the authority, in concluding that the applicant for renewal was not a fit and proper person, was entitled to have regard, in addition to a recent offence, to two speeding convictions prior to the original grant, one of which had only come to the attention of the authority after a previous renewal. Where an applicant for a taxi driver's licence had a serious previous conviction for lewd and libidinous practices and the licensing authority in their capacity as education authority used taxis to transport children, the conviction was held to be relevant—*Chief Constable of Strathclyde v East Dunbartonshire Council* unreported 9 March 1999 Glasgow Sheriff Court.

In relation to "spent convictions", s.4(1) of the Rehabilitation of Offenders Act 1974, provides that no evidence shall be admissible in any proceedings such as those conducted by a licensing authority to prove that the applicant, "has committed or been charged with or prosecuted for or convicted of or sentenced for any offence which was the subject of a spent conviction" and they cannot be asked (or if asked is not required to answer) any question which refers thereto. This is, however, subject to the proviso of s.7(3) of the 1974 Act which allows the authority to admit or require evidence where "justice cannot be done ... except by admitting or requiring evidence relating to a person's spent convictions or to circumstances ancillary thereto". The proviso does not, however, confer a dispensing power to be exercised by way of discretion by the licensing authority but is there "to ensure that spent convictions stay spent unless ... the party applying to put the spent conviction in can satisfy [the licensing authority] concerned that there is no other way of doing justice"—Sedley J in *R v Hastings Magistrates Ex p. McSpirit* [1994] 18 L.R. 20. The licensing authority must, therefore, first address and take a decision as to whether to admit or require details of such spent convictions to be put before them in evidence—*Morton v City of Dundee DC*, 1992 S.L.T. (Sh Ct) 2; *O'Doherty v Renfrewshire Council*, 1998 S.L.T. 327. This could normally be done at a "pre-hearing" at which reference might be made to the class of offence, its age and, gauged by penalty, its apparent seriousness—see further the English case of *Admanson v Waveney DC* [1997] 2 All E.R. 898 and *Cashley v City of Dundee DC*, 1994 S.L.T. 1111. An authority is entitled to consider all spent convictions which it has decided to admit after adopting the proper "two-stage test as well as unspent convictions and those convictions where the applicant has already pled guilty (or has been found guilty after trial) but has not yet been sentenced"—*R v Crewe and Nantwich BC Ex p. Baker* [1996] 7 C.L. 426. The weight that the authority puts on such convictions is a matter within its own discretion.

The fact that an applicant lied to the licensing authority might render them an unfit person (*Midlothian DC v Kinnear*, 1993 G.W.D. 3-193. In *J&J (Inns)* a person was deemed unfit inter alia because of her association with certain individuals. A decision on unfitness will often depend on the authority drawing inferences from conduct which they have found to have occurred. In *Malcolm v Aberdeen City Council*, 2004 S.L.T. (Sh Ct) 88, remarks of a sexual nature were made by a taxi driver to a female passenger. No physical contact was made. The committee had concluded that such conduct could have led a female passenger to think that physical contact or a request for sex may have followed and on that basis concluded that he was no longer a fit and proper person to hold a taxi licence. The sheriff held that the committee had made an unwarranted inference. While there had been no contact and the passenger had not been asked by the committee whether she thought that an approach was likely, it may be suggested that it could not be said that the authority were not entitled to draw such a conclusion. They heard evidence from the appellant and the passenger and it was for them to draw inferences from what they had found to have occurred. What was said was arguably enough to justify a conclusion of unfitness. A private hire car drivers' licence was suspended as a result of a non-harassment order and the suspension was upheld by a sheriff because the offence occurred while he was working: *Anderson v Glasgow City Council* unreported 20 May 2010 Glasgow Sheriff Court and also *Ritchie v Aberdeen City Council* [2011] CSIH 22; 2011 S.C. 570; 2011 S.L.T. 869.

Subparagraph 3(b): This reflects the factual situation specified in para.1(2)(b). Whether an activity is managed by or carried on for the benefit of a person of the type referred to is a question of fact but an application must be refused if the authority are of the opinion that this is the case in respect of a particular application. Ordinarily, the benefit will be a financial benefit. The authority will require to explain why the person would have been refused a licence. This must on the basis of one or other of the other grounds for refusal set out in this paragraph. For a practical example of the application of the phrase, "for the benefit of another" in respect of a street trader's licence see *Sneddon v West Dunbartonshire Council*, 1998 G.W.D. 34-1766.

Subparagraph 3(c)(i) and (ii): While suitability or convenience is in respect of the conduct of the activity for which the licence is sought, the Inner House has offered the opinion that character and location should receive a wide interpretation such as to allow consideration of amenity to neighbouring properties (*William Hill (Scotland) Ltd v Kyle and Carrick District Licensing Board*, 1991 S.L.T. 559)—see also *JE Sheeran (Amusement Arcades) Ltd v Hamilton DC*, 1986 S.L.T. 289. The relevant date for consideration of suitability, etc. is the date of the hearing of the application by the licensing authority—*Bantop v Glasgow District Licensing Board*, 1990 S.L.T. 366. It is, however, for the licensing authority to satisfy themselves that the premises are unsuitable and it is not enough if they are unable to satisfy themselves that the premises are suitable—*R&D Leisure Ltd v City of Glasgow Licensing Board* (1998) 10 S.L.L.P. 27. In *Birrell v Glasgow City Council* [2015] CSIH 21, it was held, in respect of an application for a street traders licence, that the authority was entitled to be satisfied that a pedicab was not a suitable vehicle on the ground that it did not have a three point seat belt or roll cage notwithstanding that a Vehicle and Operator's Services Agency certificate had been issued. The certificate did not prohibit the authority from taking the view that is was not suitable. It would have been failing in its duty had it not had regard to police and council official advice on the issue. In *Central Radio Taxis (Tollcross) Ltd v City of Edinburgh Council* unreported 20 March 2015 Edinburgh Sheriff Court, the sheriff rejected an argument that a private hire car booking office in Edinburgh Airport was not a suitable or convenient location by reason of alleged misleading signage which it was said could cause confusion as between taxi and private hire car operations at the airport. While the fact that planning permission for the proposed activity has been granted would not mean that the authority could not conclude that the premises were not suitable (*JE Sheeran*, above) it has been observed that in such a case they should be slow to refuse on such a ground (*Leisure Inns Ltd v Perth and Kinross DC*, 1991 S.C. 224). There would have to be some material justifying such a conclusion. "Extent" would cover the intensity of the proposed activity, e.g. the number of persons occupying or its duration. While the impact of the activity on the amenity of the area would be relevant, there would need to be some material before the authority capable of justifying a conclusion of unsuitability on that ground—*Killen v Dundee City Council* [2008] CSIH 43; 2008 S.L.T. 739.

Subparagraph 3(c)(iii): The authority must form a view as to the kind of persons "likely to be in" the premises, etc. on the basis of the information before them, whether disclosed in the application, any relevant objections or representations, as a result of their own inquiries or their own knowledge.

Subparagraph 3(c)(iv): In relation to undue public nuisance (quaere whether some lesser amount is acceptable) it is to be noted that all that is required is the "possibility" of that consequence. That is not, it would appear, a high test see *Anderson v Fife Council* unreported 22 March 2006 Cupar Sheriff Court. Past incidents involving the premises may be held to be relevant and the cumulative effect of these may be enough to justify a refusal—*McKay v Banff and Buchan Western Division Licensing Board*, 1991 S.L.T. 20. The possibility of undue public nuisance arising, notwithstanding the fact that the premises may be well managed, may be enough to cause a refusal—*Surrey Health Council v McDonalds Restaurants Ltd* [1990] 3 L.R. 23; *City of Glasgow District Licensing Board v Paglioca*, 1995 S.L.T. 180. Consideration of the conduct of persons who might be refused entry to the premises may, in certain circumstances, be relevant—*Clear v Cynon Valley BC* [1995] C.L.Y. 3149.

Subparagraph 3(c)(v): Public order or public safety is self-explanatory. Again, there must be some basis for the concern that in the light of this factor the premises are not suitable. "Public" includes those who use the premises or facility—*Sangha v Bute and Cowal Divisional Licensing Board*, 1990 S.C.L.R. 409. Safety issues are "a matter of impression" provided that the applicant is given a chance to address the licensing authority on them—*Texaco Ltd v North Lanarkshire Licensing Board*, 1998 S.L.T. 726. If a licensing authority does seek to draw an inference of undue public nuisance then it should have reasonably substantive material before it—*Richmond Inns Ltd v City of Aberdeen DC* unreported 11 June 1996 Aberdeen Sheriff Court; *City Petroleum Ltd v City of Edinburgh Licensing Board* (1998) 10 S.L.L.P. 20; *Texaco v West Fife District Licensing Board*, 1998 S.C. 470. Although a licensing authority is entitled to draw inferences it must have an adequate basis in fact. The factual material must be reasonably capable of yielding the conclusion. It has been held that they should not take into account any incidents which a sheriff in a previous appeal had already ruled as being insufficient to warrant a risk to public safety—*Clark v North Ayrshire Licensing Board*, 1998 G.W.D. 8-396.

Subparagraph 3(d): This has been described as a sweeping up provision (*Noble Organisation Ltd v City of Glasgow District Council (No.3)*, 1991 S.L.T. 213). It has been observed that some other good reason must be something other than the grounds set out in subparas 3(a), (b), and (c) above (*Noble Organisation*, above; see also *Gerry Cottle's Circus v City of Edinburgh DC*, 1990 S.L.T. 235; *Central Radio Taxis (Tollcross) Ltd v City of Edinburgh Council* unreported 20 March 2015 Edinburgh Sheriff Court). The statement of reasons for the authority's decision should make clear that this ground is being relied upon (*Calderwood v Renfrewshire Council*, 2004 S.L.T. 219). Over provision of similar facilities has been held to be a matter which would constitute other good reason (*Noble Organisation Ltd v Kilmarnock and Loudoun District Council*, 1993 S.L.T. 759). It does not include the absence of a taxi operator from an informal waiting list of potential licence holders—*Dundee Taxi Cab Co Ltd v Dundee City Council*, 2005 S.L.T. 401. Conflict with an adopted policy of the authority in respect of the relevant activity could also constitute good reason, always provided the authority did not fetter their discretion or apply the policy in a blanket fashion without considering the merits of the particular application (*Calderwood*, above). In that case it was observed that where an applicant is made aware that a policy is in issue there is a practical onus on them to address the matter. The mere number of objections to an application could not be an "other good reason" without regard to their content—*Noble Organisation Ltd v City of Glasgow District Council (No.3)*, 1991 S.L.T. 213.

Subparagraph (3A)

This was added by para.4 of the Schedule to the Civic Government (Scotland) Act 1982 (Licensing of Skin Piercing and Tattooing) Order 2006 (SSI 2006/43).

Subparagraph (4)

A certificate under para.2(4) must be submitted prior to any decision being taken on an application. This subparagraph does not apply where the application is made in respect of a house in multiple occupation used as a women's refuge.

Subparagraph (5)

A decision on an application must be notified to the applicant, the chief constable, relevant objectors or persons making representations and, in relation to premises, the fire authority.

Subparagraph (6)

This provides for a notification of the decision by the sending of a written notice or publication of a notice in a newspaper circulating in the area.

Subparagraph (7)

A licence when granted is to be made out and delivered to the licence holder. A duplicate may be issued on payment of the appropriate fee.

Subparagraph (8)

If an employee or agent has been named in the application under para.1(2)(b) or (c)(iv), the licence is to be granted jointly in the name of the applicant and the employee or agent.

Restriction on successive applications

6. Where a licensing authority have refused an application for the grant or renewal of a licence they shall not, within one year of their refusal, entertain a subsequent application from the same applicant for the grant of the same kind of licence in respect of the same activity in the same area or, where the activity consists of or includes the use of premises or vehicle or vessel, in respect of an activity consisting of or including the same use of the same premises, vehicle or vessel unless in their opinion there has been, since their refusal, a material change of circumstances.

DEFINITIONS

"licensing authority": s.2.
"licence": s.8.
"premises": ss.8, 41A(4).
"vessel": s.133.

GENERAL NOTE

This provision prohibits the authority from entertaining a subsequent application within one year of their having refused an application for grant or renewal, unless there has been, in their opinion, a material change of circumstances. This prohibits an application from the same applicant for the grant of the same kind of licence in respect of the same activity in the same area or where premises are used in respect of an activity consisting of or including the same use of the same premises. Clearly, a different applicant or an application involving a different area or different premises would escape the prohibition. The use of the word "same" suggests that the area or premises must be "identical" for the prohibition to apply. It is suggested that a marginal or de minimis alteration in area/premises would probably not be sufficient to engage the prohibition. It is clearly a question of fact whether premises are different. There must be sufficient factual material for the authority to make a decision—*Kelvinside Community Council v Glasgow District Licensing Board*, 1990 S.L.T. 725.

Temporary licences

7.—(1) A licensing authority may grant a licence to have effect for such period not exceeding 6 weeks from its being granted as they may determine, and such a licence shall be known as a "temporary licence".

(2) This Schedule shall apply with the modifications specified in sub-paragraph (3) to (5) below in relation to applications for temporary licences.

[1](3) Paragraphs 1(3), (1A), (2), (2ZA), (2A) to 4, and 5(1), (2) and (4) to (6) shall not apply, but in relation to each application for a temporary licence the licensing authority—

[1](a) shall consult the chief constable and, where the application relates to an activity wholly or mainly to be carried on—

(i) in premises to which Part 3 of the Fire (Scotland) Act 2005 (asp 5) applies, the enforcing authority;

[2](ii) in any other premises, the Scottish Fire and Rescue Service; and

[1](b) may, subject to sub-paragraph (3A) below grant it subject to such conditions as they think fit.

[1](3A) The conditions referred to in paragraph (b) of sub-paragraph (3) above shall not relate to any matter in relation to which requirements or prohibitions are or could be imposed by virtue of Part 3 of the Fire (Scotland) Act 2005 (asp 5).

(4) Paragraph 6 shall not apply so as to prevent a licensing authority from entertaining an application for the grant of a licence where they have, within one year, refused an application from the same applicant for a temporary licence for the same activity.

(5) Paragraphs 8, 9, 10 and 18 shall not apply.

(6) A temporary licence shall not be capable of being renewed but, where the holder of or the applicant for a temporary licence has also made an application for a licence under paragraph 1 above in respect of the same activity, the temporary licence, if granted, shall continue to have effect until—

(a) the licence applied for under paragraph 1 has been granted, whether as a result of an appeal under paragraph 18 below or not, or has been deemed to have been granted; or

(b) where the licensing authority have refused that application, the time within which an appeal under paragraph 18 below against that decision may be made has elapsed; or

(c) when such an appeal has been lodged, it has been abandoned or determined.

NOTES

1. As amended by the Fire (Scotland) Act 2005 (Consequential Modifications and Savings) Order 2006 (SSI 2006/475) Sch.1 para.11 (effective 1 October 2006).

2. As amended by the Police and Fire Reform (Scotland) Act 2012 (asp 8) Sch.7(2) para.53 (effective 1 April 2013).

3. As amended by the Air Weapons and Licensing (Scotland) Act 2015 (asp 10) Sch.2 Pt 3 para.5 (date yet to be appointed).

DEFINITIONS
"licensing authority": s.2.
"chief constable": s.8.
"enforcing authority": s.8.
"licence": s.8.
'premises": s.8.

GENERAL NOTE
This makes provision for the granting of temporary licences.

Subparagraph (1)

A temporary licence is to be effective for a period not exceeding six weeks.

Subparagraphs (2) and (3)

The provisions of the Schedule generally apply to the application for temporary licences, subject to specific modifications which exclude paras 1(3), 2–4 and 5(1), (2) and (4)–(6). However, the authority must consult the chief constable and, in respect of premises, either the enforcing authority or the Scottish Fire and Rescue Service and may grant a temporary licence subject to such conditions as they think fit. The authority thus has a very wide discretion in respect of conditions which may be attached to temporary licences.

Subparagraph (3A)

This prohibits imposition of conditions in respect of matters covered by Pt 3 of the Fire (Scotland) Act 2005. It and amendment to the previous subparagraph were introduced by the Fire (Scotland) Act 2005 (Consequential Modifications and Savings) Order 2006 (SSI 2006/475).

Subparagraph (4)

The prohibition on entertaining of subsequent applications by the same applicant in respect of the same activity does not apply to temporary licences.

Subparagraphs (5) and (6)

Paragraphs 8, 9, 10 and 18 do not apply. Accordingly, any challenge to a refusal of a temporary licence must be by way of judicial review—*Gerry Cottle's Circus v City of Edinburgh DC*, 1990 S.L.T. 235. A temporary licence is not renewable but if the holder of or applicant for a temporary licence has applied for a licence under para.1 in respect of the same activity, the temporary licence continues in effect until the licence applied for has been granted or, if refused, the time for appeal has elapsed and any appeal has been abandoned or determined. This has the effect of extending the life of a temporary licence beyond six weeks.

Duration of licences

8.—(1) Subject to and in accordance with the provisions of this paragraph, a licence shall come into force on being granted by a licensing authority or on such later date as they may specify as a condition of the licence and shall continue in force on being renewed by them.

(2) Subject to the provisions of this paragraph, a licence shall have effect—

(a) for a period of three years from the date when it comes into force; or

(b) for such shorter period as the licensing authority may decide at the time when they grant or renew the licence.

(3) In the event of the death of a holder of a licence (except in the case of a licence referred to in section 13 of this Act) that licence shall be deemed to have been granted to his executor and shall, unless previously revoked, suspended or surrendered, remain in force until the end of the period of 3

months beginning with the death and shall then expire; but the licensing authority may from time to time, on the application of the executor, extend or further extend that period if they are satisfied that the extension is necessary for the purpose of winding up the deceased's estate and that no other circumstances make it undesirable.

(4) Where one of the joint holders of a licence ceases to be such, the licence shall continue in force as if held by its remaining holder for a period of six weeks from the date of such cessation but, where the remaining holder has made an application under paragraph 1 above for a licence in respect of the same activity within that period of six weeks, that period shall be extended until the time specified in sub-paragraph (6) below.

(5) If an application for the renewal of a licence is made before its expiry, the existing licence shall continue to have effect until the time specified in sub-paragraph (6) below.

[1](5A) On good cause being shown, a licensing authority may, for the purposes of sub-paragraph (5), deem an application for renewal of a licence made up to 28 days before the expiry of the licence to be an application made before the expiry.

(6) The time referred to in sub-paragraphs (4) and (5) above is—

(a) the time when the licence applied for under paragraph 1 above is granted or renewed, whether as a result of an appeal under paragraph 18 below or not, or has been deemed to have been granted or renewed; or

(b) where the licensing authority have refused that application, the time within which an appeal under paragraph 18 below against that decision may be made has elapsed; or

(c) where such an appeal has been lodged, the time when it has been abandoned or determined.

(7) Where a relevant objection or representation (within the meaning of paragraph 19 below) has been made in relation to an application for the grant of a licence, that licence shall not, unless it has been deemed to have been granted under section 3(4) of this Act, come into force until—

(a) the time within which an appeal under paragraph 18 below against the grant of the licence may be made has elapsed; or

(b) where such an appeal has been lodged, it has been abandoned or determined in favour of the applicant.

(8) This paragraph is subject to paragraphs 11 to 14 below.

NOTE

1. As amended by the Criminal Justice and Licensing (Scotland) Act 2010 (asp 13) Pt 8 s.178 (effective 28 February 2011 for purposes specified in SSI 2010/413 Sch.1; not yet in force otherwise).

DEFINITIONS

"relevant objection or representation": Sch.1 para.19.
"licensing authority": s.2.
"licence": s.8.

Subparagraph (1)

A licence takes effect as from the date of grant or any later date specified in a condition attaching thereto.

Subparagraph (2)

Ordinarily, a licence is effective for three years or such shorter period as may be determined by the authority. Where an authority determines to grant a licence for a shorter period it should give a reason for so doing—*Scanlan v City of Edinburgh DC*, 1995 S.L.T. (Sh Ct) 89 at 95; *McLuskie v City of Glasgow DC*, 1993 S.L.T. 1102. It should be noted, however, that, despite the provisions of subs.(3), most licensing authorities in fact only grant licences for a period of one year.

Subparagraph (3)

Other than in the case where a licence is revoked, suspended or surrendered, where a licence holder dies the licence is deemed to have been granted to their executor for a period of three months after which it expires. There is power to extend the period upon application of the executor if the authority is satisfied that this is necessary for the winding up of the estate unless in the circumstances this is undesirable. The final 23 words were added by the Schedule to the Civic Government (Scotland) Act 1982 (Licensing of Skin Piercing and Tattooing) Order 2006 (SSI 2006/43), see pp.225–231 below.

Subparagraph (4)

Where a joint holder of a licence ceases to be such the licence continues in force as if held by the remaining holder for a period of six weeks. Provision is made for that period being extended where the remaining holder makes application for a licence in respect of the same activity under para.1 (cf. para.7(6) above).

Subparagraphs (5) and (6)

On application being made for renewal of a licence prior to its expiry it is provided that the licence continues in effect until determination of the application or of any appeal against refusal or any earlier abandonment. This may have the effect of extending the normal life of a licence pending such a determination, etc.

Subparagraph (7)

In cases where a relevant objection or representation has been made then, unless there is a deemed grant under s.3(4), no licence comes into force until any appeal against the grant has been determined in favour of the applicants, or abandoned, or the time for lodging an appeal has expired without one being lodged.

Subparagraph (8)

The provisions of this paragraph are subject to the provisions on suspension of licences.

Notification of changes and alterations

9.—(1) Where there is a material change of circumstances affecting a holder of a licence, or the activity to which the licence relates, the holder of the licence shall, in accordance with this paragraph, notify the licensing authority of the change as soon as reasonably practicable after it has taken place.

(2) The holder of a licence which relates to an activity consisting of or including the use of premises, a vehicle or a vessel shall not, unless in accordance with a requirement imposed by or in pursuance of any enactment other than Parts I or II of this Act, make or cause to be made or permit there to be made any material change in the premises or, as the case may be, the vehicle or vessel without the prior consent of the licensing authority.

(3) A notification under sub-paragraph (1) above or application for consent under sub-paragraph (2) above shall be accompanied by such fee as the licensing authority may charge under paragraph 15 below.

(4) A licensing authority, before considering whether or not to give their consent under sub-paragraph (2) above, shall be entitled to require the

holder of the licence to furnish them with specifications, including plans, of the proposed changes.

[1](5) A licensing authority, before deciding whether or not to give their consent under sub-paragraph (2) above, shall consult with the chief constable and, in the case of a change—

(a) in premises to which Part 3 of the Fire (Scotland) Act 2005 (asp 5) applies, the enforcing authority;

(b) any other premises, with the Scottish Fire and Rescue Service.

(6) Where the licensing authority have given their consent under sub-paragraph (2) above to a change in premises or a vehicle or vessel, it shall not be necessary for the holder of the licence relating to those premises or that vehicle or vessel to notify the licensing authority of that change under sub-paragraph (1) above.

[1](7) A licensing authority shall, within 7 days of their decision under sub-paragraph (2) above, send written notice of their decision to the holder of the licence and the chief constable and, where the change is—

(a) to premises to which Part 3 of the Fire (Scotland) Act 2005 (asp 5) applies, the enforcing authority;

[2](b) any other premises, with the Scottish Fire and Rescue Service.

(8) In this paragraph, a "material change" includes any material change in the particulars given or referred to in the application for a grant, or, where the licence has been renewed, the most recent application for the renewal, of the licence.

NOTES

1. As amended by the Fire (Scotland) Act 2005 (Consequential Modifications and Savings) Order 2006 (SSI 2006/475) Sch.1 para.11 (effective 1 October 2006).

2. As amended by the Police and Fire Reform (Scotland) Act 2012 (asp 8) Sch.7(2) para.53 (effective 1 April 2013).

DEFINITIONS

"licensing authority": s.2.
"chief constable": s.8.
"enforcing authority": s.133.
"licence': s.8.
'premises": s.8.
"vessel": s.133.

Subparagraph (1)

The onus is clearly placed on the licence holder to notify the authority of any material change of circumstances affecting them to which the licence relates. It is for the holder to determine whether a change is sufficiently material to require disclosure. A material change would be one of such significance as would be likely to influence the authority in determining how they would exercise their powers under the Act in relation to the licence holder or the activity to which the licence relates. However, a failure to disclose something which the authority decides is a material change and is therefore a breach of this provision could be held to be misconduct which would have a bearing on fitness to hold a licence where suspension was under consideration (para.11(4)).

Subparagraph (2)

Similarly, where the licence relates to an activity involving the use of premises or a vessel, no material change therein can be made without the prior consent of the authority. In relation to premises, the authority would require to be satisfied that any change would not render the premises unsuitable or inconvenient for the conduct of the activity in question (cf. para.5(3) above).

Subparagraph (5)

The authority must consult the chief constable or, in respect of premises, either the enforcing authority in the case of relevant premises under the Fire (Scotland) Act 2005 or the Scottish Fire and Rescue Service in the case of other premises before giving consent. This may be done informally.

Subparagraph (6)

Any consent given under subpara.(2) obviates the need to notify a change under subpara.(1).

Subparagraph (8)

This sets out a non-exhaustive definition of material change referring to the particulars given in the application.

10.—(1) A licensing authority may, at any time, whether or not upon an application made to them by the holder of the licence, vary the terms of a licence on any grounds they think fit.

(2) A licensing authority, before proceeding to vary the terms of a licence under sub-paragraph (1) above—

[2](a) shall, not later than 7 days before the day on which the proposed variation is to be considered, notify the holder of the licence, the chief constable and, where the licence relates to an activity wholly or mainly carried on in premises, the Scottish Fire and Rescue Service of the proposed variation; and

[1](b) shall give each of the persons required to be notified under sub-sub-paragraph (a) above an opportunity to be heard by the authority on that day.

[1,2](2A) Where the premises mentioned in sub-paragraph (2)(a) above are premises to which Part 3 of the Fire (Scotland) Act 2005 (asp 5) applies, that sub-paragraph applies as if the reference to the Scottish Fire and Rescue Service were a reference to the enforcing authority.

(3) A licensing authority shall have complied with sub-paragraph (2)(b) above if they have invited each of the persons whom they must notify under that sub-paragraph to attend and to be heard by the authority when the variation of the licence is to be considered.

[1](4) A licensing authority shall, within 7 days of their decision under sub-paragraph (1) above, send written notice of their decision to the holder of the licence and the chief constable and, where the licence relates to an activity wholly or mainly carried on—

(a) in premises to which Part 3 of the Fire (Scotland) Act 2005 (asp 5) applies, the enforcing authority;

[2](b) in any other premises, to the Scottish Fire and Rescue Service.

(5) A variation in the terms of a licence shall come into force—

(a) when the time within which an appeal under paragraph 18 below may be made had elapsed; or

(b) where such an appeal has been lodged, when the appeal has been abandoned or determined in favour of the variation.

(6) Sub-paragraph (5) does not apply a deemed variation of the terms of a licence under section 3(4).

NOTES

1. As amended by the Fire (Scotland) Act 2005 (Consequential Modifications and Savings) Order 2006 (SSI 2006/475) Sch.1 para.11 (effective 1 October 2006).

2. As amended by the Police and Fire Reform (Scotland) Act 2012 (asp 8) Sch.7(2) para.53 (effective 1 April 2013).

3. As amended by the Air Weapons and Licensing (Scotland) Act 2015 (asp 10) Pt 3 s.77 (date yet to be appointed).

DEFINITIONS
"licensing authority": s.2.
"chief constable": s.8.
"enforcing authority": s.133.
"licence": s.8.
"premises": s.8.

Subparagraph (1)

The authority has a wide discretion to vary the terms of a licence. It may do so *ex proprio motu*. It is not considered that the mechanism of variation may be used to substitute a new holder of the licence for the existing one, i.e. effectively to transfer a licence. To do so would have the effect of enabling transfer to be achieved where there is no express power to do so in the Act. It would also be inconsistent with the obligation to give "the holder of the licence" an opportunity to be heard in terms of subpara.(2)(b) and to give written notice of the decision to vary in terms of subpara.(4). Note however that the variation refers to the terms of the licence and not its substance so that it does not apply to a substantial alteration to, for instance, the locus at which the licenced activity is carried out from—see e.g. *Walker v City of Aberdeen Council*, 1998 S.L.T. 427. The reason why the variation does not include a change in the substance of an existing licence is that by doing so objectors would be deprived of their opportunity to object where in reality what is sought should properly be covered by a new licence application rather than a variation.

Subparagraphs (2)

Subparagraph (2)(a): The holder of the licence, the chief constable and, where appropriate, the enforcing authority or the Scottish Fire and Rescue Service must be notified by the authority of any proposed variation not later than seven days before the day when the variation is to be considered.
Subparagraph (2)(b): Those who require to be notified in terms of subpara.(2)(a) above have a right to be heard on that day (cf. disposal of an application (para.4) and *McIndoe v Glasgow District Licensing Board*, 1989 S.C.L.R. 325).

Subparagraph (2A)

This was added by the Fire (Scotland) Act 2005.

Subparagraph (3)

It is to be noted that an invitation to attend and be heard is sufficient compliance with subpara.(2)(b) above.

Subparagraph (5)

Since variation is, in terms of para.17, an appealable decision, it is provided that a variation is not to come into force until any appeal is determined in favour of the variation, or the time for lodging an appeal has elapsed. For an example of an unsuccessful appeal against a variation see *Habib v Fife Council Area Subcommittee* unreported 30 January 2008 Kirkcaldy Sheriff Court.

11.—[3](1) A licensing authority may, whether upon a complaint made to them or not, suspend or revoke a licence in accordance with the provisions of this paragraph.

[3](2) A licensing authority may order the suspension or revocation of a licence if in their opinion—

(a) the holder of the licence or, where the holder is not a natural person, any director of it or partner in it or any other person responsible for its management, is not or is no longer a fit and proper person to hold the licence;

(b) the activity to which the licence relates is being managed by or carried on for the benefit of a person, other than the licence holder, who would have been refused the grant or renewal of the licence under paragraph 5(3) above;

(c) the carrying on of the activity to which the licence relates has caused, is causing or is likely to cause undue public nuisance or a threat to public order or public safety;

(d) a condition of the licence has been contravened.

(3) A licensing authority may make an order under sub-paragraph (2)(d) above in respect of a contravention of a condition of a licence notwithstanding that there has been no conviction in that respect.

[3](4) In considering whether to suspend or revoke a licence the licensing authority may—

(a) have regard to—

(i) any misconduct on the part of the holder of the licence, whether or not constituting a breach of any provision of Part I or II of this Act or this Schedule, which in the opinion of the authority has a bearing on his fitness to hold a licence;

(ii) where the licence relates to an activity consisting of or including the use of premises or a vehicle or vessel, any misconduct on the part of persons frequenting or using the premises, vehicle or vessel occurring there or any misconduct in the immediate vicinity of the premises, vehicle or vessel which is attributable to those persons;

(b) make such reasonable inquiries as they think fit and, subject to sub-paragraph (5) below, include the results of their inquiries in the matters to which they have regard in such consideration.

(5) Where a licensing authority intend to include any of the results of their inquiries under sub-paragraph (4)(b) above in the matters to which they have regard for the purposes of sub-paragraph (4) above, they shall notify the holder of the licence of that intention.

[3](6) A licensing authority may, whether upon an application made to them or not, recall an order to suspend a licence made under this paragraph.

[1](7) A licensing authority in considering whether or not to suspend or revoke a licence may, but before deciding to do so shall, give—

(a) the holder of the licence;

(b) any person who has made a complaint relevant to the matters to be considered at the hearing;

(c) the chief constable; and

(d) where the licence relates to an activity wholly or mainly carried on—

(a) in premises to which Part 3 of the Fire (Scotland) Act 2005 (asp 5) applies, the enforcing authority;

[2](b) in any other premises, the Scottish Fire and Rescue Service,

an opportunity to be heard by the licensing authority.

[3](8) The licensing authority shall have complied with their duty under sub-paragraph (7) above if they have caused to be sent to the persons entitled under that sub-paragraph to an opportunity to be heard, not later than 14 days before the hearing, notice in writing that the authority propose to hold a hearing, together with a copy of any complaints relevant to the matters to be considered at the hearing and a note of the grounds upon which the suspension or revocation of the licence is to be considered and, where they decide to exercise their power under that sub-paragraph, they shall cause such notice, copy and note to be sent to those persons not later than that time.

[3](9) Where a licensing authority decide to order the suspension or revocation of a licence, the suspension, or as the case may be revocation shall not, subject to sub-paragraph (10) below, take effect until the expiry of the time within which the holder of the licence may appeal under paragraph 18 below against the suspension or revocation as the case may be, if such an appeal has been lodged, until it has been abandoned or determined in favour of the suspension.

[3](10) If, in deciding to order the suspension or revocation of a licence, a licensing authority determine that the circumstances of the case justify immediate suspension or revocation they may, without prejudice to their other powers under this paragraph, order that the licence shall be suspended or revocation immediately.

(11) The period of suspension of a licence under this paragraph shall be the unexpired portion of the duration of the licence, or such shorter period as the licensing authority may fix; and the effect of suspension shall be that the licence shall cease to have effect during the period of the suspension.

(12) A licensing authority shall, within 7 days of their decision under sub-paragraph (1) above, send written notice of their decision to the persons referred to in sub-paragraph 7(a), (c) and (d) above in relation to the licence and to any person who, in pursuance of sub-paragraph (7)(b) above, was heard by the authority before they reached that decision.

NOTES

1. As amended by the Fire (Scotland) Act 2005 (Consequential Modifications and Savings) Order 2006 (SSI 2006/475) Sch.1 para.11 (effective 1 October 2006).

2. As amended by the Police and Fire Reform (Scotland) Act 2012 (asp 8) Sch.7(2) para.53 (effective 1 April 2013).

3. As amended by the Air Weapons and Licensing (Scotland) Act 2015 (asp 10) Pt 3 s.78 (date yet to be appointed).

DEFINITIONS

"licensing authority": s.2.
"chief constable": s.8.
"enforcing authority": s.133.
"licence": s.8.
"premises": s.8.
'vessel": s.133.

Subparagraph (1)

This provision confers upon the authority a power to suspend or revoke a licence. The power to revoke was introduced by the 2010 Act s.69A(3). That power already exists in respect of sex shop licences under Sch.2 para.13. A licensing board also has a power to revoke a premises licence under s.39 of the Licensing (Scotland) Act 2005 where it holds a review hearing.

Subparagraph (2)

This subparagraph contains the grounds for suspension and revocation. The additional sanction of revocation will be appropriate in more serious or flagrant cases. Again, as with refusal of an application, suspension or revocation may be ordered if the authority is of the opinion that any of the specified grounds exist. Grounds (a), (b) and (c) derive from the grounds of refusal set out in paras 5(3)(a), (b) and (c)(iv) and (v). Ground (a) covers the case where, in relation to a non-natural holder of a licence, there is a change in partners, directors or managers and all or any of those persons is not fit and proper to hold a licence, as well as the case where any existing partner, etc. by reason of misconduct (see below), ceases to be fit and proper. For a case in which a suspension on this ground was upheld where it was alleged that a taxi driver was inter alia exercising control and management over a taxi licence held by another see *Ferguson v Dundee City Council* [2006] CSIH 51. In relation to ground (c) it is noted that it is the carrying on of the activity which must have caused, is causing or is likely to cause undue public nuisance, etc. before suspension can be ordered. Contrast that with para.5(3)(c)(iv) and (v) which refer to the authority having regard to the possibility of undue public nuisance or public order or safety. In the case of suspension, the authority will be likely to have material relating to how the activity has, in fact, been carried on as compared with an application for grant of a new licence where there may be no such material such that the authority could only address possibility. While the conduct of customers or persons frequenting the premises where the activity is carried out is not in terms a ground of suspension, it would be a factor to which regard may be had in terms of subpara.(4)(a)(ii). In determining whether to suspend or revoke, the authority must act proportionately. The action proposed to be taken should not be disproportionate having regard to the objective sought to be achieved by the action, the conduct in question, its extent and gravity, and any other relevant circumstances including mitigating factors. It is for the authority to weigh up the relevant considerations and determine where the balance should be struck in the public interest (see Introduction, pp.23–25 above) For example, in *Tesco Stores Ltd v Midlothian Licensing Board*, 2012 S.C.L.R. 575 the court held that suspension of a premises licence under the Licensing (Scotland) Act 2005 was disproportionate where it followed a first test purchase failure in otherwise properly run premises.

Subparagraph (3)

While contravention of a condition in a licence is an offence, conviction therefor is unnecessary before a licence can be suspended or revoked on this ground. It is sufficient that the authority is of the opinion that there has been a breach.

Subparagraph (4)

Subparagraph (4)(a): This provision sets out the factors to which the authority may have regard in considering whether to suspend or revoke on one or more of the specified grounds.

Subparagraph (4)(a)(i): Any misconduct which, in the opinion of the authority, has a bearing on fitness to hold a licence may be taken into account. The misconduct need not consist of a breach of any provisions of the Act. The authority must be satisfied that the behaviour of the holder amounts to misconduct and there must be a reasonable basis for that view. Similarly, there must be a reasonable basis for any opinion that the misconduct has a bearing on fitness to hold a licence.

Subparagraph (4)(a)(ii): Misconduct on the part of persons frequenting or using premises where the licence relates to an activity involving the use of these premises may be taken into account. This would have a bearing on whether to suspend or revoke under subpara.(2)(d) or even (a). Although the nuisance may be directly attributable to the conduct of, say, customers, it would still be possible for the authority to infer that in the circumstances the activity has caused, etc. the nuisance, etc. in the sense that, without the activity and the customers it attracts to the premises, there would be no nuisance.

Subparagraph (4)(b): As in the case of an application, the authority is empowered in respect of a possible suspension or revocation to make reasonable inquiries and to include the results of those inquiries in the matters to which they have regard. It would not appear to be necessary that the results consist of information as to misconduct such as is referred to in subpara.(4)(a)(i) and (ii).

Subparagraph (5)

The licence holder must be notified if the authority intend to have regard to the results of their inquiries.

Subparagraph (6)

The authority may, at any time, order the recall of a suspension of a licence. No grounds for a recall are specified and there is no obligation to consult with, for example, the chief constable before doing so. Recall of a suspension is not an appealable decision.

Subparagraph (7)

The licence holder, any complainer in respect of a matter to be considered at the hearing on suspension, the chief constable and, where appropriate, the fire authority may be given an opportunity to be heard where the authority is considering whether to suspend and *must* be given such an opportunity before any decision to do so is taken. In other words, if the authority decides that suspension should be ordered those persons are entitled to be heard prior to any decision actually being made. It has been held that the holder of the licence has a right to be heard on the period of suspension before it is imposed (*McIndoe v Glasgow District Licensing Board*, 1989 S.C.L.R. 325). This subparagraph was amended by the Fire (Scotland) Act 2005.

Subparagraph (8)

The authority will have complied with their duty under subpara.(7) above if, no later than 21 days before the hearing, they send to the relevant persons notice of the proposed hearing, together with copies of any relevant complaints and a note of the grounds of suspension to be considered. If the authority choose to give the relevant persons an opportunity to be heard when considering suspension, then the notice, etc. must be sent not later than 21 days before the hearing.

Subparagraph (9)

Given that there is a right of appeal against suspension or revocation it will not take effect until either the expiry of the specified time for appeal by the holder or the abandonment or determination of any appeal in favour of the suspension. Where an existing licence has been renewed it has been held that this amounts to a continuation of the previous one, carrying with it the sanction of a suspension previously imposed but delayed by the taking of an appeal against the suspension (*Basra v Cunninghame District Licensing Board*, 1995 S.C. 296; 1995 S.L.T. 1013).

Subparagraph (10)

The authority may determine that suspension of a licence with immediate effect is justified and so order. Such a decision is still appealable but the licence does not remain in effect pending any appeal.

Subparagraph (11)

The period of suspension is the unexpired portion for the duration of the licence or such shorter period as the authority determines. During that period the licence is ineffective. In other words, the holder may not carry out the activity to which the licence relates. In *Baird v Glasgow City Council*, 2003 S.L.L.P. 27 it was held that the suspension of a taxi licence for a period of six months in respect of one incident of abusive language to another motorist was, under reference to art.1 of the First Protocol to the Convention, disproportionate.

Subparagraph (12)

Within seven days of a decision to suspend, the authority must send written notice thereof to the parties referred to in subpara.(7)(a), (c) and (d) and to any complainer who was heard by the authority before any decision was made. Such persons have a right to request of the authority reasons in writing for such a decision (para.17).

12.—(1) A licensing authority shall, whether upon a complaint made to them or not, order the suspension under this paragraph of a licence if they are of the opinion that the carrying on of the activity to which the licence relates is causing or is likely to cause a serious threat to public order or public safety.

(2) In considering whether to suspend a licence under this paragraph, a licensing authority may make such reasonable inquiries as they think fit and include the results of their inquiries in the matters to which they have regard in such consideration.

(3) Where a licensing authority intend to include any of the results of their inquiries under sub-paragraph (2) above in the matters to which they have regard for the purposes of this paragraph they shall notify the holder of the licence of that intention.

[1](4) A licensing authority shall, before reaching a decision on the question whether or not to suspend a licence under this paragraph, consult the chief

constable and, where the licence relates to an activity wholly or mainly carried on—

(a) in premises to which Part 3 of the Fire (Scotland) Act 2005 (asp 5) applies, the enforcing authority;

[2](b) in any other premises the Scottish Fire and Rescue Service.

(5) An order under this paragraph suspending a licence shall have effect from the date on which it is made until whichever is the earlier of the following two dates—

(a) a date six weeks after the order was made;

[3](b) the date of any decision of the licensing authority whether or not to suspend or revoke the licence under paragraph 11 above.

(6) A licensing authority may, whether upon an application made to them or not, recall an order made under this paragraph.

[1](7) A licensing authority shall, within 7 days of their decision under sub-paragraph (1) or (6) above, send written notice of their decision to the holder of the licence, the chief constable and, where the licence relates to an activity wholly or mainly carried on—

(a) in premises to which Part 3 of the Fire (Scotland) Act 2005 (asp 5) applies, the enforcing authority;

[2](b) in any other premises, to the Scottish Fire and Rescue Service.

NOTES

1. As amended by the Fire (Scotland) Act 2005 (Consequential Modifications and Savings) Order 2006 (SSI 2006/475) Sch.1 para.11 (effective 1 October 2006).

2. As amended by the Police and Fire Reform (Scotland) Act 2012 (asp 8) Sch.7(2) para.53 (effective 1 April 2013).

3. As amended by the Air Weapons and Licensing (Scotland) Act 2015 (asp 10) Pt 3 s.78 (date yet to be appointed).

DEFINITIONS

"licensing authority": s.2.
"chief constable": s.8.
"enforcing authority": s.133.
"licence": s.8.
"premises": s.8.

Subparagraph (1)

Where the authority are of the opinion that the carrying out of the activity to which the licence relates is causing or is likely to cause a serious threat to public order or safety (cf. para.11(2)(c)) they must order suspension of the licence (cf. para.11(2), in terms of which they "may suspend"). Where the authority suspend under this provision they can do so *ex proprio motu* without any complaint having been made by, for example, the chief constable.

Subparagraphs (2) and (3)

The same power to make inquiries is given as with applications, and suspensions under para.11, and the authority must notify the holder of the intention to have regard to the results thereof with the important difference that there is no provision made for the holder being given the opportunity of being heard before the decision is taken.

Subparagraph (5)

A suspension under this paragraph takes effect immediately for a period of six weeks or until the date of any decision on suspension under para.11, whichever is the earlier.

Subparagraph (6)

Written notification of any suspension must be given to the usual parties.

Subparagraphs (4) and (7) were amended by the Fire (Scotland) Act 2005.

Supplementary

13.—(1) A holder of a licence may at any time surrender the licence to the licensing authority and it shall thereupon cease to have effect.

(2) A holder of a licence shall deliver the licence to the licensing authority—

[1](a) within 7 days after the coming into effect of a decision of a licensing authority to suspend, revoke or vary the terms of the licence or of a court, under section 7(6)(a) of this Act, to revoke it;

(b) where the licence relates to an activity which he has given up.

[1](3) A licensing authority shall, on making an order suspending or revoking a licence or on deciding to vary the terms of a licence, cause notice in writing to be given to the holder of the licence of his duty to deliver it under sub-paragraph (2) above.

[1](4) Where a licence has been surrendered under this paragraph on its suspension or revocation under section 7(6)(a) of this Act or its suspension under this Schedule and the revocation or suspension is quashed or recalled the licensing authority shall re-issue the licence.

NOTE

1. As amended by the Air Weapons and Licensing (Scotland) Act 2015 (asp 10) Pt 3 s.78 (date yet to be appointed).

DEFINITIONS

"licensing authority": s.2.
"licence": s.8.

Subparagraph (1)

Upon the voluntary surrender of a licence it will cease to have effect.

Subparagraph (2)

A licence must be delivered up to the authority following upon a decision to suspend or vary its terms by the authority or a decision to revoke by the court under s.7 and where the holder has given up the activity to which the licence relates.

Subparagraph (4)

Provision is made for the re-issuing of a licence upon the quashing of a revocation or the recall of a suspension.

14.—(1) A licensing authority shall cause to be kept a register of applications under this Schedule (in this paragraph referred to as "the register") and shall, as soon as reasonably practicable after—

(a) the receipt of each application, cause details of such receipt; and

(b) their final decision on each application, cause details of that decision

to be entered in the register.

(2) The register shall include—

(a) a note of the kind and terms of each licence granted by the licensing authority;

[1](b) a note of any suspension, revocation or variation of the terms, or surrender, of a licence.

(3) The register shall be open to the inspection of any member of the public at such reasonable times and places as may be determined by the licensing authority and any member of the public may make a copy thereof or an extract therefrom.

(4) A licensing authority may, on payment of such fee as they may charge under paragraph 15 below, issue a certified true copy of any entry in the register; and any document purporting to be certified by the proper officer of the licensing authority as a true copy of an entry shall be sufficient evidence of the terms of the original entry.

NOTE

1. As amended by the Air Weapons and Licensing (Scotland) Act 2015 (asp 10) Pt 3 s.78 (date yet to be appointed).

DEFINITIONS

"licensing authority": s.2.
"licence": s.8.
"proper officer": s.133.

GENERAL NOTE

This paragraph makes provision for the keeping of a register of applications by the authority and requires that details of the receipt of the application and the final decision thereon be kept therein. There is also to be recorded a note of the kind and terms of each licence granted and a note of any suspension, variation or surrender thereof.

Fees

15.—(1) A licensing authority shall, subject top sub-paragraph (2) below—

(a) in respect of applications made to them under this Schedule;
(b) in respect of the issue of certified duplicate licences under paragraph 5(7) above;
(c) in respect of the issue of their consideration of a material change of circumstances or in premises or a vehicle or vessel under paragraph 9 above and their disposal of the matter;
(b) in respect of the issue under paragraph 14 above of certified true copies charge such reasonable fees as they may, in accordance with sub-paragraph (2) determine different fees for different classes of business, and items of business may be classed for that purpose by reference to any factor or factors whatsoever.

(2) Subject to sub-paragraph (3) below, in determining the amount of different fees under sub-paragraph (1) above, the licensing authority shall seen ensure that from time to time the total amount of fees receivable by the authority is sufficient to meet the expenses of the authority in exercising their functions under Parts I and II of this Act and this Schedule.

(3) Sub-paragraph (2) does not apply in respect of the fees and expenses in respect of which provision is made by Section 12 of this Act.

DEFINITIONS

"licensing authority": s.2.
"licence": s.8.
"premises": s.8.
"vessel": s.8.

GENERAL NOTE

The authority is required to charge fees in respect of processing and determining, the consideration of applications, the issue of duplicate licences and other matters. Unlike fees for alcohol and cinema licences, which are the subject of statutory instrument, the matter is in the hands of the local authority and is only subject to their reasonable discretion although they must ensure that the fees are reviewed from time to time and are sufficient to cover their administrative expenses.

Sending of notice by post

16.—When a licensing authority sends by post, for the purposes of paragraphs 5(6), 9(7), 10(4), 11(12), or 12(7), written notice of its decision, it shall be treated as having been sent within the time required if it was posted so that in the normal course of post it might be expected to be delivered to the person concerned within that time.

DEFINITION
"licensing authority": s.2.

[1][**Electronic communications**

16A.—A licensing authority may determine to accept—
(a) applications for the grant or renewal of a licence under paragraph 1,
(b) objections or representations under paragraph 3,
(c) notifications of a change to a licence under paragraph 9,
by means of an electronic communication.

(2) Where a licensing authority make a determination under sub-paragraph (1) they must—
(a) specify in the determination—
(i) the form of electronic communication by which applications, objections, representations or notifications may be made or given,
(ii) the electronic address to be used for making or giving applications, objections, representations or notifications, and
(iii) any means of authentication (in addition to an electronic signature) that are acceptable, and
(b) publicise the determination as they consider appropriate.

(3) In relation to an application, objection, representation or notification made or given by means of an electronic communication, any requirement of this Schedule for the application, objection, representation or notification—
(a) to be in writing is satisfied if the communication is—
(i) in the form specified under sub-paragraph (2)(a)(i), and
(ii) sent to the address specified under sub-paragraph (2)(a)(ii),
(b) to be signed is satisfied if the communication includes an electronic signature or is authenticated by a means specified under sub-paragraph (2)(a)(iii).

(4) A licensing authority may determine to—
(a) give notices under paragraphs 5, 9, 10, 11 or 12, and
(b) give reasons under paragraph 17,
by means of an electronic communication.

(5) A licensing authority may only give a notice or reasons by means of an electronic communication if—
(a) the person to whom the notice or reasons is or are to be given has agreed to receive notices and reasons by means of an electronic communication, and
(b) the communication is sent to an electronic address, and is in an electronic form, specified for that purpose by the person.

(6) In relation to any notice or reasons given by means of an electronic communication, any requirement of this Schedule for the notice or reasons to be given in writing is satisfied if the communication is sent in accordance with sub-paragraph (5).

(7) When a licensing authority gives a notice or reasons by means of an

electronic communication then, unless the contrary is proved, it is to be treated as having been received by the person to whom it was sent on the second working day after the day on which it was sent.

(8) For the purposes of sub-paragraph (7), "working day" means a day which is not—

(a) a Saturday or Sunday,
(b) Christmas Eve or Christmas Day,
(c) a day which is a bank holiday in Scotland under the Banking and Financial Dealings Act 1971,
(d) a day appointed for public thanksgiving or mourning, or
(e) a day which is a local or public holiday in the area in which the electronic communication is to be sent.

(9) A licensing authority may make different determinations for different purposes including, in particular, for different types of licence.

(10) In this Schedule—

"*electronic communication*" is to be construed in accordance with section 15(1) of the Electronic Communications Act 2000,

"*electronic signature*" is to be construed in accordance with section 7(2) of the Electronic Communications Act 2000.]

NOTE

1. As inserted by the Air Weapons and Licensing (Scotland) Act 2015 (asp 10) Pt 3 s.83 (date yet to be appointed).

DEFINTIONS

"licensing authority": s.2.
"licence": s.8.

GENERAL NOTE

It enables an authority to decide to accept applications, objections and representations and notification of changes by electronic means. They must specify the form of communication which may be used, the electronic address to be used and acceptable means of authentication in addition to an electronic signature. Where electronic communication is accepted then any requirement under this Schedule that a document be in writing is satisfied. An authority may only give notices under the Schedule or reasons under para.17 by electronic means if the recipient has agreed to receipt in that form. Note that there is, in effect, a presumption that where a notice or reasons is given electronically, it is to be treated as having been received by the recipient on the second working day after it was sent unless the contrary is proved. The onus of proving the contrary will rest on the recipient.

Notification of decisions and giving of reasons

17.—(1) A licensing authority shall, within 10 days of being required to do so under sub-paragraph (2) below, give reasons in writing for arriving at any decision of theirs under this Schedule—

(a) to grant or renew a licence or to refuse to do so;
[3](ai) to revoke a licence or to refuse to do so;
(b) to consent or to refuse to consent to a material change in any premises, vehicle or vessel;
(c) to vary or refuse to vary the terms of a licence;
(d) in relation to paragraph 11 above—
 (i) to suspend a licence or to refuse to do so;
 (ii) as to the period of suspension;
 (iii) ordering immediate suspension;
(e) to suspend a licence under paragraph 12 above or to refuse to do so.

(2) Reasons for a decision referred to in sub-paragraph (1) above shall be given by the licensing authority on a request being made to the authority by a relevant person within 21 days of the date of the decision.

(3) Nothing in this paragraph affects the power of the sheriff under paragraph 18 below to require a licensing authority to give reasons for a decision of the authority—

(a) which is being appealed to the sheriff under that paragraph; and

(b) for which reasons have not been given under this paragraph.

(4) In this paragraph, "relevant person" means—

(a) in respect of a decision specified in sub-paragraph (1)(a) above, the applicant or any person who made a relevant objection or representation (within the meaning of paragraph 19 below) in relation to the application to which the decision relates;

(b) in respect of a decision specified in sub-paragraphs (1)(b) to (e) above, the holder of the licence or the chief constable;

[1](c) in respect of a decision specified in sub-paragraphs (1)(b) to (e) above which relates to an activity wholly or mainly carried on—

(i) in premises to which Part 3 of the Fire (Scotland) Act 2005 (asp 5) applies, the enforcing authority;

[2](ii) in any other premise, the Scottish Fire and Rescue Service.

[1](d) in respect of a decision to consent or to refuse to consent to a material change—

(i) in premises to which Part 3 of the Fire (Scotland) Act 2005 (asp 5) applies, the enforcing authority;

[2](ii) in any other premises, the Scottish Fire and Rescue Service. the appropriate relevant authority; and

(e) in respect of a decision specified in sub-paragraph (1)(d) above, any person who, in pursuance of paragraph 11(7)(b) above, was heard by the licensing authority.

NOTES

1. As amended by the Fire (Scotland) Act 2005 (Consequential Modifications and Savings) Order 2006 (SSI 2006/475) Sch.1 para.11 (effective 1 October 2006).

2. As amended by the Police and Fire Reform (Scotland) Act 2012 (asp 8) Sch.7 para.53 (effective 1 April 2013).

3. As inserted by the Air Weapons and Licensing (Scotland) Act 2015 (asp 10) Pt 3 s.78 (date yet to be appointed).

DEFINITIONS

"licensing authority": s.2.
"chief constable": s.8.
"enforcing authority": s.133.
"licence": s.8.
"premises": s.8.

GENERAL NOTE

The legal requirements in respect of reasons for decisions by statutory and quasi-judicial bodies are well settled. In *Wordie Property Co Ltd v Secretary of State for Scotland*, 1984 S.L.T. 345 at 348, Lord President Emslie explained that:

> "The decision must, in short, leave the informed reader and the court in no real and substantial doubt as to what the reasons for it were and what were the material considerations which were taken into account in reaching it."

In *Safeway Stores Plc v National Appeal Panel*, 1996 S.C. 37 it was pointed out that the adequacy of a statement of reasons will depend on the circumstances of the case. However it must deal with the substantial questions in issue in an intelligent way and not leave the informed reader or court in any real doubt as to the reasons for the decision. This was reiterated in *Trust Inns Ltd v City of Glasgow Licensing Board* [2015] CSIH 5 where it was said that the reasons need only address the "material and substantial points that arise for determination" (at [25]). In that case, the Inner House concluded that the absence from the reasons of any reference to a report by the licensing standards officer was demonstrative of the fact that no substantive points emerged from its terms. In *Robertson v City of Edinburgh District Licensing Board*, 1995 S.L.T. 107, it was explained that the phrase "informed reader" could be taken as indicating that such a person is assumed to know what took place at any hearing held by the authority. The authority are not required to produce a detailed account of their determination of the matter dealing with all the factors before it—*Noble v City of Glasgow DC*, 1995 S.L.T. 1315.

It is not necessary to set out in detail the precise thinking behind the reasons, as each member of the committee may attach different weight and significance to the considerations before them: *Ranachan v Renfrew DC*, 1991 S.L.T. 625. The reasons are normally to be taken as the final expression of the collective reasons for the decision. There is a distinction between these reasons and reasons or views expressed by individual members of the committee when arriving at a decision. The latter are to be distinguished from a fully considered statement of reasons given to an interested party and which would inform a decision as to whether there were grounds of appeal—*Ranaldi v City of Edinburgh Council*, 2000 S.L.T. 297, per Lord Justice Clerk Cullen at 298. In contrast in *Black v Dundee City Council*, 2005 S.L.T. (Sh Ct) 139 remarks by the chairman explaining the reason why he was exercising his casting vote in favour of the refusal (that in light of a limit on the number of taxi licences, the committee were bound to refuse an application) disclosed an error in law but this was not reflected in the written reasons. The sheriff held that in the circumstances the reason given by the chairman must be taken as giving the reasons why the decision was made.

If a statement is made that account has been taken of a particular submission, then in the absence of material indicating the contrary, the licensing authority must be taken as having properly addressed the relevant material so that where, for example, a policy of the authority is applicable it is likely to be sufficient if the reasons refer to the submissions made and conclude that in the light of the submissions and the material before it, the authority was not persuaded to make an exemption to the policy (*Calderwood v Renfrewshire Council*, 2004 S.L.T. 219). Note, however, that in *Ritchie v Aberdeen City Council* [2011] CSIH 22; 2011 S.C. 570; 2011 S.L.T. 869 it was observed that where the authority is balancing competing considerations in support of or against a refusal such as factors bearing on fitness and mitigating circumstances, the reasons must display how it carried out the evaluation. In that case, if the authority had regarded itself as carrying out a balancing exercise, the reasons failed to explain why it decided that the mitigating factors were outweighed by the conviction. That appears to be setting a rather higher standard than in the former case (see also *Melville v City of Glasgow Licensing Board*, 2012 G.W.D. 25-534 where the sheriff was critical of the lack of explanation for preferring one body of evidence over another where they were in conflict.) In *Donaldson v Renfrewshire Council* [2011] CSIH 66, it was held that the authority had failed to give adequate reasons in respect that it had not explained, in the context of a change in policy on street trading hours, why it had withdrawn the recognised exceptional status of the appellant in terms of his hours where there was no material to suggest any good reason for discarding his status.

It is not possible for the court to go behind the written reasons provided by the authority in respect of the maters to which they had regard, unless there is something else which indicates the contrary: *Noble v City of Glasgow DC*, 1995 S.L.T. 1315; *Christoforou v Glasgow DC*, 1998 G.W.D. 10-447. If there are gaps in the written reasons the question is whether the gaps are sufficiently formidable to justify the conclusion that the authority had failed to give due consideration to the subject matter of the gaps in reaching the decision: *RW Cairns Ltd v Busby East Kirk Session*, 1985 S.C. 110. It may be clear from the reasons given that the matters not referred to were obviously not important: *Robertson v City of Edinburgh District Licensing Board*, 1995 S.L.T. 107. The Inner House has, however, expressed its disapproval of, "bland, standard pro-forma" statements of reasons: *Din v City of Glasgow District Licensing Board*, 1996 S.L.T. 363 at 367; cf. *Mirza v City of Glasgow District Licensing Board*, 1996 S.C. 450; 1996 S.L.T. 1029. The reasons must not simply replicate the statutory grounds of refusal or suspension: see *Troc Sales Ltd v Kirkcaldy District Licensing Board*, 1982 S.L.T. (Sh Ct) 77; *Speedlift Auto Salvage Ltd v Kyle and Carrick DC*, 1992 S.L.T. (Sh Ct) 57. Where there is a partial refusal of an application, the statement of reasons should make the reasons for this clear: *Brechin Golf and Squash Club v Angus District Licensing Board*, 1993 S.C.L.R. 191; *Scanlan v City of Edinburgh DC*, 1995 S.L.T. (Sh Ct) 89. Where the period granted is shorter than usual, the statement of reasons should make this clear: *McLuskie v City of Glasgow DC*, 1993 S.L.T. 1102.

Subparagraph (1)

An authority is not *obliged* to give written reasons for any of their decisions referred to in (a)–(e) of these subparagraphs unless they are requested to do so in terms of para.17(2). Where the authority have given a reason or reasons at the time when they notified the applicant of their decision, the applicant is entitled to assume that the reason or reasons given were the only reason or reasons for their decision and they do not require to seek further reasons in terms of this subparagraph, and the licensing authority cannot then produce further reasons—*Midlothian DC v Kinnear*, 1993 G.W.D. 3-1931. Where the written reasons do not express the collective will of the licensing committee, this may constitute an error in law—see *Black v Dundee City Council*, 2002 S.L.T. (Sh Ct) 139.

Subparagraph (2)

Reasons must be given where a relevant person as defined in subpara.(4) so requests, within 28 days of the date of the decision. The time limit is directory not mandatory—*Victoria's (Licence) Ltd v Glasgow Licensing Board* (1998) 11 S.L.L.P. 15; *Mumtaz v City of Glasgow Licensing Board* 1998 S.L.T. (Sh Ct) 82; *Lamb & Gardiner Ltd v Perth and Kinross District Licensing Board* (1998) 10 S.L.L.P. 23. Any request for a statement of reasons does not require to be in writing but it is obviously preferable if it is. Since the Act does not prescribe how a statement of reasons is to be delivered, transmission of a statement by fax or, more likely nowadays electronically is sufficient to comply with the statutory requirements—*Victoria's (Licence) Ltd v Glasgow Licensing Board* (1998) 11 S.L.L.P. 15.

Subparagraph (3)

The requirement to give reasons where requested under this paragraph is quite separate from the sheriff's power to require reasons under para.18(6) where they have not previously been given.

Subparagraph (4)

This provision defines "relevant person", as being a person who has a right to request of the authority written reasons for a decision under this Schedule. It is to be noted that this includes not only persons who made a relevant objection or representation in relation to the application which is the subject of the decision but also any person who, in relation to a decision in respect of suspension of a licence, was heard by the authority, being a person who made a complaint relating to matters which were considered at the hearing in respect of the suspension. Where a person who made such a complaint was not heard by the authority when they reached their decision, they are not entitled to request written reasons.

Appeals

18.—(1) Subject to sub-paragraph (2) below, a person who may, under this Schedule, require a licensing authority to give him reasons for their decision may appeal to the sheriff against that decision.

(2) A person shall be entitled to appeal under this paragraph only if he has followed all such procedures under this Schedule for stating his case to the licensing authority as have been made available to him.

(3) A licensing authority may be a party to an appeal under this paragraph.

(4) An appeal under this paragraph shall be made by way of summary application and shall be lodged with the sheriff clerk within 28 days from date of the decision appealed against.

(5) On good cause being shown, the sheriff may hear an appeal under this paragraph notwithstanding that it was not lodged within the time mentioned in sub-paragraph (4) above.

(6) For the purposes of an appeal under this paragraph, the sheriff may, in

the case of a decision of a licensing authority for which reasons have not been given by the authority under paragraph 17 above, require the authority to give reasons for that decision, and the authority shall comply with such a requirement.

(7) The sheriff may uphold an appeal under this paragraph only if he considers that the licensing authority, in arriving at their decision—

(a) erred in law;
(b) based their decision on any incorrect material fact;
(c) acted contrary to natural justice; or
(d) exercised their discretion in an unreasonable manner.

(8) In considering an appeal under this paragraph, the sheriff may hear evidence by or on behalf of any party to the appeal.

(9) On upholding an appeal under this paragraph, the sheriff may—

(a) remit the case with the reasons for his decision to the licensing authority for reconsideration of their decision; or
(b) reverse or modify the decision of the authority,

and on remitting a case under sub-sub-paragraph (a) above, the sheriff may—

(i) specify a date by which the reconsideration by the authority must take place;
(ii) modify any procedural steps which otherwise would be required in relation to the matter by or under any enactment (including this Act).

[1](10) In considering an appeal under this paragraph against suspension or revocation of a licence the sheriff may, pending his decision on the appeal, order the recall of any order by the licensing authority under paragraph 11(10) the suspension or revocation or of any order made by the authority under paragraph 12 above but he shall not do so unless he is satisfied that all steps which in the circumstances were reasonable have been taken with a view to securing that notice of the appeal and an opportunity of being heard with respect to it have been given to the authority.

(11) The sheriff may include in his decision on an appeal under this paragraph such order as to the expenses of the appeal as he thinks proper.

(12) Any party to an appeal to the sheriff under this paragraph may appeal on a point of law from the sheriff's decision to the Court of Session within 28 days from the date of that decision.

NOTE

1. As inserted by the Air Weapons and Licensing (Scotland) Act 2015 (asp 10) Pt 3 s.78 (date yet to be appointed).

Subparagraph (1)

Persons who are entitled to require reasons in terms of the previous paragraph are, subject to the provisions of subpara.(2), entitled to appeal against the authority's decision. Where the parties are the same there is no reason why two appeals cannot be heard in a single summary application, particularly where there is an obvious connection between the two (*Wright v Renfrew DC*, 1993 S.C.L.R. (Notes) 585, dealing with the renewal of a private hire car operator's licence and a taxi driver's licence). In a case involving a late hours catering licence when the licence holder and owner of the premises leased them to a tenant, it was held that there was insufficient material to justify the conclusion that he had lost any interest to seek a further extension of late hours and proceed with an appeal to the sheriff on that matter—*Shahin v Roxburgh DC*, 1996 S.L.T. 457. It has been held that where there is no stateable ground of appeal in an appeal taken by objectors to an application for a licence in order to prevent a competitor trading there was a relevant case of abuse of process for which damages may be sought. The statutory right of appeal provides no immunity against such proceedings: *Asheden Ltd v Amber Entertainments Ltd*, 1996 S.C.L.R. 520.

Subparagraph (2)

Entitlement to appeal is subject to the condition that the person seeking to appeal has followed all available procedures under the Schedule for putting their case to the authority. This would appear to mean that where an applicant, the chief constable, a complainer in terms of para.11(7) and, in appropriate cases, the fire authority do not avail themselves of the opportunity to be heard by the authority in relation to an application, etc. or an applicant has not notified the authority of their views on any relevant objection or representation received in terms of para.4, they would not be entitled to appeal against a decision adverse to them (*Holmes v Hamilton District Council*, 1987 S.C.L.R. 407). This provision means that it is important that parties avail themselves of every opportunity to state their case to the authority prior to any decision being made.

Subparagraph (4)

Appeal procedure is by way of summary application. In relation to the hearing of the summary application and the disposal thereof, see s.50 of the Sheriff Courts (Scotland) Act 1907 and the Act of Sederunt (Summary Applications, Statutory Applications and Appeals etc. Rules) 1999 (SI 1999/929). Procedure in respect of such applications, including the allowance of adjustment of the application and any answers is at the discretion of the sheriff and "is intended to be as simple and expeditious as possible"—*Saleem v Hamilton District Licensing Board*, 1993 S.L.T. 1092 at 1094. In that case the court observed in relation to procedural disputes that it was neither advisable nor helpful to look at ordinary cause rules except in so far as expressly applied. In their application the appellant should not merely recite the statutory grounds of appeal. They must set out the basis upon which they maintain that one or more grounds of appeal are made out in the circumstances of the case—*Sutherland v City of Edinburgh District Licensing Board*, 1984 S.L.T. 241.

Subparagraph (5)

The sheriff has power to entertain an appeal lodged out of time. In *Ahmed v Chief Constable, Strathclyde Police*, 1996 S.L.T. 941 it was held that once an appeal has been timeously lodged and finally disposed of either on the merits or by being dismissed as incompetent, the right of appeal has been exhausted, and so the sheriff was not entitled to consider whether a second appeal ought to be permitted on good cause shown. The requirement to show "cause" would exclude a failure to lodge due to carelessness. Some justification for allowing it to be lodged late would be required. The fact that the statement of reasons requested under para.17 was issued late might be a good cause for hearing an appeal out of time—*Victoria's (Licence) Ltd v City of Glasgow Licensing Board* (1998) 11 S.L.L.P. 15. It is submitted that where the court is deciding this question, it should not take into account the prospects of success of the proposed appeal. That would not have anything to do with "good cause" which looks to the reason for the appeal not being timeously lodged. In *Ahmed v Chief Constable, Strathclyde Police*, 1996 S.L.T. 941 the court reserved opinion as to whether factors unrelated to the reason why the appeal was lodged out of time could be relevant—see also *HD Wines (Inverness) Ltd v Inverness District Licensing Board*, 1982 S.L.T. 73 and *Mahmood v West Lothian Licensing Board*, 1998 S.L.T. 304.

Subparagraph (6)

The sheriff's power to require reasons from the authority may be exercised either where the authority has failed to respond to a request or where no reasons were requested and therefore given and the decision was subsequently appealed. The reason for this power is because the appellant is required to found their appeal upon the stated reasons—*Christoforou v City of Glasgow DC*, 1989 G.W.D. 10-447. This provision applies only where reasons have not been given and cannot be used to amplify reasons already given—*Leisure Inns (UK) Ltd v Perth and Kinross District Licensing Board*, 1993 S.L.T. 796; *Di Ciacca v Lorn, Mid-Argyll, Kintyre and Islay Divisional Licensing Board*, 1994 S.L.T. 1150.

Subparagraph (7)

The grounds on which the sheriff may uphold an appeal are limited to the four grounds set out in subparas (a)–(d). Appeal on the merits is, therefore, excluded.

The words "may uphold an appeal" should be noted. It can be maintained that this gives a sheriff a discretion so that even if they consider that one of the grounds of the appeal has been made out in a particular case this does not mean that the appeal must necessarily succeed. In that regard it may be argued it is only where the basis on which a ground is made out is central to the authority's decision that the appeal should be upheld, hence the use of the word "may". In *Morton v City of Dundee DC*, 1992 S.L.T. (Sh Ct) 2 it was held that the authority had erred in law in considering details of the applicant's "spent" convictions before determining whether or not to admit them in evidence. However, the sheriff also found that the authority would, had it applied the law properly, have been entitled to have regard to the spent convictions by reason of an unspent conviction. In these circumstances it was held that it could not be said that the authority had exercised its discretion in an unreasonable manner and thus the appeal was refused notwithstanding the error in law made by the authority. (See also *Pancham Ltd v City of Glasgow District Licensing Board*, 1997 S.L.T. (Sh Ct) 32.) However, in *Sood Enterprises Ltd v Glasgow City Licensing Board*, 1999 S.L.T. (Sh Ct) 51, it was held that the equivalent phrase in s.39(4) of the Licensing (Scotland) Act 1976 was permissive in force rather than discretionary and simply delimited the grounds of decision. Where the sheriff has held that the authority has erred in law in a material respect in reaching their decision, it is submitted that they should refuse the appeal. If the error vitiated the decision, it should not stand. Ground (b) is predicated on the materiality of the incorrect fact. Ground (c), if established, should result in the appeal being upheld unless the breach was in respect of some issue which had no bearing on the decision reached. Ground (d) relates to the very decision under challenge and if made out should lead to the appeal being upheld. It is suggested that it is only in exceptional cases where the ground of appeal made out relates to some matter that is immaterial to the decision taken by the authority or in respect of some trivial matter that there should be any question of not upholding the appeal. If there are preliminary pleas these should be disposed of prior to consideration of the merits (*Sutherland v City of Edinburgh District Licensing Board*, 1984 S.L.T. 241) although in licensing appeals it is relatively rare for these to be argued. Such a case would be where an issue of competency arises.

Subparagraph (7)(a): An "error in law" would include an authority acting outwith its powers under this Act. Where the authority acts in breach of, or misinterprets any of the provisions of this Act, including this Schedule, in reaching a decision on an application for grant or renewal, variation, suspension or revocation of a licence, it errs in law. This would cover, for example, a failure by the authority to inform an applicant of its intention to include the results of any inquiries into matters which will be taken into account by that authority in reaching a decision; a failure to give the applicant the opportunity to notify the authority of their views on a relevant objection or representation (*Aitken v City of Glasgow District Council*, 1988 S.C.L.R. 281); taking account of an irrelevant consideration such as, for example, a purported objection that was so vague as to be meaningless, or leaving out of account a relevant one in reaching their decision (*McDowell v Cunninghame DC*, 1987 S.C.L.R. 587; *Noble v City of Glasgow DC*, 1983 S.L.T. 800; *Wordie Property Co Ltd v Secretary of State for Scotland*, 1984 S.L.T. 345); applying a policy for ulterior reasons irrelevant to the policy and its intended scope of application (*Gerry Cottle's Circus v City of Edinburgh DC*, 1990 S.L.T. 235); treating the number of objections lodged as a good reason for refusal (*Noble Organisation Ltd v City of Glasgow DC (No.3)*, 1991 S.L.T. 213); refusing an application for a taxi licence under para.5(3)(d) on the ground that the applicant had no direct control over the operation of the vehicle where the Act did not require any such direct control on the part of the applicant (*Intascot Plc v Inverclyde DC*, 1992 G.W.D. 21-1328); and receiving details of "spent" convictions under the Rehabilitation of Offenders Act 1974 before determining whether or not having regard to the circumstances of the case justice requires that these details be admitted in evidence (see pp.151–152 above). In *Killen v Dundee City Council* [2008] CSIH 43; 2008 S.L.T. 739, the authority had refused a licence for a house in multiple occupation on the ground that the premises were not suitable. The reason given was that such use was inconsistent with the designation by the council (as transport authority) as a "home zone". One of the statutory purposes of such a designation was to improve the environment of the area. The Inner House held that the committee had erred in law in proceeding on the basis that there was a necessary inconsistency but observed that had they had before them material from which they could conclude that such use would probably involve activities which were detrimental to the environment, the position would be different.

Where the authority disables itself from exercising the discretion which it is bound to exercise, by, for example, rigidly applying a policy to applications, it is acting outwith its powers under the Act (*Aitken v City of Glasgow DC*, 1988 S.C.L.R. 281; *Holt v Watson*, 1983 S.L.T. 588; *Elder v Ross and Cromarty District Licensing Board*, 1990 S.L.T. 307; *Cinderella's Rockafella's Ltd v City of Glasgow District Licensing Board*, 1994 S.C.L.R. 591). Where an authority had considered that a conviction was a conclusive reason for refusal regardless of any mitigating factors, it was held that it had erred (*Ritchie v Aberdeen City Council* [2011] CSIH 22; 2011 S.C. 570; 2011 S.L.T. 869; *Black v Midlothian Council* [2016] S.C. Edin 14). Note, however, that it has been stressed that a policy may be legitimate even where it was formulated with such precision that it could be described as a rule, always provided that the authority are prepared to listen to submissions that the policy should not be applied (*Sneddon v Renfrewshire Council*, 2009 S.L.T. 563, a case where the policy of the authority embodied in a standard condition was that all vehicles used as taxis had to be wheelchair accessible and the Inner House held that in the circumstances it could not be said that the authority had abrogated the discretion conferred upon them by s.10(2) of the Act). Where an authority had invited applications for taxi licences prior to a survey of taxis in the area it was held that they had not fettered or limited the exercise of their powers prior to the meeting at which licenses were granted as all possibilities that depended on material placed before them remained open until a decision was reached at the meeting (*Falconer v South Ayrshire Council*, 2002 S.L.T. 1033). In *Donald v City of Edinburgh Council*, 2011 G.W.D. 15-372, the sheriff held that the authority erred in law where position on a waiting list of previously unsuccessful candidates for taxi licences had been the dominant consideration in considering multiple applications. In so proceeding the authority had exceeded its powers and acted unreasonably. The sheriff opined that the Act did not expressly provide for a first come first served approach nor could such an approach necessarily be implied standing the time limits for determining applications and the limited reasons for refusal in a situation where demand exceeded availability.

Subparagraph (7)(b): There is a dearth of authority on the issue of an authority basing a decision on an incorrect material fact. It must probably be established that not only was the fact incorrect, but that it was a material one, in the sense of being significant or relevant to the decision which was reached. For this reason it would be necessary for the appellant to aver and establish that the decision was founded to some extent on the incorrect fact (*Aitken v City of Glasgow DC*, 1988 S.C.L.R. 281 at 294). An erroneous inference drawn from correct facts can be equated to an incorrect material fact—see *Art Wells (t/a Corals) v Glasgow District Licensing Board*, 1988 S.C. 289; 1988 S.C.L.R. 531. Where, however, the authority has simply preferred one body of evidence before them and reached their decision on that basis then their decision cannot be challenged as being based on an incorrect material fact. It is for the authority to assess the material or evidence before it and decide what evidence to accept or reject and the weight to attach to such material (*Khan v Aberdeen City Council*, 2005 G.W.D. 9-138; see also *Habib v Central Fife Area Regulation Sub-Committee*, 2008 S.L.T. (Sh Ct) 57).

Subparagraph (7)(c): The principles of natural justice are intended to secure fairness in the conduct of proceedings as between the parties involved. They seek to prevent what is often described as procedural unfairness or irregularity. In *Cigaro (Glasgow) Ltd v City of Glasgow District Licensing Board*, 1983 S.L.T. 549 the Lord President (Emslie), in delivering the opinion of the court, said at 553:

> "There is no magic in the words 'natural justice'. The substance of their meaning was put succinctly by the Lord President (Clyde) in *Barrs v. British Wool Marketing Board* when he said (1957 S.L.T. [153], at 157): 'The question is whether the Tribunal has dealt fairly and equally with the parties before it in arriving at that result'. Here the statute [the Licensing (Scotland) Act 1976] makes it clear that the board is not bound to hear evidence. It may do so but this is entirely a matter within their discretion and a refusal to hear evidence, whatever else it may amount to is not in itself an act contrary to natural justice."

It is essentially a matter of fairness which has been said to involve a general equality of arms and elimination of any notion of ambush in the emergence of material—*Catscratch Ltd v City of Glasgow Licensing Board (No.2)*, 2002 S.L.T. 503, a case concerning the issue of opportunity to respond to an objector's submission, where it was observed that the test under art.6 of the European Convention did not raise any different issues in that case on the question of fairness and equality of arms from those focused by the common law.

Compliance with the procedural rules relating to the notification of results of inquiries and hearings found in para.4 (above), effectively replaces the principles of natural justice so far as these might otherwise be invoked in respect of such matters. Accordingly, a breach of these provisions would ordinarily be characterised as an error in law—*Douglas v City of Glasgow DC*, 1996 S.L.T. 713. However, the principles of natural justice may be invoked where a situation arises for which no provision is made in the Act—*Jolly v Hamilton DC*, 1992 S.L.T. 28. In that case the authority learned, before the meeting at which the application was determined, that the appellant had, through no fault of his own, not been provided with the opportunity to make comments on the result of the authority's inquiries, despite attempts having been made to notify him in terms of para.4(3) and (4). The court held that in these circumstances the authority had, by not giving him the opportunity to present his views, albeit outwith the statutory period, acted contrary to natural justice. Clearly, it would be a breach of natural justice to reach a decision without giving the applicant an opportunity to comment on a matter on which the decision of the authority, so far as disclosed by the written reasons, was based (*GA Estate Agency Ltd v City of Glasgow DC*, 1991 S.C.L.R. 8; *William Hill (Scotland) Ltd v Kyle and Carrick District Licensing Board*, 1991 S.L.T. 559). Even where the statement of reasons makes no reference to such a matter, the fact that it was disclosed to the committee by the clerk may be taken as indicating that the material was considered to be relevant and taken into account (*Douglas v City of Glasgow DC*, 1996 S.L.T. 713). However, the fact that the clerk may have considered the material does not necessarily mean that the committee took account of it in reaching a decision. It may be suggested that the absence of any reference in the statement of reasons to the material—such as a statement that the material was noted or acknowledged—would tend to indicate that the contrary was the case. Equally, it would be contrary to natural justice for an authority to decide a case without giving an applicant an opportunity to comment on relevant objections which have been lodged with the application. In *Coyle v Glasgow City Council* [2012] CSIH 33; 2012 S.L.T. 1018 a submission by the police at the hearing strictly went beyond the terms of the objection in respect that it went into detail as to the circumstances of the offence of which the licence holder had been convicted. It was contended that the authority acted in breach of natural justice in taking account of the submission. The court rejected this holding that the submission was simply putting the conviction in context and, in any event, was made in response to a submission by the licence holder. In *Trust Inns Ltd v Glasgow Licensing Board* [2015] CSIH 5, the court held that where a licensing standards officer's report provided to the board had not been disclosed to the licence holder, the board had not acted unfairly or in breach of natural justice in not disclosing it. Although it had been taken into account by the board, it did not raise any substantive matters that were not already before the board in the application. There was no question of the licence holder suffering any prejudice.

An applicant has no duty to anticipate all possible objections to, e.g. the suitability of premises and it was held in *McAllister v East Dunbartonshire Licensing Board*, 1998 S.L.T. 713 to be a breach of the rules of natural justice for an applicant not to have been given notice of doubts concerning the premises which were referred to by the authority. Note, however, that in that case, it was observed that where specific objection to an application had been lodged it was appropriate for the board to approach the matter on the basis that although there was no onus on him, the applicant had to respond adequately to the objection. This approach was applied in *Chief Constable, Strathclyde Police v North Lanarkshire Licensing Board*, 2003 S.L.T. 1268, where it was pointed out that, although there was no onus on the applicant, if it were considered by the applicant that there was any need for further information there was no reason to suppose that had an approach been made to the objector it would not have been made available so that a failure to request such information was not an adequate response.

In *City of Glasgow Council v Girvan*, 1998 S.L.T. 1004, a case involving an application for a new taxi licence by a person whose late application for renewal of an existing licence the authority had earlier refused to consider, the court reserved its opinion on whether the authority should have given the applicant the opportunity to be heard on the application granted ahead of hers, before the limit in the number of licences held had been reached. Whether such a "late renewal" should be given any priority in consideration over a "completely new" application must be a matter open to question. In *McIndoe v Glasgow District Licensing Board*, 1989 S.C.L.R. 325, it was held to be contrary to natural justice not to have given the licence holder the opportunity to be heard in relation to a period of suspension imposed on him, in terms of para.11.

In a liquor licensing case a distinction was drawn between specific knowledge or private information not available to the other parties in respect of which the rules of natural justice would require disclosure (e.g. *Freeland v City of Glasgow District Licensing Board*, 1979 S.C. 226), and a board considering material submitted on behalf of an applicant and responses thereto where it makes use of its own local knowledge and experience and of the officials who advise it. The latter type of knowledge and experience was something which the board might properly rely upon in drawing inferences from such material when reaching a decision and could do so without specific disclosure (*Pagliocca v City of Glasgow District Licensing Board*, 1995 S.L.T. 180 and *Mirza v City of Glasgow District Licensing Board*, 1996 S.C. 450; 1996 S.L.T. 1029). In *Risky Business Ltd v City of Glasgow Licensing Board*, 2000 S.L.T. 923, the court acknowledged that the board was entitled to draw inferences from the material before them on the basis of local knowledge and experience and to act on its impression and knowledge of local conditions. However, that knowledge has to be identified in any reasons for the decision. In that case the court was unable to identify from the reasons the background knowledge and experience on which the board purported to rely. In *McDonald v Western Isles Licensing Board*, 2001 S.C. 628, the court held that it would be contrary to natural justice for an applicant to have to guess what issues a board may have in mind. In that case the ground of refusal of a regular extension of permitted hours on a Sunday related to Sabbath observance and was only revealed in the written reasons. It was held that in the absence of objections or any intimation of policy on the matter the issue should have been raised at the hearing by the board so as to enable the applicant to address it. It can be said that while an authority would be entitled to draw inferences from material on the basis of such knowledge, that would not entitle them specifically to determine an application on a ground said to be based on such knowledge without giving the applicant the opportunity to address it. To do so would be to act contrary to natural justice. In *Doyle v City of Glasgow DC*, 1995 S.L.T. 327, it was held that lack of notice that driving experience would be the sole criterion used to determine applications for taxi licences, as opposed to taxi driver's licences, together with the use of undisclosed criteria to allocate such licences, amounted to a breach of natural justice, at least in circumstances where the authority had imposed a ceiling on the number of licences, and there was therefore an element of competition between several applicants.

Another way in which an authority may act contrary to natural justice is if they display bias or prejudice in reaching their decision. This does not just cover actual bias or prejudice but also, and perhaps more likely, apparent bias. In relation to the latter the test was authoritatively stated in *Porter v Magill* [2002] 2 A.C. 357, per Lord Hope at [103] as being whether a fair minded and informed observer having considered the relevant facts would conclude that there was a real possibility that the tribunal was biased. He explained that this test was consistent with Scots law. In relation to the issue of bias, one is concerned with the actings of the authority's committee. One cannot necessarily impugn a decision on this ground by reason of the conduct of one member. In *Piper v Kyle and Carrick DC*, 1998 S.L.T. 267, it was observed that, "even if the views of one particular member were prejudiced this would not necessarily invalidate the decision of the committee as a whole"—see also *Matchurban v Kyle and Carrick DC*, 1995 S.L.T. 505. In *Cameron v Fife Council*, 2005 S.L.T. (Sh Ct) 115, it was held that, when two councillors who had sat on school board meetings when a licence application was discussed and where at the hearing the main objector to the licence was the rector of the school, it was contrary to natural justice to have the same two councillors sitting on the committee to determine the licence. Where the chairman of a licensing board made a private visit to an objector in premises adjoining those for which the licence was sought and, on leaving, gave a friendly wave to the objector, this was held sufficient to create in the mind of an observer the suspicion that justice was not impartial—*Mahmood v West Dunbartonshire Licensing Board*, 1998 S.C.L.R. 843. Only in the most exceptional circumstances would a plea of waiver of the rights to natural justice succeed—see *Millar v Dickson*, 2001 S.L.T. 988; *Mahmood*; *Botterills Convenience Stores Ltd v South Lanarkshire Licensing Board*, 2002 G.W.D. 34-1157. Note that a natural justice issue can be raised on appeal even if it was not argued at the original committee hearing—*Mahmood*.

Subparagraph (7)(d): In determining whether an authority has exercised its discretion in an unreasonable manner it has been accepted that the correct approach is upon the lines laid down by the Lord President (Emslie) in *Wordie Property Co Ltd v Secretary of State for Scotland*, 1984 S.L.T. 345, namely that the court will not interfere unless it is satisfied that the decision was so unreasonable that no reasonable authority could have reached it. This view has been taken, notwithstanding the fact that the approach outlined was in the context of judicial review of an exercise of statutory power by a Minister of the Crown (*Noble Organisation Ltd v City of Glasgow DC (No.3)*, 1991 S.L.T. 213, per Lord Justice Clerk (Ross) at 215; cf. Lord Morison at 217–218; *Ranachan v Renfrew DC*, 1991 S.L.T. 625). The "irrationality" test outlined in *Council of Civil Service Unions v Minister for the Civil Service* [1985] A.C. 374 is not considered to be appropriate in this context—*Latif v Motherwell District Licensing Board*, 1994 S.L.T. 414. With this ground of appeal, it is important to stress that the sheriff must not fall into the trap of substituting their own view for that of the authority. The appeal is not a review of the merits. Clearly, the authority must exercise a real discretion in reaching a decision. They must not fetter their discretion by the rigid application of a policy (for example, one limiting the number of taxi licences to be issued in respect of a particular activity in the area) without considering the merits of each individual application, including relevant personal circumstances and any argument that might be put forward to the effect that the policy should not apply to that particular application. If they do so, they err in law: *Aitken v City of Glasgow DC*, 1988 S.C.L.R. 281; *Piper v Kyle and Carrick DC*, 1988 S.L.T. 267; *Douglas v City of Glasgow DC*, 1996 S.L.T. 713. This is perhaps of particular significance in cases such as *Douglas*, where an applicant has failed to lodge an application for renewal timeously and, consequently, has required to make an application for a "new" licence, only to be faced with a limit on the number of licences held having been reached by the time that the application is considered with the result that the authority may consider refusal under s.10(3) of the Act—see also *City of Glasgow Council v Girvan*, 1998 S.L.T. 1004; *Coyle v City of Glasgow Council*, 1998 S.L.T. 453. While a policy may, of course, be followed it must be applied in a rational and fair way. The authority should not act capriciously or in an arbitrary manner—*Piper v Kyle and Carrick DC*, 1988 S.L.T. 267.

It has been pointed out above that the authority must take into account, in reaching a decision, only relevant considerations and exclude all irrelevant ones. Provided that the considerations are all relevant and material then the weight given to them in reaching a decision is a matter for the discretion of the licensing authority—*Texaco Ltd v City of Glasgow Licensing Board*, 1998 S.C. 131. The licensing authority must not apply a policy for ulterior reasons quite irrelevant to the policy—*Gerry Cottle's Circus v City of Glasgow DC*, 1990 S.L.T. 235. A consideration of relevant material only by officials and not by members of the authority would amount to a failure to act reasonably—*City Cabs (Edinburgh) Ltd v City of Edinburgh DC*, 1988 S.L.T. 184. Lapse of time between the commission of an offence and suspension would not per se be determinative of an unreasonable exercise of discretion—*Manley v Renfrew District Licensing Board* unreported 10 July 1996 Paisley Sheriff Court; cf. *McKenzie v Renfrew District Licensing Board*, 1991 S.C.L.R. 859 (Note). It has been held that an authority did not err in taking into account experience as a taxi driver in considering applications for taxi licences—*Doyle v City of Glasgow DC*, 1995 S.L.T. 327, where it was said that such experience could be relevant in undertaking the responsibilities of a taxi operator. In *City of Glasgow Council v Girvan*, 1998 S.L.T. 1004 it was held that the personal circumstances prayed in aid by the applicant for failure to renew timeously (family bereavement) were such that no reasonable authority could properly have disregarded them without consideration. In contrast, in *Coutie v Dundee City Council* [2009] CSIH 88; 2010 S.L.T. 61, it was held that it was not unreasonable for the authority, in accordance with its policy, to have imposed a condition on a taxi licence that it be accessible by disabled persons despite the fact that the applicant had contended that only he would be driving the taxi and that he suffered from a medical condition that prevented him from assisting disabled passengers. The Inner House, reversing the sheriff, held that it was reasonable for the authority to have envisaged that notwithstanding the stated intention of the applicant, the taxi would possibly be driven by others. Where the reasonableness of the policy was not challenged it could not be said that the decision was one which no reasonable authority would have reached. Where applications are granted with fairly minimal restrictions (e.g. where a late hours catering licence is curtailed for half an hour) the court may well overturn such a restriction where no apparent reason for so doing has been put forward by the licensing authority—*Ali v Banff and Buchan DC*, 1990 G.W.D. 18-1017; *Brechin Golf and Squash Club v Angus District Licensing Board*, 1993 S.C.L.R. 191.

A number of cases have concerned consideration by the authority of previous convictions of an applicant, relative to the issue of whether the applicant is a fit and proper person to hold a licence. It is settled that it is for the authority to determine whether the previous convictions bear upon the applicant's fitness to hold a licence and that it is not for the sheriff on appeal to substitute their view for that of the authority. Likewise, the weight to be attached to the convictions is a matter for the authority, not the sheriff, having regard to what it conceives to be the interests of the public as a whole (*Ranachan v Renfrew DC*, 1991 S.L.T. 625; *Hughes v Hamilton DC*, 1991 S.L.T. 628). The extent of the discretion is illustrated in *Forrestfield Hotel Ltd v Monklands District Licensing Board*, 1994 S.L.T. 823. In that case it was held that the board had not exercised their discretion unreasonably where they had refused an application for renewal of a licence on the basis of a previous conviction of a director of the applicant company which had not been brought to their attention when the licence had previously been transferred even though there had been no further convictions and no complaints. The previous conviction must, of course, be of such a nature that it could reasonably be held to be relevant to the applicant's fitness to hold the particular licence. In this regard, it was held in *Ranachan v Renfrew DC*, 1991 S.L.T. 625, that previous convictions for assault and breach of the peace were relevant to the question of fitness to hold a taxi driver's licence, and in *Hughes v Hamilton DC*, 1991 S.L.T. 628, convictions under s.62(1) of the Control of Pollution Act 1974, which prohibits the operation of a loudspeaker in a street for the purpose of advertising a trade or business, were relevant in relation to a street trader's licence. In contrast, in *McDowall v Cunninghame DC*, 1987 S.C.L.R. 587 it was held that a conviction for speeding could be of no relevance in relation to the holding of a taxi licence. However, in *Middleton v Dundee City Council*, 2001 S.L.T. 287 it was held that the authority was entitled to conclude that an applicant was not a fit and proper person to be the holder of a taxi licence on the basis of a number of convictions for driving offences. It was pointed out that in *McDowall* it was not suggested that the convictions were looked at as indicating the nature of the applicant's character. While, as has been stressed, it is for the authority to decide whether past offences bear upon an applicant's fitness, and to determine the weight to be attached to those offences, it must nevertheless act consistently in respect of the applications before it. Accordingly, in *Cashley v City of Dundee DC*, 1994 S.L.T. 1111 it was held that the authority exercised its discretion in an unreasonable manner by refusing an application on the ground that the applicant was not a fit and proper person by reason of previous convictions where, at the same meeting, licences had been granted to applicants with more serious criminal records. It may be questioned whether, in principle, *Cashley* could extend to comparing one case with the facts and circumstances in another individual case as opposed to a tract of decisions from which a policy could be deduced—*Allied Domecq Retailing Ltd v City of Glasgow Licensing Board*, 1999 G.W.D. 8-403. In *Fife Regulation and Licensing Committee v Ewing* [2011] CSIH 45; 2011 S.L.T. 1250, the court held that the sheriff ought to have declined to receive as a production a precis of previous decisions of the authority on similar applications to show that it had granted licences to applicants with more penalty points than in the instant case but having received it, should have attached no weight to it. It contained partial information and disclosed nothing about the circumstances of each case, the convictions or personal circumstances. It was said that there might be cases where on cogent evidence a sheriff could hold that the decision was unreasonable as being inconsistent with the authority's settled policy and practice but that was not the case here.

Subparagraph (8)

While evidence may be led by any party in an appeal, whatever the grounds of the appeal under the previous subparagraph, it is to be noted that the matter is within the discretion of the sheriff—"the sheriff *may* hear evidence". Accordingly, it would appear that when the sheriff is of the opinion that no useful purpose in relation to the pursuit of or opposition to an appeal would be served by leading evidence they may refuse to hear it. This would be the case where, for example, the complaint was simply that the licensing authority had erred in law. In many cases, whatever the ground of appeal, the sheriff will be in a position to determine the appeal on the basis of the material and submissions before the authority. It should usually be apparent from the terms of the application to the sheriff whether or not a party is likely to seek to lead evidence at the appeal hearing. In *Habib v Central Fife Area Regulation Sub-Committee*, 2008 S.L.T. (Sh Ct) 57 the sheriff pointed out that the evidence proposed to be led must be relevant to a particular ground of appeal. In that case it was suggested that the authority had proceeded upon an incorrect material fact. However, the provision was not intended to enable an appellant to "re-litigate" the issues decided by the authority where there was no issue that the authority had been entitled to reach the conclusion which it did on the basis of the material before it.

Subparagraph (9)

Since the licensing authority are vested with the responsibility of granting or refusing applications for grant or renewal it is appropriate that, in the event of a successful appeal, the sheriff should remit the case back to the authority for reconsideration of its decision in the light of the sheriff's determination of the appeal. It has been said that "compelling reasons" are required for removing that responsibility from the authority—*Matchurban Ltd v Kyle and Carrick DC*, 1995 S.L.T. 505. The sheriff should only take the step of reversing the decision and determining the application themselves in three situations.

The first is where the circumstances of the appeal having been sustained, there could be no other outcome than a decision to the opposite effect of that originally reached by the licensing authority. This should apply where the court, having decided that the purported basis of a decision by the authority to refuse an application could not stand, considers that there was no other material before the authority which could justify a refusal—*Risky Business Ltd v City of Glasgow Licensing Board*, 2000 S.L.T. 923 and *Speedlift Auto Salvage Ltd v Kyle and Carrick DC*, 1992 S.L.T. (Sh Ct) 57, where there were no valid reasons following appeal for refusing the application for a second-hand dealer's licence. In *Donald v City of Edinburgh Council*, 2011 G.W.D. 15-372, where the sheriff, having upheld an appeal against the authority's refusal because of the reliance on a waiting list, reversed the decision and granted the licence. He held that if the waiting list was left out of account, the applicant would have been granted a licence.

The second situation is where the authority's consideration of the application or conduct of any hearing has been so improper or so contrary to natural justice that the sheriff considers that the licensing authority cannot now be safely trusted to deal with the case again (e.g. *Coppola v Midlothian District Licensing Board*, 1983 S.L.T. (Sh Ct) 95). See also *GA Estate Agency Ltd v City of Glasgow District Council*, 1991 S.L.T. 16; cf. *Matchurban Ltd v Kyle and Carrick DC*, 1995 S.L.T. 505 and *Botterills of Blantyre v Hamilton District Licensing Board*, 1986 S.L.T. 14 at 16.

The final situation is where by reason of change of circumstances or lapse of time it would not be appropriate to remit. In *McLuskie v City of Glasgow DC*, 1993 S.L.T. 1102, where the licensing authority had failed to give reasons for a decision to grant a licence for a restricted period, the Court of Session declined to remit the case back to the sheriff with instructions to remit back to the licensing authority because it would serve no useful purpose to do so by reason of the passage of time and the licensing authority's pleadings that they did not know which facts might have influenced the committee. Any reasons given in these circumstances would have been unlikely to be based on genuine recollection. In *Doyle v City of Glasgow DC*, 1995 S.L.T. 327 at 331–332, Lord McCluskey delivering the opinion of the court said:

> "In our view, it is sufficient for the decision of the present case to point out that it is impossible, either from the point of view of the appellants or from that of the respondents, to return to the situation as it was at the time of the appellants' meeting in January 1992. Not only is it likely that membership of the relevant Committee or Sub-Committee will have changed, but it may well be that the number of taxi licences presently in operation will have altered and, in any event, the three licences which were granted in January 1992 have not been and cannot be revoked; so that the situation of the particular competition, in which eleven applicants were applying for three licences, cannot be recreated. In that situation, it seems to us that substantial justice requires that the present respondents should be granted the licences for which they applied. We appreciate that the effect of such a decision may be to cause the number of licences to exceed that established in the policy and that that may involve prejudice to existing licence holders."

See also *Douglas v City of Glasgow DC*, 1996 S.L.T. 713 at 718, when incorrect action by the authority and altered circumstances since the original decision persuaded the Court of Session not to remit to the authority for reconsideration. It may be thought that where the sheriff is of the view that the appropriate course of action is that the licensing authority's decision stands subject to modification they could simply take that step themselves. This might arise, for example, where the authority has restricted the licence to a specified area or areas, or granted it subject to certain conditions in terms of para.5(1)(b) and (2)(a). However, it can be argued that even if such restrictions or conditions as were imposed are considered by the sheriff to be so unreasonable for whatever reason, the appropriate course is to allow the authority to reconsider the matter.

On remitting, the sheriff is empowered to permit reconsideration of the decision by the licensing authority without requiring that all procedural steps required, for example, in relation to the consideration of applications under this Schedule, should be gone through again. This could cover, e.g. notification to the applicant of an intention to include the results of inquiries made under para.4. Given that any remit is purely for reconsideration of the decision, it is not thought that there is any need to go through the procedural steps again, prior to consideration, such as the giving of public notice under para.2. In *Hamid v City of Glasgow Licensing Board* (2001) 18 S.L.L.P. 8, an Extra Division reserved their opinion as to whether reconsideration under s.39(6) of the Licensing (Scotland) Act 1976 involved a hearing de novo of the application. They observed that there would clearly be circumstances where a full re-hearing would seem to be unnecessary for the purposes of a remit. This would be the case where the appeal had been allowed on the basis that the authority's reasons were inadequate in the sense of not disclosing clearly why the application had been refused but the court considered that the decision was capable of being supported and explained.

Subparagraph (10)

It might be assumed that this provision is designed to provide the licensing authority with an opportunity to be heard before any such interim order for recall is granted but that is not what the subparagraph states. The sheriff cannot make such an order unless they are satisfied that all reasonable steps have been taken with a view to securing that the authority have been given "notice of *the appeal* and an opportunity of being heard with respect *to it*". However, such an order would require to be sought by way of a motion that would require to be intimated to the authority.

Subparagraph (11)

The sheriff has a discretionary power to make an order as to expenses.

Subparagraph (12)

Appeal is to the Court of Session and is restricted to an appeal on a point of law. This would cover, for example, a sheriff misinterpreting any applicable provisions of this Act or any other relevant legislation so far as material to his decision, or effectively substituting their own views on the merits of the application for those of the authority or not properly considering the issue before them for decision—*Chief Constable, Strathclyde Police v North Lanarkshire Licensing Board*, 2003 S.L.T. 1268. In a liquor licensing case it was stated that in general the effect of s.39(8) of the 1976 Act (the equivalent of this subparagraph) is that the only appeal from the sheriff is to the Court of Session and that it was not competent to appeal to the sheriff principal either on the merits or in respect of an interlocutory decision—*Cambridge Street Properties Ltd v City of Glasgow District Licensing Board*, 1995 S.L.T. 913. It was stated that a question whether a sheriff had properly exercised their discretion was a matter of law and that any appeal on this had to be made by way of statutory appeal to the Court of Session. In *Bantop Ltd v City of Glasgow District Licensing Board*, 1996 S.C. 128; 1996 S.L.T. 552, a case where an objector purported to appeal the refusal of a sheriff to hear evidence in a licensing appeal, an Extra Division of the Court of Session held that the appeal to that court was incompetent. The court held that s.39(8) of the 1976 Act did not contain any provision whereby the right of appeal might be exercised independently of the provisions of the Sheriff Courts (Scotland) Act 1907. The appeal did not fall within s.28 of the 1907 Act. Leave to appeal had not been sought. In these circumstances a right of appeal against an interlocutory decision such as that under challenge could only be exercised in an appeal against the final judgment or determination of the sheriff in the summary application. The grounds of appeal should give proper notice of the matters to be argued (*Fife RC v Kirkcaldy District Licensing Board (No.1)*, 1991 G.W.D. 10-611; *Sutherland v City of Edinburgh District Licensing Board*, 1984 S.L.T. 241) and the absence of a competent ground of appeal or cross-appeal will disable an appellant from pursuing an argument which should have been covered by such a ground (*Chung v Wigtown District Licensing Board*, 1993 S.C. 166; 1993 S.C.L.R. 256). In *Basra v Cunninghame District Licensing Board*, 1995 S.C. 296; 1995 S.L.T. 1013, where an argument was advanced for the first time in a minute of amendment in the Court of Session and had not been the subject of written submissions before the sheriff so that the board had not had proper notice of it, the court indicated that it would not have been prepared to remit the case to the sheriff for a hearing on the matter.

The court will either allow or refuse the appeal. The Court of Session can always consider a point of competency whether or not it has been argued before the sheriff: *Wolfson v City of Glasgow District Licensing Board*, 1981 S.L.T. 17. The Court of Session is not empowered, unlike the sheriff, if so minded, to reverse or modify the licensing authority's decision. If the court affirms the sheriff's decision, that is the end of the matter. Otherwise it may remit the case to the sheriff with a direction that they remit it to the licensing authority to reconsider its decision or remit to the sheriff to proceed as accords. If the court does not consider it appropriate to instruct a remit to the licensing authority then it may remit to the sheriff with an instruction to reverse or modify the authority's decision: *McLuskie v City of Glasgow DC*, 1993 S.L.T. 1102. In relation to a matter where the sheriff has exercised a discretion the Court of Session will only interfere if their decision is wholly unreasonable: *Scotia Leisure v City of Glasgow DC*, 1991 S.C.L.R. 232. Appeal can now be taken from the Court of Session to the UK Supreme Court (formerly the House of Lords): see, e.g. *Caledonian Nightclubs Ltd v City of Glasgow District Licensing Board*, 1996 S.C. (HL) 26; 1996 S.L.T. 451. However, this can now only be done with permission of the Inner House or when that has been refused with permission of the Supreme Court (Court of Session Act 1988 s.40). In order to obtain permission the court must be satisfied that the appeal raises an arguable point of law of general public importance.

[1]Power to make provision about hearings

18A.—(1) The Scottish Ministers may by regulations make provision as to the procedure to be followed at, or in connection with, any hearing to be held by a licensing authority under this Schedule.

(2) Regulations under this paragraph may, in particular, make provision—

- (a) for notice of the hearing to be given to such persons as may be prescribed in the regulations,
- (b) about the rules of evidence which are to apply for the purposes of the hearings,
- (c) about the representation of any party at the hearing,
- (d) as to the times by which any step in the procedure must be taken, and
- (e) as to liability for expenses.

(3) regulations under this paragraph may make different provisions for different purposes including, in particular, different types of licence.

(4) Regulations under this paragraph are subject to the negative procedure.

NOTE

1. As inserted by the Air Weapons and Licensing (Scotland) Act 2015 (asp 10) Pt 3 s.79 (effective 1 December 2015).

GENERAL NOTE

It enables the Scottish Ministers to issue regulations on procedure to be followed at hearings. It is presumably intended to standardise procedures. The reference to rules of evidence and representation indicates a level of formality not hitherto employed. The ability to make provision for liability for expenses is a novel and radical step.

This paragraph came into force on 1 December 2015: Air Weapons and Licensing (Scotland) Act 2015 (Commencement No.1) Order 2015 (SSI 2015/382).

Interpretation

19.—In this Schedule, "relevant objection or representation" means—

- (a) in paragraphs 1 to 4, objection or representation which, under paragraph 3 above, the licensing authority are obliged to or intend to entertain; and
- (b) in the other paragraphs, an objection or representation which, under the said paragraph 3, they were obliged to or intended to entertain.

GENERAL NOTE

This paragraph explains the meaning of the phrase, "relevant objection or representation" under reference to the terms of para.3, which specifies the requirements which must be satisfied before the authority is obliged to entertain an objection or representation.

SCHEDULE 2

CONTROL OF SEX SHOPS AND SEXUAL ENTERTAINMENT VENUE

GENERAL NOTE

Schedule 2 contains the detailed licensing procedures and provisions for sex shops similar to those provided for Pt II licences by Pt I and Sch.1, although it should be noted that these provisions are entirely separate and have no application to Pt III licences which are wholly governed by Sch.2. Where parallels are drawn in the notes to individual paragraphs below to provisions contained in paragraphs of Sch.1 then the notes to those parts of Sch.1 should be referred to with a general caveat that any differences should be carefully noted.

Saving for existing law

1. Nothing in this Schedule—

(a) shall afford a defence to a charge in respect of any offence at common law or under any enactment other than this Schedule;

(b) shall be taken into account in any way—

(i) at a trial for such an offence; or

(ii) in proceedings for condemnation under Schedule 3 to the Customs and Excise Management Act 1979 of goods which section 42 of the Customs Consolidation Act 1876 prohibits to be imported or brought into the United Kingdom as being indecent or obscene; or

(c) shall in any way limit the other powers exercisable under any of those Acts.

GENERAL NOTE

This paragraph preserves existing criminal legislation in relation to obscene material and other offences involving similar activities. Section 42 of the Customs Consolidation Act 1876 was amended by the Statute Law (Repeals) Act 1993 s.1(1) and Sch.1.

Meaning of "sex shop" and "sex article"

2.—(1) In this Schedule "sex shop" means any premises, vehicle, vessel or stall used for a business which consists to a significant degree of selling, hiring, exchanging, lending, display or demonstrating sex articles.

(2) No premises, vehicle, vessel or stall shall be treated as a sex shop by reason only of its use for the exhibition of moving pictures by whatever means produced.

(3) In this Schedule "sex article" means—

(a) anything intended for use in connection with, or for the purpose of stimulating or encouraging—

(i) sexual activity; or

(ii) acts of force or restraint which are associated with sexual activity; and

(b) anything to which sub-paragraph (4) below applies,

but does not include any articles which are manufactured for use primarily for the purposes of birth control or which primarily relate to birth control.

(4) This sub-paragraph applies—

(a) to any article containing or embodying matter to be read or looked at or anything intended to be used, either alone or as one of a set, for the reproduction or manufacture of any such article; and

(b) to any recording of vision or sound, which—

(i) is concerned primarily with the portrayal of, or primarily deals with or relates to, or is intended to stimulate or encourage, sexual activity or acts of force or restraint which are associated with sexual activity; or

(ii) is concerned primarily with the portrayal of, or primarily deals with or relates to, genital organs, or urinary or excretory functions.

GENERAL NOTE

The definitions of both "sex shop" and "sex article" are given in this paragraph which, effectively, defines the scope of Pt III licensing.

Subparagraph (1)

Note that it is not the sale, etc. per se of "sex articles" which are covered but the use of premises by a business which consists "to a significant degree" of these activities. In England it has been held that the quantity of wares sold and their proportion to other goods sold would be relevant but no single factor is decisive and each case will turn on its facts—*Lambeth LBC v Grewal* (1986) 82 Cr. App. R. 301; *R v Peterborough City Council Ex p. Quietlynn Ltd* (1986) 85 L.G.R. 249; *Quietlynn v Southend on Sea BC* [1990] 3 All E.R. 207. In the only reported Scottish case, *Rees v Lees*, 1996 S.C.C.R. 601, the same approach would appear to have been adopted, and it was held that the Crown did not have to show that the majority of the goods sold were "sex articles". The sheriff had been entitled to infer that they formed a "significant degree" of business from evidence of the value of the goods compared with the total sales from the shop as recorded on the till receipt roll—see also the alcohol licensing cases dealing with sales ancillary to petrol sales, etc. for example *BP Express Shopping Ltd v Perth and Kinross Licensing Board*, 2005 S.L.T. 682 and *Safeway Stores Plc v City of Glasgow Licensing Board*, 2001 S.L.T. 1115. Where the "sex shop" consists of an exhibition with individual stall holders then the organiser of the exhibition may require a sex shop licence—*R v Newcastle-upon-Tyne City Council Ex p. The Christian Institute* (2001) 44 L.R.18.

Miscellaneous definitions

3.—In this Schedule—

[*Definition repealed by the Police and Fire Reform (Scotland) Act 2012 (asp 8) Sch.8 para.1 (effective 1 April 2013).*]

[2]"*authorised civilian employee*" means a person—

[1](a) appointed by the Scottish Police Authority under section 26(1) of the Police and Fire Reform (Scotland) Act 2012 (asp 12), and

(b) authorised by the chief constable for the purposes of paragraph 20 of this Schedule.

[1]"*chief constable*" means the chief constable of the Police Service of Scotland.

[*Definition repealed by the Fire (Scotland) Act 2005 (Consequential Modifications and Amendments) Order 2005 (SSI 2005/383) Sch.2 para.1 (effective 2 August 2005).*]

"*relevant objection or representation*" means—

[1](a) in paragraphs 1 to 8, an objection or representation which, under paragraph 8 below, the local authority are obliged to or intend to entertain; and

(b) in the other paragraphs, an objection or representation which, under the said paragraph 8, they were obliged to or intended to entertain.

NOTES

1. As amended by the Local Government etc. (Scotland) Act 1994 (c.39) Sch.13 para.129 (effective 1 April 1996).

2. As amended by the Criminal Justice and Licensing (Scotland) Act 2010 (asp 13) Pt 8 s.173 (effective 13 December 2010).
3. As amended by the Police and Fire Reform (Scotland) Act 2012 (asp 8) Sch.7 para.6 (effective 1 April 2013).

GENERAL NOTE

"Chief constable" and "fire authority" are defined in the same terms as those in s.8; "relevant objection or representation" is defined in the same terms as those in Sch.1 para.19. The phrase "appropriate relevant authority" was amended by the Fire (Scotland) Act 2005 Sch.13 para.129.

Requirement for licences for sex shops

[1]**4.** Subject to the provisions of this Schedule, no person shall in any area in which this Schedule is in effect use any premises, vehicle, vessel or stall as a sex shop except under and in accordance with the terms of a licence granted under this Schedule by the local authority for the area.

NOTE

1. As amended by the Local Government etc. (Scotland) Act 1994 (c.39) Sch.13 para.129 (effective 1 April 1996).

GENERAL NOTE

The sanctions for operating a sex shop without a licence are found in s.19 below.

Waivers

5.—(1) Any person who—

(a) uses in any area any premises, vehicle, vessel or stall as a sex shop; or

(b) proposes to do so,

may apply to the local authority for the area for them to waive the requirement of a licence.

(2) An application under this paragraph may be made either as part of an application for a licence under this Schedule or without any such application.

[1](3) An application under this paragraph shall be made in writing and shall contain the particulars specified in paragraph 6(2) to (6) below and such particulars as the local authority may reasonably require in addition.

[1](4) The local authority may waive the requirement of a licence in any case where they consider that to require a licence would be unreasonable or inappropriate.

[1](5) A waiver may be for such period as the local authority think fit.

[1](6) Where the local authority grant a waiver, they shall notify the chief constable and the applicant for the waiver that they have granted the application.

[1](7) The local authority may at any time give a person who would require a licence but for a waiver notice that the waiver is to terminate on such date, not less than 28 days from the date on which they gave the notice, as may be specified in the notice.

[1](8) The local authority shall give the chief constable a copy of any notice given by them under sub-paragraph (7) above.

NOTE

1. As amended by the Local Government etc. (Scotland) Act 1994 (c.39) Sch.13 para.129 (effective 1 April 1996).

GENERAL NOTE

This paragraph allows a local authority to grant a waiver when they consider that to require a licence would be unreasonable or inappropriate.

Applications for the grant and renewal of licences

6.—[1](1) An application for the grant or renewal of a licence under this Schedule shall be made in writing to the local authority.

(2) An application made by a natural person shall state—

(a) the full name and address of the applicant;

[2](b) the date and place of birth of the applicant;

[2](c) where the applicant himself is not to be carrying on the day to day management of the sex shop, the full name, address and date and place of birth of the person who is, and shall be signed by the applicant or his agent.

(3) An application made by or on behalf of a person other than a natural person shall state—

(a) the full name of the person;

(b) the address of its registered or principal office;

[2](c) the full names, private addresses and dates and places of birth of its directors, partners or other persons responsible for its management; and

[2](d) the full name, private address and date and place of birth of any person who is to carry on the day to day management of the sex shop and shall be executed by the applicant or signed by its agent.

(4) An application relating to premises shall state the full address of the premises.

(5) An application relating to a vehicle, vessel or stall shall state where it is to be used as a sex shop.

[1](6) Every application shall contain such particulars as the local authority may reasonably require in addition to any particulars required under sub-paragraphs (2) to (5) above.

NOTES

1. As amended by the Local Government etc. (Scotland) Act 1994 (c.39) Sch.13 para.129 (effective 1 April 1996).

2. As amended by the Criminal Justice and Licensing (Scotland) Act 2010 (asp 13) Pt 8 s.178 (effective 28 February 2011 for purposes specified in SSI 2010/413 Sch.1; not yet in force otherwise).

GENERAL NOTE

These provisions are similar to those contained in Sch.1 para.1.

Notification of applications

7.—(1) An applicant for the grant or renewal of a licence under this Schedule shall give notice of the application.

[1](2) Notice shall in all cases be given by publishing an advertisement in a newspaper specified by the local authority, being a newspaper circulating in their area and the applicant shall supply a copy of that advertisement to the local authority.

(3) Publication under sub-paragraph (2) above shall be not later than 7 days after the date of the application.

(4) Where the application is in respect of premises, notice of it shall in addition be displayed for 21 days, beginning with the date of the application, on or near the premises in a place where the notice can conveniently be read by the public.

(5) Every notice under this paragraph which relates to premises shall identify the premises.

(6) Every notice under this paragraph which relates to a vehicle, vessel or stall shall specify where it is to be used as a sex shop.

[1](7) Subject to sub-paragraphs (5) and (6) above, a notice under this paragraph shall be in such form as the local authority may prescribe.

[1](8) An applicant for a licence under this Schedule which is to relate to premises shall, as soon as possible after the expiry of the period of 21 days referred to in sub-paragraph (4) above, submit to the local authority a certificate stating that he has complied with sub-paragraphs (4), (5) and (7) above.

(9) An applicant shall not be treated as having failed to comply with sub-paragraph (4) above if the notice was, without any fault or intention of his, removed, obscured or defaced before the 21 days referred to in that sub-paragraph have elapsed, so long as he has taken reasonable steps for its protection and if need be, replacement; and if he has cause to rely on this sub-paragraph, his certificate under sub-paragraph (8) above shall state the relevant circumstances.

(10) Where—

(a) an applicant for a licence under this Schedule—

(i) fails to submit the certificate required by sub-paragraph (8) above;

[1](ii) in the circumstances referred to in sub-paragraph (9) above, has not, in the opinion of the local authority, taken reasonable steps for the protection or, as the case may require, replacement of the notice; or

(b) the local authority is, at any time before they reach a final decision on an application which is in respect of premises, satisfied that the notice was not displayed in accordance with sub-paragraphs (4), (5) and (7) above,

they may require the applicant to display the notice again for a period of 21 days beginning with such date as they may specify and the provisions of this paragraph shall apply in respect of such display as they apply in respect of display under sub-paragraph (4) above.

NOTE

1. As amended by the Local Government etc. (Scotland) Act 1994 (c.39) Sch.13 para.129 (effective 1 April 1996).

GENERAL NOTE

There are similarities between this paragraph and Sch.1 para.2.

Objections and representations

8.—[2,3](1) The local authority shall, as soon as an application for the grant or renewal of a licence under this Schedule is made to them, send a copy of the application to the chief constable and—

(a) where Part 3 of the Fire (Scotland) Act 2005 (asp 5) applies to the premises, vehicle vessel or stall to which the licence relates, to the Scottish Fire and Rescue Service.

(b) where Part 3 of that Act does not so apply, to the appropriate relevant authority.

[2](2) Any objection or representation relating to an application for the grant or renewal of a licence under this Schedule shall, subject to sub-paragraph (3) below, be entertained by the local authority if, but only if, the objection or representation—

(a) is in writing;
(b) specifies the grounds of the objection or, as the case may be, the nature of the representation;
(c) specifies the name and address of the person making it;
(d) is signed by him or on his behalf;
(e) was made to them within 28 days of whichever is the later or, as the case may be, latest of the following dates—
  (i) the date of submission to them of the application;
  (ii) the date when public advertisement was first given under paragraph 7(2) above;
  [1](iii) the date, if any, specified by the local authority under paragraph 7(10) above.

[1](3) Notwithstanding sub-paragraph (2)(e) above, it shall be competent for a local authority to entertain an objection or representation received by them before they take a final decision upon the application to which it relates if they are satisfied that there is sufficient reason why it was not made in the time required under that sub-paragraph.

[1](4) An objection or representation shall be made for the purposes of sub-paragraph (2) above if it is delivered by hand within the time there specified to the local authority or posted (by registered or recorded delivery post) so that in the normal course of post it might be expected to be delivered to them within that time.

[5](4A) Where a local authority have determined to accept objections and representations by means of an electronic communication made under paragraph 22A, an objection or representation is made for the purpose of sub-paragraph (2) if it is sent—
(a) to the authority by means of an electronic communication which complies with the determination, and
(b) within the time specified in sub-paragraph (2).

[5](4B) Sub-paragraph (4A) is without prejudice to sub-paragraph (4).

[1](5) Where the local authority receive notice of a relevant objection or representation they shall, before considering the application, give notice in writing of the general terms of the objection or representation to the applicant but they shall not without the consent of the person making the objection or representation reveal his name or address to the applicant.

[1](6) In considering an application for the grant or renewal of a licence under this Schedule, a local authority may make such reasonable inquiries as they think fit and include the results of these inquiries in matters they take into account, but where they intend so to include any of these results they shall notify the applicant of that intention.

[1,3](7) A local authority may, before reaching a final decision upon such an application, give the applicant and any person who has made a relevant objection or representation an opportunity to be heard by them and, where they propose to do so, must within such reasonable period (not being less than 14 days) of the date of the hearing, notify the applicant and such person of the date.

[1](8) A local authority shall not reach a final decision upon such an application—
(a) in relation to which a relevant objection or representation has been made to them, or in relation to which they intend to take into account any result of their inquiries under sub-paragraph (6) above; and
(b) in respect of which they have not, under this paragraph, given the applicant and any person who has made such objection or representation an opportunity to be heard,

unless they have given the applicant an opportunity to notify them in writing of his views on such objection or representation or, as the case may be, result within such reasonable period (not being less than 7 days) as they may specify.

NOTES

1. As amended by the Local Government etc. (Scotland) Act 1994 (c.39) Sch.13 para.129 (effective 1 April 1996).

2. As amended by the Fire (Scotland) Act 2005 (Consequential Modifications and Savings) Order 2006 (SSI 2006/475) Sch.1 para.11 (effective 1 October 2006).

3. As amended by the Criminal Justice and Licensing (Scotland) Act 2010 (asp 13) Pt 8 s.178 (effective 28 February 2011 for purposes specified in SSI 2010/413 Sch.1; not yet in force otherwise).

4. As amended by the Police and Fire Reform (Scotland) Act 2012 (asp 8) Sch.7 para.53 (effective 1 April 2013).

5. As inserted by the Air Weapons and Licensing (Scotland) Act 2015 (asp 10) Pt 3 s.83 (date yet to be appointed).

GENERAL NOTE

All references to "local authority" were substituted by Sch.13 para.22 to the Local Government etc. (Scotland) Act 1994. Subparagraphs (1) and (2) were amended by the Fire (Scotland) Act 2005 (Consequential Modifications and Amendments) Order 2005 (SSI 2005/383) para.7 and substituted by the Fire (Scotland) Act 2005 (Consequential Modifications and Savings) Order 2006 (SSI 2006/475) Sch.1 para.11(7)(a). There are parallels between this paragraph and Sch.1 paras 3 and 4. "Relevant objection or representation" is defined in Sch.2 para.3.

Disposal of applications for licences

9.—[1](1) Where an application for the grant or renewal of a licence under this Schedule has been made to a local authority they shall, in accordance with this paragraph—

[4](a) grant or renew the licence;

[1](b) grant or renew the licence subject to conditions; or

(c) refuse to grant or renew the licence.

[5](1A) In granting or renewing a licence under sub-paragraph (1)(a) a local authority may (either or both)—

(a) disapply or vary any standard conditions,

(b) impose conditions in addition to any mandatory or standard conditions to which the licence is subject.

[2,5](2) Subject to sub-paragraph (2A) the conditions referred to in sub-paragraphs (2ZA) and (1A)(b) above shall be such reasonable conditions as the local authority think fit and, without prejudice to that generality, may include conditions regulating—

(a) the hours of opening and closing of sex shops;

[6](b) displays or advertisements on or otherwise connected to or in such shops;

(c) the visibility of the interior of sex shops to passers by.

[2,5](2ZA) A variation made under sub-paragraph (1A)(a) or a condition imposed under sub-paragraph (1A)(b) has no effect in so far as it is inconsistent with any mandatory condition to which the licence is subject.

[5](2A) The conditions referred to in sub-paragraph (1A)(b) above shall not relate to any matter in relation to which requirements or prohibitions are or could be imposed by virtue of Part 3 of the Fire (Scotland) Act 2005 (asp 5).

(3) A licence under this Schedule shall not be granted—

(a) to a person under the age of 18;

(b) to a person who is for the time being disqualified under paragraph 13(10) or 19(5) below;

(c) to a person other than a natural person if any director of it or partner in it or any other person responsible for its management is disqualified under paragraph 13(10) or 19(5) below;

(d) to a person who has been convicted of an offence under paragraphs 19 to 21 below;

[3](e) to a person who is not resident in a member state of the European Union or was not so resident throughout the period of six months immediately preceding the date when the application was made;

[3](f) to a body corporate which is not incorporated in a member state the European Union;

[1](g) to a person who has, within the period of 12 months immediately preceding the date when the application was made, been refused by the same local authority the grant or renewal of a licence under this Schedule for the, vehicle, vessel or stall in respect of which the application is made, unless the refusal has been reversed on appeal; or

[1](h) to a person other than a natural person if any director of it or partner in it or any other person responsible for its management has, within that period, been refused by the same council the grant or renewal of such a licence, unless the refusal has been reversed on appeal.

[1](4) But without prejudice to sub-paragraph (3) above, the local authority shall refuse an application for the grant or renewal of a licence if, in their opinion, one or more of the grounds specified in sub-paragraph (5) below apply.

(5) The grounds mentioned in sub-paragraph (4) above are—

(a) that the applicant or, where the applicant is a person other than a natural person, any director of it or any partner in it or any person responsible for its management, is unsuitable to hold the licence by reason of having been convicted of an offence or for any other reason;

(b) that, if the licence were to be granted or renewed, the business to which it relates would be managed by or carried on for the benefit of a person, other than the applicant, who would be refused the grant or renewal of such a licence if he made the application himself;

[1](c) that the number of sex shops in the relevant locality at the time the application is made is equal to or exceeds the number which the local authority consider is appropriate for that locality;

(d) that the grant or renewal of the licence would be inappropriate, having regard—

(i) to the character of the relevant locality; or

(ii) to the use to which any premises in the vicinity are put; or

(iii) to the layout, character or condition of the premises, vehicle, vessel or stall in respect of which the application is made.

(6) Nil may be an appropriate number for the purposes of sub-paragraph (5)(c) above.

(7) In this paragraph "the relevant locality" means—

(a) in relation to premises, the locality where they are situated; and

(b) in relation to a vehicle, vessel or stall, any locality where it is desired to use it as a sex shop.

NOTES

1. As amended by the Local Government etc. (Scotland) Act 1994 (c.39) Sch.13 para.129 (effective 1 April 1996).

2. As amended by the Fire (Scotland) Act 2005 (Consequential Modifications and Savings) Order 2006 (SSI 2006/475) Sch.1 para.11 (effective 1 October 2006).

3. As amended by the Criminal Justice and Licensing (Scotland) Act 2010 (asp 13) Pt 8 s.178 (effective 28 February 2011 for purposes specified in SSI 2010/413 Sch.1; not yet in force otherwise).

4. As repealed by the Air Weapons and Licensing (Scotland) Act 2015 (asp 10) Pt 3 s.80 (date yet to be appointed).

5. As inserted by the Air Weapons and Licensing (Scotland) Act 2015 (asp 10) Pt 3 s.80 (date yet to be appointed).

6. As inserted by the Air Weapons and Licensing (Scotland) Act 2015 (asp 10) Pt 3 s.81 (date yet to be appointed).

GENERAL NOTE

This paragraph deals with the disposal of applications for sex shop licences and in subpara.(3) gives mandatory reasons for refusing a licence while subpara.(5) gives the local authority additional discretionary grounds for refusing to grant or renew a licence. For an English example of where the renewal of a sex shop licence was refused because of inappropriateness see *R v Birmingham City Council Ex p. Sheptonhurst Ltd* (1989) 87 L.G.R. 830. For a discussion of "relevant locality", see *R v Peterborough City Council Ex p. Quietlynn Ltd* (1987) 85 L.G.R. 249. In *Belfast City Council v Miss Behavin' Ltd* [2007] UKHL 19; [2007] 1 W.L.R. 1420, the authority had resolved that the appropriate number of sex shops in the particular locality was nil. A challenge to the effect that insufficient account had been taken of the applicant's art.10 right under the European Convention (freedom of expression) and his right to peaceful enjoyment of his possessions (art.1 of the First Protocol) failed. The House of Lords held that the authority exercised its powers rationally and in accordance with the statutory provisions and therefore their decision could not be described as disproportionate. For examples of licensing authority practice in relation to sex shops see *R v Rushmoor BC Ex p. Sheptonhurst Ltd, The Independent*, 3 February 1988; *R v Bournemouth BC Ex p. McCann* (1988) C.D. 3197/97; *R v Bridgenorth BC Ex p. Prime Time Promotions Ltd* [1999] C.O.D. 265; and *R v Wandsworth LBC Ex p. Darker Enterprises Ltd* (1999) 1 L.G.L.R. 1. For cases dealing with whether sexual entertainment venues should be refused having regard to the character of the locality see *R (on the application of KVP Ent Ltd) v South Bucks DC* [2013] EWHC 926 (Admin) and *R (on the application of Thompson) v Oxford City Council* [2014] EWCA Civ 94; [2014] 1 W.L.R. 1811.

All references to "local authority" were substituted by the Local Government etc. (Scotland) Act 1994 Sch.13 para.129. Subparagraph (2) was amended by and subpara.(2A) added by the Fire (Scotland) Act 2005 (Consequential Modifications and Savings) Order 2006 (SSI 2006/475) Sch.1 para.11(7)(b)(ii).

Notification of decisions and reasons

10.—[1](1) The local authority shall, in accordance with sub-paragraph (2) below, notify their decision under paragraph 9(1) above to—

(a) the applicant;

(b) the chief constable;

(c) any person who made a relevant objection or representation in relation to the application; and

[2,3](d) where Part 3 of the Fire (Scotland) Act 2005 (asp.5) applies to the premises, vehicle, vessel or stall to which the licence relates, the enforcing authority or, where Part 3 of that Act does not so apply the Scottish Fire and Rescue Service.

[1](2) Notification shall be made under sub-paragraph (1)(a), (b) or (d) above within 7 days of the decision to be notified by sending to the person concerned written notice of the decision and under sub-paragraph (1)(c) above either by so doing or by publishing within that time, in a newspaper circulating in the area of the local authority, notice of the decision.

[1](3) The local authority shall make out and deliver a licence to every person to whom a licence is granted or whose licence is renewed by the authority, and shall, when requested by any such person and on payment of such fee as they may charge under paragraph 18 below, make out a duplicate of any licence issued under this sub-paragraph and certify such duplicate to be a true copy of that original licence; and any document purporting to be so certified by the proper officer of the authority shall be sufficient evidence of the terms of that licence.

NOTES

1. As amended by the Local Government etc. (Scotland) Act 1994 (c.39) Sch.13 para.129 (effective 1 April 1996).

2. As amended by the Fire (Scotland) Act 2005 (Consequential Modifications and Savings) Order 2006 (SSI 2006/475) Sch.1 para.11 (effective 1 October 2006).

3. As amended by the Police and Fire Reform (Scotland) Act 2012 (asp 8) Sch.7 para.53 (effective 1 April 2013).

GENERAL NOTE

These provisions for the notification of reasons are paralleled in Sch.1 para.5(4)–(7).

Display of licences in sex shops

11. The holder of a licence under this Schedule shall keep exhibited in a suitable place to be specified in the licence a copy of the licence.

Duration of licences

12.—[1](1) Subject to and in accordance with the provisions of this paragraph, a licence shall come into force on being granted by the local authority or on such later date as they may specify as a condition of the licence and shall continue in force on being renewed by them.

(2) Subject to the provisions of this paragraph, a licence shall have effect—

(a) for a period of one year from the date when it comes into force; or

[1](b) for such shorter period as the local authority may decide at the time when they grant or renew the licence.

[1](3) If an application for the renewal of a licence is made before its expiry the existing licence shall continue to have effect until a final decision on the application is taken by the local authority.

[2](3A) On good cause being shown, a local authority may, for the purposes of sub-paragraph (3), deem an application for renewal of a licence made up to 28 days after the expiry of the licence to be an application made before the expiry.

[1](4) In the event of the death of the holder of a licence granted under this Schedule, the licence shall be deemed to have been granted to his executor and shall, unless previously revoked or surrendered, remain in force until the end of the period of 3 months beginning with the death and shall then expire; but the local authority may from time to time, on the application of the executor, extend or further extend that period if they are satisfied that the extension is necessary for the purpose of winding up the deceased's estate and that no other circumstances make it undesirable.

(5) Where a relevant objection of representation has been made in relation to an application for the grant of a licence, that licence shall not come into force until—

(a) the time within which an appeal under paragraph 24 below against the grant of the licence may be made has elapsed; or

(b) where such an appeal has been lodged, it has been abandoned or determined in favour of the applicant.

[1](6) Notwithstanding that an application for renewal of a licence has been refused by a local authority, the existing licence shall continue in force until—

(a) the time within which an appeal under paragraph 24 below against the refusal to renew may be made has elapsed; or

(b) where such an appeal has been lodged, it has been abandoned or determined against the applicant or, if determined in favour of the applicant, the time when the licence is renewed.

(7) This paragraph is subject to paragraphs 13, 15 and 16 below.

NOTES

1. As amended by the Local Government etc. (Scotland) Act 1994 (c.39) Sch.13 para.129 (effective 1 April 1996).

2. As amended by the Criminal Justice and Licensing (Scotland) Act 2010 (asp 13) Pt 8 s.178 (effective 28 February 2011 for purposes specified in SSI 2010/413 Sch.1; not yet in force otherwise).

3. As amended by the Police and Fire Reform (Scotland) Act 2012 (asp 8) Sch.7 para.53 (effective 1 April 2013).

GENERAL NOTE

Many of the provisions found in this paragraph are found also in Sch.1 para.8 but note that the normal period for the duration of a licence is one year and not three years as in the case of Pt II activities. All references to "local authority" were substituted by Sch.13 para.129(22)(e) to the Local Government etc. (Scotland) Act 1994.

Revocation of licences

13.—[1](1) The local authority may at any time revoke a licence under this Schedule—

(a) if, at any time of revocation, it could not, under sub-paragraph (3) of paragraph 9 above, be granted;

(b) if, in their opinion, any of the grounds specified in sub-paragraph (5)(a) or (b) of that paragraph apply; or

(c) if a condition of the licence has been contravened.

[1](2) A local authority may revoke a licence under sub-paragraph (1)(c) above in respect of a contravention of a condition of a licence notwithstanding that there has been no conviction in that respect.

(3) In considering whether to revoke a licence the appropriate authority may make such reasonable inquiries as they think fit and, subject to sub-paragraph (4) below, include the results of their inquiries in the matters to which they have regard in such consideration.

[1](4) Where a local authority intend to include any of the results of their inquiries under sub-paragraph (3) above in the matters to which they have regard for the purposes of this paragraph, they shall notify the holder of the licence of that intention.

[1](5) A local authority, in considering whether or not to revoke a licence, may, but before deciding to revoke it shall, give—

(a) the holder of the licence;

(b) any person who has made a complaint relevant to the matters to be considered at the hearing;

(c) the chief constable; and

[2,3](d) where Part 3 of the Fire (Scotland) Act 2005 (asp 5) applies to the premises, vehicle, vessel or stall to which the licence relates, the enforcing authority or, where Part 3 of that Act does not so apply, the Scottish Fire and Rescue Service,

an opportunity to be heard by them.

[1,4](6) The local authority shall have complied with their duty under sub-paragraph (5) above sent to the persons entitled under that sub-paragraph to an opportunity to be heard not later than 14 days before the hearing, notice in writing that the authority propose to hold a hearing, together with written notice of the general terms of the complaint and a note of the grounds upon which the revocation of the licence is to be considered and, where they decide to exercise their power under that sub-paragraph, they shall cause such notices and note to be sent to those persons not later than that time.

[1](7) Where a local authority decide to revoke a licence under this Schedule, the revocation shall not, subject to sub-paragraph (8) below, take effect until the expiry of the time within which the holder of the licence may appeal under paragraph 24 below against the revocation or, if such an appeal has been lodged, until it has been abandoned or determined in favour of the revocation.

[1](8) If, in deciding to revoke a licence under this Schedule, a local authority determines that the circumstances of the case justify immediate revocation, they may, without prejudice to their other powers under this paragraph, order that the licence shall be revoked immediately.

[1](9) A local authority shall, within 7 days of their decision under sub-paragraph (1) above, send written notice of their decision to the persons referred to in sub-paragraph (5)(a), (c) and (d) above in relation to the licence and to any person who, in pursuance of sub-paragraph (5)(b) above, was heard by the authority before they reached that decision.

[1](10) Where a licence under this Schedule is revoked, its holder shall be disqualified from holding or obtaining such a licence in the area of the local authority which revoked it for a period of 12 months beginning with the date of revocation unless the revocation has been reversed on appeal.

NOTES

1. As amended by the Local Government etc. (Scotland) Act 1994 (c.39) Sch.13 para.129 (effective 1 April 1996).

2. As amended by the Fire (Scotland) Act 2005 (Consequential Modifications and Savings) Order 2006 (SSI 2006/475) Sch.1 para.11 (effective 1 October 2006).

3. As amended by the Police and Fire Reform (Scotland) Act 2012 (asp 8) Sch.7 para.53 (effective 1 April 2013).

4. As amended by the Criminal Justice and Licensing (Scotland) Act 2010 (asp 13) Pt 8 s.178 (effective 28 February 2011 for purposes specified in SSI 2010/413 Sch.1; not yet in force otherwise).

GENERAL NOTE

Many of these provisions are similar to the suspension powers found in Sch.1 para.11.

Notification of changes of circumstances

14.—[1](1) Where there is a material change of circumstances affecting a holder of a licence under this Schedule or the business to which it relates, he shall, in accordance with this paragraph, notify the local authority of the change as soon as reasonably practicable after it has taken place.

[1](2) The holder of a licence under this Schedule shall not, unless in accordance with a requirement imposed by or in pursuance of any

enactment other than this Schedule, make or cause to be made or permit there to be made any material change in the premises or, as the case may be, the vehicle, vessel or stall without the prior consent of the local authority.

[1](3) A notification under sub-paragraph (1) above or application for consent under sub-paragraph (2) above shall be accompanied by such fee as the local authority may charge under paragraph 18 below.

[1](4) A local authority, before considering whether or not to give their consent under sub-paragraph (2) above, shall be entitled to require the holder of the licence to furnish them with specification, including plans, of the proposed changes.

[2](5) A local authority before deciding whether or not to give their consent under sub-paragraph (2) above, shall consult the chief constable and, in the case of a change in premises, vehicle, vessel or stall—

(a) where Part 3 of the Fire (Scotland) Act 2005 (asp 5) applies to the premises, vehicle, vessel or stall, the enforcing authority;

[3](b) where Part 3 of that Act does not so apply, the Scottish Fire and Rescue Service.

[1](6) Where the local authority have given their consent under sub-paragraph (2) above to a change in premises or a vehicle, vessel or stall it shall not be necessary for the holder of the licence relating to those premises or that vehicle, vessel or stall to notify the local authority of that change under sub-paragraph (1) above.

[1,2,3](7) A local authority shall, within 7 days of their decision under sub-paragraph (2) above, send written notice of their decision to the holder of the licence, the chief constable and either the enforcing authority where Part 3 of that Act applies in relation to the premises, vehicle, vessel or stall or, where Part 3 of that Act does not so apply, the appropriate relevant authority.

(8) In this paragraph, a "material change" includes any material change in the particulars given or referred to in the application for the grant, or, where the licence has been renewed, the most recent application for the renewal, of the licence.

NOTES

1. As amended by the Local Government etc. (Scotland) Act 1994 (c.39) Sch.13 para.129 (effective 1 April 1996).

2. As amended by the Fire (Scotland) Act 2005 (Consequential Modifications and Savings) Order 2006 (SSI 2006/475) Sch.1 para.11 (effective 1 October 2006).

3. As amended by the Police and Fire Reform (Scotland) Act 2012 (asp 8) Sch.7 para.53 (effective 1 April 2013).

GENERAL NOTE

This paragraph contains similarities to Sch.1 para.9.

Variation of licences

15.—[1](1) A local authority may, at any time, whether or not upon application made to them by the holder of the licence, vary the terms of a licence on any grounds they think fit and such variation shall come into force on such date as they may specify.

[1](2) A local authority, before proceeding to vary the terms of a licence under sub-paragraph (1) above—

[3](a) shall, not later than 7 days before the day on which the proposed variation is to be considered, notify the holder of the licence, the chief constable and the Scottish Fire and Rescue Service of the proposed variation; and

[1](b) shall give each of the persons mentioned in sub-paragraph (a) above an opportunity to be heard by the authority on that day.

[2,3](2A) Where the proposed variation is in respect of a licence which relates to any premises, vehicle, vessel or stall to which Part 3 of the Fire (Scotland) Act 2005 (asp 5) applies, sub-paragraph (2)(a) above applies as if the reference to the Scottish Fire and Rescue Service were a reference to the enforcing authority.

[1](3) A local authority shall have complied with sub-paragraph (2)(b) above if they have invited each of the persons whom they must notify under that sub-paragraph to attend and to be heard by the authority when the variation of the licence is to be considered.

(4) A variation in the terms of a licence shall come into force—

(a) when the time within which an appeal under paragraph 24 below may be made has elapsed; or

(b) where such an appeal has been lodged, when the appeal has been abandoned or determined in favour of the variation.

[4](4A) Sub-paragraph (4) does not apply to a deemed variation of the terms of a licence under section 45D(4).

[1,2,3](5) A local authority shall, within 7 days of their decision under sub-paragraph (1) above, send written notice of their decision to the holder of the licence, the chief constable and either the enforcing authority where Part 3 of that Act applies in relation to the premises, vehicle, vessel or stall or, where Part 3 of that Act does not so apply, the appropriate relevant authority.

NOTES

1. As amended by the Local Government etc. (Scotland) Act 1994 (c.39) Sch.13 para.129 (effective 1 April 1996).

2. As amended by the Fire (Scotland) Act 2005 (Consequential Modifications and Savings) Order 2006 (SSI 2006/475) Sch.1 para.11 (effective 1 October 2006).

3. As amended by the Police and Fire Reform (Scotland) Act 2012 (asp 8) Sch.7 para.53 (effective 1 April 2013).

4. As amended by the Air Weapons and Licensing (Scotland) Act 2015 (asp 10) Pt 3 s.77 (date yet to be appointed).

GENERAL NOTE

These provisions are similar to those found in Sch.1 para.10.

Surrender of licence

16.—[1](1) A holder of a licence may at any time surrender the licence to the local authority and it shall thereupon cease to have effect.

[1](2) A holder of a licence shall deliver the licence to the local authority—

[1](a) within 7 days after the coming into effect of a decision of a local authority, under paragraph 13 above, to revoke or, under paragraph 15 above, to vary the terms of the licence or the decision of a court, under paragraph 19(5) below, to revoke it;

(b) where the licence relates to a sex shop which he has ceased to use as such within 7 days of such cessation.

[1](3) A local authority shall, on revoking or varying the terms of a licence, cause notice in writing to be given to the holder of the licence of his duty to deliver it up under sub-paragraph (2) above.

(4) Where a licence has been surrendered under this paragraph on its revocation under paragraph 13 or 19(5)(a) of this Schedule and the revocation is quashed or recalled, the local authority shall re-issue the licence.

NOTE

1. As amended by the Local Government etc. (Scotland) Act 1994 (c.39) Sch.13 para.129 (effective 1 April 1996).

GENERAL NOTE

This paragraph has a parallel in Sch.1 para.13.

Register of applications

17.—[1](1) A local authority shall cause to be kept a register of applications under this Section (in this paragraph referred to as "the register") and shall, as soon as reasonably practicable after—

(a) the receipt of each application, cause details of such receipt; and

(b) their final decision on each application, cause details of that decision

to be entered in the register.

(2) The register shall include—

[1](a) a note of the terms of each licence granted by the local authority;

(b) a note of any revocation or variation of the terms or surrender of a licence.

(3) The register shall be open to the inspection of any member of the public at such reasonable times and places as may be determined by the authority and any member of the public may make a copy thereof or an extract therefrom.

[1](4) A local authority may, on payment of such fee as they may charge under paragraph 18 below, issue a certified true copy of any entry in the register; and any document purporting to be certified by the proper officer of the authority as a true copy of an entry shall be sufficient evidence of the terms of the original entry.

NOTE

1. As amended by the Local Government etc. (Scotland) Act 1994 (c.39) Sch.13 para.129 (effective 1 April 1996).

GENERAL NOTE

These provisions are similar to those in Sch.1 para.14.

Fees

18.—[1](1) A local authority shall, subject to sub-paragraph (2) below—

(a) in respect of applications made to them for the grant or renewal of a licence under this Schedule;

(b) in respect of their consideration of a material change in circumstances under paragraph 14 above and their disposal of the matter;

(c) in respect of applications made to them for the variation of a licence under this Schedule;

(d) in respect of the issue of certified duplicate licences under paragraph 10(3) above;

(e) in respect of the issue under paragraph 17 above of certified true copies;

charge such reasonable fees as they may, in accordance with sub-paragraph (2) below, determine; and the authority may under this sub-paragraph determine different fees for the different matters specified in this sub-paragraph.

[1](2) In determining the amount of the different fees under sub-paragraph (1) above, the local authority shall seek to ensure that from time to time the

total amount of fees receivable by the authority is sufficient to meet the expenses of the authority in exercising their functions under this Schedule.

NOTE

1. As amended by the Local Government etc. (Scotland) Act 1994 (c.39) Sch.13 para.129 (effective 1 April 1996).

GENERAL NOTE

The provisions for fees are similar to those applicable to Pt II licences—see Sch.1 para.15. Examples of "reasonable" fees for such establishments is found in the English case of *R v Stoke-upon-Trent City Council Ex p. Sheptonhurst Ltd* (1983) 83 L.G.R. 461.

Enforcement

19.—(1) A person who—

(a) without reasonable excuse uses any premises, vehicle, vessel or stall as a sex shop without having a licence under this Schedule for that use or there being in force a waiver under paragraph 5 above for that use or knowingly causes or permits the use of any premises, vehicle, vessel or stall as a sex shop without there being a licence for that use or there being in force a waiver under paragraph 5 above for that use; or

(b) being the holder of a licence for a sex shop, employs in the business of the sex shop any person known to him to be a person to whom under paragraph 9(3) above a licence could not be granted; or

(c) being the holder of a licence under this Schedule, without reasonable excuse knowingly contravenes, or without reasonable excuse knowingly permits the contravention of, a term or condition specified in the licence; or

(d) being the servant, employee or agent of the holder of a licence under this Schedule, without reasonable excuse knowingly contravenes, or without reasonable excuse knowingly permits the contravention of, a term or condition specified in the licence; or

(e) being the holder of a licence under this Schedule or the servant, employee or agent of such person, without reasonable excuse knowingly permits any person under the age of 18 to enter the sex shop;

shall be guilty of an offence.

(2) Any person who, in connection with an application for the grant or renewal of a licence under this Schedule, makes any statement which he knows to be false or recklessly makes any statement which is false in a material particular shall be guilty of an offence.

(3) A person guilty of an offence under sub-paragraph (1) or (2) above shall be liable, on summary conviction, to a fine not exceeding £20,000.

(4) A person who, being the holder of a licence under this Schedule, fails without reasonable excuse to comply with—

(a) paragraph 11 or 16(2) above shall be guilty of an offence and liable, on summary conviction, to a fine not exceeding level 3 on the standard scale.

(b) paragraph 14 above shall be guilty of an offence and liable, on summary conviction, to a fine not exceeding level 5 on the standard scale.

(5) Where a holder of a licence under this Schedule is convicted of an offence under this paragraph or paragraph 20 or 21 below the court by which he is convicted may, in addition to any other penalty which the court

may impose, make an order in accordance with one or both of the following paragraphs—

(a) that the licence shall be revoked;

(b) that the holder of the licence shall be disqualified from holding such a licence in Scotland for a period not exceeding 5 years.

(6) A person may appeal against an order under sub-paragraph (5) above in the same manner as against sentence and the court which made the order may, pending the appeal, suspend the effect of the order.

(7) A person may, at any time after the expiry of the first year of his disqualification under sub-paragraph (5) above, apply to the court which ordered the disqualification to remove it, and, on such application, the court may by order remove the disqualification as from such date as may be specified in the order or refuse the application, and, in either case, may order the application to pay the whole or any part of the expenses of such application.

(8) Where the holder of a licence under this Schedule is convicted of an offence under this paragraph or paragraph 20 or 21 below, an extract of such conviction and sentence (if any) shall, within 6 days after the date of the conviction, be transmitted by the clerk of the court to the local authority which granted the licence.

NOTE

1. As amended by the Local Government etc. (Scotland) Act 1994 (c.39) Sch.13 para.129 (effective 1 April 1996).

GENERAL NOTE

This paragraph provides for sanctions so that Pt III can be effectively enforced.

Subparagraph (1)

Offences are created in respect of: (a) using unlicensed premises as a sex shop; (b) employing persons in licensed sex shops who are under 18, disqualified, etc.; (c) contravening conditions of the licence; and (e) permitting a person under 18 to enter the premises. For a general discussion of statutory offences in connection with the 1982 Act, see pp.30–33 above. In *Rees v Lees*, 1996 S.C.C.R. 601, a person held to be carrying on the business of an unlicensed sex shop was erroneously convicted under s.7(1) of the Act. In respect of "persons under 18" it is presumably for the prosecution to prove the age of the person by corroborated evidence and an impression that a person is under 18 would not be corroboration—*Lockwood v Walker*, 1909 2 S.L.T. 400; *Paton v Wilson*, 1988 S.L.T. 634. None of these offences are absolute, i.e. "reasonable excuse" is allowed, see p.31. See also *Westminster City Council v Croyalgrange Ltd* [1986] 1 W.L.R. 674; [1986] 2 All E.R. 873.

Subparagraph (2)

For "falsely and recklessly" see p.32 above.

Subparagraph (3)

Note that this figure is considerably in excess of the maximum fine levied under s.7(1), i.e. level 4 or £2,000 at present—see p.32 above.

Subparagraph (4)

For standard levels of fine see Introduction, p.32 above.

Rights of entry and inspection

20.—[1,2,3](1) Without prejudice to any other provision of this Schedule an authorised officer of the local authority, an authorised civilian employee or a constable may, for the purposes specified in sub-paragraph (2) below, at any reasonable time enter and inspect any premises, vehicle, vessel or stall in relation to which a licence under this Schedule is in force or has been applied for.

(2) The purposes referred to in sub-paragraph (1) above are—

(a) where a licence is in force—

(i) seeing whether the terms of the licence are being complied with and, if they are not, obtaining information in respect of such non-compliance;

(ii) obtaining information relevant to the question whether the licence should be renewed;

(iii) seeing whether paragraph 11 above is being complied with;

(iv) ascertaining whether any person is being employed contrary to paragraph 19(1) above or whether any person under the age of 18 has been permitted to enter the sex shop contrary to that paragraph; or

(b) where the grant of a licence has been applied for, obtaining information relevant to the question whether the application should be granted.

(3) An authorised officer of a local authority or an authorised civilian employee shall not be entitled to exercise the powers which he may exercise under sub-paragraph (1) above until he has produced his authorisation to the person for the time being in charge of the premises, vehicle, vessel or stall.

(4) A constable who is not in uniform shall not be entitled to exercise the powers which he may exercise under sub-paragraph (1) above until he has produced his identification to the person for the time being in charge of the premises, vehicle, vessel or stall.

(5) Any person in charge of any premises, vehicle, vessel or stall who fails without reasonable excuse to permit a constable, an authorised civilian employee or an authorised officer of the local authority who, in pursuance of this paragraph, demands to do so to enter or inspect the premises, vehicle, vessel or stall or obstructs the entry thereto of a constable or such an officer in pursuance of this paragraph shall be guilty of an offence and liable, on summary conviction, to a fine not exceeding level 3 on the standard scale.

NOTES

1. As amended by the Local Government etc. (Scotland) Act 1994 (c.39) Sch.13 para.129 (effective 1 April 1996).

2. As amended by the Fire (Scotland) Act 2005 (Consequential Modifications and Savings) Order 2006 (SSI 2006/475) Sch.2 para.1 (effective 1 October 2006).

3. As amended by the Criminal Justice and Licensing (Scotland) Act 2010 (asp 13) Pt 8 s.173 (effective 13 December 2010).

DEFINITIONS

"authorised civilian employee": s.6.

GENERAL NOTE

The powers to enter and inspect licensed premises are similar to the provisions relating to Pt II licences found in s.5. For level of fines see Introduction, p.32 above.

Powers of entry and search

21.—(1) If a justice of the peace or sheriff is satisfied by evidence on oath that there is reasonable ground for suspecting that—

(a) any premises, vehicle, vessel or stall is being used as a sex shop; and

(b) no licence or waiver under this Schedule is in force in relation to the sex shop,

he may grant a warrant authorising any constable to enter and search the premises, vehicle, vessel or stall specified in the warrant.

(2) A constable may use reasonable force in executing a warrant granted under sub-paragraph (1) above.

(3) A constable who is not in uniform shall produce his identification if required to do so by any person in or upon any premises, vehicle, vessel or stall which the constable is about to enter, is entering or has entered under the powers conferred under sub-paragraph (1) above, and if he has been so required to produce his identification, he shall not be entitled to enter or search the premises, vehicle, vessel or stall or, as the case may be, remain there or continue to search the premises, vehicle, vessel or stall until he has produced it.

(4) Any person who fails without reasonable excuse to permit a constable, in pursuance of this paragraph, to enter and search any premises, vehicle, vessel or stall or who obstructs the entry thereto or search thereof in pursuance of this paragraph by a constable shall be guilty of an offence and liable, on summary conviction, to a fine not exceeding level 3 on the standard scale.

GENERAL NOTE

The powers to enter and search unlicensed premises are similar to the provisions found in s.6. For level of fines see p.32 above.

Sending of notice by post

22. [1]When a local authority sends by post, for the purposes of paragraph 10(2), 13(9), 14(7) or 15(5), written notice of their decision, it shall be treated as having been sent within the time required if it was posted so that in the normal course of post it might be expected to be delivered to the person concerned within that time.

NOTE

1. As amended by the Local Government etc. (Scotland) Act 1994 (c.39) Sch.13 para.129 (effective 1 April 1996).

GENERAL NOTE

This paragraph is in the same terms as Sch.1 para.16.

[1][**Electronic communications**

22A.—(1) A local authority may determine to accept—

(a) applications for the grant or renewal of a licence under this Schedule,

(b) objections or representations under paragraph 8,

(c) notifications of a change to a licence under paragraph 14,

by means of an electronic communication.

(2) Where a local authority make a determination under sub-paragraph (1) they must—

(a) specify in the determination—

(i) the form of electronic communication by which applications, objections, representations or notifications may be made or given,

(ii) the electronic address to be used for making or giving applications, objections, representations or notifications, and

(iii) any means of authentication (in addition to an electronic signature) that are acceptable, and

(b) publicise the determination as they consider appropriate.

(3) In relation to an application, objection, representation or notification made or given by means of an electronic communication, any requirement of this Schedule for the application, objection, representation or notification—

(a) to be in writing is satisfied if the communication is—

(i) in the form specified under sub-paragraph (2)(a)(i), and

(ii) sent to the address specified under sub-paragraph (2)(a)(ii),

(b) be signed is satisfied if the communication includes an electronic signature or is authenticated by a means specified under sub-paragraph (2)(a)(iii).

(4) A local authority may determine to—

(a) give notices under paragraphs 8, 10, 13, 14 or 15, and

(b) give reasons under paragraph 23,

by means of an electronic communication.

(5) A local authority may only give a notice or reasons by means of an electronic communication if—

(a) the person to whom the notice or reasons is or are to be given has agreed to receive notices and reasons by means of an electronic communication, and

(b) the communication is sent to an electronic address, and is in an electronic form, specified for that purpose by the person.

(6) In relation to any notice or reasons given by means of an electronic communication, any requirement of this Schedule for the notice or reasons to be given in writing is satisfied if the communication is sent in accordance with sub-paragraph (5).

(7) When a licensing authority gives a notice or reasons by means of an electronic communication then, unless the contrary is proved, it is to be treated as having been received by the person to whom it was sent on the second working day after the day on which it was sent.

(8) For the purposes of sub-paragraph (7), "working day" means a day which is not—

(a) a Saturday or Sunday,

(b) Christmas Eve or Christmas Day,

(c) a day which is a bank holiday in Scotland under the Banking and Financial Dealings Act 1971,

(d) a day appointed for public thanksgiving or mourning, or

(e) a day which is a local or public holiday in the area to which the electronic communication is sent.

(9) A local authority may make different determinations for different purposes including, in particular, for different types of licence.

(10) In this Schedule—

"electronic communication" is to be construed in accordance with section 15(1) of the Electronic Communications Act 2000,

"electronic signature" is to be construed in accordance with section 7(2) of the Electronic Communications Act 2000.]

NOTE

1. As inserted by the Air Weapons and Licensing (Scotland) Act 2015 (asp 10) Pt 3 s.83 (date yet to be appointed).

Notification of decisions and giving of reasons

23.—[1](1) A local authority shall, within 10 days of being required to do so under sub-paragraph (2) below, give reasons in writing for arriving at any decision of theirs under this Schedule—

(a) to grant or renew a licence under this Schedule or to refuse to do so;

(b) to revoke a licence under this Schedule or not to revoke it;

(c) to consent or to refuse to consent to a material change in any premises, vehicle, vessel or stall;

(d) to vary or to refuse to vary the terms of a licence under this Schedule.

[1,3](2) Reasons for a decision referred to in sub-paragraph (1) above shall be given by the local authority on a request being made to the authority by a relevant person within 21 days of the date of the decision.

[1](3) Nothing in this paragraph affects the power of the sheriff under paragraph 24 below to require a local authority to give reasons for a decision of the local authority—

(a) which is being appealed to the sheriff under that paragraph; and

(b) for which reasons have not been given under this paragraph.

(4) In this paragraph, "relevant person" means—

(a) in respect of a decision specified in sub-paragraph (1)(a) above, the applicant or any person who made a relevant objection or representation (within the meaning of paragraph 3 above) in relation to the application to which the decision relates;

[2](b) in respect of a decision specified in sub-paragraph (1)(b) to (d) above, the holder of the licence, the chief constable or—

(i) where Part 3 of the Fire (Scotland) Act 2005 (asp 5) applies to the premises, vehicle, vessel or stall to which the licence relates, the enforcing authority;

[4](ii) where Part 3 of that Act does not so apply, the Scottish Fiore and Rescue Service; and

[1](c) in respect of a decision specified in sub-paragraph (1)(b) above, any person who in pursuance of paragraph 13(5)(b) above was heard by the authority.

NOTES

1. As amended by the Local Government etc. (Scotland) Act 1994 (c.39) Sch.13 para.129 (effective 1 April 1996).

2. As amended by the Fire (Scotland) Act 2005 (Consequential Modifications and Savings) Order 2006 (SSI 2006/475) Sch.1 para.11 (effective 1 October 2006).

3. As amended by the Criminal Justice and Licensing (Scotland) Act 2010 (asp 13) Pt 8 s.178 (effective 28 February 2010: 28 February 2011 for purposes specified in SSI 2010/413 Sch.1; not yet in force otherwise).

4. As amended by the Police and Fire Reform (Scotland) Act 2012 asp 8 (Scottish Act) Sch.7(2) para.53 (effective 1 April 2013).

GENERAL NOTE

These provisions are similar to those found in Sch.1 para.17. Subparagraph (4)(b) was amended by the Fire (Scotland) Act 2005.

Appeals

24.—[1](1) Subject to sub-paragraph (2) below, a person who may, under this Schedule, require a local authority to give him reasons for their decision may appeal to the sheriff against that decision.

(2) A person—

(a) shall be entitled to appeal under this paragraph only if he has followed all such procedures under this Schedule for stating his case to the local authority as have been made available to him;

(b) shall not be entitled to appeal under this paragraph is his application for the grant or renewal of a licence under this Schedule has been refused on either of the grounds specified in paragraph 9(5)(c) or (d) above.

[1](3) A local authority may be a party to an appeal under this paragraph.

(4) An appeal under this paragraph shall be made by way of summary application and shall be lodged with the sheriff clerk within 28 days from the date of the decision appealed against.

(5) On good cause being shown, the sheriff may hear an appeal under this paragraph notwithstanding that it was not lodged within the time mentioned in sub-paragraph (4) above.

[1](6) For the purposes of an appeal under this paragraph, the sheriff may, in the case of a decision of a local authority for which reasons have not been given by the local authority under paragraph 23 above, require the authority to give reasons for that decision, and the local authority shall comply with such a requirement.

[1](7) The sheriff may uphold an appeal under this paragraph only if he considers that the local authority, in arriving at their decision—

(a) erred in law;

(b) based their decision on any incorrect material fact;

(c) acted contrary to natural justice; or

(d) exercised their discretion in an unreasonable manner.

(8) In considering an appeal under this paragraph, the sheriff may hear evidence by or on behalf of any party to the appeal.

(9) On upholding an appeal under this paragraph, the sheriff may—

[1](a) remit the case with the reasons for his decision to the local authority for reconsideration of their decision; or

[1](b) reverse or modify the decision of the authority, and on remitting a case under sub-sub-paragraph (a) above, the sheriff may—

(i) specify a date by which the reconsideration by the council must take place;

(ii) modify any procedural steps which otherwise would be required in relation to the matter by or under any enactment (including this Act).

(10) In considering an appeal under this paragraph against revocation under paragraph 13(8) above of a licence the sheriff may, pending his decision on the appeal, postpone the taking effect of that revocation but he shall not so postpone unless he is satisfied that all steps which in the circumstances were reasonable have been taken with a view to securing that notice of the appeal and an opportunity of being heard with respect to it have been given to the local authority.

(11) The sheriff may include in his decision on an appeal under this paragraph such order as to the expenses of the appeal as he thinks proper.

(12) Any party to an appeal to the sheriff under this paragraph may appeal on a point of law from the sheriff's decision to the Court of Session within 28 days from the date of that decision.

NOTE

1. As amended by the Local Government etc. (Scotland) Act 1994 (c.39) Sch.13 para.129 (effective 1 April 1996).

GENERAL NOTE

The procedures relating to appeals are virtually identical to those applicable to Pt II licences in terms of Sch.1 para.18. It is not a ground of refusal that a proposed event had a risk that it might make the entertainment unlawful: *McMonagle v Westminster DC* [1990] 1 All E.R. 993.

[1]Power to make provision about hearings

24A.—(1) The Scottish Ministers may by regulations make provision as to the procedure to be followed at, or in connection with, any hearing to be held by a local authority under this Schedule.

(2) Regulations under this paragraph may, in particular, make provision—

(a) for notice of the hearing to be given to such persons as may be prescribed in the regulations,

(b) about the rules of evidence which are to apply for the purposes of the hearing,

(c) about the representation of any party at the hearing,

(d) as to the times by which any step in the procedure must be taken, and

(e) as to liability for expenses.

(3) Regulations under this paragraph may make different provision for different purposes, including, in particular, different types of licence.

(4) Regulations under this paragraph are subject to the negative procedure.

NOTE

1. As inserted by the Air Weapons and Licensing (Scotland) Act 2015 (asp 10) Pt 3 s.79 (effective 1 December 2015).

Provisions relating to existing premises

25.—(1) Without prejudice to any enactment other than this Schedule it shall be lawful for any person who—

(a) immediately before the date of publication as required by section 45 of this Act was using any premises, vehicle, vessel or stall as a sex shop; and

[1](b) had before the appointed day duly applied to the local authority for a licence for the premises, vehicle, vessel or stall under this Schedule to continue to use the premises, vehicle, vessel or stall as a sex shop until

[1](i) the time within which an appeal under paragraph 24 above against any refusal by the local authority of his application has elapsed; or

(ii) where such an appeal has been lodged, it has been abandoned or determined against him.

(2) In this paragraph "the appointed day", in relation to any area, means the day specified in the resolution passed under section 45 of this Act as the date upon which this Schedule comes into effect in that area.

[1](3) A local authority shall not, before the appointed day, consider any application for the grant of a licence under this Schedule made before the appointed day and shall not grant any such application until they have considered all such applications.

NOTE

1. As amended by the Local Government etc. (Scotland) Act 1994 (c.39) Sch.13 para.129 (effective 1 April 1996).

GENERAL NOTE

These are transitional provisions relating to existing sex shops and allow them to continue trading, until any appeal against refusal of a licence has been determined or abandoned. Note that in terms of s.45 of the Act that this is an optional licensing requirement and the local authority accordingly have to pass a resolution to licence sex shops hence the reference to the "appointed day" as being the date upon which the licensing resolution takes effect.

STATUTORY INSTRUMENTS RELATING TO CIVIC GOVERNMENT (SCOTLAND) ACT LICENSING PROVISIONS

Licensing and Regulation of Taxis (Appeals in Respect of Taxi Fares) (Scotland) Order 1985

(SI 1985/2025)

[17 December 1985]

The Secretary of State, in exercise of the powers conferred upon him by section 18(6) of the Civic Government (Scotland) Act 1982 (c.45) and of all other powers enabling him in that behalf and after consultation with the Council on Tribunals in accordance with section 10 of the Tribunals and Inquiries Act 1971 (c.62), hereby makes the following order:—

Citation and commencement

1. This order may be cited as the Licensing and Regulation of Taxis (Appeals in Respect of Taxi Fares) (Scotland) Order 1985 and shall come into operation on 6th January 1986.

Application of rules

2. [1]The rules set out in the Schedule to this order shall apply to any hearing before the traffic commissioner of an appeal under section 18 of the Act.

NOTE

1. As amended by the Licensing and Regulation of Taxis (Appeals in Respect of Taxi Fares) (Scotland) Amendment Order 2011 (SSI 2011/401) art.2 (effective 1 December 2011).

Interpretation

3.[1]In this order, unless the context otherwise requires—

"*the Act*" means the Civic Government (Scotland) Act 1982;

"*hearing*" means a hearing held by the traffic commissioner in relation to an appeal under section 18 of the Civic Government (Scotland) Act 1982;

"*licensing authority*" means the licensing authority against whose decision an appeal is made;

"*the traffic commissioner*" means the traffic commissioner for the Scottish Traffic Area as constituted for the purpose of the Public Passenger Vehicles Act 1981 (c.14);

"*party*" means any person who is or would be entitled under rule 4(1) of the rules set out in the Schedule to this order to appear or be represented at a hearing.

NOTE

1. As amended by the Licensing and Regulation of Taxis (Appeals in Respect of Taxi Fares) (Scotland) Amendment Order 2011 (SSI 2011/401) art.3 (effective 1 December 2011).

SCHEDULE

Articles 2 and 3

RULES AS TO PROCEDURE IN RELATIONS IN RELATION TO APPEALS IN RESPECT OF TAXI FARES AND OTHER CHARGES

Preliminary information to be notified

1.—(1) Subject to paragraph (3) of this rule, every appeal to the traffic commissioner shall be sent in writing, stating the grounds upon which it is made, within the period of 14 days as specified in section 18(1) of the Act.

(2) Where an appeal is notified in accordance with this rule, the appellant shall at the time send a copy of the appeal to the licensing authority.

(3) Where an appeal has not been made within the 14 day period specified in section 18(1) of the Act, any appeal notified thereafter to the traffic commissioner must be accompanied by an explanation for the delay, together with a statement of reasons why the traffic commissioner should exercise his discretion under section 18(2) of the Act to hear the appeal. The traffic commissioner shall notify the appellant and the licensing authority as soon as possible as to whether or not he has agreed to exercise discretion in favour of the appellant.

Statements to be served before hearing

2.—(1) Within ten days of timeous receipt of a copy of an appeal, or notification of the traffic commissioner's decision to accept a late appeal, the licensing authority shall send to the traffic commissioner at Edinburgh two copies, and to the appellant one copy, of each of the following documents:—

(a) the newspaper or newspapers containing the advertisement by the licensing authority made in accordance with section 17(3)(b) of the Act;

(b) any written representations received by the licensing authority following upon the advertisement;

(c) all other relevant documents considered by the licensing authority prior to their decision in relation to the scales of taxi fares or other charges;

(d) a record of the proceedings, if any, in the course of which the licensing authority arrived at their decision; and

(e) a statement of the reasons for the decision of the licensing authority in relation to the scales of taxi fares and also any observations which the licensing authority propose to put forward in relation to the appeal.

(2) If he is satisfied that there is good reason to do so, the traffic commissioner may extend the time limit specified in paragraph (1) of this rule either before or after the expiry of that time limit.

Notification of hearing

3.—(1) Where the traffic commissioner decides to proceed with a public hearing, he shall, not less than seven days prior to the date of the hearing, give notice of his decision by advertisement in a newspaper circulating in the area of the licensing authority.

(2) Notwithstanding the terms of paragraph (1) of this rule, not less than fourteen days' notice shall be given to both the appellant and the licensing authority inviting them to attend and give evidence at the public hearing,

but with the prior agreement of both the appellant and the licensing authority the period of such notice may be reduced.

Appearances at hearing

4.—(1) The persons entitled to appear or be represented at the hearing shall be the appellant and the licensing authority.

(2) Any person authorised by any of the parties to the hearing shall be entitled to appear on behalf of that party whether or not that person is an advocate or a solicitor.

Procedure at hearing

5.—(1) Where two or more appeals are made to the traffic commissioner against the same scales and it appears to him to be convenient that they should be heard together he may conjoin the appeals for hearing and determination.

(2) Except as otherwise provided in these rules, the procedure at a hearing shall be such as the traffic commissioner shall at his discretion determine.

(3) The traffic commissioner may receive oral, documentary or other evidence of any fact which appears to him to be relevant to the appeal, notwithstanding that such evidence would be inadmissible in a court of law.

(4) The parties shall be heard by the traffic commissioner in such order as the traffic commissioner may decide and each party shall be entitled to call witnesses, give evidence on his own behalf and cross-examine any witness called by the other party.

(5) The licensing authority shall be entitled to call as a witness any person whose representations had been taken into account by them in reaching their decision under section 17 of the Act.

(6) If a party does not appear at a hearing, the traffic commissioner, if he is satisfied that the requirements of these rules regarding the giving notice of a hearing have been duly complied with, may proceed to deal with the appeal on the basis of the case put forward in the course of the hearing by any party present and upon the documents and information before him which he may properly consider; and a verbatim record of the proceedings at the hearing shall be taken.

(7) Except with the leave of the traffic commissioner and after consideration by him of any representations to contrary effect which may be made by or on behalf of any party to the hearing, a party shall not be entitled to advance evidence which was not before the licensing authority when the decision appealed against was made.

(8) The traffic commissioner, of his own accord or on the motion of any party, may from time to time adjourn a hearing and if the date, time and place of the adjourned hearing are announced before the adjournment, and if all parties are present or represented when such an announcement is made, no further notice shall be required.

(9) If the traffic commissioner adjourns a hearing without announcing the date, time and place of the adjourned hearing, or if all the parties are not present or represented when such an announcement is made, notification of the adjourned hearing shall be given in accordance with rule 3 of these rules.

Decisions

6.—(1) The decision of the traffic commissioner in relation to an appeal, together with the reasons for that decision shall be recorded in a document signed by him (or in the event of his absence or incapacity, by a person authorised by him in writing in that behalf).

(2) The traffic commissioner (or in the event of his absence or incapacity, a person authorised by him in that behalf) shall have power, by a certificate under his hand, to correct any clerical or any accidental error or omission in the decision document.

Giving of notices, etc.

7. Where any notice or other written matter is required under the provisions of these rules to be given or supplied by the traffic commissioner to the parties, it shall be sufficient compliance with the rules if such notice or matter is sent by post by recorded delivery to the party for whom it is intended at his usual or last known address or, if that party has appointed an agent to act on his behalf in relation to the appeal, to that agent at the address of the agent supplied to the traffic commissioner.

Disposal of appeals

8.—(1) Where the traffic commissioner so resolves he may, with the agreement of the parties intimated to him in writing before the disposal of the appeal, decide an appeal on the basis of written submissions of the parties without oral evidence and in such circumstances these rules (other than rules 3 to 5) shall apply subject to any necessary modifications in relation to any such appeal.

(2) An appeal shall be proceeded with either by way of a public hearing or on the basis of written submissions but not otherwise.

Irregularities

9. Non-compliance with any of these rules shall not render the proceedings on the appeal void unless the traffic commissioner of his own accord or on the motion of any party shall so direct.

GENERAL NOTE

Section 18 of the 1982 Act provides a right of appeal by any taxi operator to the traffic commissioner for the Scottish Traffic Area against the scales of fares and other charges for taxis fixed by the licensing authority or any review of the scales. This order makes rules as to the procedure in relation to appeals under that section.

Licensing and Regulation of Taxis and Private Hire Cars and their Drivers (Prohibited and Required Conditions) (Scotland) Regulations 1986

(SI 1986/1238)

[14 July 1986]

The Secretary of State, in exercise of the powers conferred on him by section 20(1) of the Civic Government (Scotland) Act 1982 (c.45), and of all other powers enabling him in that behalf, hereby makes the following regulations:—

Citation and commencement

1. These regulations may be cited as the Licensing and Regulation of Taxis and Private Hire Cars and their Drivers (Prohibited and Required Conditions) (Scotland) Regulations 1986 and shall come into operation on 14th August 1986.

Interpretation

2. In these regulations—

"*the 1982 Act*" means the Civic Government (Scotland) Act 1982;

"*the 1985 Act*" means the Transport Act 1985 (c.67);

"*local service*" has the meaning ascribed to it by section 2 of the 1985 Act;

"*special licence*" means a restricted PSV operator's licence granted by virtue of section 12 of the 1985 Act.

Prohibited licensing conditions

3. No licensing authority shall impose conditions under the 1982 Act on any taxi licence, private hire car licence, taxi driver's licence or private hire car driver's licence which would have the effect of—

(a) limiting the operation of a taxi or private hire car to any of the following modes of operation, namely exclusive hire, carriage at separate fares or, in the case of a taxi only, provision of a local service; or

(b) limiting the number of vehicles for which the holder of a taxi licence or private hire car licence may hold licences; or

(c) requiring the holder of a taxi licence or private hire car licence or a taxi driver's licence or a private hire car driver's licence to reside within the area of the licensing authority; or

(d) prohibiting or restricting the use of radios or other means of external communication in private hire cars or imposing additional licensing conditions on the operation of private hire cars solely because they have radios or other means of external communication; or

(e) preventing the holder of a taxi licence or private hire car licence or a taxi driver's licence or a private hire car driver's licence from engaging in an employment or business other than that for which he is licensed.

Required licensing conditions

4. Every licensing authority shall impose conditions under the 1982 Act on any taxi licence issued by them to the effect that at any time when a taxi is being used under a special licence to provide a local service which is or requires to be registered under Part I of the 1985 Act, has been previously advertised and has a destination and route which are not entirely at the discretion of the passengers, the holder of the taxi licence shall—

(a) cause to be displayed on the vehicle a notice in such form as may be prescribed by the licensing authority to indicate the nature of the service being provided; and

(b) cause to be displayed in the vehicle in such a manner that it is clearly legible to passengers a fare table containing sufficient information to enable a passenger to ascertain the fare for his journey or the manner in which that fare is computed.

Revocation

5. The Local Authorities (Prohibited Conditions for Licensing of Taxis and Private Hire Cars and their Drivers) (Scotland) Regulations 1983 (S.I. 1983 No. 1029) are hereby revoked.

GENERAL NOTE

Under s.20(1) of the 1982 Act the Secretary of State is empowered to make regulations prescribing conditions which licensing authorities shall or shall not impose in granting licences in respect of taxis and private hire cars and their drivers. These regulations prohibit certain conditions (arts 3(a)–(e)) and require the imposition of certain others (art.4). The regulation revokes and re-enacts, with amendments, the Local Authorities (Prohibited Conditions for Licensing of Taxis and Private Hire Cars and their Drivers) (Scotland) Regulations 1983 (SI 1983/1029). Section 12 of the Transport Act 1985 was prospectively amended by the Deregulation and Contracting Out Act 1994 s.81(1) and Sch.17.

Local Services (Operation by Taxis) (Scotland) Regulations 1986

(SI 1986/1239)

[14 July 1986]

The Secretary of State, in exercise of the powers conferred on him by section 12(10) of the Transport Act 1985 (c.67), and of all other powers enabling him in that behalf, and after consultation with representative organisations in accordance with section 61(2) of the Public Passenger Vehicles Act 1981 (c.14), hereby makes the following regulations:—

Citation, commencement and extent

1.—(1) These regulations may be cited as the Local Services (Operation by Taxis) (Scotland) Regulations 1986 and shall come into operation on 14th August 1986.

(2) These regulations shall extend to Scotland only.

Interpretation

2. In these regulations—

"*the 1982 Act*" means the Civic Government (Scotland) Act 1982 (c.45);

"*the 1985 Act*" means the Transport Act 1985 (c.67);

"*special licence*" means a restricted PSV operator's licence granted by virtue of section 12 of the 1985 Act; and

"*licensed taxi*" and "*taxi code*" have the meanings given by section 13(3) of the 1985 Act.

Application

3. These regulations apply to a licensed taxi which is licensed under section 10 of the 1982 Act at any time when that vehicle is being used under a special licence to provide a local service which is or requires to be registered under Part I of the 1985 Act, has been previously advertised and has a destination and route which are not entirely at the discretion of the passengers.

Prescribed provisions

4. The provisions specified in the Schedule are hereby prescribed as applying in relation to a vehicle to which these regulations apply.

SCHEDULE

Regulation 4

PRESCRIBED PROVISIONS

The 1982 Act, Part I, as it applies to the provisions hereinafter mentioned but subject to the modification that the words "condition attached to a licence" in section 7(2) shall be read as relating only to such conditions as the operator or driver of a taxi can reasonably be expected to observe at any time when these regulations apply to it.

The 1982 Act, sections 10 to 13, 16, 19, 20, 21(4) and 23.

GENERAL NOTE

By s.12 of the Transport Act 1985, provision is made for the use of taxis providing local services. Regulation 4 of these regulations prescribes the provisions of the "taxi code" (defined in s.13(3) of the 1985 Act) which apply in relation to a taxi licensed under s.10 of the 1982 Act when being so used.

Taxi Drivers' Licences (Carrying of Guide Dogs and Hearing Dogs) (Scotland) Regulations 2003

(SSI 2003/73)

[3 March 2003]

The Scottish Ministers, in exercise of the powers conferred by section 20(1) and (2A) of the Civic Government (Scotland) Act 1982 and of all other powers enabling them in that behalf, hereby make the following Regulations:

Citation, commencement and extent

1.—(1) These Regulations may be cited as the Taxi Drivers' Licences (Carrying of Guide Dogs and Hearing Dogs) (Scotland) Regulations 2003 and shall come into force on 3rd March 2003.

(2) These Regulations extend to Scotland only.

Categories of dog

2.—(1) An assistance dog is prescribed as a category of dog for the purposes of section 20(2A) of the Civic Government (Scotland) Act 1982.

(2) "An assistance dog" means a dog which—

(a) Is trained by a charity to assist a disabled person with a physical impairment for the purposes of section 1 of the Disability Discrimination Act 1995 which—

(i) consists of epilepsy; or

(ii) Otherwise affects the mobility, manual dexterity, physical co-ordination of that person or the ability of that person to lift, carry or otherwise move everyday objects; and

(b) at the time that the disabled person whom it is assisting hires a taxi, is wearing a jacket inscribed with the name of a charity.

Prescribed condition

3. The condition specified in regulation 4 below is hereby prescribed as a condition which a licensing authority shall impose in relation to taxi drivers' licences, but only in relation to those licences for which an application is made to a licensing authority on or after 3rd March 2003.

4. The condition referred to in regulation 3 above is that where the taxi has been hired—

(a) by or for a disabled person who is accompanied by a guide dog, a hearing dog or an assistance dog of that person; or

(b) by a person who wishes such a disabled person to accompany that person in the taxi,

and the circumstances specified in regulation 5 below do not apply, the driver of the taxi shall carry the disabled person's dog and allow it to remain with the disabled person and shall not make any additional charge for doing so.

5. The circumstances referred to in regulation 4 above are that—

(a) a notice of exemption in the form set out in the Schedule to these Regulations has been issued to the driver in accordance with the procedure set out in regulation 6 below and is in force;

(b) that notice is exhibited either by—

(i) affixing it in a prominent position on the dashboard facing upwards; or

(ii) affixing it to the windscreen of the taxi, facing outwards.

Notices of exemption

6.—(1) The licensing authority shall issue to a person such a notice of exemption as is referred to in regulation 5(a) above (with such deletions as it considers appropriate) if the authority is satisfied that it is appropriate on medical grounds to exempt that person from the condition specified in regulation 4 above.

(2) In determining whether to issue such a notice of exemption to a person, the licensing authority shall, in particular, have regard to the physical characteristics of the taxi which that person drives.

(3) A notice of exemption shall be issued for such period as may be specified in it.

(4) If a licensing authority requires a person to undergo a medical examination for the purpose of enabling that licensing authority to be satisfied as mentioned in paragraph (1) above, that licensing authority shall meet the cost of that medical examination.

(5) For the purpose of the discharge of their functions under this regulation, every licensing authority shall reach a final decision within 3 months of receipt of an application for a notice of exemption.

Notification of decisions and giving of reasons

7.—(1) A licensing authority shall, within the period of 7 days beginning with the day on which that decision was made under regulation 6(5) above, send written notice of their decision to the person seeking a notice of exemption.

(2) Reasons for a decision referred to in paragraph (1) above shall be given by the licensing authority on a request being made to the authority by the person seeking a notice of exemption within the period of 28 days beginning with the day on which that decision was made.

(3) A licensing authority shall, within the period of 10 days beginning with the day on which a request is received by them under paragraph (2) above, give reasons in writing for arriving at the decision.

(4) Nothing in this regulation affects the power of the sheriff under regulation 8 below to require a licensing authority to give reasons for a decision of the authority—

(a) which is being appealed to the sheriff under that regulation; and

(b) for which reasons have not been given under this regulation.

(5) For the purposes of this regulation any reference to anything done in writing shall include communication by electronic means.

Appeals

8.—(1) A person who may, under regulation 7 above, require a licensing authority to give reasons for their decision may appeal to the sheriff against a decision under regulation 6 above.

(2) A licensing authority may be a party to an appeal under this regulation.

(3) An appeal under this regulation shall be made by way of summary application and shall be lodged with the sheriff clerk within the period of 28 days beginning with the day on which the decision was made.

(4) On good cause being shown, the sheriff may hear an appeal under this regulation notwithstanding that it was not lodged within the time mentioned in paragraph (3) above.

(5) For the purposes of an appeal under this regulation, the sheriff may, in the case of a decision of a licensing authority for which reasons have not been given by the authority under regulation 7 above, require the authority to give reasons for that decision, and the authority shall comply with such a requirement.

(6) The sheriff may uphold an appeal under this regulation only if the sheriff considers that the licensing authority, in arriving at their decision—

(a) erred in law;
(b) based their decision on any incorrect material fact;
(c) acted contrary to natural justice; or
(d) exercised their discretion in an unreasonable manner.

(7) In considering an appeal under this regulation, the sheriff may hear evidence by or on behalf of any party to the appeal.

(8) On upholding an appeal under this regulation, the sheriff may—

(a) remit the case with the reasons for such decision to the licensing authority for reconsideration of their decision; or
(b) reverse or modify the decision of the authority.

(9) On remitting a case under paragraph (8)(a) above, the sheriff may—

(a) specify a date by which the reconsideration by the authority must take place;
(b) modify any procedural steps which otherwise would be required in relation to the matter by or under any enactment (including these Regulations).

(10) The sheriff may include in the decision on an appeal under this regulation such order as to the expenses of the appeal as the sheriff thinks proper.

(11) Any party to an appeal to the sheriff under this regulation may appeal on a point of law from the sheriff's decision to the Court of Session within the period of 28 days beginning with the day on which the decision was made.

Revocations

9. The Taxi Drivers' Licences (Carrying of Guide Dogs and Hearing Dogs) (Scotland) Regulations 2002 and the Taxi Drivers' Licences (Carrying of Guide Dogs and Hearing Dogs) (Scotland) Amendment Regulations 2002 are hereby revoked.

SCHEDULE

Regulation 5(a)

FORM OF NOTICE OF EXEMPTION

[*Name of licensing authority*]

[*Full name of driver*], the holder of taxi driver's licence No. [*number of licence*], is, during the period [*insert dates of beginning and end of period of exemption*], exempt from the duty to carry guide dogs, hearing dogs and assistance dogs—

(a) in the taxi having registration mark [*registration mark of taxi*] and licence number [*licence number of taxi*]*;

(b) in taxis with fixed partition segregating the driver from the passenger compartment*;

(c) in taxis without fixed partition segregating the driver from the passenger compartment*.

* delete as appropriate

GENERAL NOTE

These regulations, which supersede and revoke the previous regulations and amendment thereto (Taxi Drivers' Licences (Carrying of Guide Dogs and Hearing Dogs) (Scotland) Regulations 2002 (SSI 2002/500) and Taxi Drivers' Licences (Carrying of Guide Dogs and Hearing Dogs) (Scotland) Amendment Regulations 2002 (SSI 2002/521)), place a duty on taxi drivers, through the imposition of a condition in a taxi driver's licence, to carry a disabled passenger's guide dog, hearing dog or assistance dog. The regulations provide that the taxi driver must allow the dog to remain with the disabled person and not make any additional charge for the dog. They also prescribe certain dogs helping people with epilepsy and people with certain general disabilities listed in reg.2(2)(ii) as dogs to which this obligation applies. The regulations further provide that a taxi driver may be exempted from the obligation to carry a disabled passenger's guide, hearing or assistance dog on medical grounds and prescribe the form of exemption notice which must be displayed and the manner of its display should an exemption be allowed, as well as providing for the giving of reasons for, or appeals against, decisions of licensing authorities on applications for exemption. The notice and appeal provisions are similar to those provided for in Sch.1 of the principal Act and the annotations thereto should be referred to where appropriate.

Private Hire Car Drivers' Licences (Carrying of Guide Dogs and Hearing Dogs) (Scotland) Regulations 2004

(SSI 2004/88)

[31 March 2004]

The Scottish Ministers, in exercise of the powers conferred by sections 20(2AA) of the Civic Government (Scotland) Act 1982 and of all other powers enabling them in that behalf, hereby make the following Regulations:

Citation and commencement

1. These Regulations may be cited as the Private Hire Car Drivers' Licences (Carrying of Guide Dogs and Hearing Dogs) (Scotland) Regulations 2004 and shall come into force on 31st March 2004.

Prescribed condition

2. The condition specified in regulation 3 below is hereby prescribed as a condition which a licensing authority shall impose in relation to private hire drivers' licences, but only in relation to those licences for which an application is made to a licensing authority on or after 31st March 2004.

3. The condition referred to in regulation 2 above is that where the private hire car which the private hire car driver is driving or otherwise has charge of has been hired—

(a) by or for a disabled person who is accompanied by a guide dog, a hearing dog or an assistance dog of that person; or

(b) by a person who wishes such a disabled person to accompany that person in the private hire car,

and the circumstances specified in regulation 4 below do not apply, the driver of the private hire car shall carry the disabled person's dog and allow it to remain with the disabled person and shall not make any additional charge for doing so.

4. The circumstances referred to in regulation 3 above are that—

(a) a notice of exemption in the form set out in the Schedule to these Regulations has been issued to the private hire car driver in accordance with the procedure set out in regulation 5 below and is in force; and

(b) that notice is exhibited either by—

(i) affixing it in a prominent position on the dashboard of the private hire car facing upwards; or

(ii) affixing it to the windscreen of the private hire car, facing outwards.

Notices of exemption

5.—(1) The licensing authority shall issue to a person such a notice of exemption as is referred to in regulation 4(a) above (with such deletions as it considers appropriate) if the authority is satisfied that it is appropriate on medical grounds to exempt that person from the condition specified in regulation 3 above.

(2) In determining whether to issue such a notice of exemption to a person, the licensing authority shall, in particular, have regard to the physical characteristics of the private hire car which that person drives.

(3) A notice of exemption shall be issued for such period as may be specified in it.

(4) If a licensing authority requires a person to undergo a medical examination for the purpose of enabling that licensing authority to be satisfied as mentioned in paragraph (1) above, that licensing authority shall meet the cost of that medical examination.

(5) For the purpose of the discharge of their functions under this regulation, every licensing authority shall reach a final decision within 3 months of receipt of an application for a notice of exemption.

Notification of decisions and giving of reasons

6.—(1) A licensing authority shall, within the period of 7 days beginning with the day on which the decision was made under regulation 5(5) above, send written notice of their decision to the person seeking a notice of exemption.

(2) Reasons for a decision referred to in paragraph (1) above shall be given by the licensing authority on a request being made to the authority by the person seeking a notice of exemption within the period of 28 days beginning with the day on which that decision was made.

(3) A licensing authority shall, within the period of 10 days beginning with the day on which a request is received by them under paragraph (2) above, give reasons in writing for that decision.

(4) Nothing in this regulation affects the power of the sheriff under regulation 7 below to require a licensing authority to give reasons for a decision of the authority—

(a) which is being appealed to the sheriff under that regulation; and

(b) for which reasons have not been given under this regulation.

(5) For the purposes of this regulation any reference to anything done in writing shall include communication by electronic means.

Appeals

7.—(1) A person who may, under regulation 6 above, require a licensing authority to give reasons for their decision may appeal to the sheriff against a decision under regulation 5 above.

(2) A licensing authority may be a party to an appeal under this regulation.

(3) An appeal under this regulation shall be made by way of summary application and shall be lodged with the sheriff clerk within the period of 28 days beginning with the day on which the decision was made.

(4) On good cause being shown, the sheriff may hear an appeal under this regulation notwithstanding that it was not lodged within the time mentioned in paragraph (3) above.

(5) For the purposes of an appeal under this regulation, the sheriff may, in the case of a decision of a licensing authority for which reasons have not

been given by the authority under regulation 6 above, require the authority to give reasons for that decision, and the authority shall comply with such a requirement.

(6) The sheriff may uphold an appeal under this regulation only if the sheriff considers that the licensing authority, in arriving at their decision—

(a) erred in law;
(b) based their decision on any incorrect material fact;
(c) acted contrary to natural justice; or
(d) exercised their discretion in an unreasonable manner.

(7) In considering an appeal under this regulation, the sheriff may hear evidence by or on behalf of any party to the appeal.

(8) On upholding an appeal under this regulation, the sheriff may—

(a) remit the case with the reasons for such decision to the licensing authority for reconsideration of their decision; or
(b) reverse or modify the decision of the authority.

(9) On remitting a case under paragraph (8)(a) above, the sheriff may—

(a) specify a date by which the reconsideration by the authority must take place;
(b) modify any procedural steps which otherwise would be required in relation to the matter by or under any enactment (including these Regulations).

(10) The sheriff may include in the decision on an appeal under this regulation such order as to the expenses of the appeal as the sheriff thinks proper.

(11) Any party to an appeal to the sheriff under this regulation may appeal on a point of law from the sheriff's decision to the Court of Session within the period of 28 days beginning with the day on which the decision was made.

SCHEDULE

Regulation 4(a)

FORM OF NOTICE OF EXEMPTION

[*Name of Licensing authority*]

[*Full name of driver*], the holder of private hire car driver's licence No. [*number of licence*], is, during the period [*dates of beginning and end of period of exemption*], exempt from the duty to carry guide dogs, hearing dogs and assistance dogs—

(a) in the private hire car having registration mark [*registration mark of private hire car*] and licence number [*licence number of private hire car*]*;
(b) in private hire cars with fixed partition segregating the driver from the passenger compartment*;
(c) in private hire cars without fixed partition segregating the driver from the passenger compartment*.

* delete as appropriate

GENERAL NOTE

These regulations provide for the imposition of a condition on private hire car drivers placing a duty on them to carry a disabled passenger's guide, hearing or assistance dog in a similar manner to the preceding regulations applying to taxi drivers. An "assistance dog" has a meaning similar to that in the Taxi Drivers' Regulations and is applied to these regulations by virtue of s.20(2AA) of the 1982 Act as read with s.20(2A) of that Act. These regulations came into force on 31 March 2004 by virtue of the Private Hire Car Drivers' Licences (Carrying of Guide Dogs and Hearing Dogs) (Scotland) Regulations 2004 (SSI 2004/88).

Civic Government (Scotland) Act 1982 (Licensing of Skin Piercing and Tattooing) Order 2006

(SSI 2006/43)

[1 February 2006]

The Scottish Ministers, in exercise of the powers conferred by section 44(1)(b) and (2) of the Civic Government (Scotland) Act 1982 and of all other powers enabling them in that behalf, hereby make the following Order, a draft of which has, in accordance with section 44(3) of that Act, been laid before and approved by a resolution of the Scottish Parliament:

Citation, commencement and interpretation

1.—(1) This Order may be cited as the Civic Government (Scotland) Act 1982 (Licensing of Skin Piercing and Tattooing) Order 2006 and shall come into force on the day after the day on which it is made.

(2) In this Order—

"*the 1982 Act*" means the Civic Government (Scotland) Act 1982;

"*acupuncture*" means the insertion of needles into living tissue for remedial or therapeutic purposes;

"*cosmetic body piercing*" means the perforation of the skin and underlying tissue in order to create a tunnel in the skin through which jewellery may be inserted;

"*electrolysis*" means the removal of body hair by electrocution of the hair roots with an electrified needle;

[*Definition repealed by the Civic Government (Scotland) Act 1982 (Licensing of Skin Piercing and Tattooing) Amendment Order 2006 (SSI 2006/604) art.2(2) (12 December 2006)*.]

[1]"*regulated health care professional*" means a member of a profession regulated by a body mentioned in section 25(3) of the National Health Service Reform and Health Care Professions Act 2002;

"*skin piercing*" includes any of the following—

(a) acupuncture;

(b) cosmetic body piercing; or

(c) electrolysis; and

"*tattooing*" means the insertion into the skin of any colouring material designed to leave a semi-permanent or permanent mark including micro pigmentation.

NOTE

1. As inserted by the Civic Government (Scotland) Act 1982 (Licensing of Skin Piercing and Tattooing) Amendment Order 2006 (SSI 2006/604) art.2(2) (effective 12 December 2006).

Licensing of activity

2.—(1) The activity specified in paragraph (2) is hereby designated as an activity for which a licence under Part I of the 1982 Act shall be required, but no such licence shall be required—

(a) in respect of the carrying on of that activity before 1st April 2006; or

[1](b) for the carrying on of that activity by a regulated health care professional.

(2) The activity referred to in paragraph (1) is the carrying on of a business which provides skin piercing or tattooing.

NOTE

1. As inserted by the Civic Government (Scotland) Act 1982 (Licensing of Skin Piercing and Tattooing) Amendment Order 2006 (SSI 2006/604) art.2(3) (effective 12 December 2006).

Application of Part I of the 1982 Act

3. Part I of the 1982 Act shall have effect, subject to the modifications specified in the Schedule, for the purposes of the licensing of the activity designated by article 2.

Transitional provision

4.—[*Omitted.*]

SCHEDULE

Article 3

APPLICATION OF PART I OF THE 1982 ACT

1. Part I of the 1982 Act shall have effect subject to the modifications in paragraphs 2 to 7 of this Schedule.

2. In section 3 (discharge of functions of licensing authorities)—

(a) in subsection (1), for "6 months" substitute "12 months"; and

(b) in subsections (2) and (4), for "6 month" substitute in each place "12 month".

3. In section 6 (powers of entry to and search of unlicensed premises)—

(a) in subsections (1) and (2), after "constable" in each place insert "(or any authorised officer of the licensing authority)";

(b) in subsection (3)—

(i) after "uniform" insert "(and where the person executing the warrant is an authorised officer of a licensing authority, that officer)"; and

(ii) after "constable" where it second occurs insert "(or such authorised officer of the licensing authority)"; and

(c) in subsection (4)—

(i) after "constable" where it first occurs insert "(or authorised officer of the licensing authority)"; and

(ii) after "constable" where it second occurs insert "(or such authorised officer)".

4. In paragraph 4 of Schedule 1—

(a) before sub-paragraph (1) insert—

"(A1) Where the application for the grant or renewal of a licence which is made for the carrying on of a business which provides skin piercing or tattooing specifies the address of the premises from which the activity is to be carried on as required by paragraph 1(2)(d) above, the licensing authority shall not make a final decision upon the application unless an authorised officer of the licensing authority has visited and inspected the premises."; and

(b) in sub-paragraph (1) at the beginning insert "Without prejudice to the requirement at sub-paragraph (A1) above,".

5. In paragraph 5 of Schedule 1—

(a) in sub–paragraph (1)(a) at the beginning insert "subject to sub–paragraphs (2C) and (2D) below,";

(b) after sub–paragraph (2) insert—

[1]"(2A) Where the licensing authority is considering an application for the grant or renewal of a licence—

(a) for the carrying on of a business which provides skin piercing or tattooing; and (Licensing of Skin Piercing and Tattooing) Order 2006

(b) where the activity is to be carried out wholly or mainly in premises, the licensing authority shall not grant the licence unless it is satisfied that—

(i) in the case where the business provides only ear piercing and no other kind of skin piercing or tattooing the conditions in sub-paragraph (2BA) below are met; and

(ii) in all other cases the conditions in sub-paragraph (2B) below are met.

[1](2B) The conditions referred to in sub-paragraph (2A)(ii) above are that—

(a) separate rooms are provided for—

(i) the waiting area; and

(ii) the carrying out of skin piercing or tattooing;

(b) the waiting area has displayed a notice advising—

(i) that skin piercing and tattooing will not be carried out on any person under the influence of alcohol or drugs;

(ii) that skin piercing will not be carried out on any child under the age of 16 unless accompanied by a person who has parental rights and responsibilities in respect of that child and who has also given their consent in writing to the skin piercing; and

(iii) that tattooing will not be carried out on any person under the age of 18;

(c) the room to be used for the purposes of carrying out the skin piercing or tattooing has the following facilities—

[1](i) a wash-hand basin with hot and cold running water and which uses non-hand operated taps;

(ii) a paper towel holder containing paper towels;

(iii) a soap dispenser containing soap;

(iv) a washable bench or chair with disposable paper sheet;

(v) a dispenser containing alcohol solution;

(vi) a waste bucket with a pedal operated lid;

(vii) a sharps container for storage of needles after use; and

(viii) a first aid kit;

[1](ca) there is a general purpose sink with hot and cold running water on the premises separate from the wash-hand basin required under sub-paragraph (2B)(c)(i) above.

[1](d) unless only disposable instruments are used within the premises for skin piercing or tattooing, equipment is stored and properly maintained for use on the Premises—
(i) ultrasonic cleaners;
(ii) instrument baths; and
(iii) autoclaves and autoclaves pouches; and
(e) the premises are well ventilated and illuminated for the purposes of skin piercing and tattooing.

[1](2BA) The conditions referred to in sub-paragraph (2A)(i) above are that—
(a) a separate area with a washable chair with disposable paper sheet has been designated for the carrying out of ear piercing;
(b) the designated area has displayed a notice advising—
(i) that ear piercing will not be carried out on any person under the influence of alcohol or drugs;
(ii) that ear piercing will not be carried out on any child under the age of 16 unless accompanied by a person who has parental rights and responsibilities in respect of that child and who has also given their consent in writing to the ear piercing;
(c) the premises to be used for the purposes of carrying out ear piercing has the following facilities—
[1](i) a wash-hand basin with hot and cold running water;
(ii) a paper towel holder containing paper towels;
(iii) a soap dispenser containing soap;
(v) a dispenser containing alcohol solution; and
(vi) a waste bucket with a pedal operated lid; and
(d) the premises are well ventilated and illuminated.

(2C) Without prejudice to the generality of sub-paragraph (2) above or the requirements of sub-paragraphs (2A), (2B) and (2BA) above, where a licensing authority grants or renews a licence for the carrying on of a business which provides skin piercing or tattooing and the activity is to be carried out wholly or mainly in premises, the following conditions shall be imposed—
(a) the accommodation and facilities within the premises are to be maintained in good repair and in a good state of cleanliness;
(b) only sterile single use disposable needles may be used for skin piercing or tattooing;
(c) for the purposes of tattooing, only sterile pigment dispensed into single use pots or ink pre–packed in single use vials may be used;
(d) the activity of tattooing or skin piercing (other than acupuncture) must be carried out by an operator wearing disposable non latex gloves, which must be changed for each client;
(da) subject to paragraph (db), the activity of acupuncture must be carried out by an operator who has washed their hands immediately before carrying out the activity of acupuncture on each client;
(db) the activity of acupuncture must be carried out by an operator wearing disposable non latex gloves that have not previously been used with another client where—
(a) the operator has an open lesion on their hands;

(b) the operator is handling items that may be contaminated with blood or other body fluids;
(c) the client is bleeding or has an open lesion on an exposed part of the client's body; or
(d) the client is known by the operator to be infected with a blood-borne virus;

(e) a supply of the following must be maintained—
(i) disposable non latex gloves;
(ii) sterile single-use disposable needles; and
(iii) where tattooing is provided within the premises, disposable razors.

(f) any equipment which is not disposable shall be sterilised, if practicable, or thoroughly cleaned with fresh disinfectant after each use;

(g) skin piercing shall not be carried out on a child under the age of 16 unless accompanied by a person who has parental rights and responsibilities in respect of that child and who has also given their consent in writing to the skin piercing;

(h) any equipment which is disposable must be disposed of immediately after use in an appropriate waste receptacle;

(i) for ear piercing—
(i) a sterile cartridge for ear piercing; and
(ii) pre-sterilised jewellery supplied in packaging which indicates the part of the body for which it is intended,
must be used.

(j) for tongue piercing, a sterilised clamp must be used; and

(k) information, in an easy to understand format, must be provided to prospective clients to explain—
(i) the process of the skin piercing or tattooing;
(ii) the risks of the procedure; and
(iii) the after care requirements of the procedure.

(2D) Without prejudice to the generality of sub-paragraph (2) above, where a licensing authority grants or renews a licence for the carrying on of a business which provides skin piercing or tattooing and the activity is not to be carried out wholly or mainly in premises, the following conditions shall be imposed—

(a) disposable non latex gloves must, except for the activity of acupuncture, be worn and changed for each client;

(aa) subject to paragraph (ab), the activity of acupuncture must be carried out by an operator who has washed their hands immediately before carrying out the activity of acupuncture on each client;

(ab) the activity of acupuncture must be carried out by an operator wearing disposable non latex gloves that have not previously been used with another client where—
(a) the operator has an open lesion on their hands;
(b) the operator is handling items that may be contaminated with blood or other body fluids;
(c) the client is bleeding or has open lesions on an exposed part of the client's body; or
(d) the client is known by the operator to be infected with a blood-borne virus;

(b) the skin piercing or tattooing may only be carried out through use of disposable razors or sterile single use disposable needles;

(ba) for the purposes of tattooing, only sterile pigment dispensed into single use pots or ink pre-packed in single use vials may be used;

(c) any seating used for the skin piercing or tattooing must be washable and covered with a disposable paper sheet which shall be renewed after each use;

(d) any equipment which is not disposable shall be sterilised, if practicable, or thoroughly cleaned with fresh disinfectant after each use;

(e) any equipment which is disposable must be disposed of immediately after use in an appropriate waste receptacle;

(f) for tongue piercing, a sterilised clamp must be used;

(g) for ear piercing—

(i) a sterile cartridge for ear piercing, and

(ii) pre-sterilised jewellery supplied in packaging which indicates the part of the body for which it is intended,

must be used.

(h) skin piercing shall not be carried out on a child under the age of 16 unless accompanied by a person who has parental rights and responsibilities in respect of that child and who has also given their consent in writing to the skin piercing; and

(i) information, in an easy to understand format, must be provided to prospective clients to explain—

(i) the process of the skin piercing or tattooing;

(ii) the risks of the procedure; and

(iii) the after care requirements of the procedure.";

(c) at the beginning of sub-paragraph (3) insert "Subject to sub-paragraph (3A) below,";

(d) after sub-paragraph (3) insert—

"(3A) For the purposes of sub-paragraph (3)(a)(ii) above, where the licence applied for is for the carrying on of a business which provides skin piercing or tattooing, the licensing authority, when determining whether the applicant is a fit and proper person to be the holder of the licence, shall have regard to the knowledge, skill, training and experience which the applicant (or, where the applicant is not a natural person, those individuals who will be carrying on the activity or activities) can demonstrate in relation to the activity or activities which are to be carried on.";

(e) after sub-paragraph (7) insert—

"(7A) Where a licensing authority makes out a licence under sub-paragraph (7) above for the carrying on of a business which provides skin piercing or tattooing, the licence shall specify—

(a) the name and address of the person to whom the licence is granted;

(b) the address of the premises (if any) in which the activity is to be carried out; and

(c) where the premises are used for the carrying on of any trade or business, the name of that business.".

NOTE

1. As amended by the Civic Government (Scotland) Act 1982 (Licensing of Skin Piercing and Tattooing) Amendment Order 2006 (SSI 2006/604) art.2(4) (effective 12 December 2006).

6. In paragraph 8(3) of Schedule 1 after "Act" insert "or in the case where a licence has been granted for the carrying on of a business which provides skin piercing or tattooing".

7. After paragraph 19 of Schedule 1 insert—

"**20.** In this Schedule, "parental responsibilities" in relation to a child has the meaning given by section 1(3) of the Children (Scotland) Act 1995(**a**) and "parental rights" in relation to a child has the meaning given by section 2(4) of that Act.

21. In this Schedule—

"*autoclave*" means a pressure vessel in which the lid is sealed by the internal pressure in the vessel and which is used to steam sterilise equipment used for skin piercing or tattooing;

"*sharps container*" means a container used for holding medical waste and devices which can cause physical injury;

"*skin piercing*" and "*tattooing*" have the same meanings as in the Civic Government (Scotland) Act 1982 (Licensing of Skin Piercing and Tattooing) Order 2006; and

"*ultrasonic cleaner*" means a cleaning device which uses sound waves propagated through an aqueous medium at frequencies higher than the audible range.

GENERAL NOTE

This Order designates the activity of the carrying on of a business which provides skin piercing or tattooing as an activity for which a licence under the 1982 Act shall be required in terms of s.44(1)(b) of that Act (art.2). Skin piercing and tattooing are defined in art.1(2). An exemption from the licensing regime is provided where a registered medical practitioner carries out the activity in certain circumstances (art.2). The general licensing provisions at Pt I of the 1982 Act (including Sch.1) will apply to such licences with the important modifications as set out in the Schedule. Subparagraphs 1(2) and 2(1)(b) were amended by the Civic Government (Scotland) Act 1982 (Licensing of Skin Piercing and Tattooing) Amendment Order 2006 (SI 2006/604) art.2.

Civic Government (Scotland) Act 1982 (Licensing of Booking Offices) Order 2009

(SSI 2009/145)

[3 April 2009]

The Scottish Ministers make the following Order in exercise of the powers conferred by section 44(1)(b) and (2) of the Civic Government (Scotland) Act 1982 and all other powers enabling them to do so.

In accordance with section 44(3) of that Act, a draft of this Order has been laid before and approved by resolution of the Scottish Parliament.

Citation, commencement and interpretation

1.—(1) This Order may be cited as the Civic Government (Scotland) Act 1982 (Licensing of Booking Offices) Order 2009 and comes into force on the day after the day on which it is made.

(2) In this Order—

"*the Act*" means the Civic Government (Scotland) Act 1982;

"*relevant premises*" means the premises in relation to which a licence has been granted by virtue of article 2; and

"*relevant vehicle*" means a vehicle in relation to which a taxi licence or private hire car licence has been granted in terms of section 10 of the Act and that licence is in effect.

Licensing of booking offices

2.—(1) The activity specified in paragraph (2) is designated as an activity for which a licence under Part I of the Act shall be required, but no such licence shall be required—

(a) in respect of the carrying on of that activity before 16th November 2009; or

(b) where the number of relevant vehicles in respect of which bookings are taken does not at any time exceed 3.

(2) The activity referred to in paragraph (1) is the use of premises for the carrying on of a business which consists to any extent of the taking of bookings, by any means of communication, from members of the public for the hire of a relevant vehicle.

Application of Part I of the Act

3. Part I of the Act shall have effect, subject to the modifications specified in the Schedule, for the purposes of the licensing of the activity designated by article 2.

Transitional provision

4.—(1) A person who on or after 16th November 2009 carries on the activity designated by article 2 without a licence under Part I of the Act shall not be guilty of an offence under section 7(1) of the Act if—(Licensing of Booking Offices) Order 2009.

(a) that person made an application to the licensing authority before that date for the grant of a licence under Part I of the Act in respect of the activity being carried on by the person; and

(b) that application has not yet been finally determined.

(2) For the purposes of paragraph (1)(b), an application is finally determined—

(a) when it is withdrawn by the applicant;

(b) when it is refused by the licensing authority and the period of 28 days specified in paragraph 18(4) of Schedule 1 to the Act expires without an appeal against the refusal being made to the sheriff; or

(c) in a case where an appeal is made against a refusal by the licensing authority, when that appeal is disposed of.

(3) For the purposes of paragraph (2)(c), an appeal is disposed of—

(a) when it is abandoned by the appellant; or

(b) when a decision on it is made by the sheriff or a higher court and any period for making a subsequent appeal to a higher court expires without such a subsequent appeal being made.

SCHEDULE

Article 3

APPLICATION OF PART 1 OF THE ACT

1. Part I of the Act shall have effect subject to the modifications in paragraphs 2 to 5 of this Schedule.

2. In section 6 (powers of entry to and search of unlicensed premises)—

(a) in subsections (1) and (2), after "constable" in each place insert "(or any authorised officer of the licensing authority)";

(b) in subsection (3)—

(i) after "uniform" insert "(and where the person executing the warrant is an authorised officer of a licensing authority, that officer)"; and

(ii) after "constable" where it second occurs insert "(or such authorised officer of the licensing authority)"; and

(c) in subsection (4)—

(i) safter "constable" where it first occurs insert "(or authorised officer of the licensing authority)"; and

(ii) after "constable" where it second occurs insert "(or such authorised officer)".

3. In paragraph 5 (disposal of applications for the grant and renewal of licences) of Schedule 1—

(a) in sub-paragraph (1)(a), for "unconditionally" substitute "subject to the mandatory conditions specified in sub-paragraph (1A) below";

(b) in sub-paragraph (1)(b), for "conditions" substitute "those mandatory conditions and such conditions as are specified in sub-paragraph (2) below"; and

(c) after sub-paragraph (1), insert—

"(1A) The mandatory conditions referred to in sub-paragraph (1)(a) above are—

(a) that a record be kept of every booking for the hire of a relevant vehicle taken at the relevant premises;

(b) that a record be kept of—

(i) the registration number of the vehicle which was hired as the result of a booking taken at the relevant premises; and

(ii) the name of its driver at the time of that hire; and

(c) that the holder of the licence shall take all reasonable steps to ensure that any booking taken at the relevant premises from a member of the public for the hire of a relevant vehicle results in the hire of a vehicle which is—

(i) a relevant vehicle; and

(ii) being driven by a person who holds a licence granted under section 13 of the Act and that licence is in effect.".

4. After paragraph 19 (interpretation) of Schedule 1 insert—

"**20.** In this Schedule, "relevant premises" and "relevant vehicle" have the same meaning as in the Civic Government (Scotland) Act 1982 (Licensing of Booking Offices) Order 2009.".

GENERAL NOTE

This Order designates the use of premises for the purpose of carrying on a business, part of which consists of taking bookings from members of the public for the hire of taxis or private hire cars, as an activity for which a licence is required under the 1982 Act but does not apply if the number of vehicles for which bookings are taken is less than half. It is a "mandatory" provision and booking offices have required a licence from 16 November 2009.

[1]Knife Dealers (Licence Conditions) Order 2009

(SSI 2009/217)

[1 September 2009]

NOTE

1. Entire SSI repealed by the Knife Dealers (Licence Conditions) (Scotland) Order 2013 (SSI 2013/22) art.5 (effective 29 January 2013).

The Scottish Ministers make the following Order in exercise of the powers conferred by section 27C(1) and (2) of the Civic Government (Scotland) Act 1982 and all other powers enabling them to do so.

Citation and commencement

1. This Order may be cited as the Knife Dealers (Licence Conditions) Order 2009 and comes into force on 1st September 2009.

Interpretation

2. In this Order:

"*customer*" means a person who buys, hires, borrows or otherwise acquires any article listed in section 27A(2) of the Civic Government (Scotland) Act 1982 in a transaction with a dealer; and

"*transaction*" means where an article is sold, hired, offered or exposed for sale or hire, lent or given to the customer by a dealer.

Mandatory conditions for all knife dealers' licences

3.—(1) In granting or renewing a knife dealer's licence, a licensing authority must attach to the licence the mandatory conditions as specified in paragraphs (2) to (4).

(2) The dealer must make detailed written records on the day of the transaction with a customer and retain such records for a period of 3 years from that date stating the following information—

(a) the identity of the customer and the means by which the customer's identity was verified;

(b) the steps taken to establish that the customer was at least eighteen years of age at the time of the transaction (including any proof of age or identity sought or the means by which the customer's age was verified or reasons why such verification was not sought because it was unnecessary); and

(c) a full description of the article sold, hired, offered or exposed for sale or hire, lent or given to the customer.

(3) The dealer must ensure that any article listed in section 27A(2) of the Civic Government (Scotland) Act 1982 or display of such articles is not visible from the street or any public entrance to the premises.

(4) The dealer must display a notice which must—

(a) be displayed at all times at the point of entry to the premises, the point of sale or counter and in a position which is readily visible to customers;

(b) be at least A4 size and on which the lettering must be legible and no smaller than 5 mm in height; and

(c) contain the following wording:

(i) it is an offence to sell to a person under the age of 18 any knife or knife blade (except if the person is aged 16 or over and the knife or blade is designed for domestic use);

(ii) it is also an offence to sell to a person under the age of 18 any razor blade, axe, sword or other article which has a blade or which is sharply pointed and which is made or adapted for use for causing injury; and

(iii) a customer may be asked to provide details of his/her age and identity (which may be recorded or copied and kept for inspection for up to 3 years).

Mandatory additional conditions for swords

4.—(1) In addition to the conditions specified in article 3, a licensing authority must attach to the licence the additional mandatory conditions in paragraphs (2) and (3) where the dealer is carrying on business as a dealer in swords.

(2) The dealer must take all reasonable steps to establish from the customer and confirm the intended use of any sword.

(3) The dealer must make detailed written records on the day of the transaction with a customer and retain such records for a period of 3 years from that date stating the enquiries made of the customer or other persons or bodies as to the intended use of any sword.

GENERAL NOTE

This Order requires local authorities to attach mandatory conditions to knife dealer's licences granted or renewed under s.27C of the 1982 Act. Article 3 specifies the mandatory conditions so to be placed and art.4 specifies certain additional mandatory conditions which apply for a dealer who is carrying on business as a dealer in swords. According to the executive note issued in May 2009

> "the Scottish Government believes that the mandatory conditions represent a framework that will make it more difficult for potentially deadly weapons to fall into the wrong hands and forms a basis that can be built upon by local licensing authorities in dealing with local circumstances and individual applications".

Knife Dealers (Exceptions) Order 2009

(SSI 2009/218)

[1 September 2009]

The Scottish Ministers make the following Order in exercise of the powers conferred by sections 27A(7) and 27A(8)(b) of the Civic Government (Scotland) Act 1982 and all other powers enabling them to do so.

Citation and interpretation

1. This Order may be cited as the Knife Dealers (Exceptions) Order 2009 and comes into force on 1st September 2009.

Exception for certain articles

2. In section 27A of the Civic Government (Scotland) Act 1982 (knife dealers' licences)—

(a) in subsection (2)(a), for "those" substitute "folding pocket knives whose blades do not exceed 3.5 inches (8.91 centimetres) in length or knives",

(b) after subsection (2)(a) insert—

"(aa) daggers (other than kirpans or skean dhus whose blades do not exceed exceed 3.5 inches (8.91 centimetres) in length);".

Exceptions for certain businesses

3.—(1) Where a person (A) is teaching another person (B) the sport of fencing, the hiring, offering or exposing for hire, lending or giving of a fencing sword by A to B is not to be taken to be a business for the purposes of section 27A(4) of the Civic Government (Scotland) Act 1982 but only where A is qualified to teach B in the sport.

(2) In this Article "fencing sword" means a sword used in the sport of fencing and which may be classified as a foil, epée or sabre.

GENERAL NOTE

This Order makes certain exceptions to the requirement for a knife dealer's licence under s.27A of the 1982 Act. In art.2 folding pocket knives, kirpans and skean dhus are all exempted, provided that their blades do not exceed 3.5 inches (8.91 cm) in length. In art.3 exceptions are made for fencing teaching businesses.

Knives etc. (Disposal of Forfeited Property) (Scotland) Order 2010

(SSI 2010/214)

[25 June 2010]

The Scottish Ministers make the following Order in exercise of the powers conferred by section 27K(7) and (8)(a) of the Civic Government (Scotland) Act 1982 and all other powers enabling them to do so.

Citation and Commencement

1. This Order may be cited as the Knives etc. (Disposal of Forfeited Property) (Scotland) Order 2010 and comes into force on 25th June 2010.

Interpretation

2. In this Order—

"*the Act*" means the Civic Government (Scotland) Act 1982;

"*museum or similar institution*" means any institution to which the public are given access which has as its purpose, or one of its purposes, the preservation and display of material of historical, aesthetic or technical interest; and

"*property*" means property in the possession of the police by virtue of section 27K(2) of the Act.

[*Definition repealed by the Police and Fire Reform (Scotland) Act 2012 (Consequential Modifications and Savings) Order 2013 (SSI 2013/119) Sch.1 para.35 (effective 1 April 2013).*]

Property to which this Order applies

3.—(1) Subject to paragraph (2), this Order applies to property in respect of which—

(a) no application under section 27K(3) of the Act has been made before the end of the period of 6 months beginning with the date on which the forfeiture order was made; or

(b) such application, having been made, has been refused.

(2) Where, within the period specified in paragraph (1)(a)—

(a) an application has been made under section 27K(3) of the Act but not determined; or

(b) the person upon whose conviction the court ordered the forfeiture of the property under section 27J of the Act has appealed against the conviction or sentence,

this Order does not apply to the property unless and until that application or appeal has been refused.

Disposal of Property

4.—[1,2](1) Subject to paragraphs (4) to (6) below, rights in the property will vest in the Scottish Police Authority where either the appeal or application (as the case may be) referred to in article 3 is refused or where section 27K(6) of the Act applies (rights lost at the end of 6 months).

(2) Subject to paragraphs (3) and (4) below, property to which this Order applies must be destroyed by the police.

[2](3) Subject to paragraph (4), the Scottish Police Authority may, instead of arranging for the destruction of the property, give or sell it to a museum or similar institution but only where the Scottish Police Authority is satisfied that the property is of particular rarity, aesthetic quality or technical or historical interest.

[2](4) On application by the Lord Advocate the court may direct that any property to which the forfeiture order relates, is to vest in any person other than the Scottish Police Authority for its destruction or disposal, and may disapply paragraph (6) and make such other order relating to any proceeds as it considers appropriate.

[2](5) The title to any property given or sold to a museum or similar institution, or any other person transfers to that institution or person in accordance with paragraphs (3) or (4), and except for proceeds mentioned in paragraph (6), discharges the rights and duties of the Scottish Police Authority under paragraphs (1) and (2).

[2](6) The proceeds of any disposals under this Order (if any) are to be paid to, and vest in, the Scottish Police Authority unless a court orders otherwise.

NOTES

1. As amended by the Knife Dealer's Licence (Miscellaneous) (Scotland) Order 2010 (SSI 2010/311) art.3 (effective 28 September 2010).

2. As amended by the Police and Fire Reform (Scotland) Act 2012 (Consequential Modifications and Savings) Order 2013 (SSI 2013/119) Sch.1 para.35 (effective 1 April 2013).

Knife Dealer's Licence (Miscellaneous) (Scotland) Order 2010

(SSI 2010/311)

[15 September 2010]

The Scottish Ministers make the following Order in exercise of the powers conferred by sections 27A(8)(b) and 27K(7) of the Civic Government (Scotland) Act 1982 and all other powers enabling them to do so.

Citation, commencement and interpretation

1.—(1) This Order may be cited as the Knife Dealer's Licence (Miscellaneous) (Scotland) Order 2010.

(2) Subject to paragraph (3) this Order comes into force on 15th September 2010.

(3) Articles 2(3) and 3 come into force on 28th September 2010.

(4) In this Order "*the Act*" means the Civic Government (Scotland) Act 1982.

Exceptions for certain activities

2.—(1) The activities in this article are not to be taken to be businesses for the purposes of section 27A(4) of the Act.

(2) The hiring, offering or exposing for hire, lending or giving of an arrow by a person (A) to another person (B) where—

(a) A is teaching B the sport of archery; and

(b) A is qualified to teach B that sport.

(3) The hiring, offering or exposing for hire, lending or giving of a knife by a person (A) to another person (B) where—

(a) A is teaching B a water sport;

(b) A is qualified to teach B that sport; and

(c) the purpose of such hiring, offering or exposing for hire, lending or giving of the knife by A to B is the safety of B whilst B is undertaking that sport.

(4) The selling, hiring, offering or exposing for sale, hire, lending or giving of an arrow or a fencing sword but only where that activity is undertaken—

(a) in connection with a recognised competition; and

(b) within the vicinity of a recognised competition.

(5) In this article—

"*arrow*" means an arrow designed or adapted for use in the sport of archery;

"*fencing sword*" means a sword used in the sport of fencing and which may be classified as a foil, epee or sabre;

"*knife*"does not include a knife designed for domestic use; and

"*recognised competition*" means a competition recognised by—

(a) Scottish Fencing;

(b) Scottish Archery Association; or

(c) Scottish Field Archery Association.

Amendment to the Knives etc. (Disposal of Forfeited Property) (Scotland) Order 2010

3.—(1) The Knives etc. (Disposal of Forfeited Property) (Scotland) Order 2010 is amended as follows.

(2) In article 4(1), omit "a recovery order is granted but".

Knife Dealers (Historical Re-enactments) (Scotland) Order 2011

(SSI 2011/263)

[19 August 2011]

The Scottish Ministers make the following Order in exercise of the powers conferred by sections 27A(8)(b), 27S(1) and 27S(2) of the Civic Government (Scotland) Act 1982 and all other powers enabling them to do so.

Citation, commencement and interpretation

1.—(1) This Order may be cited as the Knife Dealer's Licence (Historical Re-enactment Events) (Scotland) Order 2011 and comes into force on 19th August 2011.

(2) In this Order "*the Act*" means the Civic Government (Scotland) Act 1982.

Exceptions for certain activities

2.—(1) The activities in this article are not to be taken to be businesses for the purposes of section 27A(4) of the Act.

(2) The selling, hiring, offering or exposing for sale or hire, lending or giving of an arrow but only where that activity is undertaken—

(a) in connection with a historical re-enactment event; and

(b) within the immediate vicinity of a historical re-enactment event.

(3) The selling, hiring, offering or exposing for sale or hire, lending or giving of an article within the meaning of section 27A(2) of the Act but only where that activity is undertaken—

(a) in connection with a historical re-enactment event; and

(b) within the immediate vicinity of a historical re-enactment event.

(4) In this article—

"*arrow*" means an arrow designed or adapted for use in the sport of archery; and

"*historical re-enactment event*" means an educational or entertainment event, to which members of the public are admitted on payment of money or money's worth, and in which participants attempt to recreate aspects of a historical event or period (which includes, but is not limited to, battle re-enactment and combat demonstrations).

Knife Dealers (License Conditions) (Scotland) Order 2013

(SSI 2013/22)

[29 January 2013]

The Scottish Ministers make the following Order in exercise of the powers conferred by sections 3A(1) and (2) and 27C of the Civic Government (Scotland) Act 1982 and all other powers enabling them to do so.

In accordance with section 3A(3) of that Act, a draft of this Order has been laid before and approved by resolution of the Scottish Parliament.

Citation, commencement and application

1.—(1) This Order may be cited as the Knife Dealers (Licence Conditions) (Scotland) Order 2013 and comes into force on the day after the day on which it is made.

(2) Articles 3 and 4 apply only to knife dealers' licences granted or renewed by a licensing authority after this Order comes into force.

Interpretation

2. In this Order, "*customer*" means a person who buys, hires, borrows or otherwise acquires any article listed in section 27A(2) of the Civic Government (Scotland) Act 1982 from a dealer

Mandatory conditions for all knife dealers' licences

3.—(1) In granting or renewing a knife dealer's licence, a licensing authority must attach to the licence the conditions specified in paragraphs (2) to (4).

(2) The dealer must make detailed written records on the day of the transaction with a customer and retain such records for a period of 3 years from that date stating the following information—

(a) the identity of the customer and the means by which the customer's identity was verified;

(b) the steps taken to establish that the customer was at least 18 years of age at the time of the transaction (including any proof of age or identity sought or the means by which the customer's age was verified or reasons why such verification was not sought because it was unnecessary); and

(c) a full description of the article sold, hired, lent or given to the customer.

(3) The dealer must ensure that any article listed in section 27A(2) of the Civic Government (Scotland) Act 1982 or display of such articles is not visible from the street or any public entrance to the premises.

(4) The dealer must display a notice which must—

(a) be displayed at all times in a position which is readily visible to customers at—

(i) the entry to the premises; and

(ii) the point of sale or counter;

(b) be at least A4 size and on which the lettering must be legible and no smaller than 5 mm in height; and

(c) contain the following wording—

(i) it is an offence to sell to a person under the age of 18 any knife or knife blade (except if the person is aged 16 or over and the knife or blade is designed for domestic use);

(ii) it is also an offence to sell to a person under the age of 18 any razor blade, axe, sword or other article which has a blade or which is sharply pointed and which is made or adapted for use for causing injury; and

(iii) a customer may be asked to provide details of his/her age and identity (which may be recorded or copied and kept for inspection for up to 3 years).

Mandatory additional conditions for swords

4.—(1) Where a knife dealer's licence permits carrying on business as a dealer in swords, a licensing authority must also attach to the licence the conditions specified in paragraphs (2) and (3).

(2) The dealer must take all reasonable steps to establish from the customer, and confirm, the intended use of any sword.

(3) The dealer must make detailed written records on the day of the transaction with a customer and retain such records for a period of 3 years from that date stating the enquiries made of the customer or other persons or bodies as to the intended use of any sword.

Revocation

5. The Knife Dealers (Licence Conditions) Order 2009 is revoked.

CINEMA LICENCES

Cinemas Act 1985

(c.13)

ARRANGEMENT OF SECTIONS

SCHEDULE 1

Amendments of Act that have effect on coming into force of s.12(11) of the Fire Precautions Act 1971.

SCHEDULES 2, 3

[*Omitted.*]

GENERAL NOTE

Cinema licensing (with the exception of safety regulations) is not one of the matters devolved to the Scottish Parliament and therefore remains under the control of the UK Parliament—see Scotland Act 1998 Sch.5 Pt II para.B5 which expressly reserves the subject matter of: "Sections 1 to 3 and 5 to 16 of the Cinemas Act 1985 which deal with the licensing of premises for film exhibition".

Control of exhibitions

Licence required for exhibitions

1.—(1) Subject to sections 5 to 8 below, no premises shall be used for a film exhibition unless they are licensed for the purpose under this section.

[1](2) A licensing authority may grant a licence under this section to such a person as they think fit to use any premises specified in the licence for the purpose of film exhibitions on such terms and conditions and subject to such restrictions as, subject to subsection (2A) and to regulations under section 4 below, they may determine.

[1](2A) Where Part 3 of the Fire (Scotland) Act 2005 (asp 5) applies in relation to the premises, no term, condition or restriction may be imposed under subsection (2) which relates to any matter in relation to which requirements or prohibitions are or could be imposed by virtue of that Part.

(3) Without prejudice to the generality of subsection (2) above, it shall be the duty of a licensing authority, in granting a licence under this section as respects any premises,—

(a) to impose conditions or restrictions prohibiting the admission of children to film exhibitions involving the showing of works designated, by the authority or by such other body as may be specified in the licence, as works unsuitable for children; and

(b) to consider what (if any) conditions or restrictions should be imposed as to the admission of children to other film exhibitions involving the showing of works designated, by the authority or by such other body as may be specified in the licence, as works of such other description as may be so specified.

NOTE

1. As amended by the Fire (Scotland) Act 2005 (Consequential Modifications and Savings) Order 2006 (SSI 2006/475) Sch.1 para.12 (effective 1 October 2006).

DEFINITIONS

"children": s.21(1).
"film exhibition": s.21(1).
"licence": s.21(1).
"local authority": s.21(1).

GENERAL NOTE

The Act provides for the licensing of film exhibitions in general (with certain important exemptions and exceptions) and this section provides for such a licensing system. Subsection (2) was amended by the Fire (Scotland) Act 2005 (Consequential Modifications and Savings) Order (SSI 2006/475) Sch.1 para.12(2).

Subsection (3) was inserted by the Fire (Scotland) Act 2005 (Consequential Modifications and Savings) Order (SSI 2006/475) Sch.1 para.12(2).

Subsection (1)

All premises used for film exhibitions require a licence and a statutory offence is created in respect of unlicensed cinemas by s.10 of the Act. "Premises" are not defined but, given the ambit of the safety regulations, the concept would appear to include the auditorium, projection rooms and all common parts of the building. Thus a multiple-screen cinema, i.e. one with several auditoria but common booking facilities, passageways, foyer, etc. would only need a single licence covering the whole building and not separate licences for each screen. A theatre is not a cinema—*Scottish Cinemas and Variety Theatres Ltd v Ritchie*, 1929 S.C. 300. Certain film exhibitions are, by virtue of subs.(5)–(8) exempted from requiring a licence, i.e. those in private dwelling houses, in premises used occasionally for film exhibitions, in moveable buildings and also non-commercial exhibitions.

Subsection (2)

A wide discretionary power to impose terms and conditions on licences is given here subject to duties imposed by subs.(3), regulations by the Secretary of State and the *Wednesbury* principle derived from the famous cinema licensing case of *Associated Provincial Picture Houses Ltd v Wednesbury Corp* [1948] 1 K.B. 223. See also *Classic Cinemas Ltd v Motherwell DC*, 1977 S.L.T. (Sh Ct) 69 where it was observed that licensing authorities, when imposing conditions, should have regard to the realities of film making and the complexities of film distribution. The conditions can include censorship separate from the British Board of Film Censors classification—see *R v Greater London Council Ex p. Blackburn* [1976] 1 W.L.R. 550. A set of model licensing conditions for the guidance of local authorities is to be found in Home Office Circular 150/1955.

Subsection (3)

Thus films which are classified as being unsuitable for children must not be shown to them and this is enforced by way of the conditions which must be imposed by the licensing authority. For the current classification system of films see Home Office Circular 98/1982.

Consent required for exhibitions for children

2.—(1) Subject to sections 5 and 6 below, no premises shall be used, except with the consent of the licensing authority, for a film exhibition organised wholly or mainly as an exhibition for children.

[1](2) Subject to subsection (2A) and to regulations under section 4 below, a licensing authority may, without prejudice to any conditions or restrictions imposed by them on the granting of a licence, impose special conditions or restrictions on the granting of a consent under this section.

[1](2A) Where Part 3 of the Fire (Scotland) Act 2005 (asp 5) applies in relation to the premises, no condition or restriction may be imposed under subsection (2) which relates to any matter in relation to which requirements or prohibitions are or could be imposed by virtue of that Part.

NOTE

1. As amended by the Fire (Scotland) Act 2005 (Consequential Modifications and Savings) Order 2006 (SSI 2006/475) Sch.1 para.12 (effective 1 October 2006).

DEFINITIONS

"children": s.21(1).
"film exhibition": s.21(1).
"licensing authority": s.21(1).

GENERAL NOTE

This section provides that premises used for film exhibitions for children are to be subject to the special consent of the licensing authority, consent being given in terms of s.3 and subject to the regulations of the Secretary of State made in terms of s.4. This provision is primarily for the safety and welfare of children and was influenced by early cinema fires in which children were the victims. The procedure for consents is contained in s.3 of the Act.

Grant, renewal and transfer of licence or consent

3.—(1) An applicant for the grant, renewal or transfer of a licence shall give to—

(a) the licensing authority,

[1](b) the appropriate fire authority, and

(c) the chief officer of police,

not less than 28 days' notice of his intention of make the application.

[1](2) The licensing authority may in such cases as they think fit, after consulting with the appropriate fire authority and the chief officer of police, grant an application for the grant, renewal or transfer of a licence notwithstanding the fact that the applicant has failed to give notice in accordance with subsection (1) above.

[1](3) In considering any application for the grant, renewal or transfer of a licence, the licensing authority shall have regard to any observations submitted to them by the appropriate fire authority or by the chief officer of police.

(4) Unless revoked under section 12 below, a licence shall remain in force for one year or for such shorter period as the licensing authority on the grant of the licence may determine.

(5) A licensing authority may transfer any licence granted by them to such other person as they think fit.

(6) Where, before the date of expiry of a licence, an application has been made for its renewal or transfer, the licence shall be deemed to remain in force or, as the case may require, to have effect with any necessary modifications until the determination of the application by the licensing authority or the withdrawal of the application.

(7) There shall be paid in respect of the grant, renewal or transfer of a licence such fees as may be fixed by the licensing authority, not exceeding—

(a) in the case of a grant or renewal for one year, £600;

(b) in the case of a grant or renewal for any less period, £200 for each month for which the licence is granted or renewed but so that the aggregate of the fees payable in any year does not exceed £600; or

(c) in the case of a transfer, £120.

(8) The Secretary of State may by order amend subsection (7) above so as to vary any sum specified in that subsection or so as to provide that any sum payable under that subsection shall cease to be so payable; and an order under this subsection may be limited to such cases as may be specified by the order and may make different provision for different cases specified in the order.

(9) An order under subsection (8) above shall be made by statutory instrument which shall be subject to annulment in pursuance of a resolution of either House of Parliament.

(10) In this Act, except where the contrary intention appears,—

[1]"*appropriate fire authority*", in relation to the building or structure, means—

(a) where Part 3 of the Fire (Scotland) Act 2005 (asp 5) applies to the building or structure, the enforcing authority as defined in section 61(9) of that Act,

[2](b) in any other case, the Scottish Fire and Rescue Service;

"*chief officer of police*", in relation to any premises, means the chief officer of police for the police area in which the premises are situated;

[*Definition repealed by the Fire (Scotland) Act 2005 (Consequential Modifications and Amendments) Order 2005 (SSI 2005/383) Sch.2 para.1 (effective 2 August 2005).*]

"*licence*" means a licence under section 1 above or a consent under section 2 above and references to a licence of either kind shall be construed accordingly;

"*licensing authority*", in relation to any premises, means the local authority in whose area the premises are situated.

NOTES

1. As amended by the Fire (Scotland) Act 2005 (Consequential Modifications and Savings) Order 2006 (SSI 2006/475) Sch.1 para.12 (effective 1 October 2006).

2. As amended by the Police and Fire Reform (Scotland) Act 2012 asp 8 (Scottish Act) Sch.7(2) para.55 (effective 1 April 2013).

DEFINITIONS

"chief officer of police": s.3(10).
"fire authority": s.3(10).
"licence": s.3(10).
"licensing authority": ss.3(10), 2(1).

GENERAL NOTE

This section provides for the grant, renewal and transfer of a cinema licence or children's performance consent. Subsection (1) was amended by the Fire (Scotland) Act 2005 (Consequential Modifications and Amendments) Order 2005 (SSI 2005/383) Sch.1 para.8 and the Fire (Scotland) Act 2005 (Consequential Modifications and Savings) Order 2006 (SSI 2006/475) Sch.1 para.12.

Subsection (1)

Thus at least 28 days' notice of an application for a licence or consent (see s.2) must be given not only to the licensing authority but also to the fire authority and the chief constable.

Subsection (2)

Notwithstanding subs.(1) the licensing authority have a discretion to grant an application even if notice has not been given, provided that the police and fire authority have been consulted.

Subsection (3)

The observations must be considered but any recommendations need not, of course, necessarily be followed.

Subsection (7)

The sums specified herein are those substituted for the original sums by the Fees for Cinema Licences (Variation) Order 1991 (SI 1991/2462). In England the Home Office expressed the view that a tariff for fees could be set which distinguished between cases on the basis of the work actually done subject to statutory maximum fees—see Association of District Councils Circular 1986/119.

Regulations by Secretary of State

4.—(1) Subject to sections 5 and 6 below, no film exhibition shall be given unless regulations made by the Secretary of State under this section are complied with.

(2) The matter for which provision may be made by regulations under this section are—

(a) safety in connection with the giving of film exhibitions (including the keeping and handling, in premises where other entertainments are being given or meetings held, of cinematograph film used or to be used for the purposes of film exhibitions or other articles or equipment so used or to be used);

(b) the health and welfare of children in relation to attendance at film exhibitions.

(3) Regulations under this section shall be made by statutory instrument which shall be subject to annulment in pursuance of a resolution of either House of Parliament.

DEFINITIONS

"children": s.21(1).
"film exhibition": s.21(1).

GENERAL NOTE

Film exhibitions (with the exception of certain categories of non-commercial exhibitions) are all subject to any regulations made by the appropriate member of the Scottish Government (this section of the Act being a devolved function within the meaning of the Scotland Act 1998) in respect of safety at film shows and, in particular, the health and welfare of children attending film shows. When s.12(11) of the Fire Precautions Act 1971 comes into effect, s.4(1) will cease to have any affect and other consequential amendments to the Act will be made. The regulations in force at the present time are in respect of subs.(2)(a): the Cinematograph (Safety) (Scotland) Regulations 1955 (SI 1955/1125) as amended by SI 1969/1575, SI 1971/471, SI 1976/1621 and 1983/367 and the Celluloid and Cinematograph Film Order 1924 (SR & O 1924/363). In respect of subs.(2)(b), the Cinematograph (Children) (Scotland) (No.2) Regulations 1955 (SI 1955/1912) apply, and a general duty to make provision for the safety of children at indoor entertainments is contained in s.23 of the Children and Young Persons (Scotland) Act 1937. The two sets of 1955 Regulations (as amended) are set out at pp.264–285, and pp.286–287 below.

Exempted exhibitions

Exhibitions in private dwelling-houses

5.—(1) This section applies to any film exhibition which—

(a) is given in a private dwelling-house,

(b) is one to which the public are not admitted, and

(c) satisfies the condition mentioned in subsection (2) below.

(2) The condition referred to in subsection (1)(c) above is that either—

(a) the exhibition is not promoted for private gain, or

(b) the sole or main purpose of the exhibition is to demonstrate any product, to advertise any goods or services or to provide information, education or instruction.

(3) The following exemptions have effect in relation to any film exhibition to which this section applies, that is to say—

(a) a licence shall not be required by reason only of the giving of the exhibition;

(b) where the exhibition is given in premises in respect of which a licence is in force, no condition or restriction on or subject to which the licence was granted shall apply to the exhibition;

(c) regulations under section 4 above shall not apply to the exhibition.

DEFINITIONS

"private gain": s.20.
"film exhibition": s.21(1).

GENERAL NOTE

This is the first of the four categories of exempted exhibition, namely film shows which are held in private houses and to which the public are not admitted provided that the show was not for private gain (with the exception of advertisements, information, educational or instructional films which may be for private gain and which are still covered by the exemption).

Other non-commercial exhibitions

6.—(1) Subject to subsections (4) and (5) below, this section applies to any film exhibition (other than one to which section 5 above applies) which—

(a) is one to which the public are not admitted or are admitted without payment, or

(b) does not fall within paragraph (a) above but is given by an exempted organisation,

and (in either case) satisfies the condition mentioned in subsection (2) below.

(2) The condition referred to in subsection (1) above is that either—

(a) the exhibition is not promoted for private gain, or

(b) the sole or main purpose of the exhibition is to demonstrate any product, to advertise any goods or services or to provide information, education or instruction.

(3) The following exemptions have effect in relation to any film exhibition to which this section applies, that is to say—

(a) a licence under section 1 above shall not be required by reason only of the giving of the exhibition unless the pictures are produced by means specified in regulations under section 4 above as means involving such risk that it is inexpedient that this paragraph should have effect;

(b) where the exhibition is given in premises in respect of which a licence under section 1 above is in force, no condition or restriction on or subject to which the licence was granted shall apply to the exhibition except so far as it relates to the matters specified in section 4(2)(a) above;

(c) a consent under section 2 above shall not be required by reason only of the giving of the exhibition;

(d) where the exhibition is given in premises in respect of which a consent under section 2 above is in force, no condition or restriction on or subject to which the consent was granted shall apply to the exhibition;

(e) regulations under section 4 above making such provision as is mentioned in subsection (2)(b) of that section shall not apply to the exhibition and regulations under that section making such provision as is mentioned in subsection (2)(a) of that section shall not apply to the exhibition unless it is given in premises in respect of which a licence under section 1 above is in force.

(4) A film exhibition is excluded from being one to which this section applies if it is organised solely or mainly as an exhibition for children who are members of a club, society or association the principal object of which is attendance at film exhibitions, unless the exhibition is given in a private dwelling-house or as part of the activities of an educational or religious institution.

(5) A film exhibition is excluded from being one to which this section applies by virtue of paragraph (b) of subsection (1) above if on more than three out of the last preceding seven days the premises in question were used for the giving of a film exhibition to which this section applied by virtue of that paragraph.

(6) In this section "exempted organisation" means a society, institution, committee or other organisation with respect to which there is in force at the time of the exhibition in question a certificate given by the Secretary of State certifying that he is satisfied that the organisation is not conducted or established for profit; and there shall be paid to the Secretary of State in respect of the giving of such a certificate such reasonable fee as he may determine.

(7) The Secretary of State shall not give such a certificate with respect to any organisation—

(a) the activities of which appear to him to consist of or include the giving of film exhibitions promoted for private gain, or

(b) the objects of which do not appear to him to consist of or include the giving of film exhibitions to which the public are admitted;

and the Secretary of State may revoke such a certificate at any time if it appears to him that, since the certificate was given, the activities of the organisation have consisted of or included the giving of film exhibitions promoted for private gain.

(8) Any certificate given by the Commissioners of Customs and Excise under section 5(4) of the Cinematograph Act 1952 before the commencement of the Cinematograph (Amendment) Act 1982 shall have effect as if given by the Secretary of State.

DEFINITIONS

"film exhibition": s.21(1).
"private gain": s.20.

GENERAL NOTE

The second category of exempt exhibitions comprises "other" non-commercial exhibitions, which themselves fall into two principal categories, namely: (a) exhibitions to which either the public are not admitted or to which the public are admitted without payment; and (b) societies or other organisations which have been exempted by a certificate of the Secretary of State notwithstanding any admission charge being made. Subsection (4) provides that the exclusions do not apply to children's clubs, etc. unless the exhibitions are in private dwelling houses or are part of educational or religious institution activities.

Exhibitions in premises used occasionally

[1]**7.**—(1) Where the premises in which it is proposed to give a film exhibition are premises used occasionally and exceptionally only, and not on more than six days in any one calendar year, for the purposes of such an exhibition, it shall not be necessary to obtain a licence under section 1 above if—

[2](a) the occupier of the premises has given to the licensing authority, to the appropriate fire authority and to the chief officer of police, not less than seven days' notice in writing of his intention so to use the premises; and

(b) he complies with any regulations under section 4 above and, subject to any such regulations, with any conditions imposed by the licensing authority and notified to him in writing.

(2) For the purposes of subsection (1) above, the giving in any premises of an exhibition to which section 5 or 6 above applies shall be disregarded.

NOTES

1. As amended by the Fire (Scotland) Act 2005 (Consequential Modifications and Amendments) Order 2005 (SSI 2005/383) Sch.1 para.8 (effective 2 August 2005).

2. As amended by the Fire (Scotland) Act 2005 (Consequential Modifications and Savings) Order 2006 (SSI 2006/475) Sch.1 para.12 (effective 1 October 2006).

DEFINITION

"film exhibition": s.21(1).

GENERAL NOTE

This is the third category of exempt exhibitions, comprising exhibitions in premises used on not more than six days in any one calendar year, provided that such use is "occasional and exceptional" and not regular, i.e. premises used only on, for example, 1 and 2 January each year would require a licence. Subsection (1)(a) was amended by the Fire (Scotland) Act 2005 (Consequential Modifications and Amendments) Order 2005 (SSI 2005/383) Sch.1 para.8 and the Fire (Scotland) Act 2005 (Consequential Modifications and Savings) Order 2006 (SSI 2006/475) Sch.1 para.12.

Exhibitions in movable buildings, etc.

[1]**8.**—(1) Where it is proposed to give a film exhibition in any building or structure of a movable character, it shall not be necessary to obtain a licence under section 1 above from the local authority in whose area the exhibition is to be given ("the appropriate authority") if—

(a) the owner of the building or structure has been granted a licence under section 1 above in respect of that building or structure by the local authority in whose area he ordinarily resides;

[1](b) he has given to the appropriate authority, to the appropriate fire authority and to the chief officer of police not less than two days' notice in writing of his intention to give the exhibition; and

(c) he complies with any regulations under section 4 above and, subject to any such regulations, with any conditions imposed by the appropriate authority and notified to him in writing.

(2) In subsection (1)(b) above—

[2]"*appropriate fire authority*", in relation to the building or structure, means—

(a) where Part 3 of the Fire (Scotland) Act 2005 (asp 5) applies to the building or structure, the enforcing authority as defined in section 61(9) of that Act,

[3](b) in any other case, the Scottish Fire and Rescue Service;

"*chief officer of police*" means the chief officer of police for the police area in which the exhibition is to be given.

[*Definition repealed by the Fire (Scotland) Act 2005 (Consequential Modifications and Amendments) Order 2005 (SSI 2005/383) Sch.2 para.1 (effective 2 August 2005).*]

NOTES

1. As amended by the Fire (Scotland) Act 2005 (Consequential Modifications and Amendments) Order 2005 (SSI 2005/383) Sch.1 para.8 (effective 2 August 2005).

2. As amended by the Fire (Scotland) Act 2005 (Consequential Modifications and Savings) Order 2006 (SSI 2006/475) Sch.1 para.12 (effective 1 October 2006).

3. As amended by the Police and Fire Reform (Scotland) Act 2012 (asp 8) Sch.7 para.55 (effective 1 April 2013).

DEFINITIONS

"film exhibition": s.21(1).

"local authority": s.21(1).

GENERAL NOTE

This is the fourth, and last, category of exempt exhibition, namely the fairly rare phenomenon of a mobile cinema, which only requires a s.1 licence in respect of the area where the owner normally resides. No indication is given of the test to be applied to "ordinarily resides" but see the examples applied by Scottish courts in the cases of *Land v Land*, 1962 S.L.T. 316 and *Reid v Inland Revenue*, 1926 S.L.T. 365. Subsection (1)(a) was amended by the Fire (Scotland) Act 2005 (Consequential Modifications and Amendments) Order 2005 (SSI 2005/383) Sch.1 para.8 and the Fire (Scotland) Act 2005 (Consequential Modifications and Savings) Order 2006 (SSI 2006/475) Sch.1 para.12.

Exhibition on Sundays

GENERAL NOTE

Section 9 applies only to England and Wales and is therefore omitted.

Enforcement

Offences

10.—(1) If—

(a) any premises in respect of which a licence under section 1 above is not in force are used for an exhibition which requires such a licence,
(b) any premises in respect of which a consent under section 2 above is not in force are used for an exhibition which requires such a consent,
(c) any premises in respect of which a licence of either kind is in force are used for an exhibition which requires a licence of that kind and are so used otherwise than in accordance with the terms, conditions or restrictions on or subject to which the licence is held,
(d) any premises in respect of which a licence under section 1 above is in force are used for an exhibition to which section 6 above applies and are so used otherwise than in accordance with the conditions or restrictions on or subject to which the licence is held, so far as they relate to the matters specified in section 4(2)(a) above, or
(e) any premises are used for an exhibition to which regulations under section 4 above apply and are so used in contravention of those regulations,

then, subject to subsection (3) below, each of the persons mentioned in subsection (2) below shall be guilty of an offence.

(2) The persons referred to in subsection (1) above are—

(a) any person concerned in the organisation or management of the exhibition,
(b) where a licence of either kind is in force in respect of the premises and the exhibition requires a licence of that kind, the holder of the licence,
(c) where a licence under section 1 above is in force in respect of the premises and the exhibition is one to which section 6 above applies, the holder of the licence under section 1, and
(d) any other person who, knowing or having reasonable cause to suspect that the premises would be used as mentioned in that subsection—
  (i) allowed the premises to be so used, or
  (ii) let the premises, or otherwise made them available, to any person by whom an offence in connection with that use of the premises has been committed.

(3) It shall be a defence for a person charged with an offence under subsection (1) above to prove that he took all reasonable precautions and exercised all due diligence to avoid the commission of the offence.

DEFINITION

"film exhibition": s.21(1).

GENERAL NOTE

This section creates a number of specific statutory offences the penalties for which are contained in the following section. For "knowingly or having reasonable cause to suspect" see Introduction, pp.31–32 above. For the defence of "due diligence" see Introduction, p.31 above.

Penalties and forfeitures

11.—(1) A person guilty of an offence under subsection (1) of section 10 above shall be liable on summary conviction to a fine not exceeding—

(a) in the case of an offence under paragraph (a) of that subsection, £20,000,

(b) in any other case, level 5 on the standard scale.

(2) Subject to subsection (3) below, the court by or before which a person is convicted of an offence under section 10(1)(a) above may order any thing produced to the court, and shown to the satisfaction of the court to relate to the offence, to be forfeited and dealt with in such manner as the court may order.

(3) The court shall not order any thing to be forfeited under subsection (2) above, where a person claiming to be the owner of or otherwise interested in it applies to be heard by the court, unless an opportunity has been given to him to show cause why the order should not be made.

DEFINITION

"level 5 on the standard scale": see p.32 above.

GENERAL NOTE

These are the penalties for contravention of the statutory offences contained in s.10. Note the power of forfeiture which could, presumably, be extended to projection equipment, films and other trade equipment.

Revocation of licence or consent

12.—(1) If the holder of a licence under section 1 above is convicted of—

(a) an offence under section 10(1) above, or

(b) an offence under section 12 of the Children and Young Persons Act 1933 (failing to provide for safety of children at entertainments) or section 23 of Children and Young Persons (Scotland) Act 1937 (the corresponding provision for Scotland) in respect of an entertainment provided at the premises to which the licence relates,

the licensing authority may revoke the licence.

(2) If the holder of a consent under section 2 above is convicted of an offence under section 10(1) above, the licensing authority may revoke the consent.

DEFINITION

"licensing authority": s.21(1).

GENERAL NOTE

This section gives the licensing authority power to revoke the licence or consent of a person convicted of an offence under the specified provisions.

Powers of entry

[1]**13.**—(1) Where a constable or an authorised officer of the licensing authority has reasonable cause to believe that—

(a) any premises in respect of which a licence of either kind is in force are being or are about to be used for an exhibition which requires a licence of that kind,

(b) any premises in respect of which a licence under section 1 above is in force are being or are about to be used for an exhibition to which section 6 above applies, or

(c) any premises in respect of which notice has been given under section 7 or 8 above are being or are about to be used for an exhibition which, but for that section, would require a licence under section 1 above,

he may enter and inspect the premises with a view to seeing whether the relevant provisions are being complied with.

(2) [*Omitted.*]

(3) A constable or authorised officer of the licensing authority may enter and search any premises in respect of which he has reason to believe that an offence under section 10(1) above has been, is being or is about to be committed if authorised to do so by a warrant granted in Scotland, by a sheriff, stipendiary magistrate or justice of the peace.

(4) Where an authorised officer of the licensing authority enters any premises in the exercise of any power under this section he shall, if required to do so by the occupier, produce to the occupier his authority.

(5) Any person who intentionally obstructs the exercise of any power conferred by this section shall be liable on summary conviction to a fine not exceeding level 3 on the standard scale.

(6) In this section "relevant provisions" means—

(a) in a case falling within subsection (1)(a) or (2)(a) above, regulations under section 4 above and the terms, conditions and restrictions on or subject to which the licence is held,

(b) in a case falling within subsection (1)(b) above, regulations under that section making such provision as is mentioned in paragraph (a) of subsection (2) of that section and the conditions and restrictions on or subject to which the licence under section 1 above is held so far as they relate to the matters specified in that paragraph.

(c) in a case falling within subsection (1)(c) or (2)(c) above, regulations under that section and any conditions notified in writing by the licensing authority to the occupier of the premises;

and in relation to any premises in respect of which notice has been given under section 8 above any reference in this section to the occupier shall be construed as a reference to the owner.

(7) [*Omitted.*]

(8) [*Omitted.*]

NOTES

1. As amended by the Fire (Scotland) Act 2005 (Consequential Modifications and Amendments) Order 2005 (SSI 2005/383) Sch.1 para.8 (effective 2 August 2005).

2. As amended by the Fire (Scotland) Act 2005 (Consequential Modifications and Savings) Order 2006 (SSI 2006/475) Sch.1 para.12 (effective 1 October 2006).

DEFINITION

"licensing authority" s.21(1).

GENERAL NOTE

This section gives a constable or authorised officer of the licensing authority the power of entry and search of cinema premises in certain specified circumstances. Subsection (2) was repealed by the Fire (Scotland) Act 2005 (Consequential Modifications and Savings) Order (SSI 2006/475) Sch.2, para.1.

Subsection (1)

For "reasonable cause to believe" see Introduction p.31 above.

Subsection (3)

For "reason to believe" see Introduction p.31 above.

Subsection (4)

For "intentionally obstructs" see Introduction pp.30–31 above.

Subsections (7) and (8)

These subsections apply only to England and Wales, and are therefore omitted.

Powers of arrest and seizure

14.—(1) If a constable has reasonable cause to suspect that a person has committed an offence under this Act (except section 9(4) above) he may require him to give his name and address, and if that person refuses or fails to do so or gives a name or address which the constable reasonably suspects to be false, the constable may arrest him without warrant.

(2) A constable or authorised officer of the licensing authority who enters and searches any premises under the authority of a warrant issued under section 13(3) above may seize and remove any apparatus or equipment or other thing whatsoever found on the premises which he has reasonable cause to believe may be liable to be forfeited under section 11(2) above.

(3) [*Omitted.*]

DEFINITION

"licensing authority": s.21(1).

GENERAL NOTE

This section gives the constable or authorised officer of the licensing authority the power to seize and remove apparatus or equipment that they have reasonable cause to believe may be liable to be forfeited under s.11(2), e.g. films, projection equipment, etc. Subsection (1) did not apply to Scotland and is, in any event, repealed. Subsection (3) has accordingly ceased to have any effect. For "reasonable cause to believe" see Introduction above.

Offences by bodies corporate

15.—(1) Where an offence under this Act committed by a body corporate is proved to have been committed with the consent or connivance of, or to be attributable to any neglect on the part of, any director, manager, secretary or other officer of the body corporate, or any person who was purporting to act in any such capacity, he as well as the body corporate shall be guilty of that offence and shall be liable to be proceeded against and punished accordingly.

(2) Where the affairs of a body corporate are managed by its members, subsection (1) shall apply in relation to the acts and defaults of a member in connection with his functions of management as if he were a director of the body corporate.

GENERAL NOTE

This section provides that where a statutory offence is committed by a body corporate with the consent and connivance or neglect of any responsible officer of the body, then that person shall also be liable. The exception of subs.(1) in relation to Sunday exhibitions does not apply in Scotland, and has been omitted.

Appeals

Appeals against decisions of licensing authority

[1]**16.**—(1) Any person aggrieved—

(a) by the refusal or revocation of a licence,

(b) by any terms, conditions or restrictions on or subject to which a licence is granted, or

(c) by the refusal of a renewal or transfer of a licence, may appeal in Scotland, to the sheriff.

(2) [*Omitted.*]

[2](3) Where the decision against which an appeal under this section is brought was given on an application of which (in accordance with section 3(1) above) notice was required to be given to an appropriate fire authority and a chief officer of police, any notice of appeal under this section against that decision shall be given to that authority and that officer as well as to any other person to whom it is required to be given apart from this subsection.

(4) Where a licence is revoked it shall be deemed to remain in force during the period within which an appeal under this section may be brought and, if such an appeal is brought, until the determination or abandonment of the appeal.

(5) Where an application for the renewal or transfer of a licence is refused, the licence shall be deemed to remain in force, or, as the case may require, to have effect with any necessary modifications—

(a) during any period within which an appeal under this section may be brought and, if such an appeal is brought, until the determination of abandonment of the appeal; and

(b) where such an appeal is successful, until the licence is renewed or transferred by the licensing authority.

NOTES

1. As amended by the Fire (Scotland) Act 2005 (Consequential Modifications and Amendments) Order 2005 (SSI 2005/383) Sch.1 para.8 (effective 2 August 2005).

2. As amended by the Fire (Scotland) Act 2005 (Consequential Modifications and Savings) Order 2006 (SSI 2006/475) Sch.1 para.12 (effective 1 October 2006).

DEFINITIONS

"licence": ss.21(1) and 3(10).

"licensing authority": ss.21(1) and 3(10).

GENERAL NOTE

A right of appeal in respect of both licences and consents is given to the sheriff and is subject to the normal summary procedure of the sheriff court. Subsection (3) was amended by the Fire (Scotland) Act 2005 (Consequential Modifications and Amendments) Order 2005 (SSI 2005/383) Sch.1 para.8 and the Fire (Scotland) Act 2005 (Consequential Modifications and Savings) Order 2006 (SSI 2006/475) Sch.1 para.12.

Subsection (1)

For general observations on such appeals see Introduction, pp.28–30 above. Note that there is no procedure for requiring a licensing authority to state reasons for its decision—see Introduction, p.28 above.

Subsection (2)

This subsection applies only to England and Wales.

17, 18

GENERAL NOTE

Sections 17 and 18 are omitted as they have no application outside of the Greater London area.

Miscellaneous and general

Music and dancing licences not required

19.—(1) A licence shall not be required for any premises under a relevant enactment by reason only of the giving of a film exhibition—

(a) which includes representations of persons playing music, dancing or singing, or

(b) which otherwise includes or is accompanied by music.

(2) For the purposes of subsection (1) above any music played at any premises by way of introduction to, in any interval between parts of, or by way of conclusion of, a film exhibition or in the interval between two film exhibitions shall be treated as music accompanying the exhibition or exhibitions, as the case may be, if the total time taken by music so played on any day amounts to less than one quarter of the total time taken by the film exhibition or exhibitions given in the premises on that day.

(3) In subsection (1) above "relevant enactment" means—

(a) [*As repealed by the Licensing Act 2003 (c.17) Sch.7 para.1 (effective 24 November 2005).*]

(b) any enactment for the regulation of places kept or ordinarily used for public dancing, singing, music or other public entertainment of the like kind.

DEFINITIONS

"film exhibition": s.21(1).

"licence": ss.21(1) and 3(10).

GENERAL NOTE

Thus a showing of, say, a "silent classic" with incidental live piano music would not require a public entertainment licence granted under s.41 of the 1982 Act.

Meaning of promotion for private gain

20.—(1) For the purposes of this Act an exhibition is promoted for private gain if, and only if,—

(a) any proceeds of the exhibition, that is to say, any sums paid for admission to the exhibition, or

(b) any other sums (whenever paid) which, having regard to all the circumstances, can reasonably be regarded as paid wholly or partly for admission to the exhibition, or

(c) where the exhibition is advertised (whether to the public or otherwise), any sums not falling within paragraph (b) above which are paid for facilities of services provided for persons admitted to the exhibition,

are applied wholly or partly for purposes of private gain.

(2) If in proceedings for an offence under section 10(1) above any question arises whether an exhibition was promoted for private gain and it is proved—

(a) that any sums were paid for admission to the exhibition or to the premises at which it was given and that the exhibition was advertised to the public, or

(b) that any sums were paid for facilities or services provided for persons admitted to the exhibition and that the exhibition was advertised (whether to the public or otherwise), or

(c) that the amount of any payment falling to be made in connection with the promotion of the exhibition was determined wholly or partly by reference to the proceeds of the exhibition or any facilities or services provided for persons admitted to it,

the exhibition shall be deemed to have been promoted for private gain unless the contrary is shown.

(3) Where an exhibition is promoted by a society which is established and conducted wholly for purposes other than purposes of any commercial undertaking and sums falling within subsection (1) above are applied for any purpose calculated to benefit the society as a whole, the exhibition shall not he held to be promoted for private gain by reason only that the application of those sums for that purpose results in benefit to any person as an individual.

(4) In subsection (3) above "society" includes any club, institution, organisation or association of persons, by whatever name called.

DEFINITION

"film exhibition": s.21(1).

GENERAL NOTE

This defines "private gain" and would appear to exclude "money's worth" such as jam jars, etc. Note the exemption provided for societies in subs.(3).

Interpretation

[1]**21.**—(1) In this Act, except where the contrary intention appears,—

[2]"*appropriate fire authority*" has the meaning given by section 3(10) above;

"*chief officer of police*" has the meaning given by section 3(1) above;

"*child*" means a person under the age of sixteen;

"*film exhibition*" means any exhibition of moving pictures other than an exhibition of items included in a programme service (within the meaning of the Communications Act 2003) that is being simultaneously received (or virtually so) by the exhibitor;

[*Definition repealed by the Fire (Scotland) Act 2005 (Consequential Modifications and Amendments) Order 2005 (SSI 2005/383) Sch.2 para.1 (effective 2 August 2005).*]

"*licence*" and references to a licence of either kind shall be construed in accordance with section 3(10) above;

"*licensing authority*" has the meaning given by section 3(10) above;

"*local authority*" means—in Scotland, a council constituted under section 2 of the Local Government etc. (Scotland) Act 1994.

(2) Any reference in this Act to an exhibition which requires a licence under section 1 above is a reference to an exhibition to which that section applies; and any reference in this Act to an exhibition which requires a consent under section 2 above is a reference to an exhibition to which that section applied.

NOTES

1. As amended by the Fire (Scotland) Act 2005 (Consequential Modifications and Amendments) Order 2005 (SSI 2005/383) Sch.1 para.8 (effective 2 August 2005).

2. As amended by the Fire (Scotland) Act 2005 (Consequential Modifications and Savings) Order 2006 (SSI 2006/475) Sch.1 para.12 (effective 1 October 2006).

GENERAL NOTE

This section contains several key definitions to terms used throughout the Act and these are, unusually, cross-references back to preceding sections. In relation to the particular terms, the definition of "film exhibition" was amended by s.203(1) of, and Sch.20, para.40 to the Broadcasting Act 1990. The definition does not include video games (see *British Amusement Catering Trades Association v Westminster City Council* [1989] A.C. 147 HL), but it does include videotaped performances, so that a public house showing videos would require a cinema licence. The definition of "licensing authority" in Scotland was amended by the Local Government etc. (Scotland) Act 1994 s.180(1) and Sch.13, para.138. For "standard scale" in Scotland see Introduction p.32 above; "appropriate fire authority" was amended by the Fire (Scotland) Act 2005 (Consequential Modifications and Amendments) Order 2005 (SSI 2005/383) Sch.1 para.8 and the Fire (Scotland) Act 2005 (Consequential Modifications and Savings) Order 2006 (SSI 2006/475) Sch.1 para.12; "film exhibition" was substituted by the Communications Act 2003 Sch.17 para.76. Other deletions were made by the Fire (Scotland) Act 2005 (Consequential Modifications and Amendments) Order 2005 (SSI 2005/383) and by the Statute Law (Repeals) Act 1993 Sch.1.

22.–24.

GENERAL NOTE

Section 22 was repealed by the Fire (Scotland) Act 2005 (Consequential Modifications and Savings) Order 2006 (SSI 2006/475) Sch.2 para.1. Section 23 (transitional provisions) is omitted as they no longer have any effect, while s.24 (consequential amendments and repeals) is omitted for the same reason.

Short title, commencement and extent

25.—(1) This Act may be cited as the Cinemas Act 1985.

(2) This Act shall come into force at the end of the period of three months beginning with the day on which it is passed.

(3) This Act does not extend to Northern Ireland.

GENERAL NOTE

The commencement date was, accordingly, 27 June 1985.

SCHEDULE 1

[*Repealed*]

STATUTORY INSTRUMENTS RELATING TO CINEMA LICENSES

Cinematograph (Safety) (Scotland) Regulations 1955

(SI 1955/1125 as amended by SI 1969/1575, SI 1971/471, and SI 1983/367)

[22 July 1955]

The Secretary of State in exercise of the powers conferred on him by ss.1, 2 and 7 of the Cinematograph Act 1909 and sections 1, 2(1)(a) and the proviso to s.5(1) of the Cinematograph Act 1952, hereby makes the following regulations:

PART 1

GENERAL REQUIREMENTS IN CONNECTION WITH CINEMATOGRAPH EXHIBITIONS

Application of Part I

1. Subject to the provisions of subsection (4) of section seven of the Cinematograph Act, 1909 and of section five of the Cinematograph Act, 1952 (which relate to exemptions in favour of certain exhibitions to which the public are not admitted or are admitted without payment), the provisions of this Part of these Regulations shall apply in connection with the giving of all cinematograph exhibitions other than those to which Part III of these Regulations applies, and to the premises used in connection with the giving of such exhibitions and to the parts thereof and the fittings, furniture, furnishings and equipment therein in this Part of these Regulations mentioned.

Exits

2.—(1) The premises shall be provided with an adequate number of exits, so placed and maintained as to afford the public ready and ample means of safe egress.

(2) In the case of premises built or substantially altered in structure after the date on which these Regulations come into operation the number of exits from each floor and tier in the auditorium shall be determined in relation to the number of persons who may be accommodated on that floor or tier and shall not be less than the appropriate number set out in Column 2 of the subjoined table.

Column 1 Number of persons	Column 2 Number of exits
1–60	1
61–600	2
601–1,000	3
1,001–1,400	4
1,401–1,700	5
1,701–2,000	6
2,001–2,250	7
2,251–2,500	8
2,501–2,700	9

(3) All exits for use by the public in leaving the auditorium shall be clearly indicated with the words "Exit" or "Way Out".

(4) All passages, courts, ramps and stairways to which the public have access, and which lead from the auditorium to outside the premises shall at all times when the public are on the premises be kept free from obstructions.

(5) Every door in the building for use by members of the public going from the auditorium to outside the building shall be so constructed and maintained as—

(a) to open outwards, unless the licensing authority shall have been satisfied that this is impracticable in the circumstances of the particular case, and

(b) to open easily and fully in such manner that the door when open does not restrict the egress of the public.

Seats

3.—(1)The seats in the auditorium shall be so arranged as to allow free access to the exits of the auditorium.

(2) All such seats shall be securely fixed to the floor except in boxes accommodating not more than eight persons.

(3) No sitting shall be allowed in the auditorium during a cinematograph exhibition except in the seats provided.

(4)(a) No standing shall be allowed in the auditorium during a cinematograph exhibition except in such places and within such numbers as may be specified by the licensing authority.

(b) Where persons are permitted to stand in any gangway, sufficient room shall be left in the gangway to allow other persons easily to pass along the gangway.

(5) Subject to the last preceding paragraph, all gangways in the auditorium shall, while the public are on the premises, be kept free from obstructions.

(6) Notwithstanding paragraphs (2), (3) and (5) of this Regulation, invalids may be permitted, with the consent of and subject to any conditions of such consent imposed by the licensing authority, to sit in the auditorium in invalid chairs, other than petrol-driven invalid chairs.

Staff

4.—(1) The licensee or some responsible person nominated by him in writing, not being a person under eighteen years of age, shall be in charge of, and present in, the premises at all times when the public are on the premises.

(2) If the licensee or the person so nominated is the operator, some other responsible person, nominated in writing by the licensee and not being a person under eighteen years of age, shall be on duty to pay special attention during the period that the operator is in charge to those matters affecting the safety of the public which the operator by reason of his duties in the projection room is unable to superintend.

(3) The number of attendants on duty to assist persons entering or leaving the auditortium shall, in any case, not be less than one for every two hundred and fifty, or part of two hundred and fifty, persons present in the auditorium; and—

(a) if the number of persons present on any floor or tier does not exceed one hundred, there shall be at least one attendant on duty on that floor or tier,

(b) if the number of persons present on any floor or tier exceeds one hundred there shall be at least two attendants on duty on that floor or tier.

(4) Every member of the staff shall be instructed by the licensee or by some person nominated by the licensee in the safety precautions to be observed in the premises so far as those precautions relate to his duties, and in the action to be taken by him in the event of fire or other emergency.

Fire precautions

5.—(1) The premises shall be provided with fire appliances suitable to the fire risks in the premises.

(2) The fire appliances shall be maintained in proper working order and be available for instant use.

(3) The licensee, persons nominated under paragraph (1) or paragraph (2) of Regulation 4 of these Regulations and at least one other member of the staff shall be properly instructed in the protection of the premises from fire, the use of the fire appliances provided, and the method of summoning the employees of the relevant authority (as defined in section 6 of the Fire (Scotland) Act 2005 (asp 5)).

(4) All curtains and similar hangings shall be of such material or so treated and maintained that they will not readily catch fire.

(5) No inflammable substance shall be used for cleaning any film or film projector.

(6) Subject to the provisions of Regulation 33 of these Regulations any inflammable film in the premises shall be kept in closed metal containers and shall be kept stored elsewhere than—

(a) in the fuel store,

(b) in any part of the premises habitually used by the licensee or members of the staff,

(c) in any part of the premises where there is a naked light, excessive heat, or any risk of fire or explosion from the electrical or heating equipment therein, or

(d) in any part of the premises forbidden to be used for the purpose in the licence granted by the licensing authority,

and the place wherein it is stored shall be kept locked.

Fire precautions, further provisions

6.—(1) No smoking shall be permitted in any projection or rewinding room or in any room in which film is stored or in which electrical batteries are installed or charged.

(2) In and immediately outside any such room notices shall be posted stating that smoking is prohibited.

(3) No readily inflammable substance, other than inflammable film, or naked light, other than arc lights in the lanterns of film projectors, spotlights, effects lamps or other electrical apparatus for the production of lighting or optical effects, shall be permitted to be in any such room:

Provided that—

(a) where an inflammable substance is used in repairing or jointing film, there may be kept in the projection and rewinding rooms not more than two fluid ounces thereof which shall be kept in a stoppered container, and

(b) there may be kept in the projection and rewinding rooms a reasonable quantity of wax for the purpose of lubricating film.

Projection and rewinding rooms

7.—(1) Subject to the provisions of Regulation 9 of these Regulations, film shall not be projected, rewound, cleaned, or otherwise manipulated except in a projection or rewinding room.

(2) Projection rooms, rewinding rooms and any part of the building to which there is direct access from a projection or rewinding room shall be well ventilated with fresh air.

(3) No doorway or hatchway of a projection or rewinding room shall communicate directly with the auditorium or any other part of the building to which the public are admitted.

(4)(a) Doorways and hatchways of projection or rewinding rooms shall be provided with doors or hatches.

(b) Such of the said doors and hatches as open upon any room lobby or space communicating directly with the auditorium or with any other part of the building to which the public are admitted shall be close-fitting so as to prevent, so far as practicable, the passage of smoke.

(c) Without prejudice to the provisions of paragraph (2) of Regulation 12 of these Regulations, all holes (other than doorways and hatchways) in the walls, ceilings or floors of projection or rewinding rooms through which smoke might pass directly into another part of the building shall be so sealed as to prevent the passage of smoke.

(5) The doors and hatches of projection or rewinding rooms, other than those communicating directly with the open air or allowing direct communication between a projection room and another projection room or a rewinding room, shall except when in immediate use be kept closed while the public are on the premises.

(6) Subject to the provisions of section four of the Cinematograph Act, 1909 (which relate to powers of entry for inspection), no person unless authorised by the person in charge of the premises shall be permitted to enter, or remain, in a projection or rewinding room while the public are on the premises.

Projection rooms

8.—(1) Projection rooms shall be large enough to enable the operators to work freely at the film projectors and any other equipment therein.

(2) The openings in the front face of a projection room—

(a) shall be fitted with windows of plate glass;

(b) shall not be larger than is necessary for effective projection and observation.

[*As repealed by the Cinematograph (Safety) (Scotland) (Amendment) Regulations 1969 (SI 1969/1575) reg.2 (effective 19 November 1969).*]

(4) The supply of electricity to the film projectors and other equipment in a projection room, not being telephone, signal or other equipment using only electricity of low energy, shall be capable of being cut off by switches or other means of control placed in the projection room.

(5) [1](a) Subject to the provisions of paragraph (1) of regulation 8a and of paragraph (7) of regulation 31 hereof, whenever a film projector is working in a projection room a competent operator who has attained the age of eighteen years shall be in charge of, and present in, the projection room."

(b) Notwithstanding sub-paragraph (a) of this paragraph the said operator may leave the projection room for a short period in case of need so long as an assistant, being a person who has attained the age of seventeen years, is left in charge of, and present in, the projection room and the operator remains on the premises.

NOTE

1. As amended by the Cinematograph (Safety) (Scotland) Amendment Regulations 1971 (SI 1971/471) reg.3 (effective 31 March 1971).

Automatic control of projectors

[1]**8A.**—(1) Notwithstanding the provisions of sub-paragraph (a) of paragraph (5) of regulation 8 of these regulations the operator in charge of a projection room may from time to time leave that projection room for a period not exceeding fifteen minutes and without leaving an assistant in charge of and present in that projection room if—

(a) there is no inflammable film in the premises other than film stored and locked up in accordance with the provisions of paragraph (6) of regulation 5 of these regulations;

(b) the said operator remains within the rooms and other places mentioned in sub-paragraph (c)(i) of this paragraph; and

(c) every film projector working in that projection room during the absence of the said operator is controlled by equipment which will automatically extinguish the source of light in the projector lantern stop the projector mechanism, and cause to sound continuously—

(i) alarm signals clearly audible in that projection room and in every room, lobby or place in the vicinity thereof commonly used or visited by an operator on duty; and

(ii) an alarm signal audible in a place in the premises where a member of the staff, not being an operator or assistant operator is normally stationed while the public are on the premises, immediately upon the untoward occurrence of any of the events specified in the next following paragraph.

(2) The events referred to in sub-paragraph (c) of the last foregoing paragraph are—

(i) the film in the projector breaking or stopping;

(ii) the projector mechanism stopping or operating at less than half its normal speed;

(iii) any switch or contractor controlling the source of light in the projector lantern or the motor driving the projector mechanism, and controlled by any such control equipment as aforesaid, failing to break in due time an electrical circuit controlled by it;

(iv) any failure of the light in the projector lantern which is not immediately and automatically made good;

(v) any failure in the supply of electricity to any such control equipment as aforesaid.

(3) Any such control equipment as aforesaid and any equipment associated therewith or controlled thereby shall be tested once a year by a competent engineer appointed by or on behalf of the occupier of the premises and a certificate stating the condition of the equipment shall, after each test, be sent to the licensing authority by or on behalf of the occupier of the premises.

NOTE

1. As amended by the Cinematograph (Safety) (Scotland) Amendment Regulations 1971 (SI 1971/471) reg.3 (effective 31 March 1971).

16mm film

9.—(1) The provisions of paragraph (1) of Regulation 7 of these Regulations shall not apply in relation to film which does not exceed sixteen millimetres in width and which is not inflammable film.

(2) No inflammable substance shall be used in repairing or jointing film in the auditorium or any other part of the premises to which the public are admitted while the public are present there.

(3) When such film as aforesaid is projected in the auditorium the following provisions shall apply:—

(a) the film projector shall be surrounded by a clear space at least three feet wide which persons, not authorised by the person in charge of the projector or under section four of the Cinematograph Act, 1909 (which relates to powers of entry for inspection), are prevented from entering by the erection of a barrier or other effective means;

(b) no smoking shall be permitted within the said clear space;

(c) the film projector shall be in the charge of a competent person who shall be present within the said clear space whenever the projector is working;

(d) (i) no illuminant, other than electric light in hermetically sealed lamps, shall be used in the film projector;

(ii) the illuminant shall be separately encased in such a way as to prevent it accidentally coming in contact with the film;

(e) electrical conductors used for the film projector shall, so far as practicable, be placed out of reach of the public.

Projectors

10.—[1](1) Unless the source of light in a film projector is an electrical discharge lamp which will not light or remain lit when the projector is not running, the projector shall be fitted with an electric shutter which, when the projector stops running, automatically cuts off the course of light from the film gate.

(4) The foregoing provisions of this Regulation shall not apply to film projectors constructed to use only film not exceeding sixteen millimetres in width and of which the illuminant complies with the provisions of sub-paragraph (d) of paragraph (3) of Regulation 9 of these Regulations.

(5) All the mechanism of a film projector shall be guarded except in so far as this not reasonably practicable in the particular circumstances.

NOTE

1. As amended by the Cinematograph (Safety) (Scotland) Amendment Regulations 1971 (SI 1971/471) reg.4 (effective 31 March 1971).

Electrical supply for projectors and other equipment

11. The supply of electricity to film projectors, spotlights, effects lamps or other electrical apparatus for the production of lighting or optical effects shall be by way of a circuit or circuits separate from any circuit used for supplying electricity for the general lighting or the safety lighting.

Sealing of walls

12.—(1) Where a pipe, duct or conductor enters a building at or below ground level, the hole through which the pipe, duct or conductor enters the building shall be so stopped as to prevent leakage of gas into the building through the hole.

(2) The holes by which pipes, ducts or conductors pass through a fire-resisting wall, floor or ceiling within a building shall be so sealed as to prevent the passage of fire and smoke.

Gas valves

13. The main valves and cocks controlling the supply of gas to the premises shall, if situated within a building, be placed as near as practicable to a door situate on the ground floor and easily accessible from outside the premises; and such valves and cocks shall if accessible to the public be secured against unauthorised interference.

Inspection of ceilings

14. All ceilings in those parts of the premises to which the public are admitted shall be inspected at least once in every five years by a competent person appointed by, or on behalf of, the occupier of the premises, and a certificate concerning the condition of the ceilings shall after each inspection be forwarded to the licensing authority by, or on behalf of, the occupier.

General lighting

15.—(1) In all parts of the building to which the public are admitted and in all passages, courts, ramps and stairways to which the public have access and which lead from the auditorium to outside the premises there shall be provided means of illumination (in these Regulations referred to as "general lighting") by electricity or gas capable of illuminating those parts clearly.

(2) All notices indicating exits from any part of the premises to which the public are admitted shall be illuminated by the general lighting at all times when the public are on the premises.

(3)(a) The means by which the general lighting is controlled—

(i) shall be so situated as to be easily accessible to those members of the staff who may be required to operate them;

(ii) shall be so situated or concealed that members of the public are unlikely to interfere with them;

(iii) shall not, in the case of electrical switchgear, be situated in a rewinding room unless that room is also a projection room;

(iv) shall not, in the case of gas taps and cocks, be situated in a projection room or a rewinding room.

(b) The means by which the general lighting of the auditorium is controlled shall, in addition to complying with the provisions of sub-paragraph (a) of this paragraph, be so constructed and arranged that when the auditorium is not clearly illuminated by the general lighting it can be quickly so illuminated.

(c) If switchgear controlling the electricity for the general lighting of the auditorium is situated in a projection room, other means of control—

(i) situated outside the projection room and also complying with the foregoing provisions of this paragraph shall be provided; and

(ii) shall be so constructed and arranged that when the auditorium is not clearly illuminated by the general lighting it can be quickly so illuminated notwithstanding that the means of control in the projection room may be switched off or inoperable.

(d) All taps and cocks controlling gas for general lighting shall, in the case of the taps of individual lamps, be secured against unauthorised interference and, in the case of all other such taps and cocks, be situated in a place to which the public are not admitted or, if this is not practicable, be secured against unauthorised interference.

Safety lighting

16.—(1) In addition to the general lighting, means of illumination adequate to enable the public to see their way out of the premises without assistance from the general lighting (in these Regulations referred to as "safety lighting") shall be provided—

(a) in the auditorium and all other parts of the building to which the public are admitted;

(b) in all passages, courts, ramps and stairways to which the public have access and which lead from the auditorium to outside the premises;

(c) for the illumination of all notices indicating exits from any part of the premises to which the public are admitted.

(2) The safety lighting shall be kept on at all times when the public are on the premises except in those parts of the premises which are lit equally by daylight.

(3) Subject to the provisions of Regulation 17 of these Regulations, the safety lighting shall be supplied from a source other than that which supplies the general lighting and shall be by electricity or gas:

Provided that the safety lighting may be by colza oil or night-lights if—

(a) electricity and gas are not both supplied to the premises, or

(b) there is a failure of the ordinary safety lighting.

(4) An electrical conductor used for the safety lighting shall not be contained in the same protective covering as a conductor used for any other purpose.

(5)(a) If the safety lighting is by electricity the means of control thereof shall be situated in a place to which the public are not admitted.

(b) If the safety lighting is by gas—

(i) the taps of individual lamps shall be secured against unauthorised interference and all other taps or cocks controlling gas for safety lighting shall be situated in a place to which the public are not admitted or, if this is not practicable, shall be secured against unauthorised interference;

(ii) taps or cocks controlling gas for safety lighting shall not be situated in a projection or rewinding room.

(6) Any circuit used for supplying electricity for use in a projection or rewinding room, other than a circuit used to supply electricity to film projectors, spotlights, and effects lamps or other electrical apparatus for the production of lighting or optical effects shall not be connected to a circuit used for supplying electricity for the safety lighting unless it is so arranged and protected that the occurrence of any electrical fault therein would not affect the last-mentioned circuit.

Batteries for safety lighting

17.—(1) Any battery supplying the safety lighting shall be fully charged before the public are first admitted to the premises on any day and, unless it is a battery mentioned in paragraph (2) of this Regulation, shall be of such capacity and so maintained as to be capable of supplying at normal voltage the full load of the safety lighting during the whole time that the public are on the premises.

(2) Notwithstanding paragraph (3) of Regulation 16 of these Regulations one or more floating or trickle-charged batteries from the same source as supplies the general lighting may be used to supply electricity for the safety lighting if—

(a) the batteries are fully charged before the public are first admitted to the premises on any day;

(b) the rate of charging the batteries is so regulated that the batteries will not discharge except on failure of the supply of electricity to the batteries;

(c) the batteries will not discharge through the supply circuit in the event of a failure of the supply of electricity to the batteries;

(d) the capacity of the batteries is sufficient to supply at normal voltage the full load of the safety lighting for not less than three hours;

(e) in the case of trickle-charged batteries, there are provided automatic change-over contractors so designed and maintained as to operate immediately and efficiently in case of need, and which are tested on each day that there is a cinematograph exhibition and before the public are admitted to the premises in order to ensure that they are in proper working order.

Batteries

18.—(1) A battery having cells or containers of celluloid shall not be permitted to be in the premises.

(2) A battery of a type which cannot be recharged to full capacity shall not be used to supply electricity for the general lighting or the safety lighting.

(3) Where batteries are used to supply electricity for either the general lighting or the safety lighting—

(a) such parts of the conductors connecting the batteries one to another or connecting the batteries to the fuses, circuit breakers, or other similar devices protecting the circuits going out from the batteries, as are situated within the room in which the batteries are installed shall not be enclosed in ducting or conduit;

(b) such parts of the said conductors as are situated within the said room shall, unless suitably insulated, be properly supported and separated so that they are kept apart;

(c) the fuses, circuit breakers and similar devices aforesaid, unless situated within the said room, shall be situated as near as is practicable to the point where the said conductors emerge from that room.

(4) Any battery used to supply electricity for either the general lighting or the safety lighting shall supply electricity only for the general lighting or the safety lighting as the case may be.

(5) Any battery used to supply electricity for either the general lighting or safety lighting shall, at least once in every six months, have its capacity tested by a person appointed by, or on behalf of, the occupier of the premises and the date and result of the test shall be entered in a register to be

kept for the purpose and available for inspection by persons authorised in that behalf by the licensing authority.

Failure of lighting

19.—(1)(a) If there is a failure of the general lighting and the general lighting is by gas, the public shall be instructed to leave the premises forthwith.

(b) If there is a failure of the general lighting and the general lighting is by electricity, the public shall, if the general lighting is not restored within one hour, be instructed to leave the premises at the end of that hour.

(2)(a) If there is a failure of the safety lighting and the safety lighting is not by electricity, all parts of the premises in which means of illumination are provided in accordance with paragraph (1) of Regulation 15 of these Regulations shall be clearly illuminated by the general lighting and the public shall be instructed to leave the premises forthwith.

(b) If there is a failure of the safety lighting and the safety lighting is by electricity, all parts of the premises in which means of illumination are provided in accordance with paragraph (1) of Regulation 15 of these Regulations other than the auditorium, shall forthwith be clearly illuminated by the general lighting and, if at the end of one hour safety lighting is not restored, the auditorium shall be clearly illuminated by the general lighting and the public shall then be instructed to leave the premises forthwith.

Fuses, switches and earths

20.—(1) Every electrical main circuit and sub-circuit in the premises shall be protected against excess current by fuses, circuit-breakers or other similar devices which will operate automatically at current values which are suitably related to the safe current ratings of the circuit and of the equipment connected to the circuit.

(2)(a) Every circuit supplying electricity for the control equipment of electric discharge-lamps having a rated electrical input exceeding 500 watts, or for electronic equipment shall, where the fuses, circuit-breakers or other similar devices aforesaid do not afford adequate protection, be provided also with electrical or thermo-electrical devices to break the circuit automatically on any dangerous rise in the temperature of the said equipment or of the transformers, chokes or smoothing devices used in connection therewith.

(b) Any such electrical or thermo-electrical devices shall be tested once a year by a competent electrical engineer appointed by, or on behalf of, the occupier of the premises.

(c) The foregoing provisions of this paragraph shall not, until the first day of January, 1958, apply in relation to electronic equipment or control equipment of electric discharge-lamps in use in the premises before the date on which these Regulations come into operation.

(3)(a) Every main circuit and sub-circuit in the premises shall be provided with earth-leakage protective devices which on the occurrence of an earth fault will disconnect the defective circuit from the supply of electricity.

(b) Sub-paragraph (a) of this paragraph shall not apply where the possible earth fault leakage current from the circuit substantially exceeds that required to operate the fuses, circuit-breakers or other similar devices aforesaid.

(4) All metal work not intended ordinarily to conduct electricity but liable to become charged with electricity if the insulation of a conductor should become defective or if a defect should occur in any electrical equipment shall be earthed.

(5) The supply of electricity to all electric signs, notices or advertising devices and to all electric discharge-lamp installations, shall be capable of being cut off by switches or other means of control so situated as to be easily accessible to members of the staff but so as not to be easily accessible to the public.

(6)(a) Every socket outlet, other than for deaf aids, in any part of the premises to which the public are admitted shall be controlled by a switch adjacent to the socket outlet.

(b) All plugs and socket outlets, other than for deaf aids, in any part of the premises to which the public are admitted shall be so constructed that the pins of the plugs and the socket outlets cannot be touched while they are live.

(7) Switchgear controlling a main circuit or sub-circuit, and not being in the auditorium shall be clearly and legibly labelled to indicate which circuit it controls.

Electric discharge-lamps

21.—(1) All electric discharge-lamp installations shall comply with the following requirements:—

(a) control equipment for electric discharge-lamps and the transformers, chokes and smoothing devices used in connection therewith shall be so placed that there is adequate ventilation and adequate access thereto for the purposes of inspection and maintenance;

(b) fixed electric discharge-lamps shall be placed out of reach of the public or so protected that if a lamp is broken no live electrode can be touched.

(2) Without prejudice to the provisions of paragraph (5) of Regulation 20 of these Regulations the supply of electricity to electric discharge-lamp installations on the outside of a building, or used within a building when the public are not admitted, and in which the voltage between any two points of the installation exceeds 650 volts shall be capable of being cut off by one or more switches or other means of control situated outside any building and so as to be accessible to employees of the relevant authority (as defined in section 6 of the Fire (Scotland) Act 2005 (asp 5)) but so as not to be easily accessible to the public.

Wiring and ventilating ducts

22.—(1) All electric wiring shall be suitably insulated.

(2) All electric wiring shall have a protective covering over the insulation thereof and, except where it is necessary that it should remain flexible, shall be kept securely fixed in position.

(3) The protective covering shall be—

(a) made of metal or other material of such rigidity as to afford substantial protection against mechanical injury;

(b) made of material which does not readily ignite or decompose;

(c) if made of metal, effectively earthed;

(d) in the case of wiring in premises which are built or wholly or mainly rewired after the date on which these Regulations come into operation, not made of lead.

(4) Where it is necessary for wiring to remain flexible its protective covering shall be flexible and the following provisions shall apply in lieu of the provisions of paragraph (3) of this Regulation:—

(a) the protective covering of such wiring used in connection with arc lamps, spotlights, effects lamps or other electrical equipment for the production of lighting or optical effects and exposed to excessive heat shall be of asbestos or other material which will prevent the heat damaging the conductor or its insulation;

(b) the protective covering of such wiring, other than that referred to in sub-paragraph (a) of this paragraph shall be such as to give a degree of protection not less than that afforded by tough rubber sheathing;

(c) the protective covering of such wiring shall not be made of lead, and if made of metal, shall be effectively earthed;

(d) such wiring shall not be longer than is necessary;

(e) such wiring shall be securely fixed, and its protective covering reinforced, at the point of entry into the equipment, plug or other fitting to which it is connected.

(5) The foregoing provisions of this Regulations shall not apply to such parts of the conductors mentioned in paragraph (3) of Regulation 18 of these Regulations connecting the batteries one to another or connecting the batteries to the fuses, circuit-breakers or other similar devices protecting the outgoing circuits, as are situated within the room in which the batteries are installed.

(6) The provisions of paragraphs (2), (3) and (4) of this Regulation shall not apply to—

(a) wiring, intended to conduct only electricity of low energy, of telephones, signal systems, deaf aids, public address equipment, depolarizer circuits for electric torch batteries and other similar equipment;

(b) audio circuit wiring;

(c) internal wiring of electric organs not intended to conduct electricity at a voltage exceeding 100 volts;

(d) conductors for electric discharge-lamp installations in which the voltage between any two points of the installation exceeds 650 volts if the conductors are so placed that they cannot be touched by the public and are suitably insulated and protected;

(e) temporary wiring if the licensing authority is satisfied that the wiring is so insulated and so protected or placed as to be reasonably safe in the circumstances.

(7) No electric wiring, other than wiring for the purpose of operating or lighting the ventilating system and having its own protective covering, shall, after the date upon which these Regulations come into operation, be placed (otherwise than by way of repair of wiring already installed) in any ventilating duct.

(8) Any lighting fittings or other electrical apparatus installed in any ventilating duct after the date upon which these Regulations come into operation shall be totally enclosed.

Generators, transformers and switchgear

23.—(1) Electricity generating plant and main supply transformers shall be placed in a room or rooms—

(a) separate from the auditorium,
(b) of substantial construction,
(c) of which the walls, floors and ceilings (except for windows, skylights and openings therein communicating directly with the open air) and doors shall be so constructed or lined as to be fire-resisting,
(d) not communicating directly with the auditorium or with any part of the building to which the public are admitted:

Provided that the provisions of this paragraph shall apply only where such equipment is installed or moved from one room to another after the date on which these Regulations come into operation, or where a room in which such equipment has been installed is altered in structure after the said date.

(2) The switchgear and fuses controlling or protecting the main supply of electricity shall be placed in a room to which the public are not admitted and any door thereof which communicates directly with any part of the premises to which the public are admitted, shall be kept locked.

Heating appliances

24.—(1) Every heating appliance used in the premises which is so situated as to be within reach of any member of the public shall be fitted with guards which comply with the standards of construction and fitting required by the Heating Appliances (Fireguards) (Scotland) Regulations, 1953, in the case of a heating appliance of a type which is so designed that it is suitable for use in a dwelling house or other residential premises.

(2) Every heating appliance used in the premises shall be situated sufficiently far from any woodwork, hangings or other materials or substances liable to catch fire for there to be no likelihood of fire by reason of their proximity to the heating appliance.

(3) Every heating appliance situated in a part of the premises to which the public are admitted shall be fixed in position.

(4) Every heating appliance situated in a projection or rewinding room shall be so constructed and enclosed that there is no likelihood of film igniting or decomposing by reason of contact with, or proximity to, the heating element.

(5)(a) No oil-burning heaters other than those forming part of boiler installations shall be used in the premises.
(b) No gas fire shall be used in a projection or rewinding room.

Electrical apparatus generally

25. Electrical apparatus and equipment in the premises shall not be used for such a purpose or in such a manner or when it is in such a condition as to cause danger of electric shock, fire or explosion.

Supervision of electrical installations

26. A person who has attained the age of eighteen years and who has received sufficient training for the purpose shall be made responsible for ensuring that the electrical installations and equipment in the projection room are maintained in a good serviceable condition.

Inspection of electrical installations

27. All electrical installations shall be inspected once a year by a competent electrical engineer appointed by, or on behalf of, the occupier of the premises and a certificate stating the condition of the installations shall, after each inspection, be forwarded to the licensing authority by, or on behalf of, the occupier of the premises.

PART II

ADDITIONAL REQUIREMENTS IN CONNECTION WITH CINEMATOGRAPH EXHIBITIONS FOR WHICH INFLAMMABLE FILM IS USED

Licence to be necessary

28. Any means of producing pictures for a cinematograph exhibition which includes the use of inflammable film is by this Regulation specified as a means involving risk such that it is inexpedient that paragraph (1) of subsection (1) of section five of the Cinematograph Act, 1952 (which provides that a licence shall not be required in the case of certain exhibitions to which the public are not admitted or are admitted without payment), should have effect in the case of cinematograph exhibitions where the pictures are produced by such means.

Application of Part II

29. Subject to the provisions of subsection (4) of section seven of the Cinematograph Act, 1909 (which exempts exhibitions in private dwelling houses to which the public are not admitted), the following provisions of this Part of these Regulations shall apply in addition to the provisions of Part I of these Regulations in connection with the giving of cinematograph exhibitions for which any inflammable film is used and to the premises used in connection with the giving of such exhibitions and to the parts thereof and the fittings, furniture, furnishings and equipment therein in this Part of these Regulations mentioned.

Fire precautions

30. All persons employed in connection with cinematograph exhibitions who may be called upon to handle or use inflammable film shall be warned of the special dangers attaching to inflammable film and shall be instructed in the special precautions applicable to their particular duties which should be taken in connection with its handling and use.

Projection and rewinding rooms

31.—(1) Separate rooms shall be provided as a projection room and as a rewinding room respectively and inflammable film shall not be projected except in the projection room, or rewound, cleaned, or (except in the ordinary course of projection) otherwise manipulated, except in the rewinding room.

(2) The walls, floors and ceilings (except for windows, skylights and openings therein communicating directly with the open air) and doors of the projection and rewinding rooms shall be so constructed or lined as to be fire-resisting.

(3) All fittings, fixtures, furniture and furnishings (other than floor coverings) in the projection and rewinding rooms shall be of metal, hardwood,

or such other material or so treated and maintained as not readily to catch fire.

(4)(a) Every communicating doorway between the projection and rewinding rooms shall be fitted with a close-fitting, self-closing door, so constructed and maintained that it can be opened easily from either side, and the door shall be kept closed when not in immediate use.

(b) Every other opening allowing direct communication between the projection and rewinding rooms shall be fitted with a close-fitting, fire-resisting hatch or shutter which shall either be secured in a closed position or be so constructed and maintained as to be self-closing.

(5) All doorways of the projection and rewinding rooms, other than communicating doorways between them, shall be fitted with self-closing doors so constructed and maintained that they will open easily on being pushed from inside and can be opened from outside the projection or rewinding room.

(6)(a) One entrance to the projection room shall be from the open air.

(b) Each projection or rewinding room shall be provided with a doorway and also, unless the licensing authority shall have been satisfied that this requirement is impracticable or unreasonable in the circumstances of the particular case, an alternative way of egress for the operators, whether a doorway hatchway or window.

(7)(a) Whenever inflammable film is being projected a competent operator who has attained the age of eighteen years shall be in charge of, and present in, the projection room.

(b) Notwithstanding sub-paragraph (a) of this paragraph the said operator may leave the projection room for a short period in case of need, so long as an assistant, being a person who has attained the age of 17 years, is left in charge of the projection room and the operator remains on the premises and within call.

(8) Subject to the provisions of section four of the Cinematograph Act, 1909 (which relate to powers of entry for inspection), no person shall be permitted while the public are on the premises to enter or remain in the projection or rewinding room unless his presence there is necessary or desirable for the purpose of the exhibition or for the purpose of instruction and is authorised in accordance with the provisions of paragraph (6) of Regulation 7 of these Regulations.

Projection room shutters

[1]**31A.**—(1) The openings in the front face of a projection room in which inflammable film is used shall be fitted with metal shutters so constructed that—

(a) they can be closed from a point within the projection room near the projectors and also from a point outside the projection and rewinding rooms which is accessible to members of the staff;

(b) they can, if required, be closed simultaneously; and

(c) when closed, they fit closely over the openings.

(2) The shutters aforesaid and the mechanism for closing them shall be tested on each day on which there is a cinematograph exhibition, and before the public are admitted to the premises.

NOTE

1. As inserted by the Cinematograph (Safety) (Scotland) (Amendment) Regulations 1969 (SI 1969/1575) reg.3 (effective 19 November 1969).

Projectors used for inflammable film

31B.—(1) A film projector in which inflammable film is used shall have a metal shutter (in addition to and operating independently of that required by regulation 10(1) of these regulations) capable of cutting off the source of light from the film gate; and the shutter shall either be such that it operates automatically when the projector stops, or that it can be readily operated by hand:

Provided that this paragraph shall not apply to—

(a) a projector in which the source of light is an electric discharge lamp which will not light or remain lit when the projector is not working; or

(b) a projector constructed only to use film and exceeding 16 mm, in width and in which the source of light is a hermetically sealed electric lamp.

(2) A projector in which inflammable film is used shall be so constructed and maintained that the film gate of that projector is not liable to become overheated.

(3) The openings above and below the film gate of a projector in which inflammable film is used shall be sufficiently narrow to prevent flame travelling upwards or downwards.

NOTE

1. As amended by the Cinematograph (Safety) (Scotland) Amendment Regulations 1971 (SI 1971/471) reg.5 (effective 31 March 1971).

Spools and spool-boxes

32.—(1) Each film projector in which inflammable film is used shall be fitted with one or more metal spool-boxes of substantial construction, and when the projector is working the film shall be made to pass from such a spool-box either to the same or to another such spool-box.

(2) The spool-boxes shall be so constructed as to prevent, as far as practicable, the possibility of flame passing to or from the inside thereof when the spool-box is closed, and they shall be kept closed when the projector is working.

(3) The spools upon which inflammable film is wound shall be substantially constructed of material which does not readily ignite or decompose with heat and shall be designed to accommodate not more than 2,050 feet of film.

Inflammable film

33.—(1) Notwithstanding the provisions of paragraph (6) of Regulation 5 of these Regulations inflammable film in current use and not exceeding 21,000 feet in all may be kept in the projection and rewinding rooms.

(2) Inflammable film in a projection or rewinding room shall be kept at all times, subject to the exigencies of its use, in closed metal containers of robust construction.

(3) Inflammable and non-inflammable film shall not be wound on the same spool.

(4) Inflammable film shall not be used if it is in such a condition as to be likely to jam or break while passing through the film projector.

Equipment in projection and rewinding rooms

34.—(1) The lighting of the projection and rewinding rooms shall be by electricity or daylight.

(2) All transformers, rectifiers, resistances, choke coils, motors and the illuminants of viewing devices for the examination of film, in the projection or rewinding rooms which are liable to attain a temperature at which inflammable film will ignite or decompose shall without preventing their proper ventilation be so guarded or enclosed as to prevent the ignition or decomposition of film by accidental contact with any of them or with any part of the equipment to which their heat may be communicated.

(3) All metal work of equipment used in rewinding film shall be earthed so as safely to discharge static electricity.

(4) No electrical equipment shall be allowed in the rewinding room except—

(a) equipment for lighting or heating the room, rewinding machines, and viewing devices for the examination of film, and

(b) telephones, signal systems, and hand torches using only electricity of low energy.

Part III

Requirements in Connection with Cinematograph Exhibitions in Premises used only Occasionally

Application of Part III

35.—(1) Subject to the provisions of subsection (4) of section seven of the Cinematograph Act, 1909, and of section five of the Cinematograph Act, 1952 (which relate to exemptions in favour of certain exhibitions to which the public are not admitted or are admitted without payment), the provisions of this Part of these Regulations shall apply—

(a) in connection with the giving of cinematograph exhibitions in an auditorium where seating is provided for not more than four hundred persons, in premises which have not been used on more than three days in any week in the current calendar year for cinematograph exhibitions (not being exempted exhibitions within the meaning of section five of the Cinematograph Act, 1952), and during which there is no inflammable film in the premises;

(b) in connection with the giving of cinematograph exhibitions in premises for which there is no licence in force, and to which subsection (2) of section seven of the Cinematograph Act, 1909, applies, and during which there is no inflammable film in the premises;

(c) in connection with the giving of cinematograph exhibitions in any building or structure of a moveable character to which subsection (3) of section seven of the Cinematograph Act, 1909, applies, and during which there is no inflammable film in the premises,

[1](d) subject to paragraph (2) of this regulation, in connection with the giving of cinematograph exhibitions in premises which are (or in a part of premises which is, as the case may be), while the cinematograph exhibition is being given, used for another purpose or purposes to which the giving of the cinematograph exhibition is incidental or subsidiary (not being exempted exhibitions within the meaning of section five of the Cinematograph Act 1952), and by

means which include the use of any electro-magnetic tape or disc recording of vision,"; and

[1](2) In the case of cinematograph exhibition to which sub-paragraph (d) of the last preceding paragraph relates (whether or not any of sub-paragraphs (a), (b) and (c) of that paragraph also relates thereto), the provisions of this part of these regulations shall apply with the exception of regulations 37, 40 and 41, and to the premises used in connection with the giving of such exhibitions and to the parts thereof and the fittings, furniture, furnishings and equipment therein in this Part of these Regulations mentioned.

NOTE

1. As inserted by the Cinematograph (Safety) (Scotland) Amendment Regulations 1983 (SI 1983/367) reg.2 (effective 11 April 1983).

Exits

36. Regulation 2 of these Regulations shall apply in connection with the giving of cinematograph exhibitions to which this Part of these Regulations applies with the exception of paragraph (5) thereof.

Seats

37.—(1) Where the audience exceeds two hundred and fifty persons all seats in the auditorium shall, except in boxes accommodating not more than eight persons, be either securely fixed to the floor or battened together in lengths of not less than four or more than twelve.

(2) Regulation 3 of these Regulations shall apply in connection with the giving of cinematograph exhibitions to which this Part of these Regulations applies, with the exception of paragraph (2) thereof.

Staff

38.—(1) A responsible person who has attained the age of eighteen years, being the licensee or some person nominated in writing by the licensee, shall be in charge of the premises at all times when the public are on the premises.

(2) At least two attendants, neither of whom shall be a person in charge of a projector, but of whom one may be the person in charge of the premises assist persons in entering and leaving the auditorium.

(3) Every member of the staff shall be instructed by the licensee of the premises or by some person nominated by the licensee in the safety precautions to be observed in the premises so far as those precautions relate to his duties, and in the action to be taken by him in the event of fire or other emergency.

Fire precautions

39.—(1) Fire appliances suitable to the fire risks in the premises shall be provided.

(2) The fire appliances shall be maintained in proper working order and be available for instant use.

(3) No inflammable substance shall be used for cleaning any film or film projector.

(4) Any metal work of a film projector liable to become charged with electricity if the insulation of a conductor should become defective or if a defect should occur in any film projection equipment, shall be effectively earthed.

16mm film

40.—(1) The provisions of this Regulation shall apply in relation to film which does not exceed sixteen millimetres in width.

(2) No inflammable substance shall be used in repairing or jointing film in the auditorium or in any other part of the premises to which the public are admitted while the public are present there.

(3) If a film projector is placed in the auditorium or elsewhere than in a projection room—

(a) the film projector shall be surrounded by a clear space at least three feet wide which persons, not authorised by the person in charge of the projector or under section four of the Cinematograph Act, 1909 (which relates to powers of entry for inspection), are prevented from entering by the erection of a barrier or other effective means;

(b) no smoking shall be permitted within the said clear space;

(c) the film projector shall be in the charge of a competent person who shall be present within the said clear space whenever the projector is working;

(d) (i) no illuminant, other than electric light in hermetically sealed lamps, shall be used in the film projector;

(ii) the illuminant shall be separately encased in such a way as to prevent it accidentally coming in contact with the film;

(e) electrical conductors used for the film projector shall be suitably insulated and provided with a suitable protective covering over the insulation and shall, so far as practicable, be placed out of reach of the public.

Projection and rewinding rooms

41.—(1) Film which exceeds sixteen millimetres in width shall not be projected, rewound, cleaned or otherwise manipulated except in a projection or rewinding room to which the public are not admitted.

(2) Projection rooms shall be large enough to enable the operators to work freely at the film projectors and any other equipment therein.

(3) Whenever a film projector is working in a projection room a competent person shall be in charge of, and present in, the projection room.

Lighting

42.—(1) In all parts of the building to which the public are admitted means of illumination shall be provided capable of illuminating those parts clearly.

(2)(a) Means of illumination adequate to enable the public to see their way out of the building shall be kept on at all times when the public are on the premises—

(i) in those parts of the building to which the public are admitted except those which are lit equally well by daylight, and

(ii) for the illumination of all notices indicating exits for use by the public in leaving the auditorium.

(b) Means of illumination provided under paragraph (1) of this Regulation may be used for the purposes of this paragraph.

(3) If at any time there is a failure of the means of illumination mentioned in sub-paragraph (a) of paragraph (2) of this Regulation, and that means of illumination is either by electricity or by gas, the parts of the building and notices mentioned in the said sub-paragraph (a) shall immediately be

illuminated by some alternative means of illumination adequate to enable the public to see their way out of the building.

Part IV

Additional Requirements in connection with Television Exhibitions

Application of Part IV

43. Subject to the provisions of subsection (4) of section seven of the Cinematograph Act, 1909, and of section five of the Cinematograph Act, 1952 (which relate to exemptions in favour of certain exhibitions to which the public are not admitted or are admitted without payment), the provisions of this Part of these Regulations shall apply, in addition to the provisions of Part I or Part III of these Regulations, as the case may require, in connection with the giving of cinematograph exhibitions by means of television equipment and to the premises used in connection with the giving of such exhibitions and to the television equipment therein.

Voltage and amperage

44. The applied voltage of electricity used in television equipment shall not exceed 150,000 volts and the prospective fault current shall not exceed one ampere at any voltage exceeding 650 volts.

Television equipment

45. Television equipment shall comply with the following requirements:—

(a) every circuit supplying electricity for high-tension television equipment shall be provided with electrical or thermo-electrical devices to break the circuit automatically on any dangerous rise in the temperature of the equipment or of the transformers, chokes, or smoothing devices used in connection therewith;

(b) the television projector shall be so screened and the projected light beam shall be so directed, screened or filtered that no person shall be subject to a radiation of X-rays of a rate exceeding 0.5 Rontgen units during seventy hours' continuous operation.

Television recording equipment

46. No inflammable film shall be used in connection with any television recording equipment in the premises.

Notice of installation

47. Television equipment shall not be installed in the premises unless two weeks' notice shall have been given to the licensing authority and shall not be used unless a reasonable opportunity shall have been given for any inspection or consultation which the licensing authority may think fit to undertake or require.

PART V

MISCELLANEOUS

Exhibition of Regulations

48. Copies of these Regulations shall be exhibited in premises used in connection with the giving of cinematograph exhibitions to which any of the foregoing Parts of these Regulations applies so that they can easily be seen by members of the staff.

Interpretation

49.—(1) In these Regulations—

"*building*" includes a building or structure of a moveable character;

"*fire-resisting*" means, in relation to a wall, floor, ceiling, door, hatch or shutter of a room, so capable of enduring fire as to be capable of preventing, for a period of thirty minutes from the occurrence, the passage of any fire which might occur in that room;

"*gas fire*" includes a gas-burning heating appliance in which the source of the gas is in liquid form or the gas is contained in a portable container;

"*general lighting*" has the meaning ascribed to it by Regulation 15 of these Regulations;

"*heating appliance*" means a gas or electric fire other than one which is so constructed that when the appliance is burning, or, in the case of an electric fire, consuming electric energy, at the maximum rate for which it is designed, the heating element and, in the case of a gas fire, any flame, is so enclosed within the body of the appliance that there is no likelihood of injury to the person from burning, or of ignition of clothing or other fabrics by reason of, in either case, contact with or proximity to, the heating element or any flame;

"*heating element*" means, in the case of a gas fire, that part thereof which is designed to be directly heated by the impingement thereon of the burning fuel, and, in the case of an electric fire, that part thereof which is designed to be directly heated by the passage of the electric current;

"*inflammable film*" means film which is more inflammable than safety film;

"*licence*" means a licence granted under section two of the Cinematograph Act, 1909;

"*licensee*" means the person or persons to whom a current licence shall have been granted, or, if there shall be no such person, then the occupier of the premises;

"*projection room*" means a substantially constructed room, separate from the auditorium, and used for the purpose of projecting moving pictures on to a screen by means of a film projector;

"*rewinding room*" means a substantially constructed room, separate from the auditorium, and used for the purpose of rewinding, examining, cleaning or otherwise manipulation film except in the ordinary course of projection;

"*safety lighting*" has the meaning ascribed to it by Regulation 16 of these Regulations.

(2) The Interpretation Act, 1889, shall apply to the interpretation of these Regulations as it applies to the interpretation of an Act of Parliament.

Repeals

50.—(1) The following Regulations, that is to say—

(a) the Regulations made by the Secretary for Scotland under the Cinematograph Act, 1909, and dated the 22nd September, 1923, and

(b) the Regulations made by the Secretary of State under the Cinematograph Act, 1909, and dated the 6th June, 1930

are hereby revoked.

(2) Section thirty-eight of the Interpretation Act, 1889, shall apply as if these Regulations were an Act of Parliament and as if any Regulations revoked by these Regulations were Acts of Parliament repealed by an Act of Parliament.

Citation and commencement

51.—(1) These Regulations may be cited as the Cinematograph (Safety) (Scotland) Regulations, 1955, and shall come into operation on the first day of January, 1956.

(2) These Regulations shall extend only to Scotland.

GENERAL NOTE

All references to the Cinematograph Act 1952 should now be read as referring to the Cinemas Act 1985. The reference to the Interpretation Act 1889 should be read as referring to the Interpretation Act 1978. These Regulations (albeit in amended form) still apply despite the changes in technology and, in particular, digital projection.

Regulation 4 was amended by the Cinematograph (Safety) (Scotland) Amendment Regulations 2003 (SSI 2003/144) reg.2.

Regulation 5(3) was amended by the Fire (Scotland) Act 2005 (Consequential Modifications and Amendment) (No.2) Order 2005 (SSI 2005/344) Sch.1 para.3.

Regulations 8(2)(c) and (3) were revoked by reg.2 of the Cinematograph (Safety) (Scotland) (Amendment) Regulations 1969 (SI 1969/1575). Regulation 8(5)(a) was substituted for the original and reg.8A added by the Cinematograph (Safety) (Scotland) (Amendment) Regulations 1971 (SI 1971/471).

Regulation 21(2) was amended by the Fire (Scotland) Act 2005 (Consequential Modifications and Amendments) (No.2) Order 2005 (SSI 2005/344) Sch.1 para.1.

Regulation 26 was amended by the Cinematograph (Safety) (Scotland) Amendment Regulations 2003 (SSI 2003/144) reg.2.

Regulation 30(7)(a) was amended by the Cinematograph (Safety) (Scotland) Amendment Regulations 2003 (SSI 2003/144) reg.2.

Regulation 31A was added by reg.3 of the Cinematograph (Safety) (Scotland) (Amendment) Regulations 1969 (SI 1969/1575). Regulation 31B was added by reg.5 of the Cinematograph (Safety) (Scotland) (Amendment) Regulations 1971 (SI 1971/471).

Regulation 35 was amended by reg.2 of the Cinemas (Safety) (Scotland) (Amendment) Regulations 1983 (SI 1983/367).

Regulation 38 was amended by the Cinematograph (Safety) (Scotland) Amendment Regulations 2003 (SSI 2003/144) reg.2.

Cinematograph (Children) (Scotland) (No.2) Regulations 1955

(SI 1955/1912)

[16 December 1955]

The Secretary of State in exercise of the powers conferred on him by sections 1, 2 and 7 of the Cinematograph Act 1909 and section 1 and section 2(1)(b) of the Cinematograph Act 1952, hereby makes the following Regulations:

1.—(1) These Regulations may be cited as the Cinematograph (Children) (Scotland) (No. 2) Regulations, 1955, and shall come into operation on the first day of January, 1956.

(2) The Interpretation Act, 1889, applies to the interpretation of these Regulations as it applies to the interpretation of an Act of Parliament.

(3) These Regulations shall extend only to Scotland.

2.—(1) These Regulations apply to cinematograph exhibitions other than exhibitions given in a private dwelling-house to which the public are not admitted whether on payment or otherwise and exempted exhibitions.

(2) In this Regulation the expression "exempted exhibitions" means exempted exhibitions within the meaning of section five of the Cinematograph Act, 1952, including exhibitions which by virtue of subsection (3) of that section are to be treated as such, but excluding exhibitions which by virtue of subsection (2) thereof are not to be treated as such.

3. No child apparently under the age of five years shall be admitted to a cinematograph exhibition unless the child is accompanied by and in the charge of a person who appears to have attained the age of sixteen years.

4. No child apparently under the age of twelve years shall be admitted after the hour of seven in the evening of any day to a cinematograph exhibition at any premises in the course of which there is to be shown any film or portion of a film which shall have been shown to the public at those premises on that day before the hour of seven in the evening, unless the child is accompanied by and in the charge of a person who appears to have attained the age of sixteen years.

5. At a cinematograph exhibition organised wholly or mainly as an exhibition for children under the age of sixteen years there shall be stationed on the lowest floor of the auditorium not less than one attendant who has attained the age of sixteen years for every one hundred persons or part of one hundred persons present there, and on each floor of the auditorium above the lowest floor not less than one such attendant for every fifty persons or part of fifty persons present there, and the number of such attendants stationed on any floor of the auditorium to which children are admitted shall not be less than the number of exits for use by members of the public in leaving that floor.

6. The Cinematograph (Children) (Scotland) Regulations, 1955, are hereby revoked.

GENERAL NOTE

These regulations provide for the welfare of children at cinematograph exhibitions and require children to be accompanied by persons of 16 or over in certain circumstances. Regulation 5 requires the provision of attendants at exhibitions organised for children.

ANIMAL LICENCES

Performing Animals Regulation Act 1925

(15 and 16 Geo. 5 c.38)

NOTE

1. Entire Act to be repealed by the Animal Health and Welfare (Scotland) Act 2006 (asp 11) Sch.2 para.9 (date yet to be appointed).

ARRANGEMENT OF SECTIONS

Restriction on exhibition and training of performing animals

1.—(1) No person shall exhibit or train any performing animal unless he is registered in accordance with this Act.

(2) Every local authority shall keep a register for the purpose of this Act, and any person who exhibits or trains animals as aforesaid on making an application in the prescribed form to the local authority of the district in which he resides, or if he has no fixed place of residence in Great Britain, to the local authority of such one of the prescribed districts as he may choose, and on payment of such fee as appears to the local authority to be appropriate shall be registered under this Act, unless he is a person, who, in pursuance of an order of the court made under this Act, is prohibited from being so registered.

(3) Any application for registration under this Act shall contain such particulars as to the animals and as to the general nature of the performances in which the animals are to be exhibited or for which they are to be trained as may be prescribed, and the particulars so given shall be entered in the register.

(4) The local authority shall give to every person whose name appears on the register kept by them a certificate of registration in the prescribed form containing the particulars entered in the register.

(5) Every register kept under this Act shall at all reasonable times be open for inspection, and any person shall be entitled to take copies thereof or make extracts therefrom.

(6) Any person entered on the register shall, subject to the provisions of any order made under this Act by any court, be entitled, on making

application for the purpose, to have the particulars entered in the register with respect to him varied, and where any such particulars are so varied the existing certificate shall be cancelled and a new certificate issued.

(7) A copy of every certificate of registration issued by a local authority shall be transmitted by the authority to the Secretary of State and shall be available for inspection at all reasonable times.

(8) A local authority may charge such fees as appear to them to be appropriate for inspection of the register, for taking copies thereof or making extracts therefrom or for inspection of copies of certificates of registration issued by them.

DEFINITIONS

"animal": s.5(1).
"exhibit": s.5(1).
"train": s.5(1).
"local authority": s.6(1).
"prescribed": s.5(1).

GENERAL NOTE

The Act applies to regulate the exhibition and training of performing animals and provides for a system of licensing of those persons who wish to train and exhibit animals. It should be noted that it is the intention of the Scottish Ministers that this legislation will be eventually superseded by orders made under the provisions of s.26 of the Animal Health and Welfare (Scotland) Act 2006 but until such time the 1925 Act remains in force—see p.26 above.

Subsection (1)

The penalty for a contravention of the Act is set out in s.4. Note that, by virtue of s.2, the courts have additional powers to prohibit or restrict the exhibition or training of animals in certain circumstances. Note also the exemption of certain categories of training and exhibition provided for in s.7.

Subsection (2)

Thus a register of all trainers and exhibitions must be kept—the prescribed form thereof is to be found in the rules made pursuant to s.5(2) of the Act. These local authorities in Scotland with which a person of no fixed abode may register are: the City of Aberdeen Council, the City of Dundee Council, the City of Edinburgh Council and the City of Glasgow Council—the Performing Animals Rules 1925 (SR&O 1925/1219) reg.2. A local authority cannot use any view formed in relation to the morality of allowing animals to perform in public as a reason for refusing registration—see *Gerry Cottle's Circus v City of Edinburgh DC*, 1990 S.L.T. 235. The provision in relation to fees was substituted for the original by the Local Government (Scotland) Act 1973 s.209(1) and Sch.25 para.7(a).

Subsection (4)

The prescribed form of the certificate of registration is provided for in the rules.

Subsections (5) and (7)

These subsections were amended and partially repealed by the Local Government (Scotland) Act 1973 s.209(1) and Sch.25 para.7(6)(c). For "at all reasonable times" see Introduction p.30 above.

Subsection (8)

This subsection was added by the Local Government (Scotland) Act 1973 s.209(1) and Sch.25 para.7(d).

Power of courts to prohibit or restrict exhibition and training of performing animals

2.—(1) Where it is proved to the satisfaction of a court of summary jurisdiction on a complaint made by a constable or an officer of a local authority that the training or exhibition of any performing animal has been accompanied by cruelty and should be prohibited or allowed only subject to conditions, the court may make an order against the person in respect of whom the complaint is made prohibiting the training or exhibition or imposing such conditions thereon as may be specified by the order.

(2) If any person is aggrieved by the making of such an order or a refusal to make such an order, he may appeal to the Crown Court.

(3) An order made under this Act shall not come into force until seven days after it is made, or, if an appeal has been entered within that period, until the determination of the appeal.

(4) Any court by which an order is made under this section shall cause a copy of the order to be sent as soon as may be after the order comes into force to the local authority by which the person against whom the order is made is registered and to the Secretary of State, and shall cause the particulars of the order to be endorsed upon the certificate held by that person, and that person shall produce his certificate on being so required by the court for the purposes of endorsement. A local authority to which a copy of an order is sent under this section shall enter the particulars of the order on the register.

DEFINITIONS

"animal": s.5(1).
"exhibition": s.5(1).
"local authority": s.6(1).
"trainer": s.5(1).

GENERAL NOTE

This section gives the court a valuable power to either prohibit or restrict by way of conditions the exhibition and training of performing animals on a complaint being made by the police or officer of a local authority and provision is made for the endorsement of the local authority's register in such circumstances. The reference to "crown court" in subs.(2) was inserted by the Courts Act 1971 s.56(2) and Sch.9 Pt 1, and the applicability of the section to Scotland is provided for in s.6(b).

Power to enter premises

3.—(1) Any officer of a local authority duly authorised in that behalf by the local authority and any constable may—

(a) enter at all reasonable times and inspect any premises in which any performing animals are being trained or exhibited, or kept for training or exhibition, and any such animals found therein; and

(b) require any person who he has reason to believe is a trainer or exhibitor of performing animals to produce his certificate.

(2) No constable or such officer as aforesaid shall be entitled under this section to go on or behind the stage during a public performance of performing animals.

DEFINITIONS

"animals": s.5(1).
"exhibitor": s.5(1).
"local authority": s.6(1).
"trainer": s.5(1).

GENERAL NOTE

In order to enforce the provisions of the Act an authorised officer of the local authority or a police officer may enter premises, inspect the animals therein and require the trainer of exhibitor to produce the certificate issued in terms of s.1(4), with the proviso that this power may not be exercised on or behind the stage during a public performance of performing animals. For "at all reasonable times", see p.30 above. For "reason to believe", see Introduction p.31 above.

Offences and legal proceedings

4.—(1) If any person—

(a) not being registered under this Act exhibits or trains any performing animal; or

(b) being registered under this Act exhibits or trains any performing animal with respect to which or in a manner with respect to which he is not registered; or

(c) being a person against whom an order by a court of summary jurisdiction has been made on complaint under this Act, contravenes or fails to comply with the order in any part of Great Britain, whether within or without the area of jurisdiction of that court; or

(d) obstructs or wilfully delays any constable or officer of a local authority in the execution of his powers under this Act as to entry or inspection; or

(e) conceals any animal with a view to avoiding such inspection; or

(f) being a person registered under this Act, on being duly required in pursuance of this Act to produce his certificate under this Act fails without reasonable excuse so to do; or

(g) applies to be registered under this Act when prohibited from being so registered;

he shall be guilty of an offence against this Act and shall be liable on summary conviction upon a complaint made by a constable or an officer of a local authority to a fine not exceeding level 3 on the standard scale.

(2) Where a person is convicted of an offence against this Act, or against the Protection of Animals Act, 1911, as amended by any subsequent enactment, the court before which he is convicted may in addition to or in lieu of imposing any other penalty—

(a) if such person is registered under this Act order that his name be removed from the register;

(b) order that such person shall either permanently or for such time as may be specified in the order be disqualified for being registered under this Act;

and where such an order is made, the provisions of subsections (2), (3) and (4) of section two of this Act shall apply to the order as they apply to an order made under that section.

(2A) Where a person is convicted of any offence under sections 28C or 28F(16) of the Animal Health Act, 1981 (c.22), or sections 19 to 24, 25(7), 29 or 40(11) of the Animal Health and Welfare (Scotland) Act, 2006 (asp 11), the court by which he is convicted has the same powers under subsection (2) in relation to such convictions as it has in relation to convictions for offences under this Act.

DEFINITIONS

"animal": s.5(1).
"exhibits": s.5(1).
"level 3 on the standard scale": see p.32 above.
"requested under this Act": s.1.
"trains": s.5(1).

GENERAL NOTE

This section provides for a number of statutory offences and the penalty therefor, and for an additional power of removal from the local authority register when a person has been convicted of certain statutory offences. Subsection (2A) was inserted by the Animals Health and Welfare (Scotland) Act 2006 (Consequential Provisions) Order 2006 (SSI 2006/536) Sch.1.

Interpretation, rules, and expenses

5.—(1) For the purposes of this Act—

The expression "*animal*" does not include invertebrates:

The expression "*exhibit*" means exhibit at any entertainment to which the public are admitted, whether on payment of money or otherwise, and the expression "*train*" means train for the purpose of any such exhibition, and the expressions "*exhibitor*" and "*trainer*" have respectively the corresponding meanings:

The expression "*local authority*" means—

[...]

The expression "*prescribed*" means prescribed by rules made by the Secretary of State.

(2) The Secretary of State may make rules for prescribing anything which is to be prescribed under this Act, and as to the execution and performance by local authorities of their powers and duties under this Act, and generally for carrying this Act into effect.

(3) Any expenses of a local authority under this Act, so far as not covered by fees, shall be defrayed.

GENERAL NOTE

The all-important definitions here are those which cover "exhibit" and "train"—note that the payment of money to view the exhibition is not a prerequisite but that there are certain statutory exceptions for training and exhibition contained in s.7. The definition of "local authority" for Scotland is given in s.6(a). The rules which were made in terms of subs.(2) are to be found as the Performing Animals Rules 1925 (SR & O 1925/1219) set out below. Power to amend subs.(3) was given by the Local Government (Scotland) Act 1966 s.42(2) and Sch.4 Pt II.

Application to Scotland

6. This Act shall apply to Scotland subject to the following modifications:—

(a) The expression "local authority" means a council constituted under section 2 of the Local Government etc. (Scotland) Act 1994.

(b) Reference to a court of summary jurisdiction shall be construed as references to the sheriff; references to an appeal to quarter sessions shall not apply; and the Protection of Animals (Scotland) Act, 1912, shall be substituted for the Protection of Animals Act, 1911.

GENERAL NOTE

Subsection (a) was amended by the Local Government etc. (Scotland) Act 1994 s.180(1) and Sch.13 para.13. In relation to courts, the sheriff court has summary jurisdiction here.

Exceptions from application of Act

7. This Act shall not apply to the training of animals for bona fide military, police, agricultural or sporting purposes, or the exhibition of any animals so trained.

DEFINITIONS

"animal": s.5(1).
"exhibition": s.5(1).

"training": s.5(1).

GENERAL NOTE

This section provides for bona fide exhibition and training of animals for a number of specified purposes and would thus exclude police dogs, sheep dogs, military horses, gun dogs, etc. from the ambit of the Act.

Short title, commencement, and extent

8.—(1) This Act may be cited as the Performing Animals (Regulation) Act, 1925.

(2) [*Omitted.*]

(3) [*As repealed by the Statute Law Revision Act 1950 (c.6).*]

GENERAL NOTE

Subsection (2) has no application to Scotland; subs.(3) was repealed by the Statutes Law Revision Act 1950.

[1]Pet Animals Act 1951

(14 and 15 Geo. 6, c.35)

NOTE

1. Entire Act to be repealed by the Animal Health and Welfare (Scotland) Act 2006 (asp 11) Sch.2 para.9 (date yet to be appointed).

ARRANGEMENT OF SECTIONS

SECTION

Licensing of pet shops

1.—(1) No person shall keep a pet shop except under the authority of a licence granted in accordance with the provisions of this Act.

(2) Every local authority may, on application being made to them for that purpose by a person who is not for the time being disqualified from keeping a pet shop, and on payment of such fee as may be determined by the local authority, grant a licence to that person to keep a pet shop at such premises in their area as may be specified in the application and subject to compliance with such conditions as may be specified in the licence.

[2](2A) Where a person is for the time being disqualified under section 28F(1) and (2) of the Animal Health Act 1981 (c.22), or section 40(1) and (2) of the Animal Health and Welfare (Scotland) Act 2006 (asp 11), notwithstanding subsection (2), a local authority shall not grant a licence to keep a pet shop to that person.

(3) In determining whether to grant a licence for the keeping of a pet shop by any person at any premises, a local authority shall in particular (but without prejudice to their discretion to withhold a licence on other grounds) have regard to the need for securing—

(a) that animals will at all times be kept in accommodation suitable as respects size, temperature, lighting, ventilation and cleanliness;

(b) that animals will be adequately supplied with suitable food and drink and (so far as necessary) visited at suitable intervals;

(c) that animals, being mammals, will not be sold at too early an age;

(d) that all reasonable precautions will be taken to prevent the spread among animals of infectious diseases;

(e) that appropriate steps will be taken in case of fire or other emergency;

and shall specify such conditions in the licence, if granted by them, as appear to the local authority necessary or expedient in the particular case for securing all or any of the objects specified in paragraphs (a) to (e) of this subsection.

[1](3A) No condition may be specified under subsection (3) of this section which relates to any matter in relation to which requirements or prohibitions are or could be imposed by virtue of Part 3 of the Fire (Scotland) Act 2005 (asp 5).

(4) Any person aggrieved by the refusal of a local authority to grant such a licence, or by any condition subject to which such a licence is proposed to be granted, may appeal to a court of summary jurisdiction having jurisdiction in the place in which the premises are situated; and the court may on such an appeal give such directions with respect to the issue of a licence or, as the case may be, with respect to the conditions subject to which a licence is to be granted as they think proper.

(5) Any such licence shall (according to the applicant's requirements) relate to the year in which it is granted or to the next following year. In the former case, the licence shall come into force at the beginning of the day on which it is granted, and in the latter case it shall come into force at the beginning of the next following year.

(6) Subject to the provisions hereinafter contained with respect to cancellation, any such licence shall remain in force until the end of the year to which it relates and shall then expire.

(7) Any person who contravenes the provisions of subsection (1) of this section shall be guilty of an offence; and if any condition subject to which a licence is granted in accordance with the provisions of this Act is contravened or not complied with the person to whom the licence was granted shall be guilty of an offence.

(8) In the application of this section to Scotland, in subsection (4) for the reference to a court of summary jurisdiction there shall be substituted a reference to the sheriff.

NOTE

1. As amended by the Fire (Scotland) Act 2005 (Consequential Modifications and Savings) Order 2006 (SSI 2006/475) Sch.1 para.2 (effective 1 October 2006).

2. As amended by the Animal Health and Welfare (Scotland) Act 2006 (Consequential Provisions) Order 2006 (SSI 2006/536) Sch.1 para.3 (effective 3 November 2006).

DEFINITIONS

"animal": s.7(3).

"keeping a pet shop": s.7(1).

"local authority": s.7(3).

GENERAL NOTE

The Act provides for the licensing and regulation of persons who keep businesses that sell pet animals and s.1 sets out the basic framework of these licensing provisions. Note the possible interrelation of these provisions to those contained in the Breeding of Dogs Act 1973 (see pp.322–331 below). Subsection (2A) was inserted by the Animal Health and Welfare (Scotland) Act 2006 (Consequential Provisions) Order (SSI 2006/536) Schedule para.3. Subsection (3A) was inserted by the Fire (Scotland) Act 2005 (Consequential Modifications and Savings) Order (SSI 2006/475) reg.2 and Sch.1.

Subsection (1)

The requirement for licensing is mandatory for both for the local authority and applicant and an offence of keeping unlicensed premises is created under s.1(7).

Subsection (2)

No prescribed form of application is provided for here, although it is presumably intended that applications shall be in writing. Persons who have been disqualified from holding a licence in terms of s.5 are not competent applicants but there is no lower age limit for applicants, notwithstanding the prohibition in s.3 on sales of pet animals to persons under 12 years of age. Note that the premises from which the business is to be operated must be specified in the application and a licence is issued subject to any conditions placed thereon by the local authority. The reference to fees was amended by the Local Government (Scotland) Act 1973 s.209(1) and Sch.25 para.26, and power to amend this subsection was contained in the Local Government (Scotland) Act 1966 s.42(2) and Sch.4 Pt II.

Subsection (3)

This subsection contains a non-exhaustive list of five matters relating to animal welfare which the local authority must take into account when considering an application and it is incumbent upon the authority to specify conditions in the licence as appear necessary or expeditious to secure these matters.

Subsection (4)

This provides a right of appeal by way of summary application to the sheriff court (by virtue of subs.(8)) in cases of refusal or in relation to conditions imposed, and the court can, on upholding such an appeal, direct the local authority to issue the licence or make directions in relation to the conditions. See also pp.28–30 above, in respect of general matters relating to this appeal procedure. For "person aggrieved" see pp.28–29 above.

Subsections (5) and (6)

A licence runs from either: (a) the date upon which it is granted to 31 December of that same year; or (b) from 1 January to 31 December of the year following upon that in which the application is made. Curiously there is no provision relating to transfers of licences on the death of an applicant and thus a new application would have to be made by the personal representatives of the deceased to cover the interim period prior to the sale of any such business.

Subsection (7)

It is an offence to keep an unlicensed pet shop or to contravene the conditions of a licence and the penalty therefor is provided for in s.5(1).

Pets not to be sold in streets, etc.

2. If any person carries on a business of selling animals as pets in any part of a road or public place or at a stall or barrow in a market, he shall be guilty of an offence.

DEFINITIONS

"animal": s.7(3).
"road": s.7(3).

GENERAL NOTE

Section 2 makes it an offence to sell pet animals in public places, roads or at market stalls or barrows and the penalty therefore is laid down in s.5(1). In *White v Kilmarnock and Loudon DC*, 1991 S.L.T. (Sh Ct) 69; 1990 S.C.L.R. 771, it was held that a local authority could not issue a licence to a person who was selling pet animals from a permanent structure in an indoor market since this constituted a market stall rather than shop. For a further discussion of "market" in the context of the Act see *R (on the application of Haynes) v Stafford BC* [2006] EWHC 1366 (Admin); [2007] 1 W.L.R. 1365. The reference to "road" was substituted by the Roads (Scotland) Act 1984 Sch.9 para.40(2), and the subsection was also amended by the Pet Animals Act 1951 (Amendment) Act 1983 s.1.

3. [*This provision, which related to the sale of pets to children under 12, was* *repealed by the Animals Health and Welfare (Scotland) Act 2006 (asp 11) Sch.2 para.9 (effective 6 October 2006).*]

GENERAL NOTE

This provision, which related to the sale of pets to children under 12, was repealed by the Animals Health and Welfare (Scotland) Act 2006 Sch.2 para.9.

Inspection of pet shops

4.—(1) A local authority may authorise in writing any of its officers or any veterinary surgeon or veterinary practitioner to inspect (subject to compliance with such precautions as the authority may specify to prevent the spread among animals of infectious diseases) any premises in their area as respects which a licence granted in accordance with the provisions of this Act is for the time being in force, and any person authorised under this section may, on producing his authority if so required, enter any such premises at all reasonable times and inspect them and any animals found thereon or any thing therein, for the purpose of ascertaining whether an offence has been or is being committed against this Act.

(2) Any person who wilfully obstructs or delays any person in the exercise of his powers of entry or inspection under this section shall be guilty of an offence.

DEFINITIONS

"animal": s.7(3).
"local authority": s.7(3).
"veterinary surgeon": s.7(3).
"veterinary practitioner": s.7(3).

GENERAL NOTE

This section provides for rights of entry and inspection to officers of the local authority and veterinary surgeons and practitioners who have been authorised in writing by the local authority to carry out these powers for the purpose of ensuring compliance with the Act and an offence for obstructing or delaying such persons is created, the penalty for which is provided for in s.5(2).

Subsection (1)

For "at all reasonable times" see Introduction p.30 above.

Subsection (2)

For "wilfully obstructs" see Introduction pp.30–31 above.

Offences and disqualifications

[1]**5.**—(1) Any person guilty of an offence under any provision of this Act other than the last foregoing section shall be liable on summary conviction to a fine not exceeding level 2 on the standard scale or to imprisonment for a term not exceeding three months or to both such fine and such imprisonment.

(2) Any person guilty of an offence under the last foregoing section shall be liable on summary conviction to a fine not exceeding level 2 on the standard scale.

(3) Where a person is convicted of any offence under this Act or of any offence under the Protection of Animals Act 1911, or the Protection of Animals (Scotland) Act, 1912, the court by which he is convicted may cancel any licence held by him under this Act, and may, whether or not he is the

holder of such a licence, disqualify him from keeping a pet shop for such period as the court thinks fit.

(4) A court which has ordered the cancellation of a person's licence, or his disqualification, in pursuance of the last foregoing subsection may, if its thinks fit, suspend the operation of the order pending an appeal.

(5) Where a person is convicted of any offence under sections 28C or 28F(16) of the Animal Health Act 1981 (c.22), or sections 19 to 24, 25(7), 29 or 40(11) of the Animal Health and Welfare (Scotland) Act 2006 (asp 11), the court by which he is convicted has the same powers under subsections (3) and (4) in relation to such convictions as it has in relation to convictions for offences under this Act.

NOTE

1. As inserted by the Animal Health and Welfare (Scotland) Act 2006 (Consequential Provisions) Order 2006 (SSI 2006/536) Sch.1 para.3 (effective 3 November 2006).

DEFINITIONS

"level 2 on the standard scale": see Introduction p.32 above.

"keeping a pet shop": s.7(1).

GENERAL NOTE

This section provides penalties for the offences created under this Act and also for additional powers to the sheriff to disqualify licence holders and to cancel licences.

Subsection (1)

This subsection contains the penalty for contravention of ss.1, 2 and 3 of the Act.

Subsection (2)

This provides the penalty for contravention of s.4(2).

Subsection (3)

This contains an additional discretionary power for the court to cancel existing licences and to disqualify persons from holding such licences for a period upon conviction for contraventions of the Act or certain other specified Acts: see also the Animal Boarding Establishments Act 1963 s.3(3) and the Breeding of Dogs Act 1973 s.3(3).

Subsection (4)

The court may grant an interim suspension of any cancellation or disqualification order pending an appeal.

Subsection (5)

This subsection was inserted by the Animal Health and Welfare (Scotland) Act 2006 (Consequential Provisions) Order (SSI 2006/536) Schedule para.3.

6. [*Omitted.*]

GENERAL NOTE

This section applied only to England and Wales.

Interpretation

7.—(1) References in this Act to the keeping of a pet shop shall, subject to the following provisions of this section, be construed as references to the carrying on at premises of any nature (including a private dwelling) of a business of selling animals as pets, and as including references to the keeping of animals in any such premises as aforesaid with a view to their being sold in the course of such a business, whether by the keeper thereof or by any other person:

Provided that—

(a) a person shall not be deemed to keep a pet shop by reason only of his keeping or selling pedigree animals bred by him, or the offspring of an animal kept by him as a pet;

(b) where a person carries on a business of selling animals as pets in conjunction with a business of breeding pedigree animals, and the local authority are satisfied that the animals so sold by him (in so far as they are not pedigree animals bred by him) are animals which were acquired by him with a view to being used, if suitable, for breeding or show purposes but have subsequently been found by him not to be suitable or required for such use, the local authority may if they think fit direct that the said person shall not be deemed to keep a pet shop by reason only of his carrying on the first-mentioned business.

(2) References in this Act to the selling or keeping of animals as pets shall be construed in accordance with the following provisions, that is to say—

(a) as respects cats and dogs, such references shall be construed as including references to selling or keeping, as the case may be, wholly or mainly for domestic purposes; and

(b) as respects any animal, such references shall be construed as including references to selling or keeping, as the case may be, for ornamental purposes.

(3) In this Act, unless the context otherwise requires, the following expressions have the meanings hereby respectively assigned to them, that is to say:—

"*animal*" includes any description of vertebrate;

"*local authority*" in Scotland means a council constituted under section 2 of the Local Government etc. (Scotland) Act 1994;

"*pedigree animal*" means an animal of any description which is by its breeding eligible for registration with a recognised club or society keeping a register of animals of that description;

"*road*" has the same meaning as in the Roads (Scotland) Act 1984;

"*veterinary surgeon*" means a person who is for the time being registered in the Register of Veterinary Surgeons;

"*veterinary practitioner*" means a person who is for the time being registered in the Supplementary Veterinary Register.

GENERAL NOTE

Certain key definitions are provided for in this section, albeit in a somewhat convoluted form.

Subsection (1)

The keeper of a pet shop is a person who carries on at premises of any nature, including a private dwelling house, a business of selling animals as pets, and includes the keeping on premises of animals destined for sale within the course of a business whether by the keeper or some other person. This all-embracing definition was held to include the keeper of animals destined for export and kept in premises to which the public did not have access—see *Chalmers v Diwell* (1975) 74 L.G.R. 173 but see also *R (on the application of Haynes) v Stafford BC* [2006] EWHC 1366 (Admin); [2007] 1 W.L.R. 1365. There are, however, two important exceptions to the basic definition in that the following are excluded: (a) persons who only sell pedigree animals or the offspring of their own pet animals; and (b) those who sell animals in the very limited circumstances provided for in s.7(1)(b) and whom the local authority deem to be not keeping a pet shop.

Subsection (2)

This provides further clarification of what is meant by the selling or keeping of animals as pets.

Subsection (3)

The definition of "local authority" in Scotland was substituted by the Local Government (Scotland) Act 1994 Sch.13 para.36, and "road" by the Roads (Scotland) Act 1984 Sch.9 para.40(3). The definition of "premises" which originally appeared in the Act was removed by the Pet Animals Act 1951 (Amendment) Act 1983 s.1(b).

Short title, commencement and extent

8.—(1) This Act may be cited as the Pet Animals Act 1951.

(2) This Act shall not extend to Northern Ireland.

(3) This Act shall come into operation on the first day of April, nineteen hundred and fifty-two.

[1]Animal Boarding Establishments Act 1963

(c.43)

NOTE

1. Entire Act to be repealed by the Animal Health and Welfare (Scotland) Act 2006 (asp 11) Sch.2 para.9 (date yet to be appointed).

ARRANGEMENT OF SECTIONS

Licensing of boarding establishments for animals

[1]**1.**—(1) No person shall keep a boarding establishment for animals except under the authority of a licence granted in accordance with the provisions of this Act.

(2) Every local authority may, on application being made to them for that purpose by a person who is not for the time being disqualified—

(a) under this Act, from keeping a boarding establishment for animals; or

(b) under the Pet Animals Act 1951, from keeping a pet shop; or

(c), (d) [*Omitted.*]

(e) under the Protection of Animals (Amendment) Act 1954, from having the custody of animals,

and on payment of such fee as may be determined by the local authority, grant a licence to that person to keep a boarding establishment for animals at such premises in their area as may be specified in the application and subject to compliance with such conditions as may be specified in the licence.

(2A) Where a person is for the time being disqualified under section 28F(1) and (2) of the Animal Health Act 1981 (c.22), or section 40(1) and (2) of the Animal Health and Welfare (Scotland) Act 2006 (asp 11), notwithstanding subsection (2), a local authority shall not grant a licence to keep a boarding establishment for animals to that person.

(3) In determining whether to grant a licence for the keeping of a boarding establishment for animals by any person at any premises, a local authority shall in particular (but without prejudice to their discretion to withhold a licence on other grounds) have regard to the need for securing—

(a) that animals will at all times be kept in accommodation suitable as respects construction, size of quarters, number of occupants, exercising facilities, temperature, lighting, ventilation and cleanliness;

(b) that animals will be adequately supplied with suitable food, drink and bedding material, adequately exercised, and (so far as necessary) visited at suitable intervals;

(c) that all reasonable precautions will be taken to prevent and control the spread among animals of infectious or contagious diseases, including the provisions of adequate isolation facilities;

(d) that appropriate steps will be taken for the protection of the animals in case of fire or other emergency;

(e) that a register be kept containing a description of any animals received into the establishment, date of arrival and departure, and the name and address of the owner, such register to be available for inspection at all times by an officer of the local authority, veterinary surgeon or veterinary practitioner authorised under section 2(1) of this Act;

and shall specify such conditions in the licence, if granted by them, as appear to the local authority necessary or expedient in the particular case for securing all the objects specified in paragraphs (a) to (e) of this subsection.

(4) Any person aggrieved by the refusal of a local authority to grant such a licence, or by any condition subject to which such a licence is proposed to be granted, may appeal to a magistrates' court; and the court may on such an appeal give such directions with respect to the issue of a licence or, as the case may be, with respect to the conditions subject to which a licence is to be granted as it thinks proper.

(5) Any such licence shall (according to the applicant's requirements) relate to the year in which it is granted or to the next following year. In the former case, the licence shall come into force at the beginning of the day on which it is granted, and in the latter case it shall come into force at the beginning of the next following year.

(6) Subject to the provisions hereinafter contained with respect to cancellation, any such licence shall remain in force until the end of the year to which it relates and shall then expire.

(7) In the event of the death of a person who is keeping a boarding establishment for animals at any premises under the authority of a licence granted under this Act, that licence shall be deemed to have been granted to his personal representatives in respect of those premises and shall, notwithstanding subsection (6) of this section (but subject to the provisions hereinafter contained with respect to cancellation), remain in force until the end of the period of three months beginning with the death and shall then expire:

Provided that the local authority by whom the licence was granted may from time to time, on the application of those representatives, extend or further extend the said period of three months if the authority are satisfied that the extension is necessary for the purpose of winding up the deceased's estate and that no other circumstances make it undesirable.

(8) Any person who contravenes the provisions of subsection (1) of this section shall be guilty of an offence; and if any condition subject to which a licence is granted in accordance with the provisions of this Act is contravened or not complied with, the person to whom the licence was granted shall be guilty of an offence.

(9) In the application of this section to Scotland, in subsection (4) for any reference to a magistrates' court there shall be substituted a reference to the sheriff.

NOTE

1. As inserted by the Animal Health and Welfare (Scotland) Act 2006 (Consequential Provisions) Order 2006 (SI 2006/536) Sch.1 para.4 (effective 3 November 2006).

DEFINITIONS

"animal": s.5(2).
"keeping a boarding establishment for animals": s.5(1).
"local authority": s.5(2).
"veterinary practitioner": s.5(2).
"veterinary surgeon": s.5(2).

GENERAL NOTE

This Act provides for a mandatory system of licensing for kennels and catteries where the main business activity being carried on is to provide accommodation for other people's dogs and cats. This section provides the basic framework for the licensing system under the Act. These statutory provisions will eventually be superseded by Orders made under the Animal Health and Welfare (Scotland) Act 2006 but remain in force until so superseded.

Subsection (1)

This is a mandatory scheme of licensing and an offence is created by subs.(8) of keeping an unlicensed establishment.

Subsection (2)

There is a degree of discretion left to the local authority here but certain persons are excluded from eligibility as applicants. Subsection (2)(c) and (d) were repealed by s.3(2) and (3) and the Schedule to the Protection of Animals (Amendment) Act 1988. Note that there is no apparent minimum age requirement for an applicant. The reference to fees was amended by the Local Government (Scotland) Act 1966 s.42 and Sch.4 Pt II which contains a power to amend this subsection.

Subsection (2A)

This subsection was inserted by the Animal Health and Welfare (Scotland) Act 2006 (Consequential Provisions) Order (SSI 2006/536) Schedule para.4.

Subsection (3)

A non-exhaustive list of matters to be taken into account in determining the granting of licences is set out here. These relate to the welfare of the animals boarded and a register must be kept (the form of register is not prescribed, but the contents are). The local authority must specify conditions in the licence which appear necessary or expedient to secure all of the objects listed.

Subsection (4)

The right of appeal in Scotland is to the sheriff by reason of subs.(9). For general observations on such appeals see pp.28–30 above. Note that there is no procedure for requiring a licensing authority to state reasons for its decision—see p.28 above.

Subsections (5) and (6)

Thus a licence runs either from the date upon which it comes into force until 31 December of that year or from 1 January to 31 December of the following year.

Subsection (7)

This makes provision for a temporary transmission of a licence to the personal representatives of a deceased licensee.

Subsection (8)

The penalty for this offence is set out in s.3.

Inspection of boarding establishments for animals

2.—(1) A local authority may authorise in writing any of its officers or any veterinary surgeon or veterinary practitioner to inspect (subject to compliance with such precautions as the authority may specify to prevent the spread among animals of infectious or contagious diseases) any premises in their area as respects which a licence granted in accordance with the provisions of this Act is for the time being in force, and any person authorised under this section may, on producing his authority if so required, enter any such premises at all reasonable times and inspect them and any animals found thereon or any thing therein, for the purposes of ascertaining whether an offence has been or is being committed against this Act.

(2) Any person who wilfully obstructs or delays any person in the exercise of his powers of entry or inspection under this section shall be guilty of an offence.

DEFINITIONS

"animals": s.5(2).
"local authority": s.5(2).
"veterinary practitioner": s.5(2).
"veterinary surgeon": s.5(2).

GENERAL NOTE

A system of entry to and inspection of boarding establishments is provided for in this section and is exercised by the officer of the local authority or by veterinary surgeons or practitioners authorised by them.

Subsection (1)

For "at all reasonable times" see p.30 above.

Subsection (2)

For "wilfully obstructs and delays" see pp.30–31 above. The penalty for the statutory offence created here is provided for in s.3.

Offences and disqualifications

[1]**3.**—(1) Any person guilty of an offence under any provision of this Act other than the last foregoing section shall be liable on summary conviction to a fine not exceeding level 1 on the standard scale or to imprisonment for a term not exceeding three months or to both such fine and such imprisonment.

(2) Any person guilty of an offence under the last foregoing section shall be liable on summary conviction to a fine not exceeding level 1 on the standard scale.

(3) Where a person is convicted of any offence under this Act or of any offence under the Protection of Animals Act 1911 or the Protection of Animals (Scotland) Act 1912 or the Pet Animals Act 1951, the court by which he is convicted may cancel any licence held by him under this Act, and may, whether or not he is the holder of such a licence, disqualify him from keeping a boarding establishment for animals for such period as the court thinks fit.

(4) A court which has ordered the cancellation of a person's licence, or his disqualification, in pursuance of the last foregoing subsection may, if its thinks fit, suspend the operation of the order pending an appeal.

(5) Where a person is convicted of any offence under sections 28C or 28F(16) of the Animal Health Act 1981 (c.22), or sections 19 to 24, 25(7), 29

or 40(11) of the Animal Health and Welfare (Scotland) Act 2006 (asp 11), the court by which he is convicted has the same powers under subsections (3) and (4) in relation to such convictions as it has in relation to convictions for offences under this Act.

NOTE

1. As inserted by the Animal Health and Welfare (Scotland) Act 2006 (Consequential Provisions) Order 2006 (SI 2006/536) Sch.1 para.4 (effective 3 November 2006).

DEFINITIONS

"boarding establishment for animals": s.5(1).
"level 1 on the standard scale": see Introduction p.32 above.

GENERAL NOTE

This section provides for the penalties for the statutory offences created by s.1(8)—see subs.(1)—and s.2(2). In addition there are powers to disqualify a person from holding a licence or to cancel an existing licence. Subsection (5) was inserted by the Animal Health and Welfare (Scotland) Act 2006 (Consequential Provisions) Order (SSI 2006/536) Schedule para.4.

4. [*Omitted.*]

GENERAL NOTE

This provision applies only to England and Wales.

Interpretation

5.—(1) References in this Act to the keeping by any person of a boarding establishment for animals shall, subject to the following provisions of this section, be construed as references to the carrying on by him at premises of any nature (including a private dwelling) of a business of providing accommodation for other people's animals:

Provided that—

(a) a person shall not be deemed to keep a boarding establishment for animals by reason only of his providing accommodation for other people's animals in connection with a business of which the provision of such accommodation is not the main activity; and

(b) nothing in this Act shall apply to the keeping of an animal at any premises in pursuance of a requirement imposed under, or having effect by virtue of the Animal Health Act 1981.

(2) In this Act, unless the context otherwise requires, the following expressions have the meanings hereby respectively assigned to them, that is to say:—

"*animal*" means any dog or cat;

"*local authority*" means in Scotland a council constituted under section 2 of the Local Government etc. (Scotland) Act 1994;

"*veterinary practitioner*" means a person who is for the time being registered in the Supplementary Veterinary Register;

"*veterinary surgeon*" means a person who is for the time being registered in the Register of Veterinary Surgeons.

GENERAL NOTE

The definition of "boarding establishment for animals" in subs.(1) would therefore exclude, e.g. a hotel keeper who provides separate accommodation for guest's cats and dogs while they are staying at the hotel. Proviso (b) was amended by the Animal Health Act 1981 s.96 and Sch.5. The definition of "local authority" in Scotland was amended by the Local Government etc. (Scotland) Act 1994 s.180(1) and Sch.13 para.61.

6. [*These ceased to have effect after 1 February 1964.*]

GENERAL NOTE

These ceased to have effect after 1 February 1964.

Short title, repeal, extent and commencement

7.—(1) This Act may be cited as the Animal Boarding Establishments Act 1963.

(2) [*Repealed.*]

(3) This Act shall not extend to Northern Ireland.

(4) This Act shall come into operation on 1st January, 1964.

GENERAL NOTE

Subsection (2) was repealed by Schedule Pt XI to the Statute Law (Repeals) Act 1974.

[1]Riding Establishments Act 1964

(c.70)

NOTE

1. Entire Act to be repealed by the Animal Health and Welfare (Scotland) Act 2006 (asp 11) Sch.2 para.9 (date yet to be appointed).

ARRANGEMENT OF SECTIONS

SECTION

Licensing of riding establishments

1.—(1) No person shall keep a riding establishment except under the authority of a licence granted in accordance with the provisions of this Act.

(2) Every local authority may, on application being made to them for that purpose by a person who is an individual over the age of eighteen years or a body corporate, being a person who is not for the time being disqualified,—

(a) under this Act from keeping a riding establishment; or

(b) under the Protection of Animals (Cruelty to Dogs) Act 1933, from keeping a dog; or

(c) under the protection of Animals (Cruelty to Dogs) (Scotland) Act 1934, from keeping a dog; or

(d) under the Protection of Animals (Amendment) Act 1954, from having the custody of animals; or

(e) under the Animal Boarding Establishments Act 1963, from keeping a boarding establishment for animals;

and on payment of such fee as may be set by the local authority grant a licence to that person to keep a riding establishment at such premises in their area as may be specified in the application and subject to compliance with such conditions as may be specified in the licence.

[1](2A) Where a person is for the time being disqualified under section 28F(1) and (2) of the Animal Health Act 1981 (c.22), or section 40(1) and (2) of the Animal Health and Welfare (Scotland) Act 2006 (asp 11), notwithstanding subsection (2), a local authority shall not grant a licence to keep a riding establishment to that person.

(3) Where an application for the grant of a licence for the keeping of a riding establishment at any premises is made to a local authority, they shall

not proceed to a decision in the matter unless they have received and considered a report by a veterinary surgeon or veterinary practitioner authorised by them to carry out inspections under the next following section of an inspection of the premises carried out by him within the period of twelve months immediately preceding the date on which the application is received by the local authority or on or after that date, being a report containing such particulars as in their view enable them to determine whether the premises are suitable for the keeping thereat of a riding establishment, and describing the condition of the premises and of any horses found thereon or anything thereat.

(4) In determining whether to grant a licence for the keeping of a riding establishment by any person at any premises a local authority shall in particular (but without prejudice to their discretion to withhold a licence on any grounds) have regard to—

(a) whether that person appears to them to be suitable and qualified, either by experience in the management of horses or by being the holder of an approved certificate or by employing in the management of the riding establishment a person so qualified, to be the holder of such a licence; and

(b) the need for securing—

(i) that paramount consideration will be given to the condition of horses and that they will be maintained in good health, and in all respects physically fit and that, in the case of a horse kept for the purpose of its being let out on hire for riding or a horse kept for the purpose of its being used in providing instruction in riding, the horse will be suitable for the purpose for which it is kept;

(ii) that the feet of all animals are properly trimmed and that, if shod, their shoes are properly fitted and in good condition;

(iii) that there will be available at all times, accommodation for horses suitable as respects construction, size, number of occupants, lighting, ventilation, drainage and cleanliness and that these requirements be complied with not only in the case of new buildings but also in the case of buildings converted for use as stabling;

(iv) that in the case of horses maintained at grass there will be available for them at all times during which they are so maintained adequate pasture and shelter and water and that supplementary feeds will be provided as and when required;

(v) that horses will be adequately supplied with suitable food, drink and (except in the case of horses maintained at grass, so long as they are so maintained) bedding material, and will be adequately exercised, groomed and rested and visited at suitable intervals;

(vi) that all reasonable precautions will be taken to prevent and control the spread among horses of infectious or contagious diseases and that veterinary first aid equipment and medicines shall be provided and maintained in the premises;

(vii) that appropriate steps will be taken for the protection and extrication of horses in case of fire and, in particular, that the name, address and telephone number of the licence holder or some other responsible person will be kept displayed in a prominent position on the outside of the premises and that instructions as to action to be taken in the event of fire, with particular regard to the extrication of horses, will be kept displayed in a prominent position on the outside of the premises;

(viii) that adequate accommodation will be provided for forage, bedding, stable equipment and saddlery;

and shall specify such conditions in the licence, if granted by them, as appear to the local authority necessary or expedient in the particular case for securing all the objects specified in subparagraphs (i) to (viii) of paragraph (b) of this subsection.

(4A) Without prejudice to the provisions of subsection (2) or (4) of this section, every licence granted under this Act after 31st December 1970 shall be subject to the following conditions (whether they are specified in the licence or not), namely—

(a) a horse found on inspection of the premises by an authorised officer to be in need of veterinary attention shall not be returned to work until the holder of the licence has obtained at his own expense and has lodged with the local authority a veterinary certificate that the horse is fit for work;

(b) no horse will be let out on hire for riding or used for providing instruction in riding without supervision by a responsible person of the age of 16 years or over unless (in the case of a horse let out for hire for riding) the holder of the licence is satisfied that the hirer of the horse is competent to ride without supervision;

(c) the carrying on of the business of a riding establishment shall at no time be left in the charge of any person under 16 years of age;

(d) the licence holder shall hold a current insurance policy which insures him against liability for any injury sustained by those who hire a horse from him for riding and those who use a horse in the course of receiving from him, in return for payment, instruction in riding and arising out of the hire or use of a horse as aforesaid and which also insures such persons in respect of any liability which may be incurred by them in respect of injury to any person caused by, or arising out of, the hire or use of a horse as aforesaid;

(e) a register shall be kept by the licence holder of all horses in his possession aged three years and under and usually kept on the premises which shall be available for inspection by an authorised officer at all reasonable times.

(5) Any person aggrieved by the refusal of a local authority to grant such a licence, or by any condition subject to which such a licence is proposed to be granted (not being one of the conditions set out in subsection (4A) of this section), may appeal to a magistrates' court; and the court may on such an appeal give such directions with respect to the issue of a licence or, as the case may be, with respect to the conditions subject to which a licence is to be granted as it thinks proper.

(6) Any such licence shall (according to the applicant's requirements) relate to the year in which it is granted or to the next following year. In the former case, the licence shall come into force at the beginning of the day on which it is granted, and in the latter case it shall come into force at the beginning of the next following year.

(7) Subject to the provisions hereinafter contained with respect to cancellation, any such licence shall remain in force for one year beginning with the day on which it comes into force and shall then expire.

(8) In the event of the death of a person who is keeping a riding establishment at any premises under the authority of a licence granted under this Act, that licence shall be deemed to have been granted to his personal

representatives in respect of those premises and shall, notwithstanding subsection (7) of this section (but subject to the provision hereinafter contained with respect to cancellation), remain in force until the end of the period of one year beginning with the death and shall then expire:

Provided that the local authority by whom the licence was granted may from time to time on the application of those representatives, extend or further extend the said period of one year if the authority are satisfied that the extension is necessary for the purpose of winding up the deceased's estate and that no other circumstances make it undesirable.

(9) Any person who contravenes the provisions of subsection (1) of this section shall be guilty of an offence; and if any condition to which a licence under this Act is subject (whether by virtue of subsection (4A) of this section or otherwise) is contravened or not complied with, the person to whom the licence was granted shall be guilty of an offence.

(10) In the application of this section to Scotland, in subsection (5) for any reference to a magistrates' court there shall be substituted a reference to the sheriff.

NOTE

1. As inserted by the Animal Health and Welfare (Scotland) Act 2006 (Consequential Provisions) Order 2006 (SSI 2006/536) Sch.1 para.5 (effective 3 November 2006).

DEFINITIONS

"approved certificate": s.6(4).
"authorised officer": s.6(4).
"horse": s.6(4).
"keeping of a riding establishment": s.6(1) and (3).
"local authority": s.6(4).
"premises": s.6(4).
"veterinary practitioner": s.6(4).
"veterinary surgeon": s.6(4).

GENERAL NOTE

The keeper of a horse-riding establishment is the person who carries on the business of hiring out horses for riding or for the purposes of riding instruction in return for payment, and in order so to do he or she requires a licence issued under the 1964 and 1970 Acts. Section 1 provides the basic framework for making and considering applications for licences, the granting and refusal of applications, mandatory licence conditions, the duration of licences and provisions for appeals. The 1964 and 1970 Acts will be superseded by Orders made under the Animal Health and Welfare (Scotland) Act 2006 but until this is done they will remain in force.

Subsection (1)

The keeper of a horse-riding establishment requires a licence and it is an offence to operate such a business without one (s.1(9)). Note the definition of a riding establishment in s.6(1), which excludes livery stables (see note to s.6(1) below), and certain exemptions contained in ss.6(1) and 6(2).

Subsection (2)

The appropriate local authority is that in whose area the premises from which the business is carried on is situated—s.6(3). Note that an applicant must be a body corporate or person over the age of 18 who has not been disqualified from keeping a riding or animal boarding establishment or from keeping a dog or having custody of animals under the specified legislation. Subsection (2)(d) was repealed by the Protection of Animals (Amendment) Act 1988 s.3(2) and (3). The reference to fees was amended for Scotland by the Riding Establishments Act 1970 s.2(1) and the Local Government (Scotland) Act 1973 Sch.25 para.33. There is no specified form of application but a suggested form appears in Home Office Circular 296/70.

Subsection (3)

Thus an inspection is a prerequisite to the granting of a licence. The scheme of inspections is set out in s.2.

Subsection (4)

This subsection requires the local authority in determining an application to have regard to a number of specified matters relating to: (a) the suitability and qualification of the licence holder; and (b) the welfare of the horses—note the "paramount consideration" referred to in sub-s.(4)(b)(i). In relation to welfare matters the local authority must attach such conditions to the licence as appear to them "necessary and expedient" for securing these objects. These conditions are without prejudice to the mandatory conditions in subs.(4A):

> "Although s.1(4) lays down matters on which a licensing authority must have regard when considering whether to grant a licence, nowhere in the Act is it stated what the general objective of the legislation which a licensing authority should have in mind when deciding the question one is therefore left uncertain as to whether the object of the legislation is the welfare of horses, the protection of members of the public using a riding establishment and perhaps something else all together" (per Sheriff AL Stewart in *McKay v Dundee City Council* unreported 22 February 1999 Dundee Sheriff Court).

Contravention of conditions is an offence in terms of subs.(9). Note that if the local authority is not satisfied that, having regard to all circumstances, it would be justified in granting a full licence, it may instead grant a provisional licence in terms of s.1 of the Riding Establishments Act 1970. Subsection (4) was substituted for the original by s.2(1)(ii) of the 1970 Act.

Subsection (4A)

This subsection, added by s.2(1)(ii) of the Riding Establishments Act 1970 requires certain mandatory conditions to be placed on all licences whether specified therein or not. These conditions relate to horses found to be in need of veterinary attention, the supervision of horses and riders, the minimum age for persons left in charge of the business, compulsory insurance cover, and the keeping of a register of all horses aged three years and under. For a discussion of the insurance provisions see Home Office Circular 296/70. Contravention of any of these mandatory conditions is an offence in terms of subs.(9). Subsection (4A) was inserted by the Animal Health and Welfare (Scotland) Act 2006 (Consequential Provisions) Order (SSI 2006/536) Schedule para.5.

Subsection (5)

An appeal against refusal of a licence or the placing upon it of any condition (provided it is not a mandatory condition in terms of the above subsection) may be made by way of summary procedure to the sheriff, by reason of subs.(10)—for general observations on such appeals, see pp.28–30 above. Note that there is no procedure for requiring a licensing authority to state reasons for its decision—see Introduction, p.28 above. The sheriff can give the local authority appropriate directions in relation to the issuing of a licence or the conditions to be placed thereon—for a practical example of this see *McKay v Dundee City Council* unreported 22 February 1999 Dundee Sheriff Court. This subsection was amended by s.2(2) of the Riding Establishments Act 1970. For "person aggrieved" see pp.28–29 above.

Subsections (6) and (7)

Licences run for a period of one year from either the date upon which it was granted or 1 January of the year following that in which the application is made.

Subsection (9)

This subsection was amended by s.2(2) of the Riding Establishments Act 1970.

Inspection of riding establishments

2.—(1) A local authority may, subject to the provisions of this section, authorise in writing any such person as the following, namely, an officer of theirs, an officer of any other local authority, a veterinary surgeon and a veterinary practitioner, to inspect any such premises in their area as the following, that is to say,—

(a) any premises where they have reason to believe a person is keeping a riding establishment;

(b) any premises as respects which a licence granted in accordance with the provisions of this Act is for the time being in force; and

(c) any premises as respects which a licence has been applied for under this Act.

(2) Any person authorised under this section may, on producing his authority if so required, enter at all reasonable times any premises which he is authorised under this section to enter and inspect them and any horses found thereon or any thing therein for the purpose (except in the case of any such premises as are mentioned in paragraph (a) of the foregoing subsection) of making a report to the local authority for the purposes of section 1(3) of this Act or for the purpose of ascertaining whether an offence has been or is being committed against this Act.

(3) A local authority shall not authorise a veterinary surgeon or veterinary practitioner to inspect any premises under this section except one chosen by them from a list of such persons drawn up jointly by the Royal College of Veterinary Surgeons and the British Veterinary Association.

(4) Any person who wilfully obstructs or delays any person in the exercise of his powers of entry or inspection conferred by subsection (2) above shall be guilty of an offence.

DEFINITONS

"keeping a riding establishment": s.6(1).
"licence": s.1.
"local authority": s.6(4).
"premises": s.6(4).
"veterinary practitioners": s.6(4).
"veterinary surgeon": s.6(4).

GENERAL NOTE

This section provides for powers of entry to and for the inspection of both licensed and unlicensed riding establishments by persons authorised by the local authority, and it is an offence to wilfully obstruct or delay such a person exercising their powers of entry or inspection.

Subsection (1)

For "reason to believe" see p.31 above.

Subsection (2)

For "at all reasonable times" see p.30 above.

Subsection (4)

For "wilfully obstructs or delays" see pp.30–31 above. The penalty for a contravention of this subsection is provided for in s.4(1).

Offences

3.—(1) If any person—

(a) at a time when a horse is in such a condition that its riding would be likely to cause suffering to the horse, lets out the horse on hire or uses it for the purpose of providing, in return for payment, instruction in riding or for the purpose of demonstrating riding;

(aa) lets out on hire for riding or uses for the purpose of providing, in return for payment, instruction in riding or for the purpose of demonstrating riding any horse aged three years or under or any mare heavy with foal or any mare within three months after foaling;

(b) supplies for a horse which is let out on hire by him for riding equipment which is used in the course of the hiring and suffers, at the time when it is supplied, from a defect of such a nature as to be apparent on inspection and as to be likely to cause suffering to the horse or an accident to the rider;

(c) fails to provide such curative care as may be suitable, if any, for a sick or injured horse which is kept by him with a view to its being let out on hire or used for a purpose mentioned in paragraph (a) of this subsection;

(d) in keeping a riding establishment knowingly permits any person, who is for the time being disqualified under this Act from keeping a riding establishment, to have control or management of the keeping of the establishment; or

(e) with intent to avoid inspection under section 2 of this Act, conceals, or causes to be concealed, any horse maintained by the riding establishment;

he shall be guilty of an offence under this Act.

(2) A person who for the purpose of obtaining the grant of a licence under this Act gives any information which he knows to be false in a material particular or makes a statement which he knows to be so false or recklessly gives any information which is so false or recklessly makes any statement which is so false shall be guilty of an offence under this Act.

DEFINITIONS

"horse": s.6(4).
"keeping a riding establishment": s.6(1).
"licence": s.1.

GENERAL NOTE

This section creates a number of statutory offences additional to those in ss.1(9) and 2(4). Subsection 3(1)(aa) was added by s.3 of the Riding Establishments Act 1970. See also s.1 of the Protection Against Cruel Tethering Act 1988.

Subsection (2)

For "knowingly or recklessly" see Introduction p.32 above.

Penalties and disqualifications

[1]**4.**—(1) Any person guilty of an offence under any provision of this Act other than section 2(4) thereof shall be liable on summary conviction to a fine not exceeding level 3 on the standard scale or to imprisonment for a term not exceeding three months or to both such fine and such imprisonment.

(2) Any person guilty of an offence under section 2(4) of this Act shall be liable on summary conviction to a fine not exceeding level 2 on the standard scale.

(3) Where a person is convicted of any offence under this Act or of any

offence under the Protection of Animals Act 1911 or the Protection of Animals (Scotland) Act 1912 or the Pet Animals Act 1951 or the Animal Boarding Establishments Act 1963, the court by which he is convicted may cancel any licence held by him under this Act and may, whether or not he is the holder of such a licence, disqualify him from keeping a riding establishment for such period as the court thinks fit.

(4) A court which has ordered the cancellation of a person's licence, or his disqualification in pursuance of the last foregoing subsection may, if it thinks fit, suspend the operation of the order pending an appeal.

[1](5) Where a person is convicted of any offence under sections 28C or 28F(16) of the Animal Health Act 1981 (c.22), or sections 19 to 24, 25(7), 29 or 40(11) of the Animal Health and Welfare (Scotland) Act 2006 (asp 11), the court by which he is convicted has the same powers under subsections (3) and (4) in relation to such convictions as it has in relation to convictions for offences under this Act.

NOTE

1. As inserted by the Animal Health and Welfare (Scotland) Act 2006 (Consequential Provisions) Order 2006 (SSI 2006/536) Sch.1 para.5 (effective 3 November 2006).

DEFINITIONS

"keeping a riding establishment": s.6(1).
"level 2/3 on the standard scale": see p.32 above.
"licence": s.1.

GENERAL NOTE

The penalties for contraventions of the various statutory offences created under the Act are set out here. Note that the delay or obstruction of an authorised officer carrying out an inspection is regarded as a less serious offence. Subsection (3) contains power for the court to cancel a licence held under the Act. Subsection (5) was inserted by the Animal Health and Welfare (Scotland) Act 2006 (Consequential Provisions) Order (SSI 2006/536) Schedule para.5.

5. [*Omitted.*]

GENERAL NOTE

This section applies only to England and Wales.

Interpretation

6.—(1) References in this Act to the keeping of a riding establishment shall, subject to the provisions of this section, be construed as references to the carrying on of a business of keeping horses for either or both of the following purposes, that is to say, the purpose of their being let out on hire for riding or the purpose of their being used in providing, in return for payment, instruction in riding, but as not including a reference to the carrying on of such a business—

(a) in a case where the premises where the horses employed for the purposes of the business are kept are occupied by or under the management of the Secretary of State for Defence; or
(b) solely for police purposes; or
(c) by the Zoological Society of London; or
(d) by the Royal Zoological Society of Scotland.

(2) Where a university provides courses of study and examinations leading to a veterinary degree to which relates an order made under section 3 of the Veterinary Surgeons Act 1966 (which section enables the Privy Council, where a university provides such courses, and it appears to the Privy Council that the courses are of the standard therein mentioned, to direct that a

holder of the degree to which the courses lead shall be qualified to be a member of the Royal College of Veterinary Surgeons), horses kept by the university for use in the instruction of students undergoing such courses shall, during the continuance in force of the order, be deemed for the purposes of the foregoing subsection not to be kept as mentioned in that subsection.

(3) For the purposes of this Act a person keeping a riding establishment shall be taken to keep it at the premises where the horses employed for the purposes of the business concerned are kept.

(4) In this Act the following expressions have the meanings respectively assigned to them, that is to say—

"*approved certificate*" means—

(a) any one of the following certificates issued by the British Horse Society, namely, Assistant Instructor's Certificate, Instructor's Certificate and Fellowship;

(b) Fellowship of the Institute of the Horse; or

(c) any other certificate for the time being prescribed by order by the Secretary of State;

"*authorised officer*" means a person authorised by a local authority in pursuance of section 2 of this Act;

"*horse*" includes any mare, gelding, pony, foal, colt, filly or stallion and also any ass, mule or jennet;

"*local authority*" in Scotland means a council constituted under section 2 of the Local Government etc. (Scotland) Act 1994;

"*premises*" includes land;

"*veterinary practitioner*" means a person who is for the time being registered in the Supplementary Veterinary Register in pursuance of the Veterinary Surgeons Act 1966;

"*veterinary surgeon*" means a person who is for the time being registered in the Register of Veterinary Surgeons in pursuance of the Veterinary Surgeons Act 1966.

GENERAL NOTE

This section contains the important definitions used throughout the Act.

Subsection (1)

Note that a riding establishment is the carrying on of a business of keeping horses for hire for payment for the purpose of riding or instruction in riding, subject to certain exemptions. It does not apply to livery stables (i.e. stables where the owners of horses pay to have those horses kept there for their own use).

Subsection (2)

This subsection was amended by s.28(8) of the Veterinary Surgeons Act 1966.

Subsection (3)

Thus it is the location of the stables which is the important factor, e.g. donkeys used for seaside rides are, for the purposes of the Act, "kept" in their home stables.

Subsection (4)

"Approved certificate" and "authorised officer" were inserted into this subsection by s.5 of the Riding Establishments Act 1970. "Local authority" was substituted in Scotland for the original definition by the Local Government etc. (Scotland) Act 1994 s.180(1) and Sch.13 para.64. "Veterinary practitioner" and "veterinary surgeon" were substituted for the original by s.28(8) of the Veterinary Surgeons Act 1966.

Orders

[1]**6A.** Any order made under this Act shall be made by statutory instrument and may be varied or revoked by a subsequent order made in the like manner.

NOTE

1. As inserted by the Riding Establishments Act 1970 (c.32) s.6 (effective 1 February 1991).

GENERAL NOTE

This section was inserted by s.6 of the Riding Establishments Act 1970. There are currently no subsisting orders.

7., 8. [*Sections 7 and 8, which related respectively to transitional provisions and repeals of existing legislation, were repealed by Sch.1, Pt. III to the Statute Law (Repeals) Act 1976 (c.16).*]

GENERAL NOTE

Sections 7 and 8, which related respectively to transitional provisions and repeals of existing legislation, were repealed by Sch.1 Pt III to the Statute Law (Repeals) Act 1976.

Short title, commencement and extent

9.—(1) This Act may be cited as the Riding Establishments Act 1964.

(2) This Act shall not extend to Northern Ireland.

(3) This Act shall come into operation on 1st April 1965.

[1]Riding Establishments Act 1970

(c.32)

NOTE

1. Entire Act to be repealed by the Animal Health and Welfare (Scotland) Act 2006 (asp 11) Sch.2 para.9 (date yet to be appointed).

ARRANGEMENT OF SECTIONS

Provisional licences for riding establishments

1.—(1) In any case in which application is made under the principal Act to a local authority for a licence to keep a riding establishment and the local authority are not satisfied that having regard to all the circumstances they would be justified in granting such licence they may grant a provisional licence which shall come into force at the beginning of the day on which it is granted and shall remain in force for three months.

(2) A local authority may on application being made to them in that behalf before the expiration of a provisional licence extend the said period of three months for a further period not exceeding three months:

Provided that they shall not under this subsection authorise a person to keep a riding establishment by virtue of a provisional licence for more than six months in any period of one year.

(3) The following provisions of the principal Act as amended by this Act shall apply and have effect in all respects as if references therein to a licence included references to a provisional licence and as if references therein to licences granted under that Act included references to provisional licences granted under this Act, that is to say, section 1(1), (2), (3), (4), (4A), (8) and (9) and sections 2, 3, 4 and 5:

Provided that in the application as aforesaid of subsection (8) of section 1 of the principal Act to the personal representatives of the holder of a provisional licence the said subsection shall be read and have effect as if for the words "one year" in each place where they occur there were substituted the words "three months".

(4) For the purposes of this section the expression "local authority" has the same meaning as in the principal Act.

DEFINITION

"the principal Act": s.7.

GENERAL NOTE

This section gives local authorities powers to grant provisional licences for three months (with a possible three months further extension) where they are not satisfied that a full licence in terms of the Riding Establishments Act 1964 should be granted. The procedure for the grant of provisional licences and their conditions contained in the 1964 Act in respect of full licences applies mutatis mutandis here.

2.–6. [*Omitted.*]

GENERAL NOTE

These sections made a number of important and consequential amendments to the 1964 Act and are omitted here as all of those amendments are incorporated into the text and notes to the 1964 Act.

Interpretation

7. In this Act the "principal Act" means the Riding Establishments Act 1964.

Short title, citation and commencement

8.—(1) This Act may be cited as the Riding Establishments Act 1970 and the principal Act and this Act may be cited together as the Riding Establishments Acts 1964 and 1970.

(2) This Act shall not extend to Northern Ireland.

(3) This Act shall come into operation on 1st January 1971.

[1]Breeding of Dogs Act 1973

(c.60)

NOTE

1. Entire Act to be repealed by the Animal Health and Welfare (Scotland) Act 2006 (asp 11) Sch.2 para.9 (date yet to be appointed).

ARRANGEMENT OF SECTIONS

SECTION

GENERAL NOTE

With effect from 30 December 1999 certain important amendments were made to this Act by virtue of the Breeding and Sale of Dogs (Welfare) Act 1999. The intention of the Scottish Ministers is that eventually the 1973 and 1993 Acts will be superseded by Orders made under s.26 of the Animal Health and Welfare (Scotland) Act 2006 but until this is done those Acts will remain in force.

Licensing of breeding establishments for dogs

1.—(1) No person shall keep a breeding or rearing establishment for dogs except under the authority of a licence granted in accordance with the provisions of this Act.

(2) Every local authority may, in application being made to them for that purpose by a person who is not for the time being disqualified—

(a) from keeping a breeding or rearing establishment for dogs; or
(b) under the Pet Animals Act 1951, from keeping a pet shop; or
(c)–(d) [*As repealed by the Protection of Animals (Amendment) Act 1988 (c.29) s.3, Sch.*];
(e) under the Protection of Animals (Amendment) Act 1954, from having the custody of animals; or
(f) under the Animal Boarding Establishments Act 1963, from the boarding of animals,

and on payment of a fee of two pounds or such sum as the local authority may determine, grant a licence to that person to keep a breeding establishment for dogs at such premises in their area as may be specified in the application and subject to compliance with such conditions as may be specified in the licence.

[1](2AA) Where a person is disqualified under section 28F(1) and (2) of the Animal Health Act 1981 (c.22), or section 40(1) and (2) of the Animal Health and Welfare (Scotland) Act 2006 (asp 11), notwithstanding subsection (2), a local authority shall not grant a licence to keep a breeding establishment for dogs to that person.

(2A) On receipt of an application by a person to a local authority for the grant of a licence under this Act in respect of any premises—

(a) if a licence under this Act has not previously been granted to the person in respect of the premises, the authority shall arrange for the inspection of the premises by a veterinary surgeon or veterinary practitioner and by an officer of the authority; and

(b) in any other case, the authority shall arrange for the inspection of the premises by a veterinary surgeon or veterinary practitioner or by an officer of the authority (or by both).

(2B) Where an inspection is arranged under subsection (2A) of this section, the local authority shall arrange for the making of a report about the premises, the applicant and any other relevant matter; and the authority shall consider the report before determining whether to grant a licence.

(3) [*Repealed.*]

(4) In determining whether to grant a licence for the keeping of a breeding or rearing establishment for dogs by any person at any premises, a local authority shall in particular (but without prejudice to their discretion to withhold a licence on other grounds) have regard to the need for securing—

(a) that the dogs will at all times be kept in accommodation suitable as respects construction, size of quarters, number of occupants, exercising facilities, temperature, lighting, ventilation and cleanliness;

(b) that the dogs will be adequately supplied with suitable food, drink and bedding material, adequately exercised, and visited at suitable intervals;

(c) that all reasonable precautions will be taken to prevent and control the spread among dogs of infectious or contagious diseases;

(d) that appropriate steps will be taken for the protection of the dogs in case of fire or other emergency;

(e) that all appropriate steps will be taken to secure that the dogs will be provided with suitable food, drink and bedding material and adequately exercised when being transported to or from the breeding establishment;

(f) that bitches are not mated if they are less than one year old;

(g) that bitches do not give birth to more than six litters of puppies each;

(h) that bitches do not give birth to puppies before the end of the period of twelve months beginning with the day on which they last gave birth to puppies; and

(i) that accurate records in a form prescribed by regulations are kept at the premises and made available for inspection there by any officer of the local authority, or any veterinary surgeon or veterinary practitioner, authorised by the local authority to inspect the premises;

and shall specify such conditions in the licence, if granted by them, as appear to the local authority necessary or expedient in the particular case for securing all the objects specified in paragraphs (a) to (i) of this subsection.

(4A) Regulations under paragraph (i) of subsection (4) of this section shall be made by the Secretary of State by statutory instrument; and a statutory instrument containing regulations made under that paragraph shall be subject to annulment in pursuance of a resolution of either House of Parliament.

(5) Any person aggrieved by the refusal of a local authority to grant such a licence, or by any condition subject to which such a licence is proposed to be granted, may appeal to magistrates' court; and the court may on such an appeal give such directions with respect to the issue of a licence or, as the case may be, with respect to the conditions subject to which a licence is to be granted as it thinks proper.

(5A) A local authority shall determine whether to grant such a licence before the end of the period of three months beginning with the day on which the application for the licence is received.

(6) Any such licence shall come into force at the beginning of the day specified in the licence as the day on which it is to come into force; and that day shall be the later of—

(a) the day stated in the application as that on which the applicant wishes the licence to come into force; and

(b) the day on which the licence is granted.

(7) Subject to the provisions hereinafter contained with respect to cancellation, any such licence shall remain in force until the end of the period of one year beginning with the day on which it comes into force and shall then expire.

(8) In the event of the death of a person who is keeping a breeding or rearing establishment for dogs at any premises under the authority of a licence granted under this Act, that licence shall be deemed to have been granted to his personal representatives in respect of those premises and shall, notwithstanding subsection (7) of this section (but subject to the provisions hereinafter contained with respect to cancellation), remain in force until the end of the period of three months beginning with the death and shall then expire.

Provided that the local authority by whom the licence was granted may from time to time, on the application of those representatives, extend or further extend the said period of three months if the authority are satisfied that the extension is necessary for the purpose of winding up the deceased's estate and that no other circumstances make it undesirable.

(9) Any person who contravenes the provisions of subsection (1) of this section shall be guilty of an offence; and if any condition subject to which a licence is granted in accordance with the provisions of this Act is contravened or not complied with, the person to whom the licence was granted shall be guilty of an offence.

(10) In the application of this section to Scotland, in subsection (5) for any reference to a magistrates' court there shall be substituted a reference to the sheriff.

NOTE

1. As inserted by the Animal Health and Welfare (Scotland) Act 2006 (Consequential Provisions) Order 2006 (SSI 2006/536) Sch.1 para.6 (effective 3 November 2006).

DEFINITIONS

"breeding establishment": s.4A(2).
"premises": s.4B(1).
"local authority": s.5(2).
"rearing establishment": s.4B(1).
"veterinary practitioner": s.5(2).
"veterinary surgeon": s.5(2).

GENERAL NOTE

Section 1 sets out the general licensing scheme for dog breeding or rearing establishments and provides for applications, the grant of a licence, relevant considerations and conditions, appeals, temporary transmission of licences on death and a statutory offence of keeping an unlicensed establishment. Note that throughout the Act the expression "dog breeding establishment", which is used in the original Act, is now, for the purposes of Scotland only, amended to read "dog breeding or rearing establishment" by virtue of the 1982 Act s.137 and Sch.3 para.3.

Subsection (1)

A person who carries on at any premises (including a private house) a dog breeding or rearing establishment, requires a licence and it is an offence, by virtue of subs.(9), to carry on such a business without a licence.

Subsection (2)

Note that the only formal qualification for a licence is that the applicant shall not have been disqualified from keeping an establishment of this or an analogous nature. There is no apparent minimum age requirement or "fit and proper person" stipulation (but this may be implied from the provisions relating to welfare of dogs here). Subsection (2) was amended by the Breeding and Sale of Dogs (Welfare) Act 1999 s.10 and Sch.1. Paragraphs (c) and (d) were repealed by s.3(2) and the Schedule to the Protection of Animals (Amendment) Act 1988. The provision with respect to fees which had already been amended for Scotland by the Local Government (Scotland) Act 1975 s.38(1) and Sch.6 Pt II para.45(a), was repealed by Sch.1 to the 1999 Act and replaced by a new s.3A of the Act—see below.

Subsections (2A) and (2B)

These subsections were inserted by s.1 of the 1999 Act and provide that where an applicant has not previously held a licence for the premises in question, a mandatory inspection of the premises by a veterinary practitioner or surgeon and an officer of the authority must be arranged by the authority and in every other case an inspection by either a vet or an officer (or both) shall be arranged. A report on the premises, the applicant and "any other relevant matter" must then be considered by the authority before determination whether or not they will grant the licence applied for. Subsection (2A) was inserted by the Animal Health and Welfare (Scotland) Act 2006 (Consequential Provisions) Order (SSI 2006/536) Schedule para.6. Subsection (2B) was inserted by the Breeding and Sale of Dogs (Welfare) Act 1999 s.1.

Subsection (3)

This subsection was repealed for Scotland by the Local Government (Scotland) Act 1975 s.38(1) and Sch.6 Pt II para.45(b).

Subsection (4)

This is a non-exhaustive list of matters to be taken into account in considering an application. Those matters listed here must be satisfied and, if they appear to the local authority to be necessary and expedient, must be the subject of specific conditions. Paragraph (d) was amended by s.2(1) of the 1999 Act and paras (f)–(i) were added by s.2(2) of that Act. For the prescribed form of records required by para.(i), see subs.(4A), below.

Subsection (4A)

This subsection was inserted by s.2(3) of the 1999 Act. This function of the Secretary of State was transferred to the Scottish Ministers by virtue of the Scotland Act 1998 (Transfer of Functions to the Scottish Ministers etc.) (No.2) Order 1999 (SI 1999/3321). For the relevant order see the Breeding of Dogs (Licensing Records) (Scotland) Regulations 1999 (SSI 1999/176) set out at pp.398–399 below.

Subsection (5)

By virtue of subs.(10) these powers are all exercised in Scotland by the sheriff by way of summary procedure. For "person aggrieved" see pp.28–29 above. For an example of how an appeal was conducted under this provision see *Hamilton v East Ayrshire Council* unreported 19 October 2004 Kilmarnock Sheriff Court where such an appeal was, apparently, treated in the same manner as an appeal under the licensing provisions of the 1982 Act. In particular it was held that a decision taken by the local authorities licensing panel and notified to the applicant could not be subsequently reviewed by the authority, whether within the three month period specified in subs.(5A) or otherwise, as it would be ultra vires to do so. There is no obligation to consider objections or representations from persons other than the statutory consultees and, although there is no requirement for the licensing authority to state the reasons for their decisions, if all other facts and circumstances favour a different decision then the court may draw an inference that there was a lack of rational reason for the decision—*Lonhro Plc v Secretary of State for Trade & Industry* [1989] 2 All E.R. 609 at 620F–620G.

Subsection (5A)

This subsection was added by s.3(1) of the 1999 Act and provides that the local authority must determine a licence application within three months of the receipt of the application. These are, however, no "deemed grant" provisions analogous to those provided for in s.3 of the 1982 Act.

Subsections (6) and (7)

Licences run for a period of one year from the date upon which they come into force. These subsections were amended by s.3(2) of the 1999 Act and replace the previous provisions which were related to calendar years. If a licence has never been issued and the refusal to grant it is subject to an appeal then it cannot be said to have expired and therefore there is still a valid point to be decided on appeal—*Hamilton v East Ayrshire Council* unreported 19 October 2004 Kilmarnock Sheriff Court.

Subsection (8)

This subsection allows the personal representatives of a licence holder to continue the business for certain limited periods and purposes.

Subsection (9)

The penalties for this offence are specified in s.3.

Inspection of breeding establishments for dogs

2.—(1) A local authority may authorise in writing any of its officers or any veterinary surgeon or veterinary practitioner to inspect (subject to compliance with such precautions as the authority may specify to prevent the spread among animals of infectious or contagious diseases) any premises in their area as respects which a licence granted in accordance with the provisions of this Act is for the time being in force, and any person authorised under this section may, on producing his authority if so required, enter any such premises at all reasonable times and inspect them and any animals found thereon or any thing therein, for the purpose of ascertaining whether an offence has been or is being committed against this Act.

(2) Any person who wilfully obstructs or delays any person in the exercise of his powers of entry or inspection under this section shall be guilty of an offence.

DEFINITIONS

"veterinary practitioner": s.5(2).
"veterinary surgeon": s.5(2).

GENERAL NOTE

This section gives authorised persons the right to enter and inspect all licensed premises. For a similar power to enter unlicensed premises see the Breeding of Dogs Act 1991.

Subsection (1)

For "at all reasonable times" see Introduction p.30 above.

Subsection (2)

For "wilfully obstructs or delays" see pp.30–31 above. The penalty for contravention of subsection is provided for in s.3.

Offences and disqualifications

[1]**3.**—(1) Any person guilty of an offence under any provision of this Act other than the last foregoing section shall be liable on summary conviction to—

(a) imprisonment for a term not exceeding three months; or

(b) a fine not exceeding level 4 on the standard scale,

or to both.

(2) Any person guilty of an offence under the last foregoing section shall be liable on summary conviction to a fine not exceeding level 3 on the standard scale.

(3) Where a person is convicted of any offence under this Act, the court by which he is convicted may (in addition to or in substitution for any penalty under subsection (1) or (2) of this section) make an order providing for any one or more of the following—

(a) the cancellation of any licence held by him under this Act;

(b) his disqualification, for such period as the court thinks fit, from keeping an establishment the keeping of which is required to be licensed under this Act; and

(c) his disqualification, for such period as the court thinks fit, from having custody of any dog of a description specified in the order.

(4) A court which has made an order under this section may, if it thinks fit, suspend the operation of the order pending an appeal.

(4A) Where a person is convicted of any offence under sections 28C or 28F(16) of the Animal Health Act 1981 (c.22), or sections 19 to 24, 25(7), 29 or 40(11) of the Animal Health and Welfare (Scotland) Act 2006 (asp 11), the court by which he is convicted has the same powers under subsections (3) and (4) in relation to such convictions as it has in relation to convictions for offences under this Act.

(5) Where a court makes an order under subsection (3)(c) of this section in relation to a description of dogs it may also make such order as it thinks fit in respect of any dog of that description which—

(a) was in the offender's custody at the time when the offence was committed; or

(b) has been in his custody at any time since that time.

(6) An order under subsection (5) of this section may (in particular)—

(a) require any person who has custody of the dog to deliver it up to a specified person; and

(b) (if it does) also require the offender to pay specified amounts to specified persons for the care of the dog from the time when it is delivered up in pursuance of the order until permanent arrangements are made for its care or disposal.

(7) A person who—

(a) has custody of a dog in contravention of an order under subsection (3)(c) of this section; or

(b) fails to comply with a requirement imposed on him under subsection (6) of this section,

shall be guilty of an offence.

(8) Where a court proposes to make an order under subsection (5) of this section in respect of a dog owned by a person other than the offender, the court shall notify the owner who may make representations to the court; and if an order is made the owner may, within the period of seven days beginning with the date of the order, appeal to—

(a) in England and Wales, the Crown Court; or

(b) in Scotland, the High Court of Justiciary,

against the order.

(9) A person who is subject to a disqualification by virtue of an order under subsection (3)(c) of this section may, at any time after the end of the period of one year beginning with the date of the order, apply to the court which made the order (or, in England and Wales, any magistrates' court acting for the same petty sessions area) for a direction terminating the disqualification from such date as the court considers appropriate.

(10) On an application under subsection (9) of this section the court—

(a) shall notify the relevant local authority which may make representations to the court;

(b) shall, having regard to the applicant's character and his conduct since the disqualification was imposed, any representations made by the relevant local authority and any other circumstances of the case, grant or refuse the application; and

(c) may order the applicant to pay all or any part of the costs, or (in Scotland) expenses, of the application (including any costs, or expenses, of the relevant local authority in making representations);

and in this subsection "the relevant local authority" means the local authority in whose area are situated the premises in relation to which the offence which led to the disqualification was committed.

(11) Where an application under subsection (9) of this section in respect of a disqualification is refused, no further application under that subsection in respect of that disqualification shall be entertained if made before the end of the period of one year beginning with the date of the refusal.

NOTE

1. As inserted by the Animal Health and Welfare (Scotland) Act 2006 (Consequential Provisions) Order 2006 (SSI 2006/536) Sch.1 para.6 (effective 3 November 2006).

DEFINITIONS

"keeping a breeding or rearing establishment for dogs": ss.4A(7) and 4B(2).

"level 2/3 on the standard scale": see Introduction p.32 above.

GENERAL NOTE

This section provides the penalties for the various statutory offences created under the Act together with the power of the court to cancel an existing licence and/or disqualify a person from holding such a licence.

Subsection (1)

The power to impose a sentence of imprisonment for all offences committed after 30 December 1999 was added by s.4(1) of the 1999 Act.

Subsection (2)

Note that the power to imprison is not given for offences committed under s.2(2).

Subsection (3)

This subsection was amended by s.5(1) of the 1999 Act, which gave the courts substantial additional powers in relation to offenders.

Subsection (4)

This subsection was amended by s.5(2) of the 1999 Act.

Subsections (5)–(8)

These subsections, which were inserted by s.5(2) of the 1999 Act, provide the court to make specific orders in relation to dogs which are or where in the custody of the offender and subs.(8) provides a right of appeal to the High Court.

Subsections (9)–(11)

These subsections, inserted by s.5(2) of the 1999 Act, provide a review mechanism in relation to the disqualification orders—note that one year must not have elapsed since the making of the order.

Fees

3A.—(1) The costs of inspecting premises under this Act and the Breeding of Dogs Act 1991 shall be met by the local authority concerned.

(2) A local authority may charge fees—

(a) in respect of applications for the grant of licences under this Act; and

(b) in respect of inspections of premises under section 1(2A) of this Act.

(3) A local authority may set the level of fees to be charged by virtue of subsection (2) of this section—

(a) with a view to recovering the reasonable costs incurred by them in connection with the administration and enforcement of this Act and the Breeding of Dogs Act 1991; and

(b) so that different fees are payable in different circumstances.

GENERAL NOTE

These new provisions, inserted by s.6 of the 1999 Act, allow for a level of fees to be imposed, which relates to the reasonable costs incurred by the licensing authorities in administering and enforcing the Act. The level of fees must be reasonable and not at such a level as to make the activity to be licensed financially unviable because of the fees sought. Subsection (3A) was inserted by the Breeding and Sale of Dogs (Welfare) Act 1999 s.6.

4. [*As repealed by the Local Government Act 1974 (c.7) Schs 7 (para.15(1)) and 8.*]

GENERAL NOTE

This section was repealed by Schs 7 (para.15(1)) and 8 to the Local Government Act 1974.

Breeding establishments for dogs

[1]**4A.**—(1) References in this Act to the keeping of a breeding establishment for dogs shall be construed in accordance with this section.

(2) A person keeps a breeding establishment for dogs at any premises if he carries on at those premises a business of breeding dogs for sale (whether by him or any other person).

(3) Subject to subsection (5) of this section, where—

(a) a person keeps a bitch at any premises at any time during any period of twelve months; and

(b) the bitch gives birth to a litter of puppies at any time during that period,

he shall be treated as carrying on a business of breeding dogs for sale at the premises throughout the period if a total of four or more other litters is born during the period to bitches falling within subsection (4) of this section.

(4) The bitches falling within this subsection are—

(a) the bitch mentioned in subsection (3)(a) and (b) of this section and any other bitches kept by the person at the premises at any time during the period;

(b) any bitches kept by any relative of his at the premises at any such time;

(c) any bitches kept by him elsewhere at any such time; and

(d) any bitches kept (anywhere) by any person at any such time under a breeding arrangement made with him.

(5) Subsection (3) of this section does not apply if the person shows that none of the puppies born to bitches falling within paragraph (a), (b) or (d) of subsection (4) of this section was in fact sold during the period (whether by him or any other person).

(6) In subsection (4) of this section "breeding arrangement" means a contract or other arrangement under which the person agrees that another person may keep a bitch of his on terms that, should the bitch give birth, the other person is to provide him with either—

(a) one or more of the puppies; or

(b) the whole or part of the proceeds of selling any of them;

and "relative" means the person's parent or grandparent, child or grandchild, sibling, aunt or uncle or niece or nephew or someone with whom he lives as a couple.

(7) In this section "premises" includes a private dwelling.

NOTE

1. As inserted by the Breeding and Sale of Dogs (Welfare) Act 1999 (c.11) s.7 (effective 30 December 1999).

GENERAL NOTE

This new section was inserted by s.7 of the 1999 Act and provides certain new key definitions, which seek to clarify and strengthen the original definitions given in the Act. Note that these definitions apply to dog breeding establishments in both England and Wales and Scotland. Section (4A) was inserted by the Breeding and Sale of Dogs (Welfare) Act 1999 s.7.

Rearing establishments for dogs

[1]**4B.**—(1) For the purposes of the application of this Act in relation to Scotland, a person keeps a rearing establishment for dogs at any premises if he carries on at those premises a business of rearing dogs for sale (whether by him or any other person).

(2) In subsection (1) of this section "premises" includes a private dwelling."

NOTE

1. As inserted by the Breeding and Sale of Dogs (Welfare) Act 1999 (c.11) s.7 (effective 30 December 1999).

GENERAL NOTE

This new section, which applies to Scotland only, was inserted by s.7 of the 1999 Act, and provides a definition of the keeper of a dog-rearing establishment. The original definition of a "breeding or rearing establishment" formerly appeared in s.5(2) of the Act and highlighted the distance between the positions in England and Wales and Scotland, the Scottish definition having been derived from the 1982 Act s.137 and Sch.3 para.3. Section (4B) was inserted by the Breeding and Sale of Dogs (Welfare) Act 1999 s.7.

Interpretation

5.—(1) Nothing in this Act shall apply to the keeping of a dog at any premises in pursuance of a requirement imposed under, or having effect by virtue of, the Diseases of Animals Act 1950.

(2) In this Act, unless the context otherwise requires, the following expressions have the meanings hereby respectively assigned to them, that is to say:—

"*local authority*" in Scotland means a council constituted under section 2 of the Local Government etc. (Scotland) Act 1994;

"*veterinary practitioner*" means a person who is for the time being registered in the supplementary veterinary register;

"*veterinary surgeon*" means a person who is for the time being registered in the register of veterinary surgeons.

GENERAL NOTE

This section contains additional definitions to those contained in ss.4A and 4B, above and was amended by s.10 and Sch.1 of the 1999 Act, which repealed certain words therein. The definition of local authority was substituted in Scotland by the Local Government etc. (Scotland) Act 1994 s.180(1) and Sch.13 para.91.

6. [*Omitted.*]

GENERAL NOTE

These transitional provisions, which were amended for Scotland by the 1982 Act s.137 and Sch.3 para.3, are no longer of any practical effect and have been omitted.

Short title, extent and commencement

7.—(1) This Act may be cited as the Breeding of Dogs Act 1973.

(2) This Act shall not extend to Northern Ireland.

(3) This Act shall come into operation on 1st April 1974.

Dangerous Wild Animals Act 1976

(c.38)

ARRANGEMENT OF SECTIONS

Licences

1.—(1) Subject to section 5 of this Act, no person shall keep any dangerous wild animal except under the authority of a licence granted in accordance with the provisions of this Act by a local authority.

(2) A local authority shall not grant a licence under this Act unless an application for it—

(a) specifies the species (whether one or more) of animal, and the number of animals of each species, proposed to be kept under the authority of the licence;

(b) specifies the premises where any animal concerned will normally be held;

(c) is made to the local authority in whose area those premises are situated;

(d) is made by a person who is neither under the age of 18 nor disqualified under this Act from keeping any dangerous wild animal; and

(e) is accompanied by such fee as the authority may stipulate (being a fee which is in the authority's opinion sufficient to meet the direct and indirect costs which it may incur as a result of the application).

(3) A local authority shall not grant a licence under this Act unless it is satisfied that—

(a) it is not contrary to the public interest on the grounds of safety, nuisance or otherwise to grant the licence;

(b) the applicant for the licence is a suitable person to hold a licence under this Act;

(c) any animal concerned will at all times of its being kept only under the authority of the licence—

(i) be held in accommodation which secures that the animal will not escape, which is suitable as regards construction, size, temperature, lighting, ventilation, drainage and cleanliness and which is suitable for the number of animals proposed to be held in the accommodation, and

(ii) be supplied with adequate and suitable food, drink and bedding material and be visited at suitable intervals:

(d) appropriate steps will at all such times be taken for the protection of any animal concerned in case of fire or other emergency;

(e) all reasonable precautions will be taken at all such times to prevent and control the spread of infectious diseases;

(f) while any animal concerned is at the premises where it will normally be held, its accommodation is such that it can take adequate exercise.

(4) A local authority shall not grant a licence under this Act unless the application for it is made by a person who both owns and possesses, or proposes both to own and to possess, any animal concerned, except where the circumstances are in the authority's opinion exceptional.

(5) A local authority shall not grant a licence under this Act unless a veterinary surgeon or veterinary practitioner authorised by the authority to do so under section 3 of this Act has inspected the premises where any animal will normally be held in pursuance of the licence and the authority has received and considered a report by the surgeon or practitioner, containing such particulars as in the authority's opinion enable it to decide whether the premises are such that any animal proposed to be kept under the authority of the licence may suitably be held there, and describing the condition of the premises and of any animal or other thing found there.

(6) Subject to subsections (2) to (5) of this section, a local authority may grant or refuse a licence under this Act as it thinks fit, but where it decides to grant such a licence it shall specify as conditions of the licence—

(a) conditions that, while any animal concerned is being kept only under the authority of the licence,—

(i) the animal shall be kept by no person other than such person or persons as is or are specified (whether by name or description) in the licence;

(ii) the animal shall normally be held at such premises as are specified in the licence;

(iii) the animal shall not be moved from those premises or shall only be moved from them in such circumstances as are specified in the licence;

(iv) the person to whom the licence is granted shall hold a current insurance policy which insures him and any other person entitled to keep the animal under the authority of the licence against liability for any damage which may be caused by the animal; and

(v) the terms of any such policy shall be satisfactory in the opinion of the authority;

(b) conditions restricting the species (whether one or more) of animal, and number of animals of each species, which may be kept under the authority of the licence;

(c) a condition that the person to whom the licence is granted shall at all reasonable times make available a copy of the licence to any person entitled to keep any animal under the authority of the licence;

(d) such other conditions as in the opinion of the authority are necessary or desirable for the purpose of securing the objects specified in paragraphs (c) to (f) of subsection (3) of this section.

(7) Subject to subsection (6) of this section, a local authority may, in granting a licence under this Act, specify such conditions of the licence as it thinks fit.

(8) Where a local authority proposes to insert in a licence under this Act a provision permitting any animal to be, for any continuous period exceeding 72 hours, at premises outside the area of the authority, the authority shall consult the local authority in whose area those premises are situated.

(9) A local authority which grants a licence under this Act may at any time vary the licence by specifying any new condition of the licence or varying or revoking any condition of it (including any condition specified, or previously varied, under this subsection); but any condition of a licence specified by virtue of subsection (6) of this section may not be revoked and any condition specified by virtue of paragraph (a)(ii) of that subsection may not be varied.

(10) Where a local authority varies a licence under subsection (9) of this section, then—

(a) if the variation was requested by the person to whom the licence was granted, the variation shall take effect immediately after the authority decides to make it;

(b) in any other case, the variation shall not take effect until the person to whom the licence was granted has become aware of the variation and had a reasonable time to comply with it.

DEFINITIONS

"dangerous wild animal": s.7(4) and Schedule.
"keep": s.7(1)–(3).
"local authority": s.7(4).
"premises": s.7(4).
"veterinary practitioner": s.7(4).
"veterinary surgeon": s.7(4).

GENERAL NOTE

The Act provides for a system of licensing of the keepers of dangerous wild animals and is designed to secure both the safety and well being of the animals themselves and also of the general public. Section 1 makes such licences mandatory and sets out the matters which the licensing authority must take into account when considering applications therefor.

Subsection (1)

Subject to the specific exemptions for zoos, circuses, pet shops and experimental animals as set out in s.5, it is mandatory for the keeper of a dangerous wild animal to have a licence therefor. The concept of "keeping" is set out in ss.7(1)–(3) but the ownership requirement of s.1(4) should also be noted. A licence can relate to more than one animal of more than one species—see s.1(2)(a). It is an offence to keep such an animal without a licence—see s.2(5).

Subsection (2)

There is no statutory form for an application, but any application must specify the number and species of the animals to be kept and the premises at which they are to be kept. The relevant licensing authority is that in whose area the premises are situated. Only persons who are 18 years old or more and who have not been disqualified from holding a licence by reason of s.6(2) of the Act are eligible to hold licences. The fees that can be charged for such applications must cover the direct and indirect costs incurred as a result thereof, so that administrative and processing costs are to be covered in addition to the direct cost of granting the application.

Subsection (3)

Before granting the licence the licensing authority must be satisfied in relation to a number of specified matters which relate: (a) to the public interest (non-exhaustively including safety and nuisance); (b) to the suitability of the applicant; (c) to the suitability of the animal's security, accommodation, welfare, food and bedding; (d) to fire and emergency provision; (e) to disease precautions; and (f) to the adequacy of exercise provision. Unless it is so satisfied in relation to all of these matters the licensing authority must refuse the application.

Subsection (4)

Except in extraordinary circumstances (undefined but for the opinion of the licensing authority) a keeper must also be the owner or prospective owner of the animal covered by the licence—see also s.7(1)–(3).

Subsection (5)

A prerequisite of granting a licence is the obtaining and consideration by the licensing authority of a veterinary report dealing with the matters specified in this subsection.

Subsection (6)

This subsection imposes a requirement upon a licensing authority, where it decides to grant an application, to make certain conditions mandatory (paras (a)–(c)) and, in addition, such other conditions relating to the welfare of the animals in terms of s.1(3)(c)–(f) as are necessary or desirable. Note that the actual keepers are to be specified. "Damage" in para.(a)(iv) is defined in s.7(4) so as to include death or injury to any person. For "at all reasonable times" see p.30 above.

Subsection (7)

Notwithstanding the above subsection, there is a general power to impose such conditions on a licence as the licensing authority thinks fit.

Subsection (8)

Although licences relate to premises only within the area of the licensing authority, power is given to make provision for the keeping of an animal in another licensing authority area subject to consultation with that other authority, the object thereof being to obviate the need for two separate licences relating to the same animals.

Subsections (9) and (10)

Subject to the provisos set out in this subsection, there is a limited power to vary and revoke the conditions of a licence, and the time when such variations come into effect is specified.

Provisions supplementary to section 1

2.—(1) Where—

(a) a person is aggrieved by the refusal of a local authority to grant a licence under this Act, or

(b) a person to whom such a licence has been granted is aggrieved by a condition of the licence (whether specified at the time the licence is granted or later) or by the variation or revocation of any condition of the licence,

he may appeal to a magistrates' court; and the court may on such appeal give such directions with respect to the grant of a licence or, as the case may be, with respect to the conditions of the licence as it thinks proper, having regard to the provisions of this Act.

(2) Any licence under this Act shall (according to the applicant's requirements) relate to the calendar year in which it is granted or to the next following year.

In the former case, the licence shall come into force at the beginning of the day on which it is granted, and in the latter case it shall come into force at the beginning of the next following year.

(3) Subject to the provisions hereinafter contained with respect to cancellation, any licence under this Act shall remain in force until the end of the year to which it relates and shall then expire:

Provided that if application is made for a further licence before the said date of expiry the licence shall be deemed to be still in force pending the grant or refusal of the said application, and if it is granted the new licence shall commence from the date of the expiry of the last licence.

(4) In the event of the death of anyone to whom a licence has been granted under this Act the said licence shall continue in force for a period of twenty-eight days as if it had been granted to the personal representatives of the deceased and if application is made for a new licence within the said period the said licence shall be deemed to be still in force pending the grant or refusal of that application.

(5) Any person who contravenes the provisions of section 1(1) of this Act shall be guilty of an offence.

(6) If any condition of a licence under this Act is contravened or not complied with, then,—

(a) the person to whom the licence was granted, and

(b) any other person who is entitled to keep any animal under the authority of the licence and who was primarily responsible for the contravention or failure to comply,

shall, subject to subsection (7) of this section, be guilty of an offence.

(7) In any proceedings for an offence under subsection (6) of this section, it shall be a defence for the person charged to prove that he took all reasonable precautions and exercised all due diligence to avoid the commission of such an offence.

(8) In the application of this section to Scotland, in subsection (1) for any reference to a magistrates' court there shall be substituted a reference to the sheriff.

DEFINITIONS

"keep any animal": s.7(1)–(3).
"licence": s.1(1).
"local authority": s.7(4).

GENERAL NOTE

This section provides for a number of supplementary administrative matters in connection with the scheme of licensing under the Act, namely: appeals; the duration of licences; transmission of licences on death; and contraventions.

Subsection (1)

A right of appeal is provided against both the refusal of the licensing authority to grant a licence and also against the imposition, variation or revocation of conditions thereof, although it would not be competent to seek to review any of the mandatory conditions imposed by virtue of s.1(6)(a)–(c). Appeal is by way of summary application and is made to the sheriff court by reason of subs.(8). The sheriff may then remit the matter back to the licensing authority with appropriate directions. For general observations on appeals in such cases see pp.28–30 above.

Subsection (2)

Licences have a maximum duration of one year and run either from 1 January to 31 December of the year following that in which the application is made or, alternatively, from the date upon which it is granted until 31 December of that same year and the applicant must choose for which period to apply.

Subsection (3)

If an existing licensee applies for a new licence before the expiry of the existing licence, then the existing licence will continue in force until the grant or refusal of the new licence but note that there is no deemed licence until the final determination of any appeal.

Subsection (4)

This subsection gives a limited right of transmission of a licence to their personal representatives on the death of a licensee.

Subsection (5)

Thus an offence of keeping an unlicensed dangerous wild animal is created.

Subsections (6) and (7)

An offence of failing to comply with the conditions of a licence is also created and this can apply to both the licensee and the person entitled to keep the animal by virtue of s.1(6)(a)(i) and who was primarily responsible for the contravention of that condition. Note that two statutory defences are created namely that all reasonable precautions were taken and that "all due diligence" was exercised (see Introduction p.31 above). Note also that there is a power of seizure of unlicensed animals or those kept in breach of conditions contained in s.4.

Inspection by local authority

3.—(1) Subject to subsection (2) of this section, a local authority to which an application has been made for a licence under this Act, or which has granted such a licence, may authorise in writing any veterinary surgeon or veterinary practitioner or such other person as it may deem competent to do so to inspect any premises where any animal is proposed to be held in pursuance of a licence for which an application has been made under this Act, or where any animal is or may be held in pursuance of a licence which has been granted under this Act; and any persons authorised under this section may, on producing their authority if so required, enter any such premises at all reasonable time and inspect them and any animal or other thing found there, for the purpose of ascertaining whether or not a licence should be granted or varied or whether an offence has been or is being committed against this Act.

(2) A local authority shall not give an authority under subsection (1) of this section to inspect premises situated outside its area unless it has obtained the approval of the local authority in whose area those premises are situated.

(3) The local authority may require the person who has applied for a licence under this Act or, as the case may be, to whom the licence concerned has been granted under this Act to pay the local authority the reasonable costs of the inspection.

(4) Any person who wilfully obstructs or delays any person in the exercise of his power of entry or inspection under this section shall be guilty of an offence.

DEFINITIONS

"licence": s.1(1).
"local authority": s.7(4).
"premises": s.7(4).
"veterinary practitioner": s.7(4).
"veterinary surgeon": s.7(4).

GENERAL NOTE

Powers to authorise qualified persons to inspect and enter premises where animals are kept or to be kept are given and an offence of wilful obstruction or delay of any person exercising those powers is created. Note that such an inspection is a mandatory prerequisite of granting a licence (s.1(5)) and that the licensee may be required to pay for the reasonable cost of such an inspection. For "wilfully obstructs or delays" see Introduction pp.30–31 above.

Powers to seize and dispose of animals without compensation

4.—(1) Where—

(a) an animal is being kept contrary to section 1(1) of this Act, or

(b) any condition of a licence under this Act is contravened or not complied with,

the local authority in whose area any animal concerned is for the time being may seize the animal, and either retain it in the authority's possession or destroy or otherwise dispose of it, and shall not be liable to pay compensation to any person in respect of the exercise of its powers under this subsection.

(2) A local authority which incurs any expenditure in exercising its powers under subsection (1)(a) of this section shall be entitled to recover the amount of the expenditure summarily as a civil debt from any person who was at the time of the seizure a keeper of the animal concerned.

(3) A local authority which incurs any expenditure in exercising its powers under subsection (1)(b) of this section shall be entitled to recover the amount of the expenditure summarily as a civil debt from the person to whom the licence concerned was granted.

DEFINITIONS

"an animal is being kept": s.7(1)–(3).
"licence": s.1(1).
"local authority": s.7(4).

GENERAL NOTE

A licensing authority can seize and either keep or destroy an animal where the keeper of that animal is not licensed to keep it or there is a breach of any licence condition, and no compensation is payable in respect of any such seizure and disposal. The cost of exercising these powers can be met from the keeper and is recoverable as a civil debt.

Subsection (1)

The power to seize can be exercised without there having been any conviction provided that the licensing authority have reason to believe that an offence has been committed and where the police consider that an offence under s.1 has or might have been committed then they are acting lawfully if they seize animals without a warrant where this is reasonably necessary to preserve evidence or maintain public safety—see *Halpern v Chief Constable of Strathclyde*, 1988 S.C.L.R. 137.

Exemptions

5. The provisions of this Act shall not apply to any dangerous wild animal kept in:—

(1) a zoo within the meaning of the Zoo Licensing Act 1981 for which a licence is in force (or is not for the time being required) under that Act,

(2) a circus;

(3) premises licensed as a pet shop under the Pet Animals Act 1951;

[1](4) a place which is the place specified in a section 2C licence within the meaning of the Animals (Scientific Procedures) Act 1986.

NOTE

1. As amended by the Animals (Scientific Procedures) Act 1986 Amendment Regulations 2012 (SI 2012/3039) reg.27 (effective 1 January 2013).

DEFINITIONS

"circus": s.7(4).

"dangerous wild animal": s.7(4) and Schedule.

GENERAL NOTE

This section provides an exemption from the licensing provisions for animals kept in certain specified premises. The wording relating to zoos was substituted for the original by s.22(1)(a) of the Zoo Licensing Act 1981. The wording in subs.(4) was substituted for the original by the Animals (Scientific Procedures) Act 1986 s.27(2) and Sch.3 para.10.

Penalties

6.—(1) Any person guilty of an offence under any provision of this Act shall be liable on summary conviction to a fine not exceeding level 4 on the standard scale.

(2) Where a person is convicted of any offence under this Act or of any offence under the Protection of Animals Acts 1911 to 1964, the Protection of Animals (Scotland) Acts 1912 to 1964, the Pet Animals Act 1951, the Animal Boarding Establishments Act 1963, the Riding Establishments Acts 1964 and 1970, or the Breeding of Dogs Act 1973, the court by which he is convicted may cancel any licence held by him under this Act, and may, whether or not he is the holder of such a licence, disqualify him from keeping any dangerous wild animal for such period as the court thinks fit.

(3) A court which has ordered the cancellation of a person's licence, or his disqualification, in pursuance of the last foregoing subsection may, if it thinks fit, suspend the operation of the order pending an appeal.

[1](3A) Where a person is convicted of any offence under sections 28C or 28F(16) of the Animal Health Act 1981 (c.22), or sections 19 to 24, 25(7), 29 or 40(11) of the Animal Health and Welfare (Scotland) Act 2006 (asp 11), subsections (2) and (3) apply as they do to convictions under this Act.

NOTE

1. As amended by the Animal Health and Welfare (Scotland) Act 2006 (Consequential Provisions) Order 2006 (SSI 2006/536) Sch.1 para.8 (effective 3 November 2006).

DEFINITIONS

"dangerous wild animal": s.7(4) and Schedule.

"keeping": s.7(1)–(3).

"level 4 on the standard scale": see p.32 above.

GENERAL NOTE

This section provides a penalty for any of the offences created under the Act and in addition allows the court to cancel a licence if the keeper has been convicted of an offence under this Act or analogous animal licensing or welfare legislation. Note that an appeal against cancellation or disqualification can be suspended pending an appeal if the court thinks fit so to do. Subsection (3A) was inserted by the Animal Health and Welfare (Scotland) Act 2006 (Consequential Provisions) Order 2006 (SSI 2006/536) Schedule para.8.

Interpretation

7.—(1) Subject to subsection (2) of this section, for the purposes of this Act a person is a keeper of an animal if he has it in his possession; and if at any time an animal ceases to be in the possession of a person, any person who immediately before that time was a keeper thereof by virtue of the preceding provisions of this subsection continues to be a keeper of the animal until another person becomes a keeper thereof by virtue of those provisions.

(2) Where an animal is in the possession of any person for the purpose of—

(a) preventing it from causing damage,
(b) restoring it to its owner,
(c) undergoing veterinary treatment, or
(d) being transported on behalf of another person,

the person having such possession shall not by virtue only of that possession be treated for the purposes of this Act as a keeper of the animal.

(3) In this Act expressions cognate with "keeper" shall be construed in accordance with subsections (1) and (2) of this section.

(4) In this Act, unless the context otherwise requires, the following expressions have the meanings hereby respectively assigned to them, that is to say—

"*circus*" includes any place where animals are kept or introduced wholly or mainly for the purpose of performing tricks of manoeuvres;

"*damage*" includes the death of, or injury to, any person;

"*dangerous wild animal*" means any animal of a kind for the time being specified in the first column of the Schedule to this Act;

"*local authority*" means in relation to Scotland a council constituted under section 2 of the Local Government etc. (Scotland) Act 1994;

"*premises*" includes any place;

"*veterinary practitioner*" means a person who is for the time being registered in the supplementary veterinary register;

"*veterinary surgeon*" means a person who is for the time being registered in the register of veterinary surgeons.

(5) the second column of the Schedule to this Act is included by way of explanation only; in the event of any dispute or proceedings, only the first column is to be taken into account.

NOTES ON SUBSECTIONS

Subsection (1)

This is perhaps the most important of the subsections in that it defines a keeper of an animal as being the person who possesses the animal or was the last person to possess the animal if it has ceased to be in the possession of a person, but note that subs.(2) provides certain statutory exemptions. The ownership proviso of s.1(4) must be read alongside this subsection, so that a keeper is normally the person who both owns and possesses the animal.

Subsection (2)

Thus a temporary custodian who holds the animal to prevent it causing damage (defined in subs.(4) below) or to restore it to its owner, or a vet or a transporter, is not a keeper.

Subsection (4)

The definition of "local authority", so far as it relates to Scotland, was substituted by the Local Government etc. (Scotland) Act 1994 s.180(1) and Sch.13 para.105. The definition of "zoo" was removed by s.22(1)(b)(i) of the Zoo Licensing Act 1981. In relation to circuses, in *South Kesteven DC v Mackie* (2000) 40 L.R. 28, the English Court of Appeal held that dangerous wild animals which performed for most of the year in a travelling circus, did not require licences under s.1(1) of the Act when kept by their owners in winter quarters during the winter months since, per Simon Brown LJ "the enlarged definition of circus within the 1976 Act was capable of encompassing the circus' winter quarters. Indeed there was no true distinction to be drawn between the winter quarters and weekend stopping places. In either event the animal animals were circus animals whose life as seen by their owners was to perform tricks or manoeuvres. That was why he kept them and the position was essentially no different whatever the season of the year".

Subsection (5)

The effect of this is that only the scientific name of the kind of animal contained in col.1 of the Schedule (e.g. orycteropidae) is to be taken into account in any dispute or proceedings and the col.2 descriptions (the common English names of the kind of animals, e.g. aardvark), is to be disregarded.

Power of Secretary of State to modify the Schedule

8.—(1) If the Secretary of State is satisfied that the scope of this Act should be extended so as to include animals of a kind not for the time being specified in the Schedule to this Act or diminished so as to exclude animals of a kind for the time being specified in that Schedule, he may by order make the necessary modifications to that Schedule and any such order may be revoked by a subsequent order under this subsection.

(2) The power conferred by the foregoing subsection on the Secretary of State shall be exercisable by statutory instrument which shall be subject to annulment in pursuance of a resolution of either House of Parliament.

GENERAL NOTE

The Secretary of State's powers have been so exercised as to substitute the present Schedule for the original one by the Dangerous Wild Animals Act 1976 (Modification) Order 1984 (SI 1984/1111).

9. [*Omitted.*]

GENERAL NOTE

This transitional provision has ceased to have any effect.

Short title, commencement and extent

10.—(1) This Act may be cited as the Dangerous Wild Animals Act 1976.

(2) This Act shall come into operation at the expiration of a period of three months beginning with the date on which it is passed.

(3) This Act does not extend to Northern Ireland.

SCHEDULE

[1]KINDS OF DANGEROUS WILD ANIMALS

NOTE: See section 7(5) of this Act for the effect of the second column of this Schedule.

Scientific name	*Common name or names*
MAMMALS	
Marsupials	
Family Dasyuridae: the species *Sarcophilus laniarius*	Tasmanian devil
Family Macropodidae: the species *Macropus fuliginosus, Macropus giganteus, Macropus robustus* and *Macropus rufus*	Western grey kangaroo Eastern grey kangaroo Wallaroo Red kangaroo
Primates	
Family *Cebidae*: all species except those of the genera *Aotus, Callicebus* and *Saimiri*	New-world monkeys (including capuchin, howler, saki, uacari, spider and woolly monkeys) *Exceptions:* Night monkeys (also known as owl monkeys) Titi Squirrel monkeys
Family *Cercopithecidae*: all species	Old-world monkeys (including baboons, the drill, colobus monkeys, the gelada, guenons, langurs, leaf monkeys, macaques, the mandrill, mangabeys, the patas monkey, the proboscis monkey and the talapoin)
Family *Hominidae*: all species except those of the genus *Homo*	Anthropoid apes (including the chimpanzee, the bonobo, the orang-utan and gorillas) *Exception:* Man
Family *Hylobatidae*: all species	Gibbons Siamangs
Family *Indriidae*: all species except those of the genus *Avahi*	Leaping lemurs (including the indri and sifakas) *Exceptions:* Woolly lemurs
Family *Lemuridae*: all species except those of the genus *Hapalemur*	Large lemurs *Exceptions:* Bamboo lemurs (also known as gentle lemurs)
Edentates	
Family *Dasypodidae*: the species *Priodontes maximus*	Giant armadillo

Family Myrmecophagidae: the species *Myrmecophaga tridactyla*

Giant anteater

Carnivores

Family *Canidae*: all species except—
- (a) those of the genera *Alopex, Cerdocyon, Dusicyon, Otocyon, Pseudalopex, Urocyon, Vulpes* and *Nyctereutes*
- (b) *Canis familiaris*, other than the subspecies *Canis familiaris dingo*

Canids (including wild dogs, wolves, jackals, the maned wolf, the dhole, the bush dog, and the dingo) other than the excepted species

Exceptions:
- (a) foxes, culpeo, grey zorro, raccoon dogs
- (b) domestic dogs

Family *Felidae*: all species except—
- (a) Felis silvestris (including the subspecies *Felis silvestris catus*), *Felis margarita, Felis nigripes, Otocolobus manul, Leopardus tigrinus, Leopardus geoffroyi* (also known as *Oncifelis geoffroyi*), *Leopardus guigna* (also known as *Oncifelis guigna*), *Catopuma badia* (also known as *Pardofelis badia*) and *Prionailurus rubiginosus*
- (b) a hybrid descended exclusively from two or more of the species described in paragraph (a)
- (c) a hybrid of which—
  - (i) one parent is *Felis silvestris catus*, and
  - (ii) the other parent is a first generation hybrid of *Felis silvestris catus* and any species not described in paragraph (a)
- (d) a hybrid descended exclusively from hybrid cats as described in paragraph (c) (ignoring, for the purpose of determining exclusivity of descent, the parents and remoter ancestors of any hybrid within that paragraph)
- (e) a hybrid descended exclusively from *Felis silvestris catus* and any one or more hybrid cat as described in paragraph (c) (ignoring, for the purpose of determining exclusivity of descent, the parents and remoter ancestors of any hybrid within that paragraph)

Cats (including the bobcat, caracal, cheetah, jaguar, leopard, lion, lynx, ocelot, puma, serval and tiger) other than the excepted species

Exceptions:
- (a) The wild cat (including the domestic cat), the sand cat, the black-footed cat, the pallas cat (also known as the manul), the little spotted cat (also known as the oncilla or tiger cat), the Geoffroy's cat, the kodkod (also known as the guina) the bay cat (also known as the Borneo cat), and the rusty-spotted cat
- (b) a cat descended exclusively from two or more of the species described in paragraph (a)
- (c) a cat of which one parent is a domestic cat and the other parent is a first generation hybrid of a domestic cat and a cat that is a dangerous wild animal
- (d) a cat descended exclusively from hybrid cats described in paragraph (c)
- (e) a cat descended exclusively from the domestic cat and hybrids cats described in paragraph (c)

Family *Hyaenidae*: all species except *Proteles cristatus*

Hyenas

Exception:

Aardwolf

Family *Mustelidae*: (a) all species of the genera *Arctonyx, Melogale, Mydaus, Taxidea, Pteronura, Aonyx, Enhydra* and *Lontra* (b) the genus *Lutra* except the species *Lutra lutra* (c) the species *Eira barbara, Gulo gulo, Martes pennanti* and *Mellivora capensis*	(a) The hog badger, the ferret badger, the stink badger, the American badger, the giant otter, the African clawless otter, the oriental small-clawed otter, the sea otter, the river otters, and the marine otter (b) the hairy-nosed otter (c) the tayra, the wolverine, the fisher (also known as the peken or fisher cat) and the honey badger *Exception:* European otter
Family *Ursidae*: all species, including the species *Ailuropoda melanoleuca* and *Ailurus fulgens*	Bears (including the giant panda and the red panda)
Family *Viverridae*: (a) all species of the genera *Civettictis* and *Viverra* (b) the species *Cryptoprocta ferox*	(a) Civets (including the African civet, the large-spotted civets, the Malayan civet and the Indian civets) (b) the fossa
Pinnipedes	
Family *Odobenidae*: all species	Walrus
Family *Otariidae*: all species	Eared seals
Family *Phocidae*: all species except *Phoca vitulina* and *Halichoerus grypus*	True seals (also known as earless seals) other than the excepted species *Exceptions:* Common seal (also known as the harbour seal) Grey seal
Elephants	
Family *Elephantidae*: all species	Elephants
Aardvark	
Family *Orycteropodidae*: the species *Orycteropus afer*	*Aardvark*
Odd-toed ungulates	
Family *Equidae*: all species except *Equus asinus* and *Equus caballus*	Horses Wild asses Zebras *Exceptions:* Donkey (also known as the ass) Domestic horse
Family *Rhinocerotidae*: all species	Rhinoceroses
Family *Tapiridae*: all species	Tapirs

Even-toed ungulates	
Family *Antilocapridae*: the species *Antilocapra Americana*	Pronghorn
Family Bovidae: all species except domestic forms of the genera *Bos, Bubalus, Capra* and *Ovis*	Antelopes, bison, buffalo, gazelles, goats and sheep *Exceptions:* Domestic cattle Domestic buffalo Domestic goats Domestic sheep
Family *Camelidae*: all species of the genera *Camelus*	Camels
Family Cervidae: all species of the genera *Alces* and *Rangifer* except domestic forms of the species *Rangifer tarandus*	Moose (also known as the elk) Caribou (also known as the reindeer) *Exception:* Domestic reindeer
Family *Giraffidae*: all species	Giraffe Okapi
Family *Hippopotamidae*: all species	Hippopotamus Pygmy hippopotamus
Family *Suidae*: all species, except domestic forms of the species *Sus scrofa* other than farmed wild boar	Old-world pigs other than animals of the excepted kind *Exception:* Domestic pig, other than farmed wild boar
Family *Tayassuidae*: all species	New-world pigs (also known as peccaries)
Hybrids	
A hybrid of a mammal specified in the first column of this Schedule where one parent is, or both parents are, of a kind so specified, but not including an excepted hybrid of the family *Felidae*	A hybrid animal with a dangerous wild animal as a parent *Exception:* A cat hybrid that is not a dangerous wild animal
BIRDS	
Cassowaries	
Family *Casuariidae*: all species	Cassowaries
Ostrich	
Family *Struthionidae*: all species	Ostrich
REPTILES	
Crocodilians	
Family *Alligatoridae*: all species	Alligators Caimans

Family *Crocodylidae*: all species	Crocodiles
	False gharial
Family *Gavialidae*: all species	Gharial (also known as the gavial)
Lizards and snakes	
Family *Atractaspididae*: all species of the genera *Atractaspis*	Burrowing asps (also known as mole vipers, or burrowing vipers)
	Stiletto snakes
Family *Colubridae*: (a) all species of the genera *Malpolon* and *Thelotornis* (b) the species *Dispholidus typus, Rhabdophis subminiatus, Rhabdophis tigrinus, Elapomorphus lemniscatus, Philodryas olfersii, Tachymenis peruviana, Xenodon severus*	(a) All rear-fanged venomous colubrid snakes of the specified genera (including montpellier snakes, the false cobra, and twig or bird snakes) (b) the boomslang, the red-necked keelback, the tiger keelback (also known as the yamakagashi or the Japanese tiger-snake), the Argentine black-headed snake, the South American green racer, the Peruvian racer (also known as the Peru slender snake), the Amazon false viper (also known as the false fer-de-lance)
Family *Elapidae*: all species	Front-fanged venomous snakes of the specified family (including cobras, coral snakes, kraits, mambas, whipsnakes, death adders and all other Australian poisonous snakes)
Family *Hydrophiidae*: all species	Sea snakes
Family *Helodermatidae*: all species	Gila monster
	Mexican beaded lizard
Family *Viperidae*: all species	Front-fanged venomous snakes of the specified family (including adders, the barba amarilla, the bushmaster, the fer-de-lance, moccasins, rattlesnakes and vipers)
INVERTEBRATES	
Spiders	
Family *Ctenidae*: all species of the genus *Phoneutria*	Wandering spiders
Family *Hexathelidae*: all species of the genus *Atrax*	Sydney funnel-web spider and its close relatives
Family *Sicariidae*: all species of the genus *Loxosceles*	Brown recluse spiders (also known as violin spiders)
Family *Theridiidae*: all species of the genus *Latrodectus*	Widow spiders and close relatives
Scorpions	
Family *Buthidae*: all species	Buthid scorpions
Family *Hemioscorpiidae*: the species *Hemiscorpius lepturus*	Middle Eastern thin-tailed scorpion

NOTE

1. As amended by the Dangerous Wild Animals Act 1976 (Modification) (Scotland) Order 2008 (SSI 2008/302) Sch.1 para.1 (effective 1 October 2008).

GENERAL NOTE

This Schedule was substituted by the Dangerous Wild Animals Act 1976 (Modification) (Scotland) Order 2008 (SSI 2008/302) Schedule. In any disputed proceedings only the scientific name in the first column of the Schedule is to be taken into account—see s.7(5) above.

Zoo Licensing Act 1981

(c.37)

ARRANGEMENT OF SECTIONS

GENERAL NOTE

This Act has been extensively amended by the Zoo Licensing Act 1981 Amendment (Scotland) Regulations 2003 (SSI 2003/174) and now reads differently to the Act applicable to zoos in England and Wales—consequently the text below applies to Scotland only. Zoo licensing is a devolved function and the powers of the Secretary of State were transferred to the Scottish Ministers by virtue of s.53 of the Scotland Act 1988.

Licensing of zoos by local authorities

1.—(1) Subject to this section it is unlawful to operate a zoo to which this Act applies except under the authority of a licence issued under this Act by the local authority for the area within which the whole or the major part of the zoo is situated.

(2) In this Act "zoo" means an establishment where wild animals (as defined by section 21) are kept for exhibition to the public otherwise than for purposes of a circus (as so defined) and otherwise than in a pet shop (as so defined).

(3) The local authorities for the purposes of this Act are—

[*(a) and (aa) repealed by the Local Government (Wales) Act 1994 (c.19) Sch.18 para.1 (effective 1 April 1996*.)]

[1](b) in Scotland, the councils constituted under section 2 of the Local Government etc. (Scotland) Act 1994.

(4) [*As repealed by the Statute Law (Repeals) Act 2004 (c.14) Sch.1 para.1 (effective 22 July 2004)*.]

NOTE

1. As amended by the Local Government etc. (Scotland) Act 1994 (c.39) Sch.13 para.124 (effective 1 April 1996).

DEFINITIONS

"circus": s.21(1).
"local authority": s.1(3)(b).
"pet shop": s.21(1).
"wild animals": s.21(1).
"zoo": s.1(2).

GENERAL NOTE

The Act provides for the licensing and regulation of zoos and this section makes it unlawful to operate a zoo without a licence. Subsection (4) was repealed by the Statute Law (Repeals) Act 2004 Sch.1 (17)(1) para.1. Subsection 3(a) only applies to England and subs.(3)(b) to Wales.

Subsection (1)

Operators of zoos (defined in the following subsection) are required to have a licence that has been granted by the local authority in whose area the whole or a major part of the zoo is situated, although certain zoos may be exempt from the requirement if a dispensation in terms of s.14 has been granted. It is an offence to operate an unlicensed zoo and penalties apply for so doing—see s.19.

Subsection (2)

This subsection defines "zoo"—curiously not included within the general definition section at the end of the Act where "circus", "pet shop" and "wild animal" are all defined. The essence of the definition of zoo is that it is an establishment that is not a circus or pet shop and where wild animals are kept for exhibition to the public, and that the establishment is kept open for eight days or more in each 12 month period. Note that whether or not an admission charge is levied is irrelevant. Words were deleted by the Zoo Licensing Act 1981 Amendment (Scotland) Regulations 2003 (SSI 2003/174) reg.4(a).

Subsection (2A)

This subsection makes the Act apply also to private licensed zoos.

Subsection (2C)

This subsection gives the definition of a "section of a zoo" and "the closure of a section of a zoo".

Conservation measures for zoos

1A. The following are conservation measures to be implemented in zoos in accordance with this Act—

(a) participating in at least one of the following—
  (i) research from which conservation benefits accrue to species of wild animals;
  (ii) training in relevant conservation skills;
  (iii) the exchange of information relating to the conservation of species of wild animals;
  (iv) where appropriate, breeding of wild animals in captivity; and
  (v) where appropriate, the repopulation of an area with, or the reintroduction into the wild of, wild animals;

(b) promoting public education and awareness in relation to the conservation of biodiversity, in particular by providing information about the species of wild animals kept in the zoo and their natural habitats;

(c) accommodating their animals under conditions which aim to satisfy the biological and conservation requirements of the species to which they belong, including—
  (i) providing each animal with an environment well adapted to meet the physical, psychological and social needs of the species to which it belongs; and
  (ii) providing a high standard of animal husbandry with a developed programme of preventative and curative veterinary care and nutrition;

(d) preventing the escape of animals and putting in place measures to be taken in the event of any escape or unauthorised release of animals;

(e) preventing the intrusion of pests and vermin into the zoo premises; and

(f) keeping up-to-date records of the zoo's collection, including records of—
- (i) the numbers of different animals;
- (ii) acquisitions, births, deaths, disposals and escapes of animals;
- (iii) the causes of any such deaths; and
- (iv) the health of the animals.

GENERAL NOTE

This section was added by the Zoo Licensing Act 1981 Amendment (Scotland) Regulations 2003 (SSI 2003/174) and gives effect to the conservation measures that zoos are required to adopt by virtue of art.3 of the Directive 1992/22/EC relating to the keeping of wild animals in zoos. Note that the section requires conservation measures to be implemented in zoos with reference to: (a) participating in research, training, information exchange, breeding of wild animals in captivity and repopulation of natural habitats; (b) public education relating to biodiversity and habitats; (c) accommodating animals humanely; (d) prevention of escape; (e) preventing the intrusion of vermin, etc.; and (f) keeping proper records.

Application for licence

2.—(1) An application to the local authority for a licence for a zoo shall not be entertained by the local authority unless, at least two months before making it, the applicant has given notice in writing to the local authority of his intention to make the application, has published notice of that intention in one local newspaper circulating in the locality and one newspaper with a national circulation and has exhibited a copy of that notice at the site and the said notice shall state that the notice to the local authority may be inspected as provided by subsection (3).

(2) Any notice given or published under subsection (1) must identify the situation of the zoo for which the application is to be made; and the notice to the local authority must specify—
- (a) the kinds of animals listed in taxonomic category of Order and approximate number of each group kept or to be kept for exhibition on the premises and the arrangements for their accommodation, maintenance and wellbeing;
- (b) the approximate numbers and categories of staff employed or to be employed in the zoo;
- (c) the approximate number of visitors and motor vehicles for which accommodation is or is to be provided;
- (d) the approximate number and position of the means of access provided or to be provided to the premises.

(3) Any notice given to the local authority under this section shall, until the disposal of the application to which it relates, be kept available by the authority at their offices for public inspection free of charge at reasonable hours.

DEFINITIONS

"animals": s.21(1).
"local authority": s.1(3)(b).
"taxonomic category": s.21(1).
"zoo": s.1(2).

GENERAL NOTE

This section deals with how applications for zoo licences are to be made to the local authority and the applicant is required to give prior notice of the matters specified in subss.(2) and (2A). For "at reasonable hours" see p.30 above. Subsection (2A) was inserted by the Zoo Licensing Act 1981 Amendment (Scotland) Regulations 2003 (SSI 2003/174).

Consideration of application

3.—(1) On the consideration of an application for a licence the local authority shall take into account any representations made by or on behalf of any of the persons mentioned in subsection (2).

(2) The persons are:—

(a) the applicant;

(b) the chief officer of police (or in Scotland the chief constable) for any area in which the whole or any part of the zoo is situated;

[1](c) the appropriate authority;

(d) the governing body of any national institution concerned with the operation of zoos;

(e) where part of the zoo is not situated in the area of the local authority with power to grant the licence;—

(i) a planning authority for the area in which the part is situated (other than a county planning authority);

(ii) [*Omitted as this subprovision relates to Wales specifically*.]

(f) any person alleging that the establishment or continuance of the zoo would injuriously affect the health or safety of persons living in the neighbourhood of the zoo;

(g) any other person whose representations might, in the opinion of the local authority, show grounds on which the authority has a power or duty to refuse to grant a licence.

[1](3) In subsection (2) "the appropriate authority" means—

(a) where Part 3 of the Fire (Scotland) Act 2005 (asp 5) applies in relation to the zoo—

(i) the enforcing authority within the meaning of section 61(9) of that Act, and

[2](ii) the relevant authority (as defined in section 6 of that Act) in whose area the zoo or any part of it is, or is to be, situated if that authority is not the enforcing authority mentioned in sub-paragraph (i);

(b) in any other case, the relevant authority in whose area the zoo or any part of it is, or is to be, situated.

NOTES

1. As amended by the Fire (Scotland) Act 2005 (Consequential Modifications and Savings) Order 2006 (SSI 2006/475) Sch.1 para.10 (effective 1 October 2006).

2. As amended by the Police and Fire Reform (Scotland) Act 2012 (asp 8) Sch.7 para.52 (effective 1 April 2013).

DEFINITIONS

"local authority": s.3(1)(b).

"zoo": s.1(2).

GENERAL NOTE

This section provides that if representations are made by or on behalf of the persons or bodies specified in subs.(2) then these representations must be taken into account by the local authority. Subsections (2)(c) and (3) were substituted by the Fire (Scotland) Act 2005 (Consequential Modifications and Savings) Order 2006 (SSI 2006/475).

Subsection (1)

Note that there is no requirement for a local authority to consult any of the persons listed in the following subsection, merely a duty to take any representations made by them into account.

Subsection (2)

The persons concerned are the applicant, the chief constable, the fire authority, the planning authority, persons falling within (f) and (g) and the governing bodies of national institutions including the National Federation of Zoological Gardens of Great Britain and Northern Ireland, the National Zoological Association, the Scottish Society for the Prevention of Cruelty to Animals and the Royal Zoological Society of Scotland. Subsection (2)(ii) is omitted as it applies only to England and Wales.

Grant or refusal of licence

4.—(1) Before granting or refusing to grant a licence for a zoo, the local authority shall—

(a) consider inspectors' reports made in pursuance of inspections of the zoo under this Act.

(1A) Before granting or refusing to grant a licence for a zoo, the local authority shall also—

(a) consult the applicant about the conditions they propose would be attached to the licence, if one were granted, under section 5(2A) and (if applicable) section 5(3); and

(b) make arrangements for an inspection to be carried out in accordance with section 9A (subject to subsection (2) of that section).

(2) The local authority shall refuse to grant a licence for a zoo if they are satisfied that the establishment or continuance of the zoo would injuriously affect the health or safety of persons living in the neighbourhood of the zoo, or seriously affect the preservation of law and order.

(2A) The local authority shall also refuse to grant a licence for a zoo if they are not satisfied that the conservation measures referred to in section 1A will be implemented in a satisfactory manner at the zoo.

(3) The local authority may refuse to grant a licence for a zoo if subsection (2A) does not apply but they are not satisfied that the standards of accommodation, staffing or management are adequate for the proper care and wellbeing of the animals or any of them or otherwise for the proper conduct of the zoo.

[2](4) The local authority may also refuse to grant a licence if—

(a) the applicant, or

(b) (where the applicant is a body corporate) the body or any director, manager, secretary or other similar officer of the body, or

(c) any person employed as a keeper in the zoo,

has been convicted of an offence under this Act or under any of the enactments mentioned in subsection (5), subsection (5A) or of any other offence involving the ill-treatment of animals.

(5) the Protection of Animals Acts 1911 to 1964;
the Protection of Animals (Scotland) Acts 1912 to 1964;
the Pet Animals Act 1951;
the Animal Boarding Establishments Act 1963;
the Riding Establishments Acts 1964 and 1970;
the Breeding of Dogs Act 1973;
the Dangerous Wild Animals Act 1976;
the Endangered Species (Import and Export) Act 1976;
Part 1 of the Wildlife and Countryside Act 1981.

[1](5A) sections 28C or 28F(16) of the Animal Health Act 1981 (c.22);
sections 19 to 24, 25(7), 29 or 40(11) of the Animal Health and Welfare (Scotland) Act 2006 (asp 11).

(6) If the local authority are not satisfied that any planning permission required under Part III of the Town and Country Planning Act 1990 or

under the Town and Country Planning (Scotland) Act 1997, for the establishment of the zoo or for the continuance of the zoo during the period for which the licence would be in force, has been, or is deemed to be, granted, they shall either refuse to grant the licence or grant the licence but suspend its operation until the local planning authority within the meaning of the said Act of 1990 or, as the case may be, 1997 have notified the local authority that any such planning permission has been or is deemed to be granted.

(7) Except as provided by this section the local authority shall not refuse to grant a licence pursuant to an application and if they do refuse to grant it they shall send to the applicant by post a written statement of the grounds of their refusal.

(8) When a licence is granted the local authority shall send it to the applicant by post and the licence or a copy of it shall be publicly displayed at each public entrance to the zoo.

NOTES

1. As amended by the Planning (Consequential Provisions) (Scotland) Act 1997 (c.11) Sch.2 para.32 (effective 27 May 1997).

2. As amended by the Animal Health and Welfare (Scotland) Act 2006 (Consequential Provisions) Order 2006 (SSI 2006/536) Sch.1 para.10 (effective 3 November 2006).

DEFINITIONS

"animals": s.21(1).
"keeper": s.21(1).
"the list": s.21(1).
"local authority": s.1(3)(b).
"zoo": s.1(2).

GENERAL NOTE

This section deals with the grant or refusal of a zoo licence and the steps which the local authority must take before doing so. Note that subss.(2) and (2A) provide the mandatory grounds upon which a local authority must refuse to grant a licence whereas subss.(3) and (4) contain discretionary grounds. In the absence of such grounds and provided that there are no adverse planning considerations, the local authority must grant the application.

In subs.(1) words were deleted and subs.(1A) was inserted by the Zoo Licensing Act 1981 Amendment (Scotland) Regulations 2003 (SSI 2003/174). Subsection (2) was amended by the Zoo Licensing Act 1981 Amendment (Scotland) Regulations 2003 (SSI 2003/174). Subsection (2A) was inserted by the Zoo Licensing Act 1981 Amendment (Scotland) Regulations 2003 (SSI 2003/174). Subsection (3) was amended by the Zoo Licensing Act 1981 Amendment (Scotland) Regulations 2003 (SSI 2003/174). Subsection (4)(c) was amended by the Animal Health and Welfare (Scotland) Act 2006 (Consequential Provisions) Order 2006 (SSI 2006/536). In subs.(5) words were deleted by the Wildlife and Countryside Act 1981 ss.73(4) and 75(14) and new words added by s.72(14).

Subsection (5A) was amended by the Animal Health and Welfare (Scotland) Act 2006 (Consequential Provisions) Order 2006 (SSI 2006/536). Subsection (6) was amended by the Planning (Consequential Provisions) Act 1990 Sch.11 and the Planning (Consequential Provisions) (Scotland) Act 1997 Sch.2.

Subsection (1)

Sections 10–12 of the Act deal with zoo inspections.

Subsection (1A)

This was inserted in furtherance of the EC Zoo Directive.

Subsection (2)

The local authority would clearly have to have information from which they could be so satisfied. If they are satisfied, this is a mandatory ground of refusal.

Subsection (2A)

Like subs.(1A) this was also inserted in furtherance of the Zoo Directive and requires the local authority to be satisfied that the conservation measures in subs.(1A) will be implemented in a satisfactory manner.

Subsection (3)

These are discretionary grounds for refusal but are unlikely to have much effect at the present day given the requirements of the Zoo Directive.

Subsection (4)

This is a discretionary power and the exercise of discretion would require the licensing authority to consider the nature and age of the convictions and their effect on the ability to run a zoo.

Subsection (6)

If planning requirements have not been met then a licence must either be refused or suspended.

Subsection (7)

There are no other mandatory or discretionary grounds for refusal and no general "catch-all" provision such as refusal, "for any other good reason". Accordingly the licensing authority, in the absence of such grounds, are obliged to grant a licence. The fact that a local authority might not care for the concept of keeping wild animals in captivity would not be a valid ground for refusal of a zoo licence—see *Gerry Cottle's Circus v City of Edinburgh DC*, 1990 S.L.T. 235.

Period and conditions of licence

5.—(1) An original licence granted under this Act shall be granted for a period of four years beginning with the date specified in the licence as that on which it is granted or any later date specified in the licence as that on which the licence is to commence.

(2) A fresh licence granted under this Act to the holder of an existing licence shall be granted for a period of six years beginning with the end of the period of the existing licence.

(2A) A licence under this Act shall be granted subject to conditions requiring the conservation measures referred to in section 1A to be implemented at the zoo.

(3) Any licence under this Act may be granted subject to such other conditions as the local authority think necessary or desirable for ensuring the proper conduct of the zoo during the period of the licence, including conditions relating to the following—

(a)–(b) [*Repealed.*]

(c) insurance against liability for damage caused by animals.

(4) In deciding what conditions to attach to a licence, a local authority shall have regard to any standards specified by the Scottish Ministers under section 9 and sent by them to the authority.

(5) The Secretary of State may, after consulting the authority, direct them to attach one or more conditions to a licence, and the authority shall give effect to such a direction.

(5A) But he may not direct the authority to attach a condition which is inconsistent with the implementation at the zoo of the conservation measures referred to in section 1A.

(6) The authority shall not attach to a licence any condition inconsistent with one they are so directed to attach.

(7) The authority shall not attach to a licence a condition which relates only or primarily to the health, safety or welfare of persons working in the zoo.

DEFINITIONS

"animals": s.21(1).
"any standards": s.9.
"local authority": s.1(2)(b).
"zoo": s.21(1).

GENERAL NOTE

The section provides for the duration of zoo licences and for the conditions to be placed upon such licences. Subsections (2A) and (5A) were inserted by and the section otherwise amended by the Zoo Licensing Act 1981 Amendment (Scotland) Regulations 2003 (SSI 2003/174).

Subsection (1)

The original licence, i.e. the first licence granted to the zoo operator, has a duration of four years.

Subsection (2)

A fresh licence is one provided for in s.6.

Subsection (2A)

The conservation measures are a mandatory condition.

Subsection (3)

The subsection allows the local authority to impose such conditions as it thinks necessary and, without prejudice to the generality, a condition relating to insurance against damage caused by animals. The Secretary of State recommended that a licence contains a sentence to the effect that its issue does not imply that the requirements of other legislation relating to the zoo have been met—Department of Environment Circular 5/84.

Subsection (5A)

The Zoo Licensing Act 1981 Amendment (Scotland) Regulations 2003 (SSI 2003/174) apply such mandatory conditions.

Renewal of licence

[1]**6.**—(1) Where application for the renewal of an existing licence is made to the local authority not later than six months before the end of the period of the licence or such shorter time as the local authority may in special circumstances allow the local authority may either—

(a) extend the period of the existing licence; or
(b) direct the applicant to apply for a fresh licence in accordance with section 2.

(1A) Before extending the period of an existing licence under subsection (1)(a) the authority shall—

(a) make arrangements for an inspection to be carried out in accordance with section 9A (subject to subsection (2) of that section); and
(b) consider the report made to them pursuant to that inspection.

(2) Where application for a fresh licence is made by the holder of an existing licence, the existing licence shall, if the application is made before the end of the period of that licence or within six months after notice of a direction given to the applicant under subsection (1)(b), continue in force until the application is disposed of or withdrawn.

(3) Any extension of the period of an existing licence under subsection (1)(a) shall be granted for a period of six years beginning with the end of the period of the existing licence; and the local authority shall take reasonable steps to secure that the holder of the licence is notified in writing of the extension.

(4) The local authority shall give notice to the holder of any licence granted by that authority, not later than nine months before the end of the period of the licence, of the latest date on which application for renewal may be made under this section.

NOTE

1. As amended by the Zoo Licensing Act 1981 Amendment (Scotland) Regulations 2003 (SSI 2003/174) reg.9 (effective 1 April 2003).

GENERAL NOTE

This section deals with the renewal of licences. Department of Environment Circular 5/84 recommends that the option provided for in subs.(1)(b), i.e. the issue of a fresh licence, be only used where there is a "good and substantial reason" and the example given, "if there have been radical changes in management since the previous licence was granted or if the types of animals kept in the zoo" have altered—see further paras 3–5 of the circular. An alteration in the licence conditions in terms of s.16 might be more appropriate. Subsection (1A) was inserted by and words in subs.(2) deleted by the Zoo Licensing Act 1981 Amendment (Scotland) Regulations 2003 (SSI 2003/174).

Transfer, transmission and surrender of licence

7.—(1) A licence for a zoo may with the approval of the local authority be transferred to another person, and in that case the transferee shall become the holder of the licence from the date specified by the authority and notified by them to the transferor and transferee.

(2) On the death of the holder of a licence, the personal representatives of the deceased are deemed to be the holders of the licence during the period of three months after the death or such longer period as the local authority may approve.

(3) The holder of a licence may at any time surrender it to the local authority who shall thereupon cancel the licence.

GENERAL NOTE

This section provides for the transfer of an existing licence (where the local authority determine and notify its expiry date), the temporary transfer upon the death of the licensee and the surrender of the licence. Words were substituted by the Zoo Licensing Act 1981 Amendment (Scotland) Regulations 2003 (SSI 2003/174).

Scottish Ministers' functions

Scottish Ministers' list

8.—(1) The Scottish Ministers shall, after consultation with the presidents of the British Veterinary Association, the National Federation of Zoological Gardens and the National Zoological Association and with such other persons as they think fit, compile a list consisting of two parts, the first part containing the names of veterinary surgeons and veterinary practitioners falling within subsection (2) and the second part containing the names of persons falling within subsection (3).

(2) The surgeons and practitioners shall have experience of animals of kinds which are kept in zoos or which in the Scottish Ministers' opinion might be so kept and shall be competent to advise about the implementation in zoos of the conservation measures referred to in section 1A.

(3) Each of the persons shall be competent in the Scottish Ministers' opinion to do all the following, namely, to inspect animals in zoos, to advise on keeping them and on their welfare, to advise about the implementation in zoos of the conservation measures referred to in section 1A, and to advise on the management of zoos generally.

(4) A person's name may be contained in both the first and the second parts of the list.

(5) After such consultation, the Scottish Ministers' may vary the list by adding names or deleting them (or both).

(6) Persons on the list may charge the licensing authority such amounts in respect of their services and expenses as the Secretary of State may from time to time determine with the approval of the Minister for the Civil Service.

DEFINITIONS

"animals": s.21(1).
"local authority": s.1(3)(b).
"zoo": s.1(2).

GENERAL NOTE

The Scottish Ministers must draw up a list of experienced persons from which inspectors may be drawn and the list can be varied from time to time. Subsections (2) and (3) were amended by the Zoo Licensing Act 1981 Amendment (Scotland) Regulations 2003 (SSI 2003/174).

"Secretary of State" references were replaced by "Scottish Ministers" by the Scotland Act 1998.

Scottish Ministers' standards

9. After consulting such persons on the list and such other persons as he thinks fit, the Secretary of State may from time to time specify standards of modern zoo practice, that is, standards with respect to the management of zoos and the animals in them.

DEFINITIONS

"animals": s.21(1).
"the list": s.21(1).
"zoo": s.1(2).

GENERAL NOTE

In May 1988 the, "Secretary of State's Standards of Modern Zoo Practice" was compiled. References to "Secretary of State" were replaced by "Scottish Ministers" by the Scotland Act 1998.

Inspections

Procedure relating to inspections before the grant, refusal, renewal or significant alteration of licences

[1]**9A.**—(1) This section applies where an inspection is to be carried out as mentioned in sections 4(1A), 6(1A) and 16(2B) and (3A).

(2) Where an inspection under section 10 falls to be carried out within the period of 12 months beginning with the date on which a local authority become required to make arrangements for an inspection to be carried out as mentioned in subsection (1)—

(a) the authority need not arrange for an inspection to be carried out in accordance with this section; and

(b) if they do not, subsections (10) to (13) of this section apply in relation to the inspection under section 10 as they would have applied in relation to an inspection in accordance with this section.

(3) Where—

(a) an application has been made under section 6(1) for renewal of a zoo's licence and the authority propose to extend the period of the licence; and

(b) one or more inspections of the zoo are required by section 16, (the authority may combine those inspections with the inspection which is required by section 6(1A)(a).

(4) Where more than one inspection is required under section 16, the authority may combine the inspections.

(5) Subject to subsection (6), where in the course of an inspection under section 10 or 12 or in accordance with this section it becomes apparent to the inspectors that a significant alteration to the licence is likely to be needed, they shall—

(a) consult the holder of the licence about that alteration;

(b) consider whether any new conditions they consider will be needed to secure that alteration are likely to be met if the licence is altered; and

(c) include their findings and recommendations in a report.

(6) Subsection (5) does not apply where the inspection is an inspection before the significant alteration of a licence, and the significant alteration the inspectors consider likely to be needed is the same or substantially the same as that which the authority propose to make or the Secretary of State proposes to direct the authority to make.

(7) An inspection required by section 4(1A)(b) or 6(1A)(a) (including an inspection required by section 6(1A)(a) which is combined with another inspection) shall be conducted by one or more inspectors nominated, after consultation with the authority, by the Scottish Ministers from the list.

(8) An inspection required by subsection (2B)(b) or (3A)(b) of section 16 (including such an inspection which is combined with another such inspection, but not including such an inspection which is combined with an inspection required by section 6(1A)(a)) shall be conducted by one or more persons who appear to the authority to be competent for the purpose and who are authorised by the authority to conduct the inspection.

(9) Before carrying out an inspection in accordance with this section, the authority shall, after consultation with the applicant or operator of the zoo (as the case may be), give him at least twenty-eight days' notice of the date on which it is proposed to carry it out.

(10) Except in the case of an inspection carried out before the grant or refusal of an original licence, the inspector shall consider whether the conditions attached to the licence are met.

(11) In the case of an inspection carried out before the grant or refusal of a licence, the inspector shall consider whether the conditions proposed by the authority under section 4(1A)(a) are likely to be met if the licence is granted.

(12) In the case of an inspection carried out before the period of an existing licence is extended, the inspector shall consider whether the

conditions attached to the licence are likely to be met if the period of the licence is extended.

(13) In the case of an inspection carried out before the significant alteration of a licence, the inspector shall consider—

(a) whether any new or varied conditions proposed by the authority under section 16(2B)(a) or by the Scottish Ministers under section 16(3A) are likely to be met if the licence is so altered; and

(b) whether the conservation measures referred to in section 1A will be implemented at the zoo if the licence is altered as proposed by the authority of the Scottish Ministers (as the case may be).

(14) Except in the case of an inspection carried out before the grant or refusal of an original licence, the inspector may require the production of all records kept by the holder of the licence in pursuance of conditions requiring the conservation measures referred to in section 1A(f) to be implemented at the zoo, and the holder shall produce the records.

(15) The inspector shall send his report to the authority, and within one month after receiving the report of the inspection the authority shall send a copy to the applicant or operator (as the case may be) and give him an opportunity to comment on it.

NOTE

1. As amended by the Zoo Licensing Act 1981 Amendment (Scotland) Regulations 2003 (SSI 2003/174) reg.12 (effective 1 April 2003).

GENERAL NOTE

These provisions were added by the Zoo Licensing Act 1981 Amendment (Scotland) Regulations 2003 (SSI 2003/174) and introduce a requirement for a zoo to be inspected before a decision is taken about the granting, refusing or renewing of a licence or when making a significant alteration to a licence. Inspectors making inspections in accordance with s.9(A) (or in circumstances described in s.9A, under s.10) must consider whether existing, and any proposed, licence conditions will be met. The references to "Scottish Ministers" were inserted by the Scotland Act 1998.

Periodical inspections

10.—(1) The local authority shall carry out periodical inspections in accordance with this section of any zoo for which a licence granted by that authority is in force.

(2) Before any such inspection the local authority shall, after consultation with the operator of the zoo, give him at least twenty-eight days notice of the date upon which it is proposed to carry it out.

(3) Inspections under this section shall be made at the following times—

(a) in the case of an original licence, during the first year and not later than six months before the end of the fourth year of the period of the licence;

(b) in the case of a renewed licence or fresh licence granted to the holder of an existing licence, during the third year and not later than six months before the end of the sixth year of the period of that licence.

(4) The following provisions apply to any inspection to be carried out under this section:—

(a) the inspection shall be conducted by the following inspectors, namely—

(i) not more than three appointed by the local authority, being persons who appear to the authority to be competent for the purpose, at least one of whom shall be a veterinary surgeon or veterinary practitioner; and

(ii) two nominated after consultation with the local authority by the Scottish Ministers from the list, one from the first part of the list and one from the second;

and the names of all persons inspecting shall be notified to the operator of the zoo;

(b) the operator may give notice to the local authority of objection to any one or more of the inspectors, and the local authority or the Scottish Ministers as appropriate may if they think fit give effect to any such objection;

(c) representatives of the operator not exceeding three in number may accompany the inspectors on the inspection; and the inspectors may require the attendance of any veterinary surgeon or veterinary practitioner employed in or retained by or for the purposes of the zoo;

(d) the inspection shall extend to all features of the zoo directly or indirectly relevant to the health, welfare and safety of the public and the animals, including measures for the prevention of the escape of animals;

(e) the inspectors shall require the production of all records kept by the operator in pursuance of conditions of the licence requiring the conservation measures referred to in section 1A(f) to be implemented at the zoo, and the operator shall produce the records.

(5) The inspectors shall send their report to the local authority, and the report may include advice on the keeping of records and recommendations for any practicable improvements designed to bring any features of the zoo up to the normal standards of modern zoo practice; and for this purpose the inspectors shall have regard to any standards known to them which have been specified by the Secretary of State under section 9.

(6) Any disagreement between the inspectors over recommendations to be made in their report relating to the welfare of the animals or any of them may be referred to the Secretary of State, who may, after consultation with such persons on the list as he thinks fit, give such guidance as he thinks proper in regard to the recommendations to be made.

(7) Within one month after receiving the report of the inspection the local authority shall send a copy to the operator of the zoo and give him an opportunity to comment on it.

DEFINITIONS

"animals": s.21(1).
"local authority": s.1(3)(b).
"the list": s.21(1).
"zoo": s.1(2).

GENERAL NOTE

The local authority is required to carry out periodical inspections of zoos upon giving the appropriate notice to the licence holder—for an interesting case arising out of the inspection regime see *R (on the application of Zoolife International Ltd) v Secretary of State for Environment, Food and Rural Affairs* [2007] EWHC 2995 (Admin). Subsection (4) was amended by the Zoo Licensing Act 1981 Amendment (Scotland) Regulations 2003 (SSI 2003/174).

References to "Secretary of State" were replaced by "Scottish Ministers" by the Scotland Act 1998.

Special inspections

11.—(1) The local authority may at any time carry out a special inspection of a zoo for which a licence granted by them is in force if they consider it appropriate to do so having regard to—

(a) any periodical report on the zoo made to them pursuant to section 10; or

(b) any representations made to them on behalf of a properly constituted body concerned with any aspect of the management of zoos or the welfare of animals; or

(c) any report on the zoo made to them pursuant to an inspection in accordance with section 9A or under the provisions of section 12; or

(d) any other circumstances which in their opinion call for investigation.

(2) A special inspection under this section shall be conducted by persons who appear to the local authority to be competent for the purpose and who are authorised by the authority to conduct the inspection.

(3) Where the purpose of the inspection relates to the health of animals, the inspectors shall include (or, if one, the inspector shall be) a veterinary surgeon or veterinary practitioner with experience of animals of kinds kept in the zoo.

(4) On appointing persons under subsection (2), the authority shall communicate to them and to the operator of the zoo the purpose and scope of the inspection.

(5) Paragraphs (c) to (e) of subsection (4) and subsections (5) to (7) of section 10 apply to a special inspection as they apply to a periodical inspection except that the references in subsections (4)(d), (4)(e) and (5) to features and records and improvements are references only to features and records and improvements relevant to the purpose and scope of the special inspection.

DEFINITIONS

"animals": s.21(1).
"local authority": s.1(3)(b).
"zoo": s.1(2).

GENERAL NOTE

Such inspections may be appropriate when the local authority wishes to check compliance with licence conditions which require improvements to be made within a specified period—Department of Environment Circular 5/84. Subsection (1) was amended by the Zoo Licensing Act 1981 Amendment (Scotland) Regulations 2003 (SSI 2003/174).

Special inspections of closed zoos

[1]**11A.**—(1) The local authority may at any time carry out a special inspection of a zoo or a section of a zoo to which section 16E applies—

(a) if they consider it appropriate to do so having regard to their function under section 16E(4) of supervising the implementation of a plan prepared under section 16E(2);

(b) if they consider it appropriate to do so having regard to their function under section 16E(6); or

(c) if they consider it appropriate to do so in order to determine whether to exercise their function under section 16E(7) or (8).

(2) Subsection (4)(c) of section 10 and subsections (2), (3) and (4) of section 11 apply to an inspection under this section as they apply to an inspection under those sections.

(3) The inspectors may require the production of all records of the zoo's collection kept by the operator of the zoo, and the operator shall produce the records.

(4) The inspectors shall send their report to the authority, and, except where the operator of the zoo cannot after reasonable enquiries have been made be found, the authority shall send a copy to the operator forthwith and give him an opportunity to comment on it.

NOTE

1. As amended by the Zoo Licensing Act 1981 Amendment (Scotland) Regulations 2003 (SSI 2003/174) reg.15 (effective 1 April 2003).

DEFINITIONS

"local authority": s.1(3)(b).
"section of a zoo": s.1(2C).
"zoo": s.1(2).

GENERAL NOTE

This section, which was inserted by the Zoo Licensing Act 1981 Amendment (Scotland) Regulations 2003 (SSI 2003/174), allows a local authority to carry out in certain circumstances a special inspection of a zoo in respect of which a zoo closure direction has been made.

Informal inspections

12.—(1) Without prejudice to sections 9A, 10 and 11, the local authority shall make such arrangements as they think fit to ensure that any zoo for which a licence granted by that authority is in force is inspected informally by an inspector once in any calendar year in which no inspection is made under those sections.

(2) The inspector shall be appointed by the authority and shall be a person appearing to the authority to be competent for the purpose of the inspection.

DEFINITIONS

"local authority": s.1(3)(b).
"zoo": s.1(2).

GENERAL NOTE

Department of Environment Circular 5/84 suggested that, inter alia, informal inspections would be appropriate to check upon management matters, compliance with conditions, the progress of carrying out recommendations in previous reports, and to see if there have been any relevant changes or new animals. The reference to "9A" was added by the Zoo Licensing Act 1981 Amendment (Scotland) Regulations 2003 (SSI 2003/147).

Special cases

Local authority zoos

[1]**13.**—(1) When a local authority is the owner of a zoo to which this Act applies, this Act shall apply with the following additions and modifications.

(2) As soon as practicable after granting a licence for the zoo, or extending the period of a licence, or receiving an inspectors' report made in pursuance of an inspection of the zoo under this Act, the authority shall send to the Secretary of State a copy of the licence, or notification in writing of the extension, or a copy of the report (as the case may be).

(3) The authority shall send with the copy of the report any comments on it which they may have.

(4) Sections 16(1A), 16A, 16B, and 18 apply as if—

(a) references to the authority were references to the Scottish Ministers; and

(b) the words "granted by them" in section 16A(1) were omitted.

(5) Section 16(1B) applies as if—

(a) for "authority shall make such alterations to the licence as they consider" there were substituted "the Scottish Ministers shall direct the authority to make such alterations to the licence as they consider"; and

(b) for "they are" there were substituted "he is".

(6) The following provisions apply in place of section 16C:—

(a) paragraph (b) applies where the Scottish Ministers are of the view that a zoo is being operated without a licence in contravention of this Act.

(b) the Scottish Ministers shall make a zoo closure direction in respect of the zoo unless—

(i) the authority inform the Scottish Ministers that in their opinion a direction should be made under section 14(1) in respect of the zoo, and the Scottish Ministers make a direction under section 14(1)(a); or

(ii) the authority grant a licence for the zoo within such period as the Scottish Ministers consider to be reasonable in the circumstances.

(7) Section 16D applies as if—

(a) references to section 16E were references to subsection (8) of this section; and

(b) the reference in subsection (2) to the authority were a reference to the Scottish Ministers.

(8) The following provisions apply in place of section 16E to a zoo to which, by virtue of subsection (7)(a), this subsection applies:—

(a) the authority shall make arrangements in relation to all animals kept in the zoo—

(i) for their future care; or

(ii) for their disposal and for their care until they are disposed of;

(b) the authority shall supply the Scottish Ministers with any information they request about the care or disposal of animals kept in the zoo;

(c) the Scottish Ministers may, after giving the authority an opportunity to be heard, give them a direction in such terms as they see fit about the care of animals kept in the zoo or their disposal, and the authority shall comply with such a direction;

(d) arrangements for the care or disposal of animals under this subsection shall not be prejudicial to the interests of the protection of wild animals and the conservation of biodiversity;

(e) the Scottish Ministers may, after giving the authority an opportunity to be heard, make a direction under this paragraph varying a direction under paragraph (c) (including such a direction as varied by a direction under this paragraph);

(f) the Scottish Ministers may, after giving the authority an opportunity to be heard, make a direction revoking a direction under paragraph (c) (including such a direction as varied by a direction under paragraph (e));

(g) where this subsection applies by virtue of section 16D(3) (read in accordance with subsection (7) above), references in this subsection and in subsections (9) and (10) to a zoo shall be read as references to that section of the zoo which is closed permanently to the public.

(9) If the Scottish Ministers consider that an inspection of a zoo to which subsection (8) applies is appropriate having regard to their function under subsection (8)(c) they may require an authority to—

(a) carry out a special inspection of the zoo to be conducted by one or more inspectors nominated, after consultation with the authority, by the Scottish Ministers from the list;

(b) obtain a report of the inspection; and

(c) send a copy of the report to the Scottish Ministers forthwith.

(10) For the purposes of an inspection under subsection (9), inspectors may require the production of all records of the zoo's collection kept by the operator, and the operator shall produce the records.

(11) Section 10(4)(c) applies to an inspection under subsection (9) as it applies to an inspection under that section.

(12) References in this Act to "a zoo closure direction" are to a direction requiring a zoo to be closed permanently to the public.

NOTE

1. As amended by the Zoo Licensing Act 1981 Amendment (Scotland) Regulations 2003 (SSI 2003/174) reg.17 (effective 1 April 2003).

DEFINITIONS

"local authority": s.1(3)(b).

"zoo": s.1(2).

GENERAL NOTE

Where a local authority is itself a zoo operator then for the purposes of inspection, etc. the licensing authority is, in effect, the Scottish Ministers. The amendments provide that the new ss.16–16G apply to local authorities. Extensively amended by the Zoo Licensing Act 1981 Amendment (Scotland) Regulations 2003 (SSI 2003/174).

Dispensation for particular zoos

[1]**14.**—(1) Subject to subsection (1A), if the local authority with power to grant a licence for a zoo inform the Scottish Ministers that in their opinion a direction should be made under this subsection because of the small number of animals kept in the zoo or the small number of the kinds of animal kept there, he may, after consulting such persons on the list as he thinks fit, direct—

(a) that this Act shall not apply to that zoo; or

(b) that sections 10 and 11 or either of them shall not apply thereto.

(1A) The Scottish Ministers may only make a direction under subsection (1) where they are satisfied that it is not prejudicial to the protection of wild animals and the conservation of biodiversity to do so.

(2) If the operator of a zoo informs the Scottish Ministers that in their opinion a direction should be made under this subsection because the number of inspectors provided for by section 10(4)(a) is too large for the zoo (having regard to the small size of the zoo or the small number of the kinds of animal kept there), the Scottish Ministers may, after consulting the local authority with power to grant a licence for the zoo and such persons on the list as they think fit, direct—

(a) that in the application of this Act to the zoo, section 10(4)(a) and (b) shall not apply; and

(b) that, instead, any inspection to be carried out under section 10 shall be conducted by such inspector or inspectors as the Scottish Ministers appoint.

(3) Subject to subsection (3A), any direction made under subsection (1) or (2) may be revoked or varied by a further direction of the Scottish Ministers made after they have consulted the local authority and such persons on the list as he thinks fit.

(3A) The Scottish Ministers may only vary a direction made under subsection (1) where they are satisfied that it is not prejudicial to the protection of wild animals and the conservation of biodiversity to do so.

(4) While a direction under subsection (1) has effect, this Act, or sections 10 and 11, or either of them, shall not apply to the zoo (depending on the terms of the direction and any variation made by a further direction under subsection (3)).

(5) While a direction under subsection (2) has effect, this Act shall apply to the zoo with the modifications specified in the direction (subject to any variation made by a further direction under subsection (3)).

(6) The Scottish Ministers shall take reasonable steps to secure that the local authority and any person who operates the zoo are notified in writing of any direction made under subsection (1), (2) or (3).

NOTE

1. As amended by the Zoo Licensing Act 1981 Amendment (Scotland) Regulations 2003 (SSI 2003/174) reg.17 (effective 1 April 2003).

DEFINITIONS

"animals": s.21(1).
"local authority": s.1(3)(b).
"the list": s.21(1).
"zoo": s.1(2).

GENERAL NOTE

The local authority may propose to the Scottish Ministers that a particular zoo is exempted from the requirement to have a licence if it is a small zoo where a limited number of animals are kept. The amendments secure that exemptions from the requirements of the Act may only be granted when they are not prejudicial to the objectives of the Zoo Directive set out in art.1 thereof (protection of wild fauna and conservation of biodiversity). Subsections (1) and (3) were amended by and subss.(1A) and 3(A) added by the Zoo Licensing Act 1981 Amendment (Scotland) Regulations 2003 (SSI 2003/174).

Fees and other charges

15.—(1) Subject to this section, the local authority may charge such reasonable fees as they may determine in respect of—

(a) applications for the grant, renewal or transfer of licences;
(b) the grant, renewal, alteration or transfer of licences;

(2) Any fee charged under paragraph (a) of subsection (1) in respect of an application shall be treated as paid on account of the fee charged under paragraph (b) on the grant, renewal or transfer applied for.

(2A) Subject to this section, the authority may charge to the operator of the zoo such sums as they may determine in respect of reasonable expenses incurred by them—

(a) in connection with inspections in accordance with section 9A and under sections 10 to 12;
(b) in connection with the exercise of their powers to make directions under this Act;
(c) in the exercise of their function under section 16E(4) of supervising the implementation of plans prepared under section 16E(2); and
(d) in connection with the exercise of their function under section 16E(7) or (8).

(2B) The authority's charge under subsection (2A)(d) shall take into account any sums that have been, or will fall to be, deducted by them from a payment under section 16F(7) in respect of their costs.

(3) In respect of any fee or other sum charged under this section, the local authority may, if so requested by the operator, accept payment by instalments.

(4) Any fee or other charge payable under this section by any person shall be recoverable by the local authority as a debt due from him to them.

(5) The local authority shall secure that the amount of all the fees and other sums charged by them under this section in a year is sufficient to cover the amount of reasonable expenditure incurred by the authority in the year by virtue of this Act.

DEFINITIONS

"local authority": s.3(1)(b).
"zoo": s.21(1).

GENERAL NOTE

The amendments enable a local authority to recover from a zoo operator their costs under the Act as amended. Subsections (1) and (5) were amended by and subss.(2A) and (2B) added to by the Zoo Licensing Act 1981 Amendment (Scotland) Regulations 2003 (SSI 2003/174).

Enforcement

Power to alter licences

[1]**16.**—(1) At any time after the grant of a licence under this Act, it may be altered by the local authority if in their opinion it is necessary or desirable to do so for ensuring the proper conduct of the zoo during the period of the licence (whether their opinion arises from an inspectors' report or an alteration of standards specified under section 9 or otherwise).

[2](1A) Subsection (1B) applies where—

(a) the authority have made a direction under section 16A(2) in respect of a zoo;

(b) the period specified in that direction by virtue of section 16A(2)(c), including such a direction as varied under section 16A(4), has expired; and

(c) the authority are satisfied that a condition specified in that direction which requires any conservation measure referred to in section 1A to be implemented at the zoo is not met in relation to—

(i) if the zoo was specified under section 16A(2)(b)(i), any section of the zoo;

(ii) if a section of the zoo was specified under section 16A(2)(b)(ii), that section of the zoo or any smaller section of the zoo included in that section.

[2](1B) The authority shall make such alterations to the licence as they consider to be necessary or desirable to ensure that the section of the zoo in relation to which they are satisfied that the condition is not met is closed permanently to the public.

(2) Before exercising the power under subsection (1), the local authority shall give the holder of the licence an opportunity to make representations.

[2](2A) Subsection (2B) applies in place of subsection (2) where the authority propose to make under subsection (1) a significant alteration to a licence (not being one to which subsection (3A) applies), except where the alteration is in accordance with the recommendations in a report pursuant to section 9A(5)(c).

[2](2B) Before making a significant alteration to a licence the authority shall—

(a) consult the holder of the licence about the alteration they propose to make to the licence;

(b) make arrangements for an inspection to be carried out in accordance with section 9A (subject to subsection (2) of that section); and

(c) consider the report made to them pursuant to that inspection.

[2](3) Subject to subsections (3A) and (3B), at any time after the grant of a licence under this Act, the Scottish Ministers may, after consulting the authority, direct them to alter the licence, and the authority shall give effect to such a direction within a reasonable time.

[2](3A) If the Scottish Ministers propose to direct the authority to make a significant alteration to a licence, they shall first notify the authority of the proposed alteration and the authority shall—

(a) consult the holder of the licence about the alteration which the Scottish Ministers propose to direct them to make to the licence;

(b) make arrangements for an inspection to be carried out in accordance with section 9A (subject to subsection (2) of that section); and

(c) send a copy of the report made to them pursuant to that inspection to the Scottish Ministers.

[2](3B) The Scottish Ministers may not direct the authority to make an alteration to the licence which is inconsistent with the implementation at the zoo of the conservation measures referred to in section 1A.

(4) An alteration under this section may be made by varying, cancelling or attaching conditions or by a combination of any of those methods.

[2](4A) Subject to subsection (3), the local authority shall secure that upon its alteration a licence contains such conditions as the authority think necessary or desirable for requiring the conservation measures referred to in section 1A to be implemented at the zoo.

(5) The authority shall secure that the terms of any condition attached to a licence are not inconsistent with the terms of a condition attached or varied in pursuance of a direction of the Scottish Ministers.

[2](6) No alteration made under this section shall have effect until written notification of it has been received by the holder of the licence; and this subsection is without prejudice to section 18(7) and (7A).

NOTES

1. As amended by the Zoo Licensing Act 1981 Amendment (Scotland) Regulations 2003 (SSI 2003/174) reg.20 (effective 1 April 2003).

2. As amended by the Zoo Licensing Act 1981 Amendment (Scotland) Regulations 2003 (SSI 2003/174) Sch.1 para.17 (effective 22 April 2003).

DEFINITIONS

"local authority": s.3(1)(b).
"zoo": s.21(1).

GENERAL NOTE

This section gives the local authority and the Scottish Ministers power to alter licences. Subsection (6) was modified by and subss.(1A), (1B), (2A), (2B) and (4A) added by the Zoo Licensing Act 1981 Amendment (Scotland) Regulations 2003 (SSI 2003/174).

Enforcement of licence conditions

16A.—(1) Subsection (2) applies where the local authority, after giving the licence holder an opportunity to be heard, are not satisfied that a condition attached to a licence granted by them under this Act is met in relation to the zoo or a section of it.

(2) Unless subsection (3) applies, the authority shall make a direction specifying—

(a) the licence condition which they are not satisfied is met;
(b) whether they are not satisfied that that condition is met in relation to—
  (i) the zoo; or
  (ii) a section of the zoo, and if so, which section;
(c) steps to be taken by the licence holder to ensure that that condition is met in relation to the zoo (or, if a section of the zoo is specified under paragraph (b)(ii), in relation to that section) within a period specified in the direction, which may not exceed two years from the date of the direction; and
(d) whether the zoo or a section of it is required to be closed to the public during that period or any part of it specified in the direction.

(3) This subsection applies if the authority have power to make a zoo closure direction under section 16B(5) and they exercise that power.

(4) The authority may, after giving the licence holder an opportunity to be heard, make a direction under this subsection varying a direction under subsection (2) (including such a direction as varied by a direction under this subsection).

(5) A direction under subsection (4) may increase the period specified in the direction under subsection (2)(c) or (d), but the period as increased must not exceed two years beginning with the date of the direction under subsection (2).

(6) A direction under subsection (2) (including such a direction as varied by a direction under subsection (4)) may be revoked by a further direction of the authority.

DEFINITIONS

"local authority": s.1(3)(b).
"section of a zoo": s.1(2C).
"zoo": s.21(1).

GENERAL NOTE

These new powers were inserted by the Zoo Licensing Act 1981 Amendment (Scotland) Regulations 2003 (SSI 2003/174) and allow the local authority to specify mandatory steps to be taken to satisfy the licensing conditions. It enables them to issue directions to licence holders requiring them to comply with licence conditions and to require the public to be excluded from the zoo or part of it for a period of time.

Zoo closure direction

[1]**16B.**—(1) The local authority shall make a zoo closure direction in respect of a zoo licensed under this Act where—

(a) they have made a direction under section 16A(2) in respect of the zoo;
(b) the period specified in the direction by virtue of section 16A(2)(c), including such a direction as varied under section 16A(4), has expired; and
(c) they are satisfied, after giving the licence holder an opportunity to be heard, that a condition—

(i) specified in that direction and in respect of which the zoo was specified under section 16A(2)(b)(i), and

(ii) which requires any conservation measure referred to in section 1A to be implemented at the zoo,

is not met in relation to the zoo.

(2) The authority shall make a zoo closure direction in respect of a zoo licensed under this Act where they are satisfied, after reasonable enquiries have been made, that the operator cannot be found.

(3) The authority shall make a zoo closure direction in respect of a zoo licensed under this Act where, after giving the licence holder an opportunity to be heard—

(a) they are satisfied that members of the public have had access to it on fewer than seven days in the period of 12 months ending on the date on which the authority determine that they are so satisfied; and

(b) it does not appear to them that it is the licence holder's intention that members of the public will have access to it on seven days or more during any future period of 12 months.

(4) The authority may make a zoo closure direction in respect of a zoo licensed under this Act where—

(a) they have made a direction under section 16A(2) in respect of a zoo;

(b) the period specified in that direction by virtue of section 16A(2)(c), including such a direction as varied under section 16A(4), has expired; and

(c) they are satisfied, after giving the licence holder an opportunity to be heard, that a condition specified in that direction, other than one which requires any conservation measure referred to in section 1A to be implemented at the zoo, is not met in relation to—

(i) if the zoo was specified in that direction, the zoo or any section of it; or

(ii) if a section of the zoo was specified in that direction, that section, any part of that section, any larger section which includes that section, or the whole zoo.

(5) The authority may, after giving the licence holder an opportunity to be heard, make a zoo closure direction in respect of a zoo licensed under this Act if—

(a) any reasonable requirements relating to the premises or conduct of the zoo notified by them to the licence holder in consequence of the report of any inspection under this Act are not complied with within such time as is reasonable in the circumstances;

(b) they are satisfied that the zoo has been conducted in a disorderly manner or so as to cause a nuisance;

(c) the licence holder (or where the licence holder is a body corporate, the body or any director, manager or secretary or similar officer of the body) is convicted of any offence mentioned in section 4(4); or

(d) any person who, to the knowledge of the licence holder, has been so convicted is employed as a keeper in the zoo.

(6) But the authority may not make a zoo closure direction under subsection (5) if a direction under section 16A(2) is in force in respect of the zoo and—

(a) when that direction was made there were grounds upon which the authority could have made a zoo closure direction under subsection (5) in respect of the zoo, but they chose not to do so; and

(b) the grounds upon which they would make a zoo closure direction under subsection (5) are the same as any of the grounds upon which they could have made a zoo closure direction when they made the direction under section 16A(2) instead.

(7) No zoo closure direction may be made under subsection (5)(a) or (b) on grounds involving the care or treatment of animals unless the authority have first consulted such persons on the list as the Scottish Ministers may nominate for the purposes of this subsection.

(8) Where the authority make a zoo closure direction in respect of a zoo under this section, the zoo's licence is revoked from the date on which the direction has effect.

NOTE

1. As amended by the Zoo Licensing Act 1981 Amendment (Scotland) Regulations 2003 (SSI 2003/174) reg.21 (effective 1 April 2003).

DEFINITIONS

"licensing authority": s.1(3)(b).
"zoo": s.21(1).

GENERAL NOTE

This section gives a local authority power to revoke a licence and make a zoo closure notice where operators have failed to obtemper an order made under the previous section, where the licence holder cannot be traced, or where the public are no longer admitted to the zoo on seven days or more in a year and for other specified reasons. It was added by the Zoo Licensing Act 1981 Amendment (Scotland) Regulations 2003 (SSI 2003/174).

Zoo closure direction for zoos without licences

[1]**16C.**—(1) This section applies where the local authority are of the view that a zoo is being operated without a licence in contravention of the Act.

(2) If the authority are satisfied, after reasonable enquiries have been made, that the operator of a zoo to which this section applies cannot be found, they shall make a zoo closure direction in respect of the zoo.

(3) Otherwise, unless the authority inform the Scottish Ministers that in their opinion a direction should be made under section 14(1) and they make a direction under section 14(1)(a) the authority shall give to the operator of the zoo at least 35 days' notice in writing of—

(a) their intention to make a zoo closure direction in respect of the zoo; and

(b) the operator's opportunity to be heard in accordance with subsection (4)(a).

(4) Where notice has been given under subsection (3)—

(a) the authority shall give the operator of the zoo an opportunity to be heard; and

(b) after the period of notice has expired, and after having given the operator an opportunity to be heard, the authority shall make a zoo closure direction in respect of the zoo unless—

(i) it appears to the authority that the view they reached as mentioned in subsection (1) was incorrect; or

(ii) notice under section 2(1) of intention to make an application for a licence for the zoo has been given to the authority before the expiration of the period of notice given under subsection (3).

(5) Where, before the expiration of the period referred to in subsection (3), notice is given to the authority under section 2(1) of intention to make an application for a licence for the zoo, but—

(a) an application for a licence for the zoo is not made by the end of a period of three months beginning on the date on which the notice was given under section 2(1); or

(b) the application for a licence for that zoo is refused and—

(i) no appeal is brought against the refusal within the time mentioned in section 18(2); or

(ii) if an appeal is brought against the refusal within the time mentioned in section 18(2), it is abandoned or the court confirms the decision to refuse the application,

the authority shall make a zoo closure direction in respect of the zoo.

NOTE

1. As amended by the Zoo Licensing Act 1981 Amendment (Scotland) Regulations 2003 (SSI 2003/174) reg.21 (effective 1 April 2003).

DEFINITIONS

"licensing authority": s.1(3)(b).
"zoo": s.21(1).

GENERAL NOTE

This section, added by the Zoo Licensing Act 1981 Amendment (Scotland) Regulations 2003 (SSI 2003/174), provides powers to close zoos similar to the previous section but in relation to unlicensed zoos.

Application of section 16E

[1]**16D.**—(1) Section 16E applies to—

(a) a zoo in respect of which a zoo closure direction has been made, from the date on which the direction has effect (in accordance with section 18(10));

(b) a zoo whose licence has expired or been surrendered, from the date of its expiration or surrender (as the case may be).

(2) This Act shall cease to apply to a zoo when the local authority have notified the operator, or, where the operator cannot be found, any person appearing to them to be responsible for the zoo, in writing that they are satisfied that—

(a) all animals which are to be disposed of pursuant to section 16E have been disposed of;

(b) satisfactory arrangements for the care of any animals kept in the zoo which are not to be disposed of pursuant to section 16E are in effect; and

(c) there are reasonable grounds for believing that satisfactory arrangements will continue to be maintained for such animals.

(3) Section 16E applies to a section of a zoo which is closed permanently to the public by virtue of alterations to the zoo's licence under section 16(1B), from the date on which those alterations have effect (in accordance with section 18(7A)).

(4) If a section of a zoo which was closed permanently to the public by virtue of alterations to the zoo's licence under section 16(1B) reopens pursuant to further alterations to the licence, section 16E shall cease to apply to that section.

NOTE

1. As amended by the Zoo Licensing Act 1981 Amendment (Scotland) Regulations 2003 (SSI 2003/174) reg.21 (effective 1 April 2003).

DEFINITIONS

"animals": s.21(1).
"local authority": s.1(3)(b).
"zoo": s.21(1).

GENERAL NOTE

This section, added by the Zoo Licensing Act 1981 Amendment (Scotland) Regulations 2003 (SSI 2003/174), specifies how s.16E (welfare of animals following closure of zoo) will be applied.

Welfare of animals following closure of zoo

16E.—(1) Subsections (2) to (7) apply to a zoo to which this section applies unless the local authority are satisfied, after reasonable enquiries have been made, that the operator of the zoo cannot be found.

(2) As soon as reasonably practicable after the date from which this section applies, the operator of the zoo shall give to the authority a plan of the arrangements the operator proposes to make in relation to all the animals kept in the zoo—

(a) for their future care; or
(b) for their disposal and for their care until they are disposed of.

(3) The operator of the zoo shall supply the authority with any information they request about the care or disposal of animals kept in the zoo.

(4) Where the authority notify the operator of the zoo that they approve a plan prepared under subsection (2), the operator shall implement it under the supervision of the authority.

(5) Except with the agreement of the authority, the operator of the zoo shall not—

(a) dispose of any animal kept in the zoo before a plan prepared under subsection (2) has been approved by the authority; or
(b) dispose of any animal kept in the zoo other than in accordance with a plan so approved.

(6) Where—

(a) the authority are not satisfied with a plan prepared under subsection (2);
(b) the authority are not satisfied with the way in which such a plan is being implemented;
(c) the operator of the zoo has not prepared such a plan within a reasonable period after the date from which this section applies; or
(d) the authority consider that urgent steps need to be taken by the operator to safeguard the welfare of animals kept in the zoo,

(the authority may, after giving the operator an opportunity to be heard, make a direction in such terms as they see fit as to the care of animals kept in the zoo or for their disposal and for their care until they are disposed of.

(7) Where—

(a) the zoo operator has not complied with a direction under subsection (6) to the satisfaction of the authority; or
(b) the authority consider that urgent steps need to be taken by them to safeguard the welfare of animals kept in the zoo,

the authority shall, after giving the operator an opportunity to be heard, make arrangements in relation to all the animals kept in the zoo for their future care, or for their disposal and for their care until they are disposed of.

(8) Where the authority are satisfied, after reasonable enquiries have been

made, that the operator of the zoo cannot be found, they shall make arrangements for the future care of the animals kept in the zoo, or for their disposal and for their care until they are disposed of.

(9) For the purpose of giving effect to arrangements under subsection (7) or (8) the authority may—

(a) care for any animal on the premises of the zoo; or

(b) remove any animal found on the premises of the zoo and either retain it in the authority's possession or dispose of it.

(10) Arrangements for the care or disposal of animals under this section shall not be prejudicial to the interests of the protection of wild animals and the conservation of biodiversity.

(11) The authority may make a direction varying or revoking a direction under subsection (6) (including such a direction as varied by a direction under this subsection), but unless they are satisfied, after reasonable enquiries have been made, that the operator cannot be found, they shall not do so without first giving him an opportunity to be heard.

(12) Where this section applies by virtue of section 16D(3), references in this section to a zoo shall be read as references to that section of the zoo which is closed permanently to the public.

NOTE

1. As amended by the Zoo Licensing Act 1981 Amendment (Scotland) Regulations 2003 (SSI 2003/174) reg.21 (effective 1 April 2003).

DEFINITIONS

"animal": s.21(1).
"local authority": s.1(3)(b).
"zoo": s.21(1).

GENERAL NOTE

This section, added by the Zoo Licensing Act 1981 Amendment (Scotland) Regulations 2003 (SSI 2003/174), provides for the welfare of zoo animals following upon closure of a zoo. It requires the operators to prepare a plan for the future care or disposal of the animals and seek the local authority's approval therefore. Arrangements must not be prejudicial to the Zoo Directive.

Power of authority to dispose of animals

[1]**16F.**—(1) This section applies where a local authority are required to make arrangements under section 16E(7) or (8).

(2) The authority may sell or otherwise dispose of any animal in relation to which arrangements are required to be made if—

(a) after making reasonable inquiries they are satisfied that the animal is owned by the operator of the zoo;

(b) after making reasonable inquiries they are unable to identify or unable to find the animal's owner;

(c) they have obtained the consent of the owner of the animal;

(d) the owner of the animal has been asked for his consent before a date specified in the request but that date has passed and the authority have not received it and the owner has not arranged to take possession of the animal or arranged for such possession to be taken by another person; or

(e) the owner has arranged to take possession of the animal or for its possession to be taken by another person, but the date for implementation of the arrangements has passed and they remain unimplemented.

(3) Where an animal is sold or given away under subsection (2) above, any person to whom the animal is sold or given shall have a good title to it.

(4) Subsections (5) to (9) apply when the authority have sold all the animals which are to be sold under subsection (2).

(5) Subject to subsection (8), the authority shall pay to the operator of the zoo a sum equal to the total proceeds of the sales of animals falling within subsection (6), less any part of the charge which the authority are entitled to make under section 15(2A)(d) which has not been paid.

(6) An animal falls within this subsection if the authority are satisfied that it was owned by the operator of the zoo immediately before its sale under subsection (2) (whether or not they were so satisfied when they exercised their power of sale under that subsection).

(7) Where an animal is not owned by the operator and the authority have identified a person whom they are satisfied was the owner of an animal immediately before its sale under subsection (2), they shall (subject to subsection (8)) pay to that person a sum equal to the proceeds of the sale of that animal, less the costs incurred by them in connection with the sale and in caring for the animal before the sale.

(8) If the person to whom the authority is required to make a payment under subsection (5) or (7) cannot be found before the end of the period of four months beginning with the date of the sale of the last animal which is to be sold under subsection (2), the proceeds of sale shall vest in the authority.

(9) Any remaining proceeds of the sales under subsection (2) shall vest in the authority.

(10) An authority must make any payment they are required to make under subsection (5) or (7) before the end of the period of four months beginning with the date of the sale of the last animal which is to be sold under subsection (2), but they shall not make such payment before the end of the period of one month beginning with the date of that sale.

(11) Nothing in this section shall prevent an authority from making arrangements, on the advice of a veterinary surgeon or practitioner, for an animal to be put down without delay where it is necessary or expedient to do so in the interests of its welfare.

(12) References in this section, other than at subsection (2)(a), to an animal owned by the operator of the zoo include an animal which is owned by the operator jointly with any other person.

NOTE

1. As amended by the Zoo Licensing Act 1981 Amendment (Scotland) Regulations 2003 (SSI 2003/174) reg.21 (effective 1 April 2003).

DEFINITIONS

"animal": s.21(1).
"local authority": s.1(3)(b).
"zoo": s.21(1).

GENERAL NOTE

This section, added by the Zoo Licensing Act 1981 Amendment (Scotland) Regulations 2003 (SSI 2003/174), gives the local authority power to dispose of zoo animals following upon the closure of a zoo.

Powers of entry

[1]**16G.**—(1) For the purpose of giving effect to arrangements under section 16E(7) or (8), a person duly authorised by the local authority for the purposes of this subsection may, on producing his authority if so required, enter the premises of the zoo for the purposes of—

(a) inspecting any animal found there to which the arrangements relate;

(b) inspecting the accommodation of any such animal;

(c) caring for any such animal;

(d) removing any such animal; or

(e) removing any records of any such animal.

(2) Subsection (1) shall not authorise entry into any part of the premises of the zoo which is used as a private dwelling.

(3) If a sheriff is satisfied by evidence on oath that—

(a) it is necessary or desirable for the purpose of giving effect to arrangements under section 16E(7) or (8) for a person duly authorised by the authority for the purposes of this subsection to enter the premises of the zoo for the purposes mentioned in subsection (1); and

(b) either—

(i) any part of the premises to which admission for any of those purposes is sought is used as a private dwelling; or

(ii) admission to the premises or any part of the premises for any of those purposes has been refused,

that sheriff may grant a warrant authorising that person to enter the premises, or (as the case may be) the part of the premises used as a private dwelling or to which admission has been refused for any or all of those purposes with or without constables and any other persons who may be necessary, and if need be by reasonable force.

(4) A warrant granted under subsection (3) shall also specify—

(a) the length of time for which it is valid; and

(b) the times at which entry may be effected,

and may contain such restrictions as the sheriff thinks fit.

(5) A person duly authorised for the purposes of subsection (3) shall, if so required, produce his authority and warrant before entering the premises of the zoo or part of the premises to which the warrant relates (as the case may be).

NOTE

1. As amended by the Zoo Licensing Act 1981 Amendment (Scotland) Regulations 2003 (SSI 2003/174) reg.21 (effective 1 April 2003).

DEFINITION

"animal": s.21(1).

GENERAL NOTE

This section, added by the Zoo Licensing Act 1981 Amendment (Scotland) Regulations 2003 (SSI 2003/174), allows powers of entry to authorised persons for the purpose of inspecting an animal or the accommodation for such an animal, caring for that animal or removing that animal and a sheriff, being satisfied by evidence on oath, has the power to issue a warrant for such entry where the zoo is in a private house or admission has been refused to the authorised person.

Revocation of licence

17. [*Omitted.*]

GENERAL NOTE

This section was repealed by the Zoo Licensing Act 1981 Amendment (Scotland) Regulations 2003 (SSI 2003/174) reg.22 (effective 22 April 2003) as being no longer necessary.

Appeals

18.—(1) A person aggrieved by—

(a) the refusal to grant a licence;

(b) any condition attached to a licence;

(c) any variation or cancellation of a condition;

(d) the refusal to approve the transfer of a licence;

(e) a direction under section 13(8)(c) or 16A(2) or any variation of such a direction;

(f) a zoo closure direction;

(g) the refusal to approve a plan prepared under section 16E(2);

(h) a direction under section 16E(6) or any variation of such a direction; or

(i) any arrangements under section 16E(7) or (8),

may appeal by summary application to the sheriff.

(2) Any such appeal shall be brought within twenty-eight days from the date on which the person wishing to appeal receives written notification of the authority's decision as to the matter in question; but an appeal may be brought under this section whether or not the authority's decision was made in pursuance of a direction of the Scottish Ministers under this Act.

(3) On an appeal under this section to a magistrates' court, the court may confirm, vary or reverse the local authority's decision and generally give such directions as it thinks proper, having regard to the provisions of this Act.

(4) On an appeal under this section to the sheriff, he shall have power (without prejudice to any other power which he may have) to confirm, vary or reverse the local authority's decision and to award such expenses as he thinks fit.

(5) The procedure on an appeal to a magistrates' court under this section shall be by way of complaint for an order, and the Magistrates' Courts Act 1980 shall apply to the proceedings.

(6) The decision of the sheriff on an appeal under this section shall be final.

(7) In so far as a condition attached to a licence (whether on its grant or later), or the variation of a condition, imposes a requirement on the holder of the licence to carry out works he would not otherwise be required to carry out, the condition or the variation shall not have effect—

(a) during the period within which the holder is entitled to appeal against the attachment or variation, or

(b) where such an appeal is brought within that period, during the period before the appeal is determined or abandoned.

(7A) An alteration to a licence under section 16(1B) has effect—

(a) if an appeal is brought under this section within the time mentioned in subsection (2), and the authority's decision is confirmed or varied, on the day following the day on which the appeal is determined, or on such other day as the court directs;

(b) if an appeal is brought under this section within the time mentioned in subsection (2) but is subsequently abandoned, on the day following the day on which the appeal is abandoned, or on such other day as the court directs; or

(c) if no appeal is brought within the time mentioned in subsection (2), on the expiration of that time.

(8) Subsection (9) applies to the following directions—

(a) a direction under section 16A(2)(d) which requires the zoo or a section of it to be closed to the public;

(b) a direction under section 13(8)(c), 16A(2) or 16E(6) which imposes a requirement on the operator of the zoo to carry out works the operator would not otherwise be required to carry out; and

(c) a direction under section 13(8)(c) or 16E(6) which imposes a requirement to dispose of any animals or any variation of such a direction.

(9) A direction to which this subsection applies shall not have effect—

(a) during the period within which the holder is entitled to appeal against it; or

(b) where such an appeal is brought within that period, during the period before the appeal is determined or abandoned.

(10) A zoo closure direction has effect—

(a) if an appeal is brought under this section within the time mentioned in subsection (2), and the authority's decision is confirmed or varied, on the day following the day on which the appeal is determined, or on such other day as the courts directs;

(b) if an appeal is brought under this section within the time mentioned in subsection (2) but is subsequently abandoned, on the day following the day on which the appeal is abandoned, or on such other day as the court directs; or

(c) if no appeal is brought within the time mentioned in subsection (2), on the expiration of that time.

GENERAL NOTE

This section gives a right of appeal to the sheriff under summary procedure. Subsections (1), (2) and (8) were amended by and subss.(7A)–(10) added by the Zoo Licensing Act 1981 Amendment (Scotland) Regulations 2003 (SSI 2003/174).

Subsection (1)

This extended right of appeal is by way of summary application. For "person aggrieved" see pp.28–29 above. Subsection (1)(a) is omitted as it applies to England and Wales only.

Subsection (2)

The period during which the appeal may be brought has been extended from the former 21 days to 28 days.

Subsection (3)

Applies only to England and Wales and has been omitted.

Subsection (4)

This subsection defines the powers which the sheriff can exercise on appeal.

Subsection (5)

Applies only to England and Wales and has been omitted.

Subsection (6)

There is no appeal to the sheriff principal or Court of Session.

Subsection (7)

Where a licence condition obliges a licence holder to carry out works the requirement to carry out the works is suspended until the appeal is determined or abandoned.

Subsection (7A)

A s.16(1B) alteration takes effect one day after the determination or abandonment of the appeal.

Offences and penalties.

[1]**19.**—(1) If a zoo is operated without a licence in contravention of this Act, the operator is guilty of an offence.

(2) If the operator of a zoo fails without reasonable excuse to comply with any condition for the time being attached to a licence for the zoo granted under this Act and held by him, he is guilty of an offence.

(3) Any person who intentionally obstructs an inspector acting pursuant to this Act is guilty of an offence.

(3A) Any person who intentionally obstructs a person duly authorised for the purposes of section 16G(1) or (3) and acting pursuant to that authorisation is guilty of an offence.

(3B) If the holder of a licence for a zoo fails without reasonable excuse to comply with a direction given under section 16A(2)(d) to close the zoo, or a section of it to the public, for a period, the holder is guilty of an offence.

(3C) If any person notified in writing of a zoo closure direction pursuant to section 19A(1) or (2) fails without reasonable excuse to comply with that direction, the operator is guilty of an offence.

(3D) If the operator of a zoo fails without reasonable excuse to comply with a local authority's request for information under section 16E(3), the operator is guilty of an offence.

(3E) If, contrary to section 16E(5), the operator of a zoo without reasonable excuse and without the agreement of the local authority disposes of any animal kept in the zoo—

(a) before a plan prepared under section 16E(2), has been approved by the authority; or

(b) otherwise than in accordance with such a plan which has been approved by the authority,

the operator is guilty of an offence.

(3F) If the operator of a zoo fails without reasonable excuse to comply with a direction given under section 16E(6), the operator is guilty of an offence.

(3G) If, contrary to section 4(8), the holder of a licence for a zoo fails without reasonable excuse to display the zoo licence or a copy of it publicly at each public entrance to the zoo the holder of the licence is guilty of an offence.

(4) A person guilty of an offence under this section is liable on summary conviction to a fine not exceeding level 4 on the standard scale for an offence under subsection (1), (2), (3A), (3B), (3C), (3E), or (3F) and level 3 on the standard scale for an offence under subsection (3), (3D) or (3G).

(5) Where an offence under this section committed by a body corporate is proved to have been committed with the consent or connivance of, or to have been attributed to any neglect on the part of, any director, manager, secretary or any other similar officer of the body corporate, or any person who was purporting to act in any such capacity, he, as well as the body corporate, is guilty of that offence and liable to be proceeded against and punished accordingly.

NOTE

1. As amended by the Zoo Licensing Act 1981 Amendment (Scotland) Regulations 2003 (SSI 2003/174) reg.24 (effective 1 April 2003).

GENERAL NOTE

This section creates a number of statutory offences to which the defence of "reasonable excuse" is available—subs.(2). For the level of fines see Introduction p.32 above. Subsections (3A)–(3G) were inserted by the Zoo Licensing Act 1981 Amendment (Scotland) Regulations 2003 (SSI 2003/174).

Subsection (5) was amended by the Criminal Procedure (Scotland) Act 1975 s.289G.

Supplemental

Directions

[1]**19A.**—(1) Where a local authority make a direction under this Act, they shall take reasonable steps to secure that the operator of the zoo is notified in writing of it.

(2) But where, after reasonable enquiries have been made, the operator of the zoo cannot be found, the authority shall take reasonable steps to secure that any person appearing to them to be responsible for the zoo is notified in writing of the direction.

(3) The operator of a zoo or other person notified in writing of a direction pursuant to subsection (2) shall comply with a direction under this Act made in respect of that zoo.

NOTE

1. As amended by the Zoo Licensing Act 1981 Amendment (Scotland) Regulations 2003 (SSI 2003/174) reg.25 (effective 1 April 2003).

GENERAL NOTE

This section, added by the Zoo Licensing Act 1981 Amendment (Scotland) Regulations 2003 (SSI 2003/174), provides that the local authority must takes reasonable steps to secure that the operator of a zoo or any person appearing to them to be responsible for the zoo is notified in writing of any direction made by them under the Act and that the operator of the zoo or person notified shall comply with a direction made under the Act.

Electronic communications

[1]**19B.**—(1) Subject to subsection (2), any reference in this Act to any document, notice, notification or statement in writing shall include a reference to that document, notice, notification or statement being an electronic communication (as defined in section 15(1) of the Electronic Communications Act 2000 (c.7)), which has been recorded and is consequently capable of being reproduced.

(2) Any notice which a local authority requires to send may be given to or served on a person by such an electronic communication only if—

(a) the person consents in writing to the receipt of a notice of the kind in question from the sender by electronic communication sent to a specified number or address; and

(b) the communication is sent to the number or address in question.

(3) In any legal proceedings, an electronic communication sent to any person under this Act shall, unless the contrary is proven, be regarded as having been received by that person on the second working day after the day on which it was sent.

(4) In subsection (3), "working day" means a day which is not—

(a) a Saturday;

(b) a Sunday;
(c) Christmas Eve;
(d) a bank holiday in Scotland under the Banking and Financial Dealings Act 1971 (c.80);
(e) a day appointed for public thanksgiving or mourning; or
(f) a day which is a local or public holiday in the area in which the electronic communication is to be sent.

NOTE

1. As inserted by Electronic Communications (Scotland) Order 2006 (SSI 2006/367) art.2 (effective 23 June 2006).

GENERAL NOTE

This section was inserted by the Electronic Communications (Scotland) Order 2006 (SSI 2006/367) in an attempt to bring the law into line with the 21st century.

20. [*Omitted.*]

GENERAL NOTE

This section is omitted as it contained transitional provisions for existing zoos and is no longer of any effect.

Interpretation

21.—(1) In this Act—

"*animals*" means animals of the classes Mammalia, Aves, Reptilia, Amphibia, Pisces and Insecta and any other multi cellular organism that is not a plant or a fungus and "wild animals" means animals not normally domesticated in Great Britain;

"*circus*" means a place where animals are kept or introduced wholly or mainly for the purpose of performing tricks or manoeuvres at that place;

"*keeper*" includes any person employed under the directions of a keeper;

"*the list*" means the list compiled by the Secretary of State under section 8;

"*pet shop*"' means premises for whose keeping as a pet shop a licence is in force, or is required, under the Pet Animals Act 1951;

"*taxonomic category*" means a group or assemblage of species recognised as an entity in scientific classification;

"*zoo*" has the meaning assigned by section 1(2).

"*zoo closure direction*" has the meaning assigned by section 13(12).

(2) Nothing in this Act and nothing done under it shall prejudice or affect the operation of any of the relevant statutory provisions (whenever made) as defined in Part I of the Health and Safety at Work etc. Act 1974.

GENERAL NOTE

This definition section was amended to include the definition of "zoo closure order" by the Zoo Licensing Act 1981 Amendment (Scotland) Regulations 2003 (SSI 2003/174). The Secretary of State expressed the view that deer, caged birds, exotic pheasants and wild fowl should be included in the category of "wild animal"—see Department of Environment Circular 11/88 para.30.

Consequential amendments

22.—(1) [*Omitted.*]

(2) For the purpose of the said Act an animal shall be treated as kept in a

zoo when it is elsewhere in the personal possession of the operator of the zoo, or of competent persons acting on his behalf.

GENERAL NOTE

Subsection (1) is omitted as its consequential amendments are found elsewhere. Subsection (2) provides for temporary cover under the Act for a zoo animal out on a supervised excursion—but see Department of Environment Circular 5/84.

22A. [*Omitted.*]

Short title, commencement and extent

23.—(1) This Act may be cited as the Zoo Licensing Act 1981.

(2) [*As repealed by the Statute Law (Repeals) Act 2004 (c.14) Sch.1 para.1 (effective 22 July 2004)*.]

(3) This Act does not extend to Northern Ireland.

GENERAL NOTE

The Act was brought into force on 30 April 1984 by the Zoo Licensing Act 1981 (Commencement Order) 1984 (SI 1984/423).

[1]Breeding of Dogs Act 1991

(c.64)

NOTE

1. Entire Act to be repealed by the Animal Health and Welfare (Scotland) Act 2006 (asp 11) Sch.2 para.9 (date yet to be appointed).

ARRANGEMENT OF SECTIONS

SECTION

NOTE

Note that from 30 December 1999 certain important amendments to this Act have been made by the Breeding and Sale of Dogs (Welfare) Act 1999. It is the intention of the Scottish Ministers to eventually replace this legislation by orders made under s.26 of the Animal Health and Welfare (Scotland) Act 2006 but until this is done the present provisions remain in force.

Power to inspect premises not covered by licence under Breeding of Dogs Act 1973

1.—(1) If a justice of the peace is satisfied by information on oath laid by any officer of a local authority authorised in writing for the purposes of this section by the authority, or any veterinary surgeon or veterinary practitioner so authorised, that there are reasonable grounds for suspecting that an offence against section 1(1) of the Breeding of Dogs Act 1973 (breeding establishments for dogs to be covered by a licence) has been or is being committed at any premises in the area of the authority, the justice may issue a warrant authorising any such officer, surgeon or practitioner to enter those premises, by reasonable force if need be, and inspect them and any animals or anything found there.

(2) No warrant shall be issued under subsection (1) above authorising entry to any premises for the time being used as a private dwelling.

(3) The reference in subsection (2) above to premises for the time being used as a private dwelling does not include a reference to any garage, outhouse or other structure (whether or not forming part of the same building as the premises) which belongs to or is usually enjoyed with the premises.

(4) A warrant issued under subsection (1) above—

(a) may authorise persons to accompany the person who is executing the warrant; and

(b) shall continue in force for the period of one month commencing with the date of issue.

(5) The power of entry conferred by the warrant may be exercised at all reasonable times and any person entering the premises in exercise of that power shall—

(a) produce the warrant if so required; and

(b) comply with such precautions (if any) as the justice of the peace may specify to prevent the spread among animals of infectious or contagious diseases.

(6) In the application of this section to Scotland, any reference to a justice of the peace shall include a reference to a sheriff and the reference in subsection (1) to written information on oath shall be construed as a reference to evidence on oath.

(7) In this section "local authority", "veterinary practitioner" and "veterinary surgeon" have the same meanings as in the Breeding of Dogs Act 1973.

DEFINITIONS

"local authority": s.5(2) of the 1973 Act.

"veterinary practitioner": s.5(2) of the 1973 Act.

"veterinary surgeon": s.5(2) of the 1973 Act.

GENERAL NOTE

The 1991 Act was "aimed at bringing to an end the abuses which occur in the so-called 'puppy farms', i.e. unlicensed dog-breeding establishments which remained outside the controls of the 1973 Act because, being unlicensed, local authority officials had no right of access or inspection" (Scottish Office Environment Department Circular No.24/91). Whether it has achieved this purpose in fact is a matter of continuing concern. This section gives local authorities powers of entry and inspection in relation to unlicensed dog breeding and rearing establishments similar to those for licensed premises covered by the 1973 Act.

Subsection (1)

For "reasonable grounds for suspecting" see p.31 above. Note that a sheriff can grant a warrant—see subs.(5).

Subsection (2)

Note the qualification relating to outbuildings contained in the following subsection. The exclusion of private dwelling houses is a curious proviso. The view expressed in Scottish Office Environment Department Circular No.24/91 is that "although it would therefore remain theoretically possible to continue breeding illegally in a dwelling house, it is unlikely that this could be done to any substantial scale".

Subsection (5)

For "at all reasonable times" see Introduction p.30 above.

Offence and disqualification

2.—(1) Any person who intentionally obstructs or delays any person in the exercise of his powers of entry or inspection under section 1 above is guilty of an offence and liable on summary conviction to a fine not exceeding level 3 on the standard scale.

[1](2) Where a person is convicted of an offence under subsection (1) above, the court by which he is convicted may make an order providing for either or both of the following—

(a) his disqualification, for such period as the court thinks fit, from keeping an establishment the keeping of which is required to be licensed under the Breeding of Dogs Act 1973; and

(b) his disqualification, for such period as the court thinks fit, from having custody of any dog of a description specified in the order.

[1](2A) A court which has made an order under or by virtue of this section may, if it thinks fit, suspend the operation of the order pending an appeal.

[1](2B) Subsections (5) to (11) of section 3 of the Breeding of Dogs Act 1973 (provisions about disqualification) apply in relation to an order made under subsection (2)(b) above as they apply in relation to an order made under subsection (3)(c) of that section.

(3) [*As repealed by the Breeding and Sale of Dogs (Welfare) Act 1999 (c.11) Sch.1 para.1 (effective 30 December 1999).*]

NOTE

1. As amended by the Breeding and Sale of Dogs (Welfare) Act 1999 (c.11) s.5 (effective 30 December 1999).

GENERAL NOTE

The Act covers, in Scotland, both breeding and rearing establishments, as does the 1973 Act. For "level 3 on the standard scale" see p.32 above. For "intentionally obstructs or delays" see pp.30–31 above. Subsection (2) was amended by the Breeding and Sale of Dogs (Welfare) Act 1999 s.5(4). Subsection (2A) was inserted by the Breeding and Sale of Dogs (Welfare) Act 1999 s.5(5). Subsection (3) was repealed by the Breeding and Sale of Dogs (Welfare) Act 1999 s.5(4).

Short title, commencement and extent

3.—(1) This Act may be cited as the Breeding of Dogs Act 1991.

(2) This Act shall come into force at the end of the period of two months beginning with the date on which it is passed.

(3) This Act does not extend to Northern Ireland.

[1]Breeding and Sale of Dogs (Welfare) Act 1999

(c.11)

NOTE

1. Entire Act to be repealed by the Animal Health and Welfare (Scotland) Act 2006 (asp 11) Sch.2 para.9 (date yet to be appointed).

ARRANGEMENT OF SECTIONS

An Act to amend and extend certain enactments relating to the commercial breeding and sale of dogs; to regulate the welfare of dogs kept in commercial breeding establishments; to extend powers of inspection; to establish records of dogs kept at such establishments; and for connected purposes.

GENERAL NOTE

Although dog breeding and rearing establishments have been licensed since the passing of the Breeding of Dogs Act 1973, and unlicensed establishments have been subject to legislation by the Breeding of Dogs Act 1991, considerable public disquiet was expressed that, notwithstanding such legislation, the problem of "puppy farms", where dogs were being subjected to cruelty and exploitation, had still not been properly addressed. Accordingly, Parliament passed this Act, whose long title is:

> "An Act to amend and extend certain enactments relating to the commercial breeding and sale of dogs; to regulate the welfare of dogs kept in commercial breeding establishments; to extend powers of inspection; to establish records of dogs kept at such establishments; and for connected purposes."

This Act, which deals with an area of law that has now been devolved to the Scottish Parliament, may well be the last UK statute to deal with a civic government licensing matter. It came into force on 30 December 1999 and note that the two sets of regulations made under the Act are Scottish statutory instruments applicable only to Scotland. The amendments made to the 1991 Act are included in the pages referring to that Act.

Licensing of breeding establishments etc.

Inspection and report before grant of licence

1. [*Omitted.*]

GENERAL NOTE

This section inserted new subss.(2A) and (2B) into s.2 of the 1991 Act.

Licence conditions

2. [*Omitted.*]

GENERAL NOTE

This section amended s.1(4) of the 1973 Act and added a new subs.(4A).

Commencement and duration of licence

3. [*Omitted.*]

GENERAL NOTE

This section made consequential amendments to s.1(6) and (7) of the 1973 Act and added a new subs.(5A).

Imprisonment for keeping unlicensed establishments, etc.

4. [*Omitted.*]

GENERAL NOTE

This section amended s.3(1) of the 1973 Act and the amended text is found above.

Disqualification

5. [*Omitted.*]

GENERAL NOTE

Subsections (1)–(5) of this section made consequential amendments to s.3 of the 1973 Act by amending subss.(1), (3) and (4) and by adding new subss.(6)–(11). Subsection (6) of this Act was a transitional provision and no longer has any effect.

Fees

6. [*Omitted.*]

GENERAL NOTE

This section added a new s.3A to the 1973 Act.

Definition of establishments

7. [*Omitted.*]

GENERAL NOTE

This important section dealing with several key definitions is incorporated into ss.4A and 4B of the 1973 Act.

Sale of dogs

[1]**8.**—(1) The keeper of a licensed breeding establishment is guilty of an offence if—

(a) he sells a dog otherwise than at a licensed breeding establishment, a licensed pet shop or a licensed Scottish rearing establishment,

(b) he sells a dog otherwise than to the keeper of a licensed pet shop or a licensed Scottish rearing establishment knowing or believing that the person who buys it intends that it should be sold (by him or any other person),

(c) he sells a dog which is less than eight weeks old otherwise than to the keeper of a licensed pet shop or a licensed Scottish rearing establishment,

(d) he sells to the keeper of a licensed pet shop or a licensed Scottish rearing establishment a dog which was not born at a licensed breeding establishment, or

(e) he sells to the keeper of a licensed pet shop or a licensed Scottish rearing establishment a dog which, when delivered, is not wearing a collar with an identifying tag or badge.

(2) The keeper of a licensed Scottish rearing establishment is guilty of an offence if—

(a) he sells a dog otherwise than at a licensed Scottish rearing establishment or a licensed pet shop,

(b) he sells a dog otherwise than to the keeper of a licensed pet shop knowing or believing that the person who buys it intends that it should be sold (by him or any other person),

(c) he sells a dog which is less than eight weeks old otherwise than to the keeper of a licensed pet shop, or

(d) he sells a dog which, when delivered to him, was wearing a collar with an identifying tag or badge but is not wearing such a collar when delivered to the person to whom he sells it.

(3) The keeper of a licensed pet shop is guilty of an offence if he sells a dog which, when delivered to him, was wearing a collar with an identifying tag or badge but is not wearing such a collar when delivered to the person to whom he sells it.

(4) In proceedings against any person for an offence under this section it shall be a defence for that person to show that he took all reasonable steps and exercised all due diligence to avoid committing the offence.

(5) In this section—

"*identifying tag or badge*", in relation to a dog, means a tag or badge which clearly displays information indicating the licensed breeding establishment at which it was born and any other information required by regulations,

"*licensed breeding establishment*" means a breeding establishment for dogs the keeping of which by its keeper (or, where more than one, each of its keepers) is licensed under the 1973 Act,

"*licensed pet shop*" means a pet shop the keeping of which by its keeper (or, where more than one, each of its keepers) is licensed under the Pet Animals Act 1951,

"*licensed Scottish rearing establishment*" means a rearing establishment for dogs the keeping of which by its keeper (or, where more than one, each of its keepers) is licensed under the 1973 Act (as it applies in relation to Scotland), and "*regulations*" means regulations made by the Secretary of State by statutory instrument;

and a statutory instrument containing regulations made under this section shall be subject to annulment in pursuance of a resolution of the Scottish Parliament.

NOTE

1. As amended by the Scotland Act 1998 (Transfer of Functions to the Scottish Ministers etc.) (No.2) Order 1999 (SI 1999/3321) art.3(1) (effective 15 December 1999).

DEFINITIONS

"knowing or believing": Introduction p.32 above.
"due diligence": Introduction p.31 above.

GENERAL NOTE

This section creates a whole new series of statutory offences in relation to the sale of dogs by the keeper of a licensed breeding establishment and is designed to provide a strict regulation of such sales. "Sale" itself is not defined but presumably would be construed in its normal meaning of the making over or exchange of the dog "for money or other valuable consideration" (*Oxford English Dictionary*). The regulations referred to are devolved regulations made by the Scottish Ministers. These regulations have been made in relation to s.8(5)—see the Sale of Dogs (Identification Tag) (Scotland) Regulations 1999 (SSI 1999/177) at pp.400–412 below. Subsection (5) was amended by the Scotland Act 1998 (Transfer of Functions to the Scottish Ministers etc.) (No.2) Order 1999 (SI 1999/3321) art.3(1).

Penalties

9.—(1) A person guilty of an offence under section 8 is liable on summary conviction to—

(a) imprisonment for a term not exceeding three months, or
(b) a fine not exceeding level 4 on the standard scale,

or to both.

(2) Where a person is convicted of an offence under section 8(1) or (2), the court before which he is convicted may (in addition to or in substitution for any penalty under subsection (1)) make an order providing for any one or more of the following—

(a) the cancellation of any licence held by him under the 1973 Act,
(b) his disqualification, for such period as the court thinks fit, from keeping an establishment the keeping of which is required to be licensed under the 1973 Act, and
(c) his disqualification, for such period as the court thinks fit, from having custody of any dog of a description specified in the order.

(3) A court which has made an order under this section may, if it thinks fit, suspend the operation of the order pending an appeal.

(4) Where a court makes an order under subsection (2)(c) in relation to a description of dogs it may also make such order as it thinks fit in respect of any dog of that description which—

(a) was in the offender's custody at the time when the offence was committed, or
(b) has been in his custody at any time since that time.

(5) An order under subsection (4) may (in particular)—

(a) require any person who has custody of the dog to deliver it up to a specified person, and
(b) (if it does) also require the offender to pay specified amounts to specified persons for the care of the dog from the time when it is delivered up in pursuance of the order until permanent arrangements are made for its care or disposal.

(6) A person who—
(a) has custody of a dog in contravention of an order under subsection (2)(c), or
(b) fails to comply with a requirement imposed on him under subsection (5),
is guilty of an offence.

(7) A person guilty of an offence under subsection (6) is liable on summary conviction to—
(a) imprisonment for a term not exceeding three months, or
(b) a fine not exceeding level 4 on the standard scale,
or to both.

(8) Where a court proposes to make an order under subsection (4) in respect of a dog owned by a person other than the offender, the court shall notify the owner who may make representations to the court; and if an order is made the owner may, within the period of seven days beginning with the date of the order, appeal to—
(a) in England and Wales, the Crown Court, or
(b) in Scotland, the High Court of Justiciary,
against the order.

[1](9) A person who is subject to a disqualification by virtue of an order under subsection (2)(c) may, at any time after the end of the period of one year beginning with the date of the order, apply to the court which made the order (or, in England and Wales, any magistrates' court acting in the same local justice area) for a direction terminating the disqualification from such date as the court considers appropriate.

(10) On an application under subsection (9) the court shall, having regard to—
(a) the applicant's character,
(b) his conduct since the disqualification was imposed, and
(c) any other circumstances of the case,
grant or refuse the application; and where an application under subsection (9) in respect of a disqualification is refused, no further application under that subsection in respect of that disqualification shall be entertained if made before the end of the period of one year beginning with the date of the refusal.

NOTE

1. As amended by the Courts Act 2003 (c.39) Sch.8 para.383 (effective 1 April 2005).

DEFINITIONS

"level 4 on the standard scale": Introduction p.32 above.

GENERAL NOTE

This section provides the penalties for the statutory offences created by s.8. In addition to imprisonment and financial penalties, the court may also cancel an existing licence and disqualify a person from keeping a breeding and rearing establishment or from having custody of a dog. Additional orders may be made in relation to dogs that are in the custody of the offender at the time when the offence was committed, or subsequently. The offences are triable summarily in the sheriff court with a right of appeal to the High Court.

Supplementary

Repeals

10. The Schedule (repeals, including repeals of spent enactments) has effect.

GENERAL NOTE

The Schedule no longer has any practical application and is omitted here.

Short title, commencement and extent

11.—(1) This Act may be cited as the Breeding and Sale of Dogs (Welfare) Act 1999.

(2) This Act shall come into force at the end of the period of six months beginning with the day on which it was passed.

(3) This Act does not extend to Northern Ireland.

GENERAL NOTE

The commencement date of this Act was 30 December 1999, it having been passed on 30 June 1999.

STATUTORY INSTRUMENTS RELATING TO ANIMAL LICENSING

Performing Animals Rules 1925

(SR&O 1925/1219)

In pursuance of Section 5(2) of the Performing Animals (Regulation) Act 1925 hereinafter referred to as the Act, the Secretary of State for the Home Department hereby makes the following Rules dated December 3, 1925:

Form of application for registration (Section 1)

1. Every application for registration under the Act shall be made in writing in the form, and shall contain the particulars set out in the First Schedule hereto.

Application by person having no fixed place of residence in Great Britain (Section 1(2))

2. If the applicant has no fixed place of residence in Great Britain he shall make his application for registration to the local authority of one of the following districts: ... In Scotland: The Cities of Aberdeen, Dundee, Edinburgh and Glasgow.

Form of Register (Section 1(2))

3. The register which the local authority is required to keep for the purpose of the Act shall be in the form set out in the Second Schedule hereto. Each registration shall be given a serial number according to the order in which it is made, and the serial number shall be inserted in the certificate of registration issued to the applicant.

4. The local authority shall either arrange the names of the registered persons alphabetically or shall keep as part of the register an alphabetical index of the names of persons registered.

Form of Certificate of Registration (Section 1(4))

5. The certificate of registration which the local authority is required to issue to each registered person shall be in the form set out in the Third Schedule hereto.

Application for variation of registered particulars (Section 1(6))

6. Applications for variation of the registered particulars shall be made in the form set out in the Fourth Schedule hereto.

Certified copy of certificate of registration

7. A local authority may issue a certified copy of any certificate of registration issued by them if satisfied that the original has been destroyed or lost, and may charge therefor the fee hereinafter prescribed: provided that such certified copy shall be issued only to the person to whose registration it relates.

Inspection of Register entries (Section 1(5))

8. The copy of the certificate of registration sent by the local authority to the Home Office shall be open to inspection on payment of the prescribed fee on each day other than Saturday on which the office is open between the hours of 11 and 12 in the morning and 3 and 4 in the afternoon.

Fees (Sections 1(2) (5) (7) and 5(3))

9. [*Omitted as is no longer applicable.*]

Short Title

10. These rules may be cited as the Performing Animals Rules, 1925.

GENERAL NOTE

These are the rules made by the Secretary of State in terms of s.5(2) of the Performing Animals (Regulations) Act 1925. The appropriate local authorities in Scotland for the purposes of r.2 would be the City of Aberdeen Council, the City of Dundee Council, the City of Edinburgh Council and the City of Glasgow Council all as constituted in terms of s.2 of the Local Government etc. (Scotland) Act 1994. Rule 9, which was amended by the Performing Animals Rules 1968 (SI 1968/1464), has ceased to have any practical effect due to the amendments made to s.1(2) of the 1925 Act by s.209(1) and Sch.25 para.7(a) of the Local Government (Scotland) Act 1973. The Schedules to the rules are set out below.

FIRST SCHEDULE

FORM OF APPLICATION

Performing Animals (Regulation) Act, 1925

I, the undersigned, do hereby apply for registration under the Performing Animals (Regulation) Act, 1925, and do hereby declare the following particulars to be true and complete to the best of my knowledge and belief.

Signature ....

Date .... 19 .

Address to which certificate of registration is to be sent ....

....

PARTICULARS

1. Full name of applicant, surname first in block capitals.				
2. Stage name (if any) used in Great Britain.				
3. Nationality.				
4. *Either* (a) address of fixed place of residence in Great Britain, *or* (b) permanent postal address in Great Britain from which letters directed to applicant will be forwarded.				
5. Address or addresses (if any) in Great Britain, other than temporary addresses while on tour, at which applicant trains or intends to train performing animals. (If none, write "None".)				
6. State whether previously registered under the Act. If so, state name of local authority by whom registered and number and date of certificate of registration.				
7. Kinds of animals proposed to be (a) trained, (b) exhibited, stating number of each kind.	To be trained		To be exhibited	
	Kind	Number	Kind	Number
8. Describe briefly the general nature* of the performance or performances in which the animals are to be exhibited or for which they are to be trained, mentioning any apparatus which is used for the purpose of the performance.				

* The description must be sufficient to give a general idea of what is done by the animals taking part in the performance, and should state the approximate duration of the performance, the number of times for which it is usually to be given in one and the same day, and the number of animals of each kind taking part in the performance. It need not give details which would divulge any professional secret.

Note.—The fee payable in respect of the registration of a person under the Act is 21*s*, which should be remitted with the application.

Second Schedule

Form of Register

Performing Animals (Regulation) Act, 1925

	Column 1			Column 2	Column 3	Column 4	Column 5	Column 6				Column 7	Column 8	Column 9
Serial No.	Name of Trainer or Exhibitor			Nationality	*Either* (a) Address of fixed place of residence in Great Britain *or* (b) permanent postal address in Great Britain from which letters directed to the trainer or exhibitor will be forwarded	Address or addresses at which animals are to be trained	Particulars of any previous Registration	Kinds of animals				Description of General Nature of Performance	Date of Registration	Particulars of any Order of Court made under Section 2 or Section 4
								To be trained		To be exhibited				
	Surname	Other names	Stage name					Kind	No.	Kind	No.			

THIRD SCHEDULE

CERTIFICATE OF REGISTRATION

Performing Animals (Regulation) Act, 1925

THIS IS TO CERTIFY THAT the person to whom the undermentioned particulars relate has this day been registered under the above Act with the Registration Authority for the—

County
County Borough
City
Burgh } of ....

Date .... 19 ....

Serial Number of Entry in Register ....

Signature of Clerk of Registration Authority or other authorised officer ....

PARTICULARS

Column 1			Column 2	Column 3	Column 4	Column 5	Column 6				Column 7	Column 8	Column 9
Name of Trainer or Exhibitor			Nationality	*Either* (a) Address of fixed place of residence in Great Britain *or* (b) permanent postal address in Great Britain from which letters addressed to the trainer or exhibitor will be forwarded	Address or addresses at which animals are to be trained	Particulars of any previous Registration	Kinds of animals				Description of General Nature of Performance	Date of Registration	Particulars of any Order of Court made under Section 2 or Section 4
							To be trained		To be exhibited				
Surname	Other names	Stage name					Kind	No.	Kind	No.			

Fourth Schedule

Form of application for variation of particulars entered in register

Performing Animals (Regulation) Act, 1925.
Application to have the particulars entered in the register with respect to the applicant, varied.

To: [*strike out words not applicable*]
The Town Clerk, ...
The Clerk of the .... County Council.
Full name of applicant ....
[*Surname first in block capitals*]

Number and date of certificate of registration

I return herewith my certificate of registration under the above Act and I hereby apply to have the particulars entered in the Register with respect to me varied, as follows:

I also request that my existing certificate may be cancelled and a new certificate of registration may be issued to me in pursuance of Section 1(6).

Date 19

Signature ....

Address ....

....

NOTE

No fee is payable for the issue of a new certificate of registration.

GENERAL NOTE

Schedule 1 provides the prescribed application form. Note that despite the detailed information which must be given, "trade secrets" need not be divulged. The reference to 21s can be ignored and the figure fixed by the local authority in terms of s.1(2) of the 1925 Act as amended should be substituted. Schedule 2 provides the prescribed form for the local authority register and Sch.3 provides the prescribed form of certificate of registration mentioned in s.1 of the Act. Schedule 4 gives the prescribed form for an application to vary the particulars entered in the register—s.1(6) of the Act. The references to "Town Clerk", etc. should be varied to correspond with the appropriate officers in the new authorities.

Breeding of Dogs (Licensing Records) (Scotland) Regulations 1999

(SSI 1999/176)

[15 December 1999]

The Scottish Ministers, in exercise of the powers conferred upon them by section 1(4)(i) of the Breeding of Dogs Act 1973 and of all other powers enabling them in that behalf, hereby make the following Regulations:

Citation, commencement and extent

1.—(1) These Regulations may be cited as the Breeding of Dogs (Licensing Records) (Scotland) Regulations 1999 and shall come into force on 30th December 1999.

(2) These Regulations extend to Scotland only.

Provisions

2. For the purposes of section 1(4)(i) of the Breeding of Dogs Act 1973, the records referred to in that section shall be in the form set out in the Schedule to these Regulations.

SCHEDULE

Regulation 2

Form of Record to be kept at Premises for each Breeding Bitch

Name	Date of birth	Address where kept	Breed	Descrip-tion*	Date of mating	Details of sire**	Details of litter								Total number in litter
							Male				Female				
							Date of birth	Weight	Descrip-tion*	Sale details***	Date of birth	Weight	Descrip-tion*	Sale details***	

* Enter name (in the case of puppies), colour, identifying features (if any) and registration number (if any).
** Enter name, address where kept, breed, colour and registration number (if any).
*** Enter date of sale, and name, address and status (for example, private/pet shop) of purchaser.

Sale of Dogs (Identification Tag) (Scotland) Regulations 1999

(SSI 1999/177)

[15 December 1999]

The Scottish Ministers, in exercise of the powers conferred upon them by section 8(5) of the Breeding and Sale of Dogs (Welfare) Act 1999 and of all other powers enabling them in that behalf, hereby make the following Regulations:

Citation, commencement and extent

1.—(1) These Regulations may be cited as the Sale of Dogs (Identification Tag) (Scotland) Regulations 1999 and shall come into force on 30th December 1999.

(2) These Regulations extend to Scotland only.

Provisions

2. In addition to the information required under section 8(5) of the Breeding and Sale of Dogs (Welfare) Act 1999 to be displayed on an identifying tag or badge, that identifying tag or badge shall also clearly display the following other information:—

(a) the date of birth of the dog; and

(b) the identifying number, if any, allocated to the dog by the licensed breeding establishment at which it was born.

Licensing of Animal Dealers (Young Cats and Young Dogs) (Scotland) Regulations 2009

(SSI 2009/141)

[30 March 2009]

SECTION

The Scottish Ministers make the following Regulations in exercise of the powers conferred by sections 26(1), (2) and (3), 27(1), (3), (4), (5)(a), (6), (7) and (8) and 51(2) of the Animal Health and Welfare (Scotland) Act 2006 and all other powers enabling them to do so.

In accordance with sections 26(5) and 27(9) of that Act, they have consulted with such persons appearing to them to represent relevant interests and such other persons as they consider appropriate.

In accordance with section 51(3) of that Act, a draft of this instrument has been laid before, and approved by resolution of, the Scottish Parliament.

Citation and commencement

1. These Regulations may be cited as the Licensing of Animal Dealers (Young Cats and Young Dogs) (Scotland) Regulations 2009 and come into force on the day after the day on which they are made.

Interpretation

2.—(1) In these Regulations—

"*animal dealing licence*" means a licence granted under these Regulations;

"*inspector*" means a person appointed as an inspector by the Scottish Ministers or a local authority for the purposes of these Regulations;

"*licence holder*" means a person who is the holder of an animal dealing licence;

"*licensing authority*" means a local authority;

"*local authority*" means the council constituted under section 2 (constitution of councils) of the Local Government etc. (Scotland) Act 1994 for the area in which an applicant or licence holder has their premises in Scotland, or, where the applicant or licence holder does not have premises in Scotland, the City of Edinburgh Council;

"*purchaser*" means a person to whom a licence holder sells a young cat or young dog;

"*sell*" means to sell or dispose of and "sells", "sale" or "sold" are to be construed accordingly;

"*veterinary surgeon*" means a person who is registered in the register of veterinary surgeons or the supplementary veterinary register provided for under sections 2 and 8 of the Veterinary Surgeons Act 1966;

"*young cat*" means a cat which is less than 84 days old; and

"*young dog*" means a dog which is less than 84 days old.

(2) Any reference in these Regulations to anything done in writing or produced in written form includes a reference to an electronic communication as defined in the Electronic Communications Act 2000 which has been recorded and is consequently capable of reproduction.

(3) An electronic communication may only be sent by the Scottish Ministers to a person if that person has consented in writing to the use of that method of communication and transmission is to an email address provided by the recipient.

(4) An electronic communication shall be taken to be received on the day after the day of its transmission.

Persons who are required to hold an animal dealing licence

3.—(1) It is prohibited for a person to carry on, without the authority of an animal dealing licence, an activity which—

(a) involves a young cat or young dog for which the person is responsible; and

(b) involves—

(i) acquiring and keeping with a view to sale; or

(ii) selling,

any such young cat or young dog.

(2) Paragraph (1) applies only in relation to the carrying on of an activity on or after 30th April 2009.

(3) But paragraph (1) does not apply—

(a) to a person who holds a breeding licence granted under section 1(2) of the Breeding of Dogs Act 1973;

(b) to a person who holds a pet shop licence granted under section 1(2) of the Pet Animals Act 1951;

(c) in relation to the sale by a person of a young cat or young dog kept at an animal sanctuary, animal rehabilitation centre or an animal re-homing centre;

(d) in relation to the sale by a person of the progeny of a cat or dog kept by that person as a pet; or

(e) to a person who sells no more than 2 young cats or 2 young dogs or one of each such type of animal in any 12 month period.

(4) It is an offence for a person, without lawful authority or excuse—

(a) to act in breach of paragraph (1); or

(b) to contravene any condition of an animal dealing licence,

and such a person will be liable on summary conviction to a fine not exceeding level 4 on the standard scale, or to imprisonment for a term not exceeding 3 months, or both.

Applications for animal dealing licences

4.—(1) Subject to paragraph (2), the licensing authority must consider an application for an animal dealing licence where—

(a) the application is made to the authority in writing; and

(b) the required fee has been paid.

(2) The licensing authority must not grant an application from an applicant who is for the time being subject to an order for disqualification under—

(a) section 5(3) of the Pet Animals Act 1951 (offences and disqualifications);

(b) section 1(1) of the Protection of Animals (Amendment) Act 1954 (power to disqualify persons convicted of cruelty to animals);

(c) section 3(3) of the Animal Boarding Establishments Act 1963 (offences and disqualifications);

(d) section 3(3)(b) or (c) of the Breeding of Dogs Act 1973 (offences and disqualifications);

(e) section 28F(1) and (2) of the Animal Health Act 1981 (deliberate infection: disqualification orders);

(f) section 34(1) and (2), (3) or (4) of the Animal Welfare Act 2006 (disqualification);

(g) section 40(1) and (2) of the Animal Health and Welfare (Scotland) Act 2006 (disqualification orders); or

(h) regulation 21(2).

Imposition of fee

5. The licensing authority must impose a reasonable fee equivalent to the amount of costs and expenses incurred in processing an application for an animal dealing licence or renewal of an animal dealing licence.

Consideration of applications for animal dealing licences

6.—(1) When considering whether to grant, renew, vary or refuse an animal dealing licence, but without prejudice to its discretion to refuse an animal dealing licence on other grounds, the licensing authority must in particular have regard to the need for securing that—

(a) a young cat or young dog is at all times kept in accommodation suitable as respects construction, size of quarters, number of occupants, exercising facilities, temperature, lighting, ventilation and cleanliness;

(b) a young cat or young dog is at all times adequately supplied with suitable food, drink and bedding material, adequately exercised and visited at suitable intervals;

(c) all reasonable precautions are taken to prevent and control the spread among such young cats and young dogs of infectious or contagious diseases; and

(d) appropriate steps are taken for the protection of a young cat or young dog in the case of fire or other emergency.

(2) The licensing authority must, before reaching a decision as to whether or not to grant, renew, vary or refuse an animal dealing licence, consider a report made to the authority by an inspector, unless—

(a) the applicant does not have premises in Scotland on the date the application is received, in which case no report will be required as no inspection will be carried out; or

(b) paragraph (5) applies.

(3) The report referred to in paragraph (2) must be made following an inspection by an inspector carried out after the application for the animal dealing licence has been received.

(4) The inspection referred to in paragraph (3) means the inspection of any such places, equipment and documents as the inspector thinks necessary for the purpose of enabling the licensing authority to satisfy itself on the matters referred to in paragraph (1).

(5) In the case of an application for a renewal of an animal dealing licence, the licensing authority may, for the purposes of paragraph (2), rely upon a report based on an inspection made in respect of that licence within a period of one year before the date of the application for renewal.

Grant or renewal of animal dealing licences

7.—(1) The licensing authority may grant or renew an animal dealing licence which must be in writing and must state—

(a) the name and home or business address of the licence holder or applicant;

(b) the address of the premises where the animals must be kept during the period referred to in regulation 15(1);

(c) the number of the animal dealing licence;

(d) the date of commencement of the animal dealing licence and of its expiry, which will be no later than 3 years from the date of its commencement; and

(e) the conditions subject to which the animal dealing licence has been granted.

(2) The licensing authority must determine an application for an animal dealing licence, or a renewal or variation of such a licence, within 3 months of the date on which the application is received.

(3) Where the licensing authority has received an application for the renewal of an animal dealing licence before the expiry date of that licence, then that licence will be regarded as continuing in force, for a maximum period of 3 months or until such time as a decision is issued on that application by the licensing authority, if earlier.

Conditions of an animal dealing licence

8.—(1) The licensing authority must when granting or renewing an animal dealing licence specify the maximum number of young cats and young dogs that may be kept by the licence holder at any one time (the "maximum permitted number of animals").

(2) An animal dealing licence must include the specified conditions.

(3) The specified conditions are that—

(a) the licence holder must not, without reasonable excuse, keep a cat or dog which is less than 8 weeks of age at any time unless that cat or dog is accompanied by its mother;

(b) the licence holder must not keep more than the maximum permitted number of animals;

(c) the licence holder must ensure that all young cats and young dogs acquired by the licence holder—

(i) receive a physical examination by a veterinary surgeon in the 24 hour period immediately after they are acquired by the holder;

(ii) have a unique number assigned to each of them for the purpose of identifying the animals individually; and

(iii) are accompanied by a written record containing information as to the matters contained in the Schedule so far as applicable;

(d) the licence holder must ensure that any disease or parasitic infection of a young cat or young dog is treated within 24 hours of identification, whether after the physical examination by a veterinary surgeon or otherwise;

(e) the licence holder must retain for no less than 3 years from the date of sale of a young cat or young dog a copy of the written record referred to in subparagraph (c)(iii);

(f) the licence holder must ensure that the licensing authority is permitted to inspect at any reasonable time any place or equipment used in, or in connection with, the acquisition, sale, transport or keeping of animals to which the licence relates and any documents held by or on behalf of the licence holder relating to such animals;

(g) the licence holder must accede to any reasonable request for information from the licensing authority relating to the undertaking by the licence holder of any activities referred to in subparagraph (c);

(h) the licence holder must provide the number of the animal dealing licence which that person holds and the name and telephone number of the licensing authority in any advertisement or information issued by or on behalf of the licence holder; and

(i) the licence holder must, prior to delivery of a young cat or young dog to a purchaser, exhibit the animal dealing licence (or a copy) to the purchaser.

(4) An animal dealing licence may be subject to such further conditions as the licensing authority considers necessary for the purposes of securing the welfare of animals for which the animal licence holder is responsible.

Revocation, suspension or variation of animal dealing licences

9.—(1) The licensing authority may at any time—

(a) revoke, suspend or vary an animal dealing licence;

(b) vary the maximum permitted number of animals;

(c) revoke, suspend or vary a condition of an animal dealing licence, other than any of the specified conditions referred to in regulation 8(3).

(2) The powers referred to in paragraph (1) may be exercised—

(a) on application by the licence holder;

(b) on a contravention of a condition of an animal dealing licence;

(c) on a contravention of these Regulations;
(d) if any information supplied by the licence holder is false; or
(e) if doing so is necessary in order to protect the welfare of any animal.

(3) Where any of the powers referred to in paragraph (1) is exercised—
(a) the licensing authority must notify the licence holder in writing of the revocation, suspension, or variation; and
(b) the licence holder must, if required by the licensing authority, return his or her licence to the authority within 21 days of receipt of such a notice.

(4) If the licensing authority vary an animal dealing licence, it must re-issue the licence as varied.

Death of licence holder

10.—(1) In the event of the death of the licence holder the animal dealing licence will be deemed to have been granted to the licence holder's personal representatives upon their application, as long as none of the personal representatives is subject to an order for disqualification under any of the provisions set out in regulation 4(2)(a) to (h), and will remain in force for a period of 3 months beginning with the date of death.

(2) A licensing authority may, on the application of those personal representatives, extend the period of 3 months referred to in paragraph (1) if the licensing authority is satisfied that the extension is necessary for the purpose of winding up the deceased's estate and that no other circumstances make extension undesirable.

Exercise of functions by inspectors

11. A licensing authority may appoint in writing an inspector (whether or not an officer of the authority) to exercise the powers conferred on an inspector by these Regulations.

The register of animal dealing licences and provision of information

12.—(1) The licensing authority must keep, in such form as it considers appropriate, a register of animal dealing licences which must include the name and home or business address of the licence holder, the address of the premises where the period referred to in regulation 15(1) will take place and the number of the licence.

(2) The licensing authority must make the register available for public inspection without charge during reasonable office hours and must allow copies of the register to be taken.

Review of a decision by the licensing authority

13.—(1) A licence holder or applicant may apply in writing to the licensing authority for a review of a decision.

(2) An application for review—
(a) must be made within 21 days after the date that notice of a decision is received by the licence holder or applicant; and
(b) may include any written explanation that the licence holder or applicant considers appropriate.

(3) A decision which is the subject of an application for review shall, unless the licensing authority direct otherwise in writing, have effect until the date of determination of that application.

(4) The application for review shall be determined by the licensing authority, in accordance with paragraphs (5) to (10).

(5) The licensing authority shall appoint a person to carry out the functions in paragraph (8) ("the appointed person").

(6) The licensing authority shall inform the licence holder or applicant in writing—

(a) of the name and address of the appointed person;

(b) of the role of that person; and

(c) that the licence holder or applicant may give a written explanation (or further explanation) to that person.

(7) Any written explanation referred to in paragraph (6) shall be given to the appointed person within 14 days after the date of intimation to the licence holder or applicant under that paragraph.

(8) The appointed person shall—

(a) examine the merits of the decision;

(b) consider any written explanation given by the licence holder or applicant;

(c) report to the licensing authority following that examination; and

(d) include in that report such recommendation (if any) for determination of the application as the appointed person shall think fit.

(9) The licensing authority shall consider the report of, and any recommendation by, the appointed person.

(10) The licensing authority shall inform the licence holder or applicant in writing of the result of the determination of the review.

(11) In this regulation "decision" means the—

(a) determination of an application for an animal dealing licence or for renewal or variation of such a licence;

(b) decision to attach a condition to a licence; or

(c) decision to revoke, suspend or vary a licence.

Appeals

14.—(1) An applicant or licence holder may appeal to the sheriff against a determination of a review by the licensing authority under regulation 13.

(2) The licensing authority may be a party to an appeal under this regulation.

(3) An appeal under this regulation shall be made by way of summary application and shall be lodged with the sheriff clerk within the period of 28 days from the day on which the determination was made.

(4) On good cause being shown, the sheriff may hear an appeal under this regulation notwithstanding that it was not lodged within the time mentioned in paragraph (3) above.

(5) For the purposes of an appeal under this regulation, the sheriff may require the licensing authority to give reasons for that decision, and the licensing authority shall comply with such a requirement.

(6) The sheriff may uphold an appeal under this regulation only if the sheriff considers that the licensing authority, in arriving at their determination—

(a) erred in law;

(b) based their determination on any incorrect material fact;

(c) acted contrary to natural justice; or

(d) exercised their discretion in an unreasonable manner.

(7) In considering an appeal under this regulation, the sheriff may hear evidence by or on behalf of any party to the appeal.

(8) On upholding an appeal under this regulation, the sheriff may—

(a) remit the case with the reasons for such decision to the licensing authority for reconsideration of their determination; or
(b) reverse or modify the determination of the authority.

(9) On remitting a case under paragraph (8)(a) above, the sheriff may—
(a) specify a date by which the reconsideration by the authority must take place;
(b) modify any procedural steps which otherwise would be required in relation to the matter by or under any enactment (including these Regulations).

(10) The sheriff may include in the decision on an appeal under this regulation such order as to the expenses of the appeal as the sheriff thinks proper.

(11) The decision of the sheriff is final.

Separation of young cats and young dogs

15.—(1) A licence holder who acquires a young cat or young dog which is to be sold must keep the animal separately from any other animal kept by him or her for a period of not less than 10 days from the date of acquisition of the young cat or young dog.

(2) A licence holder must keep a young cat or young dog referred to in paragraph (1) at the premises specified in the animal dealing licence.

(3) A young cat or young dog acquired at the same time from the same source as another such animal may be kept with that animal during the period referred to in paragraph (1).

(4) If any other animal or animals join in the same part of the premises the young cat or young dog during the period referred to in paragraph (1) a new 10 day period of separation from other animals must be commenced from the date the animals are joined together.

(5) A young cat or young dog must be examined by a veterinary surgeon during the first 24 hours of the period referred to in paragraph (1), and a licence holder must—
(a) provide such care and treatment for the animal as is reasonably required by the veterinary surgeon; and
(b) keep the animal until such time as the animal is fit to be sold.

(6) It is an offence for a person, without lawful authority or excuse, to contravene or fail to comply with any provision of this regulation, and such a person will be liable on summary conviction to a fine not exceeding level 4 on the standard scale, or to imprisonment for a term not exceeding 3 months, or both.

Transport of young cats and young dogs

16.—(1) A licence holder must transport a young cat or a young dog directly from the premises specified in the animal dealing licence to its purchaser in Scotland.

(2) It is an offence for a person, without lawful authority or excuse, to contravene or fail to comply with any provision of this regulation, and such a person will be liable on summary conviction to a fine not exceeding level 4 on the standard scale, or to imprisonment for a term not exceeding 3 months, or both.

Powers of inspectors

17.—(1) Any inspector may, on producing evidence of that inspector's authority, if so required, enter any premises except domestic premises at all reasonable times and inspect such premises and any animals found there for the purposes of preparing a report.

(2) An inspector may enter any premises except domestic premises at all reasonable times, on producing, if requested, evidence of that inspector's authority, for the purpose of ascertaining whether these Regulations or any animal dealing licence are being, or have been, complied with and, in particular, may—

- (a) inspect and copy any records (in whatever form they are held) kept under these Regulations or any animal dealing licence, or remove such records to enable them to be copied;
- (b) inspect and check the operation of any computer and any associated apparatus or material which is or has been in use in connection with the records;
- (c) for that purpose, require any person having charge of, or otherwise concerned with, the operation of the computer, apparatus or material to afford the inspector such assistance as the inspector may reasonably require (including providing the inspector with any necessary passwords);
- (d) where a record is kept by means of a computer, require the record to be produced in a form in which it may be taken away;
- (e) examine, or require the examination of, any young cat or young dog or any other animal kept on the premises; and
- (f) take on to the premises such persons to give the inspector such assistance and such equipment as the inspector considers necessary.

(3) If a sheriff or justice of the peace is satisfied by evidence on oath laid by any inspector that there are reasonable grounds for suspecting that an offence against these Regulations has been or is being committed at any domestic premises in the area of the licensing authority, the sheriff or justice may issue a warrant authorising any inspector to enter those premises, by reasonable force if need be, and inspect them and any animals or any thing found there.

(4) A warrant issued under paragraph (3) above—

- (a) may authorise persons to accompany the person who is executing the warrant; and
- (b) shall continue in force for the period of one month commencing with the date of issue.

(5) The power of entry conferred by the warrant may be exercised at all reasonable times and any person entering the premises in exercise of that power shall—

- (a) produce the warrant if so required; and
- (b) comply with such precautions (if any) as the sheriff or justice of the peace may specify to prevent the spread among animals of infectious or contagious diseases.

(6) If an inspector enters any unoccupied premises, the inspector must leave them as effectively secured against entry as the inspector found them.

Obstruction

18. If any person intentionally obstructs an inspector (or a person assisting an inspector in accordance with regulation 17(2)(f)) in the exercise of the powers conferred by regulation 17 that person is guilty of an offence and will be liable on summary conviction to a fine not exceeding level 4 on the standard scale, or to imprisonment for a term not exceeding 3 months, or both.

Offence of making a false statement

19. It is prohibited for a person for the purposes of obtaining or holding an animal dealing licence—

(a) to make a statement to the licensing authority (or someone acting on its behalf) knowing it to be false in a material particular; or

(b) recklessly to make a statement to the licensing authority (or someone acting on its behalf) which is false in a material particular,

and breach of such prohibition is an offence and will be liable on summary conviction to a fine not exceeding level 4 on the standard scale, or to imprisonment for a term not exceeding 3 months, or both.

Offences by bodies corporate

20.—(1) Where a body corporate is guilty of an offence under these Regulations and that offence is proved to have been committed with the consent or connivance of, or to have been attributable to any neglect on the part of—

(a) any director, manager, secretary or other similar officer of the body corporate; or

(b) any person who was purporting to act in any such capacity,

that director, manager, secretary or officer, as well as the body corporate, is guilty of the offence and liable to be proceeded against and punished accordingly.

(2) For the purposes of paragraph (1)—

(a) "director" in relation to a body corporate managed by its members, means a member of the body corporate; and

(b) "body corporate" includes a Scottish partnership, and, in relation to such a partnership, a reference to a director or other officer of a body corporate is a reference to a partner.

Disqualifications

21.—(1) Where a person is convicted of an offence under—

(a) these Regulations;

(b) section 28C (deliberate infection: Scotland) or 28F(16) (deliberate infection: disqualification orders) of the Animal Health Act 1981; or

(c) sections 19 (unnecessary suffering), 20 (mutilation), 21 (cruel operations), 22 (administration of poisons etc.), 23 (animal fights), 24 (ensuring welfare of animals), 25(7) (care notices), 29 (abandonment) or 40(11) (disqualification orders) of the Animal Health and Welfare (Scotland) Act 2006,

the court by which that person is convicted may revoke any animal dealing licence held by that person.

(2) Where a person is convicted of an offence under these Regulations, the court by which that person is convicted may disqualify that person from holding an animal dealing licence for such period as the court thinks fit.

(3) A court which has revoked an animal dealing licence under paragraph (1), may, if it thinks fit, suspend the operation of the order–

(a) for such period as it considers necessary for enabling arrangements to be made in relation to any animals kept or owned by the licence holder in the course of their business; or

(b) pending an appeal.

(4) A court which has ordered a person's disqualification under paragraph (2) may, if it thinks fit, suspend the operation of the order pending an appeal.

Termination or variation of disqualification

22.—(1) A person who has been disqualified under regulation 21(2) may request the court which made the disqualification to terminate or vary that disqualification.

(2) An application under paragraph (1) may not be made—

(a) before the expiry of the period of one year beginning with the date on which the disqualification was made;

(b) where there has been a previous application under that paragraph in relation to the same disqualification, before the expiry of one year beginning with the date on which the previous application was determined; or

(c) within any period specified under paragraph (5).

(3) On an application under paragraph (1), the court may—

(a) refuse the application;

(b) terminate the disqualification; or

(c) vary the disqualification so as to relax any period of disqualification imposed by it.

(4) In considering the application, the court must have particular regard to—

(a) the nature of the offence in relation to which the disqualification was made;

(b) the character of the applicant; and

(c) the applicant's conduct since the disqualification.

(5) Where the court refuses an application made under paragraph (1), the court may specify a period in excess of one year during which the applicant may not make a further application under paragraph (1).

Enforcement

23.—(1) These Regulations are enforced by the local authority.

(2) The Scottish Ministers may direct, in relation to cases of a particular description or any particular case, that the Scottish Ministers will enforce these Regulations instead.

SCHEDULE

Regulation 8(3)(c)(iii)

WRITTEN RECORD TO ACCOMPANY A YOUNG CAT OR YOUNG DOG TO BE SOLD BY A LICENCE HOLDER

Information to be completed by licence holder

1. Name and address of the licence holder.

2. Address of premises where the young cat or young dog has been kept (if different from 1 above).

3. Name of the licensing authority and the animal dealing licence number.

4. Sex and breed of the animal.

5. Date of birth of the animal.

6. Identification number assigned to the animal.

7. Date the animal was acquired by the licence holder.

8. Name and address of the veterinary surgeon who conducted a physical examination of the animal in accordance with the animal dealing licence condition under regulation 8(3)(c)(i), and the date on which that examination was carried out.

9. Details of all medicines administered to the animal prior to sale by, or on behalf of, the licence holder.

10. Date of sale of the animal by the licence holder.

11. Date of physical transfer of animal from the licence holder to the purchaser (if different from 10. above).

12. Name and address of the person to whom the animal is sold by the licence holder.

13. A statement as to the requirements of regulation 15 (separation of young cats and young dogs).

GENERAL NOTE

The regulations provide for the licensing of animal dealers who acquire and sell young dogs and cats and are therefore engaged in animal dealing and in terms of reg.3 require to hold an animal dealing licence. Applications and fees for licences are dealt with in regs 4 and 5, while regs 6–9 provide for the consideration of applications, their grant and renewal conditions, revocation, suspension and variation of licenses. The remaining regulations deal with a number of associated matters including inspection, disqualification, record keeping, transport and other issues.

APPENDIX

APPENDIX 1

Civic Government (Scotland) Act 1982 as it stands without the amending 2015 Act.

ARRANGEMENT OF SECTIONS

PART I

LICENSING—GENERAL PROVISIONS

PART II

LICENSING AND REGULATION—PARTICULAR ACTIVITIES

Licensing and regulation of taxis and private hire cars

Licensing and regulation of metal dealers

Miscellaneous licences

PART III

CONTROL OF SEX SHOPS AND SEXUAL ENTERTAINMENT VENUES

SCHEDULES

SCHEDULE 1

LICENSING—FURTHER PROVISIONS AS TO THE GENERAL SYSTEM

3. Objectors and representations.
5. Disposal of applications for the grant and renewal of licences.
7. Temporary licences.
10–12. Variation, revocation and suspension of licences.
13–14. Supplementary.
17. Notification of decisions and giving of reasons.
18. Appeals.

SCHEDULE 2

CONTROL OF SEX SHOPS AND SEXUAL ENTERTAINMENT VENUES

8. Objections and representations.
9. Disposal of applications for licences.
10. Notification of decisions and reasons.
15. Variation of licences.

Discharge of functions of licensing authorities

3.—(1) For the purpose of the discharge of their functions under this Part of this Act, every licensing authority shall consider, within 3 months of its having been made to them under paragraph 1 of Schedule 1 to this Act, each application so made and, subject to the following provisions of this section, reach a final decision on it within 6 months.

(2) On summary application by the licensing authority within the 6 month period referred to in subsection (1) above, the sheriff may, if it appears to him that there is good reason to do so, extend that period as he thinks fit.

(3) The applicant shall be entitled to be a party to a summary application under subsection (2) above.

[1](4) Where the licensing authority have failed to reach a final decision on the application before the expiry of—

(a) the 6 month period referred to in subsection (1) above, or
(b) such further period as the sheriff may have specified on application under subsection (2) above,

the licence applied for shall be deemed to have been granted or, as the case may be, renewed on the date of such expiry and shall remain in force for one year, but this subsection is without prejudice to the powers of revocation under section 7(6)(a) of this Act, of variation under paragraph 10 of Schedule 1 to this Act and of suspension under paragraphs 11 and 12 of that Schedule and to the provisions of paragraph 8(5) of that Schedule.

(5) The licensing authority shall make out and deliver the licence to the applicant to whom it has been deemed to have been granted under subsection (4) above.

NOTE

1. As amended by the Criminal Justice and Licensing (Scotland) Act 2010 (asp 13) Pt 8 s.172(2) (effective 28 March 2011).

Rights of entry and inspection

5.—[1,2](1) Without prejudice to any other provision of this Act, an authorised officer of the licensing authority, an authorised civilian employee or a constable may, for the purposes specified in subsection (2) below, at any reasonable time—

(a) enter and inspect any premises, vehicle or vessel used or to be used for an activity in relation to which a licence is in force or has been applied for under this Act;

(b) require production of and inspect any equipment, plant, apparatus or stock-in-trade which is or is to be kept or used in connection with any such activity;

(c) require production of and inspect any records or other documents required by or under this Part or Part II of this Act to be kept by the holder of the licence and take copies of or extracts from any such record or document.

(2) The purposes referred to in subsection (1) above are—

(a) where a licence is in force—

(i) seeing whether the terms of the licence are being complied with and, if they are not, obtaining information in respect of such non-compliance;

(ii) obtaining information relevant to the question whether the terms of the licence should be varied under paragraph 10 of Schedule 1 to this Act or whether the licence should be renewed or, under paragraph 11 or 12 of that Schedule, suspended; or

(b) where the grant of a licence has been applied for, obtaining information relevant to the question whether the application should be granted.

(3) Any person who—

[2](a) being a person for the time being in charge of any premises, vehicle or vessel, fails without reasonable excuse to permit a constable, an authorised civilian employee or an authorised officer of a licensing authority who, in pursuance of subsection (1) above, demands to do so to enter or inspect the premises, vehicle or vessel or obstructs the entry thereto of a constable or such an employee or officer, in pursuance of that subsection;

[2](b) being a person in respect of whom powers are exercised under subsection (1) above, on being required under that subsection to do so by a constable, an authorised civilian employee or an authorised officer of the licensing authority, fails without reasonable excuse to produce any equipment, plant, apparatus or stock-in-trade or to permit a constable or such an employee or officer, in pursuance of that subsection, to inspect any equipment, plant, apparatus or stock-in-trade;

[2](c) being a holder of a licence, on being required by a constable, an authorised civilian employee or an authorised officer of the licensing authority, in pursuance of subsection (1) above, to produce any records or other document required by or under this Part or Part II of this Act to be kept by the holder of a licence, fails without reasonable excuse to produce them;

shall be guilty of an offence and liable, on summary conviction, to a fine not exceeding level 3 on the standard scale.

[2](4) An authorised officer of a licensing authority, an authorised civilian employee or a constable may require any person who the officer, employee

or constable has reasonable ground to believe is carrying on an activity which requires to be licensed to produce his licence within 5 days of being required to do so.

[2](5) Any person who, having been required under subsection (4) above to produce a licence, fails without reasonable excuse to do so within the period of 5 days specified in that subsection shall be guilty of an offence and liable, on summary conviction, to a fine not exceeding level 1 on the standard scale.

[1,2](6) An authorised officer of a licensing authority or authorised civilian employee shall not be entitled to exercise the powers which he may exercise under subsection (1) or (4) above until he has produced his authorisation—

(a) in relation to the exercise of powers under subsection (1)(a) above, to the person for the time being in charge of the premises, vehicle or vessel; and

(b) in any other case, to the person in respect of whom the powers are to be exercised.

(7) A constable who is not in uniform shall not be entitled to exercise the powers which he may exercise under subsection (1) or (4) above until he has produced his identification—

(a) in relation to the exercise of powers under subsection (1)(a) above, to the person for the time being in charge of the premises, vehicle or vessel; and

(b) in any other case, to the person in respect of whom the powers are to be exercised.

NOTES

1. As amended by the Fire (Scotland) Act 2005 (Consequential Modifications and Savings) Order 2006 (SSI 2006/475) Sch.2 para.1 (effective 1 October 2006).

2. As amended by the Criminal Justice and Licensing (Scotland) Act 2010 (asp 13) Pt 8 s.173 (effective 13 December 2010).

Offences, etc.

7.—[1](A1) Any person who without reasonable excuse does anything for which a licence is required under section 27A without having such a licence is guilty of an offence and liable—

(a) on summary conviction to imprisonment for a term not exceeding 12 months or a fine not exceeding the statutory maximum or both;

(b) on conviction on indictment to imprisonment for a term not exceeding 2 years or a fine or both.

[1](1) Any person who without reasonable excuse does anything for which a licence is required under any provision of Part II of this Act other than section 27A without having such a licence shall be guilty of an offence and liable, on summary conviction—

(a) in a case where the licence so required is a public entertainment licence, to a fine not exceeding £20,000 or to imprisonment for a term not exceeding six months or to both; and

(b) in any other case,

to a fine not exceeding level 4 on the standard scale.

(2) If a condition attached to a licence is not complied with, the holder of the licence shall, subject to subsection (3) below, be guilty of an offence and liable, on summary conviction—

[1](a) in a case where the licence is a public entertainment licence and the condition is attached under section 41(3)(b) of this Act, to such fine or imprisonment as is mentioned in subsection (1)(a) above (or to both);

[1](aa) in a case where the licence is a knife dealer's licence, to a fine not exceeding level 5 on the standard scale; and

(b) in any other case,

to a fine not exceeding level 3 on the standard scale.

(3) It shall be a defence for a person charged with an offence under subsection (2) above to prove that he used all due diligence to prevent the commission of the offence.

[1](4) Any person who, in making an application under this Part of this Act to the licensing authority, makes any statement which he knows to be false or recklessly makes any statement which is false in a material particular shall be guilty of an offence and liable, on summary conviction,

(a) in a case where the application is for a knife dealer's licence, to a fine not exceeding level 5 on the standard scale; and

(b) in any other case, to a fine not exceeding level 4 on the standard scale.

(5) Any person who, being the holder of a licence—

(a) fails without reasonable excuse to notify the licensing authority of a material change of circumstances in accordance with paragraph 9(1) of Schedule 1 to this Act;

(b) without reasonable excuse makes or causes or permits to be made any material change in any premises, vehicle or vessel in contravention of paragraph 9(2) of Schedule 1 to this Act;

(c) fails without reasonable excuse to deliver his licence to the licensing authority in accordance with paragraph 13(2) of Schedule 1 to this Act,

shall be guilty of an offence and liable, on summary conviction, to a fine not exceeding, in the case of an offence under paragraph (a) or (b) above, level 3 on the standard scale, and in the case of an offence under paragraph (c) above, level 1 on the standard scale.

(6) Where a holder of a licence is convicted of an offence under section 5 (other than subsection (5) thereof), 6 or this section, the court by which he is convicted may, in addition to any other penalty which the court may impose, make an order in accordance with one or both of the following paragraphs—

(a) that the licence shall be revoked;

(b) that the holder of the licence shall be disqualified from holding a licence for a period not exceeding 5 years.

(7) Where the holder of a licence is convicted of an offence under this section, an extract of such conviction and sentence (if any) shall, within 6 days after the date of the conviction, be transmitted by the clerk of the court to the licensing authority which granted the licence.

(8) A person may appeal against an order under subsection (6) above in the same manner as against sentence and the court which made the order may, pending the appeal, suspend the effect of the order.

(9) A person may, at any time after the expiry of the first year of his disqualification under subsection (6) above, apply to the court which ordered the disqualification to remove it, and, on such application, the court may by order remove the disqualification as from such date as may be specified in the order or refuse the application, and, in either case, may order the applicant to pay the whole or any part of the expenses of such application.

(10) Where an offence is alleged to have been committed under subsection (2) above by an employee or agent named in a licence, proceedings in respect of that offence may be instituted against the joint licence holder who is the

employer of the employee or principal of the agent, whether or not proceedings have been instituted against the employee or agent.

NOTE

1. As amended by the Custodial Sentences and Weapons (Scotland) Act 2007 (asp 17) Pt 3 s.59 (effective 1 June 2010).

PART II

LICENSING AND REGULATION—PARTICULAR ACTIVITIES

Licensing and regulation of taxis and private hire cars

Taxi and private hire car licences

10.—(1) A licence, to be known as a "taxi licence" or, as the case may be, a "private hire car licence", shall be required for the operation of a vehicle as—

(a) a taxi; or
(b) a private hire car.

(2) A licensing authority shall not grant or renew a taxi licence or private hire car licence unless they are satisfied that the vehicle to which the licence is to relate is suitable in type, size and design for use as a taxi or private hire car, as the case may be, and is safe for that use, and that there is in force in relation to the vehicle such a policy of insurance or such security as complies with Part VI of the Road Traffic Act 1972.

(3) Without prejudice to paragraph 5 of Schedule 1 to this Act, the grant of a taxi licence may be refused by a licensing authority for the purpose of limiting the number of taxis in respect of which licence are granted by them if, but only if, they are satisfied that there is no significant demand for the services of taxis in their area which is unmet.

[1](4) A vehicle shall, for the purposes of subsection (2) above, be treated by a licensing authority—

(a) as being suitable in type, size and design if it complies with regulations in that regard made by the Secretary of State under section 20(2) of this Act in respect of their area; and
(b) as not being so suitable if it does not so comply.

(5) A taxi licence or private hire car licence shall extend to the operation of a vehicle substituted for the vehicle in respect of which the licence was granted or, as the case may be, last renewed if the licensing authority are as respects the substitute vehicle satisfied as to the matters specified in subsection (2) above, and where a taxi licence or private hire car licence extends under this subsection to a substitute vehicle, subsection (6) below shall not apply in respect of the vehicle replaced by the substitute vehicle.

(6) Subject to subsection (5) above, the holder of a taxi or private hire car licence shall within 28 days of his selling or otherwise disposing of the vehicle to which the licence relates deliver to the licensing authority his licence and any licence plate or other thing which has been issued by the licensing authority for the purpose of indicating that the vehicle is a taxi or, as the case may be, private hire car, and if without reasonable excuse he fails to do so he shall be guilty of an offence and liable, on summary conviction, to a fine not exceeding level 2 on the standard scale.

NOTE

1. As amended by the Disability Discrimination Act 1995 (c.50) Pt V s.39(2) (effective 5 February 2003).

Taxi and private hire car driving licences

13.—(1) A licence, to be known as a "taxi driver's licence" or, as the case may be, a "private hire car driver's licence", shall, subject to subsection (2) below, be required for driving or otherwise having charge of a taxi or private hire car.

(2) A private hire car driver's licence shall not be required by the holder of a taxi driver's licence for driving or otherwise having charge of a private hire car whilst in operation as such.

[1](3) A licensing authority shall not grant a licence to any person under this section unless that person has held, throughout the period of 12 months immediately prior to the date of his application, a licence authorising him to drive a motor car issued under Part III of the Road Traffic Act 1972 or a licence which would at the time of his application entitle him to such a licence without taking a test, not being a provisional licence.

(4) A licensing authority may, at any time, for the purposes of satisfying themselves that he is physically fit to drive a taxi or, as the case may be, private hire car, require an applicant for or holder of a taxi driver's licence or private hire car driver's licence to submit to medical examination, at their expense, by a medical practitioner nominated by them.

(5) A licensing authority may require an applicant for a taxi driver's licence to take a test of his knowledge of the area to which the licence is to relate, of the layout of roads in that area and such other matters relating to the operation of a taxi as the authority consider desirable, and the authority may refuse to grant a licence to a person who does not satisfy them that he has adequate knowledge of any of these matters.

(6) If a person holding a licence under this section ceases for any reason to be authorised by law to drive on a road the vehicle to which the licence relates, the licence shall cease to have effect.

NOTE

1. As amended by the Criminal Justice and Licensing (Scotland) Act 2010 (asp 13) Pt 8 s.174 (effective 11 November 2011).

Licensing and regulation of metal dealers

Metal dealers: licensing and regulation

28.—(1) Subject to subsection (2) below, a licence, to be known as a "metal dealer's licence", shall be required for carrying on business as a metal dealer.

(2) A metal dealer's licence shall not be required by a person in relation to whom there is in force a warrant under section 29(1) or (4) of this Act (referred to in subsection (3) below and in sections 30 to 37 of this Act respectively as "*an exemption warrant*" and "*a temporary exemption warrant*").

(3) Sections 30 to 36 of this Act shall not apply to a person in relation to whom an exemption warrant or temporary exemption warrant is in force.

(4) A metal dealer's licence shall, in addition to specifying the activity which he engages in, specify the premises in or from which the activity is to be carried on.

Metal dealers' exemption warrants

29.—[2](1) A licensing authority shall, on application by a metal dealer, issue an exemption warrant in relation to him if there is produced to them a certificate by the auditor of the metal dealer's business stating that, in a financial year ending in the period of 18 months immediately preceding the production to them of the certificate, the total amount received by the dealer as a principal in the ordinary course of his business in respect of metal sold or supplied by him, without any deduction being made, exceeded £1,000,000 or such other sum as may be substituted for that sum by order made by the Secretary of State.

(2) An order made for the purposes of subsection (1) above shall be made by statutory instrument subject to annulment in pursuance of a resolution of either House of Parliament.

(3) An exemption warrant shall remain in force for 3 years from the date of its issue.

(4) A licensing authority may, on application by a metal dealer, issue a temporary exemption warrant in relation to him if they are satisfied that he has not been carrying on business as a metal dealer.

(5) A temporary exemption warrant in relation to a metal dealer shall remain in force from the date of its issue or such later date as the licensing authority may specify—

(a) for a period of 18 months; or

(b) until (if earlier that the expiry of that period) the date of the grant to that dealer of an exemption warrant; or

(c) if a metal dealer's licence has been applied for by him within that period, until the date when it is granted or is deemed to have been granted or, if it is refused, until the expiry of the time within which he may lodge an appeal under paragraph 18 of Schedule 1 to this Act against that refusal or, where he has lodged such an appeal, until it has been abandoned or determined against him.

(6) It shall be a condition of a temporary exemption warrant that the dealer to whom it relates shall acquire metal only from persons selling or otherwise disposing of it in the course of trade or business.

(7) A licensing authority may revoke a temporary exemption warrant on the grounds that the metal dealer to whom it relates has contravened the condition specified in subsection (6) above.

(8) An authorised officer of a licensing authority or a constable may require any person who the officer or constable has reasonable ground to believe is carrying on business as a metal dealer without having a metal dealer's licence to produce his exemption warrant or temporary exemption warrant within a reasonable time of being required to do so; and any person who does not have a metal dealer's licence and who, having been so required to produce his exemption warrant or temporary exemption warrant within that time, fails, without reasonable excuse, to do so shall be guilty of an offence and liable, on summary conviction, to a fine not exceeding level 3 on the standard scale.

(9) An officer of a licensing authority or a constable who is not in uniform shall not be entitled to exercise the powers which he may exercise under subsection (8) above until he has produced his authorisation or, as the case may be, identification to the person in respect of whom they are to be exercised.

(10) In this section—

[1]"*auditor*" means a person who is eligible for appointment as a statutory auditor under Part 42 of the Companies Act 2006; and

"*financial year*", in relation to a metal dealer, means the financial year of his business or, if it has no financial year, the year beginning on 6th April.

NOTES

1. As amended by the Companies Act 2006 (Consequential Amendments etc) Order 2008 (SI 2008/948) Sch.1(1) para.9 (effective 6 April 2008).

2. As amended by the Civic Government (Scotland) Act 1982 (Metal Dealers' Exemption Warrants) Order 2012 (SSI 2012/324) art.2 (effective 20 February 2013).

Keeping of records

30.—(1) This section applies to metal acquired by or disposed of by the holder of a metal dealer's licence in the course of his business as a metal dealer.

(2) A metal dealer shall keep the following records, containing the particulars required by this section—

(a) in relation to each place occupied by him for the purposes of his business as a metal dealer—
(i) records of all metal to which this section applies received at that place;
(ii) records of all such metal processed at or despatched or otherwise disposed of from that place;

(b) records of all metal to which this section applies received or processed at or despatched or otherwise disposed of from any place other than a place occupied by him for the purposes of his business as a metal dealer,

and separate records shall be kept of the particulars with respect to metal received and metal despatched, processed or otherwise disposed of, respectively.

(3) A metal dealer shall keep records for the purposes of this section either by—

(a) keeping, at each place occupied by him for the purposes of his business as a metal dealer, books with serially numbered pages recording all metal to which this section applies received or processed at or despatched or otherwise disposed of from that place; or

(b) the use of a device for storing and processing information, but—
(i) where he keeps books under paragraph (a) above, he shall not have in use at any one place and at any one time more than one book for recording particulars with respect to metal received at that place and more than one book for recording particulars with respect to metal processed at, or despatched or otherwise disposed of from, that place; and
(ii) where he uses a device for storing and processing information under paragraph (b) above, he shall, by means of that device or otherwise, keep particulars of all modifications made in the records kept by the device.

(4) Records kept under subsection (3) above shall be retained by the dealer for a period of two years from the day on which the last entry was made in it.

(5) The said particulars, in the case of metal received or acquired, are—

(a) the description and weight of the metal;
(b) the date and time of the receipt of the metal;
(c) if the metal is received or acquired from another person, the name and address of that person;

(d) the price, if any, payable in respect of the receipt or acquisition of the metal, if that price has been ascertained at the time when the entry in the record relating to that metal is to be made;
(e) where paragraph (d) above does not apply, the value of the metal at the time when the entry is to be made as estimated by the dealer;
(f) in the case of metal delivered at the place in question by means of a mechanically propelled vehicle bearing a registration mark (whether the vehicle belongs to the dealer or not), the registration mark borne by the vehicle.

(6) The said particulars, in the case of metal despatched, processed or otherwise disposed of are—
(a) the description and weight of the metal immediately before its despatch, processing or other disposal;
(b) the date of despatch, processing or other disposal of the metal and, in the case of processing, the process applied;
(c) in the case of metal disposed of on sale or exchange, the name and address of the person to whom the metal is sold or with whom it is exchanged, and the consideration for which it is sold or exchanged;
(d) in the case of metal disposed of otherwise than on sale or exchange, its value immediately before its disposal as estimated by the dealer.

(7) Particulars required under this section to be recorded in respect of metal received or otherwise acquired shall be so recorded immediately after the receipt or acquisition; and particulars so required to be recorded in respect of metal disposed of shall be so recorded immediately after the disposal.

(8) Any person who fails to comply with any requirement imposed upon him by this section shall be guilty of an offence and liable, on summary conviction, to a fine not exceeding level 3 on the standard scale.

Retention of metal

31.—(1) Subject to subsection (2) below and section 35 of this Act, no metal dealer shall dispose of or process any metal acquired by him in the course of business until the expiry of a period of 48 hours (excluding any time on Saturdays or Sundays) after its acquisition.

(2) A licensing authority may, on granting a metal dealer's licence or at any time thereafter, on application by the dealer and after consultation with the chief constable, order that subsection (1) above shall not apply to such metal or classes of metal as may be specified in the order.

(3) An order under subsection (2) above may—
(a) be made subject to such conditions as the licensing authority think fit;
(b) relate to metal still to be acquired by the metal dealer to whom the order relates;
(c) be varied or revoked by the licensing authority.

(4) The holder of a metal dealer's licence may appeal to the sheriff against a decision of the licensing authority under this section and paragraphs 18(3) to (9) and (11) and (12) of Schedule 1 to this Act shall, with any necessary modifications, apply to an appeal under this subsection.

(5) Any person who fails to comply with subsection (1) above shall be guilty of an offence and liable, on summary conviction, to a fine not exceeding level 3 on the standard scale.

Receipts and invoices: itinerant metal dealers

33.—(1) An itinerant metal dealer shall obtain from each person who buys metal from him a receipt showing the weight and description of the metal, the name and address of the buyer and the price paid for the metal.

(2) Any such receipt shall be kept by the dealer for a period of 6 months from its date of issue.

(3) An itinerant metal dealer shall keep a record in respect of each sale to him of metal showing the weight and description of the metal, the name and address of the seller and the price paid for the metal.

(4) Any such record shall be kept by the dealer for a period of 6 months from the date of the sale to which it relates.

(5) Any person who fails to comply with any provision of this section shall be guilty of an offence and liable, on summary conviction, to a fine not exceeding level 3 on the standard scale.

Requirement to keep records

[1]**33C.**—(1) This section applies where a metal dealer or an itinerant metal dealer ("the dealer"), in the course of the dealer's business—

(a) acquires any metal (whether or not for value), or

(b) processes or disposes of any metal (by any means).

(2) In respect of any metal acquired, the dealer must record the following information—

(a) the description and weight of the metal,

(b) the date and time of the acquisition of the metal,

(c) if the metal is acquired from another person—

(i) the name and address of the person,

(ii) the means by which the person's name and address was verified,

(d) the price, if any, payable in respect of the acquisition of the metal, if that price has been ascertained at the time when the entry in the record relating to that metal is to be made,

(e) the method of payment of the price (if applicable),

(f) where no price is payable for the metal, the value of the metal at the time when the entry is to be made as estimated by the dealer,

(g) in the case of metal delivered to the dealer by means of a vehicle, the registration mark (within the meaning of section 23 of the Vehicle Excise and Registration Act 1994) borne by the vehicle.

(3) Where the dealer has paid for metal, the dealer must keep a copy of—

(a) the cheque, or

(b) the document evidencing the electronic transfer of funds.

(4) In respect of any metal processed or disposed of, the dealer must record the following information—

(a) the description and weight of the metal immediately before its processing or disposal,

(b) in the case of metal which is processed, the process applied,

(c) in the case of metal disposed of by sale or exchange—

(i) the consideration for which it is sold or exchanged,

(ii) the name and address of the person to whom the metal is sold or with whom it is exchanged, and

(iii) the means by which the person's name and address was verified,

(d) in the case of metal disposed of otherwise than by sale or exchange, its value immediately before its disposal as estimated by the dealer.

(5) The dealer must—

(a) keep separate records in relation to—
   (i) metal acquired, and
   (ii) metal processed or disposed of,
(b) record the information immediately after the metal is acquired, processed or disposed of,
(c) keep a copy of any document produced by a person to verify that person's name or address, and
(d) retain information recorded or documents kept under this section for a period of not less than 3 years beginning with the date on which the information was recorded or document obtained.

(6) The Scottish Ministers may by regulations—
(a) specify the means by which a person's name and address may be verified for the purposes of this section,
(b) require further information to be recorded about any metal acquired, processed or disposed of by metal dealers or itinerant metal dealers.

(7) Regulations under subsection (6)—
(a) may make different provision for different purposes, and
(b) are subject to the negative procedure.

NOTE

1. As inserted by the Air Weapons and Licensing (Scotland) Act 2015 (asp 10) Pt 3 s.70 (partially in force as of 1 December 2015).

Offences relating to metal dealing

34.—(1) Any metal dealer or itinerant metal dealer who disposes of metal to a person apparently under the age of 16 or who acquires metal from such a person, whether that person is acting on his own behalf or on behalf of another person, shall be guilty of an offence and liable, on summary conviction, to a fine not exceeding level 3 on the standard scale.

(2) In any proceedings for an offence under subsection (1) above, it shall be a defence to prove that the person to whom it is alleged the metal was disposed of or from whom it is alleged it was acquired was 16 years of age or over at the time.

(3) Any metal dealer or itinerant metal dealer who knowingly or recklessly furnishes false particulars under section 30 of this Act or, as the case may be, false information on any record or receipt which he is required by section 33 of this Act to keep shall be guilty of an offence and liable, on summary conviction, to a fine not exceeding level 4 on the standard scale.

(4) Any person who, when selling metal to or purchasing metal from a metal dealer or itinerant metal dealer, gives the dealer a false name or address shall be guilty of an offence and liable, on summary conviction, to a fine not exceeding level 3 on the standard scale.

Interpretation of section 28 to 36

37.—(1) In sections 28 to 36 of this Act—

"*itinerant metal dealer*" means a person who carries on a business which consists wholly or partly of buying and selling for scrap waste materials and old, broken, worn out, defaced or partly manufactured articles made wholly or partly of metal which he collects by means of visits from place to place and which he disposes of without causing them to be kept in a metal store or other premises (either by so keeping them himself, or by disposing of them or giving custody of them to a person who keeps a metal store);

"*metal*" means any metal (including any precious metal) and any alloy of any metals, whether old or new and includes manufactured articles, whether old or new, made wholly or partly of metal, of any of the materials commonly known as hard metal or of cemented or sintered metallic carbides;

"*metal dealer*" means a person carrying on business in terms of subsection (2) below but does not include an itinerant metal dealer within the meaning of this subsection;

"*metal store*" means a place where metal is received or kept in the course of a metal dealer's business;

"*processing*", in relation to metal, includes melting down and any process whereby the composition or form of the metal or of any article which is made of the metal is altered so as to make it substantially less identifiable than before the process, and "*process*" and "*processed*" shall be construed accordingly.

(2) For the purposes of sections 28 to 36 of this Act a person carries on business as a metal dealer if he carries on a business which consists wholly or partly of buying and selling for scrap old, broken, worn out, defaced or partly manufactured articles made wholly or partly of metal (whether the metal sold is in the form in which it was bought or otherwise), other than a business in the course of which metal is not bought except as materials for the manufacture of other articles and is not sold except as a by-product of such manufacture or as surplus materials bought but not required for such manufacture.

Exemptions

[1]**37A.**—(1) The Scottish Ministers may by regulations make provision specifying circumstances in which the provisions of sections 28 to 37 are not to apply.

(2) Regulations under subsection (1)—

(a) may make transitional, transitory or saving provision,

(b) are subject to the negative procedure.

NOTE

1. As inserted by the Air Weapons and Licensing (Scotland) Act 2015 (asp 10) Pt 3 s.70 (partially in force as of 1 December 2015).

Miscellaneous licences

Public entertainment licences

41.—(1) A licence, to be known as a "*public entertainment licence*", shall be required for the use of premises as a place of public entertainment.

[3](2) In this section, "*place of public entertainment*" means any place where members of the public are admitted or may use any facilities for the purposes of entertainment or recreation but does not include—

(a) an athletic or sports ground while being used as such;

(aa) premises in respect of which a licence is required under section 41A of this Act while such premises are being used for the purposes mentioned in that section;

(b) an educational establishment while being used as such;

(c) premises belonging to or occupied by any religious body while being used wholly or mainly for purposes connected with that body;

[3](d) premises licensed under the Theatres Act 1968, or section 1 of the Cinemas Act 1985;

[3](e) premises in respect of which there is a club gaming permit (within the meaning of section 271 of the Gambling Act 2005 (c.19)) or a prize gaming permit (within the meaning of section 289 of that Act of 2005);

[1,3](f) licensed premises within the meaning of the Licensing (Scotland) Act 2005 (asp 16) in which public entertainment is being provided during licensed hours within the meaning of that Act;

[3](g) premises in which machines for entertainment or amusement are being provided incidentally to the main purpose or use of the premises where that main purpose or use is not as a place of public entertainment; or

[3](h) such other premises as the Scottish Ministers may by order made by statutory instrument specify.

[3](2A) A statutory instrument containing an order made under subsection (2)(h) is subject to annulment in pursuance of a resolution of the Scottish Parliament.

[2](3) Without prejudice to section 3B of and paragraph 5 of Schedule 1 to this Act, a licensing authority may attach conditions to a public entertainment licence—

(a) restricting the use of the premises to a specified kind or specified kinds of entertainment or recreation;

(b) limiting the number of persons to be admitted to the premises;

(c) fixing the days and times when the premises may be open for the purposes of the entertainment or recreation.

(4) In this section, "*educational establishment*" has the meaning given by paragraphs (i) and (ii) of the definition of that expression in section 135(1) of the Education (Scotland) Act 1980 but includes a university and a theological college.

NOTES

1. As amended by the Licensing (Scotland) Act 2005 (asp 16) Sch.6 para.6 (effective 1 September 2009).

2. As amended by the Criminal Justice and Licensing (Scotland) Act 2010 (asp 13) Pt 8 s.172 (effective 28 March 2011).

3. As amended by the Criminal Justice and Licensing (Scotland) Act 2010 (asp 13) Pt 8 s.176 (effective 1 April 2012).

PART III

CONTROL OF SEX SHOPS AND SEXUAL ENTERTAINMENT VENUES

Control of sex shops

45.—(1) A local authority may resolve that Schedule 2 to this Act shall have effect in their area; and if they do so resolve that Schedule shall have such effect as from the day specified in that behalf in the resolution (which must not be before the expiration of the period of one month beginning with the day on which the resolution is passed).

(2) A local authority shall, not later than 28 days before the day specified in the resolution for the coming into effect of Schedule 2 to this Act in the

authority's area, publish notice that they have passed a resolution under this section in a newspaper circulating in their area.

(3) The notice shall state the general effect of that Schedule.

Licensing of sexual entertainment venues: interpretation

[1]**45A.**—(1) This section applies for the purposes of the interpretation of section 45B and Schedule 2 (as modified for the purposes of section 45B).

(2) "*Sexual entertainment venue*" means any premises at which sexual entertainment is provided before a live audience for (or with a view to) the financial gain of the organiser.

(3) For the purposes of that definition—

"*audience*" includes an audience of one,

"*financial gain*" includes financial gain arising directly or indirectly from the provision of the sexual entertainment,

"*organiser*", in relation to the provision of sexual entertainment in premises, means—

(a) the person ("A") who is responsible for—

(i) the management of the premises, or

(ii) the organisation or management of the sexual entertainment, or

(b) where A exercises that responsibility on behalf of another person (whether by virtue of a contract of employment or otherwise), that other person,

"*premises*" includes any vehicle, vessel or stall but does not include any private dwelling to which the public is not admitted,

"*sexual entertainment*" means—

(a) any live performance, or

(b) any live display of nudity,

which is of such a nature that, ignoring financial gain, it must reasonably be assumed to be provided solely or principally for the purpose of sexually stimulating any member of the audience (whether by verbal or other means).

(4) For the purposes of the definition of "*sexual entertainment*", "*display of nudity*" means—

(a) in the case of a woman, the showing of (to any extent and by any means) her nipples, pubic area, genitals or anus,

(b) in the case of a man, the showing of (to any extent and by any means) his pubic area, genitals or anus.

(5) Sexual entertainment is provided if (and only if) it is provided (or allowed to be provided) by or on behalf of the organiser.

(6) References in Schedule 2 (as modified for the purposes of section 45B) to the use of any premises by a person as a sexual entertainment venue are to be read as references to their use by the organiser.

(7) The following are not sexual entertainment venues—

(a) a sex shop (within the meaning of paragraph 2(1) of Schedule 2),

(b) such other premises as the Scottish Ministers may by order specify.

(8) An order under subsection (7)(b) may make different provision for different purposes.

(9) Premises at which sexual entertainment is provided as mentioned in subsection (2) on a particular occasion ("the current occasion") are not to be treated as a sexual entertainment venue if sexual entertainment has not been provided on more than 3 previous occasions which fall wholly or partly within the period of 12 months ending with the start of the current occasion.

(10) For the purposes of subsection (9)—

(a) each continuous period during which sexual entertainment is provided on the premises is to be treated as a separate occasion, and
(b) where the period during which sexual entertainment is provided on the premises exceeds 24 hours, each period of 24 hours (and any part of a period of 24 hours) is to be treated as a separate occasion.

(11) The Scottish Ministers may by order provide for—
(a) descriptions of performances, or
(b) descriptions of displays of nudity,
which are not to be treated as sexual entertainment for the purposes of this section.

(12) An order under subsection (7)(b) or (11) is subject to the negative procedure.

NOTE
1. As inserted by the Air Weapons and Licensing (Scotland) Act 2015 (asp 10) Pt 3 s.76 (partially in force as of 1 December 2015).

Mandatory licence conditions

[1]**45E.**—(1) The Scottish Ministers may by order prescribe conditions to which licences granted by local authorities under this Part are to be subject.

(2) Different conditions may be prescribed under subsection (1)—
(a) in respect of different licences or different types of licence,
(b) otherwise for different purposes, circumstances or cases.

(3) An order under subsection (1) is subject to the affirmative procedure.

(4) Subsection (1) does not affect any other power of the Scottish Ministers under this Act or any other enactment to prescribe conditions—
(a) to which licences granted by local authorities under this Part are to be subject, or
(b) to be imposed by local authorities in granting or renewing licences under this Part.

(5) The following conditions are referred to in this Part as "*mandatory conditions*"—
(a) conditions prescribed under subsection (1),
(b) conditions prescribed under any power referred to in subsection (4), and
(c) conditions imposed, or required to be imposed, by any provision of this Part.

(6) In this section and section 45F, references to licences granted by local authorities include references to—
(a) licences renewed by local authorities, and
(b) licences deemed by virtue of section 45D to have been granted or renewed by local authorities.

NOTE
1. As inserted by the Air Weapons and Licensing (Scotland) Act 2015 (asp 10) Pt 3 s.76 (partially in force as of 1 December 2015).

SCHEDULE 1

LICENSING—FURTHER PROVISIONS AS TO THE GENERAL SYSTEM

Objections and representations

3.— (1) Any objection or representation relating to an application for the grant or renewal of a licence shall, subject to sub-paragraph (2) below, be entertained by the licensing authority if, but only if, the objection or representation—

(a) is in writing;

(b) specifies the grounds of the objection or, as the case may be, the nature of the representation;

(c) specifies the name and address of the person making it;

(d) is signed by him or on his behalf;

[1](e) was made to them within 28 days of whichever is the later or, as the case may be, latest of the following dates—

(i) where public notice of the application was given under paragraph 2(7) above, the date when it was first so given;

(ii) where the application relates to a licence for an activity which is wholly or mainly to be carried out in premises and the authority have specified a date under paragraph 2(6) above, that date;

(iii) in any other case, the date when the application was made to them.

(2) Notwithstanding sub-paragraph (1)(e) above, it shall be competent for a licensing authority to entertain an objection or representation received by them before they take a final decision upon the application to which it relates if they are satisfied that there is sufficient reason why it was not made in the time required under that sub-paragraph.

(3) An objection or representation shall be made for the purposes of sub-paragraph (1) above if it is delivered by hand within the time there specified to the licensing authority or posted (by registered or recorded delivery post) so that in the normal course of post it might be expected to be delivered to them within that time.

(4) The licensing authority shall send a copy of any relevant objection or representation (within the meaning of paragraph 19 below) to the applicant to whose application it relates.

NOTE

1. As amended by the Criminal Justice and Licensing (Scotland) Act 2010 (asp 13) Pt 8 s.178 (effective 28 February 2011 for purposes specified in SSI 2010/413 Sch.1; not yet in force otherwise).

Disposal of applications for the grant and renewal of licences

5.—(1) Where an application for the grant or renewal of a licence has been made to a licensing authority they shall, in accordance with this paragraph—

[2](a) grant or renew the licence;

(b) [*As repealed by the Criminal Justice and Licensing (Scotland) Act 2010 (asp 13) Pt 8 s.172 (effective 28 March 2011).*]

(c) refuse to grant or renew the licence.

[2](1A) In granting or renewing a licence under sub-paragraph (1)(a), a licensing authority may (either or both)—

(a) disapply or vary any standard conditions so far as applicable to the licence,

(b) impose conditions in addition to any mandatory or standard conditions to which the licence is subject.

[1,2](2) Subject to sub-paragraph (2A), the conditions referred to in sub-paragraph (1A)(b) above shall be such reasonable conditions as the licensing authority think fit and, without prejudice to that generality, may include—

(a) conditions restricting the validity of a licence to an area or areas specified in the licence; and

(b) in relation to the grant of a licence, where that licence is intended to replace an existing licence, a condition requiring the holder of the existing licence to surrender it in accordance with paragraph 13 below.

[2](2AA) A variation made under sub-paragraph (1A)(a) or condition imposed under sub-paragraph (1A)(b) has no effect so far as it is inconsistent with any mandatory condition to which the licence is subject.

[1](2A) The conditions referred to in sub-paragraph (1)(b) above shall not relate to any matter in relation to which requirements or prohibitions are or could be imposed by virtue of Part 3 of the Fire (Scotland) Act 2005 (asp 5).

(3) A licensing authority shall refuse an application to grant or renew a licence if, in their opinion—

(a) the applicant or, where the applicant is not a natural person, any director of it or partner in it or any other person responsible for its management, is either—

(i) for the time being disqualified under section 7(6) of this Act, or

(ii) not a fit and proper person to be the holder of the licence;

(b) the activity to which it relates would be managed by or carried on for the benefit of a person, other than the applicant, who would be refused the grant or renewal of such a licence if he made the application himself;

(c) where the licence applied for relates to an activity consisting of or including the use of premises or a vehicle or vessel, those premises are not or, as the case may be, that vehicle or vessel is not suitable or convenient for the conduct of the activity having regard to—

(i) the location, character or condition of the premises or the character or condition of the vehicle or vessel;

(ii) the nature and extent of the proposed activity;

(iii) the kind of persons likely to be in the premises, vehicle or vessel;

(iv) the possibility of undue public nuisance; or

(v) public order or public safety; or

(d) there is other good reason for refusing the application;

and otherwise shall grant the application.

(4) A licensing authority shall not, in a case where a certificate falls to be submitted to them under paragraph 2(4) above, reach a final decision under this paragraph in respect of the application to which the certificate relates until it has been so submitted.

(5) A licensing authority shall in accordance with sub-paragraph (6) below, notify their decision under sub-paragraph (1) above to—

(a) the applicant;

(b) the chief constable;

(c) any person who made a relevant objection or representation (within the meaning of paragraph 19 below) in relation to the application; and

[1](d) where the application was for a licence for an activity wholly or mainly to be carried on —

(a) in premises to which Part 3 of the Fire (Scotland) Act 2005 (asp 5) applies, the enforcing authority;

[3](b) in any other premises, the Scottish Fire and Rescue Service.

(6) Notification shall be made under sub-paragraph (5)(a), (b) or (d) above within 7 days of the decision to be notified by sending to the person concerned written notice of the decision and under sub-paragraph (5)(c) above either by so doing or by publishing, within that time, in a newspaper circulating in the area of the licensing authority, notice of the decision.

(7) A licensing authority shall make out and deliver a licence to every person to whom a licence is granted or whose licence is renewed by the authority, and shall when requested by any such person and on payment of such fee as they may charge under paragraph 15 below, make out a duplicate of any licence issued under this sub-paragraph and certify such duplicate to be a true copy of that original licence; and any document purporting to be so certified by the proper officer of the authority shall be sufficient evidence of the terms of that licence.

(8) Where a licensing authority grant a licence in respect of which an employee or agent has been named under paragraph 1(2)(b) or (c)(iv) above, the licence shall be granted jointly in the names of the applicant and of the employee or agent, and in such a case any reference in this Schedule or in Part I or II of this Act to the holder of a licence includes a reference to one or both of those persons, as the case may require.

NOTES

1. As amended by the Fire (Scotland) Act 2005 (Consequential Modifications and Savings) Order 2006 (SSI 2006/475) Sch.1 para.11 (effective 1 October 2006).

2. As amended by the Criminal Justice and Licensing (Scotland) Act 2010 (asp 13) Pt 8 s.172 (effective 28 March 2011).

3. As amended by the Police and Fire Reform (Scotland) Act 2012 (asp 8) Sch.7(2) para.53 (effective 1 April 2013).

Temporary licences

7.—(1) A licensing authority may grant a licence to have effect for such period not exceeding 6 weeks from its being granted as they may determine, and such a licence shall be known as a "*temporary licence*".

(2) This Schedule shall apply with the modifications specified in sub-paragraphs (3) to (5) below in relation to applications for temporary licences.

[1](3) Paragraph 1(3), 2 to 4, and 5(1), (2), (2A) and (4) to (6) shall not apply, but in relation to each application for a temporary licence the licensing authority—

[1](a) shall consult the chief constable and, where the application relates to an activity wholly or mainly to be carried on —

(i) in premises to which Part 3 of the Fire (Scotland) Act 2005 (asp 5) applies, the enforcing authority;

[2](ii) in any other premises, the Scottish Fire and Rescue Service; and

[1](b) may, subject to sub-paragraph (3A) below, grant it subject to such conditions as they think fit.

[1](3A) The conditions referred to in paragraph (b) of sub-paragraph (3) above shall not relate to any matter in relation to which requirements or prohibitions are or could be imposed by virtue of Part 3 of the Fire (Scotland) Act 2005 (asp 5).

(4) Paragraph 6 shall not apply so as to prevent a licensing authority from entertaining an application for the grant of a licence where they have, within one year, refused an application from the same applicant for a temporary licence for the same activity.

(5) Paragraph 8, 9, 10 and 18 shall not apply.

(6) A temporary licence shall not be capable of being renewed but, where the holder of or the applicant for a temporary licence has also made an application for a licence under paragraph 1 above in respect of the same activity, the temporary licence, if granted, shall continue to have effect until—

(a) the licence applied for under paragraph 1 has been granted, whether as a result of an appeal under paragraph 18 below or not, or has been deemed to have been granted; or

(b) where the licensing authority have refused that application, the time within which an appeal under paragraph 18 below against that decision may be made has elapsed; or

(c) when such an appeal has been lodged, it has been abandoned or determined.

NOTES

1. As amended by the Fire (Scotland) Act 2005 (Consequential Modifications and Savings) Order 2006 (SSI 2006/475) Sch.1 para.11 (effective 1 October 2006).

2. As amended by the Police and Fire Reform (Scotland) Act 2012 (asp 8) Sch.7(2) para.53 (effective 1 April 2013).

Variation and suspension of licences

10.—(1) A licensing authority may, at any time, whether or not upon an application made to them by the holder of the licence, vary the terms of a licence on any grounds they think fit.

(2) A licensing authority, before proceeding to vary the terms of a licence under sub-paragraph (1) above—

[2](a) shall, not later than 7 days before the day on which the proposed variation is to be considered, notify the holder of the licence, the chief constable and, where the licence relates to an activity wholly or mainly carried on in premises, the Scottish Fire and Rescue Service of the proposed variation; and

[1](b) shall give each of the persons required to be notified under sub-sub-paragraph (a) above an opportunity to be heard by the authority on that day.

[1,2](2A) Where the premises mentioned in sub-paragraph (2)(a) above are premises to which Part 3 of the Fire (Scotland) Act 2005 (asp 5) applies, that sub-paragraph applies as if the reference to the Scottish Fire and Rescue Service were a reference to the enforcing authority.

(3) A licensing authority shall have complied with sub-paragraph (2)(b) above if they have invited each of the persons whom they must notify under that sub-paragraph to attend and to be heard by the authority when the variation of the licence is to be considered.

[1](4) A licensing authority shall, within 7 days of their decision under sub-paragraph (1) above, send written notice of their decision to the holder of the licence and the chief constable and, where the licence relates to an activity wholly or mainly carried on—

(a) in premises to which Part 3 of the Fire (Scotland) Act 2005 (asp 5) applies, the enforcing authority;

[2](b) in any other premises, to the Scottish Fire and Rescue Service.

(5) A variation in the terms of a licence shall come into force—

(a) when the time within which an appeal under paragraph 18 below may be made has elapsed; or
(b) where such an appeal has been lodged, when the appeal has been abandoned or determined in favour of the variation.

NOTES

1. As amended by the Fire (Scotland) Act 2005 (Consequential Modifications and Savings) Order 2006 (SSI 2006/475) Sch.1 para.11 (effective 1 October 2006).

2. As amended by the Police and Fire Reform (Scotland) Act 2012 (asp 8) Sch.7(2) para.53 (effective 1 April 2013).

11.—[3](1) A licensing authority may, whether upon a complaint made to them or not, suspend or revoke a licence in accordance with the provisions of this paragraph.

(2) A licensing authority may order the suspension of a licence if in their opinion—

(a) the holder of the licence or, where the holder is not a natural person, any director of it or partner in it or any other person responsible for its management, is not or is no longer a fit and proper person to hold the licence;
(b) the activity to which the licence relates is being managed by or carried on for the benefit of a person, other than the licence holder, who would have been refused the grant or renewal of the licence under paragraph 5(3) above;
(c) the carrying on of the activity to which the licence relates has caused, is causing or is likely to cause undue public nuisance or a threat to public order or public safety;
(d) a condition of the licence has been contravened.

(3) A licensing authority may make an order under sub-paragraph (2)(d) above in respect of a contravention of a condition of a licence notwithstanding that there has been no conviction in that respect.

(4) In considering whether to suspend a licence the licensing authority may—

(a) have regard to—
    (i) any misconduct on the part of the holder of the licence, whether or not constituting a breach of any provision of Part I or II of this Act or this Schedule, which in the opinion of the authority has a bearing on his fitness to hold a licence;
    (ii) where the licence relates to an activity consisting of or including the use of premises or a vehicle or vessel, any misconduct on the part of persons frequenting or using the premises, vehicle or vessel occurring there or any misconduct in the immediate vicinity of the premises, vehicle or vessel which is attributable to those persons;
(b) make such reasonable inquiries as they think fit and, subject to sub-paragraph (5) below, include the results of their inquiries in the matters to which they have regard in such consideration.

(5) Where a licensing authority intend to include any of the results of their inquiries under sub-paragraph (4)(b) above in the matters to which they have regard for the purposes of sub-paragraph (4) above, they shall notify the holder of the licence of that intention.

(6) A licensing authority may, whether upon an application made to them or not, recall an order made under this paragraph.

[1](7) A licensing authority in considering whether or not to suspend or revoke a licence may, but before deciding to do so shall, give—

(a) the holder of the licence;
(b) any person who has made a complaint relevant to the matters to be considered at the hearing;
(c) the chief constable; and
(d) where the licence relates to an activity wholly or mainly carried on—
  (a) in premises to which Part 3 of the Fire (Scotland) Act 2005 (asp 5) applies, the enforcing authority;
  [2](b) in any other premises, the Scottish Fire and Rescue Service,

an opportunity to be heard by the licensing authority.

(8) The licensing authority shall have complied with their duty under sub-paragraph (7) above if they have caused to be sent to the persons entitled under that sub-paragraph to an opportunity to be heard, not later than 14 days before the hearing, notice in writing that the authority propose to hold a hearing, together with a copy of any complaints relevant to the matters to be considered at the hearing and a note of the grounds upon which the suspension of the licence is to be considered and, where they decide to exercise their power under that sub-paragraph, they shall cause such notice, copy and note to be sent to those persons not later than that time.

(9) Where a licensing authority decide to order the suspension of a licence, the suspension shall not, subject to sub-paragraph (10) below, take effect until the expiry of the time within which the holder of the licence may appeal under paragraph 18 below against the suspension or revocation as the case may be, if such an appeal has been lodged, until it has been abandoned or determined in favour of the suspension.

(10) If, in deciding to order the suspension of a licence, a licensing authority determine that the circumstances of the case justify immediate suspension they may, without prejudice to their other powers under this paragraph, order that the licence shall be suspended or revocation immediately.

(11) The period of suspension of a licence under this paragraph shall be the unexpired portion of the duration of the licence, or such shorter period as the licensing authority may fix; and the effect of suspension shall be that the licence shall cease to have effect during the period of the suspension.

(12) A licensing authority shall, within 7 days of their decision under sub-paragraph (1) above, send written notice of their decision to the persons referred to in sub-paragraph 7(a), (c) and (d) above in relation to the licence and to any person who, in pursuance of sub-paragraph (7)(b) above, was heard by the authority before they reached that decision.

NOTES

1. As amended by the Fire (Scotland) Act 2005 (Consequential Modifications and Savings) Order 2006 (SSI 2006/475) Sch.1 para.11 (effective 1 October 2006).

2. As amended by the Police and Fire Reform (Scotland) Act 2012 (asp 8) Sch.7(2) para.53 (effective 1 April 2013).

12.—(1) A licensing authority shall, whether upon a complaint made to them or not, order the suspension under this paragraph of a licence if they are of the opinion that the carrying on of the activity to which the licence relates is causing or is likely to cause a serious threat to public order or public safety.

(2) In considering whether to suspend a licence under this paragraph, a licensing authority may make such reasonable inquiries as they think fit and include the results of their inquiries in the matters to which they have regard in such consideration.

(3) Where a licensing authority intend to include any of the results of their inquiries under sub-paragraph (2) above in the matters to which they have regard for the purposes of this paragraph they shall notify the holder of the licence of that intention.

[1](4) A licensing authority shall, before reaching a decision on the question whether or not to suspend a licence under this paragraph, consult the chief constable and, where the licence relates to an activity wholly or mainly carried on—

(a) in premises to which Part 3 of the Fire (Scotland) Act 2005 (asp 5) applies, the enforcing authority;

[2](b) in any other premises the Scottish Fire and Rescue Service.

(5) An order under this paragraph suspending a licence shall have effect from the date on which it is made until whichever is the earlier of the following two dates—

(a) a date six weeks after the order was made;

(b) the date of any decision of the licensing authority whether or not to suspend the licence under paragraph 11 above.

(6) A licensing authority may, whether upon an application made to them or not, recall an order made under this paragraph.

[1](7) A licensing authority shall, within 7 days of their decision under sub-paragraph (1) or (6) above, send written notice of their decision to the holder of the licence, the chief constable and, where the licence relates to an activity wholly or mainly carried on—

(a) in premises to which Part 3 of the Fire (Scotland) Act 2005 (asp 5) applies, the enforcing authority;

[2](b) in any other premises, to the Scottish Fire and Rescue Service.

NOTES

1. As amended by the Fire (Scotland) Act 2005 (Consequential Modifications and Savings) Order 2006 (SSI 2006/475) Sch.1 para.11 (effective 1 October 2006).

2. As amended by the Police and Fire Reform (Scotland) Act 2012 (asp 8) Sch.7(2) para.53 (effective 1 April 2013).

Supplementary

13.—(1) A holder of a licence may at any time surrender the licence to the licensing authority and it shall thereupon cease to have effect.

(2) A holder of a licence shall deliver the licence to the licensing authority—

[1](a) within 7 days after the coming into effect of a decision of a licensing authority to suspend, revoke or vary the terms of the licence or of a court, under section 7(6)(a) of this Act, to revoke it;

(b) where the licence relates to an activity which he has given up.

[1](3) A licensing authority shall, on making an order suspending or revoking a licence or on deciding to vary the terms of a licence, cause notice in writing to be given to the holder of the licence of his duty to deliver it under sub-paragraph (2) above.

[1](4) Where a licence has been surrendered under this paragraph on its suspension or revocation under section 7(6)(a) of this Act or its suspension under this Schedule and the revocation or suspension is quashed or recalled the licensing authority shall re-issue the licence.

14.—(1) A licensing authority shall cause to be kept a register of applications under this Schedule (in this paragraph referred to as "the register") and shall, as soon as reasonably practicable after—

(a) the receipt of each application, cause details of such receipt; and

(b) their final decision on each application, cause details of that decision

to be entered in the register.

(2) The register shall include—

(a) a note of the kind and terms of each licence granted by the licensing authority;

[1](b) a note of any suspension, revocation or variation of the terms, or surrender, of a licence.

(3) The register shall be open to the inspection of any member of the public at such reasonable times and places as may be determined by the licensing authority and any member of the public may make a copy thereof or an extract therefrom.

(4) A licensing authority may, on payment of such fee as they may charge under paragraph 15 below, issue a certified true copy of any entry in the register; and any document purporting to be certified by the proper officer of the licensing authority as a true copy of an entry shall be sufficient evidence of the terms of the original entry.

Notification of the decisions and giving of reasons

17.—(1) A licensing authority shall, within 10 days of being required to do so under sub-paragraph (2) below, give reasons in writing for arriving at any decision of theirs under this Schedule—

(a) to grant or renew a licence or to refuse to do so;

(b) to consent or to refuse to consent to a material change in any premises, vehicle or vessel;

(c) to vary or refuse to vary the terms of a licence;

(d) in relation to paragraph 11 above—

(i) to suspend a licence or to refuse to do so;

(ii) as to the period of suspension;

(iii) ordering immediate suspension;

(e) to suspend a licence under paragraph 12 above or to refuse to do so.

(2) Reasons for a decision referred to in sub-paragraph (1) above shall be given by the licensing authority on a request being made to the authority by a relevant person within 21 days of the date of the decision.

(3) Nothing in this paragraph affects the power of the sheriff under paragraph 18 below to require a licensing authority to give reasons for a decision of the authority—

(a) which is being appealed to the sheriff under that paragraph; and

(b) for which reasons have not been given under this paragraph.

(4) In this paragraph, "*relevant person*" means—

(a) in respect of a decision specified in sub-paragraph (1)(a) above, the applicant or any person who made a relevant objection or representation (within the meaning of paragraph 19 below) in relation to the application to which the decision relates;

(b) in respect of a decision specified in sub-paragraphs (1)(b) to (e) above, the holder of the licence or the chief constable;

[1](c) in respect of a decision specified in sub-paragraphs (1)(b) to (e) above which relates to an activity wholly or mainly carried on —

(i) in premises to which Part 3 of the Fire (Scotland) Act 2005 (asp 5) applies, the enforcing authority;

[2](ii) in any other premises, the Scottish Fire and Rescue Service;

[1](d) in respect of a decision to consent or to refuse to consent to a material change—

(i) in premises to which Part 3 of the Fire (Scotland) Act 2005 (asp 5) applies, the enforcing authority;

[2](ii) in any other premises, the Scottish Fire and Rescue Service; and

(e) in respect of a decision specified in sub-paragraph (1)(d) above, any person who, in pursuance of paragraph 11(7)(b) above, was heard by the licensing authority.

NOTES

1. As amended by the Fire (Scotland) Act 2005 (Consequential Modifications and Savings) Order 2006 (SSI 2006/475) Sch.1 para.11 (effective 1 October 2006).

2. As amended by the Police and Fire Reform (Scotland) Act 2012 (asp 8) Sch.7 para.53 (effective 1 April 2013).

Appeals

18.—(1) Subject to sub-paragraph (2) below, a person who may, under this Schedule, require a licensing authority to give him reasons for their decision may appeal to the sheriff against that decision.

(2) A person shall be entitled to appeal under this paragraph only if he has followed all such procedures under this Schedule for stating his case to the licensing authority as have been made available to him.

(3) A licensing authority may be a party to an appeal under this paragraph.

(4) An appeal under this paragraph shall be made by way of summary application and shall be lodged with the sheriff clerk within 28 days from the date of the decision appealed against.

(5) On good cause being shown, the sheriff may hear an appeal under this paragraph notwithstanding that it was not lodged within the time mentioned in sub-paragraph (4) above.

(6) For the purposes of an appeal under this paragraph, the sheriff may, in the case of a decision of a licensing authority for which reasons have not been given by the authority under paragraph 17 above, require the authority to give reasons for that decision, and the authority shall comply with such a requirement.

(7) The sheriff may uphold an appeal under this paragraph only if he considers that the licensing authority, in arriving at their decision—

(a) erred in law;

(b) based their decision on any incorrect material fact;

(c) acted contrary to natural justice; or

(d) exercised their discretion in an unreasonable manner.

(8) In considering an appeal under this paragraph, the sheriff may hear evidence by or on behalf of any party to the appeal.

(9) On upholding an appeal under this paragraph, the sheriff may—

(a) remit the case with the reasons for his decision to the licensing authority for reconsideration of their decision; or

(b) reverse or modify the decision of the authority, and on remitting a case under sub-sub-paragraph (a) above, the sheriff may—

(i) specify a date by which the reconsideration by the authority must take place;

(ii) modify any procedural steps which otherwise would be required in relation to the matter by or under any enactment (including this Act).

(10) In considering an appeal under this paragraph against suspension of a licence the sheriff may, pending his decision on the appeal, order the recall of any order by the licensing authority under paragraph 11(10) above that

the suspension be immediate or of any order made by the authority under paragraph 12 above but he shall not do so unless he is satisfied that all steps which in the circumstances were reasonable have been taken with a view to securing that notice of the appeal and an opportunity of being heard with respect to it have been given to the authority.

(11) The sheriff may include in his decision on an appeal under this paragraph such order as to the expenses of the appeal as he thinks proper.

(12) Any party to an appeal to the sheriff under this paragraph may appeal on a point of law from the sheriff's decision to the Court of Session within 28 days from the date of that decision.

Schedule 2

Control of sex shops and sexual entertainment venues

Objections and representations

8.—[2](1) The local authority shall, as soon as an application for the grant or renewal of a licence under this Schedule is made to them, send a copy of the application to the chief constable and—

(a) where Part 3 of the Fire (Scotland) Act 2005 (asp 5) applies to the premises, vehicle vessel or stall to which the licence relates, to the enforcing authority;

[4](b) where Part 3 of that Act does not so apply, to the Scottish Fire and Rescue Service.

[1](2) Any objection or representation relating to an application for the grant or renewal of a licence under this Schedule shall, subject to sub-paragraph (3) below, be entertained by the local authority if, but only if, the objection or representation—

(a) is in writing;

(b) specifies the grounds of the objection or, as the case may be, the nature of the representation;

(c) specifies the name and address of the person making it;

(d) is signed by him or on his behalf;

(e) was made to them within 28 days of whichever is the later or, as the case may be, latest of the following dates—

(i) the date of submission to them of the application;

(ii) the date when public advertisement was first given under paragraph 7(2) above;

[1](iii) the date, if any, specified by the local authority under paragraph 7(10) above.

[1](3) Notwithstanding sub-paragraph (2)(e) above, it shall be competent for a local authority to entertain an objection or representation received by them before they take a final decision upon the application to which it relates if they are satisfied that there is sufficient reason why it was not made in the time required under that sub-paragraph.

[1](4) An objection or representation shall be made for the purposes of sub-paragraph (2) above if it is delivered by hand within the time there specified to the local authority or posted (by registered or recorded delivery post) so that in the normal course of post it might be expected to be delivered to them within that time.

[1](5) Where the local authority receive notice of a relevant objection or representation they shall, before considering the application, give notice in writing of the general terms of the objection or representation to the

applicant but they shall not without the consent of the person making the objection or representation reveal his name or address to the applicant.

[1](6) In considering an application for the grant or renewal of a licence under this Schedule, a local authority may make such reasonable inquiries as they think fit and include the results of these inquiries in matters they take into account, but where they intend so to include any of these results they shall notify the applicant of that intention.

[1,3](7) A local authority may, before reaching a final decision upon such an application, give the applicant and any person who has made a relevant objection or representation an opportunity to be heard by them and, where they propose to do so, must, within such reasonable period (not being less than 14 days) of the date of the hearing, notify the applicant and each such person of that date.

[1](8) A local authority shall not reach a final decision upon such an application—

(a) in relation to which a relevant objection or representation has been made to them, or in relation to which they intend to take into account any result of their inquiries under sub-paragraph (6) above; and

(b) in respect of which they have not, under this paragraph, given the applicant and any person who has made such objection or representation an opportunity to be heard,

unless they have given the applicant an opportunity to notify them in writing of his views on such objection or representation or, as the case may be, result within such reasonable period (not being less than 7 days) as they may specify.

NOTES

1. As amended by the Local Government etc. (Scotland) Act 1994 (c.39) Sch.13 para.129 (effective 1 April 1996).

2. As amended by the Fire (Scotland) Act 2005 (Consequential Modifications and Savings) Order 2006 (SSI 2006/475) Sch.1 para.11 (effective 1 October 2006).

3. As amended by the Criminal Justice and Licensing (Scotland) Act 2010 (asp 13) Pt 8 s.178 (effective 28 February 2011 for purposes specified in SSI 2010/413 Sch.1; not yet in force otherwise).

4. As amended by the Police and Fire Reform (Scotland) Act 2012 (asp 8) Sch.7 para.53 (effective 1 April 2013).

Disposal of applications for licences

9.—[1](1) Where an application for the grant or renewal of a licence under this Schedule has been made to a local authority they shall, in accordance with this paragraph—

(a) grant or renew the licence unconditionally;

(b) grant or renew the licence subject to conditions; or

(c) refuse to grant or renew the licence.

[1,2](2) Subject to sub-paragraph (2A) the conditions referred to in sub-paragraph (1) above shall be such reasonable conditions as the local authority think fit and, without prejudice to that generality, may include conditions regulating—

(a) the hours of opening and closing of sex shops;

(b) displays or advertisements on or in such shops;

(c) the visibility of the interior of sex shops to passers by.

[2](2A) The conditions referred to in sub-paragraph (1) above shall not relate to any matter in relation to which requirements or prohibitions are or could be imposed by virtue of Part 3 of the Fire (Scotland) Act 2005 (asp 5).

(3) A licence under this Schedule shall not be granted—

(a) to a person under the age of 18;

(b) to a person who is for the time being disqualified under paragraph 13(10) or 19(5) below;

(c) to a person other than a natural person if any director of it or partner in it or any other person responsible for its management is disqualified under paragraph 13(10) or 19(5) below;

(d) to a person who has been convicted of an offence under paragraphs 19 to 21 below;

[3](e) to a person who is not resident in a member state of the European Union or was not so resident throughout the period of six months immediately preceding the date when the application was made;

[3](f) to a body corporate which is not incorporated in a member state of the European Union;

[1](g) to a person who has, within the period of 12 months immediately preceding the date when the application was made, been refused by the same local authority the grant or renewal of a licence under this Schedule for the premises, vehicle, vessel or stall in respect of which the application is made, unless the refusal has been reversed on appeal; or

[1](h) to a person other than a natural person if any director of it or partner in it or any other person responsible for its management has, within that period, been refused by the same local authority the grant or renewal of such a licence, unless the refusal has been reversed on appeal.

[1](4) But without prejudice to sub-paragraph (3) above, the local authority shall refuse an application for the grant or renewal of a licence if, in their opinion, one or more of the grounds specified in sub-paragraph (5) below apply.

(5) The grounds mentioned in sub-paragraph (4) above are—

(a) that the applicant or, where the applicant is a person other than a natural person, any director of it or any partner in it or any person responsible for its management, is unsuitable to hold the licence by reason of having been convicted of an offence or for any other reason;

(b) that, if the licence were to be granted or renewed, the business to which it relates would be managed by or carried on for the benefit of a person, other than the applicant, who would be refused the grant or renewal of such a licence if he made the application himself;

[1](c) that the number of sex shops in the relevant locality at the time the application is made is equal to or exceeds the number which the local authority consider is appropriate for that locality;

(d) that the grant or renewal of the licence would be inappropriate, having regard—

(i) to the character of the relevant locality; or

(ii) to the use to which any premises in the vicinity are put; or

(iii) to the layout, character or condition of the premises, vehicle, vessel or stall in respect of which the application is made.

(6) Nil may be an appropriate number for the purposes of sub-paragraph (5)(c) above.

(7) In this paragraph "*the relevant locality*" means—

(a) in relation to premises, the locality where they are situated; and

(b) in relation to a vehicle, vessel or stall, any locality where it is desired to use it as a sex shop.

NOTES

1. As amended by the Local Government etc. (Scotland) Act 1994 (c.39) Sch.13 para.129 (effective 1 April 1996).

2. As amended by the Fire (Scotland) Act 2005 (Consequential Modifications and Savings) Order 2006 (SSI 2006/475) Sch.1 para.11 (effective 1 October 2006).

3. As amended by the Criminal Justice and Licensing (Scotland) Act 2010 (asp 13) Pt 8 s.178 (effective 28 February 2011 for purposes specified in SSI 2010/413 Sch.1; not yet in force otherwise).

Variation of licences

15.—[1](1) A local authority may, at any time, whether or not upon an application made to them by the holder of the licence, vary the terms of a licence on any grounds they think fit and such variation shall come into force on such date as they may specify.

[1](2) A local authority, before proceeding to vary the terms of a licence under sub-paragraph (1) above—

[3](a) shall, not later than 7 days before the day on which the proposed variation is to be considered, notify the holder of the licence, the chief constable and the Scottish Fire and Rescue Service of the proposed variation; and

[1](b) shall give each of the persons mentioned in sub-paragraph (a) above an opportunity to be heard by the authority on that day.

[2,3](2A) Where the proposed variation is in respect of a licence which relates to any premises, vehicle, vessel or stall to which Part 3 of the Fire (Scotland) Act 2005 (asp 5) applies, sub-paragraph (2)(a) above applies as if the reference to the Scottish Fire and Rescue Service were a reference to the enforcing authority.

[1](3) A local authority shall have complied with sub-paragraph (2)(b) above if they have invited each of the persons whom they must notify under that sub-paragraph to attend and to be heard by the local authority when the variation of the licence is to be considered.

(4) A variation in the terms of a licence shall come into force—

(a) when the time within which an appeal under paragraph 24 below may be made has elapsed; or

(b) where such an appeal has been lodged, when the appeal has been abandoned or determined in favour of the variation.

[1,2,3](5) A local authority shall, within 7 days of their decision under sub-paragraph (1) above, send written notice of their decision to the holder of the licence, the chief constable and either the enforcing authority where Part 3 of that Act applies in relation to the premises, vehicle, vessel or stall or, where Part 3 of that Act does not so apply, the Scottish Fire and Rescue Service.

NOTES

1. As amended by the Local Government etc. (Scotland) Act 1994 (c.39) Sch.13 para.129 (effective 1 April 1996).

2. As amended by the Fire (Scotland) Act 2005 (Consequential Modifications and Savings) Order 2006 (SSI 2006/475) Sch.1 para.11 (effective 1 October 2006).

3. As amended by the Police and Fire Reform (Scotland) Act 2012 (asp 8) Sch.7 para.53 (effective 1 April 2013).

INDEX